Muirhead Library of Philosophy

A HUNDRED YEARS OF BRITISH PHILOSOPHY

Muirhead Library of Philosophy

MUIRHEAD

20TH CENTURY PHILOSOPHY
In 22 Volumes

I	Contemporary American Philosophy (Vol I)	*Adams & Montague*
II	Contemporary American Philosophy (Vol II)	*Adams & Montague*
III	G E Moore	*Ambrose & Lazerowitz*
IV	Ludwig Wittgenstein	*Ambrose & Lazerowitz*
V	Philosophy in America	*Black*
VI	Contemporary Philosophy in Australia	*Brown & Rollins*
VII	A History of Philosophy (Vol I)	*Erdmann*
VIII	A History of Philosophy (Vol II)	*Erdmann*
IX	A History of Philosophy (Vol III)	*Erdmann*
X	Ideas	*Husserl*
XI	The Development of Bertrand Russell's Philosophy	*Jager*
XII	Contemporary British Philosophy (Vol III)	*Lewis*
XIII	Contemporary British Philosophy (Vol IV)	*Lewis*
XIV	A Hundred Years of British Philosophy	*Metz*
XV	Lectures on Philosophy	*Moore*
XVI	Commonplace Book	*Moore*
XVII	Philosophical Papers	*Moore*
XVIII	Some Main Problems of Philosophy	*Moore*
XIX	Bernard Bosanquet and His Friends	*Muirhead*
XX	Contemporary British Philosophy (Vol I)	*Muirhead*
XXI	Contemporary British Philosophy (Vol II)	*Muirhead*
XXII	Bertrand Russell Memorial Volume	*Roberts*

A HUNDRED YEARS OF BRITISH PHILOSOPHY

RUDOLF METZ

Routledge
Taylor & Francis Group
LONDON AND NEW YORK

First published 1938 by
George Allen & Unwin Ltd

Published 2013 by Routledge
2 Park Square, Milton Park, Abingdon, Oxfordshire OX14 4RN
711 Third Avenue, New York, NY 10017

First issued in paperback 2014

Routledge is an imprint of the Taylor and Francis Group, an informa business

British Library Cataloguing in Publication Data
A CIP catalogue record for this book
is available from the British Library

A Hundred Years of British Philosophy

20th Century Philosophy: 22 Volumes
ISBN 0-415-29526-2
Muirhead Library of Philosophy: 95 Volumes
ISBN 0-415-27897-X

ISBN 13: 978-1-138-87072-7 (pbk)
ISBN 13: 978-0-415-29548-2 (hbk)

THE MUIRHEAD LIBRARY OF PHILOSOPHY

As may be seen from the original programme printed in Erdmann's *History of Philosophy* under the date 1890, the Library of Philosophy was designed as a contribution to the History of Modern Philosophy under the heads: first of different Schools of Thought—Sensationalist, Realist, Idealist, Intuitivist; secondly of different Subjects—Psychology, Ethics, Aesthetics, Political Philosophy, Theology. While much had been done in England in tracing the course of evolution in nature, history, economics, morals and religion, little had been done in tracing the development of thought on these subjects. Yet "the evolution of opinion is part of the whole evolution".

By the co-operation of different writers in carrying out this plan it was hoped that a thoroughness and completeness of treatment, otherwise unattainable, might be secured. It was believed also that from writers mainly British and American fuller consideration of English Philosophy than it had hitherto received might be looked for. In the earlier series of books containing, among others, Bosanquet's *History of Æsthetic*, Pfleiderer's *Rational Theology since Kant*, Albee's *History of English Utilitarianism*, Bonar's *Philosophy and Political Economy*, Brett's *History of Psychology*, Ritchie's *Natural Rights*, these objects were to a large extent effected.

In the meantime original work of a high order was being produced both in England and America by such writers as Bradley, Stout, Bertrand Russell, Baldwin, Urban, Montague and others, and a new interest in foreign works, German, French and Italian, which had either become classical or were attracting public attention, had developed. The scope of the Library thus became extended into something more international, and it is entering on the fifth decade of its existence in the hope that it may contribute in this highest field of thought to that Intellectual Co-operation which is one of the most significant objects of the League of Nations and kindred organizations.

GENERAL EDITOR

1930

A HUNDRED YEARS OF BRITISH PHILOSOPHY

by

DR. RUDOLF METZ

Translated by

PROFESSOR J. W. HARVEY, M.A.
PROFESSOR T. E. JESSOP, M.A.
HENRY STURT, M.A.

Edited by

J. H. MUIRHEAD, LL.D., F.B.A.

LONDON: GEORGE ALLEN & UNWIN LTD
NEW YORK: THE MACMILLAN COMPANY

FIRST PUBLISHED IN 1938
SECOND IMPRESSION 1950

PRINTED IN GREAT BRITAIN
BY NOVELLO & CO. LTD.
LONDON, W.1.

To

MY PARENTS

in

Sincere Gratitude

and Reverence

CONTENTS

EDITOR'S FOREWORD

DR. RUDOLF METZ's book entitled *Die philosophischen Strömungen der Gegenwart in Grossbritannien*,[1] of which this volume is a translation, was the first attempt to give a detailed account to his own countrymen of the development of British philosophy during the last, and the first part of this, century. The great movement of British thought in the XVIIth and XVIIIth Centuries, represented by Hobbes, Locke, Berkeley, and Hume and continued in the XIXth by Mill and Spencer, had received ample recognition in continental histories of European philosophy. Dr. Metz has himself written books on Berkeley (1925), and Hume (1929), in the series Klassiker der Philosophie. But the hardly less important revival of interest in speculative problems that was initiated by Coleridge and, after an interval, manifested itself with better resources at its command and more concentrated power in the 'sixties and 'seventies of last century with the equally powerful reactions it called forth had received scant notice. As Dr. Metz himself puts it in his Preface: "The few works which have dealt with it are either mere collections of material or treat of particular aspects only and are rough summaries and sketches." This is true even of Heinze's invaluable additions to Ueberweg's *Outline of Philosophy since the beginning of the XIXth Century*.

There can have been few men living, even in Germany, who possessed in like degree the necessary equipment for the task of supplying this gap in German philosophical literature. With complete knowledge of the movement in the philosophy of his own country which exercised so profound an influence on British thought in the latter half of the XIXth Century he combines a thorough mastery of the course of that thought itself in all its manifold windings and a personal acquaintance, cultivated in repeated visits to England, with many of the men who have themselves contributed to swell its stream.

[1] Felix Meiner, Verlag, Leipzig, 1935, 2 vols.

It was the brilliant use which he had made of these advantages in presenting a picture, at once comprehensive and detailed, sympathetic and critical, weighted with learning yet full of human interest and lively portraiture, that at once attracted the notice of readers of German in this country and suggested to several, including Mr. Stanley Unwin, the publisher of the Library of Philosophy, and myself, that it was no less fitted to fill a gap in the philosophical literature of our own country than in that of Germany. As in Germany so in England, although we have many characterizations of particular movements of thought and one or two attempts to characterize it as a whole, the former have offered only the materials for a comprehensive view, while the latter have been little more than sketches and are already out of date as records of contemporary thought.

There were difficulties financial and other to be faced in so large an undertaking. But these were overcome partly by the generosity of the German publisher and of Dr. Metz himself in showing themselves prepared to regard it as no mere matter of business but as a contribution to international understanding at a time when nothing is so greatly needed, partly by a like generosity on the side of the translators who were willing to enter on it as a pure labour of love.

We have been further aided by the author's willingness to revise the whole of the German text with the view not only of bringing the bibliographies up to date but of making valuable additions of new material. The result of this has been that the English translation amounts in reality to a corrected and enlarged edition of the German work. It would be impossible here to give a complete list of these additions. But attention may be drawn to three of the longest and most important in the section on Theodor Merz (pp. 443–46), the enlargement of the section on the Oxford Moralists (pp. 527–29), and of that on the new school of Logical Positivists (pp. 723–26).

It only requires to be further explained that the Translators with the permission of the Author have permitted themselves a certain amount of abbreviation in a few passages in which the subject dealt with is more familiar to the English than to the foreign reader. For this permission and for his invaluable co-operation with us in the production of this volume I cannot conclude this Foreword without offering Dr. Metz in the name of the Publisher, the Translators, and myself as Editor our warmest thanks.

The portions for which the translators are respectively responsible are:

HENRY STURT German, Vol. I, pp. 1–56 (par. 1). (English, pp. 29–83) (par. 2).
German, Vol. II, pp. 1–246. (English, pp. 447–704.)

T. E. JESSOP German, Vol. I, pp. 217–442 and pp. 56 (par. 2)–110. (English, pp. 83 (par. 3)–121 (par. 2), pp. 237–446.

J. W. HARVEY German, Vol. I, pp. 110–213. (English, pp. 128–234.)
German, Vol. II, pp. 247–349. (English, pp. 121–234, 705–820.)

But they have all read the whole in proof and reduced my function as Editor to little more than a nominal one.

J. H. MUIRHEAD

AUTHOR'S PREFACE TO THE GERMAN EDITION

THE following book aims at giving an account of the development of British philosophy from about the middle of last century to the present day. But in order to give a foundation to my account of the British philosophy which is contemporary in the narrower sense, it seemed indispensable to include the older ideas and to show in all directions the lines of connection which bind the present to the past in a relatively complete and manageable whole. The First Part of the book owes its origin to this consideration and it is thus that the account of modern British philosophy has been rounded off into an historical unity.

But the main interest of my book begins with the Second Part, and it is for the sake of it that this laborious work has been undertaken. While those older schools of thought have been studied adequately and are well known in their main features, the later period has never been treated comprehensively. The few works which have dealt with it are either mere collections of material or treat of partial aspects only and are rough summaries and sketches. In this field almost everything had to be done which was needed for a thorough mastery of the matter. Here it was my work to discover new country in the history of philosophy and not only to mark out the complex web of contemporary British philosophy in its outer extent, but to illuminate it from within and to present it intensively as well as extensively. I had therefore to go straight to the original sources; from them only could I get presentations of the individual thinkers, of their place in schools of thought, and of the schools of thought themselves.

When in this book I speak of 'schools of thought' I am relying, of course, upon insight into the relations of ideas. But the many-coloured fullness of life, in which the philosophic thinking of an age and a nation moves, does not always fit easily into the schema of a history of philosophy, and often conflicts with the neat labelling of all those 'isms' which once were viewed with so much favour and are so unpopular to-day. A work such as the present, if it is not to lose itself in the moving manifold of phenomena, cannot in the interests of order and consistency dispense with such labels altogether. But these should not be more than signposts in a country which at first sight seems to be trackless; they can never be a substitute for facts. They are lines of direction and points of orientation for the traveller and as such are intelligible and necessary. Therefore I regard them not as the main interest of my work, but merely as an indispensable help to inquiry. It may be that one thinker or another has been classified under a wrong category, and is partly or wholly out of place where he has been put. Such objections must not be given too much weight, if I have been successful in giving a true account of the thinker and his doctrine, and in understanding him adequately. For this reason I have taken more interest in individual thinkers than in schools of thought, and more interest in the problems of thought than in the labels by which they are identified. I have made it, indeed, my chief purpose to give an account of the various philosophers in their individual character and to present as vividly as possible their personality as thinkers. In view of this each thinker will be dealt with at *one* place only, although a treatment arranged according to tendencies of thought would have required a discussion in more than one place. This may lead to many anomalies, which are inevitable if system is not to be preferred to personality, tendency of thought to the thinker, and category to living presentation.

It may seem hazardous to trace the line of British thought right down to the present day, seeing that such an undertaking has not that distant perspective which is necessary in order to survey a movement which is not yet finished or thinkers who are still in the middle of their work, and to distinguish the essential from the unessential, the permanent from the transitory. I am fully conscious of this, and where I had to treat of contemporary matters I make no claim to that accuracy of judgment which may well be required from a historian in regard to matters where the record is closed. Here much remains in the stage of a temporary arrangement and mere approximation to that which future inquiry will settle more definitely. For this reason I could not take account of all the germinal movements which can be discerned in British thought, or of anything which so far has failed to take definite form. Moreover, it was not my purpose to strive for an absolutely complete and a perfectly inclusive record. Apart from its practical impossibility such a purpose would have been theoretically mistaken. For in the realm of ideas there is the same natural selection which the genius of Darwin has shown to be so dominant in the world of nature. What is dead and forgotten, because it has failed to maintain itself in the struggle of ideas, should not be revived by the historian, merely because it once existed. But of all that has borne the test of survival, there is scarcely anything that we can afford to overlook. The principle of selection has been applied in this respect also: that a much fuller treatment has been accorded to the great figures and prophets of philosophy than to the *di minorum gentium*. To this extent the amplitude of the treatment is in a sense an indication of inner value, although it cannot be interpreted directly as fixing the place of a thinker in the scale of values.

The question may be raised: What is the meaning and value of an undertaking such as this at a time when nations are continually closing themselves more and more against one another, and mutual understanding is continually becoming more difficult? What is British philosophy to us Germans of to-day, what can we learn from it and for what useful purpose should we concern ourselves with it? This very practical question, which the generation of our fathers would have regarded as incompatible with the meaning and purpose of genuine research, must be faced to-day. The question is one of politics or of politics and culture, and so in the present case we cannot afford to dismiss it as a matter of merely taking pleasure in the picture of British thought which is here presented or of increasing or completing our knowledge of what people are thinking across the Channel. Apart from the fact that the present condition of things can hardly be maintained permanently, it appears in view of the present political situation necessary that those bridges should be built for us from the spiritual side which are so hard to build from the political side. Less than ever can we to-day neglect anything which brings the nations together and helps them to understand each other; above all, nations so close in race as the English and the German. To cultivate and promote understanding should be our aim wherever it seems to be possible; and this enterprise has been undertaken with the express purpose of bringing the minds of the two nations nearer to each other and of encouraging mutual understanding. I turn therefore to the professional philosophers not only of Germany but of Great Britain and America and ask them to co-operate in the cultural and political purposes for which this book has been undertaken. And although I am conscious that, in view of the narrowness of my circle of readers, which is due to the nature of the subject, I can make only a modest contribution to achieving that purpose, I see nevertheless in this possibility the authorization and justification of my enterprise.

Finally, it should be mentioned that I have had the good fortune to come into personal relations with a great number of British philosophers, especially with many of those who are discussed in this book. An excellent opportunity for this was furnished by the Seventh International Congress of Philosophy which met in Oxford in September 1930, and by a long stay in England on the occasion of it. What was gained by personal intercourse and the direct exchange of ideas could not in many cases have been supplied by prolonged study of books. To all those who have helped me thus, I wish now to make suitable acknowledgment. Especially are my thanks due to my friend, R. I. Aaron, Professor of Philosophy at the University College of Wales in Aberystwyth, to Professor T. E. Jessop, of the University College of Hull, and to the late Dr. F. C. S. Schiller, of Corpus Christi College, Oxford. Their ever-ready help and their valuable advice and encouragement have contributed greatly to my book. And last, though not least, I have to thank my wife for her affectionate sympathy, constant encouragement, and active co-operation during the long years which have been spent in preparing the book. Finally, it must be mentioned that the Notgemeinschaft der deutschen Wissenschaft has furnished the material basis for the appearance of the book by a generous contribution to the expense of printing. For this the author and the publisher here express fitting thanks.

RUDOLF METZ

HEIDELBERG
November 1934

PART I

OLDER SCHOOLS OF THOUGHT XIXth CENTURY

I

THE SCOTTISH SCHOOL

THE school of thought founded by THOMAS REID (1710–96) in the second half of the XVIIIth Century was called the Scottish in accordance with its geographical place of origin and the domicile of its leading representatives. In reference to the content of its doctrine it is usually termed 'the philosophy of common sense'. It forms a branch of the stem of British empiricism although it arose from conscious opposition to the school of empirical thought represented by Berkeley and Hume. It drew nourishment from the motives and problems of that school which it set out to combat and refute. But it was able neither to explode these motives and problems from within, nor to bring to them new nourishment from without. It contented itself with surveying and distorting the traditional problems and their solutions, but it nowhere advanced beyond the results which British philosophy reached in its classical period. It did not abandon the previous line of thought, but diverged from it and pushed into a side-track. In its systematic import it is far inferior to the great classic works of British philosophy, with which it is directly connected and apart from which it is unintelligible; in its regress to healthy human understanding it implies a relaxation of the philosophic impulse and a decline of that speculative force from which Hume's mighty shock to thought issued. It was not adequate to the greatness of the historical situation in which it found itself and it was incapable of managing the inheritance which came to it from Hume. Thus Reid's brave struggle against Hume resulted in no proper victory over his opponent, and the answer which he gave to Hume's sceptical challenge was no help to philosophic thought, but brought it into a blind alley. Like Kant, Reid was awakened from his dogmatic slumber by Hume, but the powerful impulse which both experienced was made fruitful and directed into a new great movement of thought by the German thinker only. From Reid and his followers there came no creative renewal of thought. They remained the undistinguished successors of great men and made no considerable contributions to thought.

Nevertheless, the historical influence and diffusion of the Scottish school is of no small importance. Reid's doctrine established itself at the Scottish universities, was organized there into a kind of scholastic system, and drew continually fresh followers into its sphere of influence. It crossed over into France, where it inspired many of the thinkers who succeeded Maine de Biran (Royer-Collard, Cousin, Jouffroy, Garnier, Damiron, de Rémusat, and others).[1] In America its tradition was carried on by J. M'Cosh (vide infra, p. 41), Noah Porter, and others. Apart from the so-called Cambridge school, in which the Platonic renaissance of the XVIIth Century was crystallized, we here for the first time in the history of British thought encounter a real school of philosophic training. For the first time we see a unified thought-system which was incorporated into the academic curriculum and was for many decades represented, taught, and elaborated by the co-operation of a considerable body of adherents. The school which was founded by Reid in Scotland had its counterpart in England, where there arose an important school with Bentham as its centre. For a long time the two proceeded in rivalry with each other and concentrated in themselves most of the philosophic energies which were available at that time.

The early history of the Scottish school falls outside the limits of this book; its chief phases can be only lightly sketched here. Even before Reid's death the leadership of the school passed to DUGALD STEWART (1753–1828), the ablest among his early students. Stewart was an eminent academic teacher, whose rhetorically powerful lectures exercised a great educational influence upon the rising generation of Scotsmen. From 1785 to 1810 he occupied the Chair of Moral Philosophy at

[1] Vide E. Boutroux, "De l'influence de la philosophie écossaise sur la philosophie française," in his *Études d'histoire de la philosophie*, 1897.

Edinburgh, which was the spiritual centre of Scottish philosophy for many generations. At his feet sat many young men who later were destined to attain distinction in the most various spheres of political and intellectual life, e.g. no less a man than Sir Walter Scott and the future Prime Ministers Palmerston and Russell. In the main points of his doctrine he followed the footsteps of Reid, with whom he disagreed only in some special questions, and his only service in point of theory consisted in the fact that he tried to systematize his master's doctrine more thoroughly and to apply it more extensively. He was a man of high intellectual culture, who understood how to put the dry and soberly expressed ideas of Reid into a pleasing and cultured literary dress. But it is remarkable that Stewart, who at that time was the most powerful exponent of philosophic culture in Great Britain, took practically no notice of the great advance of German philosophy which took place in his lifetime. After Reid, Stewart is the chief academic representative of the Scottish system. He carried its tradition on into the XIXth Century and was so powerful and influential a representative of it that it maintained itself till Bentham took over the leadership in philosophy.

Stewart's pupil and later his successor in Edinburgh, THOMAS BROWN (1778–1820), is closely connected with the Scottish school though he did not accept fully all its ideas. His philosophic position represents a sort of compromise between the associationist tendencies of the older empiricism and the intuitionist views of Reid. He thus forms a bridge from the philosophy of common sense to the later empiricism and therefore to the psychological doctrines of the two Mills, Bain, and Spencer. His most important philosophic contributions are those which he made to the problems of perception and causality, which in part brought him into violent opposition to Reid. Although he adhered to the assumption of certain intuitive principles of belief, in regard to perception he drew nearer to sensationalist views and in regard to causality to the views of Hume, while rejecting Hume's sceptical conclusions. The latter problem was treated by him in a comprehensive work in which he entered into a critical discussion with Hume (first edition in 1805; third greatly enlarged edition in 1817 under the title *An Inquiry into the Relation of Cause and Effect*). He was a much stronger thinker than Stewart, and had good critical powers. Even then he took an interest in Kant, on whose philosophy he wrote the earliest essays in English (published in the first volume of the *Edinburgh Review* in 1802), and was, like Stewart, an honoured and successful philosophic teacher. To this circumstance is due in the main the extraordinary literary success which was gained by his Edinburgh lectures. Shortly after his premature death they were published under the title *Lectures on the Philosophy of the Human Mind* (1820) and within thirty years reached no less than nineteen editions.

Less intimate were the relations of Sir JAMES MACKINTOSH (1765–1832) to the ideas of the Scottish school; he is better known as a politician and historian than as a philosopher. The only writing for the sake of which he should be mentioned here is his *Dissertation on the Progress of Ethical Philosophy, chiefly during the XVIIth and XVIIIth Centuries* which was first published in 1830 as an introduction to the seventh edition of the *Encyclopaedia Britannica* and at once achieved great popularity (ten editions to 1870). At its appearance it attracted great attention and provoked a severe reply from James Mill (*A Fragment on Mackintosh*, 1835).

In this essay, in which Mackintosh gave a sweeping view of the English moral systems of the past two centuries, he attempted a kind of reconciliation of utilitarian and intuitionist ethics. He did not reject the principle of utility, but deposed it from its dominant position and found the bases of moral conduct more in conscience and sympathy than in usefulness.

All these thinkers and a series of others, who have long since sunk into well-merited oblivion,[1] were overshadowed by a much

[1] The following may very briefly be mentioned. John Abercrombie (1784–1844), a physician who achieved a great literary success with his book *Inquiries concerning the Intellectual Powers* (1830, twenty-one editions to 1882); James Mylne, Reid's successor in the professorship of moral philosophy in Glasgow, a distinguished and influential philosophic

more important and powerful thinker, Sir WILLIAM HAMILTON (1788–1856). Hamilton gave Scottish philosophy a new impetus, and it is mainly due to him that for the second time it came dominantly into the foreground and gained a sort of pre-eminence over all other philosophic schools. This supremacy lasted from about the thirtieth to the sixtieth year of the century. From 1836 to his death Hamilton held the professorship of logic and metaphysics in the University of Edinburgh. Even before his appointment he had established his name and fame in philosophy by numerous contributions to the *Edinburgh Review*; he was known far beyond the boundaries of Scotland and even on the Continent. Among his contributions there were three of special importance, since they contained the main substance of his thought and attracted the greatest attention from his contemporaries: *Cousin's Writings and Philosophy of the Unconditioned* (1829), *Brown's Writings and Philosophy of Perception* (1830), and *Logic* (1833). In the first are developed the main principles of metaphysics, in the second those of theory of knowledge, and in the third those of logic. Later they were reprinted in his *Discussions on Philosophy and Literature, Education and University Reform* (1852). A boundary-mark in the history of the Scottish school is furnished by the edition of Reid's works (1846, completed in 1863), with careful comments and numerous excurses and notes into which Hamilton poured the immense wealth of his knowledge. Later there came also the edition of Dugald Stewart's works (in eleven volumes, 1854–58). For the most part this finished Hamilton's literary activity, apart from his *Lectures on Metaphysics and Logic*, which were not prepared

teacher, who, however, wrote nothing; David Ritchie, Hamilton's predecessor in Edinburgh, more a divine than a philosopher; John Wilson (1785–1854), better known under his pen-name of Christopher North, who also filled a philosophical professorship in the University of Edinburgh; Thomas Chalmers (1780–1847) the great Scottish theologian, for a time professor of moral philosophy in St. Andrews, and author of *Sketches of Moral and Mental Philosophy* (1836), who shortly before his death made a vigorous attack upon German philosophy and upon Hegel's 'nihilism'.

by himself for publication and were edited after his death by his pupils Mansel and Veitch (in four volumes, 1858–60).

With Hamilton, Scottish philosophy enters upon the final stage of its course; with him begins the process of inward disintegration and transition to other lines of thought. But its finest flowering takes place just before the end, when it reaches not only its widest popularity and its most concise academic expression but also its highest achievement in criticism and speculation. But this is attained not by its own resources but by the extension of its range of problems and by the introduction of new ideas. This addition was due to the omnivorous erudition of Hamilton, whose reading in philosophical and other literature far surpassed that of all previous British thinkers and came from various sources, but mainly from the recently discovered German philosophy. How Hamilton was influenced positively by the Kantian philosophy and negatively by post-Kantian philosophy will be shown later. For the present it may be said that the opening of wider prospects, mainly through the adoption of Kantian ideas, implied the shattering of the original structure of the Scottish school. The extension and deepening of the Scottish doctrine by Hamilton was achieved at the cost of its purity.

This can be shown briefly by an example. Reid's philosophy had grown out of opposition to the phenomenalist theory of knowledge of the older empiricism and especially to Hume's sceptical conclusions from it. When we know the external world, analysis shows us the mental act on one side and the real object on the other. The object is *qua* external immediately present in perception and needs no intervening pictures or presentations to mediate for us the reality of external things. Reid therefore rejects the so-called representative theory of perception or knowledge and will have nothing to do with the whole apparatus of presentations (ideas and impressions). For that we apprehend external things immediately and directly in perception is one of those fundamental principles of healthy human understanding of which we are intuitively certain and the truth of which we have no occasion to doubt. Hamilton also begins by accepting the 'natural realism' of Reid's theory of knowledge. But his doctrine implies from the first an important advance beyond Reid, inasmuch as he tries to reach this result not through a mere appeal to the healthy human understanding of the plain man, but through a critical analysis of the process of knowledge. By rejecting expressly that appeal, he returns once more to the ground of true philosophic inquiry. In the place of Reid's dogmatism he puts Kant's criticism. But this involves a displacement of the problem. The problem of knowledge is not solved by the mere assertion that we are *immediately* conscious of material reality as something different from ourselves or our mental states. When the statement that the object as such is present in consciousness is taken to mean that its existence must be identical with the experienced quality, it is evident that in many cases this condition is not fulfilled. We need, therefore, a careful critical examination of the concept of immediacy. Such an examination tells us, e.g. that all knowledge through recollection cannot be immediate in the same way as knowledge through perception, since the object which is past is no longer present. What is immediately present is rather a memory-image from which we make inferences to the object which was formerly present. The possibility of immediate knowledge therefore exists only for sense-perception. But even here Hamilton's critical analysis shows that the naïve idea of immediacy often cannot be maintained. He therefore feels himself constrained to diverge from the original common-sense theory almost as far as the phenomenalist theories against which the common-sense theory was directed. The final result is that everything which we can know about the outer world is nothing else than contents of consciousness and that therefore consciousness is the sole trustworthy voucher for the existence of external things. Of Reid's natural realism there remains nothing but the bare knowledge that in consciousness not merely the ego and its psychic acts are disclosed, but also the non-ego and its relations to the ego. But this means that the theory of common sense which was set up by Reid as a barrier against subjectivism and scepticism was so transformed by Hamilton that it returned to the opinion that we can know nothing truly beyond the transitory phenomena of consciousness. Natural realism was bent back into that very phenomenalism to refute which it was originally invented.

It is evident that these arguments are derived not so much from Berkeley and Hume as from Kant. To this extent they are not a mere return to the theories combated by Reid, but an advance beyond them to the critical theory of knowledge of the German thinker. This is shown by the fact that with Hamilton the principle of relativity is conjoined with the theory of perception, and that it is just this principle which is the centre of gravity of his whole philosophy. In general the theory of perception had maintained that we are immediately conscious at least of the primary qualities of things and that we have the right to maintain that they exist as we perceive them. To this extent our knowledge of external things is not mediated or representative, but immediate or presentative. But the fundamental principle of the relativity of knowledge maintains that we know nothing as it is in itself and therefore that we are limited to the knowledge of phenomena and that things in themselves are hidden from us. Between the two there is evidently an irreconcilable contradiction. On closer inspection, however, it is seen that the theory of perception must be interpreted in the light of the principle of relativity, and not conversely. For the primary qualities which we know immediately and which testify to the existence of a world independent of consciousness turn out in the end to be nothing but phenomena; which means that they are relative to our capacities for knowledge and are extensively modified by them, and therefore are incapable of manifesting reality in itself. Hamilton's doctrine thus ends finally in the position that the external world, *qua* known world, has no existence independently of the knowing subject.

This theory in its consequences leads to an agnosticism which is in many respects close to Kantianism or rather with that prevalent interpretation of Kantian doctrine which lays undue stress upon the phenomenalist elements of his criticism of knowledge and neglects the metaphysical implications which are contained in it. It leads, moreover, to the rejection of all metaphysics and to renunciation of any kind of speculative knowledge of the Absolute or, as Hamilton in his famous essay of 1829 expressed it, to rejection of every "philosophy of the unconditioned". But with Hamilton this is not connected with indifference or hostility to religious beliefs as with Spencer, Huxley, and others; on the contrary it involves a more vigorous affirmation of them. The *docta ignorantia* which for Hamilton is the end of all philosophy, is also the beginning of theology. When he bids the understanding keep to its boundaries, he tries to establish faith in its just rights; a faith, the proper object of which he regards as being that which in its own nature is incomprehensible. Thus for him philosophy, so far as it keeps within its own limits and rejects the presumptuous claims of reason to absolute knowledge, is the true justification of religion.

Hamilton's doctrine, which we can follow no further here, suffers from the inconsistency which arises from trying to reduce two theories so different as those of Reid and Kant to a common denominator. The result of this is that on the one side he greatly falsifies the original intentions of Reid, and that on the other side he interprets Kant's meaning very one-sidedly. The whole is a compromise which does justice to neither side and thereby discloses its inner weakness. The historical importance and influence of Hamilton's philosophy is, however, not affected thereby. He still performed the service of being the first academic philosopher of rank to open his mind to the influence of German ideas and thereby to take a decisive step in ending the insularity of British thought. This step was the more momentous because it was made by a man who during his two decades of teaching at Edinburgh had more philosophic authority than any of his contemporaries. As head of the Scottish school, Hamilton was a sort of philosophic dictator whose authority was unbounded within his circle, whom his pupils followed blindly, and who enjoyed high consideration far outside the limits of the school. His reputation remained almost unimpaired throughout his life; no one raised any noteworthy protest against his predominance. Not till nine years after his death was an attack delivered from two directions against his doctrine. The much better known and stronger of these attacks was made by John Stuart Mill in the name of empiricism. By Mill's criticism of Hamilton, contained in the book *An Examination of Sir William Hamilton's Philosophy* (1865), which was comprehensive though in many respects unjust and based on misunderstandings, the Scottish philosophy suffered such a blow to its authority and such a setback to its influence that from thenceforward it lived with reduced vitality and was threatened with extinction. The second attack, which contributed to this result, came in the same year from quite another direction. John Hutchison Stirling, who may be said to have brought Hegelianism into Great Britain, attacked Hamilton, protesting against his negative attitude to the great post-Kantian systems, both in his epoch-making work *The Secret of Hegel* and in a separate book *Sir William Hamilton, being the Philosophy of Perception* (both in 1865). Thus the idealist movement which at once became powerful set itself from the first in opposition to Hamilton and led subsequently to an almost complete neglect of his philosophy. Hamilton's interpretation of the Kantian doctrine could no longer be accepted, since it could not be brought into harmony with the predominantly Hegelian interests of these thinkers, who never even acknowledged adequately his historical service in introducing the ideas of Kant and other Germans. Thus the year 1865 marks, not indeed the end, but the almost complete exhaustion of the line of thought initiated by Hamilton and the Scottish school.

By far the best known of Hamilton's pupils is the theologian HENRY L. MANSEL (1820–71). Ordained a priest, then Lecturer in Theology at Magdalen College, later Professor of Ecclesiastical History in Oxford, and finally Dean of St. Paul's, Mansel introduced Hamilton's philosophy into England, teaching and diffusing it with vigour and success in the University of Oxford. Besides two early books on logic, he wrote on metaphysics, endeavouring to reduce the main ideas of Hamilton's doctrine to a stricter and more systematic form than the master had given to them (*Metaphysics or the Philosophy of Consciousness*, first in 1857 in the eighth edition of the *Encyclopaedia Britannica*, later in book form in 1860; and afterwards a *Philosophy of the Conditioned*, 1866, in which he tried to defend Hamilton and himself against Mill's attack). But the most influential of his writings were his Bampton Lectures on *The Limits of Religious Thought* (1858), which attracted great attention, aroused a vigorous controversy, and made his name widely known. These lectures were mainly of interest because they made perfectly plain the attitude of the school to the religious questions which Hamilton, in spite of many indications, had left obscure. For the first time and very definitely they drew the theological conclusions which lay concealed in Hamilton's agnostic phenomenalism. Starting from the principle of the relativity of knowledge, Mansel tried to show that all our efforts to discover by means of thought anything about the absolute divine nature are doomed to failure. The absolute and infinite are completely inaccessible to man's finite understanding. Every attempt to think the absolute or to apprehend it by any rational means leads to a tangle of contradictions and inconsistencies which the intellect cannot solve. In matters of faith, thought is completely impotent and must in the end confess its bankruptcy. Mansel therefore declares that all theoretic arguments against the dogmas of religion are invalid, and thus rids himself in the quickest and simplest manner of all the enemies and contemners of faith. It is not the business of reason to interfere with holy things; and there is no occasion to be sorry for this. On the contrary, this renunciation of reason should be most warmly welcomed in the interest of religion. Thus Mansel bases all our knowledge of the super-sensuous upon divine revelation and the sole task which falls upon the critical reason in deciding whether to accept or reject religious dogmas is not concerned with the content of the dogmas but merely with the evidences which can be adduced for their divine origin. In this connection he assigns a certain subordinate importance to the moral argument. Although this is not competent to give judgment upon a revealed truth, yet from our ethical standards of value we obtain helpful indications for judging religious ideas.

Mansel thus gave the Kantian theory of knowledge a more definite turn towards sceptical agnosticism than did Hamilton and made it subserve the purposes of revealed religion. More definitely than ever since the time of Bacon the separation was made between faith and knowledge, religion and philosophy; and the old saying "Credo quia absurdum" was restored once more to its rights. From this doctrine Spencer's agnosticism gained decisive support and presents itself as nothing else than its complete secularization. It was only a short step from Mansel's revelation-theology to Spencer's indifference to religion. The procedure by which the strictest orthodoxy supplied weapons for itself from one of the most advanced schools of thought, and at the same time threw extreme discredit upon thought as such, was so extraordinary that it was attacked with vigorous criticism from the most diverse quarters. The controversy which rose out of Mansel's Bampton Lectures and was conducted with equal vigour by philosophers and theologians,[1] raised a great dust, and, although the results which came from it had but small importance, the interest of the public in the questions discussed was greatly increased, and a favourable atmosphere thus prepared for the keener pursuit of philosophy which ensued soon afterwards.

After Hamilton and Mansel, the path of Scottish philosophy runs steeply downward. Of those who issued from the school or adhered to it there are only a few names of importance who represent the doctrine in its purity. Even in JOHN D. MORELL (1816–91) those centrifugal tendencies appear which were to gain the upper hand more and more in the future. It is true that Morell was rooted in the Scottish tradition, within which

[1] Among Mansel's critics were men so distinguished as J. S. Mill, T. H. Huxley, and F. D. Maurice.

he received his early philosophic training, but he was subject to many influences from other schools of thought and was especially receptive to the German systems with which he first came into touch during a student-journey in Germany. We owe to Morell, who was, like Hamilton, a man of wide reading and catholic receptivity of mind, some works on the history of philosophy. Among them is the book *Historical and Critical View of the Speculative Philosophy of Europe in the XIXth Century* (1846), which justly attracted lively attention and contributed to widen the philosophic outlook of Englishmen, and a book on Fichte's ethics (1848). But his chief contribution was a *Philosophy of Religion* (1849) in which we can trace the influence of Schleiermacher and R. Rothe. His *Introduction to Mental Philosophy on the Inductive Method* was published in 1862.

Another thinker of Hamilton's school was JAMES M'COSH (1811–94), a voluminous philosophic writer who went to America in 1868 and took with him the philosophy of common sense and achieved for it a certain recognition. Besides many systematic works, M'Cosh wrote a full history of the Scottish philosophy (*Scottish Philosophy from Hutcheson to Hamilton*, 1875).[1]

HENRY CALDERWOOD (1830–97), at first a Scottish minister, then from 1868 Professor of Moral Philosophy in Edinburgh, began as a pupil of Hamilton. But even in his first book (*Philosophy of the Infinite*, 1854, second edition, 1861), which he published while still a student, there appeared a surprising independence towards his master who was still alive. In this book he subjected Hamilton's doctrine to a searching criticism and ruthlessly exposed its weaknesses. His purpose was to re-establish the original meaning of the doctrine of common sense by separating from it the agnostic elements introduced by Hamilton and Mansel. His chief desire was to refute Hamilton's argument that the human mind, as being finite, cannot

[1] In this connection I may refer to a bibliography of the Scottish philosophy which will appear shortly from the pen of Professor T. E. Jessop.

know the infinite. He saw in a religion which builds altars to the unknown and unknowable God, and excludes rational thinking from its sphere, nothing but mere superstition, and no true reverence for the divine nature. To the agnostic relativism, which was inherent in Hamilton but was first made into a basic philosophic principle by Mansel and Spencer, Calderwood opposed the genuine intuitionism of the earlier Scottish doctrine. We are immediately conscious of God as an all-wise, all-powerful, and all-righteous being. Such knowledge is independent of all rational considerations, transparent and certain, and therefore intuitive. Calderwood represented a similar intuitionism in the ethics which he presented in a successful handbook (*Handbook of Moral Philosophy*, 1872, fourteenth edition, 1888). While attacking naturalism and hedonism, he insisted upon the necessity of an absolute law and aim of conduct. This aim he took to be neither happiness nor pleasure, but the full and harmonious use of all our powers and talents to the fulfilment of their natural purposes.

Finally we must notice the following fact. The Scottish doctrine, which in the middle of the century had been the focus of philosophic life in England, found itself in the succeeding decades driven more and more from its commanding position and under the pressure of two powerful opponents, Darwinism and idealism, against both of which it had to defend itself. While Veitch (vide infra) undertook the defence against idealism, Calderwood concerned himself with Darwinism. In his last systematic book (*Evolution and Man's Place in Nature*, 1893, completely recast in 1896) he entered the controversy which raged over the Darwinian evolutionary systems. While recognizing the great value of the results of recent biological inquiry, he saw the weakness of their application to the general problems of philosophy. He comes to the conclusion that the animal descent of man can give no basis for explaining the rational and ethical elements of his nature and he held to the assumption of a transcendent intelligence as the common cause both of moral and of cosmic development. In this way he tried to vindicate the Scottish philosophy which had always been founded upon religion against the attack of those tendencies in Darwinism which were hostile to religion.

As the *ultimus Scotorum* in the sense of faithful adherence to the school must finally be mentioned JOHN VEITCH (1829–94), Professor of Logic and Rhetoric in the University of Glasgow. Veitch was very closely related to Hamilton. He sat at his feet as a student, later became his assistant, after his death was joint-editor of his lectures and wrote no less than three books to commemorate his personality and to explain and diffuse his teaching (*Memoir of Hamilton*, 1869; *Hamilton* in Blackwood's Philosophical Classics, 1879; *Hamilton: the man and his Philosophy*, 1884). Of his independent works we need merely mention his essay *Knowledge and Being* (1889) (a complete index of his writings is given in the book posthumously edited by R. M. Wenley, *Dualism and Monism*, 1895, vide pp. ix seq.). In this Veitch develops his own doctrine with a constant polemic against the idealist theories of the school of Kant and Hegel; he tries to defend the last positions of the Scottish tradition against the attack of the new movement of thought. But Veitch is fighting in lost positions for a lost cause and nothing reveals more plainly the complete collapse of a once powerful front than this rear-guard resistance of the last successor of a great line. Here the simplicity and superficiality of common sense are pitted against the profound thought of Kant and Hegel, and Veitch tries with his coarsely realistic theory of knowledge to discredit the works of the critique of reason and of idealist speculation. His naïve realism implies a regress to Reid or even further back; and although he came from Hamilton's school he is almost completely wanting in Hamilton's critical caution. He is wanting also in the sympathetic understanding of the real meaning of the new problems and what is required for their solution which in spite of many misunderstandings we find in Hamilton. Veitch's polemic is directed mainly against Green's theory of relations and his doctrine of the eternal self-consciousness. Against the former he sets his own simple, coarse-fibred realism (the reality which we perceive or know exists outside of our consciousness and is independent of it whether we know the reality or not, and this fact must be accepted simply as given). Against the latter doctrine he puts the fact of the real individual ego and the psychological analysis of its contents. All through he is fighting with insufficient means and measuring with an inadequate scale; and thus makes all the more evident the complete exhaustion of the Scottish philosophy.

Although the last representatives of the school (Morell, M'Cosh, Thomas Spencer Baynes, Veitch, and Calderwood) were still living and working in the 'eighties and 'nineties of the last century, the Scottish tradition cannot be said to be regularly maintained after the early 'seventies. Scottish thought disintegrates or passes over into other more powerful and new-fashioned schools. It still exerts an influence here and there, but it can no longer maintain itself independently. Such centrifugal tendencies appeared even among thinkers who are to be reckoned as members of the school. Others parted early from it and either went their own ways or joined other camps. Thus, e.g., Ferrier confessed that he had learnt more from Hamilton than from all the other philosophers together. But his own later thinking moved far away from him and involved itself in profound speculations, including a sharp polemic against Kant and Hegel (vide infra, pp. 246 ff.). A similar path was followed much later by Laurie, who also moved far beyond his Scottish origin and developed a metaphysics which has scarcely anything in common with his philosophic starting-point (vide infra, pp. 429 ff.). With Fraser, Hamilton's pupil and successor in Edinburgh, the original, still active Scottish impulse was later deflected into the paths of Berkeleyan philosophy (vide infra, pp. 228 ff.). But some principles of the Scottish doctrine passed into thought-systems which were originally unconnected with it. For example, there is intuitionism both in the ethics and the philosophy of religion of Martineau and in the philosophers of the Oxford Movement (J. H. Newman and W. G. Ward), while agnosticism, as is well known, appeared anew in Spencer's evolutionism, though with a difference. And there are connections also between

Mansel's doctrine and Balfour's theism. In these and many other ways Scottish ideas percolated into the British philosophy of the XIXth Century. The least to be influenced was the more thorough-going empiricism, owing to the wide difference of the underlying ideas. But even here occasional lines of connection may be traced. It may be noticed that James Mill in his youth was greatly impressed by Dugald Stewart, to whose lectures he owed his earliest philosophic and psychological education.

The national Scottish philosophy, so far as one can use that name, in the expansion which was given to it mainly by Hamilton had opened for itself the path by which it was destined to cross the boundary of its native country and join the great stream of European thought. At the moment when the Scottish school was moving to its end, this stream was represented in Great Britain by the idealist movement. Although no actual historical transition from the former to the latter occurred, one may say that Scottish thought, after it had fulfilled its mission, was taken up and dissolved by idealism. It is no accident that the renaissance of Kant and Hegel of the 'sixties and 'seventies was encouraged in Scotland at its first onset and later in the Scottish universities more than anywhere except in Oxford. We need only mention the Hegelian work of the Scotsman Stirling and the teaching of Caird, also a Scotsman, at the University of Glasgow. And if it was an accident that Stirling's epoch-making book (1865) and Caird's thorough and widely influential teaching in Glasgow (beginning in 1866), both in the service of Hegel and the new movement, occurred just when Hamilton's star began to set (Mill's decisive attack was in 1865), this accident has a deep significance in the history of thought. Thus in the middle of the 'sixties Hegelianism established itself firmly in Scotland and from Glasgow, where it had gained a strong position, pressed continually harder upon the native philosophic tradition. Only in the citadel of Hamiltonianism, the University of Edinburgh, was the old school able to maintain itself much longer. There the dissolution was delayed till the 'nineties. Both professorships, as there were no successors of the Scottish school available, fell into the hands of neo-Kantians. That of Hamilton, which till then was occupied by Fraser, was in 1891 given to Andrew Seth (Pringle-Pattison); that of D. Stewart, the last occupant of which was Calderwood, was given to Andrew Seth's brother, James Seth. Thereby the Scottish philosophy vacated its last academic strongholds in favour of the new school and was completely extinguished. The few ideas which it contributed to the new century are not continuously connected with it, but are occasional recurrences to one or other of its principles, and that more to those of Reid than of Hamilton. Wherever the healthy human understanding with its intuitive certainties and convictions is appealed to and is recognized as the decisive criterion of truth, wherever knowledge strives to free itself from the subtleties of an over-critical and sceptical intellect and resorts to the direct methods of natural realism, there we see plainly reminiscences of the system of the Scottish school and its founder. As such views are represented by thinkers of the new-realist school more often than by any other (plainest by J. C. Wilson, G. F. Stout, G. E. Moore, J. Laird, and C. E. M. Joad), it follows that the little which is still alive of the Scottish school must be looked for mainly in new-realism.

II

THE UTILITARIAN-EMPIRICAL SCHOOL

THE main line of British philosophy runs in a relatively continuous and self-contained course from the Renaissance to the present day. This line of thought is usually called empiricism or the philosophy of experience. More than any other it can look back upon a long tradition and in no other country has it been embodied so typically and strikingly as in the British Isles. We may therefore call it the indigenous or national or traditional school, and although it would be a crude misinterpretation of the facts to identify it simply with British thinking, yet there is a certain justification for holding that this is the most typically British school. In any case we have here not a school which has been invented by historians of philosophy, but the real existence of a single basic idea and attitude of thought, which in spite of great diversity, in spite of side-issues and by-paths, offers to our view what is essentially a unitary whole. The philosophic line which stretches from Bacon and Hobbes to Locke, Berkeley, and Hume, and thence to Bentham, Mill, and Spencer, implies a complex of coherent and harmonious principles which take on a different appearance according to the standpoint from which they are viewed, but always stand in relation to the same totality. If we wish to find suitable terms for this totality in its main aspects, we must choose empiricism or positivism to show its general philosophic position, sensationalism or phenomenalism in relation to its theory of knowledge, associationism in relation to its psychology, hedonism, eudaemonism, or utilitarianism in relation to its ethics, scepticism or agnosticism in relation to its metaphysics, deism or indifferentism (occasionally also atheism) in relation to religion, liberalism in relation to politics.

The classical empiricism of the XVIIth and XVIIIth Centuries, which we distinguish from its natural successor, the modern empiricism of the XIXth Century, culminates in the philosophy of Hume and finds a temporary ending there. The ending was temporary because Hume did not leave behind him any neat and tidy stock of doctrines which pupils and successors could have taken over to elaborate, but a complete confounding and undermining of philosophic principles which abolished all possibility of orthodox teaching and prevented all direct continuation of his doctrine or of any philosophic training akin to it. Herein lies the real meaning of what is usually in a condescending spirit called the Humian Scepticism. The line of British empiricism upon the whole runs straight forward and continuously till it reaches its highest point in Hume; is then interrupted and deflected, and does not move forward again till it receives a new influx of ideas. The break of continuity occurs just where the classical empiricism is divided from its modern counterpart and is renewed in a changed form. The interruption is marked historically by the counter-attack which was made by Reid and the Scottish school against Hume; the new incoming ideas are represented by Bentham's philosophy.

It is important that these historical connections should be clearly indicated. The later school is not immediately connected with the earlier; there is a break between them. The break is filled by the Scottish philosophy. By Reid's attack and by the Scottish movement resulting from it the traditional empiricism was so severely crippled and repressed that it took a long time to recover from the blow. The first decades of the XIXth Century are filled with the conflicts of these rivals which lasted till the famous attack by J. S. Mill upon Hamilton in 1865 brought them to an end. In this decisive encounter empiricism was victorious. The controversy between Mill and Hamilton is exactly parallel historically to that between Reid and Hume. But the fortune of arms inclined in this case to empiricism, which had gained new strength and now drove its Scottish opponent finally from the field. By re-establishing its tradition and contributing new ideas and principles of thought it showed itself to be the stronger philosophic force and the better able to survive. The rivalry between the two schools and their contest for supremacy forms the interesting and progressive factor in British thought from the middle of the XVIIIth to the middle of the XIXth Centuries, and it is remarkable that the span of time thus occupied is exactly a century, i.e. from Reid's first attack upon Hume in 1764 to Mill's final attack upon Hamilton in 1865. These two years are both dramatic climaxes in the conflict, while the intervening period is marked by less decisive encounters and skirmishes, occasionally also by truces and armistices, though also with a certain open or latent tension.

In accordance with its historical importance, modern empiricism as exemplified in its chief works from Bentham to the younger Mill shows itself to be an intellectual movement of high rank and very powerful influence. It not only formed the back-bone and driving force of the specific advance in philosophy, but like no other movement of the day it diffused its influence into the spheres of literature, culture, politics, law, social reform, and education, dominated and informed them with its spirit, and stamped its character upon them. It grew up not so much from the closets of students or from lecture-rooms as from the hard necessities of life and the fluctuating daily struggle for existence. It was not merely the concern of scientists or specialists and so, unlike the Scottish philosophy and other schools of the century, limited mainly to academic and learned circles. This was shown externally by the fact that its chief representatives were not holders of professorships or other academic posts but were mostly engaged in practical professions. From the beginning it develops itself amid the varied occupations and practical conditions of life, and this eminently practical character which is peculiar to it secures to it a much wider and deeper range of influence than is usually accorded to philosophic ideas and movements. Thus it takes over the inheritance of its classical predecessor, while increasing and enhancing it and penetrating more deeply into various provinces of life. It is not only the mirror which picks up and reflects national thought and feeling; it is also together with literature and poetry the chief moulder of its spirit. What is almost unique in this connection, it opens for philosophy a path of influence upon politics, law, Parliament, legislation, and education. It makes a positive contribution to the solution of urgent social, economic, penological, and other practical questions. In all this it is a true successor of the age of enlightenment wholly averse to the scientific ideal of pure contemplation, and entirely in the service of practice even when it works theoretically. It is pragmatic through and through, even though it has not discovered the philosophic formula for its essential character.

We get another view of empiricism if we raise the question of its intrinsic philosophical value and so test it by the criterion of its classical predecessor. Here as might be expected the comparison is to its disadvantage, although an unprejudiced study will lead to a more favourable judgment than is usually formed of it. For there can be no doubt that the empirical philosophy reached its highest speculative development in the triad Locke, Berkeley, and Hume, so that the development which followed takes in this respect a downward path. In its classical period the system of empiricism had not only established its ground-plan, but had exhausted its speculative possibilities on all points of principle. The XIXth Century was unable to make any important advances within the framework of the traditional doctrine. To this extent the later empiricism is indeed the work of thinkers who are far below their predecessors and is wanting in all true originality and power of creative thought. But the men of this philosophic generation, though inferior to its predecessors, are no mere copyists or commentators, they are not men who live upon inherited wealth and consume it; they employ themselves rather in a careful and fruitful management of their wealth; they put out their inherited capital to interest. Thus, although no real speculative results were achieved, important new positive values were created. These consist mainly in progress in differentiating and distinguishing problems, in refining methods of investigation, and finally in a vast expansion and enrichment of the empirical material and in the opening up of new fields of inquiry. This later phase of the empirical movement becomes for the first time hungry for experience in the true sense of the word. It collects eagerly masses of new material, arranges and classifies, methodizes and systematizes; in short, tries to apprehend and deal with them philosophically. But when philosophy surrenders itself in this measure to experience, it runs the risk of being mastered by it, instead of mastering it. Thus it becomes ever more forced away from the central problems, and its main interests are deflected to outlying matters. This is shown in a slackening of the properly speculative impulse, in renunciation of constructive system, in a negative attitude to the problems of metaphysics, in the transformation of theory of knowledge into psychology, and of logic into methodology and in the primacy of action. Thus modern empiricism is a movement which is extensive rather than intensive; broad rather than deep. Although this is a disadvantage upon the whole, in one sense it is an advantage. For it has done excellent service in conquering new material and provinces of inquiry. It is to the XIXth Century also that we owe a well-worked-out system of empirical logic, whereas the classical period had produced nothing more than a few suggestions, combined with a general theory of science and a methodology of knowledge which till then had been almost completely neglected. In ethics also there is now achieved for the first time a strict systematization of what in the earlier ethical doctrine had been apprehended indeed, but never reduced to a firm and permanent shape. This holds good less strikingly for psychology; while the work done in theory of knowledge in general shows a definite regress as compared with the earlier. On the other hand, new ground was broken in the spheres of law, politics, social life, education, and others belonging to practice.

Apart from the evolutionist school which will be dealt with in the next section, the main figures of modern empiricism are Bentham, James Mill, and John Stuart Mill. Upon these three thinkers rests the chief burden of the movement and in them is embodied the inheritance of the British tradition in its best and most penetrating form. Although Jeremy Bentham (1748–

1832) goes back a long way into the XVIIIth Century both in regard to his intellectual education and to his literary activity, he belongs in regard to his philosophic influence to the XIXth Century. In him we see the earliest representative of what we term modern empiricism. His work lies exclusively in the field of practical philosophy; in the first place in ethics and then in all the departments of study which are based on ethics, such as politics, social reform, legislation, jurisprudence (especially penology), international law, and education. In all these spheres he was a radical innovator and revolutionary, and by him the English thought of the XIXth Century was fertilized more deeply and shaped more intensively than by any other man. Herein he continues and revives those liberal-democratic and utilitarian views established by Locke, by which the century was dominated. No other philosopher's doctrine has had a wider field of influence; none has had more important practical results. He was withal the freest spirit of his age and country. He bowed before no authority and no tradition. He emancipated himself from all bonds of State, Church, constitution, and traditional law; from inveterate prejudices and rigid customs. He was the greatest questioner of the established order of things, both of doctrines and of institutions, the most ruthless transvaluer of traditional values, the severest critic of dead conventions; in short the 'radical philosopher' or 'philosophic radical', as his contemporaries called him. He is the founder of a new political and social ideology which in many respects is akin to that invented later by Karl Marx and may be said to have anticipated it, although it grew out of very different logical assumptions, and is, much more than Marx's ideology, based upon a popular appeal. His ideas, although they were organized into a strict doctrinal system, never aimed at mere instruction, but at the practical purpose of changing and improving existent things. Falling far and wide upon fruitful soil, they were seized upon gladly and enthusiastically by his contemporaries. Everything, in fact, which was current in England at that time among progressive liberal thinkers was attracted by Bentham's doctrine as by a powerful magnet. Thus for the first time upon British soil, rather by the diligence of pupils than by any particular concern of the master, there was established an ambitious school of philosophic training. The only parallels to it were the much feebler efforts in a similar direction by the thinkers of the XVIIth Century who formed the 'School of Cambridge' and later by the thinkers grouped around Reid. The ideas of the master were taken up by a number of diligent and devoted pupils, commented on, diffused, and applied in many and various directions. Finally they were erected into a political programme, and a political party (known under the name of 'philosophic radicals') was established to carry them out, with a literary organ to diffuse them. Therewith the doctrine transformed itself into propaganda and even entered Parliament, the proper place for transforming ideas into realities. Bentham himself did not come before the public; he lived in quiet retirement engaged in elaborating his system and left everything else to his followers. How much of his ideas was realized in this way by the great legislative reforms of the 'thirties it is not easy to say exactly. But that the spirit of his ideas infused itself into them and contributed considerably to their accomplishment is generally recognized to-day.

In the history of philosophy Bentham figures as the creator and founder of the ethical system of utilitarianism. But he is certainly not the inventor of utility as an ethical principle. This penetrates the moral doctrine of the English and French Enlightenment and is occasionally formulated and applied there. Bentham suddenly received the new insight which lighted up his thinking like a lightning flash on reading the third volume of Hume's *Treatise of Human Nature*. In his own words scales fell from his eyes, when the high importance of the idea of utility for human conduct first flashed upon him. In this creative moment the bridge was established from the classical tradition to its modern revival. Bentham's great historical service consists in this, that he took a firm hold upon this idea, made it the basic principle of his thinking and the main pillar of his system, that he built up this system with vast energy and perseverance and supplied it with an inexhaustible wealth of empirical material. There is hardly any other system of thought in which a single principle is thus thoroughly systematized and established by a wealth of experience as it is by Bentham. For not only the masses of empirical material, which he brought under his main theoretic principle, but the principle itself was also a result gained from experience. Herein we can see the sharp contrast in which this doctrine stands to the views of the Scottish school to which it was historically opposed. On one side there are *a priori* principles, innate in human nature and established as immediately evident by intuitive knowledge, on which our judgments of value rest. On the other side there is the simple thought, which is confirmed by innumerable experiences and may be verified at any moment, that all human conduct is determined by and filled with striving to obtain pleasure and to avoid pain. How Bentham from this elementary principle arrived at the universal application of the principle of utility and from thence at his famous ethical formula of the "greatest happiness of the greatest number", how he advanced to the qualification of the whole moral life and thence to the establishment of a balance of pleasure and pain in human conduct or to the so-called hedonistic calculus, how he applied these ideas to the most diverse spheres of practical life, especially to politics and social reform—none of this can be followed out further here. It must suffice to mention that he tried to bring the whole sphere of human action (both individual and social) under a single dominant principle which is all-embracing, applied with ruthless consistency and brutal disregard of counter-arguments. In this way he tried to get a rational view of the confusing multiplicity of moral phenomena and to subordinate them to a strictly reasoned system. Thus ethics (together with the other practical departments of study) was to be raised for the first time to the rank of a strict science and, like the natural sciences, added to the domain of exact inquiry. The greatness of this conception and of its execution depends upon the radical isolation of one definite and separate aspect with a magnificent neglect of all the others. Out of a complex and many-dimensional field Bentham cuts a single surface and presents it to us with all the apparatus of exact scientific investigation. This was achieved by making the principle of utility the all-important factor and by subjecting the whole moral life to a complete quantification. Thus ethics was divested not only of all qualitative elements, but of all metaphysical, religious, and other conditions, and Bentham even sought to dispense with the psychological foundation which British moralists both before and since have always considered indispensable.

The development of British thought which follows, partly in Bentham's lifetime and partly after it, is influenced entirely by the powerful, well-established, and logical system of utilitarianism. But it was inevitable that this system, which claimed to be final, should decline into dogmatism, and instead of setting minds free, should put a crippling constraint upon all who fell within its influence. For a long time, apart from the followers of the Scottish school and a few minor thinkers and eccentrics, utilitarianism claimed the adhesion of almost the whole body of English philosophers and workers in philosophy. The great problems of life and thought seemed here to be finally solved, and no room was left for the free development of philosophic powers, except for the ever more minute and detailed extension of the basic principle, and for its application to wide provinces. In moral philosophy Bentham seemed to have spoken the last word, and, as metaphysical and religious problems were completely set aside by him, the wings of speculation were clipped. The stiff orthodoxy of the school of Bentham thus came to form the strongest hindrance to further philosophic progress.

Of those contemporaries of Bentham who made independent contributions and, without being directly pledged to follow him, moved along the paths of utilitarian thought, we must mention at least Godwin, Malthus, and Ricardo. All three belong less to the philosophic movement in the proper sense than to that spiritual *milieu* which draws its nourishment from philosophy and in turn enriches philosophy. William Godwin

(1756–1836), whose famous and striking book *An Enquiry Concerning Political Justice* (1793) is the chief of his writings to be mentioned here, is a more radical and uncompromising assailant of the existing social order even than Bentham himself. He was under the direct influence of the wave of the French Revolution and is the first systematic revolutionary among British thinkers. He also regards pleasure and happiness as the motives of human action and like Bentham he demands their maximization in order to obtain the ideal Utopian condition of society to which he aspires. Reason, which he invests with sovereign rights, is for him the sole guide and liberator of man from political oppression and religious servitude. His fanatical faith in progress, his anarchism, his zeal against priestcraft and those who delude the people, his humanitarian and cosmopolitan dream of human happiness, his deification of reason, his attack upon social institutions and current ethical ideas, were all drawn from the spiritual armoury of the Enlightenment and the Revolution. By Godwin they were brought together into a closely reasoned system of thought, and as they were presented with passionate feeling, they shook men's minds with immense power, above all those of the romantic poets. Coleridge and Wordsworth, Southey and Shelley, and many others succumbed to the charm of Godwin's doctrine and saw themselves compelled to come to terms with it, in part to free themselves from it, in part to be engulfed by it.

Godwin's soaring Utopian views were attacked by THOMAS R. MALTHUS (1766–1834) in his noteworthy and notorious *Essay on the Principle of Population* (first published in 1798) which brought the matter back on to the ground of sober fact. His theory of population, which immediately on its first appearance unloosed a storm of indignation and a flood of replies, was aimed in the first place against the delusion of progress and of the ever-increasing perfectibility of man and society which was characteristic of the Enlightenment. It aimed at showing that the realization of such dreams of happiness was shattered against the iron law which the problem of population reveals to us: to the effect that population increases much faster than the means of support. Accordingly we can expect no progressive increase of happiness, but on the contrary an increase of individual and social misery due to these conditions. Malthus's doctrine, which in its consequences concurred with Bentham's line of thought, became at once a component of the utilitarian doctrine, and gave a powerful though depressing impulse to English economic thinking which left its traces in practical legislation. As a living force it maintained itself at least till after the middle of the century. Historically it was more influenced by A. Tucker and W. Paley than by Bentham; not to speak of Hume, to whose ideas on population it owed much, as Malthus himself gratefully acknowledged. Later Darwin borrowed from it the pregnant idea of the struggle for existence (the term itself occurs in Malthus) and thus obtained the point of view which dominated his biological researches.

David Ricardo (1772–1823) with strict adherence to principle and with much wider application than Malthus developed the economic doctrine of utilitarianism in his *Principles of Political Economy and Taxation* (1817). Any estimate of the surpassing importance of this book, which is a landmark in the history of British political economy, or any examination of the doctrine contained in it lies outside our present scope. It was surpassed only by the classical work of Adam Smith, with which it is closely connected, carrying on its line of thought into the XIXth Century in an independent form. Ricardo stood, mainly through the mediation of James Mill, in closer connection with Bentham's ideas than did Malthus, with whose social and political views he essentially agreed. The economic thinking of the XIXth Century, especially that of Marx, owes its basic ideas to him, and his views later became increasingly the commonplaces of the theoretic study of economic laws and facts.

After Bentham, the main stream of utilitarian thought is continued directly in James Mill (1773–1836). He is the young protégé, friend and ally of Bentham, whose doctrine he takes over and carries on like a confession of faith. He forms a bridge from the refounder of empiricism to its completer: from Bentham to his own son John Stuart Mill. Thus his position is mainly a mediating one. It is his task to guard the inheritance in order to hand it on pure and unadulterated into the hands of his greater son and successor. He was the most vocal herald and most zealous propagandist of Benthamite ideas. Round him mainly there grouped themselves those 'philosophic Radicals' who worked for the renovation of English political life in the spirit of Bentham. His literary activity directed itself mainly upon moral philosophy and the practical studies cognate with it; upon history, jurisprudence, theory of the State, politics, and political economy, in which latter study he professed himself to be the immediate follower of Ricardo. In all these provinces he drew upon the ideas of the school, which had passed into his bones and which he felt no need to question. To the utilitarian formula of the greatest happiness of the greatest number he adhered with the enthusiasm and zeal of an initiated disciple.

In one respect, however, he performed an important and necessary service for the cause of the school. Bentham had taken next to no trouble about the theoretic foundation of his doctrine, and thus there was a gap in his system which needed to be filled, especially as the opposing Scottish school had produced works of high merit which could be neutralized only by works of equal merit from the other side. Mill undertook this task in his most important book *Analysis of the Phenomena of the Human Mind* (1829, new edition by J. S. Mill, 1869). In it he laid the psychological foundation of the utilitarian doctrine. Apart from its function as a foundation, Mill's psychology has a special historical importance. For such a foundation it was necessary to have recourse to the older empirical ideas, and accordingly Mill had to pick up or effect a junction with the thread of development at the point where it had been broken by the Scottish thinkers half a century before, that is, with the association-psychology of the older classical school. Thus Mill's psychology shaped itself by recurring to the doctrines of Hume and Hartley and therefore in express opposition to the intuitionism of the Scottish school. He gave currency again to the mechanism of the mind, introduced once more the anatomizing method and with it psychic chemistry, held firmly to the analysis of mental phenomena into their simplest parts (psychic atoms), revived the law of association as the basic law of psychic life and the phenomenalist view in the theory of knowledge, and thus called afresh into existence the whole stock of ideas belonging to the classical philosophic theory. He drew nearer to Hartley than to Locke and Hume, but refrained from all physiological explanations and confined himself to the simple exploration of consciousness. He had a keen eye for analysis, kept a firm grasp upon his main principle of association, refined his method, strengthened his system, and brought in new empirical material, but never abandoned in any essential point the foundations consecrated by tradition. Here again, Mill played his characteristic part of mediator by doing the same service for theoretical studies that Bentham had done for practice, i.e. renovating thought with the spirit of classical British philosophy. His historical importance lies in the fact that he gave to psychology and theory of knowledge a stimulus which involved a long series of further results and remained vigorous at least till near the end of the century.

The work of John Stuart Mill, the greatest empiricist thinker of the XIXth Century, grew organically out of the philosophic situation created by Bentham and J. Mill. Before we pass on to him it is necessary to mention the names of some men who were born between the elder and the younger Mill and are also closely connected with them. Among the closer friends of the Mills, at first intimate with the father and later standing in paternal friendship with the son, were the jurist John Austin (1790–1859), and the historian George Grote, brother of the philosopher, John Grote, who will be mentioned later. Austin, for some years Professor of Law in the University of London, undertook a stricter systematization of the province of law from the utilitarian standpoint, and in his influential book *The Province of Jurisprudence determined* (1832) laid the foundations of a philosophy of law.[1] But his affiliation to the utilitarian circle was complicated by influences coming to him from the historical school of law and the German romantics; since in his later twenties he made a long stay as a student in Heidelberg and Bonn, where he formed acquaintance with men like Savigny, A. W. Schlegel, Brandis, and others. In this way his thought gained a wider outlook beyond the orthodox limits of Benthamism; and this showed itself in many ways, not the least being that he based the ethics of utility not upon utility itself, but tried to support it by religious sanctions. Grote, famous as the historian of Greece, had from the first more sympathy with the views of the elder Mill than Austin, and joined Mill energetically in the reforming efforts of philosophic radicalism, which he also represented in Parliament. But his system of thought was fed from other sources, above all from Greek philosophy, with which he was thoroughly acquainted (as witness his works on Plato and Aristotle). In his posthumous *Fragments on Ethical Subjects* (1876), his only systematic work, he tried to establish the social character of morality more effectively than the utilitarians had done with their predominantly individualistic views, emphasizing the primacy of society over the individual and the individual's duty to subordinate himself to the collective will of the community.

Beside Austin and Grote we may mention here SIR JOHN HERSCHEL (1792–1871) and WILLIAM WHEWELL (1794–1866). Though far away from Bentham's circle, they did important work in preparation for the logical inquiries of the younger Mill. In the *Discourse on the Study of Natural Philosophy* (1830) by Herschel, the great astronomer, Mill found not only abundant documentary material taken from the natural sciences for describing the processes of induction, but he saw here his own empirical method implicitly at work, though not yet explicitly explained. Still more valuable for him were the comprehensive researches of Whewell, based upon thorough knowledge of the theory and history of the inductive sciences

[1] From his papers were published after his death *Lectures on Jurisprudence, or the Philosophy of Positive Law* (1863).

as set forth in his two monumental works *History of the Inductive Sciences* (1837, German translation 1839–42) and *Philosophy of the Inductive Sciences* (1840). Whewell possessed a quite stupendous knowledge of the past, and in the range and thoroughness of his encyclopaedic learning surpassed even Hamilton himself, who had the reputation of being the most learned man of his time. In preparing the third book of his *Logic* ("On Induction"), Mill made full use of the material accumulated by Whewell and gratefully acknowledged that without this preliminary work he could not have been equal to his task. But at the same time he felt with sure instinct the definite methodological contrast which separated him from Whewell. In him he saw a representative of what he called the German or *a priori* view of human knowledge and its capacities. Whewell was, in fact, strongly influenced by Kant and rejected the empirical logic and theory of knowledge. Like Mill he recognized the fundamental importance which belongs to induction as the process of deducing general truths and principles from particular facts in all scientific investigation and discovery. And therefore he called 'inductive' those sciences which are usually called 'natural sciences.' In them he did not put the sole emphasis upon the observation of facts, but regarded as an equally important factor the ideas in forming which understanding plays the main part. It is quite in accordance with the Kantian doctrine that perceptions are blind without ideas, while ideas without perceptions are empty, when Whewell in the introduction to the first-mentioned work says that the essential condition of all scientific progress is the union of clear ideas with definite facts. It is called by Whewell the fundamental antithesis of philosophy that the idea must never be independent of observed fact, but that fact must ever be drawn towards the idea. This he expressed aphoristically in the following passage: "The antithesis of *sense* and *ideas* is the foundation of the philosophy of science. No knowledge can exist without the union, no philosophy without the separation, of these two elements" (*Philos. of the Inductive Sciences*, new edition, 1847, vol. ii, p. 443). Whewell's purpose in his two great works was to restore Bacon's *Novum Organum* and to bring Bacon's work up to the advanced level of modern science. Thus the study of the methodological bases of science began with Whewell and was continued directly by Mill's *Logic*, and the controversy which subsequently arose between them proved very fruitful and awakened interest in these questions both in philosophical and in scientific circles.

We come now to JOHN STUART MILL (1806–73), in whom modern empiricism reaches its conclusion, as the classical empiricism reached its conclusion in Hume a century earlier. Many persons think Mill to be the greatest British thinker of the XIXth Century. However this may be, it is certain that he was the greatest philosophic writer of his age. Like Bacon, Hobbes, Locke, Shaftesbury, Berkeley,[1] Hume, Bentham, James Mill, and later Spencer, he never held an academic post, and practised philosophy, not as a merely scientific or learned pursuit, or for the benefit of a small circle of students and experts, but as a spiritual mission to be fulfilled in obedience to an inward call and, as it were, before the eyes of the whole nation. He was the foremost philosophic voice of his time and became one of the series of great literary and creative forces that, like him, have stamped themselves upon the spiritual aspect of England in the XIXth Century. With Mill, more than with his immediate predecessors, philosophy came forth from its previous narrow circle, extended itself till it became an affair of general literature, and thus became the property of the whole intellectual élite of the nation. It was carried on in the forum of a wide and broad publicity, into which it radiates its powers, while in its turn it was strengthened by the influences of the cultural life by which it was surrounded.

In the development of British philosophy, Mill's work stands for the last great synthesis of empiricism. In it all the leading themes of empiricism unite once more into a great harmony. This occurs, not in the form of a well-fitted and strictly regulated system, as with Spencer later; but in that freer style which occupies as many provinces of experience as

[1] [Berkeley was Fellow and Tutor in Trinity College, Dublin.—ED.]

possible, in order to penetrate them with philosophic thought, but not to include them in a comprehensive unity or to subject them to the constraint of an architecturally composed system. The former and not the latter is indeed the true style of empirical philosophizing, which, because it is devoted to experience in all its manifold possibilities, cannot surrender itself directly to a simple basic idea or find satisfaction in the regimentation of a system. Systematized thought, such as later occupies a predominant position with Spencer, is an alien element which it is hard to reconcile with the principles of empiricism. As these principles are held unimpaired by Mill, we may regard him and not Spencer as the last genuine representative of the great British tradition.

This tradition had passed into his bones in early youth. His education was made according to the ideas and under the sole control of his father, far from school and university, strictly in the spirit and according to the principles of the Benthamite philosophy. He himself has described this extraordinary experiment vividly in his *Autobiography* (1873), and it is almost a miracle that he was not ruined by it. The doctrine with which he was thus inoculated under outer compulsion he accepted willingly and in full faith and thus at the age of fifteen he was a finished and perfect utilitarian, who was at home in all the doctrines of the school and had acquired all imaginable sorts of knowledge. He was so completely caught by the system that at the age of sixteen, together with some kindred spirits, he founded a philosophical society, which he called the 'Utilitarian'. It was from this use, apart from isolated earlier applications, that the term gradually gained currency. The word 'utilitarian' which Mill boyishly inscribed upon his banner became for him the symbol of all that he had acquired in philosophy through his father, i.e. the ideas of Bentham and his school.

At the age of twenty Mill was overtaken by a severe spiritual crisis, which must be noticed here, because it determined all his future life and for the first time emancipated what had been so far repressed by his artificial education, his own native character. This crisis, especially in the fruitful effects which it produced later, implied nothing else than a reaction against the doctrinaire narrowness and stuffiness of the views in which his education had imprisoned him. Already he showed a certain reaction against the eudaemonist theory of happiness, the determinist ethics, and the tyranny of the understanding. For the first time he became aware of the high importance of art and poetry as cultural influences, for the first time he recognized the need for the education of the emotions and the imagination as well as of the merely theoretic faculty of understanding; and the value of the inner culture of the individual soul besides the mere arrangement of external conditions. The new world, which now poured in upon him and which enabled him to overcome his deep spiritual shock, was first disclosed to him by his absorption in the poetry of Wordsworth. Later many helps came from other sides; at first from his occupation with the genius of Goethe, then from his acquaintance with the great romantic poet and thinker Coleridge, with whom he came into touch both through his own reading and by friendly intercourse with enthusiastic young friends of Coleridge such as Frederick D. Maurice and John Sterling, the friend of Carlyle who died young; and finally from Carlyle himself, who had then begun to reveal the spiritual world of Germany to his countrymen. By him Mill felt himself partly attracted, partly repelled. Although resisting, he could not wholly withdraw himself from his influence, which was responsible not only for the direction in which his thought was now moving, but also for the limitations within which it remained enclosed. One thing was certain to him, that he had now parted irrevocably with his father's mode of thinking.

All this was made clear in two important papers which Mill published in 1838 and 1840 in the *Westminster Review*; the first devoted to Bentham, the second to Coleridge (both included later in the first volume of *Dissertations and Discussions*, 1859). These essays deserve special attention, because in them Mill was one of the first to set forth the decisive contrast by which the spiritual life of his time was divided into two sharply opposed camps. This contrast on one side was embodied and symbolized in Bentham, who continued the traditions of the XVIIIth Century, and on the other side in Coleridge, in whom the new spiritual forces which had appeared in the XIXth Century concentrated themselves and pressed for utterance. Mill, who by origin, environment, and education was pledged to the world of Bentham and later was moved profoundly by that of Coleridge, felt the polar tensions which discharged themselves in the bearers of these two names and the dialectical forces which came to expression in them. He recognized with keen sagacity the absolute opposition between their ideas and views of life ("every Englishman to-day is by implication either a Benthamite or Coleridgian"), and he described them, on the whole correctly, by saying that Coleridge's doctrine is ontological, conservative, religious, concrete, historical, and poetic, while Bentham's is experimental, innovative, infidel, abstract, matter-of-fact, and essentially prosaic. In a wider sense he viewed the contrast as that between the XVIIIth and XIXth Centuries, or as that between the Enlightenment and the romantic period, or again as that between the British and German spirit. At the same time he felt the necessity of reconciling these contrasts with one another and balancing their tensions, and an inner call to try to effect a synthesis of them, in the conviction that "whoever could master the premises and combine the methods of both would possess the entire English philosophy of the age".

The shock which he received from Coleridge, whom Mill rightly regarded as the English interpreter of German idealism, had temporarily at least the result of carrying him far from the dogmas of Bentham's school. In the essay on Bentham he discussed the master's system and pointed out the mistakes and inadequacies of his doctrine. He dissociated himself, as he said later, "emphatically from the narrow-hearted Benthamism of his early writings". He saw plainly that Bentham's philosophy had touched only the surface of things and that the deeper and finer aspects of life remained hidden from it. These Coleridge had brought to light and from him, therefore, Mill sought enlightenment on those decisive questions in which, as he believed, he had renounced the traditional way of thinking. If now we survey Mill's later work in his chief books, all of which belong to a time *subsequent* to these two essays, the question arises to what extent the impulse from Coleridge proved fruitful and how far his standpoint was changed by it. The right answer to this question will at the same time put Mill's historical position in its true light.

First it must be said that the impulse from Coleridge, as we might briefly term the opening of Mill's mind to the currents of thought springing from Idealism and Romanticism, reached its highest point with the composition of these essays, and that in Mill's later thought there was no enhancement of its power, but rather a weakening of it. Mill himself was under this impression when towards the end of his life he looked back over this phase of his development (in his *Autobiography*) and observed that at that period he had mistakenly emphasized too much the favourable side of one line of thought (Coleridge) and the unfavourable side of the other (Bentham). Often, later, he affirmed his solidarity with the ideas of the XVIIIth Century against which he had at that time experienced a certain reaction, but had never completely given up. It is a remarkable fact that though he was introduced by Coleridge, Carlyle, and others to the world of German thought, Mill never exerted himself to master the German philosophic systems. In this respect he was far inferior to his older contemporary Hamilton. It is true that he was superficially acquainted with the poetry of Goethe and the educational theories of Pestalozzi, and later came into contact with Wilhelm von Humboldt. But what he knew of the German philosophic movement from Kant to Hegel was derived almost exclusively from hearsay, and did not get beyond some confused and vague ideas. Here Mill, whose freer spirit was in other respects widely accessible to outside influences, persisted in that insularity which is characteristic of so many British thinkers. Wherever he suspected German influences, he set himself against them and depreciated them in favour of his national tradition. German philosophy was to him a book with seven seals whose secrets he felt not the smallest desire to discover.

Nevertheless, Coleridge's impulse did not pass from him without trace. He never definitely broke away from his old associations, or arrived at a real reconciliation of the old with the new ideas. Through him the utilitarian movement became fluid once more, pressed over its narrow boundaries, and burst its dogmatic shell. Although it did not conquer much new country, it became conscious of its own limits, and there arose in it an anticipation of new ideas and fresh philosophic life. One cannot say that there was a radical renovation, but there was an important change in the traditional doctrine; a change which did not surrender the old doctrine in any important point but at many points shook it, and occasionally altered it to such an extent that it would no longer fit into the former framework. With Mill, as Paul Hensel justly says (vide *Kleine Schriften und Vorträge*, 1930, pp. 139 seq.), many ideas sprang into activity from within the fixed forms of traditional doctrine which went far beyond what these forms could include. "His whole life was a manly struggle to force his rich and individual character into the Procrustean bed of a narrow system" (ibid.).

Mill manifested his superiority to most of his contemporaries in the fact that he was willing to learn from everyone (with the exception of German philosophers) who had anything to say to him. His thinking shows almost always that conciliatory spirit which is ready to mediate between opposing schools of thought and to allow contradictory arguments to act upon each other.

As we have seen, Mill's philosophy sprang from the soil of British tradition. As an assumed possession he first takes over in ethics the utilitarianism of Bentham, in psychology and theory of knowledge the doctrines of his father, in political economy the theories of Malthus and Ricardo, in metaphysics and religion the agnosticism which was common to them all. Next from outside comes that new system of ideas which is embodied in Coleridge and Carlyle. This his philosophy, though it was shaken by it, was never able to assimilate. Another school with which rather later (*circa* 1840) Mill's philosophy comes into contact is the French positivism of St. Simon and his great pupil Comte. It was better suited than the other to Mill's way of thinking and was therefore quickly apprehended and easily assimilated. His relations with Comte, which took a personal form by exchange of letters, led to a thorough union of the two systems. Thence sprang a philosophic combination which rested on the similarity of aim and inner kinship of their views. In Mill English Empiricism and French Positivism flowed together in one wide channel. Nevertheless, from the last phase of Comte's thought Mill turned away disappointed. In its pseudo-religious rigidity he thought that the freedom of philosophic inquiry was endangered, and felt compelled to reject it. But it is the German and the Scottish schools that throughout are the main opponents.

Mill takes little notice of the deep differences between the two schools. He sees only their common opposition to his own methods. Thus the whole philosophy of his age presents itself to him under the single aspect of a tension between the German-Scottish and the British group, or between the transcendental philosophy of Kant, the common-sense theory of Reid, and Hamilton's doctrine which sprang from their union on the one side and empiricism on the other side. He finds himself continually in conflict with everything which does not spring from experience or cannot be verified through experience; against innate ideas, *a priori* truths, and intuitive certainties, whether in knowledge or ethics or anywhere else. Under this he includes everything which is supposed to be part of the secure property of healthy human understanding and therefore all those basic elements and principles of human nature which Reid's analysis had brought to light. Apriorism in all its varieties is for him nothing but a great *asylum ignorantiae*, which he makes responsible for the corruption of all true science and of all honest philosophic inquiry. In his own time the doctrine of Hamilton stood as the strongest bulwark of this intuitionist philosophy, and against it and its powerful influence he prepared himself for a final struggle. Mill's polemical book against Hamilton (1865) is the last phase of this long conflict between the opposing schools in Great Britain, and with it the strife is buried. It ends with the complete overthrow of the adversary and the triumphant affirmation of Empiricism.

Mill's work in the several departments of philosophy can be noticed here only very summarily. In the first place—not only on respect of time, but in respect of their importance—stand his services to logic. To him and no one else does Empiricism owe the establishment and development of its logical theory. Compared with him the work of his predecessors is hardly appreciable.[1] It is true that Hobbes, Locke, and Hume built the foundations, but Mill was the first to raise the edifice. He subjected the whole area of this province to a thorough systematization and, Bacon apart, he was in the main the first to make the logical foundations of the exact sciences a matter of inquiry. He makes an epoch in the history of logic, not only as regards the new methodical foundation of this study, but also as regards the vast extension of its field of work. All subsequent logic, so far as it did not move along the familiar lines of the Aristotelian tradition or follow idealist-metaphysical or mathematical paths, is more or less indebted to him. But even the traditional and idealist systems were spurred by him to new reflection upon the basis of their method. Through Mill the psychological tendency in logic gained the upper hand for many decades and its predominance was not broken till Husserl's epoch-making inquiries about the end of the century. All inquiries into the theory and method of science take their

[1] The only man who before Mill and Whewell gave a decided impulse to the study of logic, which was so much neglected all through the XVIIIth Century, was Richard Whately, Archbishop of Dublin (1787–1863). In 1826 he published his *Elements of Logic*, which went through many editions. It is a textbook of formal logic on the lines of the traditional doctrine, treating the forms and rules of inference, with special attention to fallacies. But it was merely the revival of interest in logical problems for which Mill's work was indebted to him, not for any definite suggestions from his teaching. On other logical works of the first half of the century see p. 705.

start mainly from Mill, and however far they may have departed from him subsequently, are indebted to him for their beginnings. Mill has added a whole new area to the frame of logical science in his doctrine of the method of forming scientific concepts and of exact inquiry generally. His logic of the natural sciences, which is developed in the fundamental sections on induction, is, as compared with all previous attempts of this kind, the most systematic treatment of this field, to which he added the first attempt to form a logic of the mental sciences. It is true that he was not yet able to recognize the essential differences between the methods of the two; and that he overemphasized the claim of natural science to supremacy. But he saw that there was an important logical problem here, and he was one of the first to include in the domain of logic a group of sciences which had been almost completely neglected by logicians. These facts should not be forgotten by later logicians and writers on the methods of mental science, many of whom to-day show scant respect for Mill's work. He tries to solve this problem by regarding the procedure of mental science as being strictly parallel to that of natural science; through such a parallelism alone does he think that mental studies can be made strictly scientific. In general, Mill's *Logic* (which first appeared in two volumes in 1843 under the title *A System of Logic, Ratiocinative and Inductive*) is the strictest and most comprehensive application of the principles of Empiricism which has been carried out in Great Britain. Mill has driven apriorism from its last and strongest positions and has not shrunk from drawing the most radical conclusions. Thus he goes far beyond all his predecessors, even beyond Hume. They had not ventured to attack the autonomy of logic in this place or that; they had shrunk from interfering with certain provinces consecrated by centuries of tradition. But Mill made a clean sweep. He explained the logical axioms themselves and mathematical propositions as being nothing but inductions from experience. "We see no reason to believe that there can be any object of our knowledge, whether our experience or what may be inferred from our experience by analogy, or that there is any idea, feeling, or power in the human mind which needs for its justification and its origin to be referred to any other source than to experience." This leading theme rings like a great basic harmony through the whole of Mill's *Logic*.

In the *theory of knowledge* also Mill tries to establish the empirical-psychological standpoint in its full logical purity, mainly and with comprehensive argument in his second philosophic work, his *Examination of Sir William Hamilton's Philosophy* (1865). It is the basic work of modern Empiricism on the theory of knowledge as James Mill's *Analysis* is on psychology. Mill's capacity for clear, fluent presentation and for practical, critical controversy here reaches its highest development. His doctrine of knowledge, however, is much below his logic in philosophic importance. Here there was no new province to conquer; but only a field to be cultivated anew which had already been occupied intensively by the classical representatives of Empiricism, whose work he was able to utilize. In the main he recurs to the old ideas of Berkeley and Hume, and reaches some new formulations, but no real additions to knowledge. His standpoint is that of a strictly articulated phenomenalism, the most important doctrines of which are those concerning the nature of matter and mind. The solution of the problem of the external world (or of matter) is found by him in the effort to avoid crude sensationalism, in the well-known formula of 'permanent possibilities of sensation.' Not the sensations which are immediately present to consciousness and are continually in flux and wanting in all duration and permanence, but the fact that under given conditions we expect certain sensations as possible and that these possible sensations possess stability and permanence, this seems to him to be the key to the problem. But he is not aware that the concepts 'possibility' and 'permanence' presuppose an objective arrangement of things and that therefore strict sensationalism, which dissolves all real being into feelings and their associations, is surrendered in principle. Moreover, the doctrine of the mind or ego is developed upon the same lines. In complete agreement with Hume's bundle-theory, Mill defines mind as the series of our feelings, as they actually appear in consciousness, and he extends this theory only in so far as he adds to the feelings which present themselves immediately those infinite possibilities of feeling and emotion which need merely certain conditions for their actual presentation; these conditions being always present as possibilities whether they actually occur or not. Yet he notices the remarkable fact that this bundle of feelings is aware of itself as past or future, so that we must either regard the ego as a something different in principle from a series of feelings or possibilities of feeling or must accept the paradox that something which *ex hypothesi* is merely a series of feelings can be aware of itself as a series. Mill can neither solve this paradox nor make up his mind to revise the bundle-theory in favour of a doctrine of the ego as a spiritual principle of unity. He contents himself with observing this mysterious fact, and renounces any attempt to explain it. In any case his dead stop in face of this and of other problems shows that he often had to suppress violently the illumination of his own better insight, in order to remain faithful to the traditional doctrine of his school. Though he viewed this with increasing mistrust, he never came either here or elsewhere really to break through the crust of tradition.

He failed to do so in his *Ethics*, developed mainly in his *Utilitarianism*, 1863, which must now be briefly described. Here also Mill starts from the radically utilitarian doctrine of Bentham and his own father, but, without completely giving up the principle of utility, arrives in the course of his development at a much more refined and less repellent moral theory. One may say that Mill transposed the hard and shrill tones of the Benthamite doctrine into a subtler and nobler key. His high ethical sensibility, combined with a finely appreciative feeling for value, failed to find satisfaction in a doctrine which had reduced all human action to a striving for pleasure and happiness and had expressed all feelings of pleasure and happiness in purely quantitative terms. Mill weighs feelings of pleasure and unpleasure against each other, in this respect a true utilitarian. But in his reckoning he includes also qualitative differences, estimating feelings of pleasure not only according to their quantity but according to their higher or lower value. Thus a higher kind of value can outweigh a great quantity of a lower kind, and a man may be regarded as a higher moral character if the higher kinds are more fully developed in him than the lower. When Mill prefers to speak of the welfare of mankind instead of the greatest happiness of the greatest number, when in his ethics he says more about duty and character than about happiness and utility, when he rates the ethical worth of man more highly than mere effort to obtain pleasure, and when finally he plants the ethical ideal in the all-round and harmonious development of personality, he is following out the consequences of that important correction which he made in the basic formula of utilitarianism. Similarly, he softened the extreme individualism of the school by bringing it into harmony with a moderate socialism. It is easy to see that here new wine has been poured into old bottles. The methodological bases are the same as in Mill's predecessors, but the content has been considerably changed. Mill is standing upon the threshold of a new view of life which, bound in the fetters of tradition, he is not able to seize resolutely, but of which he has a lively foreboding.

A glance at Mill's attitude to *metaphysical* and *religious* questions will round off the picture which I have been trying to sketch. His autobiography contains the following impressive passage; "I am one of the very few examples in this country of one who has not thrown off religious belief, but never had it. I grew up in a negative state with regard to it." Much later Mill wrote *Three Essays on Religion* which aroused general surprise when they were published after his death. For in them he no longer maintains his cool sceptical attitude to final questions. He discusses them in a thoroughly speculative manner, although feeling his way cautiously to positive views upon the cosmic order, upon the meaning of suffering in the world, upon the nature of God, and other metaphysical questions. In his careful examination of the path which should lead him from the empirical bases of his thought to the attempt to answer transcendental problems, he shows much sympathy with the idea of a divine world-principle. This he thinks of as a being of the highest moral perfection, but not of infinite power. Thus he finds the idea of a finite God, who in constant struggle against the negative world-principles leads the cosmic process upwards to ever higher development and thus needs the active co-operation of man, to harmonize best both with moral and with religious experience—an idea which has often shown itself fruitful in later times. Although this last phase of Mill's thought cannot be harmonized with the views on these matters which he inherited, it stands in no contradiction to his own philosophic development. It shows the more definite appearance of ideas which were latent in the general course of his thought and were not completely unfolded only because they were repressed by the system which he had inherited.

The most gifted pupil of Mill, who was one of his inner circle of friends and owed his advancement to him, was ALEXANDER BAIN (1818–1903). He was, like the Mills, of Scottish origin and held from 1860–80 the professorship of logic in the University of Aberdeen. Through him and his success as a teacher the newer empirical school received for the first time an academic representation corresponding to its importance and extended itself through the north of the kingdom where so far the Scottish school had held the field, and where recently idealism also had established itself. In Bain, Fraser, whom we may call a rear-guard leader of the Scottish school, and E. Caird the three chief schools of British philosophy in the XIXth Century were for many years represented contemporaneously at the Scottish universities; the Scottish school was in decline, the empirical at its highest point, and the idealist on the upward path.

Bain, who beside his work as a teacher, was active and versatile as a writer on psychology, logic, ethics, education, grammar, and rhetoric, is known mainly for his work on psychology. In his two great and influential works *The Senses and the Intellect* (1855) and *The Emotions and the Will* (1859), in which he treated the whole field of mental life more thoroughly and comprehensively than had ever before been done, he carried forward the direct line of British psychology by attaching his views more to the elder than to the younger Mill, who, while not neglecting this department of study, did not cultivate it systematically. John Stuart Mill himself, whom Bain had helped in the preparation of his *Logic* and with whom Bain later worked in fruitful co-operation, received important assistance from this pupil and regarded him as the proper continuer of his own work.

Although Bain's psychology grew from the tradition of the British school and adheres to it completely both in its methods of inquiry and its philosophical presuppositions, it shows in many respects an advance beyond the former position and points forward to the future period of evolutionism and voluntarism. His close connection with tradition is shown not only by his strong feeling for facts, his regard for the exact sciences, his accumulation and exploitation of great masses of materials of inquiry, but also by his analytic-descriptive method, his maintenance of the principle of association, and finally his rejection of the speculative metaphysics of the soul. In contrast to the two Mills, who limited themselves to the psychology of consciousness, he enlarged the outlook of psychology in the direction of physiology, as Hartley before him had done, though not in Hartley's obscure, half metaphysical, half exact style, but in making full use of the physiological results which were available at that time, especially of those which were furnished by Johannes Müller, putting the whole apparatus of physiology into the service of psychology. The relations of psychic phenomena to their correlates in the brain and nervous system are investigated; the higher psychic processes are referred to their instinctive foundations and organic conditions; and all this is carried through free from any speculative motive and kept within the limits of exact science. But although Bain draws no materialist conclusions and indeed expressly rejects them, he hands over the whole mental life and the whole sphere of consciousness so completely to material processes that he is always in danger of falling into the abyss of materialism, and is only secured from it because he turns psychology into an exact natural science and avoids every philosophic decision. And as Hartley's first attempt to base mental life upon physiological processes had escaped descent into materialism only because of a strong religious faith, so this second attempt of Bain escaped a like fate only because of his preoccupation with strict scientific method.

In important points Bain considerably extended and improved the association-psychology and introduced many new ideas into its rigid scheme. He advanced beyond its preoccupation with intellect by giving full recognition to the emotional factors, the impulses, instincts, affections, etc., and also recognized the decisive importance of the whole sphere of the will for the formation and course of psychic processes. Thus he was the first of his school to make the attempt to break away from the passive mechanics of association and to recognize the activity and spontaneity of mental life. He also tries to escape from the atomizing of the soul by regarding it less as a sum of associated elements than as a fluid process or continuum. In all this he took account of the element of will and of its physiological correlates, and although he is remote from evolutionary views (his first important book appeared at the same time as Spencer's *Principles of Psychology*, his second in the same year as Darwin's *Origin of Species*), he adduced in his explanations both physiological and biological factors, and made use more than hitherto had been done of the genetic method. Further elements of importance are his doctrine of attention, in which stress is laid upon the element of activity, and the revival of Hume's theory of 'belief', and his discussion of the problem of the external world in relation to the theory of knowledge. The external object is for Bain not merely the product of firmly associated series of presentations, which we passively accept, but a factor assumed in our practical behaviour, which releases in us tensional energies and upon its side sets itself in opposition to us. In the subjective feeling of such opposition lies, according to Bain, the root of our belief in an external or transcendent reality. Here also the sensationalist and intellectualist points of view are replaced by the emotional and voluntarist.

Many such details point to the later development of psychology as we have it in Spencer, Wundt, Ward, Stout, and others. Nevertheless, Bain's doctrine remains upon the whole associationist, or at least is always reverting to associationism. With him also as with Mill the fetters of the school show themselves to be stronger than the new insight. It is true that he rattles the fetters, but he cannot break them. For, though he puts the spontaneity of mental life much more in the foreground than anyone before him, it turns out that the source of this spontaneity is to be sought not so much in the soul itself as in such physiological and organic factors as muscular sensations, reflex movements, release of tension, etc., upon which he bases all psychic phenomena. The active character of psychic processes as such or specifically mental energy is never definitely recognized by him.

Bain's service, therefore, consists essentially in the fact that he gave a more modern and progressive turn to the empirical psychology. Compared with this the rest of his work, however serviceable it may have been in his day, is much inferior in historical importance. He is the last considerable representative of the school of Mill who shows a trace of his spirit and more than any other carried that tradition on for a whole generation after Mill's death. For his diligent literary activity extended to the end of the century and his life was prolonged into the new one.

Of Bain's younger contemporaries who still kept up the traditions of the school we may mention Fowler, Croom Robertson, and Sully. The philosophic activity of these successors of great men belongs mainly to the last third of the century and deals with the provinces of logic, theory of knowledge, ethics, and above all psychology. THOMAS FOWLER (1832–1904), president of Corpus Christi College and from 1873 to 1889 Professor of Logic in Oxford, worked Mill's *Logic* into a convenient and much-used textbook (*The Elements of Logic, Deductive and Inductive*, two volumes, 1869), wrote upon the classical empiricism (books on Bacon, Locke, Shaftesbury and Hutcheson) and treated ethical problems both in a popular work (*Progressive Morality*, 1884) and in one of more technical interest (*The Principles of Morals*, first part 1886, second part 1887). In the latter he went back to the ideas of the British moralists of the XVIIIth Century, in trying to distinguish clearly the sanction imposed by moral feeling from those imposed by law, society, and religion. Thereby he sought to establish the autonomy of the ethical sphere, defining that sanction as the feeling of contentment or discontent which we experience when, without any reference to an external authority, we merely reflect upon our own actions. He emphasized the progressive character of morality and ascribed this to the progressive refining and sharpening of moral sensitivity and more to the intellectual than to the emotional elements of the ethical act. Like Mill, he represented a moderate utilitarianism, recognizing the qualitative differences of feelings of pleasure and unpleasure and noticing the incommensurability of higher and lower moral motives. Instead of the coarse principle of utility he put forward the concept of welfare or well-being which he understood precisely in the sense of the Aristotelian *εὐδαιμονία*.

A thinker who was much stronger and less enslaved by tradition was the Scotsman George Croom Robertson (1842–92), a pupil and colleague of Bain in Aberdeen, who had studied in Berlin (under Trendelenburg and Du Bois-Reymond), in Göttingen (under Lotze), and in Paris, and who from 1867 to his death held the philosophical professorship at University College London, of which he was the first occupant. Robertson did good service in establishing and encouraging philosophic study at the universities and was one of the chief philosophic forces of his day, a character which he established as co-founder and for many years editor of *Mind*, by far the most important philosophical organ of the English-speaking world, which owed its foundation in 1876 to the initiative of Bain, and, one may say, is still conducted in the spirit of its first editor. At that time it served the purpose of a meeting-place for the most varied schools of thought. Prepared by his training with Bain, Robertson, who was disinclined to write books,[1] devoted himself mainly to psychology; but undertook not so much an extensive treatment of the whole field of psychic phenomena (as Bain did), as an intensive examination of separate problems. Here he had the advantage of a keen analytic mind and a great gift for criticism, enabling him to produce masterpieces of psychological analysis, such as those on perception, memory, thought-process, volition, etc., which in part went far beyond his teacher. Although he was in general an adherent of empiricism, he did not allow himself to be fettered by school-dogmas, but was always eager to enlarge his mental horizon and to deepen his knowledge of philosophy. He possessed comprehensive and thorough knowledge of the whole field of the history of philosophy and he was well acquainted with the works of the great German thinkers, especially of Kant. He was penetrated with the conviction that the English empirical philosophy needed to be revived with the added deep insight of Kant's *Critique of Reason*, and his own work, especially in regard to theory of knowledge, went mainly in that direction. He had no aversion to metaphysics, and towards the end of his life made an interesting attempt, starting from the basis of empiricism, to reach a cosmology related to Leibniz's monadism though differing from it in many points.

The true continuer of the psychology of Mill and Bain was not Robertson but JAMES SULLY (1842–1923), his successor at University College, London (1892–1903). Sully was not so much a philosopher as a scientific and diligent empirical investigator and observer, and like Bain, whom he closely resembled, he plunged into the full tide of experience, accumulated fresh masses of material or worked over the old in

[1] He himself published only a small but excellent book on Hobbes (1886) and numerous papers and essays in periodicals and collections. After his death most of his articles were published as *Philosophical Remains* (1895), including two volumes of his lectures, the *Elements of General Philosophy* and the *Elements of Psychology*, both in 1896.

accordance with the latest ideas, so widening and extending the old basis without passing beyond it or providing it with a better philosophic foundation. Whatever provinces or objects he dealt with, he always maintained the attitude of the empirical psychologist. Thus, e.g., he discussed the phenomenon of laughter to which he devoted a considerable book (*An Essay on Laughter*, 1902), not like Bergson in a philosophic or metaphysical style, but following it out in the whole breadth of its empirical development, psychological and physiological, anthropological and ethnological, biological and sociological, but unable to produce that "truly philosophic theory" which he regarded as the culmination of all these separate aspects. Much earlier he had dealt in a similar style with the problem of illusion. Here also he contented himself with a "psychological study", handing over the problem for further treatment to the philosophers, to whom the proper solution belonged (*Illusions, a Psychological study*, 1881; German edition 1884). He treated psychology itself according to the principles of Bain physiologically and by the method of association; at first in its outlines (*Outlines of Psychology*, 1884) and then in a comprehensive and exhaustive presentation as the science of the human mind (*The Human Mind*, two volumes, 1892). He regarded it as the foundation of all the knowledge which aims at leading and influencing thought, feeling, and action, and so in imitation of Bain extended it to the theory of education (in the *Outlines* which he wrote "with special reference to the theory of education" and shortly afterwards in the *Teachers' Handbook of Psychology*, 1886, of which a German translation appeared in 1898). Thus also he took up child-psychology (*Studies of Childhood*, 1895) and, in this respect going far beyond Bain and following the tendency of the age, took up also experimental psychology, of the utility of which he was convinced, especially for education. Finally, eager for experience as he was, he turned his attention to aesthetics and thus opened up for empiricism a province which was new or at least much neglected since the XVIIIth Century. But here also he kept to the psychology of aesthetic phenomena and contented himself with classifying, analysing, and describing so that he failed to lead the study into a new or philosophic path but merely applied the old method to a new kind of material (in his article on Aesthetics written for the ninth edition of the *Encyclopaedia Britannica*, 1875, and in some separate papers published in periodicals).

The empirical movement in the writers just mentioned issued mainly in special psychological inquiries. But another branch sprung from its stem, and devoted to the *philosophy of history* may also be mentioned briefly here. Interest in the mental sciences and in their methodical and logical character had been awakened by Mill and simultaneously by Comte. By transferring the strict methods of natural law and causation to the world of political and social history represented by these sciences, those thinkers thought that they were able to interpret their meaning and purpose. They tried to test and so far as possible to justify this idea by actual historical inquiry. This involved the introduction of a philosophic element into the conception of history and therefore an approximation to the historical work of the Enlightenment, which was full of philosophic ideas, especially in Voltaire and Hume. The *History of Greece* (six volumes, 1845–56) of George Grote, the pupil of Bentham and friend of Mill (vide supra, pp. 59 seq.) was written in a philosophic spirit, though not obtrusively so. By far the most talented and important attempt of this kind undertaken in England was made by THOMAS HENRY BUCKLE (1821–62), author of the famous *History of Civilization in England* (the whole work was intended to have fourteen volumes, but only the first two appeared as introduction, 1857 and 1861; German edition by Ritter, no date). Although Buckle was not the pupil of any particular master, he was strongly influenced by positivist ideas. Those of Mill and Comte equally and, earlier, those of the Anglo-French Enlightenment, formed the philosophic background of his interpretation of history. This stands in very close relation with the materialist view. For as its basic thesis it teaches the dependence of spiritual life and all cultural progress upon the physical conditions of the environment; that is, upon the factors of climate, soil, nutrition, etc. This, of course, implies the transference of the methods of natural science to the sciences of history and culture, and Buckle drew the radical conclusions which follow. The world of history is subject to the same strict causal laws as the world of nature. To the uniformity of natural process corresponds the uniformity of human nature, and in the one sphere as in the other everything comes to pass in necessary sequence. What mathematics are for natural sciences, statistics are for history; they are the exact computation of all the factors which produce and determine an historical event or social condition. Buckle was full of a quite fanatical faith in the power of statistics and it is well known what bold conclusions he drew on their evidence. He took less notice of individual personalities and their ostensibly free voluntary actions than of those uniform and general factors which are expressed in the great movements of the masses; the latter and not the former are responsible for the life which is embodied in history and culture. No greater contrast can be imagined than that between Buckle's collectivist and naturalistic way of writing history and the individualist, idealistic, and heroic way of his contemporary Carlyle. In general, Buckle's ideas are drawn from the XVIIIth Century and not without justice was he mocked by his opponents as a child of the Enlightenment a century behind the times. He fought against religion and the Church as the obscurantist forces of history; he had a fanatical belief in progress which he based not upon any hope of a moral improvement in the human race but on the growing extension of knowledge and enlightenment by reason. Although he bound spirit to nature, he believed in the subjection and conquest of nature by spirit, among the peoples by whom, through the increasing rationalization of existence by the exact sciences and by philosophical criticism (to which last he assigned a specially important cultural function) the conditions for development and progress were produced.

Buckle's ambitious, one-sided, and keenly critical interpretation of culture raised a great stir in the intellectual life of

England after the middle of the century and formed one of the strongest ferments in the evolutionist movement which began about that time, though Buckle himself was hardly affected by it. Following him there appeared other attempts at a philosophic interpretation of past epochs, such as W. E. H. LECKY's (1838–1903) *History of the Rise and Influence of the Spirit of Rationalism in Europe* (two volumes, 1865, German edition by Solowicz, second edition 1873), *History of European Morals from Augustus to Charlemagne* (two volumes, 1869), and *History of England in the* 18*th Century* (eight volumes, 1878–90), which are all inspired with the spirit of Buckle. There is also the *History of the Intellectual Development of Europe* (1862) by the scientist John W. Draper, who emigrated to America, and Leslie Stephen's (1832–1904) impressive book *History of English Thought in the* 18*th Century* (two volumes, 1876–81), which is dominated by Buckle's ideas, though it is also influenced by the idea of evolution.

We may also mention two other thinkers who are loosely connected with the school of Mill, and whose doctrines, though they also have been influenced by other ideas, belong in the main to the utilitarian or empirical school, the moralist Henry Sidgwick and the logician and metaphysician Carveth Read.

HENRY SIDGWICK (1838–1900)[1] came into prominence with his *Methods of Ethics*, his earliest (except for a pamphlet) and his most influential writing. It appeared in 1874, a year after the death of Mill and the year which saw the literary first-fruits of the Oxford idealistic movement, namely, Green's *Introductions* to Hume and Wallace's *Logic of Hegel*. Sidgwick's book, which won a considerable reputation, together with his personal presence and teaching, gave to Cambridge a quickening and intensification of philosophical interest comparable with

[1] 1859 Fellow of Trinity College, Cambridge; at first Classical Lecturer; in 1869 became Lecturer in Moral Philosophy; 1883, Professor of Moral Philosophy in the University of Cambridge. A founder and first President of the Society for Psychical Research (1882).

the renaissance effected in Oxford by the disciples of Kant and Hegel. He became the leading spirit of a movement which, while not new in essence, represented a new gathering of forces in favour of a development of the native tradition in philosophy. The impulse he transmitted, later reinforced by Ward, did not indeed give rise to a powerful and relatively determinate doctrine such as went forth from Oxford, but it certainly prepared the way for the outburst of thought after the turn of the century which we associate chiefly with the philosophers of Cambridge. It could be said that he did for ethics what Ward did for psychology; with the difference, however, that whereas Ward opened up a new stage, Sidgwick rather summed up and closed an old one.

The great reputation Sidgwick enjoyed in philosophy throughout the last quarter of the XIXth Century and even later rested entirely on his first book, with which all his other writings put together cannot be compared in importance.[1] Among the several distinguished contributions to ethics made in Britain in the second half of the century it takes a high place and ranks in fact as a classic. Its importance, however, has been overrated. To call it, as has often been done, epoch-making, is to use a threadbare word, and if the epithet is to be allowed it must be made to mean far less than it means when applied within this same period to Mill and Spencer on the one hand and to Green and Bradley on the other. For Sidgwick founded neither a new method nor a new system. The service he did consisted in sifting, ordering, revising, and evaluating an already existing stock of ideas, and in his attempt to bring these into fruitful contact with new ones.

Although some of his writings deal with the most general questions of philosophy, his interest lay almost entirely with

[1] *Principles of Political Economy*, 1883; *Outlines of the History of Ethics*, 1886 (often reprinted); *Elements of Politics*, 1891; *Practical Ethics*, 1898; *Philosophy, its Scope and Relations*, 1902; *Lectures on the Ethics of Green, Spencer, and Martineau*, 1902; *The Development of European Polity*, 1903; *Miscellaneous Essays and Addresses*, 1904; *Lectures on the Philosophy of Kant*, etc., 1905. The last five were edited from his remains.

the more practical problems, with the facts of the moral, economic, social, and political life, and with the methods and categories through which they should be investigated. His primary aim was to make of ethics a self-contained philosophical discipline, free from metaphysical, psychological, and religious prejudices, free also from rhetoric and the motive of edification. For him ethics is not precept but theory. He must be judged less as a champion of old values or as an advocate of new ones than as a cool observer looking at facts as dispassionately as they and his own nature allowed. His philosophical genius was primarily critical and analytical. In the ability and tenacity required to view a problem from the most diverse angles and follow it out through ever subtler analysis and through recurrent objection and counter-objection to its ultimate ramifications, he had scarcely an equal in his day. But this tendency to look at things microscopically hindered him from seeing a problem or field of problems as a whole. Again and again he loses himself in a maze of details, unable to see his way through to any clear conclusions; and his anxiety to avoid partisanship led him to make concessions on all sides, so that the conclusions he did reach were rather compromises than genuine solutions of the problems. In consequence, all his writings, especially his chief one, have a monotonous and tedious effect; they are too irresolute to bring the reader within the grip of compelling thought. His method is akin to that of the special sciences and is the opposite of the synthetic and speculative procedure of the Oxford thinkers. That it influenced the later philosophers of Cambridge can scarcely be doubted: the affinity between it and the method of such thinkers as Moore, McTaggart, and Broad is too close to allow us to suppose that in the same *milieu* it could be due to nothing but accident. His method has to be valued prospectively, unlike the content of his doctrine, which, as we have already noted, marks not the beginning but the end of a period.

He defines ethics as the rational determination of right action on the part of individuals. It is a normative, not a merely positive, science; its realm is that which ought to be as distinguished from that which is, and comprises the ends or dictates that practical reason sets before us. According to Sidgwick only two of the attempts that have been made to formulate the moral ideal can be regarded as rational, that which finds it in happiness and that which finds it in perfection, the former of these having two distinct forms, according as the happiness to be sought is one's own or that of other people. Ethical systems may accordingly be divided into three chief types (each of which has had historical representatives), namely, egoism or egoistic hedonism, utilitarianism or universalistic hedonism, and intuitionism.

Intuitionism is based on the conviction that there are moral axioms, principles whose validity is self-evident; for example, that I ought not to prefer a present good to a future and greater one, or a good of my own to the greater good of another person. Such propositions as that I should tell the truth and keep my promises have not the same directness of evidence, but generally acknowledged principles like prudence, justice, and benevolence include at any rate elements that are directly apprehended. Sidgwick finds intuitionism represented most distinctively by Clarke and Kant. We may add Martineau, whose theory, in its developed form, had not been published when Sidgwick first issued his book. As for hedonism, in distinguishing it sharply into two kinds Sidgwick did an important service. Egoistic hedonism, exemplified by Epicurus, makes one's own pleasure and pain the standard of conduct, supports this view with the psychological theory that the aim of all our action is in fact the securing of pleasure or the avoiding of pain, and adds the claim that pleasure and pain are susceptible of measurement and are commensurable, so that it is possible to set them off against each other and aim at a favourable balance. Utilitarianism, exemplified by Bentham and J. S. Mill, makes the standard of conduct consist in the happiness not of each but of all. In my every action I have to consider the interests of all other persons who may be affected by it. "The greatest happiness of the greatest number" is Bentham's formula. With none of these systems could Sidgwick identify himself. What he sought was a synthesis of so much as seemed to be true in each, though what he reached was only an unsatisfactory compromise. Egoism, in both its ethical and its psychological forms, appealed to him least of all, and in the end he rejected it outright, as contrary to experience and reason alike. With universalistic hedonism, on the other hand, he went a considerable way, but modified it deeply, passing beyond Mill by turning his back on the psychological hedonism on which the latter had rested it and seeking for a quite different ground. His quest lay in the direction of intuitionism, which found the moral end not in empirical induction but in direct rational insight. Whether he was here influenced by the older British moralists such as Clarke and Butler, or rather by Kant and Lotze, has been much disputed. Probably all of them affected him; but any considerable appropriation by Sidgwick of the ethics of German idealism must be ruled out, for he clung to quite essential parts of utilitarianism, only correcting, modifying, and widening this, never cutting himself away from it. Such elements as he did appropriate were only externally linked to, not organically assimilated by, his thought. As an indication of this we may refer to the hostile attitude which the newer British moralists inspired by German idealism quickly adopted towards Sidgwick, and which came to clear expression in Bradley's *Ethical Studies* (1876) and in his special pamphlet *Mr. Sidgwick's Hedonism* (1877), as well as in Green's *Prolegomena to Ethics* (1883), which makes Sidgwick a frequent object of attack. Sidgwick himself was aware of the hostility, and his own inability to do justice to the Oxford school as represented by Green is plainly evident in his posthumously published *Lectures on the Ethics of Green, Spencer, and Martineau*.

Sidgwick's own position, then, in so far as he can be said to have one, tends to be a combination of elements derived from intuitionism and utilitarianism, a reconciliation of rational and empirical ethics, of the two main currents of British moral philosophy which hitherto had been in conflict, or at any rate aloof from each other. He himself called his doctrine utilitarianism—sometimes, more explicitly, utilitarianism on an intuitionist basis—thereby drawing attention to the aspect he wished to emphasize most. It shows virtually no signs of the evolutionism of Spencer, Huxley, Stephen, Alexander, and others, all of whom made their application of the Darwinian idea to ethics after Sidgwick's book had appeared, and though in later editions of this he tried to take account of it, his position even at the end must be called pre-evolutionist or possibly anti-evolutionist. Also in the later editions he rejected the pure intuitionism of Martineau along with the idealism of Green, and these two thinkers together with Spencer became the object of special attack in the posthumously published lectures mentioned above.

In removing utilitarianism from the egoistic hedonism with which it had been connected, Sidgwick left the way open for a rational, intuitionist grounding. Not only did he find it an error of fact to hold that the only end of volition is the attainment of pleasure and the avoidance of pain; he maintained that even if it were it would be impossible to pass, by a sort of induction, from this egoism to the utilitarian principle of universal happiness. For mental facts cannot be made the determinants of ethical norms, what is of what ought to be. The origin of our moral ideas has nothing to do with their validity. With this stress on the idea of oughtness Sidgwick took a decisive step beyond all empirical ethics whatever, though, as usual, he remained in a half-way position, through identifying the object of obligation, the moral ideal, with happiness instead of with duty. It is an ideal apprehended and guaranteed by intuition, possessing a clearness and certainty as great as any possessed by a mathematical axiom, that, as a rational being, I ought to treat others as I think I should be treated under similar circumstances. This is the principle of justice. The principle of prudence—that I should prefer a future good to a present lesser one—and the principle of benevolence —that I should seek my own good only within the frame-work of the general good—are also moral axioms, objects not of induction but of rational intuition. The distinctive utilitarian command to pursue the happiness of all, not of one's self only, clearly rests on the first and last of these three principles. That is, utilitarianism is based on intuitionism, and conversely intuitionism issues in utilitarianism. The two are bound up inseparably with each other.

But utilitarianism has a further support in common sense, in the naïve moral feelings of the ordinary man. It is characteristic of Sidgwick that, despite his rejection of any empiricist determination of the moral ideal, he considered it most important to bring his theoretical views into harmony with practical experience and to avoid any clash with the established order of moral practice. While he held that philosophy must in certain respects transcend and even differ from common opinion, he was convinced that it should never wholly depart from this or contradict it. He therefore tried to show that utilitarianism and common sense are compatible; indeed, that the former is but the precise and systematic formulation of the latter, and the ideal towards which the moral life of mankind has in fact been moving throughout its history. In practice we are unconsciously utilitarian. Philosophical ethics is thus rooted in the empirical facts of the existing moral order, and has no need to go outside this for its norms and ideals. Sidgwick accordingly called the established moral laws "a wonderful product of nature", the "result of a centuries-old growth", and hated nothing so much as "that spirit of revolution" which rebels against and tries to destroy the morality of the settled customs, institutions, and orders of society. He was genuinely conservative, at the furthest remove from Nietzsche's demand for a "transvaluation of all values". In this attachment to the natural products of our historical development and in his reliance on these as important determinants of any reasonable ethical position, Sidgwick embodied the general temper and manner of thinking characteristic of his nation, and takes his place in the long line of British moral philosophers in whose doctrines that way of thinking has again and again been crystallized.

CARVETH READ (1848–1931)[1] is another thinker who moved largely within the limits of the traditional empiricism, though, being untypically speculative-minded, he went beyond it to a metaphysic. In his first two writings, which deal entirely with logic, he was confessedly in very close agreement with the empiricist theories of Mill, Bain, Spencer, and Venn. Logic has as its subject-matter not mere concepts or words but always facts and the relations between these. It is the general science of facts, or, as the later of the two writings defines it, the science of the conditions that must be fulfilled if any judgment that can be proved is to be proved. Read calls this grounding of logical principle on fact materialist logic, to distinguish it from a nominalism like Whately's and a conceptualism like Hamilton's.

In epistemology also Read's position is empiricist, at any rate in the sense that it starts from and returns to experience. It is phenomenalist, after the manner of Hume and Mill, in that it regards the world of experience as consisting entirely of data of consciousness, consciousness containing as well as unifying it. Consciousness is reality in the proper sense, and being the condition of material existence it cannot be derived from or explained in terms of this. In his explanation of things existing before there was a knowing mind to perceive them as what would have been phenomena, had there been a conscious organism present to perceive them, he follows Mill's conception of unperceived entities as permanent possibilities of sensation. It is at this point that his metaphysic begins.[2] The state of the world when there were no phenomena (because there were not yet any organisms endowed with consciousness) is called by Read, Being or absolute reality. But although not within

[1] Studied first at Cambridge, later under Wundt at Leipzig, and under Kuno Fischer at Heidelberg. After lecturing on philosophical, economic, and literary subjects in London to candidates for the Indian Civil Service, he held from 1903 to 1911 the Grote Chair of Philosophy at University College, London.

[2] *The Metaphysics of Nature*, 1905 (second edition, 1908). Also his chapter in *Contemporary British Philosophy*, edited by J. H. Muirhead, First Series, 1924.

consciousness it cannot be thought without consciousness. Reality in general, that is to say, and not merely empirical reality inorganic and organic, is conscious. More precisely, consciousness accompanies Being, and perceived facts are phenomena of Being. Thus an epistemological phenomenalism gives rise to a sort of metaphysical panpsychism.

The diverse constituents of this world-view and their relations to one another cannot be said to satisfy the requirements of philosophical theory. Reality is conceived as composed of three factors: phenomenal, conscious, and transcendent or pure being. The first of these is the world of things in space and time, the world of daily experience and of the sciences. Yet the condition of anything phenomenal—the conscious—is said to be something that comes into existence relatively late, something indissolubly tied down to the phenomenal, to matter. The result is a sharp dualism of mind and body: the latter is an empirical substance, the former an activity of absolute Being, and between them there can be no reciprocal action. Volition cannot be the cause of motion, for these two are made to belong to different orders of existence. What the will effects is a change in Being. Of this change we have a direct awareness, and the same change becomes mediately evident to us in the empirical motion we perceive. Consciousness, therefore, is made a function not strictly of the body it dwells in but of transcendent Being in so far as this manifests itself in the body. The essential nature of this true Being and of its activities is unfathomable by us. If we were to try to determine it more closely we could only do so by attributing to it some of the properties of the consciousness which is its correlative. Read conjecturally attributes to it time (or at least succession), change, co-existence (possibly not as spatial relation), and order or uniformity of change. An empiricist view of the universe clouded over with a speculative metaphysic is what he finally gives us, the weak points of which are obvious—for example, the ambiguity of a consciousness that is at one time genuine awareness and at another a completely indeterminate something attaching to all being whatever; the reduction of the material world to a phenomenal existence in knowing consciousness, and the correlative expansion of this same world beyond consciousness into a world of absolute Being; finally, the mysterious relation left between the phenomenal world and the real world, a relation that exists as it were behind the back of consciousness.

In his *Natural and Social Morals* (1909) he transfers these metaphysical ideas to the sphere of ethics. The principle of unity in this sphere is the original unity of men through brotherhood and co-operation, the fullest satisfaction of all their desires, and the recognition of a supreme end of all their strivings. This supreme good is philosophy in an extended sense, that is, culture. Philosophy is the true realization of human nature, and through it the world comes to a knowledge of itself. Only through self-knowledge can man, as the highest manifestation of conscious life and of empirical being generally, rise to ever higher levels of freedom, nobility, happiness, and wisdom. It is with the fanaticism of a genuine apostle of the Enlightenment that Read expects from the increasing illumination of man through science and philosophy, through active co-operation, and the application of eugenics, the inner liberation of man, his true happiness and salvation. He was one of the relatively few Britons who passionately believed in the efficacy of eugenic measures to stem and reverse the moral as well as the physical degeneration of the nations. This biological interest shows itself further in his latest writing, *The Origin of Man and of his Superstitions* (1920; second edition in two volumes, 1925), which keeps to the field of anthropology.

Read may be said to be the last follower of the old empirical tradition, for his relation to it, though somewhat loose, was genuine and vital. But as early as the time when his philosophical activity was beginning the tradition we have been surveying was on the decline. In J. S. Mill all the several motives and energies of the empirical movement were gathered together. In consequence his death marked a very decisive turning-point, the beginning of a slow but constant dissolution of the view of life and the world which had found in him its last imposing representative. New forces were knocking at the door of British philosophy. Within Mill's lifetime Stirling had raised his voice on behalf of Kant and Hegel, and Mill's eyes were scarcely closed when the idealism of Oxford sent forth the first of its great new works. A new age of thought was thereby inaugurated, which departed consciously from the old native forms and was resolved to seek truth in its own way. An idealism of German origin entered the lists against the British tradition and, especially within the academic circles, wrung from it place after place. But even before the onset of this new philosophical force, while Mill's star still shone brightly, other forces came into play on the side of empiricism, changing its face, giving it a new impetus, and moving it in a new direction. These forces came from the special science of biology. They constituted the great movement let loose by Spencer and Darwin in the 'fifties and 'sixties, a movement which, for all its empiricism, differed so strikingly from the empiricism typified by Bentham and Mill that we must consider it separately.

III

THE EVOLUTIONARY-NATURALIST SCHOOL

We have seen that during the first half of the XIXth Century and for some time afterwards the dominant feature of British philosophy was the antagonism between the Scottish school and the traditional empiricists, and that the latter steadily gained ground. But even before this conflict, with Hamilton and Mill as its last protagonists, had been settled in favour of the latter, a new force, destined to power, had come into play, namely, the doctrines of Spencer and Darwin. It was in the 'fifties that the idea of evolution appeared in philosophy as well as in the special sciences, the decade which saw the death of Hamilton and the rise of Mill to the height of his power. The movement instigated by Spencer and Darwin was connected intimately with what we have regarded as the traditional line of British thought. Although a new and luxuriant shoot, it sprang from the same stock and had its roots in the same soil as the old empiricism. No sharp line can be drawn between it and the movement led by Bentham and Mill; the two lines of thought cross and recross to such an extent that the assignment of a thinker to the evolutionist school can rest on nothing more than the predominance of the new impulse in his philosophy. But the new impulse soon became so powerful that from the 'sixties onwards very few thinkers were able to avoid being moved by it.

It was because the idea of evolution was in the air about the middle of the century that it appeared simultaneously from several independent sources and broke like a hurricane on the entire intellectual life of the day, sweeping everything with it. In the field of philosophy it came from Spencer, in the field of the special sciences from Darwin and Wallace, and in order of publication priority belongs to Spencer. But the emergence of the new principle from widely removed quarters at the same time—the reason of its dramatically swift and unexampled success—makes the question of priority relatively unimportant. The general point of interest is that the alliance which philosophy now entered into with biology proved to be as fruitful as that which was forged with mathematics and physics at the time of Descartes and Newton. Philosophers now appropriated and exploited the results of the special sciences, and scientists passed beyond their proper inquiries to the general philosophical consequences of these; the forces of evolution marching as it were in two columns, at first separately, later united.

Although Spencer was the first to bring the idea of evolution before the public, it was CHARLES DARWIN (1809–82) who gave it its tremendous influence, through his *Origin of Species* (1859). This book, epoch-making in the full sense of the word, was the achievement of a remarkable scientific genius distinguished by a singular combination of acuteness and patience of observation, unswerving loyalty to fact, and power of imaginative synthesis. It created more stir, was more revolutionary, and became more entangled in the strifes of parties than any other scientific discovery of the century, and its influence simply cannot be measured. Some of its details have been superseded and others are still matters of dispute, but as a whole it has entered into and remained an integral part of the patrimony of natural science; indeed, it has overflowed through a thousand channels into our general intellectual life, at its farthest remove providing, in a weakened and distorted form, a quasi-philosophical view of life and the world for the masses of all countries. Darwin himself never assumed the mantle of a philosopher, but he was aware of the revolutionary effect that his theory was bound to have on the discussion of philosophical questions. In later writings (particularly in *The Descent of Man*, 1871) he did himself occasionally bring out some of the philosophical consequences of his ideas, by applying them to psychological and ethical problems, but this was only incidental; the strictly philosophical exploitation of the theory of evolution was never his concern. Darwin was no Darwinian, but remained to the end what he had always been, a simple, retiring, faithful, and conscientious investigator of the phenomena of plant and animal life. It is deeply moving to see him letting the wild waves of Darwinism break over his work while, all unheeding, he continued undeviatingly in his chosen studies.

The elements of his doctrine—the mutability of species, natural selection, the struggle for existence, the survival of the fittest, adaptation to environment, the inheritance of favourable characters, the animal origin of man, and so on—had been severally anticipated in earlier research and speculation, but the gathering of them together into a single impressive picture of the origin and development of living creatures was Darwin's peculiar achievement and merit. For our purpose it is of interest to note that this picture was not built up on purely biological grounds but received a decisive contribution from Malthus's theory of population.[1] It was this that supplied Darwin with his famous notion of the struggle for existence, and it was this notion that enabled him to bring his biological observations and inferences into a unitary system. The service he did to science may be expressed by saying that he divined the biological relevance of Malthus's law that in human communities there is an inverse relation between population and food supply (the former increasing faster than the latter), and brought ample empirical evidence to show that this law holds good in sub-human life, thereby merging under a common principle the whole realm of life. With the general bearing of his theory on the non-biological aspects of man, however, Darwin was little concerned, only now and then touching upon it; for example, its bearing on moral ideas, the genealogy of which he traced back (as later Nietzsche, under his influence) to the evident purposiveness of animal instinct. But the task of referring back again to man the principle which had now been worked out in detail in the living realm below him, and of developing from it a general theory of man's social life and history, was obviously set by Darwin's biological doctrine. The task was taken up by Spencer, Kidd, and others, and was

[1] See above, p. 56.

carried out by them within the general context of Darwin's ideas. Through these thinkers Darwinism bore fruit in ethics, history (especially the history of primitive peoples), sociology, anthropology, and economics; that is, in the sciences distinctively concerned with man.

Once Darwinism had established itself in the biological field and had become an apple of discord throughout the world, the general view of life and the universe implicit in it could no longer be held back. Its triumphal procession was assured. As a philosophy it made the sub-human the measure or norm of the human, regarding the human no longer as having a significance of its own but simply as being the last branch of a genealogical tree reaching back into the animal and plant world. Expressed more generally, it interpreted everything not by the higher but by the lower forms of nature. It was a *naturalism* in that it made sub-human factors more emphatic than cultural ones, a *biologism* in that it construed philosophical questions through biological categories and theories, an *evolutionism* in that it viewed all things as part of a process of upward development, and a *mechanism* because it explained teleological phenomena in terms of mechanical causes and their laws. This view of the universe, varying in points of detail but retaining the same broad lines, fell like an avalanche in the last decades of the century upon every sphere of intellectual life, and became the popular philosophy of the educated, half-educated, and uneducated alike. It roused interest in philosophical problems, carried the discussion of them away from purely professional circles, and provoked to party-strife, in particular mobilizing against itself all those who could see in it nothing but an enemy to religion and morals and all hitherto accepted values. That in Britain it rarely lapsed into crude materialism and had in general a less devastating effect than it had in other countries was due not merely to the conservative temper of the British but also and primarily to a strength and depth of religious tradition greater there perhaps than anywhere else. The Church raised a vehement opposition to the new doctrine, and the strife with it lasted for several decades. In the academic circles of philosophy also it received little welcome, was treated as an outsider, though one against which one had to measure oneself. But the strongest bulwark against the flood of Darwinism was erected by the new school of Idealism, which arose at the very time the flood was rising and gradually secured a dominating position in the universities. In its first stage the idealistic movement looked upon the defeat of Darwinism as its distinctive task; indeed, it often seems as though Kant and Hegel were called in for no other reason than to help the cause of religion in its fight against the new heresy.

Naturalistic evolutionism found its specifically philosophical embodiment in the system of HERBERT SPENCER (1820–1903), a system which formed the culminating point, the fulfilment as well as the terminus of the century, so far as the philosophy that remained loyal to the native tradition is concerned. Spencer dominated the philosophical field in England in the last thirty years or so of the century in much the same way as Mill, Hamilton, Bentham, Reid, and Hume had done in their days. He is one of the few British philosophers whose fame spread beyond Britain in their own lifetime. Indeed, he acquired a universal reputation—in Russia and China and Japan, for example, as well as in Europe and America—and his works were translated into nearly all the languages of developed peoples. He owed this unique success not so much to the intrinsic merit of his writings as to the fact that he brought to a focus the several lines of thought released by the Darwinian theory and skilfully worked them up into an impressive philosophical system. His philosophy was a timely articulation of the prevailing ideas of his day.

His training was as remarkable as the fame that came to him towards the end of his life. After a scanty schooling, at the close of which he spurned the offer of a university education, he became for a short time a teacher in an elementary school, then for some years a railway engineer, and then a journalist, after which he passed to independent authorship. All his attempts to secure a congenial office having failed, he remained an independent writer to the end of his days, exhausting in the composition of his books the little energy that his shattered health left him with. His life simply consumed itself in an heroic struggle to give shape to his philosophical ideas, and it was only through an adamantine endurance and an unshakable belief in his mission that he was able to surmount all difficulties and bring his work to completion. His writings comprise an imposing array of large volumes, a number of shorter treatises, and a mass of essays. His chief work is his *System of Philosophy*, a colossal achievement running to ten volumes. The prospectus of it appeared in 1860, and it was completed after thirty-six years of unremitting toil, an undertaking almost unexampled in the history of philosophy in its comprehensiveness, its consistency of plan, and the greatness of the obstacles it had to confront.[1]

Spencer was a self-made man, in the best sense of the term. Having had no master he had no need to swear by any master's word. No prominent thinker was ever less concerned than he with the ideas of his philosophical predecessors and contemporaries, and so absorbed did he become in his thoughts that he came to occupy a position of splendid isolation in relation to his philosophical environment. The separation was furthered by the fragmentariness of his formal training, in particular by the scantiness of his acquaintance with languages other than his own, a deficiency which he never managed to make good. To the end he remained a self-taught man, unburdened with

[1] The *System* comprised *First Principles*, one vol, 1862; *Principles of Biology*, two vols., 1864–7; *Principles of Psychology*, two vols., 1870–2; *Principles of Sociology*, three vols., 1876–96; and *Principles of Ethics*, two vols., 1892–3. All these appeared in several, usually revised, editions. Before the *System* was definitively planned the *Principles of Psychology* had been published in one vol., 1855. Part I of the *Principles of Ethics* appeared earlier as *The Data of Ethics*, 1879, and Part IV as *Justice*, 1891. Most of his shorter occasional writings are contained in his *Essays, Scientific, Political and Speculative*, three vols., 1858–74.

There is a posthumous *Autobiography*, 1904. The standard *Life* is by D. Duncan, 1908. For a complete list of Spencer's works see *Herbert Spencer's Sociology*, by J. Rumney, 1934.

historical ballast, lacking the deeper culture, and wrapped up in his own problems and ideas. Of the philosophy of Greece and Germany he knew no more than he could glean from friends and from the very imperfect textbooks then current. It is odd that the man who has been thought by many to be the chief philosophical thinker of the nineteenth century should have been virtually untouched by the greatest thinker of the modern period, Immanuel Kant. We are told that his one attempt to penetrate the mysteries of the *Critique of Pure Reason* came to grief after he had got no further than the first few pages. On the other hand he had a fine sense for what was congenial to the spirit of his time, and by incorporating in his system many ideas then in vogue but still, so to speak, only in the air, he became the philosophical mouthpiece of his age. This is why the doctrine of the philosopher who was freer from historical shackles than any other entered, by something at first sight like a trick of history, more integrally than any other philosophical system into its historical context. His subjective isolation was transformed into its opposite, into a natural, automatic, inevitable absorption into the objective course of philosophical history. In the light of these considerations the obvious "datedness" of Spencer's system and its small degree of originality become intelligible. The empiricism and positivism which it took over from the past it neither expanded nor deepened; and its remaining content, taken from current scientific investigations, made it so typical an expression of a well-defined and unique historical situation that with the change of this situation it necessarily lost the greater part of its value. And since the change set in in Spencer's own lifetime, and took the form of a shift of emphasis from the biological and sociological to the mathematico-physical sciences, Spencer's system has now, only a generation after its completion, scarcely any life left in it. The latest link in a chain of thought extending back to Bacon, it has yet far more of the dust of time upon it than any other of the major links in that chain.

Nevertheless, Spencer reintroduced into British philosophy the impulse to system. There is no obvious contradiction between such an impulse and the empiricist habit of thought, but the latter has, in fact, usually shown itself unfavourable to the former. The notorious scarcity of system, not of speculation only but also of well-rounded construction, in the philosophy of Britain, does certainly seem to be due in the last analysis to a resolute adherence to experience, from which the way to synthesis is more difficult than it is from pure thought. In the early period the only considerable system-builders were Bacon and Hobbes. Then comes a long gap. Spencer was the first after Hobbes to engage on the adventure of a system, and the system he achieved was both vaster and more compact than that of any of his predecessors. In its way it stands alone in British thought. It is doubtful if he was influenced by Hegel and Comte, the only other philosophers near him in time who carried through a similar venture. Of these two Comte is the more likely to have affected him. But it is much more probable that the idea of a thorough systematization of empirical knowledge sprang from Spencer's own conception of what a philosophy should be. For he distinguished three grades of knowledge—everyday, scientific, and philosophical—in an ascending degree of generality and unity; the business of philosophy being to aim at a supreme synthesis of the partial syntheses effected in the special sciences and of such other knowledge as had not been organized at all. This conception, like that of Comte and later of Wundt, Riehl, and many others, is a positivist one, envisaging the end and method of philosophy after the analogy of the natural sciences; it expresses the mentality of an age that put its faith primarily in science and bent itself whole-heartedly to scientific advance. It was a conception born of the need to bring order and unity into an accumulation of knowledge that was growing rapidly and becoming almost unmanageable, a conception which, instead of turning away from this knowledge, would have it carried upwards to the highest level of philosophical abstraction. It stood for an empirical philosophy advanced to its highest degree. And Spencer's system realized this ideal. He was a genuine empiricist in his insatiable hunger for facts and for the ordering of them. But the desire for system and his remarkable capacity for it dominated everything. Unceasingly he abstracted, classified, generalized, deduced, moving forward to more and more abstract unifications, until he had reached the point where he could sum up the universe in a single formula. The result was a system in which everything was given its place, a system so boldly planned and so skilfully and neatly ordered that, whatever our ultimate attitude towards it may be, we cannot help admiring it. Spencer must be ranked among the greatest philosophical architects that history has known.

The leading idea throughout is that of evolution. Spencer was the first to give to this idea a really universal application, to cast it into the form in which it swept through the world triumphantly until at last it received a check through the catastrophe of the Great War. In making the idea of evolution central he had his predecessors, who go back to Heraclitus. Hegel is an obvious example, providing an idealistic counterweight to Spencer's naturalism, just as Marx forms a materialistic obverse to Hegel. But it would be an idle task to follow out these anticipations, for in Spencer the idea of evolution takes on a quite new form, which only the state of the science of his day made possible. Not that he was dependent on Darwin, for several years before the appearance of *The Origin of Species* he had already hit upon some of the most important elements of his later system, had already been considering the idea of evolution from several angles, as is evident from essays he contributed to periodicals in the 'fifties. These essays, and the fact that the first programme of his system (in which evolution is already generalized into a cosmic principle) was drawn up in January 1858, sufficiently disprove the still common supposition that without Darwin Spencer's "synthetic philosophy" would never have seen the light. But when Darwin's work appeared, Spencer recognized in it the confirmation, in a sphere of inquiry with which hitherto he had had little contact, of his own tentative (though even then well-elaborated) ideas, and the vast fruitfulness of its conclusions.

Despite his own approximate anticipation (in an essay of 1852 and another of 1857) of Darwin's theory of the origin and change of species through natural selection, Darwin's theory enabled him to fill certain gaps in his own thought and gave him that interest in biology which found its chief expression in his *Principles of Biology* (1864–7). And it must be allowed that Spencer's system would not have won its enormous success without the wave of Darwinism that carried it forward.

A full discussion of the origin of the evolutionary theory falls outside our scope, but we may indicate an interesting link between it and the philosophy of nature of German idealism. When Spencer was beginning to turn his thought to philosophical questions, his attention was drawn, through Coleridge, to Schelling's view that the development of the realm of organic life consists in a movement of increasing differentiation, organization, and individualization. This speculative doctrine was later given an empirical confirmation in the embryological investigations of K. E. von Baer, who had been influenced by the philosophy of nature of Schelling and Oken; and of this confirmation Spencer soon became aware. In Baer's law—that the structural changes that occur during the growth of an embryo exhibit a progressive development from indeterminate to determinate, from homogeneous to heterogeneous, forms—Spencer saw a significance extending far beyond biology; and his formulation in his *First Principles* (1862) of evolution as the fundamental principle of things is nothing more than an extreme generalization of it. Beyond Baer's law Spencer had no further interest in Schelling's philosophy of nature. All the remaining factors in the construction of his theory of evolution came not from philosophy but from the natural sciences in the strict sense—the nebular hypothesis of Kant and Laplace, the principle of the conservation of energy, Lyell's geological investigations, and those of Lamarck and Darwin in biology.

But this characterization of all process whatever as progessive differentiation of the relatively simple into the relatively complex was for Spencer incomplete, one-sided. He felt himself obliged to regard this movement in one direction as counterbalanced by an equal tendency in the reverse direction. Differentiation is balanced by integration, difference by unity, development by regression or dissolution; the second tendency being directed to the undoing of the work of the first. Their action is reciprocal, each completing and intensifying the other. And it is not the process of specification but the process of integration, the raising of differentiations to higher unities or wholes, that is the primary one. Every line of development, however, has an upper limit, a state of equilibrium, which is the starting-point of opposite forces making for dissolution. In its complete form, then, the most general law of evolution is this eternal rhythm of development and dissolution, a unitary and continuous process with two opposed and correlative aspects.

So far Spencer's cosmic formula is free from any metaphysical presupposition. This enters only in the final generalization that the rhythm of coming-to-be and passing-away is to be identified with the distribution and redistribution of matter and motion. From this final point of view evolution is on the one hand an integration of matter accompanied by a dissipation of motion, on the other hand an absorption or consumption of motion accompanied by a disintegration of matter. And since the total quantity of matter and motion is a constant, all this change, all change whatever, can be nothing but a varying grouping and division, regrouping and redivision of matter and motion in space, occurring in accordance with purely mechanical laws. In the end, therefore, Spencer's universe, both as a whole and in its parts, is a colossal machine, the working of which is determined throughout by causal law. The laws of matter, force, and movement are valid for all phenomena whatever, as much for the social and intellectual life of man as for the realm of the inorganic. To demonstrate this is the task of Spencer's *Synthetic Philosophy*.

Spencer saves this mechanism from crass materialism by introducing his famous doctrine of the Unknowable, which supplies an opening, a valve as it were, in his otherwise closed system. Because he expounded it at the beginning of his system, in his *First Principles*, it has often been regarded as the foundation of the system. But in reality it is only a decoration of the façade, intended to give to the structure an appearance less repellent to religious minds; it was, moreover, a borrowed doctrine, not an original one. It rests on the familiar epistemological arguments about the limitation of our cognitive capacities. We can know only the relative, the conditioned, the phenomenal. But just because we know this is so, we are obliged by a necessity of reason to posit a correlative Absolute or Unconditioned. Even though we cannot penetrate it further, we cannot avoid assuming its existence. Spencer puts this great *x* in his account and calls it the Unknowable. Somewhat inconsistently, however, he proceeds to a line of thought, nearer to metaphysics than to epistemology, by which the unknown quantity is given a quite definite characterization. He declares that we are bound to regard the world accessible to our experience and all the changes within it as the revelation of a Power which amid the change remains constant and which is infinite in space and in time. By this argument, which is certainly more consistent than the preceding epistemological argument with the foundations of Spencer's system, the Unknowable clearly loses a fair amount of its unknowableness. The idea which has so often been supposed to lie at the centre of Spencer's philosophy suffers from an inner contradiction; it was never thought out coherently.

That the doctrine of the Unknowable came from Kant is obvious. But Spencer took it over not directly but from Hamilton and Mansel, who had modified it deeply; and he did nothing to it but translate it into his own ways of speech. The phenomenalism, however, which underlay the doctrine and which Spencer did not formally establish but tacitly presupposed, was a common possession of the empirical way of thinking from Berkeley to Mill, a part of the tradition in which his mental life had developed. Finally, his characterization of the Absolute as a force constant throughout the changes of phenomenal events is clearly a transference to metaphysics of the law of the conservation of energy.

We have mentioned that Spencer's agnosticism—which is not absolute but relative, since he *affirms* the existence of a transempirical realm—sprang not out of the exigencies of his system but out of a side-glance towards religion. It enabled him to formulate the relation between religion on the one hand and science or philosophy (these two being essentially the same for Spencer) on the other. It was his opinion that the doctrine of the unknowableness of the Absolute had the positive value of showing how the age-long strife between those forces could be brought to an end. That which is acknowledged and respected in science or philosophy as the Unknowable is the same as that to which the religious consciousness is directed, one object looked at from different points of view. The sphere of philosophy is the knowable, of religion the unknowable, and so long as each keeps to its proper sphere there can be no occasion of conflict.

It would be out of place here to enter into the details of Spencer's system, to pass storey by storey and room by room through so vast a structure. A few brief indications must suffice. In his *First Principles* he has laid down the foundations. He has drawn a neat line between the knowable and the unknowable, defined the general task of philosophy, and enunciated the universal law of evolution. Beyond this he goes no further in the discussion of logical, methodological, and epistemological questions, but proceeds straightway to the testing of his basic principle of evolution in the wide spaces of experience. In the problems of pure thought he had little interest. He had, indeed, a marked gift for abstract thinking, but only exercised it when he had a large field of empirical material to work on. There could have been no question of a special treatise on logic, since the consideration of this branch of inquiry from an evolutionary point of view would have been condemned from the beginning to sterility. But he defined his attitude towards the war which was being waged in his day between Hamilton and Mill on the issue apriorism *versus* empiricism, the question whether all our knowledge rests on individual experience or whether there are any fundamental principles which attest themselves by rational necessity or self-evidence as independent of all individual experience. Spencer goes with apriorism to the extent of conceding that there are such principles, necessary in the sense that their contradictories are inconceivable, and that they must accordingly be treated as innate features of the individual mind. But it is impossible for them to be independent of all experience whatever. The individual mind inherits from the beginning the accumulated experience of its long line of ancestors, and Spencer tries to show on neurological grounds that this racial experience constitutes its original knowledge. The so-called *a priori* truths have been developed in the experience of the human race and are thus *a priori* only in relation to the individual. Obviously, the true meaning of the *a priori* is here falsified by Spencer. He has not reconciled rationalism and empiricism, but only introduced a correction into the extreme form of the latter as represented, presumably, by Mill. But the tendency to conciliate was characteristic. We have noticed it already in his attempt to compose the strife between religion and science, and it shows itself in yet other connections. In most cases, however, it leads not to decisive solutions but to compromises, and it is its operation in this way that gives rise to those vague and tenuous abstractions, those bloodless and colourless generalizations, those arid schemata, that meet us at every step in his writings, leaving the impression again and again that Spencer's philosophy is the product not of a living man but of a thinking machine.

His predominant interest being in the practical fields of knowledge, he selected for systematization by his evolutionary principle the spheres of biology, psychology, sociology, and ethics. He omitted the inorganic (although his general plan, of course, called for its inclusion), touching on its problems only occasionally, for example in an essay of 1858 on the nebular hypothesis. Gigantic as it is, his system, without the principles of physics and chemistry, remains a torso. It was conceived on too large a scale for a single man to carry out.

It was to sociology that Spencer devoted his chief interest

and his best powers. The work in which he discussed it comprises three large volumes, and yet, judged by the programme he had laid down for himself, it was incomplete. His aim was to show that social development is a phase of the universal evolutionary process, a phase most nearly resembling the organic. Society, like the individual, is a product of organic growth, though, being of a higher order, Spencer calls it super-organic. The advance of social, as of organic life, depends on its growing capacity for adjustment to natural conditions and social environment, and the adjustment is effected positively through tradition and heredity, negatively through the elimination of societies imperfectly adapted. Here, as elsewhere in the system, the Darwinian principle of selection is emphasized. It was Spencer, by the way, who matched the slogan "the struggle for existence" with the equally famous one "the survival of the fittest". The Darwinian law of animal life was thus brought back by Spencer to the sphere of human life which, through Malthus, had first suggested it. In this sphere the factor of differentiation was found to be confirmed. He saw in it the appropriate criterion for the measurement of the degree of development or culture attained by any given social organism. The richer the differentiation within a society, the greater its advance in the evolutionary scale, in other words, the greater its advantage over rival societies in the struggle for existence. The sketch Spencer gave of the course of historical development follows the same line of thought. Like Comte, he lays down a law of three stages—a primitive state of affairs in which several social types are indifferently mixed, then a militaristic type of community resting on force, and finally, growing slowly out of this through many intermediate stages ("varieties" in the biological sense), the freer social type embodied in the industrial and commercial state of modern times. It was thus that for Spencer his own age—the age of liberalism, industry, technology, science, world-trade, and peaceful competition among the nations—was the climax of man's advance. In every realm he stood for the free play of forces, for *laissez-faire* in politics, in trade, and in education, abhorring all use of force by the State, all despotism and militarism, all control of conscience, repression of free opinion, ecclesiastical orthodoxy, and such like. In all which he faithfully reflected the ideals of the expiring century, its liberalism and individualism, its dizzy progress, its illusion of freedom, its boundless faith in knowledge, and its religious indifference—features bearing plainly the stamp of the Enlightenment in which they had their origin.

Spencer crowned his system with an ethic, in which all the preceding strands of thought were to be brought together. His principles had to exhibit their truth in the treatment of man's conduct and of the moral ideas of different peoples and times, and, most of all, in the determination of what *should be* the ends and laws of moral action. The moral sphere also must be shown to reveal the regulation of the evolutionary law. The many evolutionist ethical theories that followed Spencer's all derive from this. But despite his new principle, it cannot be said that he brought about any real transformation of ethical theory. His own ethic falls quite naturally into line with the earlier British empirical systems. He accepted the basic positions of utilitarian hedonism, and within them as a framework wove his own evolutionist theory. For example, the conduct that leads to the greatest happiness is that which carries with it the greatest furtherance and enhancement of life, that which is most fitted to achieve its end, that which is fulfilled on the higher evolutionary levels. The conception of many levels of development suggested to Spencer the distinction between a relative and an absolute ethic: on the highest level only can the moral ideal be perfectly realized. This highest level he envisages as a Utopian state of affairs, in which all clashes of individual interests would disappear in a harmony so complete that not even the choice between good and evil would have any occasion for exercise. The alternatives of egoism and altruism would be transcended. This state of affairs can only come about through the complete adjustment of the individual to his environment. We may note lastly that in ethics as in epistemology Spencer played his characteristic rôle as conciliator, trying to smooth out the conflict between intuitionist and empiricist ethics by urging that there are moral laws which are *a priori* in relation to the individual but that they have been acquired in the long struggles of the race. Here, as before, he falsifies the inner meaning of the *a priori* and remains bound to the empirical position.

But although his ethic was to give the final proof of the truth of the principle of evolution, Spencer concluded this part of his system with the confession that he had not found his general principle as fruitful here as he had expected. At no other point does he express the hint of a doubt in its universal applicability. With this one exception his thought is nowhere "sicklied o'er with the pale cast" of scepticism. He wrote with the serenely confident claim that he held the key to all the problems of philosophy, to all the riddles of the universe. But, after all, nothing short of such doctrinaire certainty could have enabled him to propose to himself and carry out the vast undertaking of his synthetic philosophy, which even those who judge it to be questionable or utterly wrong cannot but admire.

It is no part of our task to follow the course of evolutionism after Darwin and Spencer in all its phases and varieties. We can do no more than illustrate its power and scope in the persons of a few of its most prominent representatives. The men who eagerly took to the new idea and elaborated it were chiefly scientists; the philosophers by profession, especially the occupants of the university chairs, for the most part kept aloof from it and followed other paths. Among the former, THOMAS HENRY HUXLEY (1825–95) was probably the most important and most outspoken advocate of the new view of the universe. A distinguished zoologist, and one of the outstanding men in the intellectual life of the Victorian age, he succeeded—through the esteem he won by his personality, the frequency of his advocacy, the vigour and liveliness of his style, and his happy coinages and formulas—in turning the ideas of Darwin into current coin circulating in every section of society. But he had too independent a mind to follow Darwin or Spencer or anyone else blindly. Whatever he took over he stamped with his own personality. Darwin's conception of the struggle for existence he did indeed accept, but was sceptical of the law of adaptation to environment and consequently of the doctrine of natural selection. In the sphere of philosophy, into which he made frequent excursions,[1] he brought about a close connection between evolutionism and the old tradition by going back to Hume, the "prince of agnostics" as he called him, with whom he agreed in general and to some extent in particular, especially with Hume's fundamental position that all real knowledge is confined to the world of experience. Hence his hostility to metaphysics, his "agnosticism", a term coined by him and quickly and widely accepted. Also like Hume he had a strong dose of scepticism in his nature, the corollary of a mobile mind which raised him above the flat-footed dogmatism of Spencer.

Yet in many respects he departed from Hume. By sharpening the thought of the latter too finely he fell back into dogmatism, or perilously near to it. By raising the question, so contrary to the mind of Hume, of the origin of sense-impressions, he provided phenomenalism with a physiological and therefore materialistic foundation; all mental states or events, he declared, are the effects of bodily causes, so that we comprehend their origin and manner of functioning by studying the changes of the nervous system. He did not shrink from downright materialistic expressions, speaking at times in the language of Cabanis and other materialists of the XVIIIth and XIXth Centuries. It was he who first characterized the mind as an "epiphenomenon", a phenomenal by-product of the brain.

On the ground of these and similar unambiguous expressions Huxley's doctrine was in fact decried as materialistic. He himself, however, protested against any such label. He tried to show that the standpoint indicated in such expressions is by no means a final one; it is to be considered not as metaphysically binding but simply as a point of departure for the

[1] *Lay Sermons*, 1870; *Hume*, 1879; *Science and Culture*, 1881; *Evolution and Ethics*, 1893; and many other addresses and papers contained in his *Collected Essays*, nine vols., 1893–4.

scientific investigation of nature, for which it is indispensable as a working hypothesis. He claimed that it contained nothing incompatible with the purest idealism, indeed that the more frankly the materialistic position is conceded, the easier it would be to show the unassailableness of idealism. Huxley had really landed himself in a difficulty which his way of thinking could not resolve. In consequence, he took refuge in agnosticism. Materialism, he urged, is just as unprovable, and on the same grounds, as idealism is; both are simply opposite poles of the absurdity of supposing that anything can be known of the essential nature of anything, whether this be matter or mind. Natural science cannot help positing the existence of the material world and along with this the primacy of sensible reality; whereas for philosophy that world must always be problematic, *its* primary reality being consciousness, so that it can only conceive matter phenomenally, as something given to and within consciousness. Huxley was at variance with himself. When the philosopher in him was uppermost he spoke almost like a Berkeleian, and when the scientist took charge he spoke as a materialist. To escape from the dilemma he donned the mantle of the sceptic, and it was this capacity or mood that he most enjoyed, bringing all philosophies under his survey but committing himself to none, using now one and now another as served his convenience. His agnosticism, unlike Spencer's, was genuinely akin to scepticism; it meant not negative judgment but no judgment at all in ultimate matters. All this notwithstanding, Huxley was more than his agnosticism. Sooner or later his primarily positive nature would grow restive under the free play of thought and drive him to philosophical affirmations.

To the evolutionary theory of morals he made a valuable contribution in his famous Romanes Lecture of 1893, *Evolution and Ethics*. Here too he went his own way, in some respects departing from current evolutionist views. While agreeing that the law of evolution holds good in the sphere of moral action as in all other spheres, he maintained that in the moral it is realized in a quite different manner. The realm of the natural is dominated by an inexorable struggle for existence in which all fight all, sheer self-assertion triumphing over co-operation and ruthless suppression over sympathy and pity. But in the social life of man, for all its natural origin and its exposure to the pressure of natural forces, a realm *sui generis* emerges, a realm with its own uniformities and norms. Man's moral life, far from being another expression of the natural principle of pitiless competitive struggle, is an open repudiation of it. With this assertion of the peculiar autonomy of the moral order which emerges with society, Huxley released evolutionist ethics from its naturalistic fetters and cleared the way for a moral idealism, an idealism which found its finest expression in Huxley's own advocacy of man's moral dignity, in the exalted language in which he spoke and wrote of it, and in the noble temper that pervaded his outlook on human life.

Connected with Huxley through personal friendship as well as common scientific aims was JOHN TYNDALL (1820–93). His interest in philosophy was less marked than Huxley's, but he too devoted himself considerably, in lecturing and in writing, to the dissemination and popularization of the new scientific ideas, especially the idea of evolution. A famous lecture of his,[1] in which he openly confessed himself a materialist, created a great stir and made him for a while a centre of philosophical interest. But his conception of what matter is was altogether different from the popular one and even from the more refined one of science. He admitted, indeed, that the matter of physics could not have generated the universe as we know it. But he believed that every structure and activity, mental as well as physical, on the earth, even our morality and art and science, were all somehow enfolded, as in a germ, in the primeval fire of the sun.

To the inorganic sciences, however, in which Tyndall was at home, the idea of evolution had little to offer. We must return to the human realm if we are to form a just estimate of the fruitfulness of the new line of thought. The important

[1] *Address Delivered before the British Association assembled at Belfast*, 1874. See also his *Fragments of Science*, 1871.

researches of SIR FRANCIS GALTON (1822–1911)[1] were conducted under the immediate influence of Darwin, who was Galton's cousin. He is known chiefly as the founder of the science of eugenics, which demands that that selection of the fit and elimination of the unfit which occurs automatically in nature should be carried out deliberately and systematically in human society. Galton's varied work—his ethnology and anthropology, his investigation of human heredity, of colour-blindness, generic images and finger-prints, and his application of statistical methods to the study of man—was all directed towards the practical problem of improving the race by the conscious control of mating and procreation. The eugenic movement now established in many countries owes to him its ideals and many of its methods. His chief disciple and continuator in Britain (also his biographer) was KARL PEARSON, whom we must treat less briefly, since he passed from science to philosophy.

In Pearson (1857–1936)[2] the scientific outlook as extended to philosophical matters had its most radical and one-sided representative. He was a scientist of distinction in several related fields, making important pioneer contributions to the mathematical treatment of biology, anthropology, and sociology. His primary interest for us lies in his famous and influential book *The Grammar of Science* (1892; third edition 1911; cheap reprint 1937), in which he gave the scientific ideal of knowledge prevailing in his day a classical formulation, glorified the spirit behind it and the achievements it had made possible, and radiated his conviction that it was destined to serve the interests and mould the culture of the future.

Its aim is to examine the basic conceptions of modern science. Taking the mathematico-physical disciplines as the type of science, he maintained that the essential nature of science lies not in explanation but in description, in giving not the "why"

[1] *Hereditary Genius*, 1869; *Inquiries into Human Faculty and its Development*, 1883; *Natural Inheritance*, 1889; *Essays in Eugenics*, 1909.

[2] Succeeded Clifford in the Chair of Applied Mathematics, London University; 1911–33 Galton Professor of Eugenics at the same university.

but the "how" of things. Its end, moreover, is to do this of everything; nothing lies outside its scope. Since, however, things cannot be comprehended in their vast totality, science has to resort to a kind of conceptual shorthand, devises symbols, formulas, and laws, and with the help of these is able to apprehend and describe reality in an economical way. In other words, an electron, for instance, must not be thought of as empirically real; it is simply a symbol or shorthand statement contrived by the scientist's imagination, and can therefore be cast aside whenever it proves inadequate for the description of the relevant facts. Further, science is not theory for theory's sake. It is an eminently practical affair, one of the most important instruments we have for adapting ourselves to our environment and succeeding in the struggle for existence. And it is just because it has this practical end that it seeks the maximum of knowledge with the simplest means, following the law of least resistance. For the same reason it rejects all superfluous and prejudicial assumptions; so that one of its chief tasks is the freeing of thought from the lumber that superstition and obscurantism have piled up in it in the course of the centuries. Theology and metaphysics are thus condemned lock, stock, and barrel. Philosophy, in so far as it has any claim to exist at all, collapses into science as above defined. Only when regarded historically, as a phase of man's intellectual development, can it be given a place of its own.

But within its proper field also science has a work of clearance to do. It must eliminate from itself everything that is inconsistent with its character as description, ordering, and classification. This means that it must get rid of the notions of causality, force, and matter, which are nothing but fetishes still hiding in the corners of even the latest science. The category of causality has neither necessity of thought nor experience to support it, but is simply a conceptual limit invented to satisfy our need of economy of statement; force is a kind, not an explanation, of motion; and matter is nothing, at any rate nothing known, so that physics does not need the idea of it. The place of all these is filled by motion, which science describes but cannot explain. Given motion, particles, and space, all which are susceptible of precise measurement, science is in a position to work out an account of everything that falls within experience.

Pearson's position is thus an extreme glorification of the omnicompetence of science. It is in the direct line of succession to Hume's empiricism and Comte's positivism, and has an exact counterpart in the philosophical side of the thought of Ernst Mach. That Mach was aware of this very close affinity is indicated by his dedication of his *Analyse der Empfindungen* to Pearson "as an expression of fellow-feeling and esteem." They agreed also in the epistemological basis of their theory of science. This, like the rest, goes back to Hume. The facts on which science works are not mysterious things-in-themselves but just phenomena of consciousness, that is, sensations and their derivatives, apart from which there is no reality. We do indeed project some of the contents of consciousness into an outer space and speak of them as physical facts, but the projection does not really carry us beyond consciousness: a so-called external thing is simply a construct, the product of linking present with past impressions. Of course, science may and does go beyond present sensations, by forming hypotheses, laying down laws, drawing inferences, and so forth, but all these conceptual artefacts are conditioned, and receive any meaning they possess, from sensations. For Pearson, as for Mach, the mind resembles a telephone exchange, which receives external impressions, arranges them, and redirects them. But in introspection as in perception, nothing beyond sensations and the images and concepts derived from them is to be looked for; there is no soul or anything like it distinct from the contents of which we are conscious. The mind is nothing but the sum of its impressions and ideas. Pearson's epistemology is clearly identical with that of Hume and Mill and Mach.

Pearson's laudation of the scientific spirit is carried to the point of apotheosis. The very mission of modern science is to revere that one God of which alone we have an irrefutable certainty, namely, the human spirit. Religion consists in serving the cause of science, and adoration is the contemplation of the achievements of man's mind. It is the discoverers of truth who are saints and priests. In the future it will no more be said *credo quia absurdum est*, but "I believe because I understand". By Pearson, then, as by Comte, science is made divine. His attitude is that of the Enlightenment; only, it is an anachronism, a hundred years out of date.

The same may be said of his ethic,[1] which makes advance in scientific knowledge a central feature of all approximation to the moral ideal. Just as he has scourged religion (as commonly understood) as a product of superstition, so now he brands the Christian ethic as a product of blind feeling. For him a genuine ethic has nothing to do with feeling but only with knowledge and the search after this. He stands for the Socratic view that only he who knows can be truly virtuous. To the "ethic of freethought" he adds as a political supplement socialism, by which he means not the revolutionary sort associated with Marx or primarily any change at all of the existing political system, but such a slow and constant development of the moral temper as will lead every individual to subordinate his conduct to the welfare of society as a whole. Such a socialism will involve the improvement of the race by eugenic measures, the emancipation of woman, the abrogation of sexual taboos ("free love"), free choice of work, and liberty of thought. These were striking anticipations, made as early as the 'eighties, of later ideas, and to make them needed a personality like Pearson's, strong, bold, filled with confidence in the omnipotence of science, holding firmly to freedom of inquiry, scornful of compromise, drawing his conclusions bluntly even when they were likely to offend his contemporaries.[2]

Outside philosophy, but near enough to its borders to warrant mention, there was an extensive application and vindication of the principle of evolution. Sir Henry Maine (1822–88), for

[1] *The Ethic of Freethought*, 1888; second edition 1901.

[2] Besides the two works mentioned see also *The Chances of Death and other Studies in Evolution*, two vols., 1897.

example, who may be regarded as the successor of Austin,[1] gave to historical and comparative jurisprudence a quite new basis in several very influential works in which he marshalled the facts of primitive social and political organization by means of that principle.[2] A somewhat similar service was done in economics, constitutional history, and political science by WALTER BAGEHOT (1826–77).[3] Being no cloistered scholar, but a man of affairs and a banker, his ideas were directed to and had some influence on practice. His debt to Darwin is described as well as acknowledged in the sub-title of his *Physics and Politics:* "thoughts on the application of the principles of natural selection and inheritance to political society." His work excited the interest of Darwin himself.

But it was in anthropology that evolutionism acquired its chief power outside biology and philosophy. SIR JOHN LUBBOCK (Lord Avebury; 1834–1913), for instance, was a staunch Darwinian. He held that primitive man was atheistic and that religion developed from fetishism through totemism, idolatry, and other forms of polytheism, to its present monotheistic stage. SIR EDWARD BURNETT TYLOR (1832–1917), Oxford's first Professor of Anthropology and England's most influential authority in this branch of study in the century, tried to prove that the higher forms of religion, and philosophy also, sprang from animism. The mantle of Tylor has fallen upon SIR JAMES G. FRAZER (*b.* 1854), the doyen of living British anthropologists, who has long enjoyed international repute. According to him the life of primitive man was ruled more by magic than by animistic beliefs; and magic, since it aims at the domination of natural forces, is more akin to science than to religion, the latter arising much later, when, the limits of magical power having been reached, an appeal was made to higher forces,

[1] See p. 59.

[2] *Ancient Law*, 1861 (many editions); *Village Communities in the East and the West*, 1871; *Early History of Institutions*, 1875; *Dissertations on Early Law and Custom*, 1883.

[3] *The English Constitution*, 1867; *Physics and Politics*, 1869; *Lombard Street*, 1873.

fear and hope and propitiation taking the place of domination. The persistence of the influence of Spencer and Darwin is particularly evident in the work of another living anthropologist, EDWARD WESTERMARCK (*b.* 1862), a Finn who settled early in England and was Professor of Sociology in the University of London 1907–30. His *History of Human Marriage* (1891; fifth edition in three volumes, 1921) is well known. In two works he deals with problems of ethics—*The Origin and Development of the Moral Ideas* (two volumes, 1906–8; second edition 1912–17) and *Ethical Relativity* (1932). In both he appears as a typical evolutionist, his genetic treatment of moral phenomena leading inevitably to ethical relativism. He regards all attempts, such as rationalism and intuitionism, to find a ground for a supposed objective validity of moral judgments as irreconcilable with the facts of moral evolution. For him, as for Hume, moral judgment is produced and controlled not by reason but by emotion, and emotion is indefeasibly subjective. He has tried to trace out the emotional conditions not only of our spontaneous moral pronouncements but even of *a priori* theories of ethics, such as Kant's. Moral emotions, distinguished from non-moral ones by their impartiality and universality, are all derived from approval and disapproval, the negative ones (among which he includes the sense of obligation) from the latter, the positive ones from the former. Always they are the causes, not the consequences, of moral judgments, and ethical principles are never anything else but generalizations of such derived judgments. Moral emotions, moreover, are in the last analysis not individual but social in character and origin. Westermarck has always emphasized the sociological aspect of ethics.

Returning from these somewhat external ramifications of evolutionism to its more distinctively philosophical expressions, we come to GEORGE HENRY LEWES (1817–78) as its most important representative after Spencer. A versatile mind, he belongs as much to literature as to philosophy. To the general reading public he is known more by his romantic union with George Eliot and by his biography of Goethe (which has been widely read in Germany) than by his philosophical work.[1] In his younger days especially he was one of Comte's most enthusiastic disciples in England, in this respect as in others finding in George Eliot a congenial spirit. His *History of Philosophy*, of little value by our present standards but so well composed that it had an extraordinarily wide circulation, providing many English readers with the only knowledge of the history of philosophy they ever acquired, was written throughout from the positivist standpoint. Incidentally, it was one of the earliest general histories of speculative thought in the language. Its aim was to expose the vanity of all metaphysical speculation; after laying the greater part of philosophical effort under an interdict, it recommended the doctrine of Comte as the culmination of human thinking. In later years he moved further and further away from Comte's system, fell for a while under the influence of Spencer, and in the end went his own way; but he never entirely left the camp of positivism.

Lewes's philosophy, as given for the most part in his last work, is a faithful reflection of his mobile and receptive mind, and of his unusually wide knowledge, which embraced biological and psychological as well as philosophical matters. It teems with ideas, many of them important, but as a whole it lacks consistency and compactness. It is difficult to trace in it a controlling principle or scheme. One is left with the impression of a thought lively and fertile but unclarified and unmatured. Like a true positivist, Lewes insists that philosophy should be scientific, meaning by this not only that it should follow the methods of the natural sciences but also that it should confine itself to the empirical as that which alone is knowable. It was he who coined the term "metempirical" for that which lies, or is supposed to lie, beyond experience. As Shadworth Hodgson has shown,[2] Lewes does not make it clear whether he denies

[1] *The Biographical History of Philosophy*, two vols, 1845–6, and often reprinted; *Comte's Philosophy of the Positive Sciences*, 1853; *Aristotle: a Chapter from the History of Science*, 1864; *Problems of Life and Mind*, five vols., 1874–9.

[2] *The Philosophy of Reflection*, vol. i, pp. 190 ff.

the existence of the metempirical, or only its knowableness, or both. On the whole he appears to admit its existence and nothing more; whatever it may reveal to intuition and faith, for knowledge in the positivist sense it can only be a negative, a limiting, concept. In the end he did make room in philosophy for metaphysical problems, but required them to be treated and resolved in a strictly scientific manner. For him as for Spencer philosophy is the science that proceeds to the highest abstractions and the widest generalizations.

For the rest, Lewes's inquiries were mostly physiological and psychological in character. They too abound in stimulating ideas, which not infrequently rise to the level of real insight, but which on the whole have remained abortive because of the wilderness of rambling, unbalanced, and confused thought in which they lie hidden. Among them is the distinction of the type of phenomenon that manifests itself as a sheer novelty in relation to its antecedents from the type that can be understood entirely through the properties of its constituent factors. The term "emergent" for the former is his own; the latter he called a resultant. Here he anticipated the "emergent philosophy" of Lloyd Morgan and Alexander, though whether there was any continuity between him and them, any influence direct or indirect, is uncertain.

Lewes's thought belongs in the main to the period of Comte and Mill, and was but little influenced by the ideas of Darwin and Spencer. On the other hand, the next generation of thinkers, whose births fall in the 'thirties and 'forties, were caught up and carried along by the new surge of doctrine at their most impressionable age. Few, however, were so profoundly under its influence as WILLIAM KINGDON CLIFFORD (1845–79), from 1871 to his early death Professor of Mathematics in University College, London.

Clifford was a unique personality endowed with brilliant intellectual gifts, precocious and versatile, scintillating with genius, a man capable of feeling and arousing enthusiasm, and exercising a strange spell, but with an unbridled audacity about him, an extravagance and eccentricity—the result being a character of contrasts which tended to consume itself. There was a Promethean strain in him, and much that reminds us of his German contemporary Nietzsche; indeed nothing could so clearly emphasize how out of the ordinary the figure of Clifford is in English thought as his intellectual kinship with that thinker who has always been and still is so foreign to the English. But Clifford's course was a full decade shorter than Nietzsche's, and he was able to bring much less to completion. What might he not have achieved had he been granted a longer life? It is an idle question; for perhaps it was his destiny to have to put forth in a torrent all that was in him during the short span of life allowed him, so that he had already exhausted his intellectual resources when his bodily powers failed him. Thus Clifford's work, divided up in his gifted way among so many different fields of study, remained a splendid torso, and he himself was more seeker than finder, giving stimulus rather than guidance, and pointing the way to tasks he did not live to complete.

Apart from his important labours in mathematics and his thorough knowledge of natural science, Clifford's achievements included work on epistemology and the theory of science, and also on metaphysics, ethics, and philosophy of religion.[1] In his theory of knowledge Clifford takes as his starting-point a doctrine closely akin to the sensationalist phenomenalism of Berkeley and Hume. The objects of the external world are given me as impressions; they represent a series of changes in my consciousness, and have no existence beyond this. But impressions of other selves are not given in like fashion, for these cannot be objects of my consciousness. They can be inferred from my consciousness, by projecting myself out of my consciousness into the "other" self. To such impressions which I project thus out of me and recognize as

[1] His writings, delivered during his lifetime mainly as lectures or published in periodical form, were for the most part collected and published posthumously; *Seeing and Thinking*, 1879 (second edition, 1880); *Lectures and Essays*, edited by L. Stephen and Sir F. Pollock, two vols., 1879 (third edition, 1901); *The Common Sense of the Exact Sciences*, edited and completed by K. Pearson, 1885.

existing beyond my "self" Clifford gives the name "ejects". Thus while *objects* are the data appearing as phenomena in my own consciousness and pertaining solely to me, *ejects* are the contents of cognitions transferred from my own and located in the foreign consciousness where they belong. This epistemological account is further complicated by considerations of an historico-evolutionary order. Belief in the existence of a consciousness other than my own is already guaranteed, independently of all theoretical argument, by the fact that man from the first is not an isolated individual, but stands in social relations to his fellows. From the point of view of historical evolution belief in the eject is thus seen to be a sort of rediscovery or recognition of a consciousness akin to myself in the being of my fellow-men. But an *object* given to my consciousness may likewise present itself from the first, even if only in instinctive fashion, as one that can be sensed by an "other" consciousness as well as by myself. An object with which this conviction is combined Clifford calls a "social object", and the impression of externality evoked by such objects means nothing but this actual or possible relation to an "other" self-consciousness. This line of argument involves the random intermingling of very diverse motives. It may be called the social proof of the reality of the external world.

Not only sensationalist and evolutionist, but also epistemological and metaphysical lines of thought are mixed in it. We cannot here exhibit the inner connections of these divergent motives, which indeed Clifford's own saltatory fashion of thought does not bring out very clearly. But all the arguments lead finally to the element in his philosophy which has become most widely known, the theory of "mind-stuff". It is first pointed out that an impression or sensation does not need to be contained in a consciousness, but may exist also independently "outside" consciousness, that is to say, it is a "thing in itself", an absolute whose existence is "for itself" and not relative to anything else. All that can be stated about it is that it is sensed (*sentitur*). It was the elements out of which every sensation is constituted that Clifford called "mind-stuff", and he was naïve enough to suppose that he had thereby finally solved the Kantian problem of the thing-in-itself. The same goal is reached by another line of argument. He tries to show that the problem of the relation between the physical and the psychical is not to be solved by referring either to the other as its source, but that there holds between the two a thoroughgoing reciprocity and correspondence, as fundamental as that between the letters of a sentence as read or spoken, on the one hand, and as written or printed, upon the other. This he takes to indicate that we have not here to do with two things radically and in principle different, but with one and the same substance, which under one aspect appears as physical and under the other as psychical. Again, he uses the term "mind-stuff" to designate this unifying substance underlying all being; and here, too, it is evident that mind-stuff must be thought of as not merely independent of all consciousness, but as antecedent to it in time. For the primeval matter pervading the chaos of the universe has first to become concentrated and integrated in ordered structures, and not till then is there any possibility of consciousness arising: so that the levels attained by consciousness are dependent upon the level reached in the evolution of the material elements. What appears to us to be *matter* must be assumed to consist likewise of mind-stuff: every atom and molecule is, apart from its materiality, also endowed with a psychic factor. It is evident that the cosmology of Spencer plays a part in these speculations of Clifford: it is also evident that this panpsychism is nothing but a thinly veiled materialism, for Clifford's "mind-stuff", a daring enough conception in appearance, is in fact a highly mixed metaphysical notion which on closer scrutiny shows itself as in no essential different from ordinary "matter".

Of greater philosophical value, though much less widely known, are Clifford's ideas on the logic and methodology of the exact sciences. In essentials they agree with those of Mach, and especially with those of Pearson, who stood in direct connection with them and constructed a system upon them. The central principle is that of the Economy of Thought, which here, as with the other two thinkers, leads to anticipations of the later pragmatic theory of knowledge.

It is in his ethics, in which Clifford felt a special interest, that the disturbing effect of the ideas of Darwin and Spencer is most noticeable. As we have seen Clifford held that our belief in the external world rests upon a sort of social instinct, and cannot be guaranteed by pure theory. So, too, with ethics; here, also, the dominating fact is that the individual is nothing in and for himself, but that his whole being consists in his membership of a social whole by which he is at once sustained and surrounded. Here Clifford introduces the central notion of the "Tribal Self"—an idea of his own devising which he was to render notable. By this term we are to understand the sense, partly inherited and partly acquired, of what conduces to the interests of the tribe or social group to which the individual belongs. The separate selves out of which the "Tribal Self" gradually develops are actuated primarily by the striving after pleasure, the urge to satisfy their individual cravings. But the individual self is extended to the Tribal Self in the measure in which it sets aside its egoistic interests and appropriates for its own those of the tribe; while this growth of the individual is at the same time a process of social evolution. But in human life private self and social self will be in perpetual conflict, and where the latter has come to be developed it will oppose the egoistic motives of the private self which run counter to the interest of society, and will cause a man to feel abhorrence of his own conduct. It is, according to Clifford, in this condemnation of the individual by the social self that the phenomenon of conscience finds expression, as the voice of the "Tribal Self" developed and refined through natural selection. Thus for Clifford's tribal or social ethic that is morally good (or bad) which is useful (or harmful) to the tribe: or, in more Darwinian terms, which promotes (or impedes) its efficiency or capacity for survival. The goal of ethics is to train the individual to become the most perfect possible member of society—that is, one who suppresses his own interests and recognizes only those of the tribe. That is to be, in Clifford's words, an efficient citizen. If we strip these ideas of their evolutionary vesture, it is evident that they contain a notable contribution to an Idealist social ethics. Clifford expressly repudiates both the ethic of Hedonism and the principle of "the greatest happiness of the greatest number"; and though he, too, had not completely freed himself from a sort of sublimated utilitarianism and remained caught in the trammels of Darwinism, yet his doctrine is manifestly a much more satisfactory solution of the ethical problem than the traditional moral philosophy of Britain was able to supply. And his ideas in this field had the greater success and won him the respect even of thinkers who were unable otherwise to follow him, from the fact that he did not propound them as arid doctrine, but infused into them the force and impassioned fire of his personality.

This impassioned eccentricity of Clifford characterized also his attitude to religion. Here he was opposed to all compromise, and abhorred any kind of deference to ecclesiastical powers, such as even thinkers indifferent to religion so commonly affect in England. He rose to a real fanaticism of unbelief, and in his denial of God had no scruple in handling the positive religions with extreme harshness, raging against Church, creed, and priesthood with the suppressed hatred of a prophet of Enlightenment. Christianity he called "a terrible plague which has destroyed two civilizations", and directed his moral indignation against the noxious influence of priests whom he held to be the real enemies of humanity, and a standing menace to the State, society, and true morality. But even this bitter enemy of everything religious did not dispense with a sort of substitute for religious faith. He found escape in worship of the universe, and stood in reverent awe before its marvellous order and regularity. He called the feeling that animated him in this connection "cosmic emotion", and recognized it, in the famous words of Kant, in presence both of the starry heavens above and the moral law within. But he put man in the place of God, and it was to the exaltation and apotheosis of man that whatever living faith he felt was directed. Like Comte, he proclaimed the Religion of Humanity, and wrote, with a touch of extravagance, of the "father man who gazes down upon us out of the twilight of history and out of the hidden depths of every soul with the fire of eternal youth, and says: 'Before God was I was.'" In a fervour of conviction he wrote at the conclusion of his essay *Cosmic Emotion* the words: "Those who can read the signs of the times read in them that the kingdom of Man has come." But the temple of this religion was for Clifford the proud edifice of science, and it was from science that he hoped that all further progress of the spirit of man would come.

The question whether any union of Darwinism and Religion was possible was not always answered, as by Clifford, with an uncompromising "No". To another of Darwin's disciples, GEORGE JOHN ROMANES (1848–94), it remained an open problem that troubled him all through his life. Pupil and close friend of the master, Romanes was first and foremost a biologist, and his independent researches earned him the name of one of the most gifted contributors to the theory of descent. But being naturally predisposed to religion, and having been brought up in a milieu of orthodoxy, he was constantly being driven beyond the limits of purely empirical inquiry to come to terms with philosophical questions as to the general interpretation of experience which were pressing for decision in the new doctrines. The conflict between his faith and his science was sometimes dormant, and sometimes broke out openly; and it was through it that he was turned into a philosopher.

It is interesting to trace the several phases through which this conflict was brought to its final issue. Thus in his earliest writing (*A Candid Examination of Theism*, 1878) we find Romanes so closely bound in naturalistic ways of thought that the firm foundation of his youthful faith becomes a quick-sand. But this does not, as with Clifford, mean an open rejection of religion, but a time of grave inward testing, in which he takes counsel with himself in order to weigh the respective claims of the rival powers. And though Science proves itself the stronger and nullifies all arguments in favour of Theism, yet we feel that, for all that it is forced into the background, Faith is in nowise utterly obliterated. For it becomes evident that even if from the standpoint of science nothing is to be saved from the wreck, yet there is another way of treating the matter which leaves a door still open for the possibility of the existence of God. This way leads to a sort of teleological metaphysic, upon the basis of which it appears possible to penetrate into a sphere beyond that of science. But here it proves necessary to assume a supreme Spirit as the ultimate cause of all things. This argument is not, however, pursued by Romanes with any genuine conviction. Rather it continually leads him into conflict with his scientific conscience, at the bar of which no such speculations can be justified. And so he falls into a peculiar seesaw vacillation between a theistic and an atheistic view of the world, from which only a radical course of criticism could set him free. Instead he takes refuge in an attitude of agnosticism so as to allay, without resolving, the conflict of conscience in which he had become entangled.

But already only a few years later we find his point of view altered. In a lecture delivered in 1885, but only published posthumously (1895) with the title *Mind, Motion, and Monism*, Romanes inclines to a monistic Pantheism after the fashion of Giordano Bruno's, and in a short paper that appeared a little later in the *Contemporary Review* (1886) "The World as Eject" (also printed in *Mind, Motion, and Monism*), he likewise develops a monistic standpoint, which, while seeking to bridge the alternatives of Materialism and Spiritualism, plainly tends in the direction of the latter. He arrives at this position by grafting on to his own views Clifford's theory of ejects, as well as by a critical examination of the latter's doctrine of mind-stuff, upon which he impresses a character the very opposite of the original one, by reducing everything to the psychical instead of to the material. In these utterances he does not yet touch on the specifically religious question, but adopts a neutral position with regard to it. In particular the

World-Eject (as Romanes terms the Absolute) is still thought of as an impersonal, abstract, purely metaphysical principle. But in the last years of his life his outlook underwent a further alteration. The notes of a work, planned but never executed, which was to have subjected the problem of religion to a fresh examination,[1] show Romanes to be fully reconciled with religious belief. This, his final testimony, is included in *Thoughts on Religion* (1896), the volume edited by Charles Gore. Romanes had found the way back to positive religion, and now represented a personal theism in the sense of Christianity, bringing his scientific convictions also into ordered relation with it. Darwinism and the doctrine of evolution retain their full validity, but in accord not in conflict with the theistic outlook on the world. The dualism between scientific knowledge and faith is thereby overcome, and a harmonious adjustment accomplished between them.

Strictly, however, this final adjustment cannot be achieved; Darwinism is not, in so far as it is honest, compatible with supernatural religion. This view is accordingly the dominant one, and is expressed by the majority of thinkers who follow Spencer, Darwin, and Huxley in dealing with the religious problem. As typical representatives of them we may mention Charles Grant Allen (1848–99) and William Winwood Reade (1838–75). A prolific writer equally fertile in science and *belles lettres*, Allen abandoned every tie with religion, and urged a view of life based on a radical uncompromising naturalism, individualist and hedonist. He was one of the few who were concerned with problems of aesthetics, and who attempted an evolutionary interpretation of them.[2] Reade became known

[1] The title was to have been, like that of the earlier one, "A Candid Examination of Religion", but the author designated himself this time not "Physicus", but "Metaphysicus".

Other writings of Romanes on evolutionary theory are: *Animal Intelligence* (1881); *Mental Evolution in Animals* (1883); *Mental Evolution in Man* (1888); *Darwin and after Darwin* (1892).

[2] Cf. *Physiological Aesthetics* (1877); *The Colour Sense* (1879); as well as *The Evolutionist at Large* (1881) and *The Evolution of the Idea of God* (1897).

as the author of *The Martyrdom of Man* (1872, many editions), a moving and deeply felt work which had a striking literary success. As its title indicates, it is inspired by a gloomy and pessimistic outlook on life, which involves the complete rejection of all transcendent values and all religious faith, for which Reade substitutes faith in the omnipotence of science and the sombre conviction that science and science alone is called to lead man up out of his past and present desolation into a better future. Like Clifford, Reade sublimates Man into a higher kind of being, not, of course, men as individuals, but Humanity as a whole, in order to draw from the perfectibility of man the new faith that is summoned to replace the old.

Thinkers of a more religious frame of mind joined issue with the new doctrine each in his own way, and the resulting variations are very numerous. Apart from Romanes, the following may be selected out of many for consideration: JAMES ALLANSON PICTON (1832–1910), JAMES CROLL (1821–90), HENRY DRUMMOND (1851–97), and SIR JOHN ROBERT SEELEY (1834–95).

Picton attached himself closely to Spencer and took over entire the metaphysics of the *First Principles*. But he went a step further in so far as he expressly identified the "unknowable" with the divine, and thereby sought to turn the metaphysical culmination of Spencer's system in the direction of religious philosophy. He made a point of showing that Evolutionism did not necessarily issue in Agnosticism or Naturalism, let alone Materialism, but that it could combine very well with genuine religious emotion, though this might be far removed from any positive belief of a credal kind. Picton therefore occupied himself with establishing a religion upon an evolutionary foundation, and it is manifest that such a religion must inevitably lead to Pantheism. It is Spinoza's identification of God and Nature that is here proclaimed with an emotional extravagance of enthusiasm as the solution of all the questions at issue in philosophy. But although God the Creator is expressly repudiated, and the self-origination and self-sufficiency of the universe maintained, Picton yet attaches great importance to his attempted demonstration that his World-religion is identical with the essential core of the historic religions, including Christianity. Thus he calls his doctrine "Christian Pantheism", and the palpable contradiction of combining two such incompatibles leaves him quite untroubled.[1]

Whereas with Picton the religious superstructure is rather a decorative trimming than a genuine surrender of Naturalism, CROLL, a Scottish geologist, ventures a decisive step beyond its border. He, too, leaves unassailed the system of Evolutionism as a whole, and adopts the most important elements in its theory, but at the same time he lays the axe to its roots and seeks to loosen its very foundations. According to the law of evolution, matter, force, and movement are the factors whereby the entire cosmic process and every change taking place within it are determined and explained. Yet no question probes beyond them, they stand as the ultimate elements of all being and becoming, themselves in need of no explanation. But to Croll this inquiry into the source and origin of the elements seems a highly significant question. The fact that force and matter exist is less important than the question of their determination—and the fundamental problem of philosophy is the problem of how the original factors of being are finally to be determined and interpreted. If every present state of the universe is prescribed through that which precedes it, and that in turn through *its* antecedent, we are confronted by an inadmissible regress *ad infinitum*. At some time or other this series must have begun, there must have been a first determination, and it is at the same time evident that force cannot ultimately be referred to force as its determining cause, nor motion to motion. Thus from the fact that something exists at the present moment it is to be concluded that a "something" must have existed from all eternity. The thought of an eternal *universe* is, however, encumbered with the absurdity of an endless succession of events. There remains, therefore, only

[1] *The Mystery of Matter and other Essays* (1873), *The Religion of the Universe* (1904), *Pantheism* (1905), and *Spinoza* (1907).

the assumption of an eternal and infinite God, as the first Determiner of the cosmic series, or as the Creator Spirit who is the ultimate cause of all being, and so, too, the Sustainer of the entire evolutionary process. Evolutionism thus, while retaining its full validity, is not a self-contained and self-subsistent theory, but in the end passes over into Theism: which is one more proof that it is no longer at ease in its shell of Naturalism, and is striving after a firm anchorage.[1]

An attempt of an independent kind to include religion within the system of naturalistic science was that made by DRUMMOND. Evangelist, theologian, and scientific investigator, Drummond won fame at a stroke by the huge, almost unexampled success of his *Natural Law in the Spiritual World*, which, published in 1883, had had 125,000 copies sold by the end of the century. Apart from the book's popular style and the easily intelligible character of its contents, this success was chiefly due to the fact that in it the new science was treated by a man of exemplary religious conviction, and not, as so generally, condemned as an enemy of religion, but presented as being in full harmony with the teaching of the Christian faith. It was through this book first that a reconciliation was effected with that wider public which was interested in the new doctrine of evolution, but felt repelled by it on religious grounds. Drummond's basic thought—simple enough, but in its simplicity to a high degree constructive—is that of extending likewise to the spiritual world the laws valid for the natural world, as Spencer had extended them to the historico-social world. By the term "spiritual world" Drummond means chiefly the world of religion. This, he held, is subject to the same strict principle of law as holds good in the natural sphere; both principles are the same in every respect. The fundamental law of all being is thus the law of continuity; the same laws pervade every grade and level of being, binding them all together into one all-embracing unity. It is the task of science to establish the naturalness of the supernatural; of

[1] Cf. *Philosophy of Theism* (1857) and *The Philosophical Basis of Evolution* (1890).

religion, to demonstrate the supernaturalness of the natural. And the spiritual becomes natural in the same degree as nature becomes spirit. The flaw in this philosophy is that *πρῶτον ψεῦδος*, the disregard of the *μετάβασις εἰς ἄλλο γένος*; it suffers from an almost intolerable confusion of heterogeneous spheres of being, an utter obliteration of all boundaries between nature and spirit. Religion disguised in the cloak of science misuses science for her own ends; and the confusion is carried so far that one may well doubt whether we have here a degradation of mind to the natural, or a spiritualizing of nature. But the inner motives of the doctrine are exposed to view when we find the final upshot to be that the spiritual has priority over the natural, that matter possesses no reality of its own, but is merely incarnation of spirit, and that only spirit exhibits the essence of reality.

Drummond's popular philosophy came to further flower in *The Ascent of Man* (1894), in which he replaces the concept struggle for existence by that of struggle for another's existence, seeking to show that ethical phenomena enter upon the scene not only in the human but far below in the animal kingdom, and that they are bound up also with the simpler processes of life. Altruistic behaviour pervades entire nature and is as potent as egoism, and the law of love or struggle for another's existence, which Drummond opposes to the Darwinian principle, flows through the whole life of the universe. Here, too, the same tendency as the earlier book showed is in evidence—that of equating different realms of being and bringing them under a single unifying, underlying principle of law.

Seeley, the well-known historian, dealt with the religious problem in two works published anonymously, *Ecce Homo* (1865: a representation of the teaching of Jesus, the appearance of which aroused violent controversy) and *Natural Religion* (1882), but his attitude is not so clear as Drummond's. The lack of definiteness in his ideas and the involved way in which they are presented leaves it a matter of doubt whether he represented a purely pantheistic religion of nature or retained room in his theory for theistic and supernaturalistic arguments. The predominant tendency of his thought is at any rate in the former direction. He also, like Drummond, was concerned to bring his conception of religion into accord with modern science and to display the laws of nature as being also the laws of God; and he was convinced that the identification of God with nature and the adoration of a higher reality *in* nature provided the man of scientific mind with an outlet for a religious emotion similar to that which in the man of devout mind is released by belief in a transcendent personal deity. Seeley was, however, much less committed in matters of belief than Drummond was. For the rest, a prominent part is played in his interpretation of religion by aesthetic factors. He held that characteristic manifestations of the religious are found in whatsoever arouses enthusiasm and stimulates wonder, whatsoever is worthy of veneration, whatsoever transports or exalts a man in wonder and admiration. Consequently, he saw the embodiments of the religious life not so much in the worship of an unperceivable transcendent Being as in disinterested devotion to truth and scientific knowledge, in the love of beauty, in warmth and purity of conscience; in a word, in every endeavour after the true, the beautiful, and the good. Thus Seeley's teaching, in which the cultural values of man are endued with a sort of religious splendour, amounts in the end rather to a religion of culture than a religion of nature; it is the expression of a highly educated personality responsive to the life of mind in all its activities rather than either the thin substitute for religion of a scientist or the faith of a soul for whom religion is a really gripping experience.

Evolutionist ethics moves in general along a narrower and more enclosed line of development than evolutionist religious philosophy, although here, too, there are a number of variations and nuances to be observed. We have already become acquainted with its main features and some of its typical forms in considering Spencer, Huxley, Westermarck, and Clifford. A number of other thinkers remain who may well be grouped together, as recognizing the problem of ethics to be one of decisive significance. By far the most important of these is SIR LESLIE STEPHEN (1832–1904), who in his chief systematic work *The Science of Ethics* (1882) made what is perhaps the maturest and best thought-out contribution to establishing morals upon the foundation of an evolutionist philosophy. Stephen was a very gifted and versatile writer whose literary work is interwoven with the intellectual life of the Victorian Age in diverse ways, bearing fruit in journalism as well as in biography, philosophical and literary history, systematic philosophy, etc. From 1882 to 1891 he was at the head of one of the greatest undertakings of British Letters, the monumental *Dictionary of National Biography*, to which he himself made numerous contributions, and chief among his other works was the *History of English Thought in the XVIIIth Century* (two vols., 1876, vide supra, p. 83), an impressive delineation of the Enlightenment in England, to be followed later by a sort of sequel for the XIXth Century (*The English Utilitarians*, three vols., 1900). Further writings of mainly philosophical content are the *Essays on Free Thinking and Plain Speaking* (1873), *An Agnostic's Apology* (1893), and *Social Rights and Duties* (two vols., 1896).

Stephen had belonged originally to orthodox circles, and had indeed been ordained for the priesthood as a young man. Later he applied himself to philosophy and under the dominating influence first of Mill, then of Darwin, and lastly of Spencer, he withdrew more and more from the Church and finally gave up his clerical status in 1875. From that time on he acknowledged his view of the world to be that of an Agnostic and Freethinker, and in religious matters he was a typical, though belated, representative of the "Enlightenment", whose views closely approximated to those of his favourite philosopher Hume. For his philosophical position upon other matters also he was quite as much indebted to the classical British Empiricism and to the Enlightenment as to the more modern thinkers, and he stood as near to Locke, Hume, and the XVIIIth-Century moralists as he had stood at first to the Utilitarianism of Bentham and the two Mills, and as he did later to the Evolutionism of Spencer and Darwin. Thus the entire thought of the British tradition, of which he had a profounder historical knowledge than most of his contemporaries, had penetrated his mind and been assimilated by him. We see the features common to this tradition constantly reappearing in his own thinking: the hostility to metaphysics, the indifference to religion (rising in his case to contempt, avowed disbelief, if not openly expressed atheism), the continually repeated appeal to experience as the sole source of our knowledge (it is in this rather than as with Spencer and others in a metaphysical doctrine that he sees the basic truth of Agnosticism); the honour paid to exact science, which he holds to be the only valid model for philosophy also and upon which he bases all human progress, the rejection of all *a priori* truths and of all deduction and construction from pure reason, and many others. But his philosophical importance is to be found not in what he has in common with his predecessors and contemporaries, but in his attempt to arrive at a formulation and a solution of his own of the problems he had inherited. But he achieved nothing of the kind except in the field of ethics.

If the foundations of an evolutionary ethic were laid by Spencer, it was Stephen who raised the edifice to its highest point. *The Science of Ethics* thus signifies not so much a mere continuation of, as a real advance upon, *The Data of Ethics*, and in it the philosophical content of that work is deepened and its value enhanced. The title of the book itself throws into relief the author's intention. Ethics admits of scientific treatment, and scientific methods should be applied to it. Ethics must consequently be set free from all metaphysical speculation and religious sanction and confine itself within the domain of experience. Moreover, it has nothing to do with moral principles presumed to be intuitively certain or derived from purely logical considerations, but its function is to describe and analyse the moral facts as they are given in experience and open to observation, in order to derive from them the general features of human conduct and human character, and it has to inquire into their genesis and the rôle allotted them in the universal evolutionary process. Ethics is therefore for the most part interwoven with biological, psychological, and sociological investigations, and it is from them that it obtains all the genuine insight that it exhibits.

The implication of the moral life with the facts of society is of special importance. Stephen attempts—and in this he goes far beyond both Utilitarianism and Spencer—to free morality from all individualist limitations and conditions and to incorporate it altogether into the social fabric. The first thing, then, to be done is to determine the relation of individual and community. The outcome is that we are to understand neither the individual as a self-subsistent atomic unit nor society as a mere sum or aggregate of such units, but that what obtains is an organic relation, such that while society as a social organism includes the separate single being as a part of its own body, the latter cannot be thought of at all outside of this relationship. In this sense Stephen uses a happy and vivid expression to designate the individual, 'social tissue', and he applies this term also to the social whole, so that the single individual is to be represented as woven into this whole fabric with every thread of his being. The upshot of this for the conduct of man is that, however much a man appears to be pursuing ends and purposes of his own, he is yet always to a definite degree under the pressure of society, and is taking cognizance of *its* interests even though he seems to be actuated by egoistic motives. For even acts that only intend the good of the agent, i.e. the satisfaction of an individual desire for pleasure or personal good, originate in the man's character which is their basis; and character is demonstrably in very large measure a product of the social fabric, almost wholly determined and shaped by factors in the community life.

The moral criterion resulting from this position is neither the individual's personal endeavour for happiness nor the demand of the greatest happiness of the greatest number, for all hedonistic and eudaemonistic theories involve ultimately the underlying assumption of the individual as a social atom. It is rather the health and efficiency of the social organism.

That act is morally good by which the life of the community is genuinely furthered and enhanced, and that community will preserve itself best in the struggle for existence in which the moral norms determining individuals are the presupposition of the social health of the whole. The final goal of all morality is the health, power, efficiency, and vitality of the social tissue, and conduct only fulfils the moral law in so far as it is directed to this end. A social system proves itself the more vital the more it is brought into and kept in a state of equilibrium, and therefore a further goal of ethics is the achieving and maintenance of social equilibrium. Expressed in terms of historical development this means that moral principles come to be adopted through a process of natural selection, and that the moral type which overcomes the others is that which is most effective, has the most potent life, and shows the best balance.

While Stephen rejects the pleasure- and happiness-theories of his predecessors, he yet seeks to do justice to the principle of utility and to find a place for it in his ethics; which thus appears as a synthesis of utilitarian and evolutionistic motives, the latter, of course, predominating. In this way the exposition given above may be made also to conform to the canon of Utility if we see in this not merely the principle of producing pleasure and happiness but also that of promoting health and maintaining life. Pleasure and health, while far from being coincident, work out in acts of at least approximately the same tendency, for wherever they are mutually opposed, the social equilibrium is impaired. Their approximation, therefore, if not their identity, will inevitably be guaranteed by evolution. But in every case utility in the sense of life-maintenance proves far more fundamental than utility in the sense of mere promotion of pleasure and happiness.

Evolution, finally, carries with it a further consequence. If certain ways of acting acquire a stronger moral weight than others through the working of natural selection, and thereby become preferred, i.e. approved by the human community, it is evident that what matters is not a single isolated action but the character from which it springs. It is therefore not only certain ways of acting but also specific characters that are bred and fostered by evolution. The training of a firm character represents a higher level of moral development than the training in this or that way of acting. This is the advance made in passing from the morality of external practice to the morality of inward habit. The more highly organized the typical moral person is, the more will he have a fixed determination of character. And the highest ethical law is therefore to be expressed not as "*do* this" but as "*be* this".

In conclusion, it is to be noted that a few years later Stephen's ethics received an extension in the earliest book of SAMUEL ALEXANDER on *Moral Order and Progress* (1889), which we shall treat of in another place (p. 624). It is a work born of the spirit of Stephen's ethics and like it in many ways, though it shows independent features.

The ethics of EDITH SIMCOX (1844–1901), which precedes Stephen's by a few years and is set out in her book *Natural Law, an Essay in Ethics* (1877), is a further variant of naturalistic evolutionism. It may be called "Perfectionism", as it sees the ideal goal of moral life and effort in the perfect unfolding of all natural human faculties. It has—and in this it is perhaps a typical feminine production—an edifying and aesthetic strain rather than the character of a scientific work. Miss Simcox connects the moral, political, and the whole higher life of the spirit with the natural powers that are developed in man, and she anchors the principle of law determining this life in the principle of natural law. The moral standard, wrought out of natural evolution and endorsed by it, is that which corresponds most to the typical character of man *quâ* man, i.e. is adapted best to humanity, while every deviation from it is felt as an imperfection and a lessening of moral values. The good of action accordingly consists in fostering and training an ideal human type by straining every natural capacity to the highest and completest achievement of which it is capable. Moral perfection is nothing but the fulfilment of natural law to which human existence is also subject. Thus the individual as an agent is summoned to active co-operation with the powers pervading the cosmos, while as a contemplative being he bows in veneration before them, to acquiesce in their governance in a spirit of religious surrender.

ALFRED BARRATT (1844–81) who, though by profession a barrister, had a passionate interest in philosophy, published when only twenty-four an ethical work (*Physical Ethics*, 1869) which agrees with the Evolutionist theories in treating of the moral being of man as a product of the development of his natural being and thus as the outcome of the physical, biological, and physiological factors and conditions which make this what it is. Barratt, too, exhibits the tendency of Evolutionism markedly to confuse the boundaries between the different levels of being, and this leads him to assign to the level of "Nature" a dominant and prerogative position over every other—the corresponding characteristic upon the side of knowledge being the predominance assigned to the natural sciences over all other disciplines. At this point the demand is put forward in the name of the unity of all knowledge that ethics, too, must be subsumed under the ideal of knowledge proper to scientific thought. This is expressed by the designation "Physical Ethics"—the foundation of the science being rational obedience to the laws of nature. In the precocity of this work of Barratt's we see evident traces of his exceptional intellectual gifts, and it contains many original features, even though as a whole it is not more than an average production. It derived a strong impetus from Spencer, whom Barratt calls the greatest philosopher of the age, but the impetus is carried forward to assume an independent form. Barratt's early death did not allow him to gather the fruits of his fervour as a thinker in a greater work. Towards the end of his life comprehensive designs for a metaphysical cosmological system were urgent in him, and what had been completed by the time of his death was published in a book entitled *Physical Metempiric* (1883). The ideas developed in this book likewise testify to the strength and force of Barratt's thought, which was moving in the direction of a monadological philosophy, with echoes of Leibniz in it, and was thus turning away from his earlier Naturalism.

Evolutionary ethics found its final expression in the XIXth Century in *The Origin and Growth of the Moral Instinct* (1898) by ALEXANDER SUTHERLAND (1852–1902), a journalist and author whose home was in Australia and who only upon this one occasion turned aside into the *terrain* of philosophy. His work, like that of Westermarck, is occupied with the empirical proof of the existence of a moral sense from the lowest animal level up to the highest types of human culture, and with the connected question of the moral progress of humanity. Sutherland finds the primary and original moral instinct in sympathy, which he makes to be rooted in mother-love. From sympathy—already exercising a decisive control over the life of primitive peoples, and variously objectified in manifold norms and maxims—there grows the idea of Duty at a higher evolutionary stage, and this in turn becoming internalized, passes into the feeling of self-respect. In other words, the fulfilment of duty is the consequence of inward self-respect and not simply for the sake of external advantage. Duty recedes into an inner conscience, and the moral life thereby attains its noblest embodiment and highest fulfilment.

After the turn of the century the most important system of evolutionary ethics which we must mention is that developed by L. T. HOBHOUSE in his book *Morals in Evolution* (two volumes, 1906). This, the last example of the school which we shall consider, will be dealt with below, when the work of this thinker will be discussed as a whole (pp. 150 ff.).

There remains to be considered a field akin to ethics, to which the new science and philosophy alike offered fertile possibilities of application, viz. sociology. Here, too, Spencer had shown the way, which other investigators were to follow further than he did. As, however, their achievements belong for the most part to specialist science, I may omit them from this study. But apart from works of more general interest already mentioned or to be mentioned later in another context attention should be drawn to a work much esteemed in its day, which attempted to extract the sociological value from Darwinism and to make it fruitful—BENJAMIN KIDD's (1858–1916)

Social Evolution (1894). This book had a success as huge as Drummond's *Natural Law in the Spiritual World*,[1] and the reasons were very much the same; the popular and impressive style and the limpid clarity of the thought were contributory to it, but the main ground for it was the fact that here a life-line was thrown to religion by one of its bitterest foes, Darwinism. This was enough to win for the book an enthusiastic reception from the general public, whereas the learned world maintained a much cooler attitude towards it.

It may be said that Kidd's sociology took over the basic contentions of the theory of descent lock, stock, and barrel—the struggle for existence, natural selection, the survival of the fittest, the inheritance of characters, etc.—the last-named less in the sense of Darwin than in that of Weismann, by whom Kidd was strongly influenced. The vital law of human existence, individual and social, and of the mutual relations also of individual and society, is the same as for the animal world: ceaseless and unremitting strife and struggle, selection and rejection, progress and development. It is not only the interests of single persons that are in opposition, but those of social organisms and finally those of entire societies in their mutual relations. All forms of society have arisen out of the struggle for existence through natural processes of selective breeding, and they remain subject to its laws. So far we have here an undiluted biological theory of society, in which, indeed, the Darwinian principle is given an exaggerated sharpness in order to be applied to social life. At this point, however, a series of motives are interwoven with this sociological pattern which give Kidd's theory its characteristic colour and to which it chiefly owed its powerful attraction. First, there is the unqualified over-emphasis of the affective factors in man, and the resulting disparagement of the rational and intellectual, to the profit of a sociology which hereby acquires an essentially emotional basis. Kidd holds that it is

[1] It passed through a long succession of impressions and editions—ten in the first year after publication—and was translated into nearly every European language.

not primarily the intellectual qualities that are bred and fostered through natural selection, and promote human development, but rather the emotional qualities, and he ascribes to the latter a much more potent social efficacy than to the former. Indeed, he even goes so far as to see in whatever is bound up with intellect, understanding, reason, science—in a word with man's rationality—a factor openly hostile to evolution and an obstacle to progress. There therefore exists for him no causal connection between higher social and mental development, and the interval separating pupils of higher and lower cultural levels is for him the result not of a difference in intellectual advance, but of the higher cultivation of emotional powers. He thus introduced a new feature into Evolutionism, hardly ever before presented or at least not in so crudely one-sided a fashion, for as expounded by all its outstanding representatives, Evolutionism had extolled knowledge and science (and therefore man *quâ* rational) as the ideal, and made all human betterment, individual and social, dependent upon them. With Kidd, on the contrary, feeling takes over the part hitherto played by science, and becomes exalted to the prime factor in social evolution—the factor which really constitutes a society. It is the opposite of reason, and in contrast to it displays a high degree of social efficacy and is shown to be the upward-driving force in evolution.

But there is a further point in his exposition, which, like the other, had never yet been thus combined with the principle of evolution. In a crude, generalizing, sketchy way that is peculiar to him, Kidd identifies the world of feeling with the domain of religion (and in a secondary sense also with that of morality). Some very strange consequences for evolution and history result from this. It should be first remarked that the concept which Kidd connects with religion shares the indistinctness of all his other concepts and formulations. At any rate, however, he understands by it an eminently social phenomenon and is never tired of stressing its emotional character as well as its ultra-rational sanction. He excludes from it every rational element as being in essential and irreconcilable contradiction to it, and he brings its ethical into greater prominence than its specifically religious aspect. Now seen from the point of view of social evolution we are led to the conclusion that religion represents the real principle of selection in the struggle for existence. It is first and foremost the ethical-religious character that is aroused by the evolutionary process, seeing that this proves itself superior in social efficacy to all others, particularly to the theoretical. No forces promote social progress so much as the moral and religious forces, no religious peoples but will overcome in the struggle for life irreligious peoples and prove themselves the fitter to survive. Religion is the greatest social force there is, and its value is shown by the fact that it proves to be the sharpest weapon in the conflicts of rival races and peoples. It acquires this pre-eminent importance especially because it arouses and cultivates in man altruistic feelings, and because it teaches him a selfless surrender to the community. All this is denied to reason, which is a destructive rather than a constructive function. The highest form of social structure is that which is based upon the highest measure of religious faith and moral will and the highest form of religious faith is Christianity, in which Kidd sees the very backbone of the entire culture of the West, the central pillar of the whole edifice. Combined with this thought is a wellnigh fanatical optimism as to progress, which, lost in uncritical admiration of the splendid advances made by the present age, ignores the defects and flaws which this very age holds hidden in the heart of it.

With this also are combined discussions bearing upon the philosophy of history, the meaning and import of Western civilization, such as Kidd also put forward in a later work: *The Principles of Western Civilization* (1902). But this is merely a lengthy reissue of his earlier arguments and contains hardly any new thoughts, and the same is true of the last work *The Science of Power* (published posthumously 1918), likewise a very successful one, written under the impress of the World War. The obstinacy with which Kidd stuck to his principles is shown by the fact that even that shattering catastrophe was unable to cure him of his delusion of progress.

We must find room here for the mention of another writer who occupied an independent, even in many respects an aloof position within the Evolutionist movement, seeing that he did not so much fit into the framework of evolutionary theory as split it. This is SAMUEL BUTLER (1835–1902), one of the most interesting men of the Victorian Age, painter, musician, philosopher, essayist, critic, translator, Homeric and Shakespearian scholar, biographer, novelist, and sheep-breeder, who, however multifarious his activities, brought a creative originality into nearly every field of interest in which he engaged. But in none of them was he a specialist or professional expert: everywhere he was a dilettante of genius, an amateur, an awakener, and stimulator who scattered his brilliant thoughts and fancies in almost prodigal profusion. He stood in conflict with nearly all the dominant opinions and forces of the time, everywhere he laid hands on the existing norms and values and went counter to everything that was in the eyes of his contemporaries sacred and valid in morality, religion and the Church, science, philosophy, and education. He was a swimmer against the current of the time, shaking the world out of its sleep, a lonely, unrecognized figure, but in spite of criticism and denial, creative and big with future meaning.

It is hard to say what was the basic interest of a personality with so many layers and facets as Butler's, but we may presume it to lie in the domain of thought. He had at any rate a philosophical brain of the first order, though he lacked the disciplined training and system of the specialist and scholar, and his thought radiated out into most of his other activities, and is there (especially in the novels) as easily to be recognized as in his more systematic discussions. One of the most alert, keen, and emancipated spirits of his age, Butler's freedom of mind was not so much that of a "freethinker" ordinarily so called, as a liberation from prejudices and from the bonds and fetters of tradition, and though in his sceptical criticism and satire he was destructive enough, Butler's thought was positive and constructive, the expression of a deeply rooted creative force.

The central idea dominating Butler's philosophy is that of evolution or development, and though he subjected this idea to far-reaching modifications and amplifications of his own, he remained to the end possessed by it. He was one of Darwin's earliest disciples, welcoming the master's doctrine with enthusiasm on its first appearance, and it signified for him an experience that determined the direction of his future thinking. But he was not the man simply to accept a doctrine passed on to him or to adhere to it merely because it was the chief fashion of the day. On the contrary, he soon found himself in opposition to it in essential points, and as he had been one of its first adherents, so now he became one of its earliest critics. Butler's critical examination of the theory of descent is certainly the most acute and penetrating that appeared in England till the end of the century, and this mainly because it did not approach the new doctrine as it were from outside with a criterion already prepared by which to judge it, but with one which, having its origin from within the theory itself, demolished and transformed it internally on its own ground. It may be said that Butler anticipated, if not expressly, at least implicitly, most of the restatements and renovations of Darwinism which only saw the light much later, whether in the work of Nietzsche or Bergson, or in Neo-vitalism, Pragmatism, and the philosophy of Emergence. Here, as in other respects, Butler was far in advance of his time, and though his life belongs to the XIXth, his mind belongs to the XXth Century.

The original intuitions which we owe to Butler—in his own day new and unfamiliar, to-day commonplace—can only be indicated shortly and in general terms. To take the most distinctive point first, Butler early recognized, with a prophetic clearness of vision, that the doctrine of evolution was in danger of foundering in the sandy desert of a materialistic and mechanistic philosophy, and all his efforts were consequently directed to bringing it back on to the paths of an idealistic and teleological interpretation of life. Here he saw an ally in the

German philosopher E. von Hartmann, with whose criticism of Darwinism he agreed in essentials, though he rejected his metaphysical speculations. He opposed the thought of a creative energy in life to the mechanism of selection and inheritance, and posited a sort of primal force or primal will pervading every part of the universe, holding the whole together in a single cosmic organism. The concept of life as a creative principle now becomes dominant—no longer the mere biological life indifferent to values, but one that possesses the emphatic worth and import which later vitalistic theories assign to it. Butler's interpretation of life is particularly interesting in his treatment of memory, which resembles that which had been already developed, though unknown to Butler, by E. Hering, and which has later become more widely known through R. Semon's doctrine of *Mneme*. According to this, we are to understand under 'life' that property of organic matter whereby it is able to remember, and matter is 'animate' in so far as it possesses this capacity. This property is already present in the germ-cell though unconscious, and it is to it that Butler refers not only conscious and purposive psychic processes but every kind of unconscious fulfilment, repetition, habituation, inheritance, and finally, the process of evolution itself. This is enough to make it clear that memory is not a merely individual phenomenon but a racial possession, and that there is a sort of tribal memory which is already functioning at the birth of the individual and is not interrupted by his death, which is nothing but a change of memories. The memory-function can thus be inherited, and as so inherited is termed instinct. A habit becomes instinct when it has been practised with sufficient frequency and regularity through a succession of generations. Instinct and intellect are different not in principle but in degree, since activities originally intellectual can sink into instincts if often enough repeated. The same thing is true also of the difference between the organic and the inorganic: there is not, according to Butler, any yawning chasm separating them, but the boundary is being continually crossed in either direction. Even inanimate matter is capable of 'remembering', and in so far as it does so may be said to be alive. All living beings are basically made of one and the same stuff and would be alike in every respect but for the divergence of their 'memories', their difference in memory-capacity, and in the actual memories deposited.

Butler's conception of memory must not, however, be understood in a mechanical sense: it is teleological through and through, as is the life which it in fact constitutes. Life is in the most fundamental sense not a mere mechanical process, a blind agitation of natural forces, but purpose, intention, will, foresight; in a word, creative design. The stream of life flows through the entire organic evolution (and even through inorganic evolution in a more expanded and less pregnant sense), uniting every living being with the unending chain of its ancestors, whose continued efficacy, functioning unaware as stored-up memory, gives it its separate individual character. The primal driving force, however, which moves in all organic life and animates it, is the will, and with this is combined the belief that gives the will power to become what it chooses; and in Butler's view the power of will is so great that if a dove resolutely willed to become a peacock, it could not be prevented from doing so by any natural selection.

We see what a transformation of Darwin's categories is involved here, and what an entirely new and alien stamp is put on the evolutionary theory. The path trodden by Butler is unmistakably that which leads from mechanism to teleology, from determinism to freedom of the will, from 'biologism' to vitalism, from naturalism to idealism, from Darwin's natural selection to Bergson's creative *élan vital* and Alexander's conception of 'emergence', and ultimately even to the psychoanalysis of Freud; and it is all nothing but the expression of his own sparkingly vivid and vital personality.[1]

[1] A straight path leads also from Butler to Bernard Shaw. The dramatist has repeatedly acknowledged this and has highly extolled the genius of his predecessor. Shaw's own thinking was in essentials fostered and determined by Butler's ideas (see the prefaces to *Major Barbara* and *Back to Methuselah*).

Butler's chief works were: *Life and Habit* (1877); *Evolution Old*

Butler's philosophy indicates the turning-point in naturalistic Evolutionism and its hour of destiny. Yet his brilliant conceptions, intuitively glimpsed rather than worked out scientifically, failed to arouse the response they deserved during his lifetime. They played only a small part in the long process by which the philosophy of evolution was recast and reforged from about the turn of the century onward. Many and varied forces belonging to diverse schools and groups shared in bringing this result about, but none was a more potent, successful, and exciting influence than that which had its source in the philosophy of Bergson. It was his *L'Évolution créatrice* that gave the decisive turn to the direction of evolutionist thought, for in it, while the form of the conception of evolution remains the same, the import and content of it has been utterly transmuted. Nothing shows more plainly the deep gulf between the older and the younger theory than Bergson's short critical examination of Spencer with which he concluded his chief book (vide *L'Évolution créatrice*, pp. 392–9, English translation 384–91). Here he explains how completely Spencer missed the real meaning of evolution, as development. Bergson's achievement has made an evolutionary philosophy in the old style henceforth an impossibility. The old forms still survive, it is true, but there is no life in them; and though we still meet even to-day isolated stragglers of the old doctrine, yet henceforward every thinker who has something real to say on these problems stands, and must necessarily stand, within the field of influence of Bergson's thought.

This is true first and foremost of the "Emergence" philosophy which has to-day entered upon the inheritance of Evolutionism. It forms a wide current in contemporary Anglo-Saxon thought and in many ways it has connections with the earlier doctrine; but what is distinctive about it is that it is penetrated through and through by Bergsonism and could not be conceived without

and New (1879); *God the Known and God the Unknown* (1879); *Unconscious Memory* (1880): *Luck or Cunning?* (1887); also the novels *Erewhon* (1872), *Erewhon Revisited* (1901), and *The Way of All Flesh* (1903).

it. Accordingly, we shall not treat of this most recent phase of Evolutionist theory in this place but shall return in other contexts to its several representatives. The chief of them, founders of the theory, if we disregard a single contribution of Lewes (cf. p. 121), are Alexander and Lloyd Morgan, and its impress is to be traced more or less deeply in the work of Hobhouse, Schiller, McDougall, Wildon Carr, and Smuts, and of the Americans Dewey, Sellars, Brightman, and Spaulding; that is, among thinkers who belong to very different schools of thought. And what has been said of the "Emergence" theory holds good also of Pragmatism, which, while it is not to be counted as really belonging to Evolutionism, has affinities with some of its variations in several of its *motifs*. But it is important to observe that the chief British representative of Pragmatism, F. C. S. Schiller, issued directly out of Darwinism, and that his mature doctrine also does not in any way belie this origin. The earliest pre-Pragmatist phase of his thought, as expressed in *The Riddles of the Sphinx* (1891), is based throughout on an evolutionist foundation, and even the theories of Darwin and Spencer found in this book expression of an independent kind, though it owes, of course, a good deal to them (see infra, p. 454). But neither did Pragmatism remain untouched by the transformation which the principle of evolution underwent, but assimilated it to its own doctrine.

This, however, does not exhaust the Bergsonian trend of thought. It penetrated—and, indeed, still penetrates—modern philosophy through countless channels. But it has divided into so many separate currents and tendencies that it cannot be any longer understood as a unified structure. And its justification lies in this—that since the influx of Bergsonism every British thinker in certain respects belongs to the Evolutionist camp or at any rate has paid his tribute in this point or in that to Evolutionism.

We conclude this section with a more detailed estimate of the philosophy of HOBHOUSE,[1] whose teaching may well be

[1] Leonard Trelawny Hobhouse (1864–1929) studied and taught from 1883 to 1897 at the University of Oxford; from 1897 to 1902

called the most notable embodiment of modern evolutionist thought. Our account will show, however, that this prolific and fruitful thinker can be neither enclosed within the narrow framework of a single principle nor assigned to a special school or trend of thought, but that he leaves these limitations far behind and requires to be measured by standards of his own. It must be emphatically underlined, therefore, that in treating of his work in this context we do not mean to anticipate any conclusion as to its character and tendency.

Hobhouse's philosophical achievement is distinguished not so much for its depth and originality as for its breadth of view, and for the comprehensive scope and wide variety of interests which it manifests. After Spencer, his is the most encyclopaedic mind among British philosophers, and he was also an investigator of high and independent standing in many and diverse fields of study,—in fact he defied the present-day spirit of specialization by mastering an astonishing wealth of both general and special knowledge and bringing it together under a single philosophical scheme of interpretation. One has, moreover, to consider that his activities as scientist and philosopher represent only a segment of his total labours, and that besides these his life was consumed in intensive work in journalism, politics, social work, organization, teaching, and the like, in order to get a just idea of his wellnigh inexhaustible energy and versatility of achievement.

he worked as a journalist in Manchester, from 1902 and onwards he combined many-sided activities in journalism, politics, applied economics, and university work, and occupied from 1907 to 1929 a chair in Sociology in London University. His philosophical writings are: *The Theory of Knowledge* (1896, third edition, 1921); *Mind in Evolution* (1901, third edition, 1926); *Morals in Evolution*, two vols., (1906; in one vol. 1923); *Social Evolution and Political Theory* (1911); *Development and Purpose, An Essay towards a Philosophy of Evolution* (1913; revised 1927); *The Metaphysical Theory of the State* (1918); *The Rational Good* (1921); *The Elements of Social Justice* (1922); *Social Development, its Nature and Conditions* (1924) (the last four works combined as *Principles of Sociology*, four vols., 1819–24); *The Philosophy of Development* (1924 in *Contemporary British Philosophy*, ed. by J. H. Muirhead, vol. i). Cf. *L. T. Hobhouse, His Life and Work* (1931), by J. A. Hobson and Morris Ginsberg.

The general character of Hobhouse's philosophical cast of mind is shown in his rooted aversion to all mere abstract speculation that is carried on in the void. His thought was always built upon the solid foundation of exact investigation into some region of empirical fact, and was constantly being rejuvenated at the well of experience; yet it never, on the other hand, stopped at the mere fact but always felt impelled to advance afresh to a philosophical conspectus and synthesis. To put the matter in a metaphor, he ploughs the empirical field and sows philosophical seeds in it, in order to reap a philosophical harvest. With this goes the close relationship which he established between philosophy and science. There is for him at bottom no real difference between the two. While the sciences seek to subject a part of reality, or reality under a single determinate aspect, to rational interpretation, philosophy strives to reach knowledge of the total reality and to subdue it to theory. Philosophy must therefore tread the path of the special sciences, and as this is the path of continual never-ending advance, philosophy also being likewise ever on the march must forgo any final conclusions. To complete the many-roomed edifice of philosophical thought in a well-rounded-off system is less important than to pursue the problems for their own sake, or for that of their factual content. The effort towards system-making which Hobhouse expressly recognizes, and which was very vigorous in his own thought, is only justified if it issues in an open system which retains and preserves the several problems in their own form, and into which a new inflow of factual material as worked out in the special sciences is always possible. Thus philosophy has first of all as its goal the synthesis of the sciences, or more precisely, a synthesis which stands in harmony with the results of specialist research, and is built upon them as a foundation. Yet it is not so one-sided as to stop at giving the scientific aspect of things an absolute validity, but comprises every sphere of experience that admits of theoretic treatment, including the realm of values within which lie the religious, aesthetic, and moral orders. It is thus in the most comprehensive sense a synthesis not only of being *quâ* scientifically known, but of being in all its orders and gradations.

The wide empirical foundation that underlies all Hobhouse's philosophical conclusions and his constant readiness to make fresh accretions of experienced matters of fact yield their fruit for philosophy, give his thought the undogmatic and loosely knit character which distinguishes it even in comparison with the philosophical doctrines that influenced him most. Just as he drew upon everything that seemed to him significant in science and life to make his own thinking more fruitful, so, too, his mind was always open in relation to the philosophical doctrines of his predecessors and contemporaries. In appropriating and assimilating the thought of another he did not bother about its school or tendency, but was concerned simply and solely with its actual value and applicability within the framework of his own system. He is thus hostile to all philosophical partisanship, and does not swear by any single master's words, but by listening to the voices of many becomes an intermediary and bridge between diverse movements mutually in conflict. This tendency to conciliation is manifested even in his earliest work, which is specially directed to reconcile the two hostile parties of traditional empiricism and reawakened idealism, and thus as early as the end of last century paved the way for that meeting of extremes which was only to show its wider and fuller effects much later. But this characteristic of Hobhouse's work may provide the reason why for all its richness and abundance it never achieved the success it deserved. The recognition he won from professional philosophers fell far short of his real accomplishment, since none of the various schools and groups could count him as belonging to them, or adopt his work in all its reach and extent.

Thus it is neither correct to call Hobhouse the best representative of the traditional British school[1] nor yet to compare his standpoint with that of Bosanquet.[2] Rather, he transcends

[1] J. A. Nicholson, *Some Aspects of the Philosophy of Hobhouse*, University of Illinois, Urbana, 1928.

[2] C. Sutton in *Logos*, vol. 16, 1927, p. 100.

both, by appropriating, or again rejecting, component elements of each, and so reaching a synthesis bearing entirely the stamp of his own mind. In this respect we find a characteristic utterance in the preface to his first work in philosophy, the *Theory of Knowledge*; it throws a clear light on the situation, and remains true for Hobhouse's later work as well as for his earlier. "The time would thus seem ripe for an unprejudiced attempt to fuse what is true and valuable in the older English tradition with the newer doctrines which have now become naturalized among us. In betaking ourselves to Lotze and Hegel, we need not forget what we have learnt from Mill and Spencer." These words seem to be aimed expressly against Green, who some twenty years before sought to direct the attention of the younger generation away from the belated systems of Mill and Spencer and introduce it to the study of Kant and Hegel (vide Green's edition of Hume's *Treatise*, vol. ii, p. 71).

It was the evolutionism of Spencer that first determined the pattern of Hobhouse's ideas. In his youth he regarded Spencer's doctrine as the last word of science, but he was soon subjecting it none the less to a radical revision, and the longer he lived the further he receded from it. He took over from Spencer the encyclopaedic character of philosophic thought and the interpretation of philosophical system-making as a synthetic conspectus of the results of scientific inquiry. With Mill he was united both by his epistemological and logical empiricism on the one hand, and by his political liberalism and individualistic theory of the State on the other. But Hobhouse owed more to the older empiricists than to those of a later day. We are reminded of Bacon not only by his general mental attitude, but by his strictly scientific method and his view of philosophy as *scientia scientiarum*; of Locke, by his epistemological realism and his general manner of treating the problem of knowledge; while his points of agreement with Hume are so many that they run like a crimson thread through Hobhouse's entire theory. The positivism of Comte also was not without influence on Hobhouse's thought. From Comte he derived his orientation towards sociology as the science of society, and from him too (or from his English disciple and apostle Bridges) he took the conception of humanity, though he did not adopt as his own the anti-metaphysical attitude of Positivism. On the other hand, the threads connecting him with the idealist movement are likewise very strong. Green's views on social and political philosophy in part accord with Hobhouse's, and in logic the latter owes almost as much to Bradley and Bosanquet as to Mill,—indeed Bosanquet particularly became, as he admitted, his intellectual guide in many respects, uncompromising as was his antagonism to Bosanquet's Hegelian theory of the State. Finally, he was influenced in the development of his realist theory of knowledge by men like T. Case and J. Cook Wilson, early precursors of the realist movement, with whom he enjoyed personal interchange of thought at Oxford.

The course of development of Hobhouse's philosophy shows that while as a young man his mind no more than that of most of his contemporaries could escape the effect of the powerful assault of the doctrines of Darwin, Spencer, and Huxley, a strong reaction set in early against their naturalistic theories of evolution, a reaction which was fostered in the intellectual atmosphere of Oxford, at that time the stronghold of Idealism. Here he encountered the full pressure and excitement of the new movement, and was for a time swept into its orbit. On the other hand he felt repelled by the too airy and abstract speculation of the Hegelians. His thirst for fact and for a close hold on reality could find no lasting satisfaction in a purely rational and intellectualist philosophy that finds its completion by soaring into the void, and he thus found himself constantly forced back upon empirical inquiry and the exact investigations of special scientific fields, or to activities of a definitely practical kind. His earliest book, which belongs to his Oxford years, upon the Labour movement (1893), testifies to his already awakened interest in social and political questions, and already in 1888 he was spending several hours a day in the laboratory of the biologist J. S. Haldane, occupied with physiological and biochemical experiments upon animals which were a preparation for his pioneer investigations in the field of animal psychology. Later he turned again to pure theory in his study of logical, epistemological, and metaphysical questions, and published as the first-fruits of his philosophical labours the *Theory of Knowledge* (1896), in which he gives a comprehensive survey of the entire field of theoretic philosophy which evinces astonishing maturity and erudition, and which forms the foundation for all his later work. After this trial flight, which unquestionably received far too little notice, although it marked the arrival of a thinker with a vigorous, tenacious, and capacious mind, and has few equals among the first books of philosophers, Hobhouse suddenly interrupted his academic career and embarked on the life of a working journalist. He only returned to university work later, by which time, apart from journalistic and other literary and practical work, he had produced two large volumes on the historical evolution of mind and morals, based on thorough specialized investigations. These books provided the basis for a coherent treatment of all the interconnected questions of philosophy. Hobhouse put the quintessence of his investigations and thought into the imposing *Development and Purpose*, a systematic exposition which was first published in 1913, but was reissued after a thorough revision near the close of his life (1927). Here he abandons the cautious circumspection with which he had previously approached metaphysical questions, and the attitude he assumes to the ultimate problems yields speculative conclusions which give a rounded unity and completeness to his philosophy. The last decade of his life was principally occupied with the furtherance of a comprehensive inquiry in sociology which he set forth in four books and combined (though more externally than inwardly) under the title "Principles of Sociology". Here, too, Hobhouse remained true to his basic principle in ascending from facts to theory, and in testing and justifying the findings of theory again and again by an appeal to facts.

We naturally cannot deal with the many ramifications of Hobhouse's activities as an investigator, which extended to fields as diverse as animal psychology, comparative and social psychology, anthropology, sociology as a special science, logic, theory of knowledge, metaphysics, ethics, philosophical sociology and theory of the State. We must be content to give a brief résumé of the essential features of the philosophical ideas in the narrower sense. Hobhouse's *theory of knowledge*, which we shall term "critical realism", begins with immediate consciousness or apprehension,—this term signifying for him much the same as "sensation" for Locke, "perception" for Berkeley, or "impression" for Hume,—the knowledge of that which is directly present or found in consciousness. All cognition begins with apprehension and returns to it in the end; "to be apprehended" is exactly the same thing as "to be the content of a consciousness". Apprehension is the cognitive act directed upon this content which is always immediately present, and it shares with all other cognitive acts the character of assertion,—namely, the assertion of the present as *being*. As regards this primary datum of knowledge all possibility of error is excluded; that of which we are immediately aware, the present given fact, remains a fact even when as viewed from a higher cognitive level it is shown to be a fiction. Apprehension decides nothing as to the status of the existent fact, but asserts this purely as present in consciousness. But this primitive datum, in principle removed from the domain of error, is yet from the first endowed with a special epistemological dignity in so far as it is at once presupposition and touchstone for all other data. Apprehension is the final court of appeal in questions as to the validity and truth of all other types of cognition. It is evident that as regards its property of being a criterion of truth apprehension exactly corresponds to Hume's "impression", the function of which consists in the justification and validation of ideas as contents of consciousness not themselves "present". Hume's fundamental principle—that ideas are validated by the impressions corresponding to them—thus also underlies not only Hobhouse's theory of knowledge, but in a further sense his entire philosophy, in so far as the demand for the verification of all philosophical intuitions through the empirical facts underlying them is one of its essential features. It is in this that Hobhouse's empiricism consists,—to be distinguished from the classical systems of English empiricism chiefly in possessing a far wider foundation in experience, corresponding to the progress made by the sciences and the amassing of cognitive material.

Empiricism with Hobhouse, as with Locke, soon takes a realistic turn, and thus finds itself opposed to Kant and all idealist theories. The contents of knowledge are given as "realiter"; all that thought has to do is to acknowledge these contents, i.e. to discover or reveal, but not to construct or produce them. This means that there is no *a priori*, but only *a posteriori* knowledge. The material of knowledge, therefore, cannot be either the confused manifold of Kant, to which the mental categories and forms of synthesis have to be applied, or the simple idea of Locke, which is a purely qualitative content, but every datum, even the apparently simple, is complex from the first, that is, besides mere quality there belong to it already relations and orderings, such as extensity, magnitude, shape, position, and even direction. In this point Hobhouse diverges from his empiricist teachers. The simple ideas of Locke or the unrelated impressions of Hume are not possible contents of knowledge; these atomistic sensations are mere abstractions of thought and there is nothing real corresponding to them. Already in the simplest apprehension the mind grasps a complex whole or a concrete fact, which involves temporal and spatial order and many other relations in addition to mere quality. This overthrow of Hume's atomism by the recognition of the given as a complex whole, which connects Hobhouse with thinkers so different from himself and one another as Green and Hodgson, opens the way for the influx of certain idealistic elements into the empirical and realistic order of ideas.

Apart from simply receiving the present content of cognition through apprehension the mind is able to perform a number of other functions upon the data, e.g. retention (by memory), analysis, construction, inference, generalization, etc. Specially significant is the process of judgment, of which Hobhouse gives a careful analysis. What is the difference between it and pure apprehension? The judgment "this is blue" consists of three factors,—the present datum ("this"), a universal content ("blue"), and the copula ("is") which effects a relation between the other two. Thus in the judgment the given is subsumed under a universal or ideal content, and this subsumption signifies the similarity of the given with every other case in which the ideal content can be realized. It is, then, this ideal content that is peculiar to the judgment,—everywhere present in the midst of the world of facts and establishing divers relations of a general character between the several data of consciousness. Thus one element of the total judgment-content is given not "realiter" but "idealiter"; the judgment relates to, or points to, a reality that lies beyond the act of judging. Hobhouse's definition of judgment even agrees verbally with Bradley's and Bosanquet's; it is the act which relates an ideal content to a reality beyond the act. This relation established between the elements of the judgment appears as acceptance or recognition in the affirmative, and as rejection or exclusion in the negative judgment. Judging therefore depends upon a synthesis of ideal and real elements. There is no need to point out in detail how clearly this theory of judgment bears the sign-manual of the neo-Hegelian logic of Bradley and Bosanquet, or further how much it owes to modern German logicians like Sigwart and Brentano.

Judgment is treated by Hobhouse, as apprehension is, among the data of knowledge, since it produces no new contents, but merely relates the given elements to one another, and asserts or rejects this relation. The second section of logic begins at the point at which the mind brings upon the scene something new over and above the given and not originally contained in the facts; to this sphere of logic he gives the general name of inference. The passage from judgment to inference is made by the imagination, through which a new content arises not present hitherto, and a new edifice constructed, though it is to be observed that the stones of the building are taken from the material of the given, or, as Hobhouse puts it, that the imagination builds with stones already shaped. The essence of inference, also, consists in obtaining a new fact as consequence (conclusion) from a given content as ground (premisses), i.e. a fact not contained in the premisses. But whereas in the case of products of the imagination the new is only suggested, in inference it is accompanied by a strong feeling of belief, on the basis of which we assert the new content as true or adequate. Inference is therefore to be distinguished from imagination as reliable assent from mere suggestion. In the factor of belief which is here introduced, and which plays a part also in the theory of judgment, of induction, and of probability, we recognize the subjective factor of Hume's theory, which in Hobhouse's is an important presupposition of these logical forms, though it is not decisive as to their objective validity. The function of thought in inference consists in so connecting up the given that knowledge of it may be extended to a further reality that is not given. The single postulate which thought must make in this is that reality is in fact a system in which the various parts are necessarily inter-connected. The activity of reason consists in relating, combining, systematizing. Up to now Hobhouse's discussion had assumed the validity of thought. The third and last part of his logical survey is taken up with the justification of its claim to validity.

In this section he moves furthest from the empiricist basis of his doctrine, and fills both hands from the storehouse of idealist thought which the followers of Kant and Hegel had transferred to England. This fact is more impressive evidence of the vigour and fecundity of the Idealist movement than is the number of dutiful votaries and disciples who adopted the Idealist standpoint rather because they found it soothing to the mind, or a stimulus to imposing phrases, or a buttress to their wavering faith than a creative impulse to revivify philosophy. Here atomic Sensationalism fades into unreality and illusion, all the weary scepticism and resigned agnosticism of which thinkers who issued from the camp of natural science had been so proud are definitely abandoned, and a line is finally drawn to exclude Intuitionism, for which the self-evidence of one proposition is alone enough to guarantee its truth. On the contrary, it is maintained that the validity of a judgment cannot consist in the fact that it is given as immediately self-evident; such an isolated judgment detached from the content of thought can never claim final, but only provisional, validity, to be established only through this context. As an isolated fact possesses no cognitive value, so, too, an isolated judgment stands on the hither side of the boundary beyond which both truth and untruth lie. It has to wait for confirmation by other judgments, and only finds its full truth in the system of knowledge as a whole. Two judgments supporting and confirming each other constitute the minimum demanded for validation. But final validation consists in the systematic interconnection of all the members of a whole with one another, and with the whole to which they have reference, and by which they are supported. The truth of knowledge is the totality, and is comparable to a democracy in which no member takes precedence over another, but where the value and truth of every single individual are indissolubly bound up with the welfare of the whole, which in turn depends upon the trustworthiness of every several member. Hobhouse uses the term "consilience" to denote the mutual dependence, interconnection, and reciprocal support of the single "members" of the cognitive whole, and their necessary relation to the total system, and it is in this that he sees the real criterion of all truth and validity. The goal of knowledge which determines the aim both of the sciences and of philosophy, and which they approach without ever completely attaining it, is the entirety perfected by the thoroughgoing consilience of all its parts and members, the completely organized system of all the judgments which support, confirm, and verify one another. But short of this every several cognition and every inquiry upon a special field, or into a special problem, must also always be controlled by the notion of consilience.

There must be continually present the thought of raising every separate and single element to continually higher levels of generality by establishing reciprocal relations between them so that they become anchored ever more firmly in the systematic whole of knowledge. The essence of all human thinking and investigation, whether of the particular sciences or of the philosophical conspectus, is not exclusiveness and finality, but always growth by an advance in consilience and coherence. The work of reason, or as Hobhouse says, of the rational impulse in man, consists in connecting together and organizing the single cognitions and separate experiences into one systematic all-inclusive structure of thought, the goal being that intellectual harmony in which the effort of the human mind comes to rest. Neither can this impulse be forced out of its path through error, for error in its turn is not in principle removed from the domain of reason, for it is partial truth, that is, a necessary stage in the systematizing of knowledge, and by its very imperfection and deficiency becomes the stimulus to ever new inquiry and to the revision of hitherto accepted results. By maintaining these positions Hobhouse's philosophy displays its widest divergence from its empiricist point of departure, and more and more appears to adopt the Anglo-Hegelian theory of truth, as developed most notably by Bradley and his disciple Joachim.

Yet at the same time there is evident a characteristic difference between Hobhouse and the Hegelians. He could make little of Bradley's Absolute, withdrawn and enthroned in dignified pre-eminence above the variegated manifold of the phenomenal world with its illusions and contradictions. He resolved the rigour and immutability of Bradley's principle into the living movement of a process which he thought of as a genuine progress to continually higher synthesis and systematic structure (though not according to the pattern of the Hegelian dialectic), with the totality of truth as its goal, so that in this matter the empiricist Hobhouse came nearer to Hegel's real intention than did the Hegelian Bradley. The way he attained this result—and here we come to an important nodal point in his philosophy—was by incorporating the notion of evolution with that of consilience, and thereby forging into a unity the two fundamental principles of his thought. The validity of our cognition increases as it progressively unfolds itself within the entirety of knowledge; it approaches complete systematic truth in the degree in which in its development it is carried higher and further by consilience. Thus truth becomes actual with advancing knowledge in the course of evolution, which is the medium of its growth into completion. Hobhouse's philosophy presents itself accordingly as a realistically applied fusion of absolutist and evolutionary elements, with Empiricism as its starting-point.

Passing from his theory of knowledge to his metaphysic we observe how here also Idealism determined and modified in essential points the empirical and realistic foundation. In particular, by extracting from Hobhouse's thought the sting of materialistic Naturalism, it gave it a basis radically different from that of the XIXth-Century systems of a scientific cast within whose orbit it had arisen. Hobhouse's extensive studies on the historical development of mind, as expounded in his *Mind in Evolution*, led him early to the conviction based upon strictly empirical research that mind is not a mere epiphenomenon of material happenings, but rather a constituent within the total reality of the highest significance and importance. With the teaching of the Idealists to strengthen the foundation laid by his own studies he came to acknowledge the spiritual principle in the world as an independent and autonomous factor not to be simply derived from matter. On the other hand, he also recognized that Reality as such is not "spiritual", but that over against the element of "spirit" or mentality, there is another non-spiritual element which he calls the mechanical principle. Mind is thus neither lord of all things, nor the chance by-product of mechanical forces, neither absolute nor epiphenomenon, but an organic impulse imposing order upon chaotic and recalcitrant elements and bringing the cosmic process into unity and harmony. The chief criterion of all spiritual or mental activity is to be found in rational purposiveness. The teleological principle takes its place alongside the mechanical, each comprising and presupposing the other, and each revealing reality under a special aspect. The fundamental conception of Hobhouse's metaphysics consists in this interpretation of reality as neither merely mechanical nor merely teleological, but as both together, that is to say, as a process of development in which the two principles stand in a relation of close reciprocity, and are, so to speak, "interwoven".[1]

Besides the mechanical and teleological principles, however, experience shows us a third that contributes to the explanation of phenomena—the organic principle. By an organism we are to understand a unity whose parts or members reciprocally condition one another; whole and parts are strictly correlated. The system of knowledge had already been shown to be such an organic structure, and now metaphysics shows that the system of reality is so likewise, the result being thus a complete harmony or correspondence between the two systems. Reality viewed as a whole is an organic system such that, despite the mutual conditioning of its parts and the reciprocal relationship of the parts to the whole, the independence of the elements and their specific function within the whole are not obliterated but preserved by the unity transcending and comprising them. There can be no part of reality that stands utterly unrelated to the rest,—which is to say that there can exist no absolutely irrational entity. From this point of view, as indeed also in other respects, Hobhouse's doctrine is a stringent rationalism, one of the most impressive embodiments of this style of thought within recent times. At every step he vindicates the rational principle in thinking and in being against the manifold irrationalist tendencies of the time, and defends himself against the fashionable philosophical maladies which asperse reason and set in its place an irrational substitute like instinct or intuition.

Of the three basic categories in terms of which reality is presented to us, the first two, the mechanical and teleological,

[1] This is the term used by Ginsberg, who has done much to interpret and commend Hobhouse's teaching.

are metaphysical forces in sheer opposition and conflict with each other. Mechanism, originally predominant, is the undifferentiated, the chaotic, and the disordered, that of which the energies intersect and annul one another because being unrelated they can give one another no mutual support. But from the beginning there is an element of mind contained in every bit of matter, which becomes effectual as order, connection, and harmony increase in the mechanical forces. At a higher stage of development these forces unite more and more in arrangements and combinations according to rational laws and ends. Evolution is accomplished by the mechanical factors being continually more and more definitely thrust into the background as the purposive elements making for establishment of order continually gain ground. Its goal is the harmonious system which it is the teleological function of mind to bring about in the course of time. The mind (or spirit) pervading the universe is continually at work to accomplish, by however slow and gradual stages, the harmonization of conflicting elements.

The third fundamental category—the organic—was much less precisely defined by Hobhouse than the other two. It is, however, maintained that it stands nearer to the category of purpose than to that of mechanism, though it admits of application to both. To the Universe as a whole, however, it is inapplicable, for this may only be interpreted teleologically. Hobhouse's metaphysic culminates in a view of the Universe as a conditional teleology, in so far as the purpose-principle can never completely attain its end, but stands always in contrast to the recalcitrant elements of mechanical matter. Hobhouse never was able to arrive at a final elucidation of the relation between the organic and the teleological. It is noteworthy how very speculative Empiricism has become in Hobhouse's philosophy, and how remote are these lofty speculations from the wide experiential basis that is their origin. This is again an example of the important influence of Idealism of the Hegelian type which gave English thought so much bolder and loftier a sweep and range.

Hobhouse's ethics, the more empirical side of which is expressed in *Morals in Evolution* and the more philosophical in *The Rational Good*, agrees in all essential points with the main principle of his philosophy. Here, too, he begins by giving an account of the historical evolution of the facts of morality based on a wide empirical survey, a sort of "genealogy of morals", and then passes on to his own philosophical interpretation of this empirical material. Here, too, the final outcome is a Rationalist, not an Empiricist, ethic, whose task is to indicate the function of reason in the sphere of practice. And here, too, he joins issue with the prejudice against rationality, and turns against the currents of irrationalism which find the only motives of our conduct in impulse, feeling, and emotion. He shows that rational elements such as purpose and deliberation play a part at least as great as, if not greater than, blind instinctive feeling. Clear thinking is as indispensable in conduct as right feeling. "The most senseless human being is not actuated simply and solely from impulse." Moreover, he is not inclined to make a sharp contrast between the world of feeling and the world of thought; the root of both is one—human nature—and they can only be isolated by an artificial abstraction. He finds the beginnings of moral rationality already in that conscious purposeful behaviour which is to be seen in the lower as well as the higher stages of the moral life. The function of the practical reason follows a course exactly parallel to that of theoretical reason, for while the latter is concerned with the correlation of single facts and cognitions by the thoroughgoing consilience of a harmonious system, the former is concerned with the unification of single impulses, promptings, and conations into the harmonious whole of feeling. Here, too, a single element—in this case a single impulse—cannot remain in isolation, but points beyond itself in a nisus towards its own supersession in the higher whole of which it is a part. The function of the will thus consists in the synthesis of single volitions, as that of volition consists in the unification of single impulses. Throughout there is a rational factor playing its part, which ultimately is manifested as *the good*. Just as in the sphere of theory faith in the victory of truth and the mastery of reason had led to Rationalism, so in the sphere of practice conviction in the omnipotence of Goodness leads to optimism. In both spheres the idea of progress supplies the impetus through which rationality realizes itself at ever higher levels, promoting the victory of truth in the domain of knowledge and of the good in the domain of conduct. The complete realization of the good is no more possible than that of the true; but the endeavour after it remains perpetual, like the corresponding everlasting progress of knowledge. The principle of rationality is operative in Ethics, as in Science, as the perpetually renewed impulse to a completed harmony, not as the final arrival at this goal.

For this ethics of harmony Hobhouse brought together elements from both empiricist and idealistic theory in the same way as he had done in his epistemology and metaphysics. He himself points out that his position is closely related, on the one hand, to Mill's Utilitarian principles, and on the other to the ethical Idealism of Green. The notion of harmony agrees with Utilitarian doctrine in so far as it comprises the general happiness as an integral component. On the other hand, Hobhouse adheres to Green's criticism of Hedonism in his psychological analysis of the springs of action, and the sting of Hedonism having been removed from Utilitarianism, the principle of the greatest happiness of the greatest number becomes transformed into the postulate of the harmonious social whole. The numerous points of contact with idealist ethics need not be further dwelt upon. Where Hobhouse's ethics deviates notably from that of Green or Kant, is in maintaining that the practical reason must not be thought of as floating high above the life of feeling and impulse, nor this treated as a negligible quantity, but as somehow included or taken up in the synthesis of the rational good.

Hobhouse's *political theory* falls to some extent outside his system, in so far as on this field he was consciously and intentionally barricading himself against the onset of idealistic ideas, so that here he stands altogether within the range of the native tradition, i.e. he is a typical representative of the liberal, democratic, and individualistic idea of the State as we meet it in the doctrine that runs, a single strand, from Locke to Mill. But in my opinion we should not esteem his ideas on this subject as highly as the other parts of his doctrine. For Hobhouse's political theory, as expounded in the mainly polemical work *The Metaphysical Theory of the State*, does not spring from the scientific objective study which characterizes the rest of his work, but from the hate-impregnated and envenomed atmosphere of the World War, to which even a thinker of so steady and objective a judgment fell a victim. He could see nothing in Hegel's theory of the State—renewed on English soil half-heartedly through the work of Green, and in a more whole-hearted and thorough way by Bosanquet—except the establishment of that reactionary mentality which had (in his view) led via the Bismarckian power-politics to German militarism and so to the World War. The Hegelian Absolute State means for Hobhouse not only the violation of the freedom and autonomy of the individual, but the subordination of Ethics to Politics, whereby the moral bonds between the peoples are abolished and naked force replaces right. In opposition to this, Hobhouse represents the view that individuality is a supreme ultimate value which is not to be absorbed without remainder into the State. The State organization cannot be an end in itself, but must always be a means, that is, one of the many possible forms of association in which human beings freely combine in order to be able to develop their potentialities and fulfil their moral obligations. Only the individual can be considered to be an end in his own right, and all forms of society—the State in particular—are to subserve the well-being and interests of individuals. The State is morally responsible to other States, as the individual is to other individuals, and no theory can relieve it of this responsibility. Here we see a typical form of bourgeois Liberalism, defending itself against the omnipotence of the State because it feels its freedom threatened thereby. The attack on Hegelianism abandons all fairness and objectivity; so far from penetrating into the profundities of Hegel's conception of the State, Hobhouse embellishes his pages with catch-phrases and arguments born of the heat and passion of the hour. And it is all the more regrettable that he adopted such arguments to establish his theory of the State from the fact that not a few of the strongest roots of his power spring from the very Idealism against which he here swears such bitter enmity.

In conclusion, there is the field of *Sociology*, in which Hobhouse's comprehensive studies were much more fruitful and positive in their outcome. Here, too, he combines the thoroughness of the specialist with the insight of the philosopher, and the points of view from which he lays down principles are arrived at from a wide survey of the facts. We must be content with the briefest indication of his conclusions. It was important to make the notion of evolution which flows like a subterranean stream through Hobhouse's entire philosophy yield fruit also in the field of sociology. But there could be for Hobhouse no question of simply taking over such an idea as Darwin's biological theory of the struggle for existence provided. He recognized earlier than many others that biological methods and points of view could not be successfully transferred to the sphere of social relationships, without critical examination. Rather, the principle of evolution needs to be subjected to manifold discriminating modifications according to the field to which it is applied. What is true enough of the life of plants and animals does not hold good without qualification for human society. What, then, does evolution mean in social life? Certainly not mere struggle for existence, and the survival of the socially stronger at the cost of the socially weaker. At the level of beings endowed with reason rational purposiveness takes the place of the irrational chance that dominates in nature, and this shows us that the higher evolution of humanity is advanced not by a conflict of all against all, but on the contrary by the organization of mutual assistance, and by the effective alliance of individuals. The highest type of Society is that in which in place of the war of all against all, there is the active co-operation of all in the war against hostile forces, and progress means essentially the growing realization of such co-operation. We recognize in this conception of co-operation which becomes the *leitmotiv* of Hobhouse's sociology, the consilience in accordance with which the members of a whole—be it a scientific discipline or a philosophical system, or a social community—mutually support and have reference to one another, and only fulfil their true being in such reciprocal association. Thus the single branches of Hobhouse's doctrine are bound together by their basic unifying concept into a strictly enclosed philosophical system—enclosed not, however, in the sense of shut off from facts, but rather open to the continual pressure of empirical material waiting for the work of philosophy to set it in its due place in the system of knowledge. The notion of consilience is closely bound up with that of evolution as the second fundamental *motif* of Hobhouse's doctrine. And in this he has the merit, which cannot be too highly rated in view of the biological aberrations of philosophical Darwinians (among whom Spencer is certainly the most notable), of giving to the idea of evolution an independent meaning according to the domain within which it is applied, and of thereby freeing it from the barrenness and hazardousness of an empty schematism professing to be a method of explaining everything in the world, and raising it to the status of a genuine methodological principle of investigation.

APPENDIX TO SECTION III

English Positivism

Chief dates and writings

1843 J. S. Mill: *System of Logic.*

1845–6 G. H. Lewes: *Biographical History of Philosophy.*

1849 Congreve's first visit to Comte in Paris.

1853 Lewes: *Comte's Philosophy of the Positive Sciences.*

1853 Harriet Martineau: *The Positive Philosophy of A. Comte, freely translated and condensed* (third edition in three vols., 1896).

1854 Congreve's second visit to Comte.

c. 1855. Harrison's visit to Comte.

1858 Congreve: *The Catechism of Positive Religion translated.*

1864 Spencer: *Reasons for dissenting from the Philosophy of A. Comte.* (In *Essays, Scientific, Political and Speculative*, vol. ii.)

1865 Bridges: *Comte's General View of Positivism.*

1865 J. S. Mill: *Auguste Comte and Positivism.*

1866 Bridges: *The Unity of Comte's Life and Doctrine, a Reply to J. S. Mill.*

1867 Founding of the London Positivist Society by Congreve. (Place of meeting from 1870, Chapel Street.)

1869 T. H. Huxley: *The Scientific Aspects of Positivism* (in *Fortnightly Review*).

1870–1900 Congreve: *Essays, Political, Social and Religious* (three vols.).

1875–9 *Comte's System of Positive Philosophy*, translated by Bridges, Harrison, Beesly and Congreve.

1878 Cleavage of the movement into the groups of Congreve (Chapel Street) and Harrison (later Newton Hall).

1881 Opening of Newton Hall by Laffitte.

1882 Bridges: *Five Discourses on Positive Religion.*

1885 E. Caird: *The Social Philosophy and Religion of Comte.*

1887 J. Cotter Morison: *The Service of Man.*

1892 *The New Calendar of Great Men.* Edited by Harrison.

1893–1925 *The Positivist Review*, edited by Beesly, later by S. H. Swinny, finally by F. J. Gould.

1899 Death of Congreve.

1906 Death of Bridges.

1907 Bridges: *Essays and Addresses.*

1915 Death of Beesly.

1916 Reuniting of the two groups (place, Chapel Street).

1923 Death of Harrison.

If we leave out of account that foreign influence in XIXth-Century England which was far the most potent—German Idealism—certainly no other doctrine was so enduring in its effect as the Positivism of Auguste Comte. There is, however, an important difference between the spheres of influence of these two foreign movements. That of Idealism was academic—it impressed itself decisively first and foremost upon professional philosophers, and led their thought into new paths. Positivism, on the other hand, fertilized rather the general intellectual life of the time and met with little esteem among professional philosophers. Moreover, Positivism owes its comparatively wide sphere of influence to the fact that it was organized in a strictly sectarian way quite in the spirit of Comte, and was propagated with great emphasis from its centres of organization. In spite of this the English Positivist movement does not properly belong to philosophy in the narrower sense. The doctrine of Comte did not give a new impetus to English thinking as those of Kant and Hegel did, so as to produce a new phase of development, but where it was accepted at all it remained stuck in the rigid dogmatic form in which the master had left it. In becoming crystallized by the pupils—or rather, the disciples—into a formulated creed it forfeited every claim to the vitality and engendering power of a genuine philosophic system. It is not therefore surprising that the ranks of the English apostles of Comte include no philosophic mind of the first order, but chiefly scientific specialists, men of letters, and philanthropists who saw in Comte's philosophy a new religion which they felt called upon to proclaim to their age. The philosophic movement, therefore, of the second half of the XIXth Century (the period in which Positivism came to its fullest growth and bloom) gained little or nothing in spite of—or because of—the real enthusiasm and missionary propagandist zeal of its adherents. Comte's teaching was taken over as dogma and preserved as dogma, and the Positivists never got beyond swearing by the words and dicta of the master.

In English Positivism, then, we have to do not with a new

doctrine, nor even with a new nuance or continuation or amplification of an old one, but simply with the transplantation of the philosophy, or, better, the religion, of Comte on to foreign soil. In what follows, therefore, we shall be content to assume as familiar the doctrine in its content, which is just that of Comte, and confine ourselves to reporting the most important dates and phases of this movement. As early as the 'forties, when Comte stood at the height of his achievement, some weighty voices were raised to indicate the exceptional significance of this philosopher. Naturally, these voices came from that school of thought which stood nearest to Comte's doctrine in virtue of a common origin,—the Empiricist school. Both Positivism and Empiricism spring from Hume as intellectual ancestor, and Comte had himself called the great Scottish thinker his real philosophical predecessor. And so J. S. Mill, who had been in active literary correspondence with Comte since 1841,[1] spoke in his *Logic* (1843) of the Frenchman as one of the first thinkers of Europe. G. H. Lewes, also, indicated the rank that belongs to Comte in the movement of modern philosophy, when in his *Biographical History of Philosophy* (a widely read book first published in 1845–6) he named him the greatest of modern thinkers, and called his doctrine the crown of all the philosophical development that had preceded it (vide supra, pp. 119 ff). Lewes, a zealous admirer of Comte, wrote a few years later a book of his own on *Comte's Philosophy of the Positive Sciences*, and in other ways, too, pleaded Comte's cause. Through him "George Eliot", later his wife, also became acquainted with Comte's doctrines; her novels, as has often been noted, show plainly the traces of Comtian influence. In the same year in which Lewes's book on Comte appeared Harriet Martineau (1802–76), sister of James Martineau, the philosopher of religion, published a translation, or rather paraphrase, of the *Cours de Philosophie Positive*, which by skilful selections gives a good conspectus of it. This work gave the English public Comte's masterpiece

[1] See *Lettres inédites à Auguste Comte*, publiées par L. Lévy-Bruhl, 1899.

in a compendious form freed from all superfluous ballast, and it was Miss Martineau's devoted labours that really introduced Comte into England and brought him to the notice of a wider public. Comte himself was highly delighted with this admirably worked-out presentation of his system. It was translated back into French, and had a wide vogue in France also, where for a time it even competed seriously in popularity with the original work.

More important for the dissemination of Comte's thought in England was the sincere admiration with which J. S. MILL responded to it. It is no coincidence that one and the same year saw Stirling proclaiming the philosophy of Hegel to the English almost like a new gospel, and Mill pointing with no less impressiveness to the figure of Comte. And in the same year (1865) also Mill gave to the public the outcome of his great critical controversy with Hamilton as the chief representative of the Scottish school. Mill had from the beginning followed the Frenchman's development as a thinker with the greatest interest; he had come into personal touch with him in an extensive correspondence, and had even given him generous pecuniary help when he was in straitened circumstances. He set down his attitude to Comte point by point in his book *Auguste Comte and Positivism* (1865), in which he declared himself in agreement with Comte's philosophy in its main features, and accepted the Humanity-principle of the Comtian religion, but adopted a critical attitude of rejection both towards the strange apparatus of religious cult and dogma through which that principle was moulded into a kind of positive faith, and towards the credulous acceptance of authority and the overstressed altruism which threatened to submerge the uniqueness of the individual and the freedom of thought. The more orthodox Positivists felt therefore that this book of Mill's was an attack upon the true meaning of the Comtian doctrine; Bridges entered the lists with a book written to answer Mill's, in which he sought to defend the unity of Comte's doctrine and life.

After Comte's name had won a certain reputation in England

controversial criticisms of him became more frequent. A thinker such as SPENCER, who by his own admission owed much to Comte, adopted in a series of essays an attitude of dissent towards important parts of his doctrines (*vide* especially *Reasons for dissenting from the Philosophy of Comte* (1864), included in the second volume of *Essays, Scientific, Political and Speculative*). Some utterances of HUXLEY were still more uncompromising in their rejection. He declared the positive philosophy of Comte to be not only meaningless for science, but even hostile to science, and put it in this respect on the same level as the Roman Church. He characterized Comtism in a happy phrase that attained a wide celebrity, as "Catholicism minus Christianity", and directed his attack upon the formula of Congreve, according to which Positivism was nothing but "Catholicism plus Science".

JOHN RUSKIN was another who took a hand in the conflict about Comte. In *Fors Clavigera* (Letter 67, May 14, 1876), he joined issue with Harrison and protested in the name of art and beauty against the gospel of steam engines and factories, against industrialism, and the fanatical trust in progress and other things whose champions he took the Positivists to be. Harrison defended himself very ably against such misunderstandings born of ignorance of Comte's writings, both in the *Fortnightly Review* for 1876 and also in the columns of *Fors Clavigera*, which Ruskin himself put at his critic's disposal (*vide* McGee, *A Crusade for Humanity*, 1931, pp. 96 ff.). For the other side, again, there were two further critical examinations of Comte, both published in 1885. One was by JAMES MARTINEAU, the philosopher of religion, who devoted a chapter of detailed argument to Comte in vol. 1 of *Types of Ethical Theory*, in which, while confessing to admiration of the Frenchman in matters of detail, he rejected Positivism taken as a whole, since he could not reconcile it with his theistic point of view. The other was by EDWARD CAIRD, the Hegelian, who criticized Comte from the idealistic standpoint in his penetrating book *The Social Philosophy and Religion of Comte*, and later in *The Evolution of Religion* (vol. 1, ch. xii, 1893). Negative as all these voices might be, they yet bear witness to the serious attention that was being given to Comte's philosophy in England in the 'sixties, 'seventies, and 'eighties of last century.

The founder and driving force behind the Positivist movement in England was RICHARD CONGREVE (1818–99). While a Fellow of Wadham College, Oxford, he went to Paris in 1849 and made Comte's personal acquaintance, paying him a second visit in 1854. The impression made upon Congreve was so overpowering that he determined to give up his teaching work in Oxford in order to dedicate his whole life to the service of Comte's Religion of Humanity. In 1855 he migrated to London, and by this important step inaugurated the new movement. In 1858 he published a translation of the *Catéchisme positiviste*,—the work in which Comte transformed his philosophical doctrine into the Positivist religion. While still Fellow and Tutor of Wadham Congreve had at the beginning of 1850 gathered about him a group of talented young men of that College and introduced them to the spirit of Comte's philosophy. This Wadham group included Frederic Harrison, John Henry Bridges, and Edward Spencer Beesly, and with Congreve as teacher it became the germ-cell of the later movement. After the young men had left the University their ways at first diverged for a time, but years after they again found themselves actively engaged in the same cause.

FREDERIC HARRISON (1831–1923) was one of the most striking personalities of the Victorian age. He was a man of extraordinarily many-sided interests and aptitudes, an expert in many fields, connected in many and varied ways with the literary, social, and political life of the time, and standing in personal relations with wellnigh all the great minds of the age. His influence everywhere made for the bridging of differences and the toning-down of what was too harsh or too rigorous. His mind was lucid, practised in criticism, nimble and quick to take up new ideas, and he had an astonishing faculty of literary expression, so that he was enabled to react promptly to all the important questions of the day, and by throwing his assured judgment and manly forthright personality into the scale where matters of moment were at stake, to exercise considerable influence upon the issue. His literary output was almost unbounded and covered an enormous range of subject-matter. All mere specialist learning and scholarship was alien to him, and the whole of his literary and scientific work was pragmatist in the best sense of the word, for he always kept his eyes wide open to the problems and questions at issue in all their richness and amplitude. His aim was always to further the victory of the deserving cause, improving what was at fault, elucidating what was obscure, and softening the brunt of antagonisms. He is the typical "universal" writer, the genuine *homme de lettres* in Voltaire's sense. The structure of his mind seems in many respects akin to that of Voltaire, of a smaller pattern certainly, and at a less eminent level, but exhibiting at that lower level a like universality of culture, dexterity of verbal expression, breadth and intensity of effective activity. Perhaps the only respect in which this man, so pre-eminently equipped for intellectual leadership, exhibited narrowness of mind, was in his ardent confession of faith in Comtism which became for him the criterion and guiding thread both in thought and conduct. But even in this respect he is to be distinguished from the other Positivists, in that his mind was rich and wide enough to refuse to accept Comte's maxims as a rigid and dead structure of dogma, taking them instead as a measuring and testing instrument with movement and life in it. He is thus the least narrowly doctrinaire of the English disciples of Comte, the one of them all who made Comtism irradiate life in all its fullness without prepossession or limitation. Only upon political matters did his close unity with his French master and his predilection for things French occasionally confuse his judgment, and lead him to be unfair to the interests of other peoples. As he continually used to raise his voice in warning against the politics of power and imperial expansion of the English, so, too, he protested against the ostensible violation of France by Prussia in the war of 1870–1, demanding, as the other Positivists also did, the active intervention of

England on the French side, and so, too, in the World War he held that the side of the allies alone represented the cause of right and humanity, and assented to an overthrow and enslavement of the German people, which had been fighting for its existence with such surpassing valour, as complete and extreme as that demanded by the greed and blind hatred of the French.

JOHN HENRY BRIDGES (1832–1906), who likewise conceived his enthusiasm for Comte's work when a student at Wadham under the dominating influence of Congreve, later studied medicine in London, then emigrated to Australia, where he practised for a time as a doctor, continuing to do so also after his return home. Besides his professional work and his efforts, pursued with great zeal, in the cause of public health, he displayed great range as an author, his writing extending to historical, philosophical, and literary subjects. (He devoted, for example, many years to the editing of Roger Bacon's *Opus Majus* in three volumes.) But above all he enlisted, both by the spoken and the written word, in the cause of Positivism and the spreading of Comte's doctrines. As early as 1865 he brought out an edition of a large part of the first volume of the *Système de Politique Positive*, the second main work of Comte, in an English translation,[1] which was completed in the years 1875–9 by the co-operative labours of himself, Harrison, Beesly, and Congreve. He had previously defended *The Unity of Comte's Life and Doctrine* (1866) against an attack of Mill, at a later date issued the *Five Discourses on Positive Religion* (1882), and took an eager share in the *New Calendar of Great Men* published by Harrison in 1892. He contributed alone 194 biographies to this last-named work, an English counterpart of Comte's *Calendrier Positiviste*. After his death his *Essays and Addresses* were collected and published (1907). Bridges' endowment as a thinker surpassed that of Harrison, but he was more a contemplative scholar of wide erudition, and lacked the reforming zeal and energy in action which Harrison possessed in so marked a degree.

EDWARD SPENCER BEESLY (1831–1915), the third member of

[1] *Comte's General View of Positivism.*

the alliance, after leaving the University worked for a time in a teaching post, and in 1860 was appointed professor of history in University College, London. His main energies were directed to the struggle against the oppression of the weaker social classes. By lectures, pamphlets, and periodical articles he represented the cause of public right and social justice on their behalf with the genuine zeal of a reformer. He also published some literary works, and took a share in the English edition of the *Politique Positive* and the *Calendrier Positiviste*.

It was thus out of the seed sown at Wadham College that the Positivist movement in England grew. It had its centre in the *London Positivist Society* founded in 1867, after the pattern of the Positivist Society founded by Comte in 1848. In 1870 the Society acquired premises in Chapel Street (Lamb's Conduit Street) which still belong to it, and which were promptly transformed into a Positivist temple in the way Comte had prescribed. There were placed the busts of great men, the saints of Humanity, representing the thirteen months, and in the front of the building a tablet was set up inscribed with the sacred formula of Positivism:

In the Name of Humanity;
Love for Principle
and Order for Basis;
Progress for end.
Live for Others. Live Openly.

Regular services were held here with a prescribed liturgy, Positivist hymns and sermons. Special solemn ceremonies took place on the feast-days of Positivism, e.g. the anniversaries of Comte's birth and death, not very different from the French originals on which they were modelled.

The organization of religious worship constituted, however, only one side of the varied activities of the Positivists. Apart from their literary activities already mentioned they exercised an influence also on educational, social, and political movements. Youth groups were formed, evening classes were instituted, and occasionally attempts were made to establish a Positivist type of schooling. In the political field they sought to obtain a lasting influence by public protests, open letters to the Government, pamphlets, etc., issued at times when momentous decisions were to be taken on home and particularly on foreign affairs. Politically a cause with which they especially identified themselves was the trade union movement, for which they helped to secure statutory recognition. Other social and political movements in which they played a more or less successful part were the feminist movement, the struggle for freedom in Ireland, the opposition to imperialist power-politics, the introduction of universal compulsory school-attendance, and Parliamentary reform.

The London Positivist Society, as constituted in Chapel Street, was from the first incorporated in the complete structure of the Positivist world-organization, which soon after Comte's death had started upon its work with France as its centre. The first High Priest of Humanity was the Frenchman Pierre Laffitte, Comte's intimate friend, who after the founder's death assumed the leadership of the entire movement, and to whom Congreve and his adherents accordingly became subordinate. The connection with the Mother Church was, however, a fairly loose one, consisting in the payment of contributions to the central fund, and in the similarity of their institutions and activities. Certain differences of view now began to form within the English group, especially regarding the question of a centralized organization of a strictly ecclesiastical kind. Congreve, its founder, a personality of great energy and individual force, was haunted by the idea of turning the movement wholly into a Church; on the other hand, the younger adherents wished to be satisfied with looser formulas and ceremonies. For the same reason a conflict broke out between Laffitte and Congreve, which in the end led to an open breach and thereby to the secession of the English group from the French headquarters. But this step had as its inevitable consequence a split within the English movement, for the younger members refused to follow the leader because of his breach with Laffitte, maintained and confirmed the connection with the French organization, and thenceforward constituted an independent group under Laffitte's leadership. None the less, Congreve held on his own way, winning over to himself a portion of the Positivist community, and continuing to hold his religious services and ceremonials in Chapel Street. The Laffitte-group won the adherence of Bridges, Harrison, and Beesly, and Bridges became the first president of the newly founded London Positivist Committee. The schism took place in 1878. In 1880 Bridges resigned the presidency, and his place was taken by the purposeful personality of Harrison, who led the group until the year 1904. They lost no time in acquiring a home of their own in London, which was called Newton Hall, and was solemnly opened by Laffitte in person on May 1, 1881.

Thus from 1878 on there were two independent Positivist groups in England, pursuing in essentials the same aims and developing the same activities, of which the one had made itself completely self-sufficient, while the other maintained official relations with the Paris centre and supported it financially. We will call the first of these the Congreve-group, the second the Harrison-group, after their respective leaders. Common to both is the fact that they displayed their greatest strength and vigour of growth in the 'eighties and 'nineties. At the turn of the century a rapid process of decay set in which nothing could arrest, and under which the whole movement languished and slowly died away. Both groups had some successes in the provinces, though mostly of a transient nature: "cells" of Positivists were formed in Liverpool, Manchester, Newcastle, and some other towns. But essentially the movement remained confined to the Metropolis. The Congreve-group was deprived of its driving power by the death of Congreve in 1899, and the loss of its leader led to its break-up. Henry Crompton took over the succession, and after him Alfred Haggard, Henri Dussanze, and Philip Thomas, but none of these had the outstanding qualities of the first English founder of Positivism. The Harrison-group showed greater vitality, and it was from its ranks that the "New Calendar of Great Men" already mentioned was compiled and published, while in addition the group brought into being an organ of its own in *The Positivist Review*, established in 1893 and edited first by Beesly, then by S. H. Swinny, and finally by F. J. Gould. Harrison gave up the presidency of the group in 1904, but continued thereafter to give the movement his support, by counsel and act, the written and the spoken word. Even when an octogenarian, nay, a nonagenarian, he did battle for his ideas with almost as much fire and zest as he had shown in youth, and was always coming to the front where he thought a right had been violated, or a wrong was to be righted. The keen old warrior passed away at ninety-one, and with him passed the last representative of a movement into which he had breathed the best life he had, and which will always remain first and foremost bound up with his name. Harrison's countless essays, speeches, discussions, and lectures spoken or written in the service of Positivism over more than half a century, are collected in the following volumes, which apart from *The Positivist Review* are the real quarry for the study of the movement: *Creed of a Layman* (1907), *The Philosophy of Common Sense* (1907), *National and Social Problems* (1908), *Realities and Ideals* (1908), *The Positive Evolution of Religion* (1913). To these must be added his *Autobiographic Memoirs* (1911) in two volumes, in which he tells the story of his rich and full life with characteristic freshness and vividness. An exact and exhaustive account of his writings will be found in J. E. McGee's *A Crusade for Humanity* (1931, pp. 241–5), in which the history of organized English Positivism is presented for the first time in compendious form. We owe to this most useful work the greater part of the facts recounted in this section.

The president of the Positivist Society appointed to succeed Harrison was S. H. SWINNY (1905), who had been for a long time editor of their journal. A year later Bridges died, and nine years later still Beesly. Then at length in the middle of the World War (1916) after the failure of several earlier attempts, reconciliation was brought about between the two opposed camps, and they were reunited. But this external strengthening of the Positivist phalanx came too late to arrest the definitive downfall of the movement now grown weak with age. From this time their meetings again were held in Chapel Street, Newton Hall having been long since (1902) lost to the movement, and the followers of Harrison having perforce sought other premises for their meetings. The years after the war completed the break-up of the movement. In 1920, on the retirement of P. Thomas, T. S. Lascelles assumed the presidency; in 1923 Harrison and Swinny died; and in 1925 the periodical (which had been for two years edited by Gould under the title *Humanity*) ceased publication. The movement may be thereby said to be virtually ended, even though there is still (1937) a London Positivist Committee, which is the owner of a room in Chapel Street.[1]

[1] For these and other details see *London for Heretics*, W. Kent (1932).—ED.

IV

GROUPS INTERESTED IN RELIGIOUS PHILOSOPHY

THE account to be given in this section of the religious philosophy of the earlier part of our period is confined to those thinkers, or groups of thinkers, who have independent importance outside the currents of philosophy with which we have hitherto been dealing. We are not here concerned, as in former sections, to trace the development of a single unified and relatively self-contained movement of thought, but rather to glean and assemble in one inclusive presentation whatever seems important or valuable in religio-philosophical theory—that is, in thought directed to religious questions—wherever it is to be found. We are, however, far from intending to present anything like exhaustively the religious life of England in the XIXth Century, even so far as it is comprised in its deposit of theory. For such a deposit was naturally much more the outcome of work in the theological than in the philosophical field, and, though the frontiers between these two are constantly being obliterated, yet we must, as far as possible, confine our account to the latter. Our brief estimate deals merely with what has genuine relevance for philosophy, and even from this we can give only selections.

Now from this point of view we are bound to take first into consideration the movement which made a deeper impress upon the religious life of England in the last century than any other, the Oxford Movement of the 'thirties and 'forties, whereby so much of contemporary religion was (so to speak) ploughed up and transmuted. Both in philosophy and in the general intellectual life of the time it meant a reaction against most of the tendencies then dominant, against Rationalism and Intellectualism, confidence in knowledge and pride of reason, the ethic of happiness and the delusion of progress, free thought and Liberalism, the reduction of existence to external fact and secular values, religion rendered shallow and the life of the

Church stagnant, in a word against the spirit of the Enlightenment as it had been rescued from the debacle of the XVIIIth Century and set firmly upon its throne in the XIXth. This movement, which, like the neo-Idealistic movement a generation later, started in the University of Oxford and was carried forward by such men as J. H. Newman, J. Keble, E. B. Pusey, W. G. Ward, and R. H. Froude, among others, was certainly directed in the first instance to the renewal and deepening of the religious life, but it also contained within itself and liberated important philosophical forces. And the same man who was its soul as a religious movement, was also its leading philosophical mind, the great and noble figure of Cardinal Newman.

John Henry Newman (1801–90) belongs beyond dispute to the first rank of the great intellectual leaders and awakeners of England in the XIXth Century. His pre-eminent place is based not only on the power of his personality, his rare character, and the nobility of his mind, but also on his breadth of mind, scope of erudition, depth of thought, and not least his potent and deeply rooted faith, to which an elevated humanity and a rich intellectual endowment equally contributed. In him were focussed the spiritual energies of the Anglo-Catholic movement, of which, though he was not its founder, he became in the course of its development the most powerful exponent. But the sphere of his influence extended far beyond this movement to include strata of thought and of religious life that had nothing in common with it. Newman is the greatest apologist of Roman Catholicism that England has produced since the cleavage between the Churches. He did more than anyone before him to reveal to the British world the glory and greatness of this Church, its faith and its tradition, its dogmas and institutions, its inner as well as its outer life, so that men could feel the living breath of its spirit. And all this because his faith was not merely a doctrine to be taught but a life to be lived, because he was himself the visible embodiment, beheld far and wide, of all that message which from a sense of inward vocation he had to deliver to his age. The only parallel in a later time is F. von Hügel, who had a similar mission to perform for the England of the last generation, though he was denied the authority and wide field of influence of his greater predecessor.

Newman's philosophy, so far as it can be detached from the rest of his work, is not only the deposit and justification of his religious belief, though of course it is that first and foremost: it is also the manifestation of the genuine impulse to knowledge and quick activity of mind which were fundamentally characteristic of his nature. He was not content to proclaim the faith which from first to last was his firm unshakable possession, but was equally concerned to establish and buttress it in theory. And in this task he did not turn back, as might have been expected, to take up the scholastic philosophy in order to renovate it. On the contrary, his whole cast of mind was very remote from Scholasticism, with which he had far fewer points of contact than points of divergence, so that it is entirely wrong to connect his doctrine with the neo-Scholastic movement, or to designate it, as is often done, as the precursor of this movement. It is rather a construction that bears no other stamp than Newman's own, of which the religious content is rooted in the Patristic teaching rather than in Thomism and the theory chiefly in the British (which is also the classical) tradition.

Newman's philosophical writings constitute only a relatively small part of his voluminous literary output.[1] The most important are *An Essay on the Development of Christian Doctrine* (1845) and *An Essay in aid of a Grammar of Assent* (1870), to which may be added *The Idea of a University* (1852), —though the purpose of this book, in which Newman develops his programme of university education, is not exclusively philosophical—together with some of his university sermons and the famous *Apologia pro Vita Sua* (1864).

The central point of Newman's theoretic philosophy is taken by the intellectual act of "assent" and the antecedent act of "apprehension": its guiding principle is to be found in

[1] Collected in thirty-six volumes, 1868–81, subsequently enlarged by the addition of some others.

the fundamental distinction between real and conceptual apprehension (and real and conceptual assent), which forms the basis of all Newman's genuine contributions whether to the theory of knowledge or later to the philosophy of religion and theology. We can call it also the primary experienced fact of his philosophy, for nearly all his thoughts flow from its source.

What, then, is to be understood by the contrast between 'real' and 'conceptual' apprehension? Apprehension, in the sense of the psychological attitude or response to any given fact, occurs in different degrees of strength and intensity, according to the character of the given apprehended by us or apprehending us. The strength of apprehension depends upon the power immanent in the object, and emanating from it to us. Now it is a fact of human nature that concrete things seize upon us much more than do abstract ideas, that what genuinely *is* in the emphatic sense of possessing real concrete existence impresses our mind more deeply than what is merely thought, inferred, deduced, or derived from the real, in a word, than anything abstract or conceptual. Real apprehension is thus more potent than conceptual apprehension inasmuch as the things that are its objects manifestly impress and affect us in an altogether greater degree than the images which are the object of conceptual apprehension. There is a corresponding distinction between the 'assent' which we make on the one hand to the concrete and real, on the other to the abstract and conceptual.

The contrast between real and conceptual apprehension is supported also by that between direct or immediate and indirect or mediate knowledge. The former occurs intuitively in the medium of imagination, an important faculty of cognition to which Newman assigns a rôle in the apprehension of realities not less significant than that given it by Hume, and more completely still in the medium of perception, whether external or internal. In perception the thing itself or at least a part or aspect of it is given us bodily and palpably, it stands directly confronting us as a concrete individual and challenges us to complete our realization of it in living experience. Perception and imagination are never utterly cut off from reality, and, wide though the interval may be between them and it, yet the real is never beyond their reach. It enters perceptual apprehension by the medium of the image; the function of perception is imaginative as well as representative (or imitative)—imaginative not indeed in the sense of indulgence in fantasy and fiction but in the sense of shaping an image that shall be a genuine constituent of reality. Real apprehension is apprehension by way of the concrete image, and however manifold may be the images or aspects of an object in the perceptual function, they mediate the reality (and therewith the essential truth) of the object they image. In the image—be it adequate or inadequate, an accurate or inaccurate rendering of the object—reality is always none the less imparted and can be brought to completion in it. And even where apprehension seems to be far removed from reality and even utterly sundered from it (as in the imaginative work of the poet and fabricator of fiction), the note of reality can yet be clearly detected, and there is always something real (always in the sense of individual, concrete, intuitable, etc.) as its underlying basis. But it is always by means of images that knowledge enters into possession of reality, and therewith attains truth; and from this point of view the inscription upon Newman's grave at Rednal, near Birmingham (*Ex Umbris et Imaginibus in Veritatem*) reveals its deeper meaning. Finally, we have to add to perception and imagination a third organ of real apprehension, namely the memory. Here, too, what we have is a concrete image-like kind of knowing giving contact with real being, so that the remembered event is throughout analogous to the perceived and imaged object, with the single difference that it occurs in the mode of past time.

Conceptual apprehension differs *toto caelo* from all real apprehension. It moves not in the medium of *image* but in that of symbol and sign. It stands in no connection with the real nature of things, but erects above this a world of its own, that of *ratio* and intellect, constituted by concepts and abstractions, logical inferences and deductions—in short, by unreal symbols. It is the indispensable aid to all scientific knowledge, and within the realm of science it is both wholly legitimate and indeed demanded. Its pretensions are only to be rejected when it trespasses upon other territory, as happens in epochs that tend towards Intellectualism. It is clear that Newman confines the power of Reason within narrow limits and does not do justice to the significance of the concept. He invariably displays a preference for the concrete and individual, the object of clear perception, the non-rational and directly experienced fact, and he indulges his preference at the cost of the rational, the universal, the abstract, that which is mediated or inferred by logical processes.

Now what is true of the act of apprehension is true also *mutatis mutandis* of the act of assent. Here, too, the same contrast is found, between real and conceptual assent, or between assent absolute and inference. There is no need for this to be further developed in detail, for the discussion throughout takes a parallel course. Newman understands by assent a mental act in which the intellectual is by no means the only side of our nature functioning, but in which rather our whole personality is involved, the emotional and volitional factors, indeed, much more powerfully than the rational. Assent is a sort of total reaction to some factual situation or special circumstance; logical processes may play a part in it, but this will be a subordinate one. Assent is an immediate concrete act, wholly personal and not further analysable, and essentially one and indivisible, and it admits therefore of no gradations or differences of degree of strength. Rather in every instance it is absolute, and even where it is doubtful the element of doubt is contained not in the act of assent but in the proposition or the fact to which assent is directed. It is quite otherwise with inference, which is always conditioned and mediated, and passes through different degrees of assurance while never getting beyond the relative certainty of probability to the absolute certainty of assent. But this passage from probability to assent must be made if we are to have a share in truth, and no conceptual abstractions or logical chains of proof and inference are any help in making it. What is needed is rather a sort of concrete feeling or instinct for truth, which is thus referred wholly inward to the subjective certitude of the individual spirit, to the personal decision of the perceiving and judging mind. Such a decision is not the result of extensive and intricate logical operations, but is based on a kind of intuitive apprehension which has behind it not only a man's faculty of thought or his understanding, but his entire personality. For "what is a proof for one understanding is none for another, and the certainty of a proposition consists really in the certainty of the mind that considers it".

This subjective capacity for apprehending truth, inclusive of so much more than all our intellectual faculties, is called by Newman the "illative sense". Under this term we are to understand that genuine method of inference which does not proceed by mere logical abstractions and conceptual processes but by means of which none the less we are enabled to apprehend truth itself in all its richness and vitality, concrete and individual. But here we have to do with a personal gift, demanding the intervention of the whole man and not an artificially isolated faculty that is never of itself able to recognize reality or attain to truth. "There is no final criterion of truth apart from the witness with which the mind itself confronts truth." And since the only standard of truth is the subjective certitude of the individual mind, the objectivity of truth is founded upon this subjectivity, i.e. upon the unconditional trustworthiness of that illative sense whereby it is apprehended.

The above sketch of the central ideas of Newman's theory of knowledge shows clearly how mistaken it is to bring this doctrine into any connection with scholastic theory. It would be truer to say (though the point need not be discussed in detail) that it is rooted in the classical systems of British empiricism, and that while it derives much from Locke, Berkeley, Butler, and Hume, it displays a free creative reshaping of what is taken over from these sources rather than the faithful dependence of a disciple. Everything in it is coloured and filled with Newman's own characteristic spiritual quality, and the tradition in which he stands supplies not so much the food he assimilates as the mental atmosphere he breathes. To that extent it may be said that the empirical tradition here underwent a renewal, but at the hands of a thinker not primarily akin to it but inwardly and fundamentally far removed from it.

Lines of connection may also be drawn—though with corresponding qualifications—with subsequent as well as with antecedent types of theory, with the "philosophy of life" of a Bergson and with the Pragmatism of a James; but in these directions Newman's teaching has only found an occasional echo. Furthermore, as Theodore Haecker has shown, Newman's careful and penetrating descriptive analyses of the phenomena of apprehension, assent, probability, and certainty, point by anticipation to Husserl's phenomenological descriptions, without it being possible to prove any historical connection between the two thinkers. We conclude from all this that Newman's theoretic philosophy had hidden within it not a few thoughts pregnant with meaning for the future, which were only to come to explicit birth at a much later date, and that, for all the depth of its roots in the past, it performed a notable work in preparation for the subsequent development of thought.

But Newman's critique of knowledge is misrepresented if regarded as having a merely theoretic purpose. From the first its aim is a practical one, namely, the establishment of religious faith. It takes its place, therefore, in a wider context in which alone it comes to its full meaning. "Theory of knowledge" forms the foundation and first stage of "theory of religion", into which it finally passes. But here, too, in the new problem that now confronts him Newman is concerned first and foremost with the subjective side of religion, that is with the apprehension of the divine in human consciousness. We must, however, emphasize that this does not mean that religion has been subjectivized or deprived of objectivity, but simply that the main interest of this thinker finds expression in the subjective side. Religion as objective fact is throughout presupposed, and, constituting as it does the unshakable foundation of all faith, it does not require any separate theoretical buttressing. The philosophical problem before Newman leads on, then, to the question: in what way does the human mind partake of divine reality, and by what cognitive means is it enabled to apprehend that reality?

When Newman somewhere remarks that for each of us there are ultimately only two reals, our own self and God, he is setting down the two primary realities with which religious thinking is concerned—the soul of man and the Divine Being. These two are to be distinguished from every other entity in respect of the character of the reality that is theirs on the ground that nothing else possesses in such high degree personality, concreteness, individuality, and vitality. For by "real" Newman does not mean every existent simply as such; he always employs the term in the emphatic sense which the four words just used indicate. From this standpoint the reality of God is manifestly the highest to which our experience has access, for it is concreteness raised to the highest power.

It is now immediately evident from the point of view of Newman's theory that the apprehension of (and assent to) such a reality takes place in the same fashion as that of concrete reality in general, that is of oneself, other selves, and the external world. But that means that in this matter nothing, or at best very little, can be achieved by the intellect and its rational functions alone, and that once again we need the intervention of the whole personality and especially of its practical side, if the soul is to come into possession of the divine reality. "In the concrete situation with which I have to do, logical demonstration is impossible," writes Newman in this context. The being of God cannot be ascertained by a process of inference, cannot come to light as the last link in a chain of syllogisms. It demands that utterly direct "real apprehension", that intuitive "illative sense", through which all our powers are brought into play and every capacity of understanding we possess is released. We are not here concerned with a specifically religious faculty, nor indeed with a *special* faculty of any kind such as might be set free to function in detachment from the personality taken as a whole. It is rather an activity in which the several parts of this whole are brought into such accord that the man's total being reaches its highest possible capacity of apprehension. Rational factors are included in this, although the value assigned to them is small, and feeling also, though Newman to be sure regards feeling with profound suspicion in so far as it is advanced as the basis of religious faith ("Religion as mere feeling is for me a dream and a mockery").

The first place in Newman's doctrine is given neither to Understanding nor to Feeling, but rather to the Conscience. And it is thus plain that his religious theory is determined predominantly by ethical motives. He had a fine sensitiveness for the autonomy of the moral life, and he did not let his profound need for a religious faith impair it; indeed, though he succeeded in bringing morality and religion into harmonious accord, his endeavour was to anchor the latter in the former and not vice versa. This is the best way to interpret the pessimistic strain in Newman's nature; he experienced more profoundly than most of the religious thinkers of his time the polar antithesis that characterizes the basic facts of the moral life, the sharp opposition between good and evil, right and wrong. And he was reluctant too lightly to bridge the gulf of this antithesis by having recourse to the divine love and the divine goodness. He felt the full brunt of the evil and suffering in the world, and suffered thereby all the pain of an exceptionally sensitive soul. He was fond of painting his picture of the world in gloomy colours, but his pessimism was not so much contempt of the world as renunciation of it, and his ascetic escape from the world expressed rather compassion and suffering resignation than belittlement and depreciation.

It is, then, in the primacy given to conscience that the ethical orientation of Newman's religious teaching is seen. Conscience first and foremost is the organ whereby the individual soul comes to know and apprehend the divine, the gate of entry of the divine into human nature. The "God that is in Conscience" is for Newman a fact of no less moment than the God of Revelation and the God of the Church; subjective religious experience matters as much or even more to him than objective religion. God is to be sought on the path that leads up from the human soul, and here, too, as always, his point of departure is the individual, personal and concrete. This path is the same from the standpoint of ethics; it is not because there is a God that moral obligation is real; but on the contrary God is recognized as existing because we feel the binding force of moral obligation. Conscience is at once the medium and the sanction of the divine principle, and Newman therefore makes a special point of analysing the facts of conscience with the greatest philosophical precision so as to bring out its real character in contrast to other activities of the human soul. It is a fully warranted instrument of cognition, as important for the disclosure of transcendent deity as is perception for the knowledge of the external world. Like perception it is a real apprehension, but the apprehension of another object, namely the highest and most concrete reality there is, the divine life. It is accordingly rooted not in the dark obscurity of feeling or in the casual play of mood, but in the bright clear light of thought; only this thought is not the abstract mediated thought that is alien to Reality, but concrete, intuitive thought, close to life and having its fulfilment *in* Reality.

Thus for Newman, as has to be repeatedly emphasized, religious faith is primarily a wholly personal and subjective concern of each several soul, which is able to attain to the divine directly of itself and have a share in a sort of natural knowledge of deity. From this starting-point Newman should logically have been led to extreme Protestantism or even to Mysticism, whereas in fact he took the opposite direction that led him into the bosom of the Roman Church. This may at first seem very strange, and we may be led to suspect a fissure running right through Newman's teaching. But the logical discrepancy to be detected in Newman's thought—that in it the most personal religious conviction goes hand in hand with the firmest attachment to an external authority—is hardly from his own point of view of great moment. The fact is rather that Newman was able to complete the passage from inner to outer, from individual autonomy to external authority, from personal experience to Church and dogma, without committing a *sacrificium intellectus* or diminishing the rights of either of the two contrasted sides. He thus acknowledged the necessity of *two* sources of religious belief, the God of Revelation as well as the "God in the Conscience", the authority and organization of the Church as well as the experience of the soul, an objective binding attachment to dogma as well as subjective conviction. It is the special note of Newman's religious philosophy that it gives equal weight to both factors and brings the two together in a harmonious synthesis.

In the *Grammar of Assent* Newman is merely concerned with the subjective side of religion, in his much earlier book upon the development of Christian doctrine he deals chiefly with its objective aspect. The dominating thought that here steps into the foreground is, that the truth of religion cannot be detached from its history; and thus the idea of development (evolution) becomes the *leitmotiv* of this discussion of what religion is, considered objectively. Now it must be emphasized at the outset that Newman's concept of development not only belongs chronologically to the pre-evolutionary epoch but has also in fact so little in common with the principle of evolution of Darwin and Spencer that it is even in contradiction to this in the point of crucial importance. To link up Newman's concept of development with historical parallels, we should have to consider rather the form which this concept assumed in the systems of Aristotle, Leibniz, and Hegel. But the historical relations of the idea will be here disregarded, not least the question—the most interesting one in this connection—of the possible (but not very probable) influence of the theory of Hegel; for Newman's ideas are original discoveries belonging first and foremost to himself and needing no sponsor to speak for them.

The philosophical basis for the development of Christian doctrine is given in an argument which is first of all concerned with the development of ideas in general. The problem is thereby from the outset transferred to the mental field, and in this very fact we see a fundamental difference between Newman's conception and those of subsequent naturalistic systems. It is with mental constructs or ideas as it is with corporeal perceived things: according to the direction from which it is seen a "thing" discloses at first only this or that aspect of its substance, it presents itself to us in manifold delineations and silhouettes which combine more and more to give a "total aspect" of the thing according as observation is keener and more prolonged. So with the idea: it is commensurable with the totality of its possible aspects, widely as these may vary for the individuals who apprehend it, and its power and its depth stand in a definite relation to the abundance and diversity of the aspects under which it is presented. No aspect is deep enough to exhaust the content of a concrete idea, nor is there any linguistic expression capable of defining it in the fullest meaning. But all these varying aspects may be related to the idea as their common point of reference, and merge in it, and however dissimilar and diverse they may be at a first glance, yet the more intense and prolonged the consideration we give them the more clearly do they testify to the reality and integrity, the originality and power, of the idea to which they belong. Newman, then, calls this process, in the course of which, whether it be short or long, the outlines and adumbrations of an idea inwardly coalesce and so approximate to their essential meaning, the mental development of the idea. But we cannot apply to this process the similitude of the stream that is clearest near its source. On the contrary, an idea gains in purity, richness, and power as the bed of the stream from which it was drawn becomes fuller and deeper. This figure of speech suggests that the historical beginnings of an idea cannot be turned into a criterion of its value and purport. It will be the more perfect the more, and the more profoundly, it fulfils itself in the course of time, and though in one sense it remains the same idea through all its transformations, yet it comes nearer to completion in its final form than at its first appearance or at any intermediate stage.

The centre of gravity in this account of historical development thus lies, in sharp contrast to the naturalistic point of view, not in the primitive but the more advanced stages of the process, not in its beginning but at its end. The meaning of an idea (by which we are to understand always a concrete construction or living power of the mind which has a significant historical mission to fulfil) cannot when it first comes upon the scene arrive at so full and effective expression as in epochs of higher and riper culture. The reason lies not so much in the idea as such as in the nature of its apprehension by the human mind,—an apprehension perpetually incomplete, inadequate to the whole truth of the idea, and only able to disclose the full wealth of aspects included within it by a gradual process of growth and advance. Time, therefore, is a necessary factor in the growth of an idea; or—what amounts to the same thing—for its comprehension and elucidation by those who receive it. This process of clarification is only accomplished in the course of its history, and increasingly in the measure in which the understanding of it, on the part of those who entertain it, ripens and deepens. Accordingly, a distinction has to be drawn between the apprehension or realization of an idea by the recipient mind and the idea itself; the former passes through many transformations and is subject to development, whereas the latter is from the beginning and throughout all these phases of transition fundamentally one and the same. If its truth is progressively disclosed in its history, this is only because this was from the start comprised within it. Its history and essence belong necessarily to one another, and the different aspects in which it unfolds itself, and the synthesis of which determines its final form, are merely "moments" or emanations of what essentially belongs to it. They are not brought to it from without but grow out of it organically from within. Otherwise expressed, the idea in its essential nature persists amid its varying aspects; its external representation is modified and developed but it does not itself change. It will thus be seen that development in Newman's sense is something different in principle from the "evolutionary" meaning the word bears for Naturalism. It has nothing to do with mechanical-causal processes of change in the world of matter, nor yet with biological growth and the formation of organisms through a perpetually rising series of levels of ever greater differentiation. Rather it means something purely mental or spiritual, the realization of the essence of ideas in the march of their history, the unfolding of that essence in the growing understanding of the apprehending mind, as first this and now that aspect of the underlying identical meaning becomes prominent.

The application of these conceptions to the history of the Christian religion and the Christian Church, which was Newman's main concern, may now easily be made. Christian doctrine is just such an idea which has passed in the course of centuries through many modifications, to disclose in them its essence ever more richly, fully, and profoundly. In these modifications we have not merely a succession of capricious and unconnected alterations in the doctrine as it was originally revealed; on the contrary, the history of Dogma shows that everything has here proceeded with the greatest regularity and in a single direction predetermined by the idea itself. The Christian idea has grown organically; without its essential meaning having been thereby affected, it has passed through a genuine process of development from its beginning down to our own day; it has revealed continually new forms and sides of its being to mankind's growing and deepening understanding, becoming thereby not poorer and weaker but more mature, more complete, and more potent. It has kept pace with the general advance of civilization to the higher levels of intellect and culture, and proportionately to the height attained it has gained in substance and fullness, in power and clarity. For in this not least is manifested the inexhaustible wealth of Christianity, that its idea-content cannot be apprehended all at once or once for all, but that time (in the sense of Bergson's *durée*) must become creative in it, to enable all that it includes to grow out of it organically and to unfold itself gradually into view. The more complex and concrete an historic idea is, the longer the period of time over which it will extend, and Newman for his part cannot doubt that the Christian idea far surpasses all others in complexity and concreteness, and therefore in fecundity in its historical development. This basic thought proved particularly effective in regard to the history of Dogma, to which Newman applied it most fruitfully, and to him first and foremost it is due that the rigid concept of Dogma gave place to a more living and organic point of view, which, though it did not venture to shake the obligatoriness and authority of Dogma, and its claim to contain a supratemporal truth, yet gained acceptance for its historical relativity and therewith for its vital connection with the development of the mind.

Newman's theory of the development of ideas in general, and of Christian doctrine in particular, was completed in a way that preserves it alike from doctrinaire rigidity and empty schematism. The further element in his theory is the important distinction he draws between genuine or sound, and spurious or wrong development. Newman terms the latter the corruption of the idea, and he devotes the larger second part of his book to a detailed and abundantly documented discussion of the relation between genuine developments of doctrine and corruptions of doctrine. He is here concerned with the question of the criteria by which we may distinguish the genuine from the spurious development, the fact of real progress from the fact of retrogression, and he sets out a theory of these criteria in some detail. There are in particular seven marks to indicate that an idea is growing organically and has not yet been infected with corruption. This is the case (1) where the idea preserves one and the same typical form; (2) where it exhibits continuously maintained principles; (3) where it preserves a power of assimilation; (4) where its first beginnings anticipate its later phases; (5) when its later aspects serve to defend and to further its earlier ones; (6) when it is able to maintain its original content and thereby to revive it to constantly new life; and finally (7) when it possesses an enduring vitality through all its phases. The fact that Christianity (and especially that idea of Christianity championed by the Roman Church) fulfils these requirements in a higher degree than any other spiritual movement in history, and that hitherto it has got the mastery over all tendencies making for its dissolution and victoriously overcome all corrupting influences—these are for Newman proof enough that in the future also Christianity will preserve its generative force, and furthermore be manifested as the living power of the mind, whose historical mission in the past stands as its most eloquent and searching witness.

Apart from Newman, who was the sole thinker of the front rank among the men of the Oxford Movement, only one personality within it had strong leanings to and aptitude for philosophy—William George Ward (1812–82). Belonging to the more radical section of the movement, Ward's influence was strong for detaching it from the Anglican Church, and his final conversion to Roman Catholicism took place even earlier than Newman's (September 1845). Ward attempted to give strict and systematic formal expression to what was for Newman a philosophical discovery lifted into clear thought out of the depths of his soul. Ward was no more tempted than Newman to go back to Scholasticism for inspiration; but he was more closely connected with contemporary tendencies of thought, with which he stood in intimate *rapport*, whether he was opposing the ideas of the time or seeking to avail himself of their help. He unfolded his religious programme in his book *The Ideal of a Christian Church* (1844), a work parallel to Newman's *Development of Christian Doctrine*. This book gave, if not the earliest, the weightiest formulation of the catholicizing tendencies in the Oxford Movement, and therefore marked a turning-point in its history. It prepared uncompromisingly for the schism that took place a year later. What drove Ward and those who fell with him into continually sharper opposition to Protestantism was the ideal of ascetic piety, the notion of the Christian life turned inward and made holy, which possessed them through and through, and not unnaturally their opposition finally led to their open confession of that form of faith, and to the Church in which they saw these ideals realized most purely. Ward's philosophical views are chiefly to be found set out in two later publications, in the treatise *On Nature and Grace* (1860) and in a lengthy series of essays which appeared in the *Dublin Review* (of which he was himself editor) between 1867 and 1882, and were issued in two volumes after his death with the title *Essays on the Philosophy of Theism* (1884), edited by his son Wilfrid Ward. These essays contain the great controversy of the Oxford Movement with the Empiricism of J. S. Mill and his school as the thinkers at that time most representative of secular philosophy. They are a sort of counterpart to Mill's *Examination of Hamilton*, and at the same time form a reply to Mill's attack, inasmuch as Ward's thought had close affinities with certain points in the teaching of the Scottish thinker.

Ward's criticism is aimed at the central thesis of the empiricist Philosophy, that all our knowledge is derived from experience and that this is the sole legitimate source of certainty and truth. We have only to pass a single step beyond the immediate data of consciousness, we have only, for instance, to consider in place of these data recollected ideas supplied to us mediately by memory, to see how untenable is the standpoint of mere experience, or, as Ward mostly calls it in relation to Mill's position, pure "phenomenism". For in remembering, we are not concerned with the present impression we have of a past event, but with the actual existence of this event in the past. The fact that we do remember is enough to show that the cognitions of our memory have no guarantee in direct experience; rather, to account for memory we have to assume cognitions that are not obtained by the way of Empiricism. But a similar conclusion holds good with regard to all knowledge, which Empiricism wishes to refer to pure experience and induction. Cognition is not based merely upon what is *de facto* experienced, but always also upon a form of knowledge which is unrelated to experience either directly or indirectly and is, in fact, fundamentally different from it. This is Intuition; and the objects known by it are not the phenomenal data of consciousness or their derivatives but universally valid, necessary, *a priori* truths of which we have immediate self-evidencing insight. Thus Ward's basic conviction leads him to assert that all human knowledge has its starting-point *not* in experience but in certain self-evident and therefore absolutely trustworthy truths which can be immediately apprehended and the certainty of which is in themselves and underived. Whatever man's cognitive faculties declare to be indubitably certain, is thereby from the first known as unconditionally true; subjective certitude is the standard by which we measure objective truth. And in whatever other way we may be able to reach knowledge, whether by experience and observation, or logical deductions, or by any way besides, intuitive knowledge is always presupposed and forms an indispensable preliminary. With these truths, so clearly recognized, Ward was building a bulwark against the then dominant Empiricism not unlike that constructed by the philosophers of the Scottish school, and, in fact, his doctrine took its place within the strong Intuitionist trend of thought into which before (and, in part, during) the rise of the Idealist movement the forces making against Empiricism were gathering without combining in a single common front. In this connection there is at any rate an inner kinship between the thinkers of the Scottish school (Hamilton, Mansel, M'Cosh), those of the Oxford Movement (Newman and Ward), and those other groups of which Martineau's was the most important.

The opposition between Empiricism and Intuitionism, however, is something more than a conflict in epistemological theory. Viewed in a wider perspective, it is seen to be based on the far-reaching philosophical contrast of Theism with Anti-Theism. For the establishment of Theism, which was Ward's main concern, and to which his intuitionist theory of knowledge was to be merely preliminary, meant likewise a sharp antagonism to the religious indifferentism of the sceptics and agnostics, recruited mainly from the empiricist camp. He combated the secularizing of philosophy, for which he held the empiricist doctrine primarily responsible, and in contrast he saw in the establishment of religion the real and most important task that lay before philosophy. Thus all his theoretical labours had ultimately no other aim or issue than the justification of his religious faith. Of this the chief constituent was the belief in personal deity in the sense taught by Christian doctrine (i.e. by Catholic dogma), and Ward's philosophical arguments for the existence of God were in essential agreement with those of other Catholic thinkers like Newman, L. Ollé-Laprune, and J. Kleutgen, by whom he had been lastingly influenced. Like them he laid special stress upon the moral argument and made it the main foundation of his apologetic. As a matter of pure theory, however, he was able to find a place in his philosophy for the existence of God without doing violence to his thought only in so far as he recognized in the fact of God's existence one of those necessary *a priori* truths which, because of their self-evidence, carry with them absolute certainty. The being of God is guaranteed neither through facts of experience nor by logical proofs but through immediate insight.

Finally, the principle of intuition is also maintained when applied to ethics. Ward's views on this subject, while they were the natural outcome of his own epistemological premisses, only reached explicit expression towards the close of his life when he had become acquainted with the ideas of Ollé-Laprune, the father of the "Modernist" movement, whose treatise *De la Certitude Morale* (1880) made a deep impression upon him and did much to further his own thought on the subject. For Ward, as for Ollé-Laprune, the problem of moral certainty occupies a central place. Just as there are necessary theoretic and metaphysical truths, so too there are moral insights, unconditionally certain because of their compelling self-evidence. The ideas of good and evil, right and wrong, of virtue and perfidy, etc., are utterly simple and admit of no further dissection or analysis. It is to me a matter of purely intuitive certainty, requiring no further consideration, that the treachery of my friend was a bad thing and to be disapproved as such; here I acknowledge a self-evident and so necessary moral truth. But the self-evidence of such ethical certainties compels recognition of a second self-evidence implied in it, namely, that they are grounded in the being of God. For once again it is a matter of immediate insight that the ethical axioms —the approval of good and the reprobation of bad actions— have their source in a higher type of being than that of man. Morality is rooted in God as the supreme law-giver of moral standards and is at the same time the best argument for His necessity and therefore for His existence.

This position in conclusion throws a bright light upon the problem of freedom. Like most representatives of Intuitionist ethics, Ward avows himself an Indeterminist, and thus here, too, he finds himself in natural opposition to Empiricism with its mechanistic and deterministic outlook. Again, it is chiefly with Mill that he crossed swords. According to Ward, the problem of the freedom of the will turns primarily upon the question whether a man has or has not the capacity to resist his natural voluntary impulses. For the answer to this question Ward relies, in contrast to his usual practice, upon the facts of experience. These show that a being endowed with reason in fact does possess this power in a high degree—that he can limit himself and offer resistance to the spontaneous promptings of the will—and that in so far as he has this power, his actions are truly free, it being immaterial whether or not in any special case the power is exercised. This simple appeal to experience which goes straight to the heart of the problem seems thus to be a sufficient proof of indeterminism. But the problem has another side as well; it includes not only the negative thesis that the human will is *not* determined at every point, but also the positive, that man is himself an original source of volition or a self-determining cause of voluntary action. At this point the threads connecting morality with religion become entwined. There are only two such original springs of causation not externally determined, the divine and the human will. For whereas God as ultimate and supreme cause is the originator of every event and therefore of human willing also, yet human volition is in no way immediately determined by the divine will. God's creative power has, rather, made man into a centre of volition on his own account. He has transferred of His own free choice to His creature the freedom proper to Himself alone, conferring upon the creature the power of causation, which enables man within certain limitations to free himself from the causal nexus binding him to God and to act independently of the divine will. God has thus in a certain limited degree renounced control over human willing and acting, and to that extent man is free, in the sense of possessing freedom of choice between right and wrong, good and evil. And thus is found a natural solution of the antinomy between morality and religion to which the problem of freedom gives rise, a solution which while it does full justice to the autonomy of the moral world yet brings it into connection with the divine law.

In this context mention should be made of FRANCIS WILLIAM NEWMAN (1805–97), the Cardinal's younger brother, who although he remained outside the Oxford Movement, held views not unlike those of his famous brother. He was a very versatile and fertile writer, but his disposition was rather that of the quiet scholar than that of the combatant or leader in religious controversy. He was the victim of all kinds of whims, and spun round himself an idea-world of his own, without feeling the need of any intellectual fellowship with others, and without the noble passion and profound conviction of faith that inspired his brother. He was far inferior to the latter, whether as a personality or as regards the depth and clarity of his thought, the purity of his will, and the strength of his faith, and it would appear in every respect perverse to set him above the great figure of the cardinal or even (as Pfleiderer did) to put him beside Schleiermacher. His religious and philosophical opinions are mainly set down in three works: in *The Soul* (1849), a sensitive and sincere book that breathes throughout a mystical fervour; in *Phases of Faith* (1850), his autobiographical account of his own spiritual pilgrimage which led him from the doctrines of Christianity to a theism detached from all positive ecclesiastical connections,—a parallel work to his brother's *Apologia pro Vita Sua*; and finally in the book *Theism, doctrinal and practical* (1858), which gives a more systematic presentation of his theological standpoint.

This is, like that of J. H. Newman, individualist as well as anti-intellectualist; but F. W. Newman's Individualism concentrates upon the wholly personal relations of the soul with God far more intensively and one-sidedly even than that of his brother. A man's own soul is the one and only source he has for the knowledge of the life of God; it is the inner sense that discloses the divine to us, the organ whereby we are enabled to approach and unite ourselves with the Divine Being. There is a strong strain of Mysticism apparent here, and combined with it is the rejection of all outward means of grace, and of every binding authority whatever, whether that of Church and dogma, the Bible, or even the mediation of Christ. The one article of belief remaining is the mystical deity as revealed and grasped in the living experience of the soul. But deep and sincere as the experience was from which it sprang, this attempt at a theism purified of all dross means in effect that the genuine substance of religion has been diluted or emptied away. In comparison with J. H. Newman's ardour and vitality, with his firmly held faith rooted in the actual institutional life of the Church, it suggests a solitary soul revelling in its own emotions, and we feel that religious thought has retreated upon the ego complacently mirroring itself and upon experience of a purely subjective personal type.

We have seen that a prominent feature of the religious philosophy of the Oxford Movement, as represented by J. H. Newman and W. G. Ward, is what we might have called its "moralism". In it the moral consciousness was displayed with all possible emphasis as not only the root of religion but as the touchstone of its reality. It was the natural presupposition of the Oxford teaching—and at the same time an indication of how deeply it was anchored in the firm foundations of the British tradition—that religion has its starting-point in morality and that all genuine development of the religious consciousness includes within it the effort towards moral perfection. The same underlying thought is even more prominent and dominant in another system also, the ethical Idealism of MARTINEAU. This, to be sure, is independent of the Oxford Movement, but the aims it pursued and the tendencies it exhibited have a certain similarity, and in its philosophical doctrine in particular it is in several points closely akin. After Newman, Martineau was certainly the most potent awakener and renewer of the life of the spirit in the spheres of morality and religion which the British nation produced in the XIXth Century. Like Newman, he belongs to the front rank of the great spirits of the Victorian Age.

The philosophy of Martineau[1] is more the expression and the confession of a great personality than a doctrinal theory in the narrower sense. It was not so much the product of any special philosophical school or current as the outcome of the general intellectual forces and movements which gave the Victorian Age its special stamp and character. Through his personal and literary relationships Martineau was more deeply immersed in these movements than most other thinkers of his time, not least because of the length of his life, which, beginning the year after Kant's death and not closing till beyond the threshold of the new century, included nearly three generations in its span and thus witnessed the rise and passage of many different currents and movements of thought. His mental development therefore reaches back far beyond the epoch we are here presenting into the 'twenties of last century, then

[1] James Martineau (1805–1900) worked as a Unitarian minister from 1828 to 1840, first in Dublin, then in Liverpool, and last in London. From 1840 to 1885 he was Professor at the Manchester New College which was transferred in 1853 to London, at first holding the chairs of Philosophy and Political Economy, from 1857 those of Moral and Religious Philosophy, and from 1869 he was Principal of the College. The most important of his numerous works are *Types of Ethical Theory* (two vols., 1885, third edition, 1891); *A Study of Religion* (two vols., 1888, third edition, 1900); *The Seat of Authority in Religion* (1890, third edition, 1891), as well as the collected *Essays, Reviews and Addresses* (four vols., 1890–1).

follows it for a considerable part of its course, to attain its real culmination only in the full and luminous maturity of a rarely gifted old age. In fact, those works upon which Martineau's philosophical reputation almost exclusively rests are the works of a very old man,[1] and there can surely be no other case of a man's highest creative productivity falling between the eighth and ninth decades of his life. To that extent, however, Martineau's achievements and his influence belong mainly to the period which is the subject of this part of our study, though his work as a thinker started so much earlier.

The special interest of Martineau's development as a philosopher is that it mirrors that of the mind of his age as a whole in its typical features. He gives an account of it in the preface to the *Types of Ethical Theory*. In his youth and early manhood he was deeply enmeshed in the empiricist and deterministic ways of thinking that belonged to his own home circle, and he became in succession a willing adherent of the doctrines of Locke, Hartley, Collins, Edwards, Priestley, Bentham, and James Mill. But even at that time occasional doubts occurred to him as to the soundness of these systems, though his close friendship with the younger Mill set his misgivings for a time at rest. Later, however, a profound transformation began which came to a temporary end about the year 1840 and led to an open breach with the type of thinking he had hitherto accepted. This change was manifestly more the result of an inward growth than of external influence. Deep meditation upon the problems of inner experience had revealed to Martineau a factor that until then he had not noticed, the autonomous function of the mind both in willing and knowing, involving a something different from and independent of the flux and play of phenomena and impulses, and retaining the identity in this flux unchanged. It was in particular the problems of the moral consciousness that troubled him. He began

[1] This is not quite true. His chief philosophical works were not published till after he resigned the Principalship of the College, but for many years before their contents had formed the material of his lectures.—ED.

to realize the deeper meaning of notions like responsibility, guilt, desert, and duty, and was brought face to face with the question whether there is not above and beyond every empirical existent an ideal realm of what "ought to be", and whether this does not provide the point of view from which alone the real meaning of human willing and acting is discernible. Naturalism did not enable him to give any answer to these perplexing questions, and he therefore abandoned a view of the world which insists that not only every external but every internal event is determined according to strict causal law. A critical examination of the causal problem led him then to a thorough revision of the doctrine hitherto accepted, and prepared the way for the discovery which was later to become one of the central motives of Martineau's thought.

Martineau had thus by the age of forty already got the better of Naturalism in certain essential points, but his final reversion to Idealism was the outcome of the first-hand sympathetic acquaintance he acquired of German philosophy on the occasion of a period of study at Berlin in the winter of 1848–9. He himself in his old age regarded this experience as having been of great importance for his own mental development. He spoke of "a kind of second education in Germany" through which he had been led "mainly under the admirable guidance of the late Professor Trendelenburg", and described its effect as "a new spiritual birth". This contact with the Aristotelian Trendelenburg, however, whose lectures upon Logic and the History of Philosophy he attended, did not furnish him with any ready-made philosophical system which he could have made his own in its entirety, and Trendelenburg's own metaphysics was unacceptable to him. What it did do was to give him for the first time a deeper understanding of the whole development of philosophical thinking from the time of the ancient Greeks to the modern Germans, enabling him to discern the inner connections and spiritual forces that are active in all the great systems of the past and unite them all one with another. In this way he obtained what he had not before, the intellectual equipment out of which the various theoretical, ethical, and religious ideas that were moving in his mind and struggling into explicit expression could coalesce in a single philosophical conspectus. He himself wrote from Berlin (February 25, 1849): "Trendelenburg's lectures on the history of philosophy have precisely hit my wants, not imposing a system upon me . . . but affording faithful guidance to sources of both ancient Greek and modern German systems, and presenting in the best way an occasion for the review and correction of my own opinions" (*Life and Letters of James Martineau*, by J. Drummond and C. B. Upton, vol. 2, p. 331). Thus he was not only stimulated to a renewed study of the writings of Plato and Aristotle, but also to immerse himself thoroughly in the wealth of ideas of the German Idealists, especially Kant and Hegel, from whose pages, as he says, the obscurity began now for the first time to be lifted. It was this mutual illumination of German through Greek and Greek through German systems of thought that gave rise to the new insights which were to combine to form Martineau's own philosophy, though it was only to find its mature exposition a generation or more later. This philosophy belongs, therefore, to no special school of doctrine, but unites within itself the fundamental motives of idealistic thought of all times and peoples, that of the religious systems (of Christian doctrine in particular) as well as that of the systems of philosophy. Religious and Christian teaching had, in fact, as great a part in shaping Martineau's thought as philosophical theory, and they were a continual source of fresh power in framing his general outlook upon the world.

Martineau had thus revised his own way of thinking from its foundations by direct contact with German philosophy some time before the neo-idealistic movement began in the 'seventies, and the Greek thinkers had been of service to him in this process of renewal very much as they were to be later to the Oxford disciples of Kant and Hegel. He had in his own person anticipated the development of British philosophy by about twenty years, but he remained at first an isolated figure, able neither himself to liberate a movement of thought nor to find one to which to attach himself. The reasons for this comparative lack of influence were twofold. The doctrine that had taken shape within him, though it had found literary expression in occasional minor publications, had not as yet been treated systematically in a major work: and he had no intellectually alert and receptive milieu in which to proclaim it—such as the University of Oxford later became. Afterwards, when the Kantian and Hegelian renaissance started in Oxford and proceeded on its victorious course, Martineau and his disciples at first greeted the new movement, so akin as they felt it to be to their own outlook, with the warmest sympathy. Green won in a special degree Martineau's admiration, and the two men became united in a friendship valuable to both. They found a common basis for their philosophical labours not only in the many points of agreement that marked their two theories, but also in the interest in religion which characterized the elder adherents of the Oxford Idealism much as it did Martineau. Moreover, the fact that they were fighting the same enemies—the materialistic, naturalistic, and agnostic tendencies of the time—drew them into alliance. But later on the good relations of the earlier years were noticeably impaired, and Martineau and those of his way of thinking found themselves in sharp opposition especially to the younger Hegelians. The differences between them consisted, on the one hand, in their fundamentally different treatment of the problems of freedom and personality (the most momentous postulates in Martineau's doctrine), and, on the other hand, in the ever-growing progressive secularization of thought through the absolutist systems of the later Hegelians. By way of contrast Martineau's teachings came to have many points of contact with those neo-Idealists who—like Pringle-Pattison, Rashdall, and Sorley—represented a more "personalist" type of doctrine and whose point of view was nearer that of Lotze than that of Hegel. In fact, Martineau's philosophy as a whole is in many respects akin to that of Lotze, and had a similar mission to accomplish in England to that of Lotze in Germany.

When Martineau's large systematic works (*Types of Ethical*

Theory, *A Study of Religion*, and *The Seat of Authority in Religion*) at length became known to the public in the 'eighties and 'nineties they aroused eager interest and won warm approbation especially outside the ranks of professional philosophers. But they came too late to form a milestone in the history of British thought. The neo-Idealist movement had taken the wind out of their sails, and they had no longer the importance of a force driving forward the development of thought, but only that of a reaffirmation and consolidation of positions that had already received trenchant expression years before. They exerted their influence rather as the literary testament of a widely acknowledged and much revered leader, the witness of a lofty moral personality that lived as well as taught life in the power of mind, than through the actual content of the doctrines they had to propound.

Martineau's philosophical aptitude and interests extended mainly over the field of ethics and philosophy of religion, and for him the treatment of purely theoretic problems is not an end on its own account but a means to prepare and establish his moral and religious philosophy. The discussion of such problems he made therefore incidental to his inquiry into the nature of religion (in vol. I of the *Study of Religion*) and did not devote special writings to them. The two problems to which he devoted particular attention were the problems of knowledge and causation. The first of these we do not here discuss, as Martineau's treatment of it is not specially characteristic. The theory of causality, on the other hand, leads directly to the great problems of metaphysics.

Causality signifies in the first place the relation between two factors, the "cause" and the "effect", and according to the prevalent theory represented by naturalistic systems, which dominates scientific thought through and through, the causal process takes place wholly in our world of appearances. Both cause and effect are phenomena, they stand to one another in serial relation and in necessary connection, the cause preceding the effect in time and (as it were) releasing it. The two factors are entirely homogeneous and have the same existential character.

Causality thus is the temporal succession of phenomena connected according to some law. The outcome of this is the theory of Determinism, i.e. of the complete determination of every inner and outer event according to causal law, to which the human will also is in strict subjection.

In contrast to this interpretation of causality Martineau lays stress upon the noumenal character of the cause; which instead of being one phenomenon among others is a genuine productive force. The effect does not proceed out of it by merely causal sequence but is brought about or engendered by it. Causality thus comes to mean origination or production, i.e. the cause is not homogeneous with the effect but heterogeneous. The ground of all appearances itself lies not in the phenomenal but in a non-phenomenal world of productive causes. And Martineau now goes on to try to show that the only true cause we know is the activity of the will, and that the essence of causality is thus identical with the will. But the will is to be found first and foremost in one's own Self or in human personality. In asserting my will I am strictly aware of myself as a power able to originate phenomena, a genuine cause capable of altering the world of appearances. But while the force issuing from the act of volition is an indispensable antecedent condition for such alternative, there is nothing in this alone to make it evident why one change occurs and not another. The essence of the act of volition therefore consists not merely in an outflow of force but in the fact that the will is capable of choosing one way of operating from among the two or more alternative possible ways presented to it, to decide upon this and to direct upon it the release of force that brings the change about. In this sense causality is nothing but the expression of a will, but it is clear that the will of man cannot be the only cause in the world as a whole. Above and beyond it extends the objective or cosmic will, which is none other than the will of the divine spirit which created the world and brings about all changes in it except such as are found in the restricted region reserved for human activity. The essential reality of the world is thus will in the sense of free causation, and the external world or nature becomes a manifestation of the supreme will of the Spirit of God.

The two great postulates at the heart of Martineau's theory of causality, the two massive pillars upon which the edifice of his metaphysic is founded, are the postulate of the freedom of the human will and the belief in the authority of God. The former constitutes the keystone of his ethics, the latter is the core of his philosophy of religion. With the belief in the divinity of the supreme principle is connected the thought of its incarnation both in the realm of nature and in the human soul. With the postulate of freedom is connected the doctrine of the uniqueness, genuine individuality, and infinite value of the human soul, to which is added finally as a third postulate belief in its indestructibility and continued existence in an everlasting future life.

Martineau's ethics stands and falls with the notion of freedom —moral freedom—which is to be combined with the concept of an autonomous personality conscious of responsibility and endowed with reason. The moral personality is free not only in relation to the world of natural happenings but also in relation to the will of God. For though it shares in the eternal Spirit that created it and is alive within it, yet this entails no loss to its independence and essential integrity. Its freedom is, however, not its own original possession but is transmitted to it by the will of God, and it is the gift of freedom that enables the human person to decide between possible alternatives for action and therewith to achieve full responsibility for what he does. In this way there is no restriction upon either the divine or the human will: God has freely created the human world and endowed it with freedom, so that man so far as he is a moral personality enjoys a liberty that renders him independent of the divine will. The two spheres, the human and the divine, are thus sharply distinguished, and by this separation of man from God the autonomy of the finite is harmonized with the absoluteness of the infinite being, and Theism reconciled with Indeterminism. The price to be paid is, of course, the admission of a dualism that pervades the entire system, and is not confined to the original duality of man and God, but characterizes Martineau's thought as a whole, with its preference for unqualified contrasts, sharp lines of demarcation and schematic subdivisions.

It will be by this time obvious that this doctrine stands in clear contrast to the absolutist systems of the Hegelians, and we can see why Martineau and his followers joined battle with such energy against that development of philosophical Idealism. For Martineau the whole of Hegelianism was for all its constant use of the word freedom nothing but Determinism in disguise, which involved the extinction of the "personality" it professed to value in the might of the Absolute. And this Absolute could not but appear to him as an abstract and complicated metaphysical scheme, in contrast to which he set the living and concrete personality of the divine Absolute. At the same time he felt repelled from Bradley's metaphysic because in his opinion it opened the door to Pantheism and Mysticism and thereby obliterated all the boundaries which his own sober and candid mind felt obliged to draw.

Martineau's ethics, as presented in the *Types of Ethical Theory*, is the outcome of a comprehensive examination of the various theories to which the history of moral philosophy has given rise. This interesting attempt to frame a doctrine of ethical types in some respects resembles Sidgwick's method of procedure, though it leads to very different results. Ethical systems are first divided into the two main groups of psychological and unpsychological, the basis of the division being whether, on the one hand, the fundamental ethical assumptions are reached from within—through self-knowledge—and thence extended to provide an interpretation of the objective world, or the contrary procedure is followed, in which latter case there are two subordinate groups, according as the clue to the human moral problem is found in the postulation of metaphysical entities or in mere phenomena and their laws. Of these the former are termed metaphysical theories (to be further subdivided into transcendental (Plato) and immanent (Descartes, Malebranche, Spinoza)), and the latter physical, of which Comte is the chief representative. The psychological types of theory are in turn divided into idiopsychological and heteropsychological, of which the former is founded on the intuitions of the individual moral consciousness, the latter on some psychic faculty other than this. And this heteropsychological type may again take three directions, according as it seeks to derive the essence of the moral fact from sense, reason, or aesthetic experience. To the first of these subdivisions belongs every form of hedonistic ethics (represented chiefly by Epicurus and Bentham), whether utilitarian or evolutionary; the second, termed "dianoetic ethics", has typical representatives in Cudworth, Clarke, and Price; while the third, the "aesthetic" type, is exemplified by Shaftesbury and Hutcheson. Martineau's own theory, finally, is that which adopts the "idiopsychological" method.

As regards its historical pedigree this theory cannot be precisely determined. Martineau himself indicates its close kinship on the one hand with Butler, on the other with Kant, and there can be no doubt that he owes more to these two thinkers than to any others. His agreement with Butler mainly concerns his method, that with Kant mainly concerns the content of his thought. Of less importance are his relations with the Scottish school of Reid and Hamilton (and, indeed, the earlier Scottish moralists also), to which critics have sometimes given prominence, though it cannot be denied that the intuitive factor, the doctrine of the immediate self-evidence of moral value-judgments, which plays a great part in Martineau's theory, points to Scottish influences. And finally it must not be forgotten that the source out of which Martineau continually renews his intuitions is the Christian ethic as proclaimed in the Sermon on the Mount.

Martineau's point of departure is the individual consciousness or inner experience upon the basis of which we have a direct insight into moral facts and qualities. He thus presupposes an original moral sense or special moral faculty which is fundamentally different from every other faculty (as that of reason or aesthetic susceptibility). In this basic assumption he is in essential agreement with Butler and his doctrine of the moral sense. We call this position ethical intuitionism, and Martineau may be considered its chief modern representative. The fundamental ethical fact, then, consists in our having *quâ* human beings an irresistible propensity to approve some things and disapprove others, and to pronounce corresponding judgments upon them. And it becomes evident at once that the objects of our moral acknowledgments and rejections are persons only and not things, and this leads to the intuition, which underlies so much else, that our moral valuations are always directed to the inner motives of an action and not to its outward consequences. Martineau, in fact, lays the whole weight on inner motive, whereas the external result, be it never so beneficent, is to him ethically irrelevant and simply to be considered as a sign or indication of the inward springs of action. If, then, we recognize moral quality in and only in the motive for action, every moral judgment must clearly arise from observation of our own motives, and is rooted in inner experience or in self-consciousness. Only from this starting-point can we arrive at value-judgments on the conduct of another; we transfer to it by analogy the procedure we have already applied to our own case. The moral life is thus displayed exclusively in the sphere of the will, and it is only actions born of the will that have any meaning for morality.

To make his account more precise, Martineau distinguishes between "spontaneities" and "volitions". In acting spontaneously we are normally prompted by a single impulse, while volition involves the presence of at least two. Plurality of impelling motives is the indispensable condition of moral judgment, and they must furthermore appear simultaneously not successively. But the Self cannot be simply the arena in which these impulses break in together and struggle for mastery; they are rather simply possibilities for the Self upon whom alone it depends which is to be followed. The Self must be the master of the impelling motives, not their slave. Moral judgment stands or falls with the ascription to the Self of a selective power enabling it to decide between two or more possibilities, and the Self must accordingly be free in its choice of motives. "Either free will is a reality or moral judgment is a delusion."

The doctrine of motivation provides the psychological basis for the postulate of the freedom of the will. If the will is free to follow one motive and reject another, if therefore a man might have acted in given circumstances otherwise than he in fact did, the question faces us whether there is any order in which motives may be ranked, which will justify a decision for this or that in particular cases. Martineau holds that there is such an order. We may consider the springs of action from two different points of view, according to their respective strengths and according to their respective excellence. We may then say that he who surrenders to the strongest impulse acts from prudence, while he who obeys the highest acts from duty, for the moral ranking depends upon the worth of the motive, the prudential upon its strength, the former being in essence universal, constant, and obligatory for everyone, the latter individual and variable according to person and circumstance.

Martineau then develops in detail a theory of the springs of action, classifying and enumerating them carefully according to systematically applied principles of division. He makes a most impressive attempt to cover this whole field of inquiry in its full extent and reduce it to order and system. There are many fine and penetrating psychological observations here, but the discussion also shows the author's pronounced propensity to formal schematization and classification, which results in many cases in forcing the phenomena to fit the logical scheme. This inquiry concludes by setting out a moral scale of values, from which we may at once read off the rank of the motive actuating us. It comprises thirteen levels: at the bottom are the so-called secondary passions, such as vindictiveness, censoriousness, suspiciousness, at the top the primary affection of compassion and the primary sentiment of reverence. Like Goethe, Martineau saw in this last the crown and completion of human character.

This is the most important and original part of Martineau's

ethics, and here as elsewhere its intuitionist character is evident, for here, too, it is to the specifically moral consciousness or ethical sense that we owe the objective ranking of moral values, and through which we are able to apprehend as immediately self-evident and with intuitive certainty the range of motive-values from highest to lowest and the different places of specific motives on the value-scale. Theoretical considerations, rational processes of inference, comparison, etc., do not here come into play, but merely our innate consciousness of moral value, which as it grows in acuteness and refinement affords us a more exact and reliable criterion to apply both to our own decisions and to the judging of the conduct of others. Martineau has, of course, to admit that the intuitive process is only fully valid for relatively simple and uncomplicated motivations, whereas where the situation is more complex the original insight into value may be capable of correction by some process of reflective thought. He speaks in this case of a "quasi-intuitive" consciousness, i.e. one that is completed by rational consideration. But it is in any case firmly maintained that there is a graduated scale of principles of action, making possible a comparative analysis of moral motives and values, and that we carry within us this scale and can read off its gradations immediately. It follows from this that all moral judgment has a comparative character. We cannot simply say that this or that course of conduct is right or wrong, good or bad, we can only maintain that it is relatively better or worse than another which the will would have been equally able to adopt. Accordingly, an action is to be esteemed right which follows a higher motive when a lower is also present. But since we bear within us the consciousness of the relative grade of value of two motives impelling us to a decision, there is already included the obligation to choose the higher motive. Martineau calls this the Canon of Principles or Obligation and distinguishes from it the Canon of Consequences: the former gives "the true *moral criterion* for determining the *right* of the case", the latter "the *rational criterion* for determining its *wisdom*". "The former suffices for the estimate of character; but for the estimate of conduct must be supplemented by the latter." But the former has in all circumstances precedence over the latter, for mere consideration of the consequences of an action for the general welfare carries in itself no moral obligation—a point that Martineau substantiates against Sidgwick—the obligation arising rather from the fact that in the conflict of motives the altruistic ones show themselves to have the higher worth. We have thus always to refer to the scale of springs of action before proceeding to estimate consequences.

This draws a sharp line of division between Martineau's ethical doctrine and every form of Hedonism, Eudaemonism, and Utilitarianism. Martineau's, like Kant's, is an ethic of conscience and duty, of responsibility and binding moral law. None of his British contemporaries has proclaimed the moral dignity of man, the elevation and integrity of personality, the freedom of the will, and the sovereignty of the moral law, with greater power of conviction than he. His doctrine formed one of the strongest bulwarks in the struggle against the naturalistic and materialistic tendencies of the time, against the flood of Darwinian and evolutionary systems, against the secularization of life, and much besides. It was all the more potent because it was backed by his great and noble personality and because the lofty spiritual life that was its message was realized in himself.

The same ideal aims pursued in his ethics were also the burden of his Philosophy of Religion. Although in making moral action an entirely inward matter he had liberated it from social ties as well as from the fetters of natural existence, he did not suppose it could be set in complete independence but sought to anchor it in that higher principle whose sphere is religion. We saw that the starting-point of Martineau's doctrine is in self-consciousness. There are, however, two ways in which the self passes beyond its own boundaries—in the act of perception, whereby it apprehends the external world of nature, and in the fact of conscience whereby it participates in the Divine Being. In both cases it is aware of itself in an Other, and again of this Other in itself; in the latter case it transcends itself to pass into a higher Self. The necessity of the passage from the moral to the religious sphere is more clearly to be seen in the conception of authority. What is the origin of the authority which makes us prefer the higher to the lower motive and recognize in this preference the real moral act? Do we somehow fashion it out of our consciousness, where it is first manifested? Would not the conflict of motives then be nothing but a struggle between our personal wants? That cannot assuredly be the import of the experience of obligation; rather, this signifies that we are becoming aware of something higher than ourselves which, because it makes claims upon us, cannot be a part of our Self. Rightly interpreted this experience of authority forces us outside our own boundaries to recognize over against our Self a being of a higher order. But since we are persons and personality implies a higher type of being than mere thinghood, this still higher order of being must be a person different from, but surpassing and transcending oneself, that is, it must be the infinite or divine personality. Thus the moral consciousness is more than a part of our Self; in it we acknowledge an objective authority or law over us which we did not make, and by it we enter into direct communion with the divine life.

The relation between ethics and religion is accordingly to be defined in the following way. The former is antecedent to the latter and requires antecedent treatment as moral rules are at first independent of any religious belief, which they precondition rather than presuppose. All higher religion is anchored in the moral consciousness and it is in the moral sphere that its most momentous achievements have their origin. On the other hand, ethics cannot be maintained within the boundaries of the merely human. It points beyond, and demands completion in the direction of religion, else it falls back to the level of Hedonism.

How strong for Martineau is the ethical orientation of religion is seen further when he comes to deal with the proofs of the existence of God. He is mainly concerned to develop two arguments. First the metaphysical argument, touched upon already, follows from the theory of Causality; since Causality is, as we have seen, identical with Will, and human volition is more or less narrowly restricted in scope, and since further there can be in the phenomenal world no genuine cause in the sense of origination, we infer from the human to the divine Will as the primordial sustainer of the whole world of nature. Thus the metaphysical argument leads straight to God as the ultimate cause or the supreme intelligent Will. More important is the moral proof for the existence of God; —or, more accurately, the attempt to exhibit God in the sphere of ethics. Here the mediating organ is conscience, whereby the Divine Being is revealed as certainly as the external world is revealed by sense-perception. In conscience we apprehend that highest Cause as at the same time supreme Law, and God as the all-righteous Law-giver, as the source of all moral values, as the origin of the authority of obligation which we cannot fashion out of our selves, and finally as the bestower of our own freedom of will, the *sine quâ non* of all moral conduct. God as upholder of an absolute moral law is the supreme moral personality, living and concrete, with whom we may as persons enter into direct communion, and no mere metaphysical "absolute".

But this communion of man with God extends far beyond the domain of ethics. While in the moral consciousness we reach assurance of the Divine Being, becoming directly aware of Him especially in the fact of conscience, Deity confronts us at first as a transcendent sovereign power exalted immensely far "above" us, to whom we owe obedience and submission. But this does not exhaust the relationship of the finite to the infinite, which is far closer and more intimate, personal, and direct than can be known in the moral consciousness. The supposition of a specifically religious sense or faculty is thus shown to be necessary, a faculty different not only from the intellectual or the aesthetic faculty, but also more particularly from the moral. Martineau recognizes this in the first place in that primary feeling of reverence to which he had assigned the highest rank of all in his moral scale of values. It is reverence that first draws us up into the higher sphere and enables us to look upward, to cross the frontier dividing merely phenomenal from true reality and to compass the ideal. What at the level of morality was submission and obedience to the divine commandment now becomes the consciousness of profound consent and assured love. In the feeling of reverence we are delivered from the incessant battle of conflicting motives and lifted up into "communion with the life and love of God". The moral finds its final fulfilment and completion in the sacred, and the finite soul enters into and is assimilated to the infinite being. And so Martineau's philosophy of religion dies away in a strain of thought which if not sheer mysticism at least comes close to it. That which had formed the substantial core of his ethics—the conception of the inviolability and independence of the individual soul—is gravely imperilled in his religious philosophy. Complete accord between the two spheres is not attained, nor indeed could be in a system which in its original intention was based upon the polar tension of the contrast between man and God, and only subsequently attempted to resolve this tension and bring the two poles closer together.

A thinker who stands in close connection with Martineau, while introducing important modifications into his doctrine in the direction of Lotze's philosophy, was CHARLES BARNES UPTON (1831–1910: from 1875 Professor of Philosophy at Manchester College). Upton developed an ethical Theism in which morality and religion are brought into close interconnection. The meaning of ethics consists not so much in the fulfilment of an autonomous moral law as in directing man onward to religious faith. Upton therefore combated the "ethicists" who aimed at depriving morality of all its "higher" attachments and basing it simply on the personal satisfaction of individual wants and desires. His ideas on metaphysics and philosophy of religion were fairly completely drawn from the teaching of Martineau and Lotze, from the latter of whom he took over the general theory of the universe as developed in the *Microcosmos*. Lotze, indeed, he regarded as the man who really brought German Idealism to completion, and he found in him his strongest ally against the powers hostile to religion which the natural sciences had unchained. Upton himself had been trained in the exact sciences, and his endeavour was to reconcile the mechanical view of the world with freedom of the will. Like Martineau he set the doctrine of the immediate consciousness of God against the basis for religion provided by Rationalism. We are aware of God's existence directly as it is revealed in feeling, in intuitive acts of apprehension, and in comparison with this intimacy our knowledge of Him by rational proof and theoretic reasoning has never more than a secondary value, important as it may none the less be. The chief difference between Upton's doctrine here and the mainly similar one of Martineau is the stronger element of Mysticism apparent in the former.

Finally, Upton was one of the first to recognize the danger threatening ethical Idealism from the side of Hegelian Absolute Idealism, namely, the suppression of the moral freedom and responsibility of the individual, the destruction of genuine liberty of choice between possible alternatives, the depreciation of fundamental realities like evil and sin to the rank of mere appearances, the exclusion of the immediate action of the divine upon the human soul, etc. As the Anglo-Hegelian movement, which in its earliest phase had made for the defence of religion and of the Church, was turning more and more into a doctrine at best indifferent to religion, Upton demanded that the Hegelian school should change its course and turn towards the philosophy of Lotze as the only one in which moral and religious experience could be truly reconciled. Such a religious philosophy undertakes the double task of doing full justice to human personality and freedom while at the same time demonstrating the immanence of God in nature and human life.[1]

[1] See *Religion and Ethics* (1891; included in *Religion and Life*, edited by R. Bartram); also *Lectures on the Bases of Religious Belief* (1894), and *Dr. Martineau's Philosophy* (1905).

The following thinkers also are closely related to Martineau's school of thought.

Richard Holt Hutton (1826–97), journalist and theologian, came no less early into touch with German philosophy and theology. He studied under Martineau in Manchester, then with him in Berlin (previously at Heidelberg), and a strong friendship united the two men. Later he won high repute as editor of and collaborator in various periodicals. He followed the lead of Martineau, finding in his teaching much the most important contribution which the XIXth Century had made towards justifying and embodying in systematic form the view of the world and philosophy of life implicit in Christianity. As regards theology he, like Martineau, began as a Unitarian, but subsequently (mainly under the influence of F. D. Maurice) he passed over to the Established Church. His theological ideas coincide in essentials with those of Maurice.[1]

William Benjamin Carpenter (1813–85), a distinguished physiologist and a Unitarian likewise, tried to establish Martineau's doctrine of causality and free will more securely by arguments from physiology and to corroborate it by exact physiological research. The philosophical background of his special inquiry approximated to the fundamental positions of Martineau.[2]

Joseph Estlin Carpenter (1844–1927), son of the above, Unitarian theologian, from 1875 to 1915 lecturer and Professor of Comparative Religion in Manchester New College, London, later Manchester College, Oxford, represents also a doctrine closely related to Martineau's ethical Theism, both on its theological and on its philosophical side.[3]

[1] His writings are mostly collections of essays, of which the following may be mentioned: *Essays Theological and Literary* (1871); *Modern Guides of English Thought* (1887); *Criticisms on Contemporary Thought and Thinkers* (1894); *Aspects of Religion and Scientific Thought* (1899).

[2] See *Principles of Mental Physiology* (1874) and *Nature and Man, Essays Scientific and Philosophical* (1888).

[3] See his *James Martineau, Theologian and Teacher* (1905); *Comparative Religion* (1913); and *Ethical and Religious Problems of the War* (1916).

As a final representation of the Unitarian standpoint we may mention the well-known champion of women's rights and prolific authoress of some thirty volumes, FRANCES POWER COBBE (1822–1904). She was influenced even more than by Martineau by Theodore Parker, the leader of American Unitarianism, and also by F. W. Newman and the ethics of Kant. Her many-sided literary activity was concerned mainly with the discussion of theological, ethical, and social questions.[1]

The strongest speculative forces in the field of the philosophy of religion in the XIXth Century were grouped about these two centres, the Oxford Movement and the Unitarianism of Martineau. But interest in the problem of religion remained continually alive also within definitely philosophical movements of thought, particularly, we have seen, among thinkers of the Scottish school, and to a less degree in Evolutionist circles, though these were concerned rather to criticize and reject than to construct in a positive sense. But for the Idealist movement also the problems of religion stood at the focus of interest, though much more in its beginning in the 'seventies and 'eighties than in its later stages. For further mention of all these contributions we refer the reader to the relevant sections of this book, while we omit as falling outside the field of our survey such religious thought as had its growth within the Churches and sects, and had a theological rather than a philosophical purport. We only mention in this connection as specially important the work of FREDERICK DENISON MAURICE (see also p. 248), one of the greatest and most influential religious leaders of his time, well known through his activity in the "Christian Socialist" reform movement. In addition may be mentioned the notable figure of Bishop CHARLES GORE (1853–1932), and the volume of essays by various authors edited by him under the title of *Lux Mundi* (1889). Gore, like

[1] See *The Theory of Intuitive Morals*, anonymously (1855); *Religious Duty* (1864); *Studies Ethical and Social* (1865); *Darwinism in Morals and other Essays* (1872); *The Hopes of the Human Race* (1874); *The Scientific Spirit of the Age* (1888); *Life; by herself*, two vols. (1894), etc.

Maurice, was a Christian Socialist and Reformer, and he was educated at Balliol, the fountain-head of British Idealism. He is to be specially mentioned in this connection for having attempted to guide the strict "Puseyist" orthodoxy of the Oxford Movement on to Modernist paths and to instil into it a spirit of liberal criticism. While as regards creed and ecclesiastical authority his point of departure was the same as Pusey's, he undertook the task of harmonizing the principle of religious authority with scientific and philosophical principles by drawing a boundary between their respective spheres of influence. He wished to anchor the Christian faith in modern science and criticism and to bring it into living relation with modern ethical and social problems.[1]

Another name that should be mentioned here is that of MAX MÜLLER (1823–1900), a pioneer investigator in the field of the scientific and historical study of religions, and one of the greatest scholars of his time. German by birth, the son of the poet Wilhelm Müller, he came to England in 1846 and occupied chairs at Oxford, in Modern Languages from 1850 to 1868, and in Comparative Philology from 1868 until his early retirement in 1875. His studies fill a long line of volumes and covered wide and varied fields, Comparative Religion, Philosophy, Biography, Comparative Mythology, Philology, Oriental Studies, Linguistics, etc. They won him a world-wide reputation, especially in India, Japan, and China, and brought him many honours. To him belongs a prominent share in the opening-up to Western scholarship of Oriental, and particularly Indian cultures and religions, and he applied the comparative method fruitfully to the study of religion, culture, and myth. He held that religion and language proceed hand in hand at least at the primitive level and can be made to throw light upon one another, and accordingly made the investigation of speech serve to further the scientific study of religion. But he was an investi-

[1] See his Bampton Lectures: *The Incarnation of the Son of God* (1891); *The Creed of the Christian* (1895); *The New Theology and the Old Religion* (1908); *The Philosophy of the Good Life* (Gifford Lectures, 1930; cheap edition, 1935), and numerous other works on theology and philosophy of religion.

gator rather than a thinker, a philologist rather than a philosopher; his very many-sidedness prevented his achieving a single unified philosophical doctrine.

He understood by religion the becoming aware of the infinite, in so far as its influence can determine the moral character of man, and he distinguished three stages in the evolution of the religious life—the physical, the anthropological and the psychological. He saw in Christianity the consummation of all religion, and the entire history of religion appeared to him to be an unconscious progression towards this supreme goal. We owe to him also a complete translation of Kant's *Critique of Pure Reason* (1881), an enterprise that had been planned but not executed half a century earlier by Schopenhauer. Müller's translation had a predecessor in that of Meiklejohn (1855), and it has in turn been now superseded by that of Norman Kemp Smith (1929), which leaves both the others far behind in exactness and philosophic insight alike.[1]

Two writers on philosophy may be added here who cannot be counted as belonging to any special group, and who were occupied with other sorts of problem besides the problem of religion,—the Scotsmen FRASER and FLINT.

ALEXANDER CAMPBELL FRASER (1819–1914) was from 1856 to 1891 successor to Hamilton in the Chair of Logic and Metaphysics in Edinburgh, and his philosophical importance lies not so much in any systematic thought of his own as in his long and successful activity as a teacher and in his qualities as editor of the works of Locke and Berkeley whereby their doctrines were made more widely known and given new life in critical and popular statements. For more than a generation the youth of Scotland sat at his feet and derived lasting impressions and suggestions from his lectures, which aimed less at committing

[1] The following of Müller's many works may be mentioned as bearing on our subject: *Introduction to the Science of Religion* (1873); *Lectures on the Origin and Growth of Religion* (1878); *Science of Thought* (1887); *Natural Religion* (1889); *Physical Religion* (1891); *Anthropological Religion* (1892); *Theosophy or Psychological Religion* (1893). The last four were delivered as Gifford Lectures at the University of Glasgow.

the hearer to any definite system than at infecting him with an impulse to philosophy through the spirit of freedom and enthusiasm they evinced, and so stimulating him to active thought on his own account. "Fraser neither taught a system nor founded a school; he aroused and stimulated thought without determining it in his own direction." (Sorley.)

He owed his philosophical training chiefly to Sir William Hamilton, his teacher and later his friend, and through him he grew up at first wholly in the Scottish philosophical tradition. He fell before long under the influence of Thomas Brown and his theory of Causality, then became attracted and indeed agitated to the core by the Scepticism of Hume with all its perilous alluringness, until finally, after a grave crisis, he found in the Idealism of Berkeley liberation from doubt and unrest, and at the same time found there his true self, as he recounts in his autobiographical work, *Biographia Philosophica* (1904). The subsequent development of Fraser's own philosophical thought is to be traced in essentials to Berkeley's doctrine, though it never belies his Scottish descent (Reid and Hamilton). He not only renewed Berkeley's philosophy for his own thought, but virtually rediscovered it for his contemporaries. His meticulously careful scholarship yielded to be sure nothing that could be called "Neo-Berkeleianism", but it did give rise to a general interest in the personality and teaching of the Irish Bishop, which was fruitful at least as a ferment and often in more systematic fashion, and provided a counterweight to the climbing ambition of the Hegelian school. He was responsible, among other works, for the standard edition of Berkeley's works (1871, second edition 1901), as well as the still authoritative biography (*Life and Letters of Berkeley*, 1871) and an excellent edition of Locke's *Essay* (two vols., 1894).

Fraser had originally been a minister of religion, and he could never in his philosophical writings altogether belie his theological descent. Thus what specially attracted him in Berkeley was the philosophical establishment and justification of the Christian religion as a Theism in which God stood at the centre as Creator, while the world came into its rights simply and solely as the Divine Creation. For the systematic exposition of this thought we have to thank instigation from without rather than any inner prompting, namely, Fraser's appointment as Gifford Lecturer, whereby, though not in the least himself inclined to systematic philosophical speculation, he was led to produce something very like a system of his own (*The Philosophy of Theism*, two vols., 1895–6, second edition in one vol., 1899). In this he adopts Berkeley's fine thought of Nature as the divine language, and expands it fruitfully to a universal symbolism. Averse as he was to all extremes, he thought he had by the development of his Theism based upon religious faith found a *via media*, on the one hand, between Atheism and Pantheism, and, on the other, between a despairing scepticism and an over-sanguine confidence in knowledge. He discerned such a despair in the sceptical Agnosticism of Hume, in whom—rather than, as was then usual, in Kant—he rightly saw the true father of the modern Agnosticism of Huxley, Spencer, and others. On the other hand, he found the opposite extreme of optimism in the overweening intellectualist Gnosticism of Hegel and the neo-Hegelians. Thus he substituted "faith" for Hume's theoretic "belief", and sought to steer between the two extremes, doing justice to the restricted scope of human knowledge while safeguarding it from exaggerations in either direction. In the same way, he detested every interpretation that exalted into absolutes the three original given types of being—man, the world, and God—for as such he, with Martineau, regarded them. The three sorts of Monism resulting from turning these data into absolutes are Panegoism (or Solipsism), Pan-Materialism, and Pantheism: these Fraser termed untheistic speculations and he subjected them to criticism and refutation from his standpoint as a Theist.

In his own doctrine he attempted a compromise to harmonize these three given entities: he abandoned to the special sciences the "world", in the sense of nature, thereby depreciating, indeed neglecting, its philosophic import, and identified the human sphere with ethics and the divine with religion. But he viewed "God" mainly from the moral side as the personification of infinite goodness, and likewise "man" as the specifically moral being, i.e. a moral "person", while "things" he regarded as existing merely for the sake of persons. And so Fraser's Theism is based on ethics like Newman's and Martineau's, and his Idealism is, like Berkeley's, spiritual and personalist, and thereby a bulwark against the naturalistic tendencies of the time. It is interesting to note in this connection that German philosophy only affected his thought to a slight and quite secondary degree. But while wellnigh exclusively following the native British Idealist tradition, he had surmounted certain current prejudices in the school of Hamilton (notably with regard to Kant), and even attempted to interpret Hegel (more or less in the sense of the Hegelian "right") and to assimilate his teaching. When we remember that Fraser's philosophical roots reached back to a time long before the revival of German Idealist systems in England, it is not surprising that after this revival he was unable to achieve a thorough reorientation of his thought, despite considerable sympathy with the new movement.

ROBERT FLINT (1838–1910) was, first, a minister of the Scottish Church, then (1864) Professor of Moral Philosophy at St. Andrews, and later (1876–1903) Professor of Theology at Edinburgh. His active work as a thinker was carried out in two fields, the Philosophy of History and the Philosophy of Religion, on both of which we owe to him a series of writings of wide scope and distinguished for exact scholarship and wide knowledge.

A special importance must be attributed to Flint's work in the first field, for the reason that the Philosophy of History (and, next to it, Aesthetics) has among all philosophical disciplines been that most neglected by British thinkers. Only in exceptional cases has it aroused any strong interest. It may almost be said that history has never become a philosophical problem at all for the English, and for this reason the revival of the philosophical attitude towards history upon the Continent —in Germany, France, and Italy—has hardly found an echo in England. Even among the ranks of the Anglo-Hegelians it cannot be said that there was any active recognition of the problem of history or any large interpretations of the historical process such as Hegel himself put forward. Flint thus has the merit of being one of the few English thinkers who have seen that history is a subject not merely to be investigated empirically but to be interpreted philosophically. History must pass over into the philosophy of history, if it is to understand itself aright, and the further historical thinking progresses the more philosophical will it be, for a philosophical meaning is essentially contained in the facts of history. Historical events do not succeed one another capriciously or by chance, they are not abandoned to anarchy and chaos; rather, a system of order and law can be discerned in them, whereby they are interconnected and one occurrence grows out of another. Yet this regular order in the course of history is not to be thought of on the analogy of scientific causation, but is manifested by a type of conformity to law peculiar to the historical process and the life of the spirit. This means that the philosophy of history as the rational interpretation of the true character and real relations of historical facts is a part of history itself, is indeed history at a higher level of cognition. History as science and history as philosophy are not two separate and mutually independent disciplines but boughs from one and the same main trunk.

It was in this spirit that Flint's monumental work on the Philosophy of History in Europe was written, a work spacious in plan and exhibiting profound learning, which indeed so far exceeded this great scholar's energy for labour, great as that was, that it unfortunately was left a mere torso after two attempts to complete it.[1] The finished portions include the philosophical theories of the French and Germans from the time of Bodin and Leibniz, and the later version of 1893 gave an account of special penetration that has not yet been superseded, of the theories of French, Belgian, and Swiss thinkers. The earlier version (1874) is specially noteworthy for having

[1] *The Philosophy of History in Europe*, vol. 1, *The Philosophy of History in France and Germany* (1874); *History of the Philosophy of History*, vol. 1, *Historical Philosophy in France and French Belgium and Switzerland* (1893). Three other volumes on Germany, England, and Italy were planned but not written.

brought the German idealistic movement from Kant to Hegel for the first time to the notice of English readers in a single conspectus that shows a comparatively high degree of understanding. Even Hegel is treated here in a thoroughly critical way; while rejecting his teaching in the main, Flint writes of him with surprising admiration. "However far one may be from being a disciple of Hegel, it is impossible to refuse to acknowledge that a richer treasure-house of philosophical thoughts scarcely exists than that formed by his eighteen volumes."

But in general Flint's interpretations agree more with the French than with the Germans—whence the brilliant success of his book in France—and he identified his own position in the philosophy of history, which he never further developed, closely with that of Renouvier. Thus he rejects those theories which treat of history as a mechanical product or as a struggle for existence between individuals and societies or as a simple organic growth or as a dialectical movement, and discerns instead in the history a creative process essentially moral, the education of the freely acting individual up to a genuine humanity in which the moral law comes to its true form and fulfilment.

The second side of Flint's intellectual production lies in the sturdy part he played in the struggle between agnostic-naturalistic tendencies and Christian theology which was being fought out in the last third of the XIXth Century. His writings on this issue, *Theism* (1877, thirteenth edition 1929), *Anti-Theistic Theories* (1879, ninth edition 1929), and *Agnosticism* (1903), which had a wide vogue, defended the cause of religious faith against unbelief with the weapons of a wide and deep erudition. Recognizing that the attitude of religious circles to modern science had hitherto been one of almost complete rejection, Flint felt that his mission as *defensor fidei* was, in contrast to this, one of reconciliation, to bridge the antagonism between orthodox theology on the one hand and naturalistic philosophy and the scientific investigation of nature on the other. He tried to avert the threat to the Christian faith contained in the teachings of Darwin, Spencer, Huxley, and their followers by blunting the points of their anti-theistic argument and adapting the results of their inquiries in as wide a measure as possible to establish his own theistic view of the world. For a proof of the existence of God he had recourse to the old ontological, cosmological, and moral arguments, which had in the meantime been generally discredited, referring especially to the necessity of a rational foundation for religion, which is (he held) much more a matter of the intellect than of feeling or the will. It is, indeed, characteristic of Flint's predominating rationalistic standpoint that he neglects the element in religion peculiar to faith and over-emphasizes its intellectual side, and the same trait is strongly evinced in other ways. It hindered rather than promoted the effectiveness of his writings in defence of Christian doctrine.

In this field also Flint put forward a programme with characteristic thoroughness, the completion of which was far beyond his power, for it aimed at nothing short of an entire system of natural theology worked out in detail. It was to treat in particular of four problems: (1) to display the evidence we have for believing in the existence of God; (2) to refute anti-theistic theories, Atheism, Materialism, Positivism, Pessimism, Pantheism, and Agnosticism; (3) to delineate the Being of God as revealed in nature and history; (4) to trace the origin and development of the idea of God in the history of theistic speculation. It was only granted him to carry out this programme in part, and, as we have seen, it was the second task (2) that he discharged most thoroughly. For the rest, and to sum up, Flint was a scholar of the first rank with interests mainly in history and theology (he was called the most learned man of his time in Scotland), with a wide power of survey, and a genuinely critical and objective mind; but he was to a much less degree an independent thinker with a position of his own. But as the historian of the Philosophy of History and as a champion against Naturalism in the last quarter of last century, his name is to-day still mentioned with respect. His last work was *Philosophy as Scientia Scientiarum and a History of Classifications of the Sciences* (1904).

PART II

RECENT SCHOOLS OF THOUGHT

END OF XIXTH AND BEGINNING OF XXTH CENTURIES

I

THE NEO-IDEALIST MOVEMENT

I. ORIGIN AND GENERAL COURSE

BY the neo-idealist movement we mean the influx of German philosophical Idealism into British thought. The influx did not become considerable until the 'sixties and 'seventies of last century, a full generation after the death of Hegel. If the characteristic of British philosophy up to the beginning of this movement is that it kept to the firm lines of a native and relatively isolated tradition, and was as unsympathetic to violent incursions from without as it was to revolutions from within, the significance of the new movement is precisely that with it a complete change set in, entirely new forms and contents of thought being seized and held fast, and a foreign and hitherto unknown stock of ideas being added to the store of British thought. Neo-Idealism, making its way into England at an important turning-point, thereby stands not merely for an immense widening, enrichment, and deepening of doctrinal content, but also and fundamentally for a complete recoil from the old ways, a turning of the philosophical rudder in an entirely new direction.

This view that the infiltration of German Idealism into England led to a breach with the native philosophical tradition contradicts a view occasionally expressed (on the English side particularly) that it was all a matter of the rousing of slumbering forces which had been present in British thought from the beginning. The latter thesis has its most impressive statement in a work by J. H. Muirhead[1] (one of great value and instructiveness for our survey), in which the attempt is made to show that a continuous stream of idealistic thought runs through the whole history of British philosophy, and that the idealistic movement was simply a widened and deepened stretch of

[1] *The Platonic Tradition in Anglo-Saxon Philosophy*, 1931.

that stream. The historical facts, however, give no support to this view. Whatever idealistic systems and motives may have appeared in the earlier centuries, the movement that broke out in the second half of the XIXth Century was neither directly nor indirectly connected with them. For this movement expressly linked itself with German philosophy from Kant to Hegel, and never harked back to any earlier British heritage; and that it could not have sprung directly from a native tradition is proved by the entire absence of any continuing idealistic current in the development of English philosophy, at any rate in the century immediately preceding the movement, that is, from about the death of Berkeley (1753) to the appearance of Stirling's work on Hegel (1865). It is of just this period that one can least allege an idealistic trend in Great Britain; nor can it be claimed that so powerful a movement as the one we are considering could have been kindled and made so mightily effective through the influence of a few scanty and scattered essays.

We must continue to believe, then, that the philosophical renaissance in England after the middle of the century was a late off-shoot of German Idealism, that it nourished itself on German sources, and was penetrated by the German spirit, or, to speak more prosaically, that it was essentially a German commodity. This is intended simply as a statement of fact, not as a judgment of praise or blame. We are saying nothing at the moment of the changes to which the foreign article was subjected after it had become established on British soil, of the extent to which it was linked to native lines of thought, or of the new forms that grew out of it. Indeed, we must emphasize the fact that the incursion of the German stream of thought was not brought about in a purely external fashion, for example, by scholastic interests or by intrigue, but happened when it did because of an inner necessity. For there can be no doubt that at that time the conditions for the acceptance of the new seed were specially favourable, and that the deciding factors were several and various.

First of all the mental atmosphere was prepared for the

reception of an idealistic view of the world by means of poetry and literature generally. The preliminary work performed in the first half of the century by outstanding poets and other writers outside professional philosophical circles, and for the most part in opposition to them, was a very important factor in the release of the strictly philosophical movement. It was out of the poetry of the Romantics that the new view of the world and attitude to life grew up which superseded the antiquated forms of thought of the Enlightenment. The earliest indications of the new spiritual content, which much later was to break its way through into philosophy also, are to be found in the poems of Shelley and Keats, of Wordsworth and Coleridge. Of these, however, only SAMUEL TAYLOR COLERIDGE (1772–1834) has any special importance. He was not only an inspired poet, but also a man of genuinely philosophical endowment, always striving to give his vision of the universe a theoretical as well as an artistic articulation. In the process his extremely receptive and restless mind passed through many changes, submitting itself at one time or another to the influence of Hartley, Berkeley, Spinoza, Plato, Plotinus, Kant, Schelling, and others. After various confusions and revulsions he finally arrived at a kind of spiritualistic metaphysics which found expression more in brilliant aphorisms and fragments than in strictly systematic form. In these he sharply opposed the prevailing philosophical views of his time and country, especially the empiricist Utilitarianism of Bentham, which was then coming into vogue. That Coleridge introduced into British philosophy a new spirit which had next to nothing in common with the current dogmas was occasionally noticed even in strictly philosophical circles (as in J. S. Mill's articles of 1838 and 1840 on Bentham and Coleridge, reprinted in his *Dissertations and Discussions*, vol. 1; see also above, p. 64). Still, of any intrusion of this new spirit into academic circles there is no trace at all either during the lifetime of the poet, or even for a generation after his death—which is the best proof that the time had not yet come for a comprehensive idealistic renovation of British thought.

In another respect the philosophy of Coleridge is of importance for our survey. With it a broad stream of German Idealism first flowed into England. Whether the central ideas of his view of the world had already shaped themselves in the poet's mind before he came into contact with the German systems,[1] or whether they only did so as a consequence of that contact, is a question difficult to settle; but all that concerns the history of thought is the fact that such a contact did happen, that it was an extremely close one, and that with it German philosophy entered into the mental perspective of the English for the first time.[2] We know that Coleridge studied in detail the doctrine of Kant, and that this left evident traces on his own thought. Still deeper, however, was the influence of Schelling, whose cosmological and aesthetic doctrines attracted and shook him and at times almost overwhelmed him. Recent research has shown that he studied various writings of Fichte and Hegel as well, and made marginal comments on them, although the influence of these thinkers is less noticeable in his published works (see footnote, *Coleridge as Philosopher*, 1930, p. 271). In addition, Lessing, Herder, Goethe, and Schiller acted decisively on his thought. In Coleridge, therefore, we have the spectacle of an early and extremely striking invasion of English spiritual life

[1] This contact occurred first during his visit to Germany in 1798–9, and thereafter through intensive study of German literature and philosophy.

[2] On the introduction of Kantianism into Britain see *Kant in England*, by R. Wellek, 1931 (Princeton).

The first books in English on Kant were: *General and Introductory View of Professor Kant's Principles*, by F. A. Nitzsch, 1796; *Principles of Critical Philosophy*, by J. S. Beck, trans. by J. Richardson, 1797; *Elements of Critical Philosophy*, by A. F. M. Willich, 1798.

The earliest English translations of Kant were—*Essays and Treatises on Moral, Political and Various Philosophical Subjects*, two vols., 1798–9; *Metaphysic of Morals*, 1799; *Logic*, 1819; *Prolegomena to Every Future Metaphysic*, 1819; the last two reissued with *Enquiry . . . into the Grounds of Proof for the Existence of God*, 1836. All these were translated by J. Richardson. J. W. Semple's version of the *Metaphysic of Ethics* first appeared in 1836. The first translation of the first *Critique* was by Francis Haywood, *Critick of Pure Reason*, 1838 (second edition, 1848). Haywood published in 1844 *An Analysis of Kant's Critick of Pure Reason*.

by German idealistic thought, along with a sharp reaction against the mental attitude of the XVIIIth Century and the persistence of this throughout the first decades of the XIXth Century in the native philosophy. The empiricist current of Utilitarianism, which found in J. S. Mill a new champion, was able to dominate the field until after the middle of the century, with the result that Coleridge's profound insights remained scattered and unable to find almost anywhere soil in which to strike root. In one disciple only was the seed he sowed to spring up. This disciple was the surgeon Joseph Henry Green (1791–1863), the poet's intimate friend for many years, and eventually his literary executor. In this latter capacity he had the task of sorting Coleridge's philosophical remains and putting them into systematic shape, a task to which he selflessly devoted the greater part of his later years, without bringing it to completion. Out of the writings, memoranda, marginal notes, and conversations of the poet, however, he built up a sort of Coleridgean system of philosophy, which was posthumously published under the title *Spiritual Philosophy, founded on the teaching of the late S. T. Coleridge* (1865, two vols.). Despite the change that had set in since Coleridge's death this work appeared and remained unnoticed, being overshadowed by Stirling's book on Hegel, which appeared the same year; and thereafter men went straight to the German sources without troubling themselves about Coleridge and his disciple. Only a few of them besides Green kept Coleridge's thoughts alive, for instance, F. D. Maurice and S. H. Hodgson; the latter's *Philosophy of Reflection* (1878) is dedicated to him as the author's "Father in philosophy". It is only recently that Alice D. Snyder (*Coleridge on Logic and Learning*, 1929; *Coleridge's Treatise on Method*, 1934) and J. H. Muirhead (*Coleridge as Philosopher*, 1930) have won the merit of subjecting the great romantic poet's philosophy to historical investigation.

One of the literary contemporaries and acquaintances of Coleridge who felt himself drawn to the philosophy of Germany was Thomas De Quincey (1785–1859). He studied enthusiastically the writings of Kant, Fichte, and Schelling, and tried to rouse interest in and to popularize their ideas; but, despite an occasional insight of surprising penetration, he lacked the understanding requisite for such a task, and introduced more obscurity than light. It cannot be said that he was an important agent in the opening up of German thought. Nevertheless, he was one of the few men in the England of the 'twenties and 'thirties who had any knowledge of it at all.[1]

After Coleridge none preached the message of Idealism more publicly and impressively than THOMAS CARLYLE (1795–1881). To him more than to anyone else belongs the merit of inducing the complete change of temper that occurred in his day, and of making the soil ready for the new seed. Less gifted and schooled philosophically than Coleridge, but with more conviction, and at once steadier and more venturesome, he inwardly appropriated the spiritual values of German literature and thought, and gave them forth again in the weighty pathos of his prophetic tones. It was his complete belief in his message that gave his utterance its impressiveness, and evoked the strongest echoes of his words. He was the first leader of the decisive reaction against the XVIIIth-Century tradition, and whatever of it had survived into the XIXth —against the Enlightenment, which in his view had Hume as its intellectual sovereign, against the hankering after doubt and unbelief, against Common Sense and Utilitarian morality, against dissolving criticism and the lordship of reason. Amid these signs of spiritual ruin in his country he tried to implant the new values brought out by the classical philosophy and literature of the Germans, and in this way became a living bridge between German and British culture, an ambassador or representative more truly than Coleridge had ever been of the German spirit in his own land. And yet, despite all this, he had no specifically philosophical interest; philosophy as erudition or pure contemplation had no meaning for him. He embraced Idealism more from the practical and religious than

[1] He published several essays on Kant and translations of portions of his works in popular periodicals. For details see R. Wellek, *Kant in England*, 1931, pp. 171–80.

from the theoretical side, more as a vital force and an attitude of mind than as a theory or a body of knowledge. Instead of thinking philosophy he simply lived it, in order to preach its spiritual values and apply them to and embody them in life, dynamically conceived. With such an attitude he learned far more from Kant and Fichte than from Schelling and Hegel, and most of all from Fichte, to whom he owed the greater part of the philosophical side of his thought; and he never tired of referring his contemporaries to Herder, Novalis, Jean Paul, Schiller, and the towering Goethe, as heralds and shapers of new and yet eternal practical values.

In America EMERSON (1803–82) had a mission similar to that of Carlyle, though he was not so closely guided by German precedents. Since his writings exercised a considerable influence in England as well, he cannot be passed over without mention.

It was from these directions rather than from strictly philosophical circles that the new movement received its strongest impetus. Within these circles there were occasional anticipations, but for the most part they amounted to nothing more than taking cognizance of and interest in the German philosophers, and only rarely showed any real understanding of them; and all of them alike were more or less isolated, never combining sufficiently to have the force of a movement. Not one of them, moreover, achieved a comprehension of German Idealism as a whole. In the precipitation of the idealistic movement they played either no part at all, or a very negligible one. We must, however, single out for mention the work of SIR WILLIAM HAMILTON (see above, pp. 33 ff.) and his school, which dominated the philosophical field, especially in Scotland, round about the middle of the century. Hamilton was the first professional philosopher of Britain to acquire and utilize a deep and extended knowledge of the philosophical literature of Germany: in voracity of reading and profundity of erudition he excelled all his contemporaries. The names of the great German thinkers meet us repeatedly in his writings. His own doctrine may be described as an attempt to reconcile or synthetize Scottish and Kantian thought, or, more accurately, as the grafting of a Kantian scion on the stock of Reid's common-sense philosophy. What Hamilton took over from Kant, however, was primarily the agnostic phenomenalism of the Critical epistemology, the doctrine that human knowledge is limited to appearances, to the finite, the conditioned, the relative. By thus bringing to the forefront only the theoretical part of Kant's doctrine, and only the negative side of that, he made it seem as though this were the whole, or at any rate the essence of the Transcendental philosophy, and through this utterly one-sided and misleading picture cut off both himself and his fellow-countrymen from an integral vision and genuine understanding of Kant's thought, at the same time blocking the way to the post-Kantian systems. Of these he had, indeed, a close knowledge, but was quite unable to make anything of them, and wasted himself in a barren and uncomprehending polemic against the "philosophy of the Unconditioned". He outlawed the great metaphysical systems that had developed out of Kant's criticism of reason, and the great weight of his authority made this sentence the prevailing opinion for a long time. This is why one of the most pressing of Stirling's tasks in laying the foundations of his new structure had to be a strong protest against Hamilton's superficialities and distortions, and a denial of the genuineness of his conception of German philosophy; for he was convinced that Hamilton's failure to do justice to this had held up the progress of British thought for a generation. Nevertheless, we are obliged to give Hamilton credit for having, through his wide erudition, rescued British philosophy from the blind alley in which it had settled, by opening up new sources and feeding it with the stream of contemporary thought abroad. Before Stirling no other philosopher had so great a share in breaking down the insularity of his country's philosophy.

After Hamilton's death the outstanding leader of philosophy in Britain, indeed the only representative and widely read thinker Britain had in the period immediately following the middle of the century, was John Stuart Mill, in whom all the currents of philosophical thought then really alive met. So complete was his sovereignty that no one could at that time count on a hearing who went against him. Of those who ventured to swim against the empiricist current we may mention first JOHN GROTE (1813–66), Professor of Moral Philosophy at Cambridge. His thinking, solitary and virtually independent, moved within the ambit of Idealism—but not the idealism of Hamilton, with its agnostic relativism. This latter he explicitly rejected, espousing instead a doctrine for which "knowledge is the sympathy of intelligence with intelligence, through the medium of qualified or particular existence".[1] The truly real, the thing-in-itself, is reached in knowing, and the reason is that its nature is the same as that of the mind that knows it. With this doctrine Grote combined a penetrating criticism of Phenomenalism or Positivism, confining his criticism, however, to its claim to be the last word, or the whole of philosophy. The knowledge of phenomena is a useful form of knowledge, and, within its proper sphere in the natural sciences, is a true sort of abstraction; but an abstraction it nevertheless is, taken out of a context much wider than itself. It is only preliminary to strictly philosophical knowledge. Consequently the phenomenalistic point of view has to be supplemented and completed by the idealistic point of view; indeed, only in so far as we think idealistically is our thinking really philosophical, for by philosophy Grote meant concern, not with the object of knowledge, but with the fact or process of knowledge itself. To any full clarification of his position, however, he never came; all he did was to recognize the inadequacy of the theories dominant in his day and to grope uncertainly after new lines of thought. Some sort of objective or metaphysical Idealism was in his mind, but, set in an environment oriented in an entirely different way, he was too solitary to be able to work out a really substantial system. In consequence he met with scarcely any immediate response, and only much later did the few fertile thoughts that he sowed find here and there suitable soil. The only philosophical

[1] *Exploratio Philosophica*, part 2, p. 296.

writing he himself published (*Exploratio Philosophica*, part 1, 1865) appeared in the same year as Stirling's work on Hegel: the rest[1] appeared posthumously and attracted little attention.

Like Grote, JAMES F. FERRIER (1808–64; Professor at St. Andrews) was one of the few who about the middle of the century refused to pass under the yoke of either Hamilton (whose intellectual gifts and virile character he greatly admired) or Mill. He went his own way, and put forward an idealistic doctrine, which, however, had far clearer outlines than the loose sketches of Grote, and contained much more of the movement which was soon to develop. His chief work, the *Institutes of Metaphysic* (1854), identifies philosophy with speculative science, and unfolds this science in a strictly systematic way, in the form of theorems each of which is deduced from what precedes it, much as in the *Ethics* of Spinoza. It is divided into three parts: (*a*) Epistemology, or theory of knowing; (*b*) Agnoiology, or theory of ignorance; and (*c*) Ontology, or theory of being. His first theorem, which as such bears the whole weight of the system, is a formulation of the fundamental law of all knowledge: "Along with whatever any intelligence knows, it must, as the ground or condition of its knowledge, have some cognizance of *itself*" (third edition, p. 79). Here already we see an evident point of agreement with Kant. Indeed, Ferrier was probably the first British thinker to reach a sympathetic understanding of German philosophy, and to make a positive use of it in the service of his own doctrine. He felt its influence during an early visit to Germany, and later remained in intimate contact with it. His two articles on Schelling and Hegel in the *Imperial Dictionary of Universal Biography* (1857–63)[2] are probably the first really understanding writings on these thinkers in the English language. His attitude to Hegel is particularly interesting. He always repudiated the supposition that he was an Hegelian. However

[1] *An Examination of the Utilitarian Philosophy*, 1870; *A Treatise on the Moral Ideals*, 1876; *Exploratio Philosophica*, part 2, 1900.

[2] Reprinted in his *Lectures on Early Greek Philosophy and other Philosophical Remains*, 1866, vol. 2.

that may be, we have his own admission that he wrestled tenaciously, though usually without success, to understand Hegel. For him, as later for Stirling, Hegel was the great mysterious Unknown, ringed about with a sort of magical awe, and of whose greatness he had not an intellectual conception, but a feeling and premonition. Again, as with Stirling, we find in Ferrier (*Institutes*, pp. 91 f.) expressions which hint that the still unconquered giant will break in like a Fate upon the hallowed traditions of British philosophy.

Ferrier's system, an absolutism with a purely theoretical motive, rests on an idealistic doctrine of knowledge and on a very original theory of ignorance. At a time when British speculation had sunk to its lowest ebb it was abstract, speculative, and constructive to a high degree. In this liberation of the speculative impulse, and also in both the structure of the system and particular trains of thought, we see the influence of Germany. But Ferrier dug also in the native mine, returning to Berkeley and building into his own system important elements from the latter's philosophy;[1] and since Berkeley was at that time virtually forgotten in England, we must give Ferrier the further credit of having discovered him afresh,[2] and of having given the first impetus to the renaissance of Berkeleianism ushered in by Fraser, Collyns Simon, Rashdall, and others. Finally we must note that he was probably the first of the Scots to revolt against the tradition of the Scottish school.[3] For him common sense could not be the criterion of philosophical truth, for everyday thinking, far from having any claim to be rational thinking, has to subject itself completely to its decisions. Herein also, then, Ferrier was a herald and prophet of things to come. But our chief concern is to

[1] Less the historical Berkeley than Berkeley seen through German spectacles, and, like everything he took over, transformed by the peculiarity of Ferrier's own mind.

[2] In his article "Berkeley and Idealism" in *Blackwood's Magazine*, 1842, vol. 51 (reprinted in his *Lectures on Greek Philosophy, etc.*, 1866, vol. 2).

[3] In calling his own philosophy "Scottish to the core", he meant that it was thoroughly original, a native product and not a foreign borrowing; and in this he was right.

adduce him as a pioneer of the idealistic movement, to which his writings, which won a considerable contemporary reputation, contributed both stimulus and content.

The last to be mentioned of those who were sensitive to German influence before the movement proper began is the theologian FREDERICK DENISON MAURICE (1805–72). He was Professor of English History and Literature (1840) together with Divinity (1846) at King's College, London, until 1853, when he was relieved of his office because of his excessively liberal views. From 1866 until his death he held the Chair of Moral Philosophy at Cambridge. He was deeply imbued with the spirit of Coleridge, being one of the latter's few disciples, but he never succeeded in penetrating and raising to the level of clear thought the obscurity and nebulosity of the poet-philosopher's Mysticism. In addition he returned through Coleridge to the direct study of the German philosophers and theologians, and derived from them various suggestions. His chief activity, however, lay outside philosophy, to which he gave only occasional attention.[1] (See above, p. 226.)

The renaissance of Idealism in England, then, had its way prepared by literary currents, and was announced by a few isolated philosophers. But two further factors helped to originate and precipitate it, firstly religious and theological interests, secondly the cultivation of classical studies in the older universities.

In the first half of the century the traditional tension between philosophy and religion, between knowledge and faith, had not passed into open conflict. Except for a few occasional clashes the respective partisans had tolerated one another and preserved a more or less benevolent neutrality. On the whole, philosophy was too indifferent to religion to make a real problem of it, concerning itself with other questions, and leaving theology alone. After the middle of the century this state of affairs underwent a fundamental and fateful

[1] See chiefly his large historical work *Moral and Metaphysical Philosophy*, two vols., 1871–2 (expansion of an article in the *Encyclopaedia Metropolitana*, 1848).

change. The rise of Darwinism drove philosophy into an explicitly hostile attitude towards religion. Naturalism and Materialism grew up luxuriantly among the followers of Darwin, and penetrated, with destructive effect, further into the mind of the general public than into the circles of the learned. Religion was thereby seriously threatened, and accordingly theology entered the lists as its appointed guardian. But the fight against Materialism could not be carried on with only theological weapons; the enemy would have to be struck down with his own weapons, that is, with philosophical ones. In this matter the native philosophy had completely failed; no new weapons could be forged out of it; indeed, it had in part gone over with flying colours into the enemy's camp. The perilous nature of the situation led to the heeding of those philosophical voices which for some time had been speaking from Germany. Orthodox circles in particular recognized the great importance for the coming struggle of an alliance with philosophical Idealism. Thus the opening of the door to the German invasion was not prompted, least of all in the first stages, by purely philosophical interests, but rather by the desire to confirm orthodox theology and revivify the imperilled faith, against Agnosticism, Naturalism, religious indifference, and open unbelief; and it was the constructive metaphysic of Hegel, not Kantianism, that was utilized first and foremost, just because Kant, in consequence of the one-sided interpretation put upon him by Hamilton's school, was himself suspected of being an Agnostic. This tendency can be seen quite plainly in the pioneers of the movement, in Stirling no less than in Green, Wallace, and the two Cairds: for all these, and for many others, philosophical Idealism, whatever other significance it had for them, meant the support and defence of religion. As we shall see, Stirling confesses this with praiseworthy candour, and even when the motive is not so openly avowed it is none the less operative. The mistaken and unjust interpretations which grew out of that motive do not concern us here; it is sufficient to stress the fact that to that motive the movement in its earliest stages owed its chief driving force. As the movement developed, however, the motive weakened: in Nettleship it is already less dominant, and with the later adherents either virtually disappears (Bradley and Bosanquet), or passes into its opposite (McTaggart). The orthodox in religion, who had greeted the first phase of the movement with enthusiasm, watched its later phases with anxiety and disappointment.

The second factor lay in a quite different sphere. The universities of Oxford and Cambridge had always cherished the humanistic spirit and the classical languages, and to that extent were guardians of the philosophical heritage of Greece. Greek philosophy, especially that of Plato and Aristotle, had long been one of the chief educational instruments for the communication of classical culture, and through it the Greek spirit passed into every department of intellectual life, exercising a fruitful influence on philosophy as on the rest. In this sense we may understand the phrase about a continuous "Platonic Tradition in Anglo-Saxon Philosophy" (Muirhead), not in the sense that some form or other of Platonism was active all through the history of British thought (the Cambridge Platonists were an isolated phenomenon, and no similar movement has since occurred). After the middle of the XIXth Century there was a new and important outburst of the study of Greek philosophy at Oxford, connected chiefly with the name of Benjamin Jowett (1817–93). Although primarily a theologian, Jowett was a man of wide culture and many-sided activity, one of the leaders of the Broad Church party, and the driving force behind the movement for the reform of the universities. Survivors of the older generation still remember him as the outstanding and most influential university teacher of his day. His teaching career was spent entirely in Oxford: in 1838 he became a Fellow of Balliol College, four years later Tutor, and in 1870 Master, besides occupying the Chair of Greek from 1855 to 1893. His chief title to fame lies in his having renewed classical studies in and through the spirit of Greek philosophy in a career of teaching and writing lasting more than half a century, and attended throughout with striking success. His translation of Plato's *Dialogues*, equipped with admirable introductions, is still reckoned as unsurpassed. It may be called classic in that through it Plato became for the first time a really vital educational force and a secure possession of the nation. It did for England what Schleiermacher's version had done for Germany. Of less importance, because less prompted and informed by sympathy with the originals, are Jowett's translations of Thucydides (1881) and of Aristotle's *Politics* (1885).

This renewed and deepened interest at Oxford in the philosophy of classical antiquity was timely and congenial in view of the turn that British thought was then taking. The affinity between Greek and German Idealism was patent, and in Oxford more than anywhere else the younger generation of scholars recognized the urgent necessity of lifting British thought out of its narrowness and servility to its own tradition and leading it back to the great stream of European philosophy. The rebirth of Platonic studies inaugurated by Jowett thus became the rallying-point of the philosophical influences which were coming from Germany. Moreover, in Jowett himself these twin forces, Greek and German, meeting each other at Oxford in fruitful reciprocity, were brought into the unity of a common direction.

It was as early as 1844 and 1845, during two summer holidays in Germany, that Jowett came into direct contact with the Idealism of that country. He visited the aged Schelling in Berlin, but was not at all impressed (in a letter of the time he speaks of him as an "old twaddler"). He also saw J. E. Erdmann and discussed with him "the best method of approaching the philosophy of Hegel". After his return to England he plunged more deeply into the study of Hegel, and even began to translate the *Logik*, a task he never finished. The earnestness with which he wrestled to grasp Hegel's meaning resembles Stirling's struggle some ten or fifteen years later. "Concerning Hegel," he wrote in a letter of 1845, "I have only a glimpse of his meaning, but feel restless until I can get deeper into it"; "One must go or perish in the attempt, that is to say, give up metaphysics altogether. It is impossible to be satisfied with any other system after you have begun with this." Unlike Stirling, however, he did not swallow Hegel entire. His was too mobile and elastic a nature to be carried completely away by Hegel, or by anyone else. Even in those early years, and in later years to a still higher degree, he preserved a characteristic intellectual independence.

What most concerns us is that he incited a select circle of his students to the study of Hegel's writings, and thereby became the first mediator of German thought at the university where British Idealism was later to have its home. It was through Jowett more than anyone else that Hegelianism was zealously studied and discussed in Oxford as early as the middle of the century, and became an intellectual force of increasing power. The seed he sowed in the minds of his pupils was to bear a rich philosophical fruit. The credit due to him in this respect is in no way affected by the circumstance that his own attitude to Hegel underwent many fluctuations, and that at no time could he be called a thoroughgoing and genuine Hegelian. The more he came to steep himself in the thought of the Greeks the more he moved away from his first philosophical master. Still, in the ripeness of his old age he looked back with reverent admiration at what Hegel had once meant for him, and wrote: "It is more than forty years since I began to read Hegel's writings, and I think in those days my mind received a greater stimulus from him than from anyone. And though I see that philosophy of that kind is not destined to be permanent, I still retain a great reverence for my old teacher and master."[1]

Of the pioneers of British Idealism, many, indeed the most important, passed through his hands, notably Green, Edward Caird, and Nettleship, who as members of Balliol College stood nearest to his work and personality. In his own writings the influence of German philosophy is plainest in his introduc-

[1] Letter of 1884. This and the preceding quotations from his letters are taken from *Life and Letters of Jowett*, by E. Abbott and L. Campbell, two vols., 1897.

tions to his translation of Plato's *Dialogues* (first edition 1871). To conclude, Jowett's importance lies in his having introduced and for many decades watched over, stimulated interest in, and taught that philosophical spirit out of which the new movement of Idealism in Britain was born.

The real awakening of British Idealism, however, did not come from the academic circles of Oxford, where the new ideas only reached literary expression after a long period of incubation, but from the courageous and memorable initiative of a hitherto unknown Scottish layman, J. H. Stirling, who published a two-volume work on Hegel in 1865 (see pp. 259–268). In the 'seventies the movement was in full swing with Green's *Introductions to Hume* (1874), Wallace's *Logic of Hegel* (also 1874), Bradley's *Ethical Studies* (1876), and Edward Caird's first book on Kant (1877). The revival also led to the founding of an important periodical, *Mind* (1876; still the leading one), which, though hospitable to all shades of thought, supplied a medium of expression for the new movement. In the 'eighties the movement consolidated its position, and brought forth another series of important works—John Caird's *Philosophy of Religion* (1880), Edward Caird's *Hegel*, Green's *Prolegomena to Ethics*, Bradley's *Logic*, the *Essays in Philosophical Criticism* (all 1883), A. Seth's *Hegelianism and Personality* (1887), Bosanquet's *Logic* (1888), and Edward Caird's larger work on Kant (1889). In the *Essays in Philosophical Criticism* the idealistic trend first reached the form of a common manifesto, and included the contributions of its youngest representatives, some of whom were later to become well known (A. Seth, Haldane, Bosanquet, Sorley, Henry Jones, Ritchie). The work was dedicated to Green, who had died the year before. In the preface Edward Caird expresses the general intention of the group as follows: "The writers of this volume agree in believing that the line of investigation which philosophy must follow, or in which it may be expected to make most important contributions to the intellectual life of man, is that which was opened up by Kant, and for the successful prosecution of which no one has done so much as Hegel." They wish, he adds, to give to the works of Kant and Hegel "a fresh expression and a new application"; they recognize that a literal acceptance of these thinkers in a different country and a different generation "would not be possible if it were desirable, or desirable if it were possible"; and they aim at showing "how the principles of an idealistic philosophy may be brought to bear on the various problems of science, of ethics, and of religion". The essays accordingly deal with problems of logic, epistemology, methodology, philosophy of history, aesthetics, social philosophy, and philosophy of religion, and thus embrace the entire sphere of philosophical inquiry as widened by German Idealism.

The greater part of the achievements of the school (for it is right to speak of a school at this stage) emanated from Oxford, which was the real stronghold of the movement, and remained so even after Green's premature death had made the first serious breach in the ranks of the pioneers. From Oxford the students who had imbibed Kant and Hegel passed out to other parts of the country, and gradually came to occupy chairs and other teaching posts in the remaining universities. The University of Glasgow was another important centre: there, through the brilliant work of Edward Caird and his brother John, the new doctrines were established very early and supplanted the hitherto dominant Hamiltonianism. Like a triumph the wave of Idealism swept everywhere, and quickly left its impress on the greater part of the philosophy pursued and taught at the universities. To this radical change and reorientation there is no parallel in the entire history of British thought. In no other country, moreover, was Idealism so splendidly revived and made so potent a spiritual influence as in Great Britain in the last third of the XIXth Century. It is very strange that of this profound transformation of English philosophy through the agency of Kant and Hegel Germany has scarcely ever become aware and has never received back from it any returning influence.

The movement advanced in several stages. The first was concerned with assimilating the content of the incoming ideas with a view to passing it on through translations, commentaries, etc., and so incorporating it in the ordinary matter of academic instruction and exploiting it in the combat against the old and still prevalent doctrines. This was the chief work of the 'seventies, and was carried out by those whom I call the pioneers—Stirling, Green, Edward Caird, Wallace, and others. Although primarily exegetic, it was done with a marked independence of mind, certain basic lines of thought being struck out which anticipated important features in the subsequent development. The imported ideas were thus transformed, or at any rate elaborated as they were transmitted. At a later stage creative criticism and independent construction came into play to consolidate and extend the ground won by the pioneers; and once the critical and speculative spirit had been unleashed, old forms could be shattered and thinking could start on new flights. The Hegelian movement thereby gave rise to a number of independent and original attempts at new solutions of the old cosmic problems. However far these efforts departed from their starting-point, with whatever other ways of thinking they came to join hands, nevertheless it was from the new idealistic movement that they received their first impulse. The two strongest speculative minds that emerged from the school were undoubtedly Bradley and McTaggart, but Bosanquet, Pringle-Pattison, Ward, Sorley, Haldane, and others, proceeded to constructive work and achieved results of some importance.

Which of the great German Idealists had the profoundest effect on British thought? Without a doubt, Hegel; so that the movement may rightly be called, as it often is in fact, Neo-Hegelian or Anglo-Hegelian.[1] This, however, should not

[1] All the chief works of Hegel have been translated into English. The following are the most important versions:—*The Phenomenology of Mind* (J. B. Baillie), 1910, two vols.; second edition, revised, one vol., 1931. *Science of Logic* (W. H. Johnston and L. G. Struthers), two vols., 1929; part ii of this larger *Logic* has also been translated by H. S. Macran—*Doctrine of Formal Logic*, 1912; *Logic of World and Idea*, 1929. *Logic of Hegel* (W. Wallace), 1874; second edition, revised, 1892; *Philosophy of Mind* (W. Wallace), 1894. These two are parts i and iii of the *Encyclopaedia*; part ii (on the Philosophy of Nature)

blind us to the fact that Kant also exercised a deep and powerful influence, liberating the critical just as Hegel liberated the speculative impulse. But all the German idealistic systems were usually regarded together as a single whole, exhibiting an organic and necessary development from Kant to Hegel, even though these two were now and then played off against each other. Fichte and Schelling were also formative forces, not merely objects of interest and inquiry; and so, too, though to a much less degree, were Herbart, Schopenhauer, and E. v. Hartmann. But of the Germans who followed the classic days of Idealism none was more zealously studied, more deeply respected, and more frequently plundered (*sit venia verbo*) than Lotze. His influence was immeasurable, less only than that of Kant and Hegel. His *System of Philosophy* (Logic and Metaphysics) appeared in translation in 1884, and was followed in the next year by a translation of his *Microcosmus*; and since Idealism was then at its height both works aroused immediate and intense interest.[1] Many Britons even came into personal relation with Lotze; indeed, at one time it was almost a fashion to spend a period of study at Göttingen University, so as to receive philosophical wisdom from the master's own lips. His striking success in England was due to the far greater ease with which his writings could be read and digested as compared with the impenetrability of Hegel and the sluggishness of Kant. Besides, he was looked on as the last living

has not yet been translated. *Philosophy of Right* (S. W. Dyde), 1896. *Lectures on the Philosophy of History* (J. Sibree), 1857. *The Philosophy of Fine Art* (F. B. P. Osmaston), 1916–20, four vols. *Lectures on the Philosophy of Religion* (E. B. Speirs and J. B. Sanderson), 1895, three vols. *Lectures on the History of Philosophy* (E. S. Haldane and F. H. Simson), 1892–5, three vols.

[1] The English version of the *System* was initiated by Green, who assumed the editorship. After his death in 1882, Bosanquet took his place. Among the translators were, besides Green and Bosanquet, Nettleship, Conybeare, and A. C. Bradley. The *Microcosmus* was translated by Elizabeth Hamilton (daughter of Sir Wm. Hamilton) and E. E. Constance Jones; it passed into a fourth edition in 1894. One set of Lotze's lectures was translated by F. C. Conybeare, *Outlines of a Philosophy of Religion*, 1892 (third edition, 1903). Another indication of interest was Henry Jones's *Critical Account of the Philosophy of Lotze*, 1895.

representative of the great age of thought that had closed with Hegel. It was consequently supposed that he provided the best way to Hegel's mysterious world, a way that could be more easily trodden than the approach through Kant; and many who were repelled by Hegel's rigid Monism found satisfaction in the looser system of Lotze. All those who in the controversy between absolute and personal Idealism felt themselves drawn to the latter turned away from Hegel and followed the banner of Lotze, who thus became the rallying-point of a number of thinkers who broke loose from the more strictly Hegelian school and achieved a freer expression of their idealistic world-view. His influence was consequently greater outside Hegelianism than within it. Even Pragmatists linked themselves with him, regarding him as one of their forerunners. Finally, much later than Lotze, Rudolf Eucken found a way into English thought. Many of his works were translated and widely read, and had a big popular success, chiefly in the decade before the Great War; but in professional philosophical circles he was scarcely noticed.

About the turn of the century the new idealistic movement reached its zenith. Until that time it held the philosophic field in almost undisputed sway: not a single notable rival arose after the old adversaries—Associationism, Common Sense, Utilitarianism, Sensationalism, Agnosticism, Naturalism, Darwinism, etc.—in fighting which it had developed its strength, and whose defeat was a part of its unexampled achievement. True, the further it moved away from its starting-point the more it lost that intense concentration and singleness of system which marked its first stage; but it gained in variety and complexity, enlarging itself into a wealth of new possibilities. The first reactions against it developed but slowly and hesitantly, and emerged mostly from its own camp, for instance Adamson's gradual transition to Realism and Naturalism, and Cook Wilson's cautious turning to Realism. The latter is of some importance because he belonged to Oxford, the stronghold of Idealism, and gathered about him there a small group of younger men. Only at the beginning of the new century, however, did the forces appear that were to launch against Idealism a powerful and in many respects successful counter-movement. With the rise of the new Realism and of Pragmatism, Idealism was faced with a war on two fronts, in the course of which it was driven more and more to assume the defensive, and lost increasingly its dominating position. Of those two opponents Pragmatism was certainly the weaker, and the fight with it—chiefly with its one notable representative in England, F. C. S. Schiller—was not even a serious affair, still less a real danger, for it petered out in a passionate and witty duel between Bradley and Schiller which for a couple of decades excited and amused philosophical readers. The attack from the side of the new Realism, however, was much more dangerous, for, unlike Pragmatism, it did not stop at direct controversy, but passed on to new issues, and justified itself and won ground in virtue of positive achievements of its own. To mention but one reason of its superiority, it was in close sympathy with the natural sciences, and thereby responded to a need of the day which Idealism had all too long neglected.

After its long decline the idealistic movement has almost come to an end within the last ten years or so. Obviously worn out and having no reserve of fresh creative energy, it has tended more and more to withdraw from encounters with its opponents, to abandon construction along its own lines, and to find its feet in other ways of thinking. This inner exhaustion has coincided with a swift succession of losses through death of its ablest leaders—Bosanquet in 1923, Bradley 1924, McTaggart and Ward 1925, Haldane 1928, Pringle-Pattison 1931, Sorley 1935, Mackenzie 1936. There are few survivors of the day of greatness; the movement has now almost entirely receded into history. The future, however, will not only give it an honourable niche, but will also look back upon it with respect and pride as the age when the British mind, wedding itself to those of Kant and Hegel, produced a mighty revolution and renewal of thinking, which even yet lives on as a quickening and fructifying force in the very different philosophy prevalent in Britain to-day.

2. THE PIONEERS

JAMES HUTCHISON STIRLING (1820–1909)

[Studied medicine at Glasgow and practised in Wales for a few years until 1851; travelled in France and Germany until 1857; in 1860 settled in Edinburgh, where he died. He twice applied unsuccessfully for a Chair in Philosophy (1866 Glasgow, 1868 Edinburgh) and never held an academic post. *The Secret of Hegel*, two vols., 1865 (new edition in one vol., 1898); *Sir William Hamilton: Being the Philosophy of Perception*, 1865; *As Regards Protoplasm*, 1869 (new edition 1872); *Lectures on the Philosophy of Law*, 1873; *Text-book to Kant*, 1881; *Philosophy and Theology* (Gifford Lectures), 1890; *Darwinianism: Workmen and Work*, 1894; *What is Thought?* 1900; *The Categories*, 1903; also a translation, *Schwegler's Handbook of the History of Philosophy*, 1867, with many later editions. See *J.H. Stirling, His Life and Work*, by Amelia H. Stirling (his daughter), 1912.]

As we have seen, German Idealism was brought in various ways to the notice of the English as early as the first half of the XIXth Century, but always too occasionally and fragmentarily to kindle a great intellectual movement and naturalize the foreign world-view in strictly philosophical circles. The credit for achieving this must be given to a single and singular writing of one man, namely *The Secret of Hegel* by Stirling. With this brilliant work Stirling really did rouse British philosophy from its dogmatic slumber and gave it a new impulse and a new direction. Of no other philosophical writing of the century can one say with equal emphasis that it provoked a revolution and founded an age. The historical importance of Stirling's book cannot be set too high: it rooted German philosophy in British soil for the first time.[1]

[1] How his enthusiasm for Hegel was aroused is described in his daughter's biography, pp. 114 ff. It was a fairly lengthy stay in Heidelberg in 1856 that more than anything else deepened an interest which he had already felt, led him to make a systematic study of Hegel's works, brought him definitively under the spell of German thought, and started him on the monumental work on Hegel to which he devoted close on ten years of intensive and painstaking labour.

Quite independently of Stirling, another early disciple of Hegel,

The book is the work not of a diligent scholar (though it does contain a fair amount of erudition), but of a man in the grip of a passion, with a sense of a mission and conscious of all that the mission involved. It is a personal confession quivering with powerful feeling; it is the product of a profound personal experience clamouring irresistibly for expression; it is athrob with the ardent adventurousness of the discoverer, and the hard toil of a pioneer has gone to its shaping. Every page of it bears traces of a tenacious and restless struggle with its subject-matter. Only because of all this did it attain to that power and depth of vision which it had to have in order to sweep men off their feet with enthusiasm and set going a new movement of thought.

Stirling's painful approach to Hegel—he himself says he *fought* his way—was attended with the magical awe one feels in the presence of something mysterious and overpowering, and whose greatness and significance are apprehended only in a premonition that needs time and labour to turn into clear conception. His book is shot through with a wonder at Hegel's strange immensity that breaks out, according to his mood, at one time in deep despair or sceptical questioning, at another in happy confidence or even in bursts of sheer exultation. The discordant expressions and judgments are to be taken only as registering his mood as his struggle is now condemned to failure and now crowned with success. On the whole the attitude of confidence, positive assertion, and rapt enthusiasm prevails, and in the end leads him triumphantly to the desired goal, the discovery of the secret of Hegel.

A few characteristic quotations may help to realize the quality of his awe of Hegel. "Hegel, indeed, so far as abstract thought is concerned, and so far as one can see at this moment, seems to have closed an era, and has named the all of things

Charles Edward Appleton (1841–79), founder and editor of *The Academy*, came to his discipleship in Heidelberg. He studied there under Eduard Zeller, and later under Michelet in Berlin, and also came into contact with A. Ruge. He was one of the first to lecture on Hegel in Oxford. One of his literary intentions was the recasting of Hegel's *Logic*, but he died too soon to carry it out.

in such terms of thought as will, perhaps, remain essentially the same for the next thousand years. To all present outward appearance, at least, what Aristotle was to ancient Greece, Hegel is to modern Europe."[1] "The philosophy of Hegel is the crystal of the universe: it is the universe thought, or the thought of the universe."[2] "All questions which interest humanity have been by him subjected to such thought as, for subtlety, for comprehensive and accurate rigour, challenges what best thought has ever yet been so applied."[3] "Shall I be able to conduct you through this vast Cyclopean edifice—this huge structure—this enormous pile—this vast mass—that resembles nothing which has yet appeared in France or England or the world? One of those vast palaces, it is, of Oriental dream, gigantic, endless—court upon court, chamber on chamber, terrace on terrace,—built of materials from the east and the west and the north and the south—marble and gold and jasper and amethyst and ruby,—old prophets asleep with signet rings—guarded by monsters winged and unwinged, footed and footless, there out in the void desert, separated from the world of man by endless days and nights, and eternally recurrent and repeating solitudes,—lonely, mysterious, inexplicable,—a giant dreamland, but still barbaric, incoherent, barren!"[4] Out of such superlatives and hyperbole doubts and suspicions start up, whether after all this colossus is only a logical juggler and swindler, "a brassy adventurer who passes himself off as a philosopher",[5] a babbler who deceives us with words. "The fact is, it is all maundering, but with the most audacious usurpation of authoritative speech on the mysteries that must remain mysteries".[6] Stirling even lets fall the hard saying, "There is something *unbefangenes*—simpletonish—in him: he is still the Swabian lout!"[7] But these reproachful expressions are quickly withdrawn—they are not judgments,

[1] Vol. 1, pp. 144 f. (1898 edition, p. 97).
[2] Vol. 1, p. 156 (1898, p. 105).
[3] Ibid.
[4] Vol. 1, p. 60 (1898, pp. 38 f.).
[5] Vol. 1, p. 71 (1898, p. 46).
[6] Vol. 1, p. 73 (1898, p. 47).
[7] Vol. 1, p. 77 (1898, p. 50).

but only the groans of a man exploring "this mysterious and puzzling labyrinth"—and Hegel remains "the greatest abstract thinker of Christianity, and closes the modern world as Aristotle the ancient".[1]

Hegel's position in the history of philosophy, here made parallel to that of Aristotle, is made clearer by a consideration of his relation to his German predecessors, especially Kant. For Hegel cannot be understood by himself; to fathom his secret we must go back to Kant, who holds the clue. The two thinkers who came between, Fichte and Schelling, whatever their importance, may be left out of account. It was Kant who laid the foundations of modern Idealism, and to understand any step that goes beyond him we must understand him. It was Kant, "the good, honest, sincere, moderate, and modest soul" (i, p. 115; 1898, p. 77), who made the principle of Idealism intelligible, and it was with this principle, thus clarified, that Hegel staked out his world and built his system. Hegel renamed, reclassified, and systematized everything, but in Kant it was all already prepared, so that it is with him that the study of metaphysics which Great Britain has to do all over again must begin. Stirling represents Kant as the more genuine, original, and profound, though simpler and more modest, Hegel as the bolder and more brilliant, but less reliable and more exotic, who built a gorgeous edifice out of the rich materials he had inherited from others. As Stirling happily puts it, Kant was "the quarry of [Hegel's] whole wealth" (i, p. 115; 1898, p. 77). A reproach that Stirling brings constantly against Hegel is that he deliberately removed all traces of his heavy indebtedness to Kant by continually attacking him, and thereby leaving the false impression that he was diametrically opposed to him, whereas in fact he was in every respect Kant's follower and continuator. It is on this point that Stirling's suspicion of the genuineness of Hegel's scintillating façade wells up again and again, though always to sink back again at a fresh vision of Hegel's colossal riches.

The line of philosophical evolution, then, runs from Kant

[1] Vol. 1, p. 116 (1898, p. 78).

through a few intermediaries to Hegel. To Kant, however, it came from Hume. For Stirling Hume was primarily the high priest of the Enlightenment and its only really great thinker, one of those vessels in which philosophical thought as it flows through time deposits itself and takes shape. But Hume's day passed, his mission ended as soon as Kant, appropriating his legacy, liquidated the whole business of the Enlightenment. Hume's vessel, then reduced to emptiness, could yield no more nourishment; evolving thought had taken a turn away from him to settle in a new and better vessel. He marks both the fulfilment and the supersession of the Enlightenment. Thus for Stirling there is no straight line through Hume, no continuation of the Enlightenment *quâ* Enlightenment, so that the way followed by English thought in the XIXth Century was only a blind alley. British philosophy had missed the march of time, and was feeding itself out of an empty vessel. "Hume is our Politics, Hume is our Trade, Hume is our Philosophy, Hume is our Religion,—it wants little but that Hume were even our Taste" (1, lxxiii; 1898, lxii). Stirling's proclamation of the philosophical mission of the Germans was thus at the same time a crusade against the dull decadence of his fellow-countrymen, against the shallow and antiquated "rationalism" with which they had misunderstood an age great in its day, and brought it to ruin. With all the passion of his nature he took every opportunity of flinging scorn at Strauss, Renan, Feuerbach, Buckle, and suchlike, and never tired of calling them the corrupters of the philosophical spirit. Buckle in particular he regarded as the most characteristic representative in Britain of these decadents, in whom, taking a phrase of Schelling's, the *Aufklärung* was perverted into an *Ausklärung*. He felt even greater contempt for the latest representatives of this "retrograde reaction", the Darwinists and Evolutionists, who called themselves advanced thinkers, and yet left us nothing but our animality. Stirling returned to Darwinism in *As Regards Protoplasm* (1869), which is directed against Huxley, and much later, in *Darwinianism* (1894), he subjected it to destructive criticism.

Stirling's verdict that genuine thinking had been neither continued nor understood in England since Hume was made to cover even those few British thinkers who *claimed* that they had understood and made their own the philosophy of Germany, that is Sir William Hamilton and his school. He exposes the worthlessness of the claim by showing that they had not rightly understood even the simplest of Kant's and Hegel's distinctive terms, and that, far from having mastered the German thought, they had mutilated and destroyed it, or at any rate left only its shallows. Hamilton, too, then, is pushed aside. Besides giving him many a thrust in the *Secret*, he crossed swords with him in a special work which appeared in the same year.

Stirling was thus unable to find among the British philosophers of his day a single ally in his struggle against the Enlightenment. Outside philosophy, however, he saw spiritual forces at work directed to the same end, for example the Romantic poetry of Wordsworth, Coleridge, and Shelley, and most of all the literary activity of Emerson and Carlyle, both of whom owed to German agency their awakening to an idealistic view of the world. Indeed, Carlyle directly influenced Stirling himself, as is evident on nearly every page of the latter's writings. Stirling was swept off his feet by Carlyle's *Sartor Resartus*, and at once fell under the spell of the prophet's originality and linguistic power, even to the extent of himself lapsing into the emotional and bombastic rhetoric which was a natural feature of Carlyle's more forceful and pithy and metaphorical style. Also from Carlyle he got his prophetic attitude, his exalted ardour, his gloomy thunder, and his hero-worship, which last led him to try his hand at rehabilitating the reputations of misunderstood geniuses (among them Aristotle, on whom he sang a paean in a later work). And he had the same readiness for enthusiasm, the same swollen style, the same caustic wit and biting scorn, the same robust and gnarled and angular personality, as Carlyle, one perhaps natural to the Scottish soil from which they both sprang. We may say that they had a similar mission: the one set out to do in the field of abstract thought what the other attempted in the world of letters.

To return to *The Secret of Hegel*: what did Stirling mean by his somewhat sensational title, and how did he set about the task of making the secret plain? There is probably a grain of truth in the wag's saying that if Stirling knew the secret of Hegel he knew how to keep it to himself. Anyhow, it is my belief that Stirling's service lay less in the unveiling of an actual secret than in his having in fact for the first time brought to the very forefront of attention the unknown genius, whose name indeed was being more and more mentioned in England, but of whom no one was able to form an even approximately concrete and clear idea. Naturally, the light that Stirling shed round Hegel was so dimmed by the peculiar manner of his own hard capture of him as to leave enough of the mysterious veil which he was seeking to remove to excite curiosity and encourage further attention to the matter in hand. A work of pure erudition would scarcely have produced this effect. What Stirling did, then, was not so much to contribute to the understanding of the content of Hegel's doctrine as to help to make evident its intellectual quality and form; and this, given the condition of British philosophy at the time, was the greater of the two. He invented a Hegel-myth, which only several decades of sober, impartial, and rigorous investigation could secularize and purify.

Stirling himself, however, believed that he had in fact, and once and for all, torn away the veil round Hegel's secret. At the very beginning of his lengthy work he expresses compendiously what he thought this secret to be: "As Aristotle—with considerable assistance from Plato—made *explicit* the *abstract* Universal that was *implicit* in Socrates, so Hegel—with less considerable assistance from Fichte and Schelling—made *explicit* the *concrete* Universal that was *implicit* in Kant."[1] An even more cryptic statement is the following: "The Secret of Hegel is the tautological reciprocity of the Logical Notion, which is a concrete in itself."[2] Somewhat clearer is his indi-

[1] Vol. 1, p. xi (1898, p. xxii). [2] Vol. 1, p. 315 (1898, p. 214).

cation of the essence of Hegel's doctrine as the concrete concept within which dialectic is confined, in the sense that when the universal thinks itself it posits its negative, the particular, and then returns upon itself as the individual. This is the path that thought takes; it can also be expressed as the movement from the concept through the judgment to the *syllogism*, or from logic through nature to spirit. The key to Hegel's philosophy, then, lies in the concrete concept, since this contains both the dialectical movement of the elements and their relatedness to the whole of knowledge. Stirling emphasizes again and again the concreteness of the Kantian and Hegelian thought, and the difficulty of struggling away from the abstractions of the understanding to this concrete thinking of reason, in which the truth of a concept comes about through the simultaneous contemplation of its opposing factors. It is precisely here that the strength of Kant and Hegel lay; their thinking never moved in airy and empty abstractions, but always kept both its feet on the solid ground of the concrete.

On the whole, Stirling's picture of Hegel seems to me to be rightly drawn. When we remember that he was entering into entirely new territory, we are astonished again and again at his profound insight into the essentials, an insight only possible in a mind with a kindred and sympathetic imagination. His exposition, often in clear and palpable imagery, often obscure and abstruse, often discursive and exuberant, illuminates the problems like a medley of searchlights. The fundamental ideas are, as it were, hammered in, and the reader simply forced to understand. One quite extraordinary difficulty in the way of exposition was set by Hegel's terminology. To get English equivalents a new philosophical vocabulary had to be created, and Stirling's heroic attempt to provide it was both a solid contribution to the later achievement and an astonishing achievement in itself, even though, despite daring images and coinages, he did not quite succeed in re-embodying Hegel's meanings.

In one respect, however, his picture of Hegel was certainly wrong. His theistic interest dominated his exposition far too much, and led him to read into Hegel too much theological orthodoxy. Stirling as philosopher was a theologian in disguise, having no use for a philosophy that did not have the care of religious interests as its chief end. Consequently he had to ask even of Kant and Hegel whether their doctrines could give us a clearer and firmer conviction of God's sovereignty and of our participation in it; and he only counted those thinkers worthy of the deep study he devoted to them because he thought he could answer that question affirmatively. Hence he never tired of extolling Hegel as the philosophical champion of Christianity. "The Hegelian system supports and gives effect to every claim of this religion"; his views "conciliate themselves admirably with the revelation of the New Testament".[1] Hegel, like Kant, directs every step of his system to proving the immortality of the soul, the freedom of the will, and the existence of God.

This coupling of philosophy with religion was of the greatest importance in the reception of Hegel into England. Hegel's philosophy only attracted because it could be harnessed to the theological chariot, and led into the field against Naturalism, Materialism, and Darwinism. It was hoped that it would lead the despisers of religion, more especially those in educated circles, back to the camp of orthodoxy. Because it took account of this attitude, Stirling's work on Hegel had a striking success; naturally among the orthodox most of all, but it also won the enthusiastic support of others who stood somewhat loosely to orthodoxy, such as Emerson, Carlyle, Jowett, Green, and Edward Caird, and even excited the admiration in Germany of Hegelians like J. E. Erdmann, Rosenkranz, and Arnold Ruge.

Stirling's importance within the idealistic movement stands and falls with his first work, *The Secret of Hegel*. Although he prolonged his activity as a philosophical writer into the new century, none of his many other works approached his first one in historical interest and in personal directness and power—neither his critical skirmishes with Hamilton, Huxley, and

[1] Vol. 1, pp. 148 f. (1898, p. 100).

Darwin, nor his admirable textbook on Kant (a parallel to his book on Hegel), nor his lectures on the philosophy of law, nor his bombastic and baroque Gifford Lectures. To the end he remained a loyal Hegelian. In his last two works, published when he was an octogenarian, he is still expounding, and recruiting for, the philosophy of Hegel.

THOMAS HILL GREEN (1836–82).

[1860, Fellow of Balliol College, Oxford; 1878–82, Professor of Moral Philosophy, Oxford. The "Mr. Gray" of *Robert Elsmere.* Introductions to Hume's *Treatise*, 1874 (in vols. 1 and 2 of *Philosophical Works of David Hume*, edited by Green & Grose).

Posthumous: *Prolegomena to Ethics* (edited by A. C. Bradley), 1883. *Works* (edited by R. L. Nettleship), three vols, 1885–8. Includes Introductions to Hume, and Lectures on Kant, on Logic, and on Principles of Political Obligation. The last published separately 1895.

See "Memoir of Green", by R. L. Nettleship, 1888, in vol. 3 of Green's *Works*, separately published 1906; *The Philosophy of T. H. Green*, by W. H. Fairbrother, 1896; *The Service of the State: Lectures on the Political Teaching of Green*, by J. H. Muirhead, 1908; *Introduction to Green's Moral Philosophy*, by W. D. Lamont, 1934.]

On the foundations laid by Stirling no one built more energetically and successfully than T. H. Green. While the former, never holding an academic post, could only propagate the newly discovered world of ideas through published writings, the latter was able to work through example and teaching as well, and was quickly rewarded with an enthusiastic response not merely in Oxford, which had been mentally prepared, but also elsewhere. It was with Green, and not before him, that German Idealism really began its mission on Anglo-Saxon soil; only through him did it win a second and abiding home in the country whose philosophy had hitherto closed itself most firmly against foreign influences and followed with extreme consistency the paths of a long native tradition. It was he who opened the carefully guarded philosophical frontier, and thenceforward no barrier opposed the free entry of the new ideas.

When Green began his career at Oxford, soon after the middle of the century, there was not a single philosophical teacher of any eminence in the venerable university. In philosophy Oxford followed John Stuart Mill, whose writings, especially his *Logic*, were read zealously by the students, and —apart of course from the constantly prescribed Plato and Aristotle—almost exclusively determined the direction of their thought. In Green's student days orthodox theology had H. L. Mansel (later Dean of St. Paul's) as its most powerful representative. At Magdalen College and afterwards as holder of the Waynflete Chair, Mansel lectured on philosophy, and his early work on *The Limits of Religious Thought* (1858; see above, p. 39) was much talked about. Being a zealous exponent of the ideas of Hamilton, who had recently died, he made Kant known in Oxford; but, of course, it was Kant on his negative side only, as an Agnostic in epistemology. Here, then, the young Green received no stimulus (except, perhaps, that which comes from opposition) or help towards his future philosophical mission. The stimulus came rather from the powerful personality which for nearly two generations dominated the intellectual life of Oxford, Benjamin Jowett (see above, p. 250), who was appointed Regius Professor of Greek in the same year as that in which Green went up to Balliol (1855). While still a student Green came into contact with this great teacher, had him indeed as a tutor, and there can be no doubt that it was Jowett who turned his thinking in the direction towards which he himself was shortly to give English philosophy a new impulsion, that is to Kant and Hegel.

To make clear Green's unique position in the development of English thought in the XIXth Century we must first and foremost determine his relation to the great thinkers of Germany. However much his thought in all its expressions moved in the atmosphere of German Idealism—and almost every line he wrote, indeed almost every word, did this—nevertheless he was aware that the historical situation into which he was born precluded any mere acceptance or reproduction of the German systems. Again and again he emphasized the need of each generation to state the philosophical problems afresh in its own way: "It must all be done over again."[1] What we have in Green, then, is no mere taking over or refurbishing of foreign ideas in the interests of erudition or of anything else, but a genuinely new beginning, a creative experience of a weighty mind which was fertilized and nourished by an external movement of thought congenial to his own. What he took over from this was formed and transformed by both his personal experience and the historical situation in which he was placed.

But how far could the work of building on the foundations laid by Stirling proceed so long as the native tradition, centuries-old and deeply rooted, held unbroken sway? From the first Green recognized that this tradition was the obstacle to be removed, that the new could not simply be put in the place of the old, but that the old must first be disrupted and dissolved. There had to be a life-and-death struggle between the naturalistic or utilitarian philosophies of Bentham, Mill, Lewes, Buckle, Spencer, Darwin, Huxley, Bain, and Sidgwick on the one hand, and the Idealism of Kant, Fichte, and Schelling on the other. Consequently, in nearly everything he wrote, in the lectures left among his remains as well as in what he published or prepared for publication, there is a continued and passionate polemic against the naturalistic group. Even his first work, his famous Introductions to Hume, bears this characteristic mark, the proclamation of the new being inseparably connected with a declaration of war against the old. Green always had an opponent before him; only so could he think effectively. At the early stage of German influence represented by him, therefore, the new constructive work had not yet begun, considerable as his preparatory contributions were. Green's mission in the history of philosophy was primarily to clear away the old systems and prepare the ground for a new synthesis of an idealistic kind. The full fruition of his work does

[1] E. Caird, in preface to *Essays in Philosophical Criticism* (1883), p. 5.

not appear until we come to the systems of Bradley, Bosanquet, McTaggart, and the rest.

In clearing the ground Green did not confine his attention to the naturalism of his contemporaries; he also and chiefly went behind them, laying his axe at the far-reaching historical roots of this way of thinking, at the great empirical systems, that is to say, of the XVIIth and XVIIIth Centuries. Hence his two Introductions to Hume's *Treatise*, which are a radical criticism of the theoretical and practical doctrines of the empirical movement from Locke to Hume. It is odd, by the way, that they were inserted in an edition of the works of this movement's classical representative. Green was guided by the Hegelian idea that philosophy advances in a dialectical manner, along the line of an increasingly rational conception of things, the systems of the past being the several steps in this advancing process. Empiricism, of course, was one of these necessary steps, and in Green's eyes the significance of the Humean doctrine in the history of philosophy consisted in its marking the end of this step, the dialectical movement of thought then rising to a new and higher stage in Kant. Looked at from this higher stage the empiricist systems from Locke to Hume do indeed appear as errors, but, in so far as they helped to invoke, in Kant, a new truth, they made a decisive contribution to the progress of thought. The *Treatise* acts as a bridge to the first *Kritik*, and is at the same time the most important turning-point in the history of modern philosophy. Hume and Kant are thus brought into close connection; the one asked a question which the other answered. By the radical character of its questioning attitude Hume's Scepticism raked thought to its depths, and thereby paved the way for a new kind of answer, which was supplied in Kant's *Kritik*. Kant is therefore the true successor of Hume. The evolution of philosophy after Hume, then, is to be found not in the straight line that leads to his XIXth-Century followers, but in the dialectical deflection that precipitated the great idealistic movement of the Germans. England had no genuine successors to Hume, for there his searching questions, which went to the very roots of knowledge, far from being answered were not even any longer understood: such philosophy as existed was decadent and lifeless, thought running on emptily without any creative impulse, and therefore without any possibility of progress. It was because the philosophical spirit that lived on in the classical English systems had passed over into Germany that Green said again and again to the younger generation of his countrymen: "Close your Mill and your Spencer and turn to Kant and Hegel." And with this *ceterum censeo* of Green's the history of English philosophy began a new chapter.

Green's doctrine accordingly bears in content and expression alike the characteristic mark and savour of that Idealism which has lived on almost unbroken from the Greeks to the moderns, and is a genuine part of it. In the construction of it he drew on the idealistic systems of Plato and Aristotle, on the ethics of Christianity, on Berkeley's theocentric metaphysic (empirical only in its disguise), and most of all on the critical Idealism of Kant and the absolute Idealism of Hegel; also in some measure on Fichte, Herbart, F. C. Baur, and Lotze. Of chief interest, naturally, is his relation to Kant and Hegel, and the frequently discussed question to which of these two he was indebted the more. Looked at externally, Green appears to be predominantly a Kantian. In epistemology as well as in ethics he did in fact owe a vast amount to Kant: over quite long stretches he is plainly following Kantian themes and arguments; his thinking often starts from the Kantian point of view, and bases itself on Kantian presuppositions; and his conclusions often coincide with, or at least closely approximate to, those of Kant. Kant's name meets us frequently in all his writings, whereas Hegel's occurs only rarely, in some of his works not at all (e.g. in the *Prolegomena to Ethics*). Nevertheless, Hegel's influence is powerfully at work in the entire background of Green's thought, unmistakably evident, even though it is difficult to put one's finger on it. It shows itself most of all in the interpretation Green gives of Kant, an interpretation which, in diametrical opposition to that given by Hamilton and his school, takes him in the direction of Hegel's absolute Idealism. Occasionally an expression can be found which suggests some hostility on Green's part, such as, "I looked into Hegel the other day and found it a strange *Wirrwarr*"[1]; but such expressions do not upset the fact that Hegel was one of the determining factors of Green's thought. In short, Green was primarily a Kantian, but one who read Kant with Hegelian spectacles.

Incomplete though it was in its literary expression, Green's thought forms a systematic whole, which falls into three parts —metaphysics, ethics, and political philosophy. Of these the ethical part is the central one, as we should expect in a mind predominantly moral in its bent. It bears the weight of the system, and is preceded and worked up to by the metaphysics (which is itself preceded by a theory of knowledge), and issues in a doctrine of the State, of the moral conditions of social and political life. Put in another way, the system takes up successively the following questions, each of which when answered leads to the next: What is real? What is man's real nature and place in reality? What ought he to do if he is to fulfil his vocation? And what will the tasks of a community be if in and by it man is to be led to his moral vocation? The last question of all, which Green did not discuss explicitly, would concern the highest reality or God, as the ground of all creaturely existence. Green's system, then, is about the nature of reality, man as a person or moral being, society or the State as a multiplicity of such beings, and God as the being from whom all the rest derive their meaning.

The theory, or, as Green characteristically calls it, the metaphysic of knowledge, is developed through opposition to the sensationalistic atomism of the Empiricists, especially of Hume, and to the realism and materialistic atomism of contemporary science. For both these the object of knowledge is an aggregate of unrelated particulars—of sensations, of material entities independent of consciousness, or of atoms, as the case may be. In all these cases the subjective factor in

[1] Hurly-burly. Quoted in *Mind*, N.S., vol. 10 (1901), p. 19.

knowledge is left entirely out of consideration: and not only subject and object, but also objects themselves are left unrelated. Hume, who always pressed on to extreme conclusions, dissolved even the self into the sequence of data, into a "bundle of impressions", and thereby reduced all reality whatever to impressions. But it is impossible to see how atomic sensations could act on each other, or enter into any other kind of connection, least of all how they could come together into that ordered whole as which the world appears to us in knowledge. Such talk is the end of any theory of reality; it is thinking landed in a blind alley, from which nothing but a radical change can rescue it. The Humean sensation corresponds to nothing real; it is an artefact, a pure *abstractum*.

Green transcends this atomism by means of his famous and much-disputed doctrine of relations, which is the heart of his metaphysic of knowledge. Whereas Hume had argued that such ideas as those of substance, causality, externality, and identity are mere fictions of the mind because they are not given in any impression, Green showed that it is precisely such "unreal" relations that make possible any knowledge at all. Whether anything is real or not depends not on any fact or datum in itself, or on the possibility or otherwise of deriving ideas from this or that fact, but entirely on the relation to each other in which the facts stand, or into which they can enter. "The 'mere idea' of a hundred thalers . . . is no doubt quite different from the possession of them, not because it is unreal, but because the relations which form the real nature of the idea are different from those which form the real nature of the possession."[1] Things are not shut up in themselves, finished once and for all, and independent of one another, but rather are real only in so far as they come out of their isolation and point to something else. That is, things stand in manifold relations to each other, condition or act on each other reciprocally, are similar or dissimilar, conflict with each other, are connected in space or time, and so on. This does not mean that things exist first in a pure givenness and isolation, and

[1] *Prolegomena to Ethics*, p. 24.

thereafter enter into relations with each other, but that apart from such relations they just cannot be conceived or have any meaning or interest for us. Take away from things their relations and virtually nothing remains. Hence Green's doctrine that the reality of things consists in nothing but the relations that bind them together. This view, reached through epistemological considerations, is then transformed, without any further and more specific proof, into a metaphysical principle.

The considerations that follow are also marked by the simple transference of an epistemological principle to metaphysics. The exaggerated formula that relations constitute reality only acquires, according to Green, an intelligible meaning when it is added that relations are not given in and with things, but can only be instituted or laid down by some uniting principle. This principle cannot be anything but the activity of mind. Things are constituted by relations, and relations presuppose the mind's relating function. That which institutes relations, however, is fundamentally different from that which is related: it is not one thing among other things, or one datum among other data, but the very condition of the possibility of data at all and of any existence whatever, for without the uniting and shaping function of the understanding we could never rise above the mere chaotic stuff of sensation. It is easy to recognize here the basic ideas of Kant. The relating act of the understanding is just Kant's synthetic unity of apperception, and Green's view that it is this relating act that constitutes reality includes Kant's dictum that the laws of nature are prescribed to nature by the understanding.

Naturally there quickly appears the tendency to pass beyond Kant's epistemological position and to draw metaphysical conclusions, these being in the direction taken by the post-Kantians, especially Hegel. Green's chief effort was to overcome the Kantian dualism of appearance and thing-in-itself. With his doctrine of ubiquitous and constitutive relations he could not, of course, rest content with two unrelated worlds. Against this dualism he shows that the notion of the thing-in-itself contains a contradiction similar to that contained in

Hume's notion of the impression, for how can that which *ex hypothesi* is unknowable enter into any relation with a knowing mind? If the thing-in-itself be the cause of appearances, it must be itself appearance, which is precisely what it is defined not to be; and if it be the raw, entirely unformed material of experience, it must be destitute of any rational determination. A sensory material utterly independent of thought-determination would be an unrelated *x*, and as such could be neither an object of knowledge nor a real fact. "Pure sensation" is an expression that corresponds to nothing in reality; it is a product of artificial abstraction. Green thus puts himself in extreme opposition to Sensationalism, and detects an unremoved residuum of this even in Kant's doctrine of the thing-in-itself. He maintains that we are bound to attribute to sensation some determinateness, namely sequence and intensity, and that these are impossible without a determining subject; from which it follows that thinking is the necessary condition of the existence of such determinate facts, and that pure sensation cannot be a constituent of the actual world.

Now what is this subjective principle which is the ground and condition of all objective being? Here again Green quickly leaves epistemology—Kantianism in its narrower meaning—and proceeds to a speculative application in which Hegelian and Berkeleian themes begin to appear. The correlate of nature—nature as a system of related things—is spirit, meaning by spirit neither the individual subject taken psychologically nor a consciousness-in-general taken epistemologically, but a universal metaphysical principle, or, as Green preferred to call it, an eternal consciousness. The universe as a system in which every element is correlative to every other and both presupposes and is presupposed by every other, requires for the condition of its being a universal and all-inclusive consciousness. This is the unity of the manifold, the identity in all change of appearance, the relation of the fleeting contents of perception to the system of thought, the relation too of particular things and facts to the world-system in its totality. It is the systematic principle which establishes unity and all order, the whole in which every part finds its logical place, the universal towards which every particular strives, and which it needs in order to complete itself and without which it is nothing, the divine unity which bears and sustains everything and in which everything lives and moves and has its being. It is the absolutely spiritual, above and beyond and before everything natural, neither in space nor in time, immaterial and immovable, eternally one with itself. Clearly, Green's first principle has many aspects, now the Kantian Reason, now the Hegelian Spirit, at another time the Berkeleian God. Because of his theistic bent the last of these appears frequently, especially in his notion of the presence and sublimation of all things (or ideas, as Berkeley would say) in God; and for this reason his doctrine provided a welcome weapon for orthodox theology in its fight against the Materialism and Naturalism that sprang from natural science. It has often been observed that the renewal of Idealism in England arose out of religious and ecclesiastical interests, as a means of defence against the faith-destroying influence of Darwinism and Evolutionism. This feature of the idealistic movement in its beginnings should not, however, blind us to the fact that the renewal of English thought, however much it was made to serve ends of a non-theoretical character, owed its origin just as much to a genuinely philosophical impulse. And this impulse is certainly present in Green, even though it failed to receive from him a purely theoretical foundation, and was primarily the expression of his predominantly moral and social interest, in which religious motives also may naturally have played a part.

The metaphysic of knowledge and the metaphysic of being, which by Green are looked at from a single point of view, issue in an ethic as soon as the finite consciousness comes to be considered. Despite the criticism sometimes made (e.g. by A. E. Taylor, *The Problem of Conduct*, pp. 59 f.) that there is nothing but a gap between Green's metaphysic and his ethic, the latter is an organic part of his system. That which for the eternal consciousness is a whole is for a finite consciousness in the first instance something divided and broken, and apprehensible only in the succession of time; but in so far as the finite consciousness is aware, however imperfectly, of the whole, so far it participates in the divine consciousness. Man is accordingly the meeting-point of the two centres of consciousness, the temporal and the eternal, the changeful and the absolutely unchanging. The relation between these two is one of the gravest problems of Green's philosophy, and it cannot be claimed that he arrived at any satisfactory account of it. The individual consciousness is said to be the medium or instrument of the universal consciousness, and to have some sort of participation in the latter, but of the manner of this participation we are told nothing more than that the eternal consciousness is communicated to us under the limitations imposed by our bodies. From the dualism evident here Green, always monistic in conviction, tried to escape by making the supposition that the apparently double consciousness does not in fact exist, and that the semblance of it arises wholly out of the inability of the finite understanding to apprehend the one and indivisible consciousness in a single presentation. But obviously this supposition, far from overcoming the dualism, only glosses it over.

We have the same situation in the ethics proper of Green. Indeed, here dualisms are even less resolved than in any other part of his system, the reason being that in his ethics he is more fully under the influence of Kant than he is in his metaphysics. He takes as his starting-point those bare needs, such as impulses and instincts, that correspond in the moral realm to bare sensations in the cognitive realm, and finds that they too require for their completion or fulfilment a principle that transcends them. In the human sphere we never in fact have bare needs, but always in addition an awareness of them and of the things connected with them. Here, too, then, as in cognition, that which is alleged to be purely objective includes from the start a reference to something subjective, and the transition from the bare need to the awareness of the thing needed presupposes that the need is present to a subject distinguished from it fundamentally by remaining constant throughout the succession of changing needs. And again as before, the subject is different from the process or sequence presented to it, is not itself a stage or series of stages within this sequence, but something abiding and changeless beyond this, something to which the particular stages are anchored.

A mere need, then, is nothing of itself, but always points to something higher, namely, to moral action, to that which we ascribe to ourselves, and for which we feel ourselves to be responsible. Green sharply distinguishes moral action from merely instinctive action, and calls the latter the negation of the former. He shows that while the conditions of our actions may spring from the natural sphere our motives cannot. What moves us to action is always an act of self-consciousness, and this belongs not to the natural but to the moral sphere. It is the responsibility we assume for it that makes an action moral, even when the action is evoked or precipitated by a purely animal need. We attribute the action to our character, and character is the unity of our temporally sequent needs; that is, in all our actions an identical consciousness operates on needs of an animal origin, and lifts them into a moral sphere. All these considerations, which cannot here be followed out in detail, have as their aim the sharp separation of the moral realm from the natural conditions out of which it arises, and in which it remains embedded.

The subject of moral action is man. It is even more important for ethics than it is for metaphysics that man is a citizen of two worlds, a child of nature as well as a creature of God. The doctrine of the empirical and intelligible aspects of man is another of the Kantian features integral to Green's ethics. Because a divine principle is at work in him, man cannot rest content with the merely natural side of his life, but strives increasingly after the higher life that is in him. The indwelling infinite forces him to realize his true self and achieve his moral vocation through continual struggle. The presupposition of all moral life is consequently the divine principle that comes to self-realization only in human personalities. The essence of finite personality consists in its being, like the eternal consciousness, a free cause. Every natural event is imprisoned in a causal system, is the effect of an earlier and the cause of a later event. Not until we come to the level of knowing do we get an experience of free causality, that is, of a cause that can produce effects without being itself the effect of an earlier cause. Involved as he is on his animal side in natural conditions, man as a knowing being can raise himself above nature and determine himself. In so far as man, as distinguished from brutes, has received the gift of knowledge and of self-knowledge (i.e. knowing himself as knowing), so far is he a free agent. It is evident once more that Green has not solved the problem of the relation of human to divine freedom. He merely affirms human freedom after the analogy of the divine; "We have to content ourselves with saying that, strange as it may seem, it is so", he says resignedly.[1]

When he comes to the concrete tasks and ends of the moral life, Green keeps to the path marked out by Kant and Fichte. The absolute value of human personality is his first principle, from which follows the requirement of the equality and brotherhood of all men. No one should strive after any good, whether his own or anyone else's, by means that are likely to prejudice the good of other people. No one should judge different people by different standards. Since every human person is of absolute value, the humanity in each individual should always be treated as an end, never as a means. The true good can only be fulfilled when each person has his *suum* which every other person is under an obligation to recognize and respect. Moral progress consists in our increasing grasp of the truth that the real end of man lies, not in external goods, and therefore not in the virtues by which these are attained, but entirely in virtuous activity regarded as an end in itself. So far as man is concerned the only object of essential and absolute value is perfection of moral character understood as realization of the true self. Green was aware that the basic idea of this ethical ideal, which in modern times had found its highest expression in German Idealism, was both present

[1] *Prolegomena to Ethics*, § 82

and potent in both Plato and Aristotle (to whom, indeed, he expressly refers); but despite the high value he set on the philosophy of the Greeks, he recognized that Christianity, through its postulate of human equality and brotherhood (its distinctive social idea), while not altering the Greek ideal had significantly widened the moral sphere. Consequently, he gave the place of honour to the Christian ideal, and regarded it as marking an extremely important step forward.

In the development of philosophy in England Green's ethic represents a deeper breach and a more radical change than anything he achieved in the more narrowly theoretical sphere: in it he struck a note that had never before been heard in Britain. As in his theory of knowledge, so also in his ethic he attacked Empiricism, and regarded his crusade against the hedonistic morality as being, alongside the positive working out of his own ideas, his special task and service to his time. How could the lofty end of the moral ideal be attained if one's conduct sprang from no other source than the pursuit of pleasure and the avoidance of pain? Pleasure as such is as irrelevant to morals as need as such, and only acquires a moral bearing when it enters into relation with a consciousness that knows it as pleasure; and then it ceases to be mere pleasure, is transformed and raised to a higher level, and becomes an element of the moral life. Similarly, the mere addition of pleasure to pleasure and the balancing of one sum against another is a meaningless undertaking, indeed an impossible one, for pleasure as such, abstracted from the object to which it attaches and the conditions in which it emerges, is entirely indeterminate, and therefore as inapprehensible as pure sensation. Pleasure may in fact attend the attainment of a desired object, but it cannot be itself the object of the desire; and the pleasantness of an attained good depends on the goodness of this good, not the goodness on the pleasantness it brings. Green thus rejects Hedonism entirely, as unsatisfactory in theory and pernicious in practice.

After this sharp rejection of Hedonism it is all the more strange to find Green acknowledging the high practical service that Utilitarianism had rendered to morality. Unable to accept the Utilitarian's identification of the highest good with the greatest possible quantity of pleasure, he nevertheless agreed with Bentham's postulate of the greatest happiness of the greatest number, and believed that through this postulate Utilitarianism had got rid of class-distinctions, developed the social sense, and contributed to the solution of the problems of social and political betterment. He even envisaged a version of the utilitarian theory cleansed of its hedonistic basis. This remarkable change-over from the Kantian ethic with its exclusive stress on disposition to the utilitarian evaluation in terms of consequences is made in the fourth book of the *Prolegomena*, the earlier parts having scarcely any trace of it. It may have been occasioned by external influences. Anyhow, in the contemporary work and person of John Stuart Mill, Utilitarianism had found an embodiment at once distinguished and noble, and therefore completely acceptable to an idealistically minded thinker, especially to one with Green's social and humanitarian leanings. Green's ethical Idealism, then, despite its strong opposition on epistemological and metaphysical grounds to utilitarian Eudaemonism, coincided with the latter when it came to consider ethical demands in the concrete; and both were permeated with a genuinely humane and social spirit.[1] Nevertheless, we cannot but feel that Green's concessions to Utilitarianism, however noble the impulse behind them may have been, introduce something foreign and inharmonious into the general structure of his philosophy; that the man who had started from a percep-

[1] To assert, as Hobhouse does (in his *Metaphysical Theory of the State*, 1918), that it was in despite of his metaphysical Idealism that Green retained his humanity, betokens so grotesque a misunderstanding of the real spirit of Idealism that it can only be attributed to a war-time mentality. J. H. Muirhead had already tried to counter that misunderstanding: "It is not in Hegelianism," he wrote in 1915 (*German Philosophy in relation to the War*, p. 39), "but in the violent reaction against the whole Idealist philosophy that set in shortly after his death, that we have to look for the philosophical foundations of present-day militarism." (See also *Mind*, vol. xxxiii, 1924, pp. 23 f.—ED.)

tion of the inadequacy of the native philosophy and set out to announce to his fellow-countrymen a truth quite new to them, which he felt profoundly, was after all unable to break completely the chains of the past in his own mind. The very foe he was out to meet, and which he had attacked with brilliant success, remained in his own breast not fully conquered. Not Green, but his younger contemporary Bradley, in his *Ethical Studies* (1876, but little noticed at the time), was the first to draw a sharp distinction between the idealistic ethic of Germany and the native Utilitarianism.

Green's political philosophy, unlike his ethics which we have in a work intended and largely prepared by him for publication, has come down to us in the form of lectures edited by another hand from his remains. It is consequently less important philosophically. His doctrine of society and of the State is simply an extension to the facts of communal life of the basic principles of his ethics. Individual and State presuppose and condition each other; moral personality can only be realized in and through society. But although he strongly emphasized the social factor and amply recognized the importance of the State, here again Green characteristically stopped short in a half-way position. The immensely deepened notion of moral personality which he had taken over from Kant and Fichte did not prevent him from falling back into the typical individualism of the English; he still put the individual, conceived as independent and free, before all individuals of a higher order, such as society, the State, and the nation. Not fully liberated from the fetters of the native tradition, he shrank from such radical consequences as Hegel had drawn. The astonishingly small influence Hegel had on his political philosophy is explicable only in the light of the political situation of England. For an unreserved acknowledgment of the Hegelian theory of the State we have to wait until Bosanquet and other younger members of the school.

Still, Green went considerably beyond the current English ideas of the State. In particular he insisted that the State rests not on force, but on the free volition of its members. Force is indeed operative in the formation of states, but always on the basis of rights both pre-existent and pre-acknowledged. The two ideas are inseparable: force springs out of rights and leads to further rights, and is consequently only a means to the creation and maintenance of rights. For the rest, the end of the State is the protection and ensuring of the moral life of its members by maintaining the circumstances in which moral persons can thrive and realize themselves, and laws are the necessary conditions of this fulfilment of man as a rational and moral being. It is not surprising, then, to find in Green a pacifist and cosmopolitan trend. That war is still resorted to as an instrument of State policy was for him not a proof of its necessity, but simply of the degraded level of international life. As for Cosmopolitanism, far from seeking to destroy the State, it comprehends Nationalism within itself, and the more a nation approximates to the ethical ideal of the State the less does it need to involve itself in war with other nations, for the same moral laws that govern the lives of individuals in society hold good equally of the political interrelations of nations.

Green's outstanding position in the earliest phase of the idealistic movement and the powerful influence he exerted were due to the fascination of his great personality and to his brilliance as a university teacher. He animated the movement with his own intellectual energy, and its doctrine with nobility and moral power, and thereby raised what might have been merely a theory into a living spiritual force. So much of his influence as proceeded directly from his personality was harshly interrupted by his premature death. Since he himself had published nothing of any length except his Introductions to Hume, it seemed desirable to collect and make available his literary remains. This task fell to his most intimate disciple, RICHARD LEWIS NETTLESHIP (1846–92), who added to the edition a sketch of Green's life and work. Nettleship, too, was an enthusiastic teacher of the new Idealism, having as it were imbibed it with his mother's milk, for he entered Jowett's and Green's college as a scholar and remained there as a Fellow until his death. He shared Jowett's affection and reverence for Plato, and had the same sympathy with the spirit of the Platonic philosophy, a sympathy which led him to explore it out of no purely academic interest, but for the intellectual quickening of his hearers and readers. For him Plato was one of the exemplars among men, a guide to uprightness, nobility, and wisdom of living, the enunciator of a world-view still and forever valid, and which each generation, to possess it, must think out afresh. In philosophical system his position was like that of Green, not only in general, but also to a large extent in detail. The moral and intellectual forces that radiated from Jowett and Green were more genuinely and actively embodied in him than in anyone else, and, as with them, his best work lay in his oral teaching, in the warmth and searchingness of his utterance and the distinction of mind that showed through it. His influence has been far greater and more persistent than one would infer from the sparseness of his writings. He himself published, besides his edition of the works of Green, only an essay on "The Theory of Education in Plato's *Republic*" (in *Hellenica*, 1880). All his other writings were edited from his remains after his premature and tragic death at the same age as his master, Green; they were published, with a biographical sketch, by A. C. Bradley in 1897.[1]

[1] *Philosophical Lectures and Remains*, two vols. (vol. 2 re-edited 1898 as *Lectures on the Republic of Plato*; vol. 1, 1901, as *Philosophical Remains*, second edition). Nettleship translated part of the volume on Logic in the English version of Lotze's *System of Philosophy*, edited by Bosanquet (1884).

3. THE HEGELIANS

EDWARD CAIRD (1835–1908)

[Educated at Glasgow, St. Andrews, and Balliol College, Oxford. 1864–6, Fellow and Tutor of Merton College, Oxford; 1866–93, Professor of Moral Philosophy, Glasgow; 1893, succeeded Jowett as Master of Balliol; retired 1907. *A Critical Account of the Philosophy of Kant*, 1877 (revised edition in two vols., 1889, under title *The Critical Philosophy of Kant*); *Hegel*, 1883 (Blackwood's Philosophical Classics); *The Social Philosophy and Religion of Comte*, 1885; *Essays on Literature and Philosophy*, two vols, 1892; *The Evolution of Religion* (Gifford Lectures), two vols., 1893; *The Evolution of Theology in the Greek Philosophers* (Gifford Lectures), two vols., 1904, German translation, 1909.

See *The Life and Philosophy of Edward Caird*, by Sir Henry Jones and J. H. Muirhead, 1921.]

After Green the next great pioneer of Idealism in Britain was Edward Caird. He was of nearly the same age as Green, while still a student at Oxford became Green's friend, and began his teaching career only a few years later than Green. His appointment to Glasgow in 1866 was consequently of the greatest importance for the extension of the idealistic movement, giving it two vigorous centres; for it was Caird who made Glasgow a stronghold of Idealism in Scotland. Something like an encircling movement against the prevailing philosophies thus began, Oxford attacking primarily the empiricist and evolutionary thought of Mill, Bain, Spencer, Darwin, and Huxley, Glasgow directing itself chiefly against the Hamiltonianism then dominant in the Scottish universities. Here Caird effected a revolution. When after twenty-seven years of successful writing and teaching he left Glasgow to succeed Jowett as Master of Balliol, a whole generation of young Hegelians had grown up, who took over and extended the territory he had staked out. And by returning to Oxford he at last filled the gap left by the premature death of Green, brought the movement back to the college where it had started and reinforced it here with the weight of his personality and the lustre of his reputation.

The task that fell to Caird in the naturalizing of German thought was a peculiar one. The first pioneer work had already been done by Stirling, but the agony of his struggle to get the sense and find an English equivalent for the idiom of Hegel, left the veil that shrouded Hegel's thought unlifted for all but a narrow circle of discerning minds. Green was too independent a thinker to be able to give a clear and faithful account of the Kantian and Hegelian doctrines. These had in one way or another entered into the structure of his system, but it is hard to distinguish them there either from one another or from the ideas that came to Green from other sources, or from his own reflection; and his obscure and heavy style made him difficult to read in any case. The later representatives of the movement, such as Bradley, Bosanquet, and McTaggart, extended and transformed the German thought too much for us to regard them as mediating its content to the British with anything like purity. It was Caird, much less bound than these to systematic ideas of his own, who became the true mediator or channel of the thought of Kant and Hegel. But instead of fulfilling this task with the cold objectivity of a pure historian, he threw into it the enthusiasm and verve of a genuine disciple and apostle, handled magisterially the treasure committed to him, and minted it into current coin that could thereafter be used by anybody. Indeed it is in Caird that we first find almost all the idealistic formulae and turns of expression made use of by the whole generation of British Kantians and Hegelians, and ridiculed by their opponents. He had to a remarkable degree the gift of expressing difficult and obscure matters in lucid, easy, and beautiful language, and by dissolving Kant's contortions and Hegel's enigmas into his own luminous and fastidious style he increased the philosophical expressiveness of the English tongue, and set his fellow-countrymen an example of the way in which such matters could be spoken and written about.

To crown all he had an unusually gifted and superb personality rich in the qualities that attract and hold youthful minds —verve, passion, intense devotion to a great cause, ease and warmth of utterance, and the brilliant literary capacity we have just referred to. He is the ideal type and purest embodiment in Britain of the Hegelian spirit, to some extent also of the letter. Avoiding any attempt to give to Hegel's system a dogmatic fixity, to press it to the point of violence, or to distort or dissipate it, he aimed simply at declaring and passing on to others its breath and quintessence—which he had caught and assimilated almost more than anybody else—with no other interest than to serve the truth and awaken philosophy to new life. His own mind had too much vitality and too much wealth of both native power and acquired culture for him to swear by the letter of any single master. Hegel to him was only the last and ripest expression of an idealistic outlook which had lived on ever since the Greeks, and not in the great philosophers only, but also in the creators of literature. His *Essays on Literature and Philosophy* and his Gifford Lectures on the theology of the Greek philosophers testify to the breadth of his conception of Idealism as an enduring spirit in which all that is lofty and noble and lovely in man and the universe finds its recognition and its highest realization, a spirit alive alike in pagan antiquity and Christianity, in Dante and Goethe, in Rousseau and Wordsworth and Carlyle. Hegel's Idealism was something he lived as well as taught, not a dead letter or a system of abstract thought, but one of the powers of life, that was to renew man from within. The final victorious sweep of the British idealistic movement only began when Caird, its acknowledged leader after the death of Green, gave it the quickening breath of his own noble mind, proclaimed it far and wide with his more intelligible speech, and gathered about him a circle of disciples, who, imbued with the same spirit, ensured the continuance of his work. No philosophical teacher of the time sowed so much fruitful seed, roused so much enthusiasm, and received so much admiration and respect as Edward Caird.

When we look at his writings, what strikes us first of all is that about 2,000 pages are devoted to Kant, whereas on Hegel there is only a small and somewhat popular book. The reason of this curious fact is his conviction that what was most important in Hegel could first be more clearly discerned in Kant. Windelband's well-known saying that to understand Kant is to go beyond him expresses Caird's conviction, if we add that the going beyond must be in the direction of Hegel. At every point he measured Kant's doctrine by the Hegelian standard, stretched it on the Procrustean bed of the Hegelian categories, and showed where it was still burdened with older lines of thought, and where it was pregnant with the hidden seeds of absolute Idealism. The main direction of his criticism of Kant was against the dualisms that run right through the Kantian system, against the facile distinction and separation of the elements of experience and thought, and the abstractions and delimitations that are its superficial characteristics. On the other hand, he saw that what Kant was really seeking was not these unrelated elements and unresolved oppositions and antinomies, but their reconciliation and supersession in a higher unity of thought; though the more Kant sought this the more it escaped him. It was in this constant conflict between Kant's real aim and his achievement, between his striving after unity and his clinging to duality, that Caird saw the tragedy of the Kantian system; and the emancipation from this conflict he found in the magnificent system of Hegel.

We thus pass from critical to absolute Idealism. The unity that Kant sought and so rarely reached (as in his transcendental apperception) is not the abstract unity that lies beyond all difference, but a unity that only expresses itself in and through difference. Without the great idea of identity in difference thought cannot take a single step forward towards philosophical truth. If we set being and not-being, or any other correlatives, in opposition to each other, we cannot say either that they are different or that they are identical. Their truth lies in neither their difference nor their identity, but in their identity in difference. The difference is as essential as the unity, for the unity sought in philosophy is an individual unity that maintains itself not simply despite the underlying difference, but in and through it, overcoming contrasts and conflicts only to dissolve again into higher ones, and then to recover itself at a still higher level. It is the organic unity which we are obliged to think the universe to be. It is the spiritual principle immanent in all things; it is the Absolute.

It is the Absolute understood not as something rigid, utterly complete, closed within itself and incapable of any development, but as a living or dynamic process which unfolds itself dialectically. By taking over from Hegel his dialectic and regarding it as the living pulse of all being and all thought, Caird put himself in sharp opposition to the younger group of Hegelians led by Bradley, who found the dialectic to be just that part of Hegel of which they could make nothing and who in consequence conceived the Absolute as static. Bradley's "block universe" was as unacceptable to Idealism, as Caird understood it, as it was to the Pragmatism that came into vogue towards the end of his life. The idea of a continually creative renewal of the universe is common to him and the Pragmatists; and it is the same idea that Bergson propagated so seductively shortly before Caird's death. We see the reason, then, why the notion of development or evolution became increasingly important in Caird's philosophy, in his last two writings obviously dominating it. For the same reason he could not pass over the vast philosophy of evolution of his contemporary Spencer without a certain sympathy, however much he was opposed to the greater part of it and to the whole line of British Empiricism of which Spencer was the last considerable representative. He felt a close affinity between the dialectical ascent of the Hegelian categories and Spencer's conception of differentiation and integration, of the continual re-grouping and re-ordering of the elements of things. In his own definition of development we can easily detect the synthesis he sought of Hegel and Spencer, or, to speak more truly, his Hegelianizing of Spencer: "development is a process at once of differentiation and integration, i.e. a process in which difference continually increases, not at the expense of unity but in such a way that the unity also is deepened."[1] Again: "Development is a process which it is difficult to describe in logically consistent language, because in it difference and unity interpenetrate each other so closely and inextricably."[2] His attitude also to Comte and Positivism, which he expounded both in a separate monograph and in a special chapter of his *Evolution of Religion*, has in it a certain sympathy and benevolence. Although he could not accept Positivism as a final view of things, he conceded that it was a step towards one, or part of the foundation. But to Empiricism new as well as old, and to the common-sense philosophy of Reid and Hamilton, he conceded nothing.

Besides the dialectic and the frequent use of its triadic organization of ideas, we also find in Caird Hegel's triumphant optimism concerning our power of cognition, the gnostic boldness of thinking to which no limits can be set and which even dares to tear away the veil of secrecy from the Absolute itself. An unreserved confidence in the powers of reason runs through all his philosophizing and gave him a freshness and vitality which led him to despise the weariness of Scepticism and the resignation of Agnosticism. Mysticism also, with its short cut to the Absolute, was repugnant to him. Where the light of reason illuminates everything the shrouding cloud of Mysticism has no place.

With few exceptions Caird's writings deal with the history of philosophy—his monumental work on Kant (the most thorough, comprehensive, and weighty ever written in English); his small but valuable monograph on Hegel; his luminous critique of Comte; a fairly large work on the Development of the Idea of God in the Greek philosophers; and a few short essays on Dante, Goethe, Rousseau, and Wordsworth, which, with an article on Cartesianism,[3] were collected in his *Essays* (1892). None of these is a mere exercise in erudite reporting; in all of them the subject is measured against the Hegelian doctrine and the treatment charged with the Hegelian spirit.

[1] *Evolution of Religion*, vol. 1, p. 175. [2] Ibid., p. 171.

[3] First published in the ninth edition of the *Encyclopaedia Britannica*, vol. 5, 1876; reprinted in the eleventh edition.

His more systematic writings comprise only a treatise on Metaphysics[1] and his Gifford Lectures on the evolution of religion. These last express his philosophy of religion, of which we must indicate the fundamental ideas.

Like most of the earliest Hegelians, and in particular like his brother John, he aimed at giving a theistic turn to the Hegelian metaphysic and using it in the service of religious faith. Unlike the later Hegelians such as Bradley, Bosanquet, and McTaggart, he was of a deeply religious nature and believed in Christianity as the highest realization of the religious consciousness. Nevertheless, he kept himself aloof from narrow and one-sided orthodoxy, preserving even in religious matters the freedom of thought proper to a true philosopher. Although his philosophy of religion is grounded in and expressed through Hegelian ideas, Spencer's conception of evolution, though given an Hegelian dress, also plays a strong part. He defines religion as the more or less developed consciousness of that infinite unity which lies beyond all the cleavages of the finite, especially its cleavage into subject and object. God is accordingly defined as the principle of unity in all things, and as a self-conscious and self-determining being. He is the Absolute and the Infinite, not, however, in an unknowable transcendence (here Caird is rejecting Max Müller's Infinite as well as Spencer's Unknowable) but lying entirely within the realm of rational knowledge. For an Infinite that is good is not the mere negation of the finite or determinable only negatively as that which transcends the finite, but is the positive presupposition and fulfilment of the finite, and is therefore certainly accessible to thought. Only in the Divine Being do finite things attain true reality and significance as elements in the revelation and self-realization of the supreme principle. Religion is on a higher level what science and philosophy are on a lower level, namely a striving after the universal beyond the particular, or the one beyond the many. Man as a rational being is therefore a religious being. In every rational con-

[1] First published in the ninth edition of the *Encyclopaedia Britannica*, vol. 16, 1883, and reprinted in his *Essays*.

sciousness the idea of God as the ultimate unity of being and knowing is present and operative. Besides the capacity to look outwards in perception of the world about him and inwards in self-knowledge, man has also the capacity to look upwards to the Divine Being which unites the outer and inner worlds and announces itself in both. The religious is essentially the rational; at any rate in its highest form, for when it springs from feeling or from blind faith it has not yet reached the fulfilment of its true Idea, which is possible only at the level of reason. It is the Hegelian reason, here as everywhere in Caird determinant. His religion, therefore, is *pro tanto* a pantheism, however little he willed it. The world is God and God is the world. God is not the transcendent power of the positive religions, not a Beyond, an Other, whom we grasp by faith, but the culmination of a theoretical view of the universe, the highest concept of speculative philosophy. In this wholly rational religion we miss the sense and awe of a Beyond, which Caird, despite his genuine faith, could not cast around his idea of God. His Hegelianism was stronger than his own experience.

Hegelianism determined also his theory of the evolution of religion. The varied forms of religious life revealed in history are steps in the development of the religious Idea, phases the Idea passes through in its process of becoming through times and peoples. Three stages of the religious consciousness are distinguished—the objective, the subjective, and the absolute, corresponding to three stages in the evolution of man, in which he is successively determined by the idea of the object, the idea of the subject, and the idea of God as the uniting principle of these two. Historically regarded, the three stages are represented by polytheism, pantheism, and Christianity respectively. The religion of Jesus is the supreme fulfilment of the religious Idea, the stage in which the religious consciousness comes to itself, the phase in which all other phases are included, absorbed, and sublimated. In basic principle and detail alike Caird here, as elsewhere, was clearly following the great German master, to proclaim whom was the end and meaning of his life.

JOHN CAIRD (1820–98)

[Brother of Edward Caird. Minister of the Church of Scotland. 1862, Professor of Divinity, and 1873, Vice-Chancellor and Principal of Glasgow University. *An Introduction to the Philosophy of Religion*, 1880; *Spinoza*, 1888 (Blackwood's Philosophical Classics), German translation, 1893.

Posthumous: *University Addresses*, 1898; *University Sermons*, 1898; *The Fundamental Ideas of Christianity* (Gifford Lectures), with memoir by E. Caird, 1899.

See *Memoir of Principal Caird*, by C. L. Warr, 1926.]

Edward Caird's much older brother, John, an influential theologian and a powerful preacher, also came forward as an ardent Hegelian in his *Introduction to the Philosophy of Religion*, the most important of his philosophical writings. He even preached Hegelianism from the pulpit, and its penetration into the theological circles of Scotland was doubtless due to him in no small degree. Like his brother he was a brilliant speaker and writer, and had an even greater skill in freeing Hegelian ideas from the armour in which Hegel had encased them and giving them an untechnical and popular expression. In doctrine, too, the brothers were alike. John's philosophy of religion kept wholly to Hegelian lines. It championed the speculative adventure of thought against the agnostic renunciations of Hamilton, Mansel, and Spencer; and, against the empiricist attempt to define religion in terms of its earliest and lowest forms insisted that only by the highest Idea of religion can the worth of any religion be measured. This Idea is prior and fundamental to all the forms in which the religious life has shown itself, so that the history of religion cannot be understood except in the light of it. Such subjective and irrational elements as fear and hope, emotion and superstition, which for Empiricism are essential constituents of religion, fall behind the rational element in value, whatever historical or other importance they may happen to have. The specifically religious capacity is reason. It is not by intensity of feeling but by knowledge and clear insight that the character and nature of religion have to be determined. Here John Caird's rationalism is more pronounced than his brother's.

He rejects the notion of an extramundane God, a God who created and still rules the world from outside it. God is rather the world's most intimate essence, including and penetrating all finite things as the absolute spirit. Man is both a finite being and a participant in the life of God and is therefore a citizen of two worlds, of the spiritual as well as of the natural. Hence the perpetual disquiet and discord of his nature, without parallel in the animal world. This rift in human nature may find a provisional healing in the moral life, but not a final one, for in the moral life we get only the beginning of that extinction of the individual self and identification of our life with an ever-increasing sphere of spiritual life beyond it which nothing but religion can promote and perfect. Religion is the sphere in which the opposition between the natural and the spiritual, the actual and the ideal, has finally disappeared, in which the infinite ideal has ceased to be an unachievable end and become in actuality fulfilled. All Caird's religious thinking aims at the reconciliation and unification of faith and knowledge, religion and philosophy; most of all at the perfecting of the religion of Jesus through Hegelianism. The profound differences between these two were left unnoticed.

In John Watson (*b.* 1847), Professor of Moral Philosophy at Queen's University, Kingston (Canada), we have a disciple of the two Cairds. Like them he was a Scot. His many writings, all published in Glasgow, confine themselves for the most part to the presentation and development of the idealistic outlook and to the exposition of its outstanding German representatives. His systematic works (*Christianity and Idealism*, 1896; *The Philosophic Basis of Religion*, 1907; *The Interpretation of Religious Experience*, 1912, 2 vols., Gifford Lectures), are concerned chiefly with the philosophy of religion, in which, as in the rest, he stands nearer to the Cairds than to anyone else.

WILLIAM WALLACE (1844–97)

[Educated at St. Andrews and Balliol College, Oxford. 1867, Fellow of Merton College, Oxford; 1882–97, Green's successor in Chair of Moral Philosophy, Oxford. *The Logic of Hegel*, translated from the *Encyclopaedia of the Philosophical Sciences*, 1874 (second edition in two vols., 1892–4); *Epicureanism*, 1880; *Kant*, 1882 (Blackwood's Philosophical Classics); *Life of Schopenhauer*, 1890; *Hegel's Philosophy of Mind*, translated from the *Encyclopaedia of the Philosophical Sciences*, with Five Introductory Essays, 1894.

Posthumous: *Lectures and Essays on Natural Theology and Ethics*, edited with biographical introduction by E. Caird, 1898.]

Wallace, another Scotsman, belonged to the early generation of students of Hegel who gathered in the 'sixties round Jowett, Green, and Edward Caird. These teachers, besides largely controlling his philosophical education, helped to determine the direction and content of his later thought. One of the earliest and ablest of the translators and interpreters of Hegel, he played a prominent part through his lectures as well as his writings in the interpretation of German Idealism. The task of making the Hegelian corpus reliably available for English students, only recently finished with a version of the larger *Logic*,[1] began with his translation of the smaller *Logic*, which he followed up much later with the *Philosophy of Mind* (parts 1 and 3 of the *Encyclopädie*). His popular books on Kant and Schopenhauer brought the ideas of these thinkers before a wider circle of readers. He had the rare gift of taking philosophical arguments out of the confusing and pretentious language in which specialists express them and re-expressing them in an easy and pleasing literary style. Although he was one of the most loyal of the disciples of Hegel he never shrank from altering his text to make the meaning clearer. Probably no one smoothed the way as much as Wallace did to the study of Hegel in Britain. He gave Hegel a new dress, which made him more acceptable and intelligible to a nation which dislikes and distrusts heaviness, obscurity, and abstractness of language.

[1] *Hegel's Science of Logic*, translated by Johnston and Struthers, two vols. 1929. Cf. above, p. 255.

But although he followed Hegel on the whole, he had a much too independent mind to feel at home in a tight-laced system. He lacked the speculative urge which many of the Anglo-Hegelians had got from Hegel, choosing rather to examine and clarify a single idea by looking at it from many angles instead of gathering a number of ideas into a system. This comes out strongly in his exegesis of Hegel, which takes the form of extremely acute and lively but often fragmentary and unrelated investigations of particular problems, pursued and tested in every possible way. In consequence, the unity and compactness of Hegel's thought are not made evident enough. Despite, however, his independence and his lack of any desire to establish dogmas, and his acknowledgment that there may be many paths leading to Idealism, his belief in the truth of the idealistic outlook was firm and deep. He felt that the insular narrowness of English philosophy could not be overcome by French "ideologies" or by the shallow notions of the Enlightenment, but only by the more powerful medicine of Idealism in the form it had reached in Germany. "The example of the Germans has served to widen and deepen our ideas of philosophy: to make us think more highly of its function, and to realize that it is essentially science, and the science of supreme reality."[1]

None of the work he himself published is systematic. Such doctrine as he had is known to us only through his posthumously edited lectures and essays, which deal chiefly with ethical, political, and religious philosophy. In the first of these fields his central idea was social co-operation. In the second he favoured a free democracy with marked socialistic tendencies, the State being for him the supreme organization uniting and including all lower forms of social grouping. In the philosophy of religion he stood very near to the two Cairds, more especially to John's speculative interpretation of Christianity. The Incarnation, which he regarded not as a unique historical fact but as an eternal truth, meant for him the

[1] *Prolegomena to the Study of Hegel's Philosophy*, second edition, p. xiii.

visible manifestation of God's immanence in man, of the spiritual in the material, of the eternal in the temporal. Man is neither a mere offshoot of nature, as Materialists will have it, nor a pure child of heaven, as the Platonists say, but the joint product of natural and spiritual factors. But nature and spirit are one and the same reality viewed now from without and then from within. The "potential divinity" which lives in man lifts him above the natural order of which he is a part and gives him mastery over and freedom from it. Thus with Wallace, as with most of the older Hegelians, Idealism issues in Theism and appears as the support and instrument of religion.

DAVID GEORGE RITCHIE (1853–1903)

[Educated at Edinburgh and Balliol College, Oxford. 1878, Fellow of Jesus College, and 1882–6, Tutor of Balliol, Oxford; 1894–1903, Professor of Logic and Metaphysics, St. Andrews. "The Rationality of History", in *Essays in Philosophical Criticism*, edited by A. Seth and R. B. Haldane, 1883; *Darwinism and Politics*, 1889; *Principles of State Interference*, 1891; *Darwin and Hegel, with other Philosophical Studies*, 1893; *Natural Rights*, 1895; *Studies in Political and Social Ethics*, 1902; *Plato*, 1902.

Posthumous: *Philosophical Studies*. Edited with memoir by R. Latta, 1905.]

Ritchie was one of those who owed their conversion to Idealism to personal contact with Green. He received his first philosophical education at the hands of Fraser and Calderwood in Edinburgh, but his thought did not settle in its final direction until he entered the intellectual life of Oxford about the middle of the 'seventies. At the time Arnold Toynbee (1852–83), the economist and social reformer, was active there, and his ardent confession of Socialism, made not only in the lecture-room but also in self-sacrificing service outside it, put before the new generation of students and dons a shining example of social responsibility. In the company of Toynbee and Green, and primarily through them, Ritchie's mind, akin to theirs in temper and ideals, ripened in the direction of the more practical fields of inquiry, such as moral, social, and political philosophy, to which his writings are almost entirely devoted. His primary aim was to illuminate and organize these fields with the categories and principles of the new Idealism. Not that he neglected the problem of a theoretical basis. In this matter he was a much stricter Hegelian than Green. From the latter he received the impetus that led him to Idealism in general, but for the specific content of his own Idealism he went for the most part straight to Hegel himself. This is evident even in his first publication, in which he took up the problem of the "rationality of history", or the possibility of a philosophy of history—a problem rarely approached by the English—and discussed it throughout from a strictly Hegelian point of view; though he never developed the essay afterwards. He was also at pains to clarify philosophically the relation of origin and value, of historical and logical method, and repeatedly pointed out that questions of fact and questions of value should always be kept severely apart, the genetic explanation of a fact being irrelevant to its worth. He regarded this principle as of fundamental importance in all thinking about morality, religion, society, and the State, but applied it chiefly in his criticism of Evolutionism: the Evolutionists, concerned exclusively with the origin of a thing and the temporal sequence of its states, were almost impotent to grasp its significance.

In his logical, epistemological, and ontological views he stood nearer to Absolutism than to the pluralism of Personal Idealism, agreeing very considerably with Bradley's doctrines of the one and the many, the individual and the universal, appearance and reality, degrees of reality, and so forth. In his theory of the State he opposed the prevalent individualism of the native school. For him the State is an organic whole, entitled to primacy over society and individuals and to interfere extensively with the affairs of the latter. Though subscribing to a democratic form of government he was not blind to the weakness of liberal parliamentarianism and of universal suffrage, and demanded that responsible statesmen should be chosen by the aristocratic standard of integrity and ability. On other details he shared Green's strong leaning to Socialism, grounding it, of course, not on any utilitarian ethic but on the principle of man's moral worth, and deriving it from the idealistic doctrine of the social self and this self's responsibility to the community. His message was not welfare and happiness, but social temper and social action.

Since, as is obvious, Ritchie's thinking moved almost entirely within the problems and solutions typical of British Hegelianism, the preceding sketch might suffice. But a further matter must be noted because it marks a departure from type. From the first the idealistic school had vehemently attacked Darwinism and the systems based on this; Stirling's work on Hegel had given the word for the attack, and many of those who followed him regarded the defeat of Darwinism as their specific duty to their time and country. Ritchie's essay "Darwin and Hegel",[1] in which he brought the two protagonists together, created something like a sensation in philosophical circles. The daring attempt to exhibit an intrinsic relation between the biological and the Hegelian ideas of evolution and thus to incorporate Darwinism in the system of Idealism was naturally condemned to failure from the start. Ritchie's particular problem was the theory of natural selection, which he tried to connect with Hegel's theory of the rationality of the real. The survival of the fittest means that only that is actual or real which has a certain value, that is, a certain measure of rationality; and the extinction of the weaker corresponds to the supersession of the negative factor in the Hegelian dialectic. Without a doubt Ritchie's attempt to harmonize the two most powerful intellectual forces of the century went very wide of the mark. His interest in Darwin, however, gave him a true insight into one point. He saw that the application of biological categories to the social life of man cannot be made without a critical consideration of the specific relations that hold in the new sphere. However useful or significant the application of the principle of selection may be, we have to remember that in

[1] First printed in *Proceedings of the Aristotelian Society*, vol. 1, 1891, and reprinted 1893 in his book with the same title.

human society there is no simple struggle for existence such as we see in the animal world, but a quite different and much more complexly conditioned struggle. The analogues in the human sphere of the biological principle are industrial and commercial competition, the technological organization of the conditions of living, social conditions, education, and such-like. Social evolution rests on co-operation, not on the extermination of the weaker by the stronger. Along this line Ritchie rose above the naturalistic to what he called an idealistic evolutionism, and by this, taken in the large, made a much more fruitful contribution to subsequent thought than by his particular attempt to expand Idealism through the unnatural linkage of Hegelian and Darwinian argumentation.

SIR HENRY JONES (1852–1922)

[Educated in Wales and at Glasgow University under E. Caird; 1883, Lecturer in Philosophy, Aberystwyth; 1884, Professor of Philosophy, Bangor; 1891, Professor of Logic and English, St. Andrews; 1894, succeeded E. Caird in Chair of Moral Philosophy, Glasgow. "The Social Organism", in *Essays in Philosophical Criticism*, edited by A. Seth and R. B. Haldane, 1883; *Browning as a Philosophical and Religious Teacher*, 1891; *A Critical Account of the Philosophy of Lotze*, 1895; *Idealism as a Practical Creed*, 1909; *The Working Faith of a Social Reformer*, 1910; *Social Powers*, 1913; *The Principles of Citizenship*, 1919; *The Life and Philosophy of E. Caird* (in collaboration with J. H. Muirhead), 1921; *A Faith that Enquires* (Gifford Lectures), 1922.

See *Old Memories* (autobiography), 1922; *Life and Letters of Sir Henry Jones*, by H. J. W. Hetherington, 1924; "Memoir", by J. H. Muirhead, in *Proc. Brit. Acad.*, vol. x; *Dictionary of National Biography*, 1922–30.]

Jones's philosophy, in so far as it had any definite content, was Hegelian Idealism in the form given to it by Caird. The moment when, as a young student come to Glasgow from Wales, he sat at the feet of this great teacher, he became a convert to the new movement and threw himself into it with the full vigour of his enthusiastic nature. All his life he remained a true disciple of Caird, to whom he owed almost everything. Well aware that he was not an original thinker, he regarded himself as the steward and guardian of a precious treasure, the idealistic outlook on all things, which he had to make known and inculcate in as many minds as possible. Idealism was the one philosophical certainty, to be preserved inviolate, though its foundations might be widened and its content fruitfully applied to more and more fields of human activity. To effect this widening and application was the task Jones set himself, a task he achieved best in religious, social, and political philosophy.

Probably no one has preached Idealism with a more daring abandonment and passion and a more genuine enthusiasm than Jones. He was less concerned with demonstration than with eloquent pleading and living conviction, all philosophy being for him an attitude to life and a spiritual dynamic rather than a system of theoretical doctrine. What Caird had worked out and won through laborious and technically rigorous thinking he seized in the warmth of direct personal experience, changing it from investigation into faith, from doctrine into feeling, not infrequently into *Schwärmerei*. Idealism was a part of practical living, a confession of faith, a gospel, something he lived in and believed in and announced as the one thing needful. In a word, in Jones Hegelianism became emotional. He is its prophet and apostle, and bore it like a missionary to the farthest frontier of the Empire when in 1908 he gave by invitation a course of lectures in the University of Sydney on "Idealism as a Practical Creed", an occasion not unlike Hegel's famous inaugural lecture at Heidelberg in 1816.

It is not surprising, then, that he sought the distinctive content of idealistic philosophy outside professedly philosophical works, and found it in the moral note in man's practical activities, in the confession of a religion (especially of the Christian religion), and most of all in the creative and sustaining factor of great works of literature. Poets express in beautiful form what philosophers put in the language of abstract concepts. Jones accordingly drew freely for the confirmation and reinforcement of his doctrine from the great literary artists:

Lessing and Goethe, Wordsworth and Browning declared in their own way the view of the universe conceptually expressed in the philosophy of Kant, Fichte, Hegel, and their English followers. In Browning's poetry in particular he discerned a lofty expression of idealistic sentiment and purpose, and described him, in an admirable book devoted wholly to him, as a genuinely "philosophical and religious teacher". For the same reasons he felt a close affinity with Carlyle, whose prophetic disposition and passionate eloquence found in Jones a new embodiment.

Into the content of his philosophical teaching we do not need to enter in detail, since it scarcely went beyond that of the older Hegelians whom we have already considered. In him we meet again, cleverly rehandled, all the familiar items of doctrine—the correlativity of thought and being, of the ideal and the real, of the spiritual and the natural; the reconciliation of opposites in the superior and all-comprehending unity of the Whole; the spiritual structure of the universe; the extirpation of all dualisms as false abstractions; the explaining away of the contingent and irrational; the idea of coherent system; the absolute with all its characteristic qualities and functions; the immanence of God in nature and man, the identification of Him with the absolute; the personality of God; the fulfilment of morality in religion; facile metaphysical optimism; and so forth.

It only remains to be noted that in Jones the difference between the earlier and later tendencies of the Hegelian school become more evident and more acute. Again and again he felt himself obliged to criticize Bradley's and Bosanquet's distortions and falsifications of orthodox Hegelianism. Against Bosanquet in particular he repeatedly and very sharply distinguished his own position. The chief point of difference lay in the opposition of Monism and Dualism. The position taken up by Bradley and Bosanquet can certainly be described as in a way monistic, but from the point of view of those like Caird and Jones who pressed the demand for unity to its ultimate consequences it appeared plainly to be a dualism. Jones therefore set about a veritable hunt for the dualities in Bradley and even more in Bosanquet, the dualities of appearance and reality, of finite and infinite, of relative and absolute, most of all the duality that sundered human nature in twain. For Jones man has no need to pass out of himself to reach the ideal; no transformation of his self by absorption into the absolute is required, for then his self would be annihilated. Rather must he become himself, realize the possibilities latent in him, and then he has already grasped the infinite, indeed *is* the infinite in its process of becoming. Jones thus substituted for Bosanquet's self-transcendence, self-realization and self-perfection. Similarly he held that the absolute is not a state in which all movement is brought to quiescence and which rests in itself blessed for ever, but a dynamic and eternally advancing process, in which time is a real factor, not a mere appearance. Here we have a contrast between Jones's activistic and pragmatic disposition, which often reminds one of Fichte, and the more contemplative and quietist attitude of the Absolutists.

There was one further point of difference. Jones thought he detected in the subjectivistic, almost solipsistic, epistemology of Bradley and others, and the subtilizing or evaporation of reality that followed from it, a grave symptom of disease, which he set himself to combat; and as he held Lotze, whose influence in English thought was very extensive, responsible for the origination of the disease, he devoted to the criticism of Lotze's theory a special work which is one of the best of his writings. His contention was that neither subjectivism nor objectivism gives a satisfactory solution of the main problem of the theory of knowledge. Mind is not independent of objects or objects independent of mind; what we have in knowledge is the movement of an objective and real world in the medium of thought. Instead of conceiving knowing as an attempt to catch reality in a net of presentations and concepts we have to conceive reality as an active principle that unveils itself to us in the process of thinking. Subject and object, thought and reality, do not need to be brought together; they are together from the beginning, as the two poles within which what we call our world lies. The ideal and the real are not two separate worlds but inseparable elements within a single universe. Jones's thought is thus dominated by the monistic idea.

JOHN HENRY MUIRHEAD (*b.* 1855)

[Educated at Glasgow and Balliol College, Oxford. After various university posts, Professor of Philosophy and Political Economy, Birmingham, 1897–1921 (retired). *The Elements of Ethics*, 1892 (fourth edition 1932); *Chapters from Aristotle's Ethics*, 1900; *Philosophy and Life and other Essays*, 1902; *The Service of the State*, 1908; *German Philosophy in Relation to the War*, 1915; *Social Purpose* (in collaboration with H. J. W. Hetherington), 1918; *The Life and Philosophy of Edward Caird* (in collaboration with Sir Henry Jones), 1921; "Past and Present in Contemporary Philosophy", in *Contemporary British Philosophy*, first series, 1924 (of this and the second series Muirhead was editor); *The Use of Philosophy*, 1928; *Coleridge as Philosopher*, 1930; *The Platonic Tradition in Anglo-Saxon Philosophy*, 1931; *Rule and End in Morals*, 1932; *Bernard Bosanquet and His Friends*, 1935.]

Muirhead's philosophical origins go back to the older generation of Hegelians. He received his education at the two centres of the movement, Glasgow and Balliol College, Oxford, studying under Caird and Green respectively, who together gave his thinking its special stamp and determined the direction it afterwards followed. From Caird he took over Hegelianism in the form it assumed under the original British Hegelians of the 'seventies; Green was responsible rather for his interest in its application to the problems of ordinary life. His systematic works deal chiefly with problems of morality and social and political life, the more purely theoretical branches of philosophy being treated only occasionally and even then more with reference to the practical branches than out of any interest in them for their own sake. So far as the theoretical grounds of his thought are concerned, he is in virtually complete agreement with the philosophy of his teacher Caird, which he has indeed tried to widen, but not to alter.

But although Muirhead has not introduced any really new

feature into British Idealism, he occupies among the men who have acted as stewards of the legacy of Caird and Green an outstanding position. He has kept the very impulse that originated the movement alive and fresh to the present day, carrying it through a changing atmosphere into a time when philosophy is being moved by influences from very different quarters, and when Idealism itself, almost but not quite extinct, has variously and deeply modified its original character. He remains as one of the very few survivors of the memorable days when British thought entered on a new stage of its development.

But he has not preserved Idealism as a dead tradition, to be given dogmatic fixity. His special service and merit lie in his having been always mindful to retain its vital and productive virtue by adapting it to the changed circumstances of the time. He has consequently thought his way into the more recent problems and attitudes, and has tried to expand the older forms and doctrines as far as possible to make them receptive of so much as is true in the new ideas. This disposition is exemplified in the mediating attitude he has adopted in the ethical controversies of his time. For Hedonism the end and criterion of moral action is pleasure. Eudaemonism makes an important correction by declaring that the *summum bonum* is not pleasure but happiness, not a mere aggregate of feelings each regarded as independent of the rest, but these feelings bent to the service of a whole that transcends any particular self. Not that Eudaemonism can give a satisfactory solution of the ethical problem, but, Muirhead argues, it is a salutary counterweight to that other theory, the ethic of duty, which lays an equally one-sided stress on the rational element of human nature. The ethic of duty for duty's sake subjects the moral life to a merely formal and abstract law, and thereby robs it of everything that is dear and precious to us. Duty is never duty *in abstracto* or utterly absolute, but always refers to a determinate object of human interest. The ideal of a world in which every act is deliberately directed against our desires and interests, and the ideal of a world without a sense of duty at all, are equally repellent. Muirhead accordingly defines morality as free obedience to a law that man, as a self-conscious unity, imposes on the many and various subordinate elements of his nature. In addition Muirhead has attempted to make the idea of evolution, like the idea of happiness, fruitful in ethics, though he has, of course, opposed the moral theories of the Evolutionists. The fact that moral standards change with time and place does not mean that for moral actions there is no universal norm. What evolution exhibits is rather that the factual differences of moral judgment presuppose a single evaluating principle from which they derive their normative intention, and that the various standards are to be regarded as stages in the development and self-realization of a single moral ideal. From this point of view the different standards of the past and present can be ranged in an ascending order of value, from which the degree of moral advance can be read off.

The undogmatic and receptive character of Muirhead's Idealism has enabled him also to smooth down the opposition between the earlier and later expressions of the idealistic movement, to gather the forces of Idealism into a common direction and thus to enrich the common stock of the school with valuable ideas taken from the many and varied absolutistic and personalistic systems which the movement produced. With his "open system" he has also been able to keep pace with and to some extent absorb the anti-idealistic currents of Pragmatism and Realism which set in about the turn of the century. He has recognized the justice of the Pragmatists' reproach that Hegelianism, especially in its absolutistic form, excessively neglected the conative and purposive element of experience and set a rigid Idea above a supple and living ideal. Idealism, he says, can accept this criticism, and when it has done so there remains no opposition between it and a rational pragmatism. And in the presence of such movements as the new Realism, suggested by natural science and bringing philosophical reflection to bear upon its results, he has admitted that Idealism must accommodate itself to scientific thought. The world-view that had done so much for the philosophy of mind could not be allowed any longer to renounce or neglect the philosophy of nature, and the intellectual culture of Idealists must accordingly be given a wider basis; for only in this way will Idealism as a philosophy be able to keep itself alive amid the burning questions of the new age, and enter as an equal partner into the agreement which is being prepared between physics and metaphysics and which is likely to determine the future course of thought. Muirhead has, as it were, summoned philosophers to sink the differences that divide schools and systems, and has given the summons a practical form in the *Library of Philosophy*, edited by him, a series of volumes by contemporary thinkers, foreign as well as native, of the most different shades of thought, and also in his *Contemporary British Philosophy* (corresponding to the German *Selbstdarstellungen*), in which for the first time the many and varied representatives of present-day philosophy in Britain have come together to give personal summaries of their views.

Finally, Muirhead has made a distinguished contribution to the history of the idealistic movement. Placing the movement in a wider intellectual setting, he has sought to understand its origin and development as well as its total significance. He traces what he calls the "Platonic tradition in Anglo-Saxon philosophy" to its very beginnings and exhibits, in opposition to the usual accounts, a unitary and uninterrupted stream of idealistic thought, flowing, if only at times as an undercurrent, through the entire history of British philosophy;[1] and shows how the XIXth-Century renewal under the influence of Germany was being prepared for on English soil long before its obvious outburst, firstly through the romantic poetry of Shelley, Keats, Wordsworth, and Coleridge (on the last of these Muirhead has written a very penetrating monograph), then through the literature of such Victorians as Carlyle, Emerson, Tennyson, Browning, and Arnold, and finally through the general change in ideas and institutions which marked the latter half of the century. Having been an eye-witness of the outburst of the movement in the 'seventies, and an active

[1] On this view see above, p. 237.

participant in it ever since, Muirhead was better fitted than anyone else to look back upon it in the eventide of his long life, see it as a whole, and disclose to the younger generation both the story of its development and the riches of its doctrinal content.

JOHN STUART MACKENZIE (1860–1935)

[Educated at Glasgow, Cambridge, and Berlin. 1890, Fellow of Trinity College, Cambridge. 1895, Professor of Logic and Philosophy, Cardiff; retired 1915. *An Introduction to Social Philosophy*, 1890, replaced by *Outlines of Social Philosophy*, 1918 (second edition, 1921); *Manual of Ethics*, 1893 (sixth edition, 1929); *Outlines of Metaphysics*, 1902 (third edition, 1929); *Lectures on Humanism*, 1907; *Elements of Constructive Philosophy*, 1917; *Ultimate Values in the Light of Contemporary Thought*, 1924; "Constructive Philosophy", in *Contemporary British Philosophy*, edited by J. H. Muirhead, first series, 1924; *Fundamental Problems of Life*, 1928; *Cosmic Problems*, 1931.

Posthumous: *John Stuart Mackenzie*, autobiography edited by his wife, 1936.

See "John Stuart Mackenzie", by J. H. Muirhead, *Proc. Brit. Acad.*, 1936.]

Like Jones and Muirhead, Mackenzie was one of those who owed their early interest in philosophy to Edward Caird. To the end he remained loyal to his great teacher, confessing himself in his last work as "a humble follower of the line of idealistic speculation in which I consider my earliest teacher, Edward Caird, to have been, on the whole, the safest guide".[1] His first work dealt with social philosophy, his next with ethics; in his later years he occupied himself chiefly with the major problems of metaphysics and, in connection with these, the problem of values. In common with most Hegelians he had little interest in epistemology and psychology, and logic also he neglected.

Metaphysics he defines as "the methodical study which seeks to take a comprehensive view of experience, with the

[1] *Cosmic Problems*, p. vi.

view of understanding it as a systematic whole".[1] By experience he here means the universe as such or reality as a whole, which he calls the Cosmos, of which the spatio-temporal universe is a partial and one-sided aspect. As the designation Cosmos indicates, he makes the idea of order essential. The world that is familiar to us is far from having the perfect order that constitutes a cosmos; on the other hand, it cannot be regarded as a mere chaos, since it contains a considerable degree of order, and since the factors that make for order on the whole predominate over those that make for disorder. This being so, we are justified in making the assumption that our own world is but part of a larger whole which has the perfect order of a cosmos. Examples of the factors that make for disorder are the accidental and the changeful; more importantly, misfortune, suffering, pain, and evil. The existence of evil in our world is the chief obstacle to belief in the perfect harmony of a cosmos, and it cannot be denied that from our limited point of view "something of the nature of evil" necessarily remains; but this does not contradict the supposition that from the point of view of the whole there may be entire harmony. In the following passage Mackenzie states these ideas with great conciseness: "The apparent contingency, change, and evil that we find in the universe as we know it, might all be regarded as compatible with the reality of a perfect order, if we could suppose that the whole is in its essence spiritual, that it realizes itself through a process of change, involving in its initial stages a certain lack of order and consequent appearance of contingency and evil, but advancing by degrees to a complete unity, in which the process is eternally and consciously retained."[2]

The distinction of the Cosmos and the spatio-temporal universe implies that the former is infinite and the latter finite, and Mackenzie saw in the newer physics a confirmation of the second of these. These very general ideas, "necessarily of a highly speculative character",[3] are developed and supported

[1] *Outlines of Metaphysics*, third edition (1929), p. 11.

[2] *Elements of Constructive Philosophy*, p. 392.

[3] *Contemporary British Philosophy*, edited by Muirhead, vol. 1, p. 242.

in a detailed account of the special kinds of order and their relations to each other—the spatial, temporal, qualitative, and causal orders, and the orders of consciousness, of value, of the logical, of the ethical, and so on. This part of his theory corresponds roughly to the doctrine of the categories.

In his latest metaphysical speculations Mackenzie emphasized much more than in his earlier ones the positive nature of the accidental and the contingent. He had fallen under the influence of certain ideas of F. C. S. Schiller and D. Fawcett.[1] He now postulated as the ultimate ground of things a creative intelligence, conceived not as an individual person but as a universal mind, which reveals and expresses itself in finite minds. This, it is obvious, is the Absolute of the Hegelians, no longer, however, static and remote and changeless as with Bradley, but moving with a creative impulse in the world-process, as with Fawcett. A corresponding shift in his point of view leads him to put imagination alongside reason, and connected with it as an important philosophical faculty. Clearly, Mackenzie is here forging a false alliance, for between Hegelianism and the philosophical fantasies of Fawcett there is nothing in common. In other places, too, we find him breaking up the hitherto consistent structure of Hegelianism by assimilating to it heterogeneous ideas taken from the latest currents of English thought.

The same tendency shows itself in Mackenzie's ethics, which he worked out with care and detail in an admirable manual.

[1] Muirhead, in his admirable memoir of Mackenzie (*Proceedings of the British Academy*, 1936), thinks that the idea of the world as a creature of imagination had been conceived by Mackenzie long before it was developed by Fawcett. This is confirmed by certain passages in which Mackenzie attributes the idea to Edward Caird (*Outlines of Metaphysics*, third edition, preface, and *Cosmic Problems*, p. 45). Still, I think it is right to say that the increased emphasis he laid on creative imagination, together with his attachment to the idea of contingency, in his later writings was consequent upon the influence of James, Schiller, and Fawcett, especially the last. Mackenzie seems to admit so much in the two passages just referred to. It remains true, of course, that between him and Fawcett there are very important points of difference.

In its original form it rejected Kant's formalism and rigorism, expounded the moral ideal as the realization of the rational self, and regarded the idea of the good as the highest of all values. These, of course, are the leading ethical ideas of the older school of Hegelians. Later, however, Mackenzie's ethic, under the influence of G. E. Moore and others, underwent a marked change, which carried it far from its starting-point. The good ceased to be the supreme value and became simply one value among others, along with truth and beauty. Indeed, Mackenzie was inclined to give the highest place to the last of these. This sprang from his increasing tendency to round off his system, from an aesthetic desire to articulate all philosophical problems into a perfect order.

Two of Mackenzie's books are devoted wholly to social philosophy. His leading idea is co-operative creation as the essential foundation of social life in all its forms, the subjugation of the animal impulses in our make-up, and the development of our rational and spiritual nature; to which correspond three aspects or functions of the State, the economic, the political or legislative, and the educative or spiritual. Mackenzie was here influenced by Steiner's conception of an organism with three members. He refused to accept the national State as either the sole or the supreme form of communal organization, advocating instead a single brotherhood embracing all nations. There is an obvious connection between this Cosmopolitanism and his metaphysical Cosmism.

As we have indicated, what is characteristic in Mackenzie is his breaking up the hard soil of the older Hegelian school and his increasing receptivity to new, even the most recent, ideas. The generous openness of his mind, the unfixed and undoctrinaire manner of his philosophizing, the cautious disposition that kept him from any claims to finality, specially fitted him to act as mediator among different currents of thought, and signify the extent to which British Hegelianism had freed itself from even the modest rigour and fixity of dogma it early acquired. He is the clearest example of what Bosanquet called "the meeting of extremes in contemporary philosophy", and his own epigram that in philosophy all dogma is heresy is the best summary of his attitude. From all quarters he took in new ideas, weighed and tested them, and retained the best. But he did not by any means succeed in fusing the new into the old. How could he when the new comprised such heterogeneous matters as Fawcett's soaring fantasies, the finical and over-subtle analysis of Moore, the activism of the Pragmatists, the emergent Evolutionism of Alexander, the dry Mysticism of McTaggart, and the scientific exactitudes of the newer physics? All these cannot be brought under a single roof. Hence the general impression we get of eclecticism, of a certain weariness of thought, and of indecision, which accounts for the fact that Mackenzie never comes to grips with his problems and lets them drag him along instead of dominating them himself. All which was due to a superabundance of knowledge, and an excess of conciliatoriness which desired to do justice to everything and to assimilate whatever was true and honourable and of good report. Mackenzie was thus a refined and lovable rather than a strong and determined thinker.

RICHARD BURDON HALDANE (1856–1928)
(FIRST VISCOUNT HALDANE OF CLOAN)

[Educated at Edinburgh and Göttingen. 1912–15 and 1924 Lord Chancellor; 1911 created Viscount. "The Relation of Philosophy to Science", in *Essays in Philosophical Criticism*, edited by A. Seth and R. B. Haldane, 1883; *The Pathway to Reality*, two vols., 1903–4; *The Reign of Relativity*, 1921 (fourth edition, 1922); *The Philosophy of Humanism and other Subjects*, 1922; "The Function of Metaphysics in Scientific Method", in *Contemporary British Philosophy*, edited by J. H. Muirhead, first series, 1924; *Human Experience*, 1926; *An Autobiography*, 1929, German translation 1930; Also translation, with J. Kemp, of Schopenhauer's *World as Will and Idea*, 1883–6.]

Although Lord Haldane's philosophical work formed but a small part of his astonishingly able and many-sided achievements—as jurist, parliamentarian, statesman, university reformer, philosopher, writer—we are forced to regard it as the centre of his life, of which all his other activities were radiations. He himself tells us, in his *Autobiography*, that his philosophical Idealism accompanied him in all his practical activities, that he really lived it and injected it into every aspect of his varied life. Of the British Hegelians of his generation he was the frankest in admiration, and the most loyal in discipleship, of the great German thinker, taking over his doctrine almost entire. The most ardent confessions of Hegelianism in the English language, outside Stirling, are to be found in his writings. "All that is in these lectures I have either taken or adapted from Hegel. . . . No one else has so much to tell to the searcher after truth": Hegel is "the greatest master of speculative method that the world has seen since the days of Aristotle".[1] And scarcely any other of the school could have said so unreservedly of himself: "I am content to say that I am a Hegelian and wish to be called so."[2] In addition he had a profound comprehension of and sympathy with German life and culture generally: none of his British contemporaries exceeded him in this respect, and only a few approached him in width of training and in mental grasp. Alongside Hegel his chief veneration went to the deep but clear wisdom of Goethe, and these two, the great philosopher and the great poet, were the guiding stars of his life; he had their portraits reproduced in his *Pathway to Reality*. In philosophy, next to Hegel he owed most to Aristotle, and always considered his own thought to be in the grand idealistic tradition which runs from the early Greeks through Plato and Aristotle to Kant, Hegel, and Lotze. While he was a student at Göttingen, at the age of seventeen, he met Lotze, who quickened his interest in philosophy and whose fascinating personality influenced him deeply for the rest of his life. Slightly earlier, at Edinburgh, he became acquainted with Stirling, and with the writings of Green and Caird, which, he testifies, "impelled me in the direction of Idealism".[3]

[1] *Pathway to Reality*, one volume edition, 1926, pp. 309, 310, 311.
[2] Ibid., p. 407.
[3] *Autobiography*, p. 7.

As we should expect with a man of such mental width, Haldane drew for the enrichment of philosophy on practical life and art, on religion, and on poetry and science. In this respect a spiritual kinsman of Hegel, he even exceeded the latter by his close interest in the natural sciences and by his incorporation of their results in his system, his aim being to renew Hegelianism with the help of the added and more accurate knowledge that had become available since Hegel's time. The zeal and understanding with which this widely busy man even in advanced years tried to penetrate the secrets of the new physics, especially the Theory of Relativity, and bring its principles to bear on philosophical problems, are astonishing. Relativity was one of his central ideas, which he argued out on purely philosophical grounds before the publication of Einstein's theory, in his *Pathway to Reality* (1903–4). Seeing later what he took to be its confirmation in Einstein's theory, he elaborated it further, chiefly in his *Reign of Relativity*. Reality is one, but its oneness or totality is not at first evident to the human mind, which sees only partial aspects of it and considers these in their particular structure and manner of being from a particular point of view. The point of view of the physicist is different from that of the biologist, and this from that of the philosopher. The physicist's knowledge is therefore as partial as the realm of objects he studies, and his categories cannot be extended to the biological realm. Every particular point of view is merely relative when considered in the light of reality in its wholeness. This, roughly, is the general and purely philosophical principle of relativity, of which, according to Haldane, Einstein's principle is only a special application. This position may be called relationism, to distinguish it from the position commonly called relativism, with which it has nothing in common.

The principle of relativity demands an intimate connection between philosophy and the special sciences, between the total aspect and the partial aspects, and Haldane made the demand explicit in his earliest philosophical essay (*The Relation of Philosophy to Science*), in which almost all the important ideas of his later thought appear. The law of relativity is at bottom the same as Hegel's dictum that truth is the whole. The special points of view of the sciences are certainly preserved in the whole of knowledge, but it is just as important to add that only within this do they have their place and enter into relation with one another. To make any partial aspect absolute, to hypostatize any department of knowledge into something independent of the other departments and of the whole, would contradict the principle of the totality of truth and the unity of reality. In its ultimate essence reality is spirit, which at the several levels of being and knowing is conceiving only itself and coming to itself, passing through the dialectical process of its self-apprehension. It is the concrete whole, the identity of knowing and being, of truth and reality.

All this involves the idea of the concrete universal, which plays as important a part in Haldane as in other Hegelians. It stands for the essence of thought and embraces the specificities of its factors, that is, the merely general and the merely particular, which in isolation are as utterly abstract as the subjective and objective taken separately. The idea of the concreteness of thought means the fusion of its one-sided and arbitrarily abstracted aspects; the one-sidedness being overcome through thought's dynamic or dialectical activity, which advances from aspect to aspect until, in a concrete whole that holds them all, it reaches truth.

Everywhere Haldane's fundamental ideas are Hegelian. His view that everything real is instinct with meaning from the beginning, that meaning is of the essence of reality, is of course Hegel's rationality of the real once more. Again, reality is conditioned by relation to thought, is possible only within knowledge. Epistemologically this is the Hegelian doctrine that thought has no limits which it does not itself set and cannot surmount. Finally, for Haldane as for Hegel, philosophy as the coming to self-consciousness and self-realization of the absolute spirit is possible only as system; and in the second volume of his *Pathway to Reality* he lays its foundations, displaying the several aspects of spirit in both the finite and the absolute stages of its development.

Viewed as a whole Haldane's position may be described as a wedding of Hegelianism with the Theory of Relativity, or, better, as an enrichment of the former by the latter. In this independent renewal of itself in a special field of knowledge so alien to it as the new theoretical physics, the Hegelian philosophy gives another sign of its unfailing productivity; since, for Haldane, Einstein's theory is simply an admission that Hegel's fundamental principle is the true principle of all science whatever, the knowledge recently brought to light being simply a new illustration and enrichment of the doctrinal framework laid down by Hegel.

SIR JAMES BLACK BAILLIE (*b.* 1872)

[Educated at Edinburgh and Trinity College, Cambridge. 1902–24, Professor of Moral Philosophy, Aberdeen; 1924, Vice-Chancellor of Leeds University; knighted 1931. *The Origin and Significance of Hegel's Logic*, 1901; *An Outline of the Idealistic Construction of Experience*, 1906; *Hegel's Phenomenology of Mind* (translation), two vols., 1910 (second edition, in one vol., 1931); *Studies in Human Nature*, 1921; "The Individual and His World", in *Contemporary British Philosophy*, edited by J. H. Muirhead, first series, 1924.]

Baillie's pre-war writings are in the tradition of British Hegelianism; it was said of him, indeed, that he was "in many respects the most orthodox of present-day Hegelians".[1] His later writings, under the shock of the war, follow a quite different direction. His philosophical work, therefore, falls into two distinct and to some extent opposed parts.

He has ranged himself with Hegel not only as an expositor and translator—in two valuable books he did much to promote Hegelian studies in Britain—but also in his first systematic work. This, the *Outline of the Idealistic Construction of Experience*, though independent in the working out of detail, is essentially little more than a free paraphrase of the leading

[1] Hoernlé in *Mind*, vol. 16 (1907), p. 549.

ideas of Hegel's *Phenomenology of Mind*, which Baillie held to be "the great masterpiece of idealistic reflection in modern philosophy". In close dependence on Hegel's book it exhibits the way in which human experience rises from stage to stage, at each higher stage developing further and richer structures, until at the level of self-consciousness it attains the oneness of subject and object in which the lower levels of sense, perception, and understanding transcend themselves and achieve their highest unity. Here Hegel's dialectic, usually neglected in British Hegelianism, is done full justice to, the Idea appearing not as a rigid or static principle, as in Green, Bradley, Bosanquet, and others, but as a living and dialectically advancing process. This merely imitative renewing of Hegel's thought was a generation too late, in the sense that it came when the Hegelian movement in Britain had passed far beyond the letter of Hegel to independent construction.

There is scarcely any connection of ideas between the absolute Idealism of the earlier work and the utterly different position that meets us in his post-war *Studies in Human Nature*. The chief reason of the remarkable change is undoubtedly a deeply felt experience of the tragedy and meaninglessness of the World War, in face of which, with its immense chaos and destruction of human relations, belief in the Hegelian world-reason was so deeply shaken as to be no longer susceptible of justification. Baillie therefore turned away to the investigation of human nature. We may say that he passed backwards from Hegel to Hume, in that he now made the concrete individuality of man his central philosophical interest. Points of contact with Hume do in fact appear; for example, strong emphasis on the non-rational factors in thinking and knowing, and an entirely anthropocentric and anthropomorphic conception of all philosophical problems. For Baillie philosophy is now no longer the search for universal truth or the coming to self-consciousness of reason, but an entirely personal affair of each thinker, directed chiefly to the satisfaction of his individual theoretical needs; it is the search for the highest degree of satisfaction that thinking can give to an individual. The sole end of truth is to bring man's mind to harmony and peace. The consequence of this doctrine, which shows in addition a pronounced pragmatistic strain, is a complete subjectivizing, individualizing, and psychologizing of thought, a radical reversion, that is, of the absolute Idealism which Baillie had formerly, and with deep conviction, stood for. Science, too, is similarly viewed anthropomorphically, as a human invention expressing an urgent human activity. This last phase of his teaching, in which he burns almost all the bridges from his own philosophical past, thus comes to rest in the native tradition of thought. It is the only example of such a development, and was determined not by intrinsic considerations but by external circumstances.

JOHN ALEXANDER SMITH (*b.* 1863)

[Educated at Edinburgh and Balliol College, Oxford. 1896–1910, Lecturer in Philosophy, Balliol College; 1910, Waynflete Professor of Moral and Metaphysical Philosophy, Oxford; retired 1935. *Knowing and Acting*, Inaugural Lecture, 1910; "Philosophy and Progress as an Ideal of Action", in *Progress and History*, edited by F. S. Marvin, 1920; *The Nature of Art*, 1924; "Philosophy as the Development of the Notion and Reality of Self-Consciousness", in *Contemporary British Philosophy*, edited by J. H. Muirhead, second series, 1925; Editor, with W. D. Ross, of the *Oxford Translation of Aristotle*, eleven vols., 1908–31; translated *De Anima* in this series, 1931.]

We cannot without incompleteness pass over J. A. Smith, with whom the line of Hegelians closes. Like so many of his predecessors he was trained at Oxford, and at the college from which the movement sprang, where he came early into personal contact with its outstanding representatives, Jowett, Edward Caird, and Nettleship, the last being his tutor. The Hegelian stock of ideas came to him also, though in a less faithful form, through Bradley and Bosanquet. At the same time, however, following the Oxford tradition, he immersed himself in the study of the Greek writers, devoting to Aristotle prolonged and intensive research. For many years he has been known as one of the leading Aristotelian scholars in Britain.

and as such shared in the editorship of the important Oxford translation of Aristotle, which was completed in 1931 with his own version of the *De Anima*. The fulfilment of this task, and his considerable influence as a teacher, are his chief contributions to philosophical inquiry.

In comparison with this his own philosophy is unimportant, and it is difficult, in view of the sparseness of his writings, to give a just picture of it. It underwent too many oscillations and changes to enable us to bring it under any single designation. Its lack of fixity is, indeed, its most striking mark. Smith himself throws much light on this in his personal statement of his philosophical development in *Contemporary British Philosophy*. Here, with a candour amounting to *naïveté*, he makes the singular confession that only when he was appointed to a chair of philosophy—one of the most important in the country—did he come to realize the necessity of thinking out a system. A happy accident came to his aid, the lighting on Croce's works during a stay in Naples. From that time onwards he felt it his task to ally himself with the doctrine of the Italian Hegelians (with Gentile as well as Croce) and secure its recognition in Great Britain. His efforts resulted, in the years immediately following the war, in something approaching a vogue for Croce,[1] especially in Oxford (where it was quickened by a visit from Croce himself), but this soon died down. In several of his own writings he identified himself with a kind of Crocean idealism, with some strands from Gentile, and thereby, at least for a time, found something like a position of his own.

The basic idea of this Idealism, which he unfolded chiefly in his *Philosophy as the Development of the Notion and Reality of Self-Consciousness*, is to be found in his doctrine of the historical character of reality. According to this, reality in its essence is not static and immovable but dynamic and change-

[1] Bosanquet and Wildon Carr also tried in the post-war years to bring British philosophy into relation with that of the Italians. On the efforts of the former I can now refer to *Bosanquet and his Friends*, edited by J. H. Muirhead (1935), pp. 253–303.

ful; it has the character of a process, is genuinely an event, is in all its parts and expressions historical. Its historicity, however, is timelessness in the sense of the supreme fulfilment of time, that is, eternity. Further, it is spiritual through and through, and outside of it there is nothing spiritual and therefore nothing in the full sense real. What we call "Matter" or "Nature" is unreal. Expressed positively, reality is a self-creating activity, and, being spirit, expresses itself most freely and fully in self-consciousness. The proper activity of self-consciousness, therefore, is philosophy understood as the self-development of spirit. The whole of reality falls within its province and is, at any rate in principle, open to penetration by it. Once more we here see utilized afresh the Hegelian thought of the rationality of the real, now directed, in sharp reaction, against the Absolutism of Bradley and all Subjectivism and Pragmatism (though the seductions of Pragmatism, which he called "un-philosophy",[1] were occasionally too much for him). Smith's philosophy is objective and dialectical Idealism in the Hegelian sense, with the typical variations which Hegelianism received at the hands of its modern Italian representatives.

[1] *Contemporary British Philosophy*, edited by J. H. Muirhead, vol. 2, p. 230.

4. THE ABSOLUTE IDEALISTS

FRANCIS HERBERT BRADLEY (1846–1924)

[Educated at University College, Oxford. 1870–1924, Fellow of Merton College, Oxford. *The Presuppositions of Critical History*, 1874, reprinted in *Collected Essays*; *Ethical Studies*, 1876 (second edition, 1927); *Mr. Sidgwick's Hedonism*, 1877, reprinted in *Collected Essays*; *The Principles of Logic*, 1883 (second edition in two vols. 1922); *Appearance and Reality*, 1893 (second edition, with Appendix, 1897, often reprinted; German translation, 1928); *Essays on Truth and Reality*, 1914; *Collected Essays*, two vols., 1935 (reprints articles and reviews, and includes two unpublished papers).

See "F. H. Bradley", memoir, by A. E. Taylor, in *Proc. Brit. Acad.*, vol. xi (1924–5), pp. 458–68; *The Platonic Tradition in Anglo-Saxon Philosophy* (chaps. v–ix), by J. H. Muirhead, 1931; *Dictionary of National Biography*, 1922–30.]

Bradley stands next only to Green and Caird in the importance of his contribution to the elaboration and propagation of Idealism in Great Britain. But with him we are in the main stream of a new phase of the movement. All that had been done hitherto was simply more or less preparatory labour, the presentation of the new world of ideas in the form of translation, exegesis, exposition, imitation, and criticism. Except in Green there had been no independent shaping and elaboration of the new material worth speaking of. With Bradley, however, British Hegelianism became fully fledged, and started on a flight of its own. He was the first to handle it creatively, to dare to plant a system of his own on the newly conquered ground. Nay, more, he was one of the few great builders of system, and one of the boldest and most original and speculative thinkers that Britain has ever produced. In modern British thought he takes a high, perhaps the highest, rank. Although there is still, and may long be, considerable and heated controversy about his philosophical work, scarcely any other thinker has done so much as he in the rousing of a genuinely philosophical vitality.

The great success of Bradley's philosophy was achieved entirely through his work as a writer, for though he was a

Fellow of an Oxford college for more than half a century, he never undertook the work of teaching, but lived in his college almost like a hermit, accessible to none but a few friends and absorbed in the working out of his ideas, a seclusion forced on him by ill-health. The high esteem in which he was held outside philosophical circles as well as in them was publicly marked shortly before his death by the royal award of the Order of Merit, which he was the first philosopher to receive. His brother philosophers honoured him in the pregnant dedication prefixed to the second volume of *Contemporary British Philosophy*: "To F. H. Bradley, O.M., to whom British philosophy owed the impulse that gave it new life in our time."

His special place in Anglo-Idealism may be indicated firstly by noting that he remained virtually untouched by Kant, owing almost everything that came to him from without to Hegel. His relation to the latter has always been a matter of controversy. He himself often refused to be called an Hegelian, on the ground that he did not know what or how much he owed to Hegel. A footnote in which he acknowledges a debt to Hegel and then adds "but the reader must bear in mind that only I am responsible for what I say" is characteristic.[1] Considering the matter very generally we may say that it was from Hegel that he received the initial impulse to independent thinking and that his philosophy, both as a whole and in detail, is deeply penetrated by the Hegelian thought, but that everything he took over, whether from Hegel or from others, was melted in the crucible of his own mind and given a distinctive form. That Hegel's influence weakened as Bradley's system grew and matured goes without saying.

In addition Spinozistic motives have been alleged with some justification. Bradley himself recommended Herbart as a needful antidote to Hegel, and certain parts of his metaphysics show that he followed his own advice. With Schelling he had some affinities and for Schopenhauer a certain preference, even though he took very little from him. Other German philosophers

[1] *Ethical Studies*, second edition, p. 148, note; cf. p. 23, note.

influenced him in special fields, for instance Lotze and Sigwart in logic, Vatke in ethics, and Volkmann in psychology.

But none of these influences was in any way decisive. It cannot be too strongly emphasized that Bradley's philosophy was of his own coining, sprang from a genuine originality of thought, grew and ripened on its own stem. For all his modest repudiations of originality, which at times strike one as a little mannered, we cannot help regarding him as an extremely independent thinker, indeed a capricious and obstinate one. This is evident in every line he wrote, in the pithiness and ruggedness of his style, in his rough and almost brutal way of disposing of his opponents, and in the way he composed his books, which give the impression not of a calm, objective, and precise presentation but of a soliloquy, or an unrestrained conversation with the reader, sometimes perfectly simple and straightforward, sometimes broken with dry and blunt or caustic wit, grotesque and ironical asides, splenetic sallies, and derision of his opponents or of himself. He loved paradox, preferred the uncommon, moved among opposites and rejoiced in contradictions, soared high but rarely let his feet leave the solid earth, was a sophist, sceptic, dogmatist and mystic all in one. Hence his philosophy had all the variety and iridescence of life itself, and its elusiveness too, so that any reproduction of it can scarcely retain its peculiar consistency and flavour. In addition his thought was extraordinarily mobile, preferring transitional positions to finished results and ever dissolving and reconstituting them in the dialectic of his unquiet mind. In all his thinking there is a strong dose of scepticism, the scepticism not of a destructive but of a lively and highly cultivated mind, which rises freely above things and enjoys playing a game with them, instead of laying hold of them and running off into just one truth which nevertheless cannot be final. One is often reminded of Hume's blithe and irresponsible way of tackling his problems. With the Hegelian dialectic understood as a precise philosophical method, Bradley had little to do, but it is implicitly applied in his looser way of passing continually from position to position. We may call his procedure dialectical so long as we take this to mean the mounting to successively higher levels of thought by a mind too restless to remain content with supposedly certain results. The joy of searching and finding is for Bradley greater than possession. "In philosophy we must not seek for an absolute satisfaction. . . . Philosophy is the exercise and enjoyment of but one side of our nature."[1] The only legitimate scepticism is renunciation of the hope of ever reaching a final possession of truth. What usually goes by the name of Scepticism he called suicidal Dogmatism.

But, through the same mobility and vitality we have been stressing, Bradley often expresses a quite different attitude: truth "is that which satisfies the intellect" and "philosophy aims at intellectual satisfaction, in other words, at ultimate truth".[2] This is the attitude that guided him in his metaphysical speculations—the need of security and order, the theoretical striving to overcome whatever is chaotic and contradictory in order to reach a harmonious world-view in which the mind shall find its peace. This seems to me to be the emotional background of Bradley's sublime metaphysic of the Absolute. It is with an entirely mystical fervour that he tries to apprehend and contemplate the Absolute as the resting-place of the soul, and with a ritual solemnity and slightly weary resignation which stand in marked contrast to the facile and mobile scepticism which we have indicated as the other side of his nature.

It is in the light of the above that we must see the bitter hostility with which the Pragmatists persecuted Bradley's doctrine and made a caricature of it. The root of the quarrel was the utter difference of temperament and attitude underlying the two philosophies; the opposition between the adventurous and combative mentality that loves to roam about the world and change it, and the wearied mentality intent on peace and security, that encloses itself in a system and keeps to the broad highway of absolute truth. The difference is obviously fundamental, and the long and bitter controversy

[1] *Essays on Truth and Reality*, p. 13. [2] Ibid., pp. 1 and 11 f.

between Bradley and Schiller is to be regarded as the expression of it.

We shall consider Bradley's philosophical work in the temporal order of its development, first his ethics, then his logic, and finally his metaphysics. His book on ethics is one of the earliest works of the idealistic school, appearing soon after Green's introductions to Hume and Wallace's translation of Hegel's smaller *Logic* and shortly before Edward Caird's first book on Kant. Preceding the publication of Green's *Prolegomena* by seven years, it was the earliest writing to mediate the ethics of German Idealism to the British, and was thus a milestone in the historical course of the moral philosophy of Britain. "For many of us," wrote Bosanquet, many years afterwards, "the publication of Mr. F. H. Bradley's *Ethical Studies* was an epoch-making event."[1] It is in his ethics that Bradley's Hegelianism is most genuinely and purely expressed, and the deep personal experience with which he had fastened on the Hegelian doctrine most immediately evident, despite the little use he makes of Hegel's terminology. It is here, too, that he refers in a striking passage to the German philosophy as the true philosophy and the only one fitted to lead British thought out of its perilous insularity. It is again here that we find the first destructive criticism with Hegelian weapons of the traditionally hallowed moral philosophies of Utilitarianism, Hedonism, and Empiricism generally. And finally, in this early book on ethics he reveals himself, with all his dependence on Hegel and the other Germans, as an independent thinker of the first rank, one who is destined to work out and carry forward the new impulse he had received from others.

For Bradley the ethical end is primarily the fulfilment and realization of the self. But what is this self? It is certainly not the human self, a mere collection or series of particular emotions or volitions or sensations. It shows itself from the outset as a single or systematic whole, as a concrete universal, of which the various and sequent particulars are simply phases or factors. The self that is relevant to ethics is a higher self,

[1] In *Contemporary British Philosophy*, vol. 1, pp. 57 f.

a universal one, standing above this or that self, mine or yours or anybody else's. Hence the ethical maxim " 'realize yourself as an infinite whole' means 'realize yourself as the self-conscious member of an infinite whole, by realizing that whole in yourself.' "[1] From this position Bradley shows how little the ethical end of Hedonism, pleasure for pleasure's sake, expresses the real meaning of morality. His argument is a classical disposal of all shallow ethics of pleasure, happiness, and utility, as represented by Mill, Spencer, Stephen, and Sidgwick, the last of whom he attacked in a special pamphlet published the year after his *Ethical Studies*. He also dismisses the contrasted ethical end of duty for duty's sake, as being equally one-sided in an opposite way, since it only substitutes for the purely particular the purely universal, an entirely abstract and formal principle which can never serve as a guide to action. It is useless to be told that we ought to do the right for the right's sake when nothing is said about the concrete content of the right. Bradley is here obviously striking at the formalism and rigorism of the Kantian ethic, though he admits that the theory criticized is not so much one that has actually been held as one set up for a polemical purpose. His criticism of this ethic is virtually identical with Hegel's.

These two one-sided theories, pleasure for pleasure's sake and duty for duty's sake, must be transcended from a higher point of view which Bradley calls the standpoint of "my station and its duties". This at bottom has the same meaning as the maxim about self-realization, for in so far as a man is not a mere individual detached from and independent of society—such an individual is a meaningless abstraction—but a social being, he can only realize his true self, the good or communal will which is to be distinguished from his purely personal pleasure-seeking self, when he has found his station and its duties, his function within a social whole. Bradley here destroys the ground of the ethical individualism that runs through the moral philosophy of the English from Locke to Spencer. At the same time he disposes of the Kantian dualism

[1] *Ethical Studies*, second edition, p. 80.

that cleaves an unbridgeable gulf between what is and what ought to be. The duty my station lays upon me cannot be an unending process in which a perpetual "ought" is accompanied by an everlasting "not yet", but must have its fulfilment here and now. The ethical ideal must be realizable in the temporal order of existence, in the satisfaction that comes through the actual fulfilment of duty. In this destruction of the tension between the "ought" and the "is" Bradley places the moral life in a gentler and kindlier atmosphere, in which love keeps company with duty and helps it.

What, then, is the moral end, if it is not the remote and unattainable ideal of the Kantian ethic? Since Bradley finds the standard of moral conduct in the society in which we happen to live, in its customs and laws and institutions, and regards it as undesirable to wish to rise above these, he so far remains embedded in the tradition of his country, which excludes the sovereignty of the individual and subjects him firmly to the moral standards of society. For the same reason Bradley rejects both the ethic of the superman and the ethic of a Utopian society as figments of the brain which can have no authority over the practical conduct of daily life.

But Bradley proceeds to erect above this real and actual morality an "ideal morality", a moral order of a higher level in which the self is no longer imprisoned within its social environment. In part abandoning the position he has reached, he gives us a glimpse of a world of values for which direct relation with the social environment is not necessary. Its values have to be sought only for their own sake, such as the effort after truth and beauty. Here, then, Bradley admits a sphere of non-social perfection. Nevertheless, this higher level cannot hover in mid-air over the lower but must be grounded in the latter and grow out of it. Ideal morality rests on social morality. Bradley's thought is thus in complete harmony with the sensibility of his own people: he embodies the idea of the British gentleman, which tolerates no break with social and national barriers. On this point he is much nearer to Hume than to Hegel.

By regarding the moral demand as something that has to be fulfilled in present reality, Bradley surmounted, Hegelian-fashion, the Kantian dualism. But even this higher position turns out to be only preliminary, to be cast in its turn into the whirlpool of his ceaseless dialectic. The old resolved dualism of "ought" and "is" breaks out afresh when it is seen that the moral idea can never be completely realized. A contradiction lies in the notion of oughtness or obligation: where there is no imperfection there is no obligation, and where there is no obligation there is no morality. Of this problem of the disparity between the moral as something really fulfilled or susceptible of fulfilment and as an ideally desirable end there can be no direct solution; which indicates that to emerge from it we must leave the sphere of morality and think our way forward into a supramoral sphere in which the notion of obligation is no longer present. This higher sphere is religion, which is the fulfilment or transcendent completion of morality in the sense that in it the ideal self which in morality for ever remains something we ought to be is now realized and truly is. These ideas lead onwards to speculations to which Bradley did not pass until, many years afterwards, he came to formulate his metaphysic. When we come to this we shall see that the good to which a self-contradiction is attached has no claim to reality in the strict sense but belongs only to the unreal world of appearance. Even in passing beyond itself to religion, therefore, it finds still a merely preliminary resolution or fulfilment. Only in the Absolute, as the true reality, does the good—along with its opposite, evil—come to its final rest, after losing its proper nature in a complete transformation. The completion of Bradley's ethic thus lies in his metaphysic of the Absolute.

With his *Principles of Logic* (1883) Bradley effected in logic a revolution comparable with the one he effected in ethics with his *Ethical Studies*, breaking in that field also the almost complete dominance of the Empiricists and opening up in England new lines of investigation. William James, Bradley's opponent, described the later book, just as Bosanquet described the earlier, as "epoch-making": "I have just read, with infinite zest and stimulation, Bradley's *Logic*. . . . It is surely 'epoch-making' in English philosophy. Both Empiricists and pan-Rationalists must settle their accounts with it. It breaks up all the traditional lines."[1]

Although Hegel is behind his logic too—more remotely and less evidently—Bradley confessed that he was indebted primarily to Lotze, secondarily to Sigwart and other German logicians. With their help he drew up a great counter-statement against the psychologism of the British empiricist logicians. His first task was to lay the axe at the root by exposing the falsity of the psychological foundation of the empiricist logic, namely, the doctrine of association, according to which knowing is the linking together of mental items that are individual or atomic in character. But how, Bradley demands, can an isolated fact that no sooner appears than it disappears be the occasion of the revival of a presentation? Of what kind are the elements so linked together in perception that when one reappears in consciousness it brings the others with it? What comes up afresh into consciousness cannot possibly be the same as it was before. Every element of mind holds within itself a certain novelty, for it enters into new relations and thereby changes its character, if only through the new point of time of its reappearance. The association of the contents of presentations must rest on something common or identical in the contents; it could not occur among pure and fleeting particulars. Hence Bradley lays down the thesis that all association is between universals. This important idea, destructive of all the associationism from Hartley and Hume to Mill and Bain, Bradley confessedly owed to Hegel, and, again confessedly, was led by it out of darkness into light. Its significance at the stage British psychology and logic had then reached can hardly be realized by us now, after several decades of Hegelianizing thinkers have completely accustomed us to it. When Bradley issued the second edition of his *Principles* after an interval of about forty years, he was able to regard any further examination of his earlier opponents as superfluous, and to say simply, in reference to

[1] *Letters of William James* (1920), vol. 1, p. 258.

a few belated stragglers of the Empiricist camp, "Let the dead bury their dead."[1]

Even on an external view Bradley's book differs from the usual treatises on logic. It is not formal or mathematical or Empiricist logic, but a very original and entirely personal investigation into the laws of thought and of logical forms. It is directed sharply and chiefly against the logic of the Empiricists, and its historical influence lies in its having broken the powerful influence of Mill and chased his doctrine from the field for several decades; it was not until very recently that a certain reaction slowly set in, somewhat in favour of Mill. The logic of Bradley is best called a metaphysical logic, in the sense that metaphysical assumptions are operative in it, or at any rate in the background. But it corresponds only in a general way to the type of logic most purely embodied in Hegel, with which it has only occasional points of contact and whose essence, the dialectic, it rarely utilizes, avoiding altogether the dialectical ascent from category to category. Moreover, its relations with the traditional Aristotelian doctrine are rather strained, even though it builds in part on its findings; the doctrine of the concept is deliberately left out, and the doctrine of the syllogism severely criticized.

As against the usual triple division of logical doctrine into concept, judgment, and inference, Bradley confines himself to the last two. He begins with the judgment because he regards this, not the concept, as the primary logical form or the original unit of thought. From the outset he declares that the judgment cannot be the connection of an idea with sensation or with another idea, on the ground that psychological factors are here irrelevant. What we are concerned with in the judgment is its meaning, its ideal and universal content, which is fundamentally different from any mental event or fact. The meaning or logical idea remains one and the same throughout the changing data; it is that part of the content of consciousness which the mind has arrested and thereby taken out of the time-order. While the mental event is particular and unique and actually

[1] Vol. 1, p. 354.

existent, the meaning is not in the order of existence at all, but is ideal and universal. Bradley's logical theory is thus an attempt to separate clearly the logical from the psychological sphere, the ideal and universal and *a priori* factors from the bare facts of cognitive experience; and its leading idea is that there can be no judgment or any other form of knowledge without a self-identical factor persisting through the flux of data. All this is expressed in Bradley's well-known and much-controverted definition of the judgment as "the act which refers an ideal content (recognized as such) to a reality beyond the act".[1] Every judgment necessarily includes such a reference or relation, and every relation presupposes in addition to the elements related a unity that holds these together. The criticism of Associationism thus leads to a doctrine of judgment.

For all his attack on psychologism, however, Bradley has not himself escaped from it. For at one time he defines judgment as an act, that is, as something mental; at another time as what the act intends or means, that is, as the logical proposition. This failure to carry far enough the separation of logic and psychology precludes us from counting him among the representatives of pure logic, and his vacillation between the two was the point his critics fastened on, first Cook Wilson, then Stout and Russell and others.

When he came later to develop his metaphysic, Bradley found a new point of view from which to define judgment. Distinguishing the real and the ideal as the "that" and the "what" respectively, as substantive and adjective, he considered the judgment as the qualification of a "that" as subject with a "what" as predicate, as the application to reality of an adjective which is not a fact but an idea; the subject being factual existence. The truth of the judgment is conditioned by the kind of reality of which the assertion is made; and in his metaphysic Bradley shows that factual existence is always fragmentary and contradictory, expressing but a partial aspect of a larger whole. Any judgment that refers to given fact, therefore, is always infected with error, and can at most reach

[1] *Principles*, second edition, vol. 1, p. 10.

only a partial or relative truth. The perfect judgment is one whose subject is in the long run the whole of reality, or the Absolute. Bradley, like Hegel, thus incorporates his logic in his metaphysic.

In his doctrine of inference Bradley again attacks deeply-rooted traditional prejudices. Averse from all blind acceptance of authority he dismisses the entire theory of the syllogism as pure superstition. The syllogism claims to be the model of all logical inference and proof, but there are many forms of inference and proof that cannot be fitted into it. For instance, Bradley gives examples to show that the major premise is often superfluous.[1] It is to Bradley's credit that he adduced a number of non-syllogistic forms of inference which the traditional logic had scarcely ever noticed.

The distinction between inference and judgment is that the latter stands much nearer to direct apprehension, to the sensory material. Before there can be any inferring, the raw stuff of knowledge must undergo a certain amount of organization, and this work is done chiefly in the judgment. In a rudimentary form judgment begins already in sensory experience, whereas inference presupposes an intellectual ground. This does not mean, however, that inference begins where judgment ends, for Bradley emphasizes the fact that primitive forms of inference are recognizable in the very beginnings of judgment, at the lowest levels of cognitive life. But explicit judgment, if not psychologically, is certainly logically prior to explicit inference, though both are aspects of the same process. Bradley's doctrine thus anticipates Bosanquet's (which is closely akin to it) in prescribing to logic the task of exhibiting the growth of thought and in tracing logical processes through the several stages of their development.

When inference is analysed, three elements can be distinguished—the data, the intellectual activity of inferring from these, and the result. The active element is a synthesis, an ideal construction; and in the further linkage thus added to the original connectedness of the data these suffer a change

[1] Op. cit., vol. i, pp. 247 f.

and pass into a new unity. For where nothing new emerges there is no inference. In the second edition of his *Principles* Bradley moved away considerably from this view of inference, preferring to regard it as essentially the self-development of an objective content.

Throughout he maintains his emphasis on the radical difference of the three spheres of the physical, the mental, and the logical, and never tires of attacking the psychologistic confusion of the last two of these. The logical idea has a quite different mode of being from the physical thing and the mental event; it does not exist, cannot occur, if by these terms we mean entering into the order of phenomena. It is ideal content, essence, the universal meaning as distinguished from fact or event. The logical, therefore, cannot apprehend, still less comprehend, the manifold and inexhaustible wealth of particulars and individuals that concrete reality presents. The colourful variety of life falls outside its province.

In the second edition of the *Principles*, some forty years later than the first, Bradley reprinted the original text with the addition of a commentary in the form of notes at the end of each chapter and a series of terminal essays. The added matter both corrects and goes beyond the text in more than unessentials. The greater part of it derives from Bosanquet, who had critically examined Bradley's *Principles* in 1885 (*Knowledge and Reality*) and three years later published his own *Logic*, which took its starting-point from Bradley. Bradley acknowledges the debt frankly and without reservation.

The great historical importance of Bradley's achievements in ethics, psychology, and logic has been several times noted above. They met with a large measure of agreement and quickly became part of the patrimony of British thought. His metaphysical views, however, as developed in his chief work *Appearance and Reality*, have provoked far more controversy. The work has been an apple of discord in modern British philosophy. Opinions about it show every variation from unmeasured praise through stupid indifference to bitter ridicule and downright contempt. Edward Caird spoke of it as the greatest event since Kant, and Muirhead has said that "nothing like it had appeared since Hume's *Treatise*. Like Hume's work it roused men of all schools from their dogmatic slumbers".[1] Its opponents, chiefly the Pragmatists, fell on it ferociously and distorted it into a scarecrow. Others regarded it as a whimsical medley of earnestness and jesting, and could not take it seriously. One wit suggested that its title should be altered to "The disappearance of reality".[2] Nevertheless, no other work has so deeply troubled the present-day philosophy of Britain, provoked so much reflection, and exercised so much influence both positive and negative, as Bradley's *Appearance and Reality*.

In metaphysics Bradley proceeded to the construction of a system. Not, however, by an irresponsible soaring above experience, but, in accordance with the demand he had laid down in the preface to his *Principles of Logic*, by critical (sceptical if you will) investigation into first principles. His aphorism is well known: "Metaphysics is the finding of bad reasons for what we believe upon instinct, but to find these reasons is no less an instinct."[3] For him, as for Schopenhauer, man is an *animal metaphysicum*. Metaphysics is his best antidote against both the dogmatic superstition of orthodox theology and the commonplaces of Materialism. It is the weapon of an intellectually free and active mind which is seeking an escape from the fetters of hardening doctrine. It is more an attitude than a theory, more a raising of and rummaging in problems than a solution of them. Hence we may even make a game of it, and it will retain some value if it issues in complete scepticism; for in Bradley the sceptical tendency is as operative as the speculative.

He assigns to metaphysics two tasks, firstly to seek a knowledge of reality in distinction from mere appearance, secondly to conceive the universe not fragmentarily but somehow or

[1] *Platonic Tradition*, p. 274.

[2] According to A. W. Benn, *History of English Rationalism in the 19th Century*, vol. 2, p. 421.

[3] Preface to first edition of *Appearance and Reality*.

other as a whole. Here we have the central ideas of his theory. Turning to the first it is obviously important to determine the meaning of the two terms involved. What is appearance? Initially at least it is not the phenomenal—whether understood as what is given to consciousness or as the opposite of the thing-in-itself—or any determinate field of being or thought distinguished from any other. Perhaps it is indeed all these, but primarily it is what we have whenever we come across a discrepancy between what exists and what is thought, whenever thought is entangled in contradictions or when it is able to grasp only a part instead of a whole, a multiplicity instead of a unity, a relative instead of an absolute; it is the relational, the fragmentary, whatever becomes and changes, the negation of meaning and of value; it is where error is and evil and sin, wherever we are driven about in restless search, wherever in our longing for the higher and better we only consume ourselves instead of reaching satisfaction.

Appearance is thus defined almost exclusively in negative terms. What then is reality? It is that which is opposed in all respects to appearance, so that to express its nature as Bradley conceives it we have only to substitute for the above negative characteristics their positive correlates. Deferring fuller description for the moment, we may preliminarily define reality as that which is free from contradiction, as unity, wholeness, rest, harmony, as the all-comprehensive, as complete truth; in short, as the Absolute.

What does Bradley assign to the sphere of appearance? The core of his teaching is to be found in his chapter on relation and quality. For Green and the older school generally, it will be remembered, the category of relation was of fundamental importance: it was that which, by linking things together, constituted them as real. Bradley tries to prove the contrary. When, he argues, we examine theoretically our ordering of facts according to their relations and qualities, we fall into unexpected difficulties and contradictions. Relation and quality presuppose each other. Qualities are nothing without relations, and we have relations whenever we distinguish, judge, or think in any way at all; as he says somewhere, when thinking ceases to be relational, it commits suicide. Of course, when we go behind thought to the unbroken unity of feeling we have got away from relations and qualities. But we cannot think of qualities without thinking of determinate features distinguished from one another, or of these without thinking of relations among them. Qualities without relations are therefore meaningless; the two are only distinguishable in thought, not separable in fact. Similarly, there cannot be relation without quality, for without qualities as terms there would be nothing to relate. When any term is taken by itself it is therefore inconceivable. But unfortunately even when terms are taken in conjunction with each other they are still unintelligible, for when we try to conceive the relation between the original relation and the quality or term, we start on an endless progress, since every new relation between the original relation and the term has itself to be related to the term. From all which Bradley draws the conclusion that whenever thinking moves in relations it becomes, by the standard of knowledge, a substitute or compromise, unable to reach truth or fathom the reality of things. Relational or discursive thinking necessarily involves itself in contradictions, and therefore refers only to the world of appearance. As we said earlier, contradictoriness is the proper criterion of the appearance-status of a thing or concept.

After getting rid of the concept of relation Bradley reduces all the other primary concepts of thought to relations which similarly do not touch their terms except through an infinite and therefore impossible series of intermediate relations. In consequence, his world of appearance is crowded to a hitherto unknown degree. The whole of the first part of his book is directed to showing that the categories and other concepts of thought and the content of experience all suffer from the unresolvable contradiction inherent in relation and therefore belong to the realm of appearance. In these chapters Bradley the sophist and sceptic lets himself go in an orgy of razor-like distinctions and subtle arguments which raise an enormous cloud of dialectical dust, so that it is not to be wondered at that in his hands things crumble away, leaving at the end nothing but a world of ruins. One after the other the following are swept into his dialectical whirlpool—qualities primary and secondary, thing and attribute, quality and relation, space and time, motion and change and succession, causation and action and passion, the substance and identity of things, even the identity of self, all natural science, error, evil, and good, indeed religion and God.

We need not follow these out singly. We will, however, select the case of the self to illustrate the procedure, since it shows most fully the extent to which Bradley would depart, when his principle required it, from the positions of such older Idealists as Green and Wallace. Nowhere else can we see more clearly how much the imposition of a schema predetermines the result and closes Bradley's eyes to a solution that is both near at hand and demanded by the problem itself. Without making even an attempt to resolve the problem of personal identity by a direct analysis of the experiential facts, he simply considered the confusing number and variety of theories about it and concluded that a concept so varying and ambiguous as that of the self could not satisfy the requirements that must be fulfilled before it or any other concept could be regarded as real. He therefore numbered it with appearances. The self, however, is a classical case for the criterion of reality which Bradley himself considered to be of great importance, namely, the harmony of the one and the many, of difference within a synthetic unity. By denying the unity of self-consciousness he equated the self with the sum of its experiences instead of with the unity of these, and thus ended with the view that it is simply a bundle of discrepancies, thereby approximating closely to the Humean theory which he had expressly pronounced to be unsatisfactory. More seriously he thereby abandoned the view he had worked out in his ethics (above, p. 326). In addition he debarred himself, as we shall see, from making any use of the category of personality in the determination of the Absolute. His theory of the self, then, as expounded in his metaphysical work, represents a relapse into Empiricism (with which, indeed, he had strong ties), and is an example of the way in which so acute a thinker did violence to a problem for the sake of a principle.

So far we are left with a dualism, with a huge gulf between appearance and reality. The matter obviously cannot rest there, and in the second part of his book Bradley sets himself to heal the wounds he has made in the first. He now shows that the two dialectically sundered realms cannot exist apart, that each involves a reference to the other. After all, an appearance is a something, not a nonentity, and therefore must somehow belong to reality. On the other hand, reality taken in and by itself would be a nonentity. It must then, in some way, include appearance; for, to say the least, it cannot be less than this. Hence Bradley's conclusion that appearance needs reality to complete itself and reality needs appearance to give itself content and actuality. The question then arises in what way appearance belongs to reality, or, as Bradley usually calls it, the Absolute. At the end of his book he says (referring with approval to Hegel) that reality is spiritual. In view of the general course of the argument this seems to be more a rhetorical peroration than his real view, for he has declared that relational thought (and he knows no other kind of thought) cannot in any way express the nature of the Absolute, and in particular that the Absolute cannot be conceived after the analogy of a self or personality, since thought and self alike belong to the realm of appearance. His real view, indicative once more of a lingering Empiricism in his thinking, is that the Absolute is sentient experience; a single, harmonious, and all-comprehending system, of course, but with sentient experience as its content. Within it all differences are resolved into concord; are, in Hegel's language, sublimated (*aufgehoben*).

This identification of the Absolute with sentient experience, and the consequent exaltation of this over the experience organized or attained through thinking, are disconcerting after the lofty standard he has set for the Absolute. Clearly there is no experience by which we can directly apprehend the

Absolute. Perhaps Bradley felt the difficulty, for he looked for an analogy to make his meaning more evident, and in the end refers us to the intimate experience we have in the immediacy of pure, completely undifferentiated feeling. This he takes as a sort of prototype or lower form of the Absolute experience, in virtue of its unbroken wholeness. The two are parallel, differing only in the respect that the one, not yet having been subjected to the discursive activity of thought, lies on the nearer side of the contradictory world of appearance, whereas the other lies beyond it, beyond it not in the spatial sense, but in the sense that it has surmounted the divisions and oppositions introduced by thought and recovered the original unbroken experience at a higher level. This absolutism of feeling, which at times intoxicates Bradley, leads him to make startlingly radical assertions, of which the following is a sample: "Nothing in the end is real but what is felt, and for me nothing in the end is real but that which I feel. . . . The real, to be real, must be felt."[1] In feeling we experience the many as one, the parts as a whole; we are below the division into subject and object and the opposition between the true and false. This most rudimentary of our experiences has the unity in multiplicity that Bradley denies to the most developed experience, self-consciousness. But the unity is only "enjoyed", and at once disappears when thought is turned upon it. We cannot even put it into words. We can only feel that it is a reflection of that higher experience through which we participate in the Absolute.

The general outline of Bradley's world-view is now clear. It depicts three levels. The lowest is the realm of immediate feeling, the pre-relational experience of undivided and undifferentiated wholeness. The next is the dialectical level, the realm of thought, in which the original unity of feeling is broken up by relations, and things are appearances only and not real. The third is the realm of reality, of the Absolute, in which the unity and wholeness lost at the second stage are reconstituted in a higher synthesis. Bradley's meaning may be faith-

[1] *Essays on Truth and Reality*, p. 199.

fully expressed in a more concrete and human way. By eating of the Tree of Knowledge we have lost our pristine unity, and all our striving aims at recovering it. To our original state, however, we can never return; the earthly Paradise is closed to us eternally. But perhaps, when we have sustained our torn and restless life here, we may find unity again in a higher and better world; and whether we are able or not to apprehend this, to it all our present longing will be directed. Man passes from the pure innocence of naïve feeling through the guilt of knowledge to redemption in the Absolute.

In this respect Bradley's Absolute appears as the product and imagined fulfilment of a wish. There are, indeed, passages in his book where we can plainly detect the deep emotion, rising at times to mystical ardour, with which he searches after it to become one with it. After all, the Absolute is no empty and tedious monotony, for all the wealth and manifoldness of the individual and the particular have entered into and are preserved within it. At the lowest it cannot be poorer than the sensible world of appearance; nay, it must be infinitely richer than anything our present experience affords. In it nothing is lost. "Every flame of passion, chaste or carnal, would still burn in the Absolute unquenched and unabridged, a note absorbed in the harmony of its higher bliss."[1] But how do appearances enter into the Absolute and form part of its nature? Certainly not in the forms by which we now know them, not with the disquiet and discontent of their present state, but somehow transfigured and reborn for the higher and more perfect life. How this is effected in each case we cannot say, but are thrown back entirely on conjecture and surmise. The elements of experience will be there, feeling and will as well as thought, but no longer at strife. There must be will where the ideal is made reality. Thought, however, must undergo a profound metamorphosis: it will be present as a higher intuition and thus lose its distinctive character, devouring itself in the attainment of its ideal, itself transcended in the finding of that transcendence the search for which is its very essence. By

[1] *Appearance and Reality*, p. 172.

thought Bradley here means, of course, relational and discursive thought, the finite activity of understanding, not the absolute activity of reason: had he but expanded this narrow and one-sided conception of thought in the direction of Hegel's Idea, he would have found what here he is seeking in vain.

From the great process of transformation by which the finite categories and appearances are submerged in the Absolute, error and evil are not excepted. So far as the first of these is concerned, this means that there can be no radical opposition between truth and error but only a more or less of one or the other. Indeed, error *is* truth, truth partial and imperfect, truth seen from the point of view of our limited and eccentric understanding. In the experience of the whole it corrects itself and disappears. It is obvious that here a very grave problem is not solved but clouded over and explained away. The violent attacks that have been made, especially by the Pragmatists, on Bradley's theory of error have certainly struck at an extremely weak point of his system.

Pain and evil, like error, are found to be compatible with absolute perfection. That they in fact exist he does not deny, but what he is concerned with is only the manner of transformation they could undergo. He resorts to an analogy. It is a common experience that a smaller pain may be absorbed and thereby extinguished by a greater joy. True, the intensity of the latter is then reduced, but the feeling as a whole may still be joyful. It is, then, at any rate possible that in the total reckoning pain is overbalanced by and submerged in pleasure and joy. This mere possibility, it seems, removes for Bradley the last obstacle to the perfection of the Absolute. Passing now to the problem of evil, he argues that evil exists only in moral experience and that moral experience is essentially full of contradiction and has the dialectical urge to surmount this in a higher—that is, a supramoral—sphere of being. Thus evil enters into the service of the good, pursuing, albeit unwillingly, the realization of the latter. Here, too, as with error, the opposition disappears if the sphere of reference be made wide enough. "All that we need to understand here is that 'Heaven's design', if we may speak so, can realize itself as effectively in Catiline or Borgia as in the scrupulous or innocent."[1] The easy optimism with which Bradley slides over these grave problems, and his distortion of facts into a picture nearer to his heart's desire, make one doubt whether the Absolute can provide that *theoretical* satisfaction for which he invented it.

As we saw earlier,[2] the supramoral sphere towards which the moral life presses is religion. With religious matters Bradley had no close or vital relation, and what he says about them strikes one as superficial, as the product not of experience but merely of arm-chair thinking. Although, he argues, with respect to morality religion is an absolute, with respect to the Absolute it is simply appearance. The inner contradictions that Bradley finds in it drive it beyond itself into the perfection of the higher metaphysical whole. What, then, is the relation of God to the Absolute? God is God only in so far as He is all in all, but in this sense He is not the God of religion, who is less than the Absolute. Thus, after all the other concepts, the concept of God too is drawn into the dialectical vortex; He is not the whole but only an aspect and therefore mere appearance, so that He, and with Him religion, must suffer the transforming plunge into the ultimate metaphysical One. With Bradley's system this peculiar solution—or dissolution—is, of course, inevitable. After regarding personality as a bundle of contradictions and therefore as a reality of a lower order, he had no choice but to ascribe to the Absolute a suprapersonal nature and to characterize it in terms of consistency and harmony. Religion for him was a practical affair; its images and concepts, being wholly concerned with the fulfilment of practical ends, do not need to be free from theoretical contradictions. That most religions represent the supreme being as a person is simply a consequence of the pragmatic need they express. Anyhow, such a representation, says Bradley, cannot meet the requirements of the metaphysical principle which he calls the Absolute, and therefore falls below it.

The Absolute, then, is the ultimate end which all things seek,

[1] *Appearance and Reality*, p. 202.

[2] P. 329.

and for which they would rather sacrifice their own nature than linger on in their present unregenerate state. It is therefore the supreme criterion of all value, that which makes the true true, the beautiful beautiful, and the good good. "The Absolute is there to secure that everywhere the highest counts most and the lowest counts least."[1] It is the real in an emphatic or exalted sense, the real as value. Everything in the realm of appearance is on the contrary alienated from its own true nature and is consequently always in the process of passing from its finitude to its true perfection. They are all in continual flux and change, and neither achieve perfection in themselves nor bear within themselves the meaning of their own true being.

But is not this unending movement towards perfection and idealization tantamount to a monstrous depreciation of the true and proper value of things, an utter annulment of all that they are and do here and now? And all the more so since the ideal is left so thoroughly indeterminate and indistinct as not to afford a sufficient compensation for all this extreme sacrifice of things completely ceasing to be themselves. Bradley himself felt this difficulty, and tried to mitigate it in a chapter (often felt to have no real connection with his main doctrine) on "degrees of truth and reality", and in certain supplementary elaborations in his *Essays on Truth and Reality*. Here we are told that all things are not indifferently cast into the pit of the Absolute. Even within the gloomy and imperfect world of appearance there is a distinction of degrees or levels defined by nearness to or remoteness from the ideal set by the Absolute, the distance of any appearance from the ideal—that is, its degree of reality—being measured by the amount of transformation required to bring it within the system of the real. With reference to the Absolute all things are relative, but there are degrees of relativity and therefore in a sense degrees of absoluteness or reality, and this makes possible the ranking of things. Body and mind, for example, are alike only appearances, but mind comes nearer to reality. Taken at its own level

[1] *Essays on Truth and Reality*, p. 348.

each thing is thus acknowledged to have a relative value of its own, assessed according to the extent to which it contains and expresses the nature of the concrete whole which is reality. Similarly with truth: viewed from the higher levels of knowledge the lower ones appear as incoherent, contradictory; but when they are taken by themselves and measured by their own order of evidence they are consistent and true. Here Bradley comes nearer to the deeper meaning of the Hegelian doctrine of dialectical stages, and gives a more satisfactory account of the real meaning, not only in his own but in all idealistic systems, of the fundamental distinction of appearance and reality.

BERNARD BOSANQUET (1848–1923)

[Educated at Balliol College, Oxford. 1871–81, Fellow and Lecturer at University College, Oxford; 1903–8, Professor of Moral Philosophy at St. Andrews. Having private means, spent most of his life independently in writing, lecturing, and social service. "Logic as the Science of Knowledge", in *Essays in Philosophical Criticism*, edited by A. Seth and R. B. Haldane, 1883; *Knowledge and Reality*, 1885; *Logic, or the Morphology of Knowledge*, two vols., 1888 (second edition, 1911); *Essays and Addresses*, 1889; *A History of Aesthetic*, 1892 (second edition, 1904); *The Civilization of Christendom and other Studies*, 1893; *Companion to Plato's Republic*, 1895; *Essentials of Logic*, 1895; *Psychology of the Moral Self*, 1897; *The Philosophical Theory of the State*, 1899 (fourth edition, 1923); *The Principle of Individuality and Value* (Gifford Lectures), 1912; *The Value and Destiny of the Individual* (Gifford Lectures), 1913; *The Distinction between Mind and its Objects*, 1913; *Three Lectures on Aesthetic*, 1915; *Social and International Ideals*, 1917; *Some Suggestions in Ethics*, 1918; *Implication and Linear Inference*, 1920; *What Religion Is*, 1920; *The Meeting of Extremes in Contemporary Philosophy*, 1921; *Three Chapters on the Nature of Mind*, 1923; "Life and Philosophy", in *Contemporary British Philosophy*, edited by J. H. Muirhead, first series, 1924.

Posthumous: *Science and Philosophy and other Essays*, edited by J. H. Muirhead and R. C. Bosanquet, 1927.

Also editor and part-translator of Lotze's *Logic and Metaphysics*, 1884; translator of Hegel's *Introduction to the Philosophy of Fine Art*, 1886.

See *Bernard Bosanquet, a Short Account of His Life*, by Helen Bosanquet, 1924; *B. Bosanquet and His Friends*. Letters illustrating the Sources and Development of his Philosophical Opinions, edited by J. H. Muirhead, 1935; *Dictionary of National Biography*, 1920–30.]

The most striking feature of Bosanquet's philosophy is its close kinship with that of Bradley. It is almost as if the two men were partners, with Bradley as the originating, initiating, and fertilizing mind and Bosanquet as on the whole the more receptive and executive mind. But it is going too far to say, as has been said recently, that the two may almost be regarded as a single philosophical personality. Despite the considerable agreement between them, detailed as well as general, we cannot rightly call Bosanquet's philosophy a mere reproduction of Bradley's. It represents an independent re-creation, extension, and application of Bradley's doctrine on the part of a genuine thinker who happened to be congenial with him and who scarcely fell below him in ability. The one is not merely the giver and the other the receiver; between the two there was a fruitful interchange of ideas, in which Bradley not infrequently was the beneficiary.

The lives of the two, which almost coincided in time, differed greatly, and the difference is reflected also in their mentality and manner of philosophizing. Bradley's nature was brooding and solitary; he occupied no teaching post and had no duties worth speaking of; he had no longing for practical activity but remained closed within himself, wholly given up to the *vita contemplativa*, living all his life within the walls of his college in a self-imposed banishment from the world. Bosanquet, on the contrary, had an active and practical nature and an enormous capacity for work, and could only for a while put up with the narrow limits of the life of a college lecturer. After ten years of this kind of life he found a wider and more concrete field of work in London, assisting in the organization of social services and lecturing to philosophical societies and to classes then being formed under the new movement for adult education. While Bradley published but four works of any size Bosanquet, one of the most productive and versatile philosophical writers of his day, published about a score. Bradley's retirement from life was paralleled by his great mental reserve; his thought was wrapt in itself, blunt, rough, and uncompromising, and almost closed to new influences. Bosanquet's mind was obliging and companionable, conciliatory, open to new knowledge and experience, and adaptable to new situations; in width of culture and erudition and in many-sidedness of interest he excelled his partner, though he lacked the latter's penetration, depth, and sheer original creativity.[1] The joint influence of the two on contemporary British philosophy is immeasurable, and to this day, when the idealistic movement is on the decline, still powerful. The movements opposed to them have grown up on them, and sharpened their weapons through controversy with them. On the Continent their doctrines have received little attention, and Bosanquet is a virtually unknown name. Of their writings none has been translated except Bradley's *Appearance and Reality* (German, 1928).

In Bradley and Bosanquet Absolute Idealism found its specifically English embodiment. The former developed it intensively, the latter extensively. It is Bosanquet's special merit that he gave to Bradley's world-view a much broader basis, applying it and exhibiting its fruitfulness in the entire circle of philosophical discipline, in aesthetics and the philosophy of religion, law, and the State, as well as in psychology, logic, epistemology, and ethics. In this encyclopaedic trait he comes closer than Bradley to Hegel, and is in general a more orthodox and consistent disciple. We may say that he turned the doctrine of Bradley back to its ultimate Hegelian starting-point, the reason being not simply that he was less dogmatic but also that he was less sceptical than Bradley. It has been rightly pointed out that he everywhere changed Bradley's abrupt "either-or" into the gentler "both-and", seeking to smooth out the oppositions between the schools instead of emphasizing and sharpening them. Nothing is more charac-

[1] On this oppositeness of attitude and temperament see Muirhead in his *B. Bosanquet and His Friends*, pp. 246 f.

teristic than the programme of one of his latest works, reflected in its title *The Meeting of Extremes in Contemporary Philosophy*, in which he did his best to find a common basis from which the various schools could all start in a co-operative attack on the problems of philosophy. Here, and also, when he felt obliged to differ, in the chivalry with which he treated his opponents, his generous and distinguished mind found a typical expression. This chivalry, it must be admitted, often led him to make concessions incompatible with his own position.

It may be said that in Bosanquet Idealism felt the need of further experience and added to its territory large tracts of thought. The special fields into which he penetrated are too numerous for us to follow him everywhere he goes: it will suffice if we can in a few of them bring out the main drift of his thought. His literary activity may be roughly divided into three periods. In the first he was concerned chiefly with the logical grounds of his system, in the second with the problems of aesthetics, ethics, and the philosophy of the State, and in the last he rounded off his world-view with a constructive metaphysic and an application of this to the sphere of religion.

Idealistic logic was considerably deepened and enriched by Bosanquet. In this field he was influenced not only by Hegel, Bradley, Lotze, and Sigwart,[1] but also, despite his opposition to them, by Mill and Jevons. His own *Logic*, which was later supplemented by studies of particular problems, gives, as the sub-title indicates, a "morphology of knowledge", that is an account of the growth and intrinsic connection of logical forms. It was a departure from the merely enumerative and classificatory procedure of the formal logicians. From the outset he was concerned with the dynamic of logical thought and its essential relation to system. For him logical thought does not consist of subjective acts but owes its distinctive character to its reference to the objective order of things which is independent of such acts; it apprehends reality and becomes one with

[1] An English translation of Sigwart's *Logik* appeared in 1895. In the same year the translator, Helen Dendy, became Bosanquet's wife.

it. Logic has thus the same content as metaphysics, and in the former as in the latter the Hegelian dictum holds good that truth is always the whole. This idea runs through all Bosanquet's teaching. Truth lies exclusively in system, so that its essential mark is coherence, the concordant relatedness of all parts in a systematic whole, not, as the copy-theory has it, extrinsic correspondence of thought and reality. "Pure facts" have neither reality nor truth until they have been linked up with other facts and seen in their place in the order of the Whole.

For Bosanquet as for Bradley the judgment, not the concept, is the first and fundamental logical form, the concept having no place in actual thinking except as an organic part of a judgment. Judgment is an organic whole of meaning and can therefore be understood only in the light of the functional unity of its parts: to enumerate or to analyse these is to tear up its living tissue. And every act of judging refers to a reality lying outside itself. The most ordinary perceptual judgment must be counted a partial expression of reality; the perfect judgment would be nothing less than an assertion of the whole of reality in its most general form. Reality as such is therefore ultimately the proper subject of every true judgment. The totality of things is always in one way or another presupposed, even though in the judging process we apprehend it but fragmentarily. Since, then, judgment is the effort of thought to determine reality, it will vary not only with the several qualitative kinds of reality it from time to time determines, but also with the degree of success it achieves in the determination. Whether as mathematical equation, logical definition, or judgment of value, its paramount specific character is settled by the underlying whole that it apprehends.

The traditional formal logic and the inductive logic of the Empiricists are alike inadequate when measured by the idea of the logical as a function of system and a factor through which the real is constituted. This comes out more clearly in Bosanquet's doctrine of inference, which, besides its treatment in the *Logic*, is worked out profoundly in his short *Implication and Linear Inference*. He here distinguishes two possible views of inference, the linear and the systematic. The procedure of the syllogism, typical of all deduction, is in accordance with the former view—linking a predicate with a subject, taking the result as a new subject and linking another predicate with it, and so on after the manner of a chain. Most so-called inductive inferences also follow the same pattern. Over against these Bosanquet sets the view of inference as systematic, implicative instead of linear, implication being the interweaving of parts into a systematic whole which is prior to them and which, as prior, directs and penetrates the entire inferential process. In all genuine inference, whether in scientific or in everyday thinking, we survey a system of facts, see it in relation to a larger system of reality, and directly or indirectly read off the implications; and the fuller and more comprehensive the connections of system are in any piece of knowledge the higher the knowledge is.

In connection with this contention that all logical processes rest on systematic, not on linear, inference, it is of interest to note the influence of Husserl.[1] Husserl's work generally, but his method of intuition of essences in particular, led Bosanquet to the idea that in all logical processes the direct manifestation of relating functions or implications plays a much greater part than inferring on the ground of previous experience. There is operative an intuitive factor, which enables us to look as it were into the innermost essence of things and directly read off their connections within a system, and Bosanquet unhesitatingly declares that that intuition, far from being alogical or irrational, is the essence of all higher forms of inference. We may also note that for him implication in this sense is the same as dialectic. Since he does not seem to have known that there was, in fact, a close historical connection between Hegel's dialectic and Husserl's intuition of essence, his detection of their intrinsic relation is a mark of the sureness of his instinct.

In his political philosophy Bosanquet stands in the great idealistic line of Plato, Aristotle, Rousseau, Hegel, and Green.

[1] See *B. Bosanquet and His Friends*, pp. 149, 171, *et passim*.

After the timid essay of Green he was the first thinker in Britain to undertake a determined revival of the idea of the State as conceived by Hegel, as against the native liberal theories of Bentham, Mill, and Spencer. Where Green had stopped short, Bosanquet went the whole way with Hegel, and was the first to do so. It may be said without reservation that his working out of the theory of the State was the most considerable and the most important within the British idealistic movement.

The fundamental problem is the relation of the individual to society, which is quickly taken up into the metaphysical problem of the relation of the part to the whole. The atomic individual hitherto taken as the starting-point by almost all British political theories (Bosanquet appropriately calls them "theories of the first look") cannot be the individual in society or the State whom we know and with whom we are in this branch of philosophy concerned; nor can the supposition that men are by nature individuals of such a sort, isolated or even opposed to each other, who are brought together into a community only at a later stage and artificially or externally, be other than false. Rousseau took a great step forward and made himself the forerunner of the idealistic theory of the State by his distinction of the *volonté de tous* and the *volonté générale*. The former is simply the sum of the particular wills, whereas the latter involves the idea of organic unity. Bosanquet illustrates the distinction with the apt example of a fortuitous crowd and a well-disciplined army, the one united by nothing but association, the other by an organization through which the members are determined by a systematic whole that permeates and lives in them. The individual, thus permeated by the general will, is rescued from his isolation, ceases to be an atom, is raised to a higher level, attaining to the genuine individuality that belongs to a self organic to the communal whole. With this deeper conception of individuality Bosanquet destroys the foundation of the individualism of the Empiricist theory of the State.

Looked at ethically, the particular self is the egoistic one, living entirely by natural impulse, while the organic self is the moral or rational one. The essence and end of the State can now be defined. The State is the general or rational will, a continuous and self-identical being, permeating a multiplicity of particular individuals in and through whom alone it has existence and meaning. The supreme end of the State is the same as that of the individual, namely the realization of the best life possible, or—it is the same thing—the raising of our nature to complete unity with the social whole. In other words it is a moral end. In its immediate task, however, the State has the more negative function of removing obstacles to the fulfilment of the moral end; and since these obstacles cannot always be removed by purely moral influence the compulsion of force has often to be applied. Force is thus an original and essential part of the nature of the State, for the selfish in their inertness and most of us in our animal nature have to be compelled to realize the true self. In this doctrine the Kantian dualism of an empirical and intelligible self is obvious. It is the task of the State to free the intelligible self from its empirical fetters and raise it, if necessary force it, to freedom; for freedom is the realization of the true self, living the best life possible to us, being one with the whole. The compulsion imposed upon us by the general will is in ultimate analysis simply the demand made by our true and better self on our lower and refractory self, and it is unavoidable as long as we have no idea, or only an imperfect one, of the necessity of the demand. This is the basis of the right of the State to punish its wrongdoers. Punishment is the requital of the injustice done to the community by the disturbance of its legal order, the negation of the anti-social will of the wrongdoer. The wrongdoer is himself a member of the wronged community, and as such has in a sense the right to be punished, lest he should be deceived about the nature of social living. His payment of the penalty is his reincorporation in the society from which by his wrongdoing he had outlawed himself. Bosanquet has here followed Hegel's theory which defines punishment as retribution.

These various tasks are best fulfilled, in Bosanquet's opinion, by the national State. The idea of humanity, of course, points beyond this, but since it does not lend itself to realization in an institution or organizing whole it has no significance in relation to the practical handling of social tasks. The morality of State action has not to be judged by the standards that hold for the action of individuals, because the ends to be realized are higher, making the State, as an individual of a higher order, *sui generis*. The force inherent in its nature, and which it has often to use against its own members, may sometimes have to be used also against other States, when the highest interests of a nation are at stake. This and similar views, as we noted when considering Hobhouse,[1] met with sharp opposition during the World War, when a blinded wartime mentality saw in the Hegelian theory of the State, which it utterly distorted, the spiritual origination of the catastrophe. To-day, however, a quieter mood having supervened, it is being recognized afresh that no English philosopher has grasped and expounded the nature of the State more profoundly than Bosanquet, an Hegelian.

Metaphysics is the beginning and end of Bosanquet's thought, and also all that lies between. The transition to it from his philosophy of the State is effected through the recognition that the social spirit, of which the State is the highest embodiment, is not the final form of individuality but only one of its preliminary forms. Beyond the institutions and activities of political life there are realms that contribute far more to the realization of the self which the State has but consolidated and made secure. In its growing apprehension of the world the human spirit rises above the State to higher systems which lead it nearer to absolute reality, namely, art, religion, and philosophy. With this last we come to metaphysics, the doctrine of the Absolute.

Although Bosanquet's metaphysical speculations, which are to be found in his Gifford Lectures, depart from and go beyond Bradley's in both content and terminology, the changes

[1] Pages 138 ff.

concern little more than nuance and flavour. In all fundamentals he follows in the direction indicated by Bradley. We need therefore only draw attention to the respects in which he seems to pass beyond Bradley.

His ideas centre in the problem of individuality. His task is to grasp the nature of individuality not in any special sphere, such as the ethical or the social, but in its ultimate metaphysical signification. This signification, as understood by Bosanquet, is in extreme opposition to the common view of the individual as something separate, peculiar, unique. His attitude to history illustrates this: unlike certain modern German philosophers, for whom history is the proper sphere of the individual, he called it a hybrid form of experience characterized by the merely temporal and accidental succession of events, and in consequence attached no importance to it. For him too, indeed, the individual is something entirely peculiar and unique, not however in the sense of being a particular uniquely distinguished from other particulars, but in the sense that there is only one thing that clearly and completely expresses the nature of individuality, namely the Absolute. The unities of mathematics and the natural sciences, such as numbers and atoms, stand at an extreme distance from the individual in Bosanquet's pregnant sense; they are abstract unities, mere repetitions of similarities, whereas the truly individual is a concrete universal identity within a richly differentiated systematic whole.

Individuality as the concrete universal, as the truly infinite in Hegel's sense, thus reaches its highest stage in the infinite experience of the Absolute. In finite experience, however, we find anticipations of it, individuals of a lower order, of which the work of art, for example, the human personality, and the social community may be taken as the most finished types. In the case of man this must not be misunderstood. In common language a man is said to possess individuality in proportion as he ceases to be a mere specimen of his kind and comes to be a personality, that is, distinguished by his own qualities and achievements. Indeed, in philosophical thought also the notions of individuality and personality are often treated as inseparable,

Rashdall being, among the more recent British philosophers, the most consistent and typical representative of this personalistic view. Bosanquet dissents from this view; he will not have it that personality is a necessary ingredient of individuality, and insists repeatedly that what maximal individuality in its true sense demands is not reached in the human individual, but has to be sought beyond the level of the personal and the finite. The human individual is a mere fragment of a larger whole, is nothing apart from this, and needs to be completed in it; is incomplete and imperfect so long as he remains in his own finitude; is not truly an individual so long as he is a person. He is initially only a multiplicity and a manifold, which strives to become a single whole. Hence he has to find a compromise or reconciliation between what he is and what he wishes or ought to become. The constitutive feature, then, of the finite self is self-transcendence. In Bosanquet's doctrine this notion is of central importance.

The notion dominates the second part of his Gifford Lectures, in which he attempts a metaphysical exposition of the "value and destiny of the individual". He finds three stages that man in his march towards his destiny must traverse, namely, the "moulding of souls", their "hazards and hardships", and their "stability and security". Man's peculiar position in the Cosmos is that he stands between the two poles of Nature and the Absolute, the finite and the infinite, so that he has a twofold character, is a finite-infinite entity. He arises out of the natural conditions of existence and is in the first instance bound up with these and subject to them in every fibre of his being. In so far as he is a pure product of Nature, however, he cannot realize the true meaning and purpose of his existence. But from the beginning he has an urge towards a higher perfection beyond his merely natural character. This urge produces a convulsion of his self, a disturbance of the compact harmony that marks the assurance of animal instinct, so that he falls into the turmoil of existence, into struggle and need, danger and affliction, finding nowhere an abiding place. He cannot, however, persist in this endless oscillation between the finite and the infinite, and strives unceasingly after the higher form of existence in which alone he can find his true self, his perfection. In this advance his finite individuality, with all its disquiet and disharmony, must be set aside; all that he has hitherto been must disappear in a radical transformation; and only when this has been achieved is he delivered from the inadequacy and imperfection, the pressure and torments, of his natural life, and raised to stability, security, peace, perfection. His self passes transfigured into the eternal peace of the Absolute. The belief in immortality means, if it has any meaning at all, not that we carry into the future world our present self, but that in that world we may somehow persist in a changed form.

We must avoid reading any religious significance into these ideas. Bosanquet was as little religious, in the narrower sense, as Bradley was, and like him regarded religion, however valuable and indispensable in its own sphere, as ultimately only a stage preliminary to metaphysics, and God as not the all-comprehending Real but as an appearance, the highest of all appearances but still falling short of the Absolute. The transformation spoken of above is to be understood rather in a purely metaphysical sense, that is as the individual's transcending himself not in a world beyond this one but in his daily life here and now. Bosanquet declares that the re-ordering of our experiences through the inclusion of them in a fuller whole of experience is something that can be verified by us at any time: the Absolute enters into our finite life and manifests itself in whatever we think and do. "A careful analysis of a single day's life of any fairly typical human being would establish triumphantly all that is needed in principle for the affirmation of the Absolute."[1]

For Bosanquet, then, as for Bradley, the Absolute, on whose altar he sacrifices man's personal individuality, is simply the product of a longing. It is the ideal we strive after, our highest value, our guiding star in the ascent of our nature. Consequently, it does not lie above a far horizon but is among us; we

[1] *Principle of Individuality and Value*, p. 377.

have only to stretch out our hands to seize it and bring it into our own being. Without doing violence to its meaning we might even call it, in Nietzsche's language, the Superman, and Bosanquet himself uses Nietzsche's expression "the transvaluation of all values" to describe the finite's transcendence of itself. The heroic character of his world-view has occasionally been emphasized. Nevertheless, it would be a mistake to go too far along this line, for Bosanquet's ideal is too much a safe refuge and a comfortable resting-place, a too passive and changeless principle, to be brought into harmony with Nietzsche's tragic struggle for the enhancement of our nature; and so, too, are his facile optimism and his conception of human life as sinking quietly to rest in the blissful harmony of the Absolute. In these respects he follows Bradley.

Although, as we saw, Bosanquet made the problem of individuality the centre of his thought, it is as evident in him as it was in Bradley how little his absolutism grew out of it. For if the ideal can only be reached by the surrender of the self, is not human personality destroyed in its innermost core? If this personality must completely transform itself to find its true self, what is left of its own distinctive value? Do we not value personality first and foremost because of what it is here and now and not because of an ideal of it whose realization would require the destruction of all that is dear to us? And anyway is not the idea of the submergence and inclusion of one individual in a higher individual extremely difficult to conceive? Truly Bosanquet in dealing with individual personality carries the devaluation of it to such lengths that there can no longer be any question of grasping its essential character. His doctrine is faced with two alternatives: either the ideal remains unfulfilled or the real is destroyed. This is the consequence of straining the ideal too far beyond the reality.

There is neither space nor need to treat the metaphysics of Bosanquet with anything like exhaustiveness. We may conclude by noting that in it the problem of value is made much more prominent than it is by Bradley, possibly through the influence of Lotze and the later German philosophy of value. But the frequent use of expressions taken from the sphere of value has not, in fact, altered anything essential in the matter, so that in this connection also we cannot say that Bosanquet succeeded in making any real advance on Bradley, who made far less use of the terminology of value. Bradley's emphatic and heightened use of the term "reality" shows that this was for him at bottom a value-concept. This being so it was an easy matter to re-express certain parts of his doctrine in the language of value. This is what Bosanquet did. For him the Absolute is not only the highest truth and the supreme reality but also the highest value, the criterion of all worth. Also he recognized levels of value as well as levels of individuality and reality. The criterion of the worth of a phenomenon lies in its logical inevitability and freedom from contradiction, or—it is the same thing—in the organic interconnection and harmony of its parts. Clearly his notion of value, and his world-view in general, were determined chiefly by logical and aesthetic motives. The influence of the logical is evident in his quest for theoretical satisfaction through the removal of everything contradictory and irrational, and the influence of the aesthetic in the harmonious rounding-off of his system in a symphony of the Absolute in which all discords find their final resolution.

On Bosanquet's contribution to aesthetics we can only touch briefly. He was one of the very few British philosophers of recent times who have occupied themselves with this field. He thereby drew attention to a part of the legacy of Hegel which the Hegelian school had, curiously enough, scarcely attended to. Besides his debt to Hegel he owed much to Ruskin and William Morris. His chief work in this connection is his comprehensive *History of Aesthetic*, which traces the development of art and of aesthetic theory from the Greeks down to the XIXth Century. Permeated with the spirit of Hegel, it is an historiographical achievement of the first rank, uniting a high level of culture with wide erudition and penetrating understanding of artistic and aesthetic problems, and unfolding large and profound surveys of spiritual situations and figures. His account, for example, of the aesthetic significance of the German movement from the beginning of the XVIIIth Century through Classicism, Romanticism, and Idealism to the post-Hegelian schools is alone a testimony to an astonishing breadth of reading. It is not too much to say that Bosanquet was the only Englishman of his time who could have risen to such a high and dominating level of observation. His own aesthetic views, which he only worked out in a very small book, fall naturally within the general outline of his system, though these appear only incidentally and in no way impede the free development of his ideas. He saw in beauty a basic type of the higher unity, a reconciliation of the particular and the general, the natural and the spiritual, necessity and freedom. He conceived it as widely as he had conceived goodness and truth, thus making it include ugliness as its lowest level or manifestation. The harmonious perfection we enjoy in a work of art is the most perfect premonition of that ultimate unity which in metaphysics we contemplate as the Absolute.

HAROLD HENRY JOACHIM (*b.* 1868)

[Educated at Balliol College, Oxford. 1892–4, Lecturer in Philosophy at St. Andrews; 1894–7 same at Balliol College; 1897–1919, Fellow and Tutor, Merton College, Oxford; 1919, Wykeham Professor of Logic, Oxford; retired 1935. *A Study of the Ethics of Spinoza*, 1901; *The Nature of Truth*, 1906; *Immediate Experience and Mediation*, Inaugural Lecture, 1919; also translator of *De gen. et corr.* in Oxford Translation of Aristotle, 1922.]

Joachim's theory of truth, worked out on the basis of the Absolutism of Bradley and Bosanquet, excited considerable attention as soon as it appeared, and provoked a lively discussion in which Russell, Moore, Schiller, Dawes Hicks, and others took part. The reason for such interest in such a relatively small book was that in it certain difficulties latent in absolutism were for the first time frankly and publicly admitted by a representative of the absolutist school, and certain consequences explicitly drawn which the leaders of the school had hitherto concealed, but which their opponents had already detected. Besides, Joachim put into systematic form ideas that Bradley had barely indicated, or developed but loosely.

The theory is that truth is to be understood exclusively as truth of system, as coherence within a larger, ultimately within the entire, whole of knowledge or being. We may call this the theory of immanent coherence. Joachim distinguishes it from three other theories then current. Firstly, truth is not the correspondence of thought and reality, the ideal representation of a fact, the true copy of an original beyond it. Secondly, it is not a property of entities independent of consciousness, existing in and for themselves and therefore unrelated to the knowing mind. And thirdly, it cannot be a direct, intuitive apprehension of objects, even though it may often assume this form; and when truth does take this form it is true not because of but despite such immediate givenness. Against these theories Joachim maintains that truth exhibits itself in rational mediation within a system. Every judgment is a member of a general structure of meaning, apart from which it is nothing; it is continuous as it were with a background from which its own determinate meaning is derived. This background is, as we have said, the whole of knowledge or being. Even such a simple, apparently self-evident proposition as $2 + 2 = 4$ only acquires meaning, and, *a fortiori*, truth, when considered in the light of the entire system of numbers, which in turn is only a section or fragment of the whole of reality. The greater the background of meaning, the truer the judgment, for its truth is a function of the degree to which the coherence of the system is realized in it. Similarly every particular experience is embedded in the ideal all-comprehending experience. This ideal experience has not to be conceived statically, as a rigid structure, a finished whole reposing in itself, but as a living and self-realizing process. Here Joachim, like Bradley, makes room for the possibility of a scale of truth between the extremes of completely systematized and therefore absolute truth on the one hand and utterly isolated facts on the other. Again in agreement with Bradley—and with Spinoza, too, whom Joachim had studied closely—error is declared to be defective truth or the shadow cast by truth; it is the negative element in the heart of things, an ugly discord which will disappear in the harmony of the Absolute, a merely fragmentary phase or factor in the endless dialectic of truth. In its ultimate metaphysical meaning it is the falling away of the finite from the infinite, the breaking off from the whole of a part that would assert itself as independent. This breaking off of one of its own factors is grounded in the very nature of truth; the fragment is its negative, its other, emerging from its womb, though only to return to it, since otherness is absorbed by oneness and surmounted by it. There is here quite plainly an element of Spinozistic mysticism, present also in Bradley but absent from Bosanquet.

After all this, developed with considerable acuteness and conviction, Joachim makes the interesting confession that the coherence theory cannot provide a satisfactory solution of the nature of truth and that it is condemned to shipwreck. He sees that it is only applicable to an ideal truth that human knowledge can never reach. Our finite knowledge is always discursive, always "about" something other than itself, and consequently any theory of truth devised by us can only be a theory "about" a truth older than itself. The notion of coherence, therefore, can never rise above the level of a knowledge that even at the last attains to nothing more than truth as correspondence. Indeed, it follows also that the coherence theory itself cannot be perfectly true, for we cannot prove, but only surmise, that it is a sign of absolute truth. Hence Joachim admits the collapse of his own theory, even though he maintains that it enters more deeply into the problem than any of the others. Such a conclusion cannot be satisfactory, and indicates that there is something wrong with the philosophical grounds out of which it has grown. The trouble lies in the unbridgeable nature of the gulf that Bradley had set between appearance and reality and which Joachim retains in the form of a too great separation between human knowledge and absolute truth. The ideal is suspended too high above the actual to be able to have in this its expression and embodiment. The keen hostility of Absolutism to Pragmatism, for example, rests at bottom on the opposition between a doctrine oriented towards the ideal and one exclusively centred in the sphere of human experience.

The influence, direct and indirect, of Bradley's doctrine was so powerful that scarcely any thinker of importance was left untouched by it. It runs through the whole of contemporary British philosophy, evident in followers, opponents, and neutrals alike. Only in very recent years has it begun to decline. Among the closest of his followers we must include along with Bosanquet and Joachim, A. E. TAYLOR, who in his earliest writings was deeply indebted to Bradley. Since Taylor, however, afterwards followed other lines of thought and struck out into lines of his own, all widely removed from Bradley's, we must consider him in another place.[1]

[1] Pages 412 ff.

5. MCTAGGART'S PLURALISM

JOHN McTAGGART ELLIS McTAGGART (1866–1925)

[Educated at Trinity College, Cambridge. 1891–1925 Fellow, 1897–1923 Tutor, of same college. *Studies in the Hegelian Dialectic*, 1896 (second edition, 1922); *Studies in the Hegelian Cosmology*, 1901 (second edition, 1918); *Some Dogmas of Religion*, 1906 (second edition with biogr. introduction by C. D. Broad, 1930); *A Commentary on Hegel's Logic*, 1910 (new edition, 1931); *The Nature of Existence*, vol. 1, 1921 (vol. 2, edited by C. D. Broad, 1927); "An Ontological Idealism", in *Contemporary British Philosophy*, edited by J. H. Muirhead, first series, 1924.

Posthumous: *Philosophical Studies*, edited by S. V. Keeling, 1934.

See *McTaggart*, a Memoir, by G. Lowes Dickinson, 1931; *McTaggart*, Memoir, by C. D. Broad, in *Proc. Brit. Acad.*, 1927, pp. 307–34 (mostly reprinted in Broad's introduction to 1930 edition of *Some Dogmas of Religion*); *Examination of McTaggart's Philosophy*, vol. 1, by C. D. Broad, 1933, vol. 2, 1938; *Dictionary of National Biography*, 1922–1930.]

After Bradley, by far the most independent and thoroughgoing Idealist was McTaggart. Within the general movement he must be assigned to the Hegelian group. True, he was in many respects much further removed from Hegelian orthodoxy than Bradley and Bosanquet, but he was much nearer to it in the important respect that his thought grew out of an intensive and profound study of Hegel's philosophy, which, however much he went beyond it along lines of his own, remained the presupposition of his own system. His distinctive place within British Hegelianism is that he took the final and decisive step in the dissolution of that allegiance with theology which had marked its earliest phase, by developing from Hegelian grounds an atheistic doctrine. He thus belongs, within Hegelianism, to the extreme Left, at the furthest remove from such thinkers as Stirling, Green, and Caird. He is distinguished from Bradley and Bosanquet, who also may be assigned to the Left, in so far as they adopted a more or less neutral attitude towards the alliance with theology, by his utter independence and originality. The most striking difference between him and those whom we have hitherto considered lies in the pluralistic turn he gave to their strongly monistic tendency.

Whatever may be decided in the controversy whether McTaggart was or was not an Hegelian, it is indisputable that he made an almost unparalleled effort to understand Hegel, and that Hegel's philosophy determined his own at many points. But it is only with considerable reservations that he can be called an Hegelian. The impression one gets is rather that the forced and wilful methods of interpretation that he brought to Hegel would have had the same or similar results if applied to other thinkers—at any rate to Plato, Leibniz, Spinoza, and Berkeley—namely, the construction of a philosophy of his own and the destruction of any other. Certainly it is as easy to pass from any of these thinkers to McTaggart's system as it is from Hegel. It has been observed that his teaching, though flying so to speak the Hegelian flag and cruising in Hegelian waters, nevertheless issued, unconsciously, in a kind of Platonism; also he has been called, with considerable justification, a modern Spinoza; and his close affinity with Leibniz's monadology and Berkeley's spiritualism has been equally emphasized and is indeed obvious. But all this, true as it is, only serves to show that his system is a thoroughly personal one, utilizing the ideas of others not as material but simply as vehicles and instruments. Whatever may be thought of its worth or importance, it is certainly one of the boldest and most imposing and original attempts to think the world as a whole that have been made in Britain. Among the modern system-builders of his own country he takes a rank shared only with Bradley, Alexander, and Whitehead. To the shaping of his rigid and exclusive system he brought a remarkable clearness and economy of thought, a severe and inevitable logic, constructive power, speculative depth, and mystical vision.

We may begin by indicating in what way Hegel is reflected in McTaggart. He himself says that Hegel's thought was the chief object of his inquiry for more than twenty years, and he devoted three books to the critical sifting and exposition of it.

At the end of the last he gave his considered judgment: "Hegel has penetrated further into the true nature of reality than any philosopher before or after him."[1] Not that this high estimate warrants our stopping where he stopped. "The next task of philosophy should be to make a fresh investigation of that nature by a dialectic method substantially, though not entirely, the same as Hegel's."[2] In the greater part of his discussions he believed himself to be in agreement with Hegel, and simply wished here and there to draw out a consequence inherent in Hegel but left implicit: only occasionally did he express himself critically and divergently. But in so self-willed a thinker all this apparent agreement was only effected through forced exegesis, distortion, and displacement; he adapted Hegel's lines of thought to his own by reading into or out of them his own prior ideas. In effect he mined Hegel's system and blew it up from within, leaving at the end nothing but ruins, which he used but sparsely in the construction of his own new system.

For McTaggart the heart of Hegel's philosophy, and the ground of its abiding value in the history of thought, is its logic and the dialectic connected with this. The many applications of the logic to the peripheral parts of the system, however, such as art, religion, history, law, and the State, he regarded as conditioned by the circumstances of Hegel's own day and as unessential, though he recognized the wealth of ideas and the great stimulus that came from them. His primary concern in this connection was to defend Hegel against the misunderstanding, still widely current, that Hegel spun the world out of pure thought, moving entirely among merely formal abstractions and constructions, without any regard for the concrete content of experience. He repeatedly emphasized the concreteness of Hegel's thought. The dialectic, far from contradicting experience, presupposes it throughout. Experience rests, of course, on immediate data of sense, which cannot be produced by pure thought, but are the conditions of its existence. Hegel, according to McTaggart, was fully aware of all this, knew and

[1] *Commentary on Hegel's Logic*, p. 311. [2] Ibid., p. 311.

meant that the dialectical movement of thought can only be fulfilled within that concrete whole of experience in which the data of sense are independent factors correlative to thought.

McTaggart's special studies in the Hegelian dialectic led him to the view that the ascent of the categories is a process not of increasing abstraction but of increasing approximation to the concrete whole. He shows that the final synthesis, reached in the absolute Idea, is the logical *prius* of all the preceding categories, that the many pairs of opposites and the higher ideas into which they are successively taken up and overcome are all produced by abstraction from that supreme category, the richest of all, in which they terminate and find their completion. The movement from category to category and from synthesis to synthesis is thus not an advance in the sense of the positing of new, hitherto non-existent content, but a reversal of the process of abstraction, a recovery of the concrete unity from which the abstractions were made. Dialectic in this sense is the only true and fruitful method of philosophy. True, some of Hegel's particular transitions are neither logically necessary nor convincing, but this does not involve any derogation of their value, for—here McTaggart takes up a thoroughly un-Hegelian position—the transition from one category to another is not in fact restricted to a single logically inevitable direction but leaves room for several possibilities. Further, the dialectical method is not rigid, fixed once and for all, but is itself subject to development, a development that can be reduced to a general law. Lastly, McTaggart contends that in the dialectical process as a whole the moment of negation plays but a very small part. It is of importance only in the initial stages, dropping more and more into the background as the ascent increases. It is accidental, not essential. In thinking, each category does not spring out of an antecedent opposition, but expresses the true significance of the lower category and itself achieves its own true nature in a higher category. Where no opposition is present there is no need of reconciliation, of a resolving synthesis of contradictions, but only of an unfolding of what before has been left implicit. Dialectic is like organic growth: the higher stages grow out of the lower as a plant grows out of a seed. The moments of opposition and negation indicate what is imperfect and faulty in the process; the moment of positive development is what expresses the true nature of thought. Consequently the meaning or end of the dialectical method is fulfilled in proportion as the negative element is displaced by the positive. McTaggart held that this interpretation of dialectic could be found in or derived from Hegel, but here, as elsewhere, he was guilty of an unconscious error. Without being fully aware of it he slipped into positions that were not always merely incapable of being fitted into Hegel's doctrine but were sometimes directly contradictory to it.

Looked at in the light of his philosophical work as a whole, McTaggart's studies in Hegel appear as a détour he had to make to come to himself. Why he had to make it it is difficult to say. During the formative period of his life Hegel was at the height of his reputation in Britain and to read him had become an established vogue. But perhaps the chief reason was a need to try out and exercise his powers on one of the greatest of the masters of thought and climb up on the master's shoulders. Nevertheless, there seemed to be no intrinsic necessity for the détour, for the impulse to fashion a world-view of his own was in him from the start, and the main lines of the one he later worked out are quite evident in the first of his books. Apparently he needed only further reflection and the maturing that time brings to shape and complete his own world-view. His philosophical development followed as it were the dialectical pattern: Hegel's doctrine was the moment of opposition he had to encounter to rise to his own true thought, the lower category that had first to be understood but then surmounted in his own system.

This last appeared in a peculiar and imposing work which was originally to bear the title "The Dialectic of Existence" but was later re-christened *The Nature of Existence*. It is the ripe product of a whole life's unwearying and unsparing thought. It is all cast in a single mould, bearing everywhere the stamp of its maker. Seen in the setting of modern British philosophy it appears foreign—like a solitary light shining from a remote and uninhabited island—and it is almost an enigma how it could have arisen in such an environment. It deserts all the familiar and well-tried and trusted ways of thought. Rarely has a thinker made such severe and unyielding demands upon himself, and set himself so high a task. His ideas progress with logical inexorability to the very end, without a trace at any point of relaxing discipline or flagging energy. The excruciating care with which he thought and wrote is revealed by the fact that he always drew up not less than five complete drafts before he would commit anything to the press. Word and thought entirely coincide: the one, laboriously and delicately chiselled, provides a perfect body for the other. And yet we detect no trace of the struggle for perfect expression; in the five-fold sifting it has all been left behind. The total impression we get of the book is of a conceptual system thought out to the end with austerity, unsparingness, lucidity, economy, and precision. But along with this we find also empty formalism and verbalism, the frequent reading out of terms of what has earlier been smuggled into them, the mere play of ideas, hair-splitting distinctions, and over-subtle definitions. To the marble-cold system of McTaggart's system, Bradley's oft-quoted phrase, "an unearthly ballet of bloodless categories", is entirely appropriate. This, however, is only one aspect—though it is the prevailing one—of McTaggart's thought and manner of exposition. Now and then we feel behind the studiously correct façade an agitation of mind, a hidden fire of deeply-lived experience, the pulse and seething of a vital personality breathing its own life into the apparently marmoreal edifice. This is the mystical side of McTaggart breaking through the texture of abstract concepts and suffusing them with livelier colours and a more concrete kind of content. But we must not suppose that these two sides of his nature stood in inevitable opposition to each other, sustaining a lasting strife between "mysticism and logic" (to borrow the happy title of one of Russell's books). In his mind they lay close together and sprang from the same root, the mysticism giving pulse and warmth to the logic, the logic dominating and disciplining the mysticism. McTaggart himself gives us the key to the understanding of this twofold aspect in the concluding sentence of his first work: "All true philosophy must be mystical, not indeed in its methods, but in its final conclusions."[1]

The title of his main work expresses its chief problem. What can be said of the characteristic marks of whatever exists or of existence as a whole? Existence as a concept falls below the concept of reality inasmuch as there are realities that do not necessarily exist while there is no existent that is not necessarily real. Reality and existence, by the way, are declared to be alike indefinable. In the distinction between existent and non-existent reality a purely theoretical interest may well fasten on the latter; but since the former is of such great importance for our practical interests, McTaggart sets himself the narrower task of investigating this—his problem is the nature of *existence*. His method is deductive and *a priori*. The general character of existence is first brought out and then the special problems of empirical existence are discussed. The two parts correspond respectively to the two volumes of the work. In the first part, a masterpiece of rigorously methodical thinking, the supreme triumph of his acutely logical mind, McTaggart stands alone among the British philosophers of every period. Since the earlier part of the XIXth Century, it is true, British philosophy has done much in the sphere of formal logic, and in the logical calculus the most abstract of all disciplines reached the summit of virtuosity. But no thinker before McTaggart had the daring in metaphysics to thrust experience contemptuously aside and construct a purely *a priori* account of the universe. It is not surprising, then, that his venture, though occasionally admired for its strangeness and novelty, was met at the outset with distrust and had no following. It was denied the widely echoing repercussion that, for example, Bradley's philosophy secured, although in clearness,

[1] *Studies in the Hegelian Dialectic.*

economy, precision, and acuteness of thought it was far superior to this.

His method of absolute demonstration, followed in the *a priori* part of his metaphysic, has a certain measure of similarity with Hegel's dialectic, but it is so individual and so wholly devised for the special ends of his own philosophy that a comparison of the two methods would give little result. McTaggart himself, despite his tendency to adhere to Hegel, was aware of this, admitting that his own method was "not characteristically Hegelian",[1] though he held that it was nearer to Hegel's than to anyone else's. There is, indeed, in McTaggart a chain of successive logical determinations, but it does not follow the triadic pattern of Hegel's categories, the transition from one stage to another is not always logically necessary (in some cases the possibility of other determinations is left open), and the lower categories are not regarded as necessarily infected with falsity, their relative truth rather than their falling short of absolute truth being stressed.

The basic difference between Hegel's thought and McTaggart's is that the former is concrete, saturated with experience, whereas the latter is abstract, remote from experience. McTaggart was always anxious to preserve the *a priori* purity of his formal determinations from any clouding by empirical material. Of course, he could not achieve this throughout. It appears that a twofold appeal to experience is necessary in order to set the deductive process going. Pure being or pure existence may be initially posited and its marks deduced *a priori;* but whether in fact anything exists at all can only be known by consulting experience. The proposition that there is something that exists rests on sense-perception and is the fundamental premiss of all subsequent deduction. Its evidence is therefore empirical, but its certainty is no less than that of *a priori* evidence. Now, for McTaggart, to say that something exists is to say that a substance exists, and the question arises whether there are many substances or only one, whether, in other words, substance is differentiated or not. This question could, in

[1] *Nature of Existence*, p. 47.

McTaggart's opinion, be answered by pure deduction—the differentiation of substance follows from the *a priori* certainty that substance cannot be simple—but he prefers to resort to empirical proof and shows that a single sense-perception is enough to demonstrate that substance is differentiated. Substance, then, exists, and is not one but many.

But *what* is it? To existence quality must be added. Whatever exists must also possess a quality. Quality, however, cannot be defined; we can only point to particular examples of it. Relation must be added too, and it also is indefinable. Since there is a multiplicity of substances there must be relations between them. Relation is therefore essential to existence. McTaggart attached considerable importance to this concept and subjected the particular relations to an acute and penetrating investigation. Relations differ from qualities in that while these inhere in things, the former as it were lie between them. A substance is accordingly described (not defined) as that which has qualities and stands in relations without being itself either a quality or a relation. Further, every substance is different from every other; the description of it cannot be applied to any other. And substances are ordered into groups, which can be formed of any substances whatever. For instance (the examples are McTaggart's own), not only do the Presidents of the United States, or the citizens of England, constitute a group, but so also do such utterly heterogeneous things as, say, the desk at which I am writing, the oldest rabbit of Australia, and the last medicine Louis XIV took. These can be grasped in some sort of a unity, if only the unity of their threeness or of my arbitrary bringing of them together. We cannot question whether the group really is a group, but only whether it is appropriate or of any use. Formal deduction apart, this line of thought has a metaphysical bearing in the sense that everything in the universe is somehow related to everything else, and in some way, however infinitesimally, acts upon everything else.

The substance that includes all others as its parts is the universe. The concept of the universe is necessary as the unity to which the plurality of substances has to be referred. Since it comprises the entire content of everything that is, there can only be one universe; two universal substances would have exactly the same content and would therefore be unthinkable. Everything that exists is thus enclosed within the unity of a fully determinate system. Every substance is connected with every other, in virtue of their common relation to the all-comprehending unity of the universe; the relation of the parts of the universe both to one another and to the whole is that of reciprocity or co-operation. The universe is an organic unity.

Specially important from the theoretical point of view is the idea of the infinite divisibility of substance. That nothing is absolutely simple is attested even at the level of perception, and for pure thought the proposition is completely evident and finally true. Now if all substances and all their parts, and all the parts of these parts, and so on, have no limit to their divisibility, we have an infinitely complex and differentiated and hierarchically organized structure with an infinite number of relations between the whole and its parts and among the parts themselves. The instrument with which thought is to master this exceedingly complex system of an infinity of relations is introduced by McTaggart under the name of "determining correspondence". With this—a causal relation (we have no space to expound it further)—and this alone, McTaggart believed, can the contradiction otherwise involved in the idea of infinite divisibility be avoided and the entire content of the universe ordered in a logically satisfactory way. When thus ordered this content appears as a hierarchical system, with the original substance at the head as the primary whole, this being divided into primary parts which are subdivided into secondary parts of the first grade and so on indefinitely. All these superordinate and subordinate wholes, together with their parts, are in a relation of mutually determining correspondence, so that a substance is only adequately described when all its parts and their relation both to one another and to the whole have been indicated. McTaggart calls this system of substances resting on determining correspondence the fundamental system of the universe.

From a purely theoretical point of view the system may be regarded equally well as monistic or as pluralistic, according as we concentrate on the unity of substance or the multiplicity of its parts. In regarding the latter as the more fundamental, McTaggart certainly cannot justify his choice on *a priori* grounds; it was determined, as we shall see later, by empirical and practical considerations. It is evident that within the multiplicity the primary parts are assigned a greater metaphysical importance than the secondary parts of all species and than the primary whole itself.

Those who take less pleasure in the formal play of concepts than in genuine metaphysical vision will get more out of the second volume of his main work (and out of the relatively popular *Some Dogmas of Religion*, which anticipates it) than out of the first. In it McTaggart at last descends from the ether of pure thought into the actual world of our experience, bringing his general results to bear on certain empirical problems and trying them out there both theoretically and practically. The important metaphysical ideas that result, and which together constitute a complete world-view, are exhibited as the necessary consequences of the *a priori* foundation. With the introduction of new problems and new material the conceptual apparatus is developed and consolidated still further, so that we have to pass once more through long stretches of desert land before we can pluck the fruit of the tree of life. Since some of McTaggart's metaphysical ideas appeared in germ in his earliest work and all the essential ones appeared in his book on religion quite independently of the logical foundation we have been considering, we are probably justified in inferring that the conceptual apparatus was thought out subsequently. If this is so, we cannot share McTaggart's belief that his metaphysical conclusions are conditioned by his *a priori* scheme, but must hold on the contrary that this is conditioned by his conclusions and was devised later to ground and strengthen them. In other words, his chief metaphysical positions have a value independently of the abstract scheme, and are grounded in themselves.

Of the many problems that present themselves in the second part we can single out only a few, in order to indicate at least the general direction of his thought. The best known is his theory of time. He first distinguishes two kinds of temporal sequence, the one passing from the past through the present to the future, the other constituted by the relations of "earlier than" and "later than". In the first, which he calls the A series, the terms are continually changing, passing into each other; in the second, which he calls the B series, they are constant, resting on persistent relations, for when an event happens earlier than another and later than yet another, the temporal order is given once and for all. The A series, therefore, is the proper series of time, since it includes the changefulness that is the essential mark of time. It appears, however, after a rather long and hair-splitting discussion, that the A series contains a contradiction, and consequently, from the point of view of true reality, simply cannot exist. Nothing real, then, is past, present or future, or subject to any change. We do, indeed, perceive things in time, and cannot help doing so, but this only shows that perception does not seize things in their real character. Whatever is in time is so far mere appearance.

This idea, so characteristic of Idealism, is given a positive expression in McTaggart's conceptual apparatus by the addition to the A and B series of a C series. This represents the real relations of things, embodies the truth falsely stated in the temporal relations of the two other series, and in all statements of spatial relations as well, for space too is mere appearance. It expresses the relations of things as one of logical inclusion. It is a series of inclusions with a determinate direction which is clearly more fundamental than the reverse direction, in that it passes from what has a poorer to what has a richer content. At the one extreme is nothing, at the other the whole. The "earlier than" of the B series is here replaced by "included in", the "later than" by "inclusive of". The final member of the series, not being included in anything, is thus inclusive of everything. Nothing can be added to it. It is obviously the absolute Idea of Hegel, and the advancing inclusiveness within the C series is obviously the counterpart of Hegel's dialectical development of the categories.

McTaggart's theory of time thus leads—and its special interest lies in this point—to the same result as Bradley's philosophy, though resting on very different presuppositions; namely, to the distinction of appearance and reality. The criterion by which these are distinguished is the *a priori* scheme of determining correspondence. Whatever cannot be brought into this is at once degraded to the status of appearance and whatever can is counted as real. By this test, matter, together with all sense-data, is relegated to appearance. If matter existed, it would be infinitely divisible, and its infinitesimal parts would fall under the principle of determining correspondence; but, it appears, such an endless dividing of matter cannot be carried out, so that matter cannot exist. For the natural sciences, however, the existence and the non-existence of matter are alike irrelevant, both being metaphysical hypotheses which touch neither science nor daily life. McTaggart, like Bradley, on whose arguments in this connection he draws considerably, rejects the assumption of the existence of matter simply on the ground that it is bad metaphysics.

We now come to the heart of McTaggart's metaphysic, the doctrine that reality is in essence spiritual. Whatever exists is spirit and nothing but spirit, in the full and strictly metaphysical sense of spiritual substance, as understood, for example, by Berkeley. All further determinations of the metaphysical nature of the world henceforward follow from the *a priori* deductions of the first part of the book. The equation of the primary substance with reality as such or the Absolute involves the correspondence of the primary parts to those spiritual beings we call persons or selves, and since selves are primarily percipients of the secondary parts to the perceptions of these selves. Selves thus possess a special metaphysical dignity. True, we must conceive them as gathered together in the unity of the absolute Substance, as the primary differentiation of this; but, it is argued, the nature of reality is more profoundly revealed in the differentiations than in the supreme unity. McTaggart's favourite illustration of the relation of the Whole and its parts is the analogy of the relation of a college and its members: both are spiritual beings, but only the members are persons in any genuine sense, whereas the college, though a spiritual unity of persons, is not itself a person. In ultimate analysis, only persons really exist, only they constitute the ingredients, metaphysically understood, of the universe. The pluralistic aspect, here as in the *a priori* section, is held to be more fundamental than the monistic. The Absolute, then, is a unity of persons, a system of selves, related to each other as the parts of substance were shown to be in the first section.

In no other contemporary system are the nature and value of finite personality more deeply apprehended and grounded than in McTaggart's. The thought that there is nothing truly real except finite persons may be said to be McTaggart's primary philosophical conviction. His entire system is organized round it, and all his other conclusions follow from it. Hence the feeling we get that underneath all the logical armour of his *a priori* deductions there is an inner agitation of mind which points to a deeper layer of thought than the formalities and abstractions that predominate in his writings. This feeling is intensified by the further properties he attributes to personality. The self is an independent entity and *sui generis*, a spiritual substance existing entirely in its own right, and completely individual, so that each is fundamentally different from every other. Consequently it is an ultimate and absolute certainty that the self cannot be included in any other self or part of a self, especially in that higher unity called in philosophy the Absolute and in religion God. The supreme metaphysical dignity of the self lies in its being in its essence subject to no change: and as thus existing from eternity to eternity, having neither beginning nor end in time, it cannot ever have been created or ever be destroyed. Given the thought of a self the thought of a creator is impossible; and if there is a God, He cannot have created the self since this exists in the same eternity as He. The self is thus immortal, in the sense of existing in a timeless eternity. Inevitably, then, it is pre-existent as well as post-existent. For its identity does not consist in continuity of consciousness or of memory but in the changelessness of its spiritual substantiality. Consciousness, indeed, is not part of the essential nature of a person and can be lost without disturbing this. Nor would the loss of memory in any way prejudice immortality, for our present life appears to us entirely valuable despite our having neither any recollection of a previous life nor any idea of any future one. Nor is it really an objection that on the above contention we have probably passed through in the past and may probably pass through in the future many stages corresponding to that which in our present existence begins with birth and ends with death. The idea of a plurality of lives, of recurrent death, far from being meaningless, is highly probable.

The doctrine of immortality leads to a position very distinctive of McTaggart, which at first sight seems paradoxical but which follows necessarily from the premisses, namely, that belief in immortality, for all its frequent connection in religion and philosophy with belief in God, can exist and remain without this. There is no logical connection between them. Neither is there between Idealism and Theism. As we have seen, there cannot be any higher level of personality than that of finite selves, in which they might be included; the Absolute, whatever it may be positively, is certainly impersonal; and to call this impersonal principle God would be obviously inappropriate. If, however, we do not identify the Absolute and God, what ideas remain to be attached to the latter? In view of the evil in the world, as well as on other grounds, the conception of the perfect goodness and omnipotence of God cannot be justified. We could only save the moral character of God by supposing His power to be limited, and the resultant conception of a God striving after the good and victoriously reaching it is, indeed, much more satisfying than that of a perfectly good God, and more probable as well. Again, God cannot be the Creator, for, as we have also noted, finite persons are eternal. The only conception, then, that seems susceptible of any justification, is of a God who is neither omnipotent nor creative, and the only reason why we should not believe in the existence of such a God is that there is no rational ground for doing so. This is a typical sample of McTaggart's method of arguing, and the purport of it is clearly that the idea of the existence of God, while certainly not contradictory, is an utterly superfluous assumption. With the probity and courage of thought characteristic of him, which shrank from any *sacrificium intellectus* and from any concession to popular views, he drew the atheistic consequence of his system. But his atheism is, of course, wholly different from the doctrines that commonly parade under that name. It is, for instance, impossible to call it irreligious. It is compatible with some forms of religion, such as Buddhism and other Oriental systems; as is also indicated by the fact that its presuppositions—the idealistic conception of the spiritual nature of the world, and the belief in the immortality of the human soul—have hitherto always been associated with a theistic world-view.

The final theme in McTaggart's metaphysic is another indication that his atheism is not irreligious. So far the self has been considered in and by itself. What of the relation of persons to one another? The autonomy of the self, raised in McTaggart's system to the highest degree, does not mean that persons are isolated, each abiding in his own selfhood. They are on the contrary related to one another vitally, profoundly, and reciprocally. The most important relation of all among them—the bond, therefore, that unites all things—is love, the emotion one self feels for another. It springs from a sense of the closest connection and community with other selves. The connection is a metaphysical one, immanent in the essence of personality, not something that has to be brought about or instituted. Love, therefore, arising out of the ultimate nature of selfhood, cannot be anything superficial or external but is deep, intrinsic, essential, and thereby charged with a singular intensity and passion. It is the greatest good that we human beings possess and the highest value that the universe embodies. It expresses the complete harmony the world has reached in its last stage, the stage of selfhood, and is the only guarantee that the essence of the world is good and not bad.

In our present life, love does not, of course, find its perfect form. This is reached only in that existence towards which all our striving is directed, and which McTaggart, retaining his abstract schema to the very end, calls the final stage of the C series. But this logical form is now nothing but a phantom, pale and empty, ill able to hold the inner fire and transport with which the thinker, now turned mystic, depicts that consummation. The final stage, which has a beginning but no ending, is the stage of absolute reality. Its value is greater than that of all the preceding stages put together; in it truth has its final triumph over error, joy over pain, goodness over evil. It is not, indeed, entirely free from evil, but this has faded into such a tenuous semblance of itself that it now appears only as an echo, a pain sympathetic with the evil in the antecedent stages. So great has love now become that it penetrates and dominates everything, and in it all things live and move and have their being. In absolute reality every self will love every other that it directly perceives. This perfect love is not the love of truth or goodness or virtue; it is not sexual affection; it is not even man's love of God; it is a passionate, all-devouring power. It is "so direct, so intimate, and so powerful that even the deepest mystical rapture gives us but the slightest foretaste of its perfection".[1] It is subject to no external determination; no cause of it can be assigned. It is best described by saying quite simply and directly that through it two beings belong to each other and become one. It is the love whose paean the poets have sung: most purely Tennyson in his *In Memoriam*, and Dante in his *Vita Nuova*, and in his *Divina Commedia*,

L'amor che move il sole e l'altre stelle.[2]

[1] *Nature of Existence*, vol. 2, p. 479.

[2] "The love that moves the sun and the other stars"—the last line of the *Comedy*.

6. THE PERSONAL IDEALISTS

ANDREW SETH PRINGLE-PATTISON (1856–1931)

[Educated at Edinburgh and in Germany. 1880–3, Fraser's Assistant at Edinburgh; 1883–7, Professor of Philosophy, Cardiff; 1887–91, Professor of Logic and Metaphysics, St. Andrews; 1891–1919 same at Edinburgh. Changed his name from Andrew Seth in 1898 as a condition of succeeding to an estate. *The Development from Kant to Hegel*, 1882 (part 2 reprinted in his *Philosophical Radicals*); "Philosophy as Criticism of the Categories", in *Essays in Philosophical Criticism*, edited by A. Seth and R. B. Haldane, 1883 (reprinted in his *Philosophical Radicals*); *Scottish Philosophy: A Comparison of the Scottish and German Answers to Hume*, 1885 (fourth edition, 1907); *Hegelianism and Personality*, 1887 (second edition, 1893); *Two Lectures on Theism*, 1897; *Man's Place in the Cosmos and other Essays*, 1897 (second edition, 1902); *The Philosophical Radicals and Other Essays*, 1907; *The Idea of God in the Light of Recent Philosophy* (Gifford Lectures), 1917 (second edition, 1920); *The Idea of Immortality* (Gifford Lectures), 1922; *Studies in the Philosophy of Religion*, 1930.

Posthumous: *The Balfour Lectures on Realism*, edited with a Memoir by G. F. Barbour, 1933 (lectures delivered in 1891).

See *A. S. Pringle-Pattison*. Memoirs by J. B. Baillie and J. B Capper, in *Proceedings British Academy*, vol. 17.]

Pringle-Pattison, a Scot, whose philosophical activity was contemporaneous with that of Bosanquet, played a prominent part in the appropriation, elaboration, and consolidation of the idealistic heritage from Germany, and was one of the ablest of the second generation of British idealists. He was not, however, markedly original. He lacked the deep intellectual forcefulness of Bradley, the comprehensive interest and culture of Bosanquet, the radical and esoteric temper of McTaggart, and Ward's training in the natural sciences. To all these he was indebted. But he attached himself to no one of them, following instead a path of his own which led through them all by a criticism and mutual adjustment of their several doctrines. The result was what may be called a normal Idealism, gathering together the various tendencies and avoiding the more radical and controversial tenets. It was through such adjustments within the school, critical encounters with its opponents, and wide investigations into the history of philosophy, that Pringle-Pattison thought out his world-view, and did so rather under the external stimulus of his appointment as Gifford Lecturer and the internal stimulus of a critical mind than out of a deeply felt urge for speculation and system. His world-view commands respect, but, with its avoidance of Monism and Pluralism, Absolutism and Personalism, and all other "isms", it is a compromise, not an original creation.

Of his earliest works, which go back to the 'eighties, two have a more than passing significance. The *Essays in Philosophical Criticism*, edited by him and his friend Haldane, constituted a common declaration or platform of a number of younger men, then little known, who adhered to the new movement, and represented the first mobilization of the forces of idealism. Pringle-Pattison contributed the opening essay, sketching the outlines of a philosophy essentially Hegel's but not tied down to him, rather moving freely through the whole line of thought between Kant and Hegel. In his first work, which had appeared in the previous year, he had shown that the development of this philosophy from Kantianism to Hegelianism proceeded by an immanent logical necessity.

Having thus appeared as the standard-bearer of Hegelianism, he created a considerable surprise when, only a few years later, he published a book in which Hegelianism was made the subject of sharp criticism and pronounced to be unsatisfactory at certain points. The book, *Hegelianism and Personality*, was not, however, directed so much against the Hegelian movement as such as against certain speculative developments of it on the part of its absolutist wing. Still, it represented something like a revolution within the high quarters of the camp, and called into being an opposition movement to which all those who were unable to support the Absolutism of Bradley and Bosanquet eventually rallied. The aim of this opposition was to purify Idealism from certain Hegelian elements by looking forward to Lotze as well as backward to Kant. At the same time it signified a revival of Theism as an integral element of Idealism, and so far a return to the older Hegelian school and its alliance with religion. Pringle-Pattison's strongly theological interests were here doubtless a deciding factor, and it is no accident that his book found a lively echo in the circle of Martineau.

The centre of this criticism of Hegel was the problem of the self, of personality. Kant's doctrine of the self, it is contended, is to be understood in its original epistemological bearing. The transcendental unity of self-consciousness is simply the logical unity of thought, the purely formal factor of knowing. It was Fichte who began the process of converting Kant's epistemology into a metaphysic of the Absolute, a process continued by Hegel and further by the British Kantians and Hegelians—for it is no more evident in Fichte than in Green's transformation of the synthetic unity of apperception into a universal spiritual principle or divine consciousness. In Hegel also logic and metaphysics are not clearly separated: the concept is hypostatized into a real essence, the categories are identified with forms of existent things, the world is constructed logically out of pure thought. But this grandiose attempt never succeeds in reaching the real data of experience, the concrete and the individual, never gets beyond the abstract and formal realm of concepts. The real cannot be produced by thought but is given to it. Thought can describe only what is already there to be found, and this is always individual and factual, and therefore alogical, irrational. By the persistent ignoring of factuality Hegel's world shrank to the logical process, in which concrete individual things became nothing but foci of formal categories.

Hegel's panlogism, Pringle-Pattison continues, is particularly inadequate with regard to that form of individuality which we call personality. It leaves no room for the reality of persons. Hegel's error, shared with him by Green and the British Hegelian school in general, of identifying human and divine consciousness and placing both in a single universal self, is a consequence of the tendency to substitute a mere form for a real being. In the purely formal self or absolute both are extinguished, robbed of their distinctive nature as individual personalities. As against this absolutism, Pringle-Pattison emphasizes the numerical and qualitative uniqueness of each genuine person, its complete utter exclusion of all other persons, its impenetrability, in comparison with which the impenetrability of matter is only a faint analogue. No self can be contained in or permeated by another. Only when regarded as a knowing subject is the self primarily a synthetic or unifying principle; regarded metaphysically, as an existent, its primary mark is separateness. Even before God the human person is relatively independent, having a centre of its own. God himself has to be conceived, not as an abstract category as Hegel's Absolute is, but as a self-conscious personality, into which a finite person can no more penetrate than God can penetrate into a finite person. Hegel's Absolute Spirit or Green's universal consciousness is in this reference a *cul-de-sac*, leading neither to finite nor to infinite personality. Hegelianism and personality are incompatible.

We need not consider how far Pringle-Pattison's criticism of Hegel's philosophy, especially his charge that it is a purely formal scheme, was justified. We have seen that a decade later McTaggart, who had an even closer knowledge of the Hegelian text, took an entirely opposite view, though it is interesting to note that he and Pringle-Pattison nevertheless came to the same conclusion in their own thinking about personality. But Pringle-Pattison's criticism has the historical interest of finding its justification not so much in the past as in the future development of British Hegelianism, that is, in the complete renunciation that ensued of Bradley's and Bosanquet's Absolutism in regard to personality. He put his finger on a wound that only began to gape afterwards, saw beforehand a coming danger, and thereby erected against it a bulwark behind which all those could take their stand who could not allow the independent right and value of finite personality to be diminished or denied. He thus divided the Hegelian camp into two opposed groups, absolutists and personalists, a division which persisted throughout the later history of the movement. To have been the first within the school consciously and firmly to maintain the indefeasible value of personality, thereby starting a line of thought which later bore fruit in various forms, is his special service in the development of British Idealism.

Hegelianism and Personality marks Pringle-Pattison's farthest departure from Hegel. In his later writings, while he retained and gave a systematic grounding to the attitude he had adopted on the question of personality, he moved back towards his original Hegelian starting-point. The tendency first became evident in a detailed critical examination of Bradley's *Appearance and Reality*,[1] in which he approached this "new theory of the Absolute" much less aggressively and negatively than his earlier attitude would have led one to expect. Finding in Bradley the opposed tendencies, one of which he calls Hegelian and the other an echo of Spinoza and Schelling, he accepted the first and rejected the second; in other words he rejected both the view that makes of the Absolute an empty undifferentiated unity in which oppositions are not genuinely overcome but simply smoothed over, and the un-Hegelian dualism of appearance and reality, and accepted the doctrine of degrees of truth and reality, which he regarded as the core of abiding value in Hegel's philosophy. Despite much criticism of detail, his general attitude towards the new Absolutism, in Bosanquet even more than in Bradley, is a favourable one. Bosanquet in particular seems to have contributed outstandingly to the final form of his metaphysic; at any rate, in the *Idea of God* it is through his frequent encounters with Bosanquet that he clarifies his own ideas. Since the question of the agreement and difference of these two thinkers is a domestic affair of the school we need not enter into it.

We find no systematic rounding-off of Pringle-Pattison's ideas into a world-view until we come to his two series of Gifford Lectures, the *Idea of God* and the *Idea of Immortality*, the first of which is in all respects the more substantial and

[1] *Contemporary Review*, 1894; reprinted in his *Man's Place in the Cosmos*.

important. Here, as before, his central interest is metaphysical. For him, as for the other Hegelian system-builders, the task of philosophy is to think reality in its wholeness, to trace out its rational synthesis as a closed and coherent system, to interpret all its parts and phases in the light of a single fundamental principle, on the supposition, which cannot be proved but must inevitably be posited, that reality is through and through rational, that things stand in an order and that this order is in principle knowable. The idea of the organic connection of the parts with both one another and the whole is the dominating theme of Pringle-Pattison's system and its Hegelian dowry; and in the light of it he discusses the relation of nature and man, the individual and society, the world and God, finite and Divine Being, and so on.

Nature is organic to man and man to God. There is no nature as a fact independent and complete in itself, such as mechanical science would have us believe. On the contrary, every natural event is directed towards man as a rational being. Man is indeed a child of nature, flesh of her flesh and bone of her bone, rooted in her and gradually ascending out of her. But he is the organ of what developed him, the instrument through which Nature first attained to consciousness of herself and enjoyment of her own being. Each is organic to the other.

When this is recognized the problem of knowledge can be attacked and solved. As a knowing being, man is still a member or organ of the universe. We have therefore to close up the gulf that philosophers have made between the knowing and the known, between subject and object, and to regard them both in their unity as members of the same system. Man as knowing subject is within the world he knows, is continuous with his objects. It follows that the reality of an object is not constituted by the knowing act but presupposed by it and in this sense independent of it—independent, that is, in an epistemological sense, not in the metaphysical sense of existing *per se*, out of all relation to mind, as matter is often alleged to be, and the other unjustifiable fiction of the thing-in-itself.

The problem of knowledge, then, cannot be solved either by an Idealism of the Berkeleian type or by a materialism of the kind associated with natural science, for the former loses the object in the subject and the latter the subject in the object; nor can it be solved by the Kantian dualism of noumena and phenomena, since this issues in Agnosticism. The solution can only be found through a realism that does justice to both the correlated factors. Since such a realism would in all essentials coincide with the unsophisticated view, Pringle-Pattison calls his view natural realism. It does not, of course, conflict at all with the fundamental idealistic thesis of the spiritual nature of the world, and can enter organically into the system of metaphysical Idealism.

Pringle-Pattison's metaphysic is idealistic, with Nature, Man, and God as its foci. Its Idealism is not so much a doctrine within it as the general basis of the whole. Its driving force lies in the idea that Nature just cannot be thought as self-existent but only as a factor in a larger whole through which spiritual values come to be expressed: the rejection of any form whatever of naturalistic philosophy is necessitated on moral grounds. But Idealism cannot be demonstrated. It rests at bottom on an absolute conviction, the rationality of which is supported less by positive argumentation than by the irrationality of the naturalistic hypothesis opposed to it. Consequently it is no cold theory but a living power and a faith, the faith that Nature, far from being the *terminus a quo* of spirit, has spirit as its *terminus ad quem*.

In this sense, Pringle-Pattison's system is anthropocentric; it centres not in origin or starting-point but in end or goal. This teleological character becomes more and more prominent, first in his doctrine of man, later and supremely in his doctrine of God. The conception of man he expounded in *Hegelianism and Personality* is now widened and deepened, without any alteration of essentials. His fundamental opposition to absolutism appears again, this time through criticism not of Hegel himself and the first Anglo-Hegelians but of the later Hegelians, primarily Bradley and Bosanquet. As against these, Pringle-

Pattison's point of view stands nearer to those of McTaggart, Sorley, and Rashdall. It may be outlined as follows. Every finite self is a unique individual, has his centre within himself and is a world to himself, an unrepeated focus of the universe. He is not, as Bradley held, a mere bridge to an absolute reality that swallows and transforms him; on the contrary, he has a being and value of his own, and his nature is what he is here and now, not what he may conceivably become. He cannot be sunk in a higher whole, cannot realize himself in extinction. He is not, to use Bradley's expression, an adjective of the Absolute, but has substantival (though not substantial) status. He is a centre in which a manifold content acquires the inner unity of a unique self. From the ethical point of view, he is a formed, settled, and determinate will, the source of his own actions, for which, in consequence, he bears the entire responsibility. He is not a point of passage or intersection of alien forces, but the shaper of his own destiny, creative and free. Freedom belongs to the core of his nature, being the fundamental condition of any moral life. *That* we are free is irrefutable, a fact which all the difficulties of the *how* cannot affect. This freedom is the miracle of the universe, which we must simply accept. Individualism, with freedom at the heart of it, is the basic principle of the real world.

This doctrine of human personality—its autonomy, freedom, and indestructibility—is the centre of Pringle-Pattison's system; everything else is related to it and determined by it. Even the idea of God, however integral the discussion of it may be to any metaphysic, is illumined and given its place by it. God, like Nature, is not the *terminus a quo* of man; He is here defined, by contrast with most theistic systems, as the *terminus ad quem* of man. The exaggerated emphasis on finite personality, which in McTaggart was to lead to atheism, in Pringle-Pattison, who was much more strongly religious, thus led to the adjustment of the idea of God to the idea of man. On the relation of God to the world, each is stated to be organic to the other: God is not a transcendent creator who, when He had brought the world into being, left it to its fate, that is, to work itself out mechanically, but is immanent in the world and is Creator in the sense that He eternally reveals Himself in it, eternally pours into its finitude and transitoriness the inexhaustible riches of His infinite nature. The finite and the divine exist only in reciprocity, in continual organic interpenetration.

Similarly, man and God are not two independent facts, but derive their significance from each other. God needs man as much as man needs God. God has no meaning if we set Him outside all relation to our personal life, and neither has man when cut off from his creative ground. The meaning and worth of the universe cannot lie in the self-surrender of finite individuals for absorption in the infinite, which would derive from it no deepening or enrichment of its nature. The existence of individual centres of thought and action is itself and already here and now an enrichment and enhancement of the Whole, and the brighter and purer the flame of individual life the greater and more intense is the enrichment. The ruin of even a single individual life would lessen the value of the universe. The supreme values are realized only in the lives of persons and communities of persons, that is, in the communion of finite persons with one another and with God. For this reason the Absolute could not of itself become a true self. The Absolute or God is only realized in His full meaning, is only truly God, when finite individuals are left in complete integrity beside Him, to enter into community with Him and thereby enhance His worth.

The enhancement of the divine by human personality logically involves man's primacy over God. Dr. Temple's comment on Pringle-Pattison's book is that God is reduced to an adjective of the universe;[1] it would be even truer to say that He is reduced to an adjective or function of man. Another objector from the side of religion is Baron von Hügel.[2] Pringle-Pattison's theism, however deep the faith from which it sprang, is at bottom only a pseudo-theism, a compromise, incapable

[1] In *Contemporary British Philosophy*, edited by J. H. Muirhead, First Series, pp. 415 f.

[2] *Essays and Addresses*, vol. 2, pp. 135–54.

of giving theoretical satisfaction. Its exaltation of human personality precludes from the start the idea of God as this has been generally understood, and for its more consistent working-out we have to turn to Bradley with his doctrine of an impersonal Absolute and to McTaggart's Atheism. Pringle-Pattison's position is a half-way one, with no firm ground beneath it, and failing at the very point which he has made the speculative climax of metaphysics, namely, the definition of the nature of God.

JAMES SETH (1860–1924)

[Educated at Edinburgh and in Germany. 1883–5, Fraser's Assistant at Edinburgh; 1886–98 Professor successively at Dalhousie, Brown, and Cornell Universities; 1898–1924, Professor of Moral Philosophy, Edinburgh. *Freedom as Ethical Postulate*, 1891; *A Study of Ethical Principles*, 1894 (seventeenth edition, 1926); *English Philosophers and Schools of Philosophy*, 1912.

Posthumous: *Essays in Ethics and Religion, with Other Papers*, edited with a memoir by A. S. Pringle-Pattison, 1926. Includes complete bibliography.]

James Seth developed in the same philosophical environment as his brother Andrew. Both grew up in the Scottish capital, which in philosophical matters was dominated for several decades by Fraser and Calderwood, the occupants of the two chairs in philosophy at the University. Although these were little affected by the neo-idealistic movement, they made the ground favourable for the reception and growth of the new ideas; Fraser by his revival of Berkeley's Idealism, Calderwood by his rejection of Hamiltonianism, at that time generally accepted in Scotland. Both were theists, and so far stood near to the Hegelian idealists. The new Idealism entered the Scottish capital about the beginning of the 'eighties from Glasgow, where Edward Caird was its influential ambassador. About the same time a University Philosophical Society was founded in Edinburgh, with such gifted young men as Adamson, Sorley, Haldane, Ritchie, and the two Seths among its members;

and through their discussion of the new ideas the idealistic movement took root in the city, where, by the way, the original pioneer of British Hegelianism, Stirling, was then residing. By the 'nineties the two university chairs were occupied by representatives of the new tendency: Andrew Seth succeeded Fraser in 1891 and James Seth succeeded Calderwood in 1898. Both continued their teaching activity, with unusual power and fruitfulness, until after the Great War.

To a community of blood and calling the two brothers added a community of doctrine. In all essentials they were in agreement. But while Andrew's chief interest lay in metaphysics, James's lay in ethics. In this field he gave to his brother's ideas a wide application and not infrequently a more rigorous and precise formulation. In his essay, highly thought of at the time, on *Freedom as Ethical Postulate*, he defended the autonomy and integrity of moral personality against the destructive tendency of the Hegelians, thereby writing a sort of ethical sequel to his brother's *Hegelianism and Personality*. Of the two sides from which the autonomy of the person, the basis and presupposition of all moral life, was threatened—namely, Naturalism, which dissolved it in Nature, and Absolutism, which dissolved it in God—he regarded the latter as the more dangerous. But both jettisoned freedom, which is so closely bound up with the idea of personality that with it man as a distinctive being stands or falls.

The task of ethics is to define man's peculiar position in relation to natural events on the one hand and the Divine Power on the other. Ethics, therefore, cannot be a merely positive science, an empirical investigation of moral phenomena and their origins, as it remains in naturalism and evolutionism (with Leslie Stephen as its typical representative), but must press forward in one direction to the philosophy of nature, in another to metaphysics and theology. In these further fields James's system is in general the same as his brother's. Philosophy is the supreme synthesis of the three metaphysical realities—nature, man, and God. But in the synthesizing it must bring out their differences as well as their positive relations, and in particular guard against any engulfing of one by another, by giving due weight to the proper status and worth of each. The crucial metaphysical problem is the relation of man as a free moral person to God. To solve this, however, without burking any of its difficulties, is beyond the capacity of thought: the two factors seem incompatible, and yet neither can be abandoned in favour of the other, as is done, for example, religiously in mysticism and philosophically in idealistic absolutism. Man only reaches the idea of a supreme being through the conviction of his own superiority over nature and of his moral freedom and autonomy. A worthy conception of human nature is consequently the only proper guarantee of a worthy conception of God: to merge and lose man's personality in God's would be simply to lose God's greatness too. For these reasons man cannot be regarded as a mere passive instrument in the hands of God. The essential note of his life as the free shaping of his own destiny is activity, and the highest view he can take of his relation to God is that of active co-operation, in which, by identifying himself with the divine ends, he becomes himself a contributor to the advancement of the world-process. With this attractive idea is linked the view that evil is a positive and real force, which we must recognize in all its tragic gravity. In this connection, as in the matter of personality, Seth again shows his opposition to the Hegelians, whose facile optimism only shelved rather than solved the problem of evil.

These ethical views, taken with their metaphysical implications, are obviously nearer to the Kantian than to the Hegelian spirit. They also have a close kinship with the ethics of Martineau. But Seth's chief debt, besides that to his brother, was by his own admission to the *Ethica* of his fellow-countryman, Laurie, who was teaching at the same time in the University of Edinburgh and who neither then nor later received much attention in professionally philosophical circles.[1]

In a later and extremely successful book, *A Study of Ethical Principles*, Seth elaborated his ideas into a comprehensive

[1] On Laurie, see pp. 429 ff.

ethical system. Against the naturalists he treated ethics as a normative science, having as its main end the discovery of the moral ideal, of the supreme criterion of moral value. Among the various solutions of this cardinal problem two opposed types may be distinguished, the Hedonism of the Epicureans and the Utilitarians, whose criterion is feeling, and the Rigorism of the Stoics, of Intuitionists, and of Kant, whose criterion is reason. A mediating theory is needed between these two extremes, one that shall do full justice to both feeling and reason and keep them together in the unity of man's total nature. This more comprehensive attitude Seth calls Eudaemonism, or the ethics of personality, meaning by this not the happiness theory of the British empirical moralists of the XVIIIth and XIXth Centuries but the idealistic attitude most purely embodied in Plato and Aristotle, in Butler and Hegel, in Goethe's *Faust*, and in the poetry of Tennyson, Browning, and Arnold. While the motto of Hedonism is self-satisfaction and of Rigorism self-sacrifice, that of Eudaemonism is self-realization. The moral imperative is directed to neither feeling nor reason, but to the total self, which is both, at a free personality regarded in every one of its activities and relations, at a self with all its capacities harmonized and living a moral life in which the real and the ideal have been brought into organic connection. The moral self is the synthetic unity of apperception looked at from the ethical point of view. The moral law, then, is that we should develop out of natural individuality the genuine ideal self of personality. And to become a person is to be free. The law of all rational beings is accordingly autonomy.

After thus determining the moral ideal he proceeds to a detailed application of it to individual and social life. He ends with a metaphysic of ethics in which he treats of freedom, God, and immortality. Here, as we have already noted, he does not go beyond the programme laid down in his first writing, or depart in anything essential from the views of his brother.

WILLIAM RITCHIE SORLEY (1855–1935)

[Educated at Edinburgh and Trinity College, Cambridge. 1883, Fellow of Trinity College, Cambridge; 1888–94, Professor of Logic and Philosophy, Cardiff; 1894–1900, Professor of Moral Philosophy, Aberdeen; 1900, Professor of Moral Philosophy, Cambridge, (succeeding Sidgwick); retired 1933. "The Historical Method", in *Essays in Philosophical Criticism*, edited by A. Seth and R. B. Haldane, 1883; *The Ethics of Naturalism*, 1885 (second edition, 1904); *Recent Tendencies in Ethics*, 1904; *The Moral Life and Moral Worth*, 1911 (fourth edition, 1930); *Moral Values and the Idea of God* (Gifford Lectures), 1918 (fourth edition, 1930); *A History of English Philosophy*, 1920; "Value and Reality", in *Contemporary British Philosophy*, edited by J. H. Muirhead, second series, 1925.

See *W. R. Sorley*, Memoir, by F. R. Tennant, in *Proc. Brit. Acad.*, 1936.]

Sorley joined the new movement early: a discussion by him of the historical method is in the *Essays in Philosophical Criticism*. His later writings dealt chiefly with ethical matters, which he criticized and systematized from the idealistic point of view. In close connection with his ethical studies he investigated, more thoroughly and deeply and with greater result in his system than most members of the school, the problems of the philosophy of value. His attachment to Kant and Hegel was on the whole looser than was usual among his fellow-idealists, but he retained Kant's cleavage of being into a realm of nature and a realm of ends, and with Hegel sought after system and regarded always the whole, thus meeting all dualisms with the attempt to surmount them in a higher unity.

In his first two books, *The Ethics of Naturalism* and *Recent Tendencies in Ethics*, he subjected the various forms of naturalistic ethics to penetrating criticism, showing firstly, taking over an idea of Lotze's, that the origin of moral ideas and judgments can settle nothing about their validity, there being no way from fact to value, from 'is' to 'ought', and secondly, that in an evolutionary process the lower stages have to be understood in the light of the higher, not vice versa. His full system was worked out later in his chief work, *Moral Values and the*

Idea of God, and is summarized in his essay "Value and Reality."

The whole of being, to grasp which is the task of philosophy, comprises two very different realms, the realm of the merely factual or existent and the realm of the valuable. Valuations as well as sense-perceptions are among the original data of experience. Both valuing and perceiving acts are indeed subjective, but not the objects intended by them. In what sense, then, are values objective? Sorley's answer is, in so far as they are a constitutive mark of personality. Persons belong to the objective order of things and are at the same time bearers of the values that appear in their lives and characters, and thus belong to both the realms just mentioned.

These ideas, due originally to Kant, acquired a specific colour from their connection with Lotze and with the philosophy of value, derived from him, of the Baden school, and almost completely coincide with Rickert's doctrine. This same line of thought, otherwise but little attended to in Britain, strongly influenced Sorley in other parts of his system: his exposition of the methodology of the sciences, for example, was taken over from Rickert, in particular the conception of the generalizing procedure of the natural sciences and the individualizing one of the historical sciences, and of the former as abstracting from value, of the latter as bound to it. Since values have their home in individuals and individuals are marked by qualitative and numerical uniqueness, these marks belong to the essence of the valuable.

When he came to elaborate his theory of value Sorley brought moral value increasingly to the forefront and at length gave it the primacy over all others, as the purest and most comprehensive, and as attaching to every other. He distinguished instrumental and intrinsic values, the former belonging even to physical objects in so far as they enter into relations with persons, the latter values in the full sense, belonging only to persons as their bearers. Only through their connections with persons do they enter into the structure of the universe.

On this theory of value he erected his metaphysic, which,

having a synoptic end, has as its most important task the overcoming of the duality of the two orders of being, the existent or natural and the valuable or moral. It has to find the unitary source from which they proceeded and into which they may again come together. Since the two orders meet in man that supreme unity, the Absolute or God, can only be conceived under the category of personality. If we are to achieve the total view that does full justice to values as well as to natural facts, we cannot dispense with the idea of God. He is required not simply as creator of the existent universe but also as the essence and source of all value.

We can only hint at the metaphysical consequences of this view. Sorley laid down two metaphysical postulates, the individual freedom of man and the universal purposefulness of nature. The former raises the grave problem of the relation of man to the omnipotence and omniscience of God. The existence of evil, the happenings that cannot tolerably be attributed to the Divine will, man's ability to act against the moral law, these and similar facts can only be explained on the supposition that God imposes a limitation on His omnipotence and that His self-limitation is an essential part of His nature. Sorley prefers this position to the neo-Hegelian reduction of things and persons to mere modes of appearance of the Absolute, in which, from the ultimate point of view, they lose everything that makes them what they appear to be.

Sorley's Idealism, since it rests on a system of values with moral value at its head, may be called an ethical Idealism. Since it accords a greater metaphysical dignity to persons, as the bearers and agents of values, than to the natural world of purely material facts, it stands nearer to the Idealism of Berkeley than to that of Plato. It is an Idealism of individual persons ranged under a divine spirit which is also conceived as a person. It is a theistic Idealism, more akin to the thought of Rashdall than to any other contemporary system; and Rashdall's system similarly goes back to Berkeley, where however, it is much more deeply rooted than Sorley's in the specifically spiritualistic side of Berkeley's metaphysic. It is directed against the absolute Idealism of the stricter Hegelians, moving more on Kantian than on Hegelian soil. Sorley did not work out an epistemology of his own, his main interest lying in ethics and metaphysics.

HASTINGS RASHDALL (1858–1924)

[1888–95, Fellow of Hertford College; 1895–1917, of New College, Oxford; 1917, Dean of Carlisle. "The Ultimate Basis of Theism", in *Contentio Veritatis*, by Six Oxford Tutors, 1902 (reprinted in *God and Man*, 1930); "Personality, Human and Divine", in *Personal Idealism*, edited by H. Sturt, 1902; *The Theory of Good and Evil*, two vols, 1907 (second edition, 1924); *Philosophy and Religion*, 1909; *The Problem of Evil* (Deansgate Lecture), 1912; *Ethics*, 1913; *Is Conscience an Emotion?* 1914; *The Moral Argument for Personal Immortality*, 1920.

Posthumous: *Ideas and Ideals*, edited by H. D. A. Major and F.L. Cross, 1928; *God and Man*, edited by Major and Cross, 1930.

See *Life of H. Rashdall*, by P. E. Matheson, 1928. With chapter on Rashdall as Philosopher and Theologian, by C. C. J. Webb.]

In Rashdall, one of the most influential leaders of religious modernism in Britain, Idealism took on a singular stamp. He probably got his first impulse towards the idealistic view of the world from the Oxford group (as a student he had attended the lectures of Green), even though quite early he felt himself repelled by the Absolutism of Bradley and Bosanquet and turned more to Lotze, whom he regarded as the only prominent modern philosopher whose thought was profoundly and without limitation Christian. But with his clearness and probity of thought, mixed with a strong dose of common sense, he could never make much of the obscure depths of the Hegelian philosophy, and oriented his thought towards Berkeley instead, whose religious metaphysic appealed to him both as a theologian and as a philosopher with an idealistic leaning. By his appropriation of the fundamental ideas of Berkeley's epistemology and metaphysics he made himself the real reviver —the only radical reviver—in the XXth Century of Berkeleian theism; for the earlier attempts by Ferrier, Fraser, Collyns Simon, and others had received only passing attention.[1]

To absolute he opposed a personal idealism. His philosophy sprang from and remained anchored in a conviction of the individual and unique character of a person, whether the person be human or divine. The passion, amounting almost to fanaticism, with which he contended for this belief made him blind to the claims or merits of any theory of a super-individual or universal entity that might prejudice the sanctity and absoluteness of personal selfhood, and led him to make his philosophical début in the company of a band of writers which included pragmatists, with whom he had scarcely anything in common beyond his opposition to Absolutism. His contribution to the collection of essays edited by Henry Sturt and entitled *Personal Idealism* expresses the main lines of his thought, which he later applied and elaborated on the theological and ethical sides but never carried further in any essential respect.

In close agreement with Berkeley he declared that there can be no matter without mind, no corporeal things existing in themselves. Mind exists in the form of knowing and willing persons, and whatever is not mind in this sense exists only in relation to mind. The realm of the intrinsically real consists of finite minds and the infinite mind which is God, the latter being required to give an utterly objective ground to the external things which first (in the order of knowledge) appear in the consciousness of finite minds. Mind is indefeasibly individual, always realized in an independent consciousness, impervious to any other consciousness. Persons, that is, exclude each other. Rashdall applied this conception, the basic idea of all his thinking, to the relation of finite persons to the Divine person, and concluded to the impossibility of any absorption of the former by the latter. Here he expressed his opposition to any form of mystical enjoyment or intuitive apprehension of God, as involving a blurring or removal of the boundaries of personality. What he desiderated was a purely rational

[1] Cf. above, p. 247.

demonstration of the foundation of religion, and he did not in the end shrink from accepting the logical consequences of his principle of the independence and impenetrability of personality, namely, the finitude of God. The power of God is limited by the existence of human persons. Absolute reality is not God but a community of personal spirits of whom God is one, though chief. This doctrine is similar to McTaggart's.

His *Theory of Good and Evil* is one of the most thorough and comprehensive of modern British treatises on ethics. He describes his position, which is nearer to Sidgwick and Moore than to Green and Bradley, as "ideal utilitarianism". According to this the ideal life has three basic categories, namely, value, pleasure, and happiness (his insistence that his theory is anti-Hedonistic is mitigated by his inclusion of pleasure in man's true good). Ethics is, of course, a sphere *sui generis*, but it is nevertheless continuous with metaphysics and involves metaphysical postulates, in particular the following three: (*a*) All moral actions must be attributed to the individual self; (*b*) the ground of the objectivity of ethical judgment is the existence of God; (*c*) immortality. Rashdall's ethic thus starts from individual persons and ends with God. Regarding evil he insists that it is no mere appearance but is as real a part of the nature of things as good is; he avoids the easy optimism of the absolutists. Owing to the positive reality of evil we are again obliged to reject the omnipotence of God.

In general his philosophy, which resembles Sorley's more nearly than anyone else's, may be described positively as a belated revival of Berkeleianism, with special attention to the view of personality that Berkeley obviously held but left implicit, and negatively as a reaction against Bradley's Absolutism, so prejudicial to the sanctity of personality. His ethics followed the British tradition in important respects and leaned chiefly towards the empirical Utilitarianism of Mill, Sidgwick, and Moore. The philosophical impulse he originally received from the Oxford Hegelians thus drifted back to the native heritage of thought, idealistic, however, as well as empirical.

6. THEISTS AND PHILOSOPHERS OF RELIGION

JAMES WARD (1843–1925)

[Educated at the Congregational College, Birmingham, and at Berlin, Göttingen, and Trinity College, Cambridge. 1875, Fellow of Trinity College; 1897, Professor of Mental Philosophy and Logic, Cambridge. "Psychology", article in *Encyclopaedia Britannica*, ninth edition, 1886 (reprinted with supplement in tenth edition, 1903; revised article in eleventh edition, 1911; and revised in book form, 1918, under title *Psychological Principles*, second edition, 1920); *Naturalism and Agnosticism* (Gifford Lectures), two vols, 1899 (fourth edition in one vol., 1915); *The Realm of Ends, or Pluralism and Theism* (Gifford Lectures), 1911 (third edition, 1920); *Heredity and Memory* (Sidgwick Lecture), 1913 (reprinted in his *Essays*, 1927); *A Study of Kant*, 1922; "A Theistic Monadism", in *Contemporary British Philosophy*, edited by J. H. Muirhead, second series, 1925.
Posthumous: *Essays in Philosophy*. With a memoir by O. W. Campbell (his daughter), edited by W. R. Sorley and G. F. Stout, 1927; *Dictionary of National Biography*, 1922–30.]

In Ward, a thinker influential and highly esteemed in Britain but almost unknown abroad, Idealism, breaking loose from its original connections, assumed a form essentially different from any of the systems we have so far considered. It is looser and more flexible than these, not being bound down to Hegelianism of either the older orthodox or the younger and liberal school or to any school or system whatever. It was hospitable and responsive to many and varied influences, but though through this eclecticism it gained in width, it lost the firm consistency and unity of the other systems. It is one of the clearest expressions of the departure British Idealism was making from its first Hegelian source and inspiration. Ward's thought sprang primarily not from an original and compelling philosophical urge but out of specialized scientific investigations and an inner religious conflict which he felt and recognized quite early as such. These two factors, empirical science and theology, were well adapted to exercise a determining influence on the world-view which in his later years he came to develop.

He broke away from theology after acute mental struggle, resigned from the Nonconformist ministry, and devoted himself to an academic career. His first new studies took the form of intensive scientific research in the fields of biology and psychology. The latter soon engaged his chief attention and he had already established his reputation as one of the leading British psychologists when, relatively late (in the 'nineties), he turned to specifically philosophical questions. His work in psychology, now generally acknowledged to have been of a pioneer character and of immense importance in the subsequent development of this science, is far superior to his work in philosophy. We must give a little space to the consideration of it, if only because it has a philosophical interest and affected not unessentially his own philosophy. It is contained in his famous article of 1886 in the *Encyclopaedia Britannica*, subsequently twice revised and then reaching its final form in his *Psychological Principles* (1918), which has the status of a classic.

As he himself indicates, his psychology owed most to the Germans Herbart, Lotze, Wundt, and Brentano. Although in many respects it was still rooted in the native tradition, it launched into a new path by turning away from the intellectualism of the British school and by rising above the old associationism and faculty-psychology. In agreement with Locke and his successors Ward insisted that psychology is the science of *individual* experience, on the ground that every mental event has its *locus* in an individual life. He insisted further that the experience which psychologists have to study is not merely cognitive or receptive but is predominantly determined by practical interests operating through feeling and volition. To be subject to the will and ministrant to our behaviour is the only function of experiences, and the recognition of this is the key to psychological understanding. But experience, though essentially conative rather than cognitive, can never be wholly subjective. From the outset it has two factors: a real and active self and its other, a real world, the two being related reciprocally as organic and co-operative parts of a single whole, so that they are only distinguishable in thought, not separate in fact.

Consciousness—to whose constituents Ward gave the general designation "presentations"—is not a chaotic manifold but a unity, and its unity takes the form of an objective continuum, a *totum objectivum*. The course of experience is marked by the progressive differentiation of this continuum through changes in the constituent presentations. "At any given moment we have a certain whole of presentations, a 'field of consciousness', psychologically one and continuous; at the next we have not an entirely new field but a partial change within the old field."[1] Every new experience is not an addendum but a modification of a pre-existent whole, introducing into it some fresh complexity: there are no discontinuous presentations. Consciousness is therefore not an aggregate of distinct and independent units but a continuous process in which a presentational field undergoes constant differentiation. In this way Ward surmounted the mechanistic view of the Empiricists, according to which the psychologist has only to analyse (like the anatomist or the chemist) the content of experience into its elements and then examine these separately. Such distinctions of process as differentiation, assimilation, and retentiveness Ward spoke of as expressive of the "plasticity" of the presentational continuum.

All this takes the bottom out of the theories, then fashionable, of association and mental faculties. Association is not a passive and quasi-mechanical process in which the contents of consciousness call up and enter into new relations with each other automatically, but is controlled throughout by a purposive subject which selects and chooses this or that experience because of its suitability to its own ends. This emphasis on purposive selection led Ward to make attention the central function of consciousness and the characteristic note of his psychology. He went the length of considering every mental activity under the aspect of attention and of widening this term to include everything that had hitherto been brought under the term consciousness. Consciousness is always a

[1] *Psychological Principles*, p. 77.

greater or less degree of attention to what is new in the presentational continuum, and, as we have already noted, far from being of a purely cognitive character, it is an intentional apprehension and selection of such data as are needful for the purposive activity of the subject. Attention thus replaces the old distinct and for the most part isolated faculties and becomes the one basic function that controls them. Its own distinctions are distinctions of degree, and all its activities are in the service of interests. The resultant psychological concept, expressed generally, is of an active attentive subject as the necessary correlate of the various kinds of presentation.

Later Ward widened this conception by connecting it with his metaphysic and by defining experience, already characterized by him primarily in terms of selective interest, as a process of self-preservation and thus as co-extensive with life itself. Cognitive activity is inextricably interwoven with all the conditions of life of the cognitive subject and can only be understood in its relations to these. A purely theoretical subject is a sheer abstraction. Ward accepted Kant's synthetic unity of apperception, but held that no synthesis would be possible without some practical interest in things, some motive to action. Experience is a living and concrete unity functioning as a whole, and of its distinguishable aspects it is the practical and not the theoretical that is the more fundamental. Because of this central contention Ward may be numbered among the early forerunners of the *Lebensphilosphie* that later became current. In particular he prepared the way for the pragmatist movement and exercised a lasting influence on such of its leaders as James and Schiller, an influence not less real because not always obvious; for, by the time pragmatism made its appearance, about the turn of the century, Ward's ideas had become common property. In his theory of time he also anticipated Bergson; he distinguished the abstract time of physics, which has no intensity, from time as experienced by us, and called the latter, because it is an intensive quantity, duration. Although Ward propounded this theory in his article of 1886 and Bergson did not publish his theory until

1889 (in his *Données immédiates de la conscience*), quite probably the two were independent.

Ward's new ideas evoked in the field of psychology a revolution the magnitude of which can scarcely be exaggerated. Henceforward it was no longer possible to follow the hallowed path of Empiricism, of which Bain was the last important representative. To avoid being considered out-of-date a psychologist had to follow Ward, and to the present day British psychology has in everything essential remained in the path marked out by him. Of his pupils, G. F. Stout is the most distinguished. In America a movement in the same direction was taking place about the same time under the lead of William James's voluntaristic psychology. The revolution effected by Ward, it must be added, took the form not of a radical departure from the traditional methods of psychological investigation but of a quiet correction of the general point of view from which the phenomena and structure of mental life had usually been regarded. His methods were much the same as those of Locke and Hume, that is, introspective. He left no room in his writings for experimental or physiological or pathological psychology, and only occasionally and cautiously made use of the comparative method, as a way not of discovering conclusions but of illustrating them. Like Brentano he started from inner perception and described the immediate data of individual consciousness.

Ward's philosophical system was fed from many sources—from Leibniz, Berkeley, Kant, Lotze (by whom he was strongly influenced during his student days at Göttingen), and all the contemporary philosophy of his own country. In the first of his chief metaphysical works he treats of the realm of nature and the naturalism and agnosticism that had arisen through the contemplation of it; in the second his subject is the realm of ends and the pluralism and theism to which this gives rise. The contrast is based, of course, on the similar Kantian dualism, and in general Ward's thought lies much nearer to Kant's than to Hegel's.

Ward thus sought in the first place a philosophical understanding of the world presented to us in the natural sciences. The result was one of the profoundest and most comprehensive examinations that the naturalism and agnosticism of the time ever received. He pursued them in all their tendencies and ramifications possible as well as actual, and hunted them out in their most secret hiding-places, exposing the common source of mechanism, evolutionism, and psycho-physical parallelism, and the insufficiency of any such theories for a philosophy that passes beyond all partial aspects to the Whole. "There is more in heaven and earth than is dreamt of by the naturalistic philosophy",[1] he cries to his opponents, a cry which in a measure holds the net result of his remarkably penetrating and impressive critique.

The mechanistic view of the world, which according to Ward lies at the basis of all scientific investigation, is one huge abstraction, the product of a radical one-sidedness which picks out a partial aspect of reality, systematizes it and follows it out to its last consequences. This narrow concentration is the ground of its magnificence and success, and the ground also of its utter falseness as a world-view. It expresses everything in terms of measured quantity, and works itself out in mathematical symbols. Everything individual and concrete, everything that gives content and pulse and colour to life, slips through the wide meshes of this net of abstract concepts. This "colourless movement of atoms", this "spectral woof of impalpable abstractions", this "unearthly ballet of bloodless categories",[2] cannot be reality. Even if it contains a faint reference to the concrete world from which it has been abstracted, it cannot, out of its own content and structure, answer the question what the real nature of the concrete world is. In a scheme that deals with nothing but homogeneous points of force only mechanically related to one another, it is meaningless to look for, and impossible to find, significance and values and ends.

In this severe criticism of mechanism, Ward obviously failed to keep sufficiently distinct natural science as such and

[1] *Naturalism and Agnosticism*, 1889, vol. 2, p. 80.

[2] Bradley, *Principles of Logic*, Bk. III, Pt. ii, c. iv, § 16.

the naturalistic world-view commonly based on it, thereby "emptying out the baby with the bath water", condemning even strictly scientific thinking on the ground that it has in fact often given rise to philosophical conclusions of extremely doubtful validity. This is strange, seeing that Ward himself had started his academic career as a scientist and had used the methods of science with great success. But the strangeness makes it significant: he had to adopt a radically critical attitude to the distinctive view-point and methods of natural science in order to be able to bring within the sphere of philosophical interest another field of knowledge which had hitherto been grossly neglected in British philosophy, namely, history. In the historical sciences, by contrast with the natural sciences, we encounter individual and concrete beings, which answer to what we mean by realities in that they set themselves ends, realize values, and form an integral part of life's concreteness and actuality. Like Sorley, Ward was here indebted to the investigations into the methodology of knowledge made by Heinrich Rickert, to which scarcely any other British philosophers seem to have paid any attention.

We have, then, within the whole of being, a sharp opposition of two realms. On the one hand is nature, the world of mechanical events, dominated by uniformity, by empirical necessity, a world of generalities and abstractions with no possible room for concrete individuals, or for spontaneity, initiative, values, and ends. On the other hand is the realm of values and ends, the world of history, of the concrete and individual, in which alone moral action is possible and in which the enchainment of mechanical causality is replaced by human purpose and freedom. But this sharp demarcation cannot be taken to involve their ultimate separateness. From a higher point of view they are seen to be partial views of a single world and must therefore somehow be brought together in thought into a unity. To discover this unity and also to determine which of the two aspects of it is the deeper and more comprehensive, is the affair of philosophy.

As we would expect, Ward made the natural a derivative of

the spiritual world. One proof of this is that Nature, when approached with the apparatus of rational science, answers the questions we put to her, and thereby verifies the rightness of the means man has devised to dominate her. Are we not justified, then, in inferring from the intelligence of the inquiring spirit to the intelligence of Nature, or at any rate to an underlying intelligent principle? Besides, the more recent researches of science have shown that organic life reaches much further down into the supposedly inorganic realm than we have hitherto been inclined to believe, and there is no proof that we have yet found the lower limit of life. Considerations such as these led Ward in the end to the supposition that Nature is animated and individualized through and through. Ward calls this panpsychism "spiritualistic monism", to indicate its direct opposition to the materialistic monism of the agnostics, evolutionists, and other naturalists. Nature is through and through teleological—a realm of ends. *Natura naturata* is itself in reality *natura naturans*.

Spiritualistic monism, however, is only a general position. It says nothing of how in particular things are made, whence they come and whither they go, what value they have and what ends they serve, and so on. To answer such questions we must start all over again, and in doing so proceed in a "radically empirical" fashion (Ward uses this phrase of William James's). From this radical point of view, reality appears to us immediately in a plurality of experiencing centres which are reciprocally related. Ward calls these units monads or entelechies, and the lowest of them that we can conceive elementary or bare monads, sometimes psychoids. These latter arise out of a matrix, perhaps an undifferentiated continuum, common to all monads and forming, so to speak, their environment. All monads are to be thought of as individuals, none being like any other, yet never in isolation but always acting and reacting on each other and, especially at the higher monadic levels, forming themselves into social groups. They must be regarded further as essentially striving after ends, with self-preservation as their highest end or law.

We need not follow this monadology any further, since it agrees with that of Leibniz in all important respects except that it gives the monads windows and leaves out the doctrine of pre-established harmony. Ward usually speaks of it as pluralism, and among modern systems it is with James's pluralistic philosophy that it has most points of contact. It forms as it were the lower storey of his metaphysical edifice. Here, with a multiplicity, we cannot remain. As far as it goes, pluralism is a thoroughly consistent position, and can satisfy our intellectual needs for a while, but it is an incomplete one, one which at both its lower and its upper limits points beyond itself to a higher position. There cannot be a plurality of finite beings without a unity that underlies and includes them. True, we are unable to verify this unity scientifically; it takes us beyond the realm of fact. For this reason the radical empiricist will deny its reality, but this is only a sign that he has not yet risen to a truly philosophical point of view. Philosophy proper has no direct dealings with facts: it is sufficient if it avoids contradicting experience. The Whole which philosophy is an attempt to understand does, indeed, include facts, but any theory that discovers the unity of the entire manifold and elicits its general meaning is philosophically justified, even if it cannot be empirically verified.

Pluralism finds its completion in theism. This crowning position of his system Ward reaches with a bold speculative leap from the finite and relative plurality of monads to an infinite and absolute unity. The existence of the many is grounded in and aims at the divine; God is both their source and their end. Theism is thus at once the basis and the crown of pluralism.

The ultimate metaphysical questions now receive their treatment and solution—the idea of evolution, the problem of freedom, immortality, the nature of God, and most of all the problem of the relation of finite beings to the Absolute. Of Ward's detailed consideration of these questions we can only give a few general indications. God is spirit, possessed of intelligence and will, and therefore personal. He is the creator, sustainer, and governor of the world. In creating the world, however, He imposed a limitation upon Himself, but this does not, of course, mean that He therefore made Himself finite in essence. As creator He transcends the world, but not in the deistic sense of standing outside it. Creation can only be understood as the abiding presence of the creative principle in the creature, so that God is equally immanent, moving the world from within. Between the transcendence and the immanence Ward could find no conceptual link, but he held to both because his deeply religious sense made him shrink from a pure pantheism on the one hand and from deism, with its idea of God as withdrawing from the world when He had made it and taking so to speak a holiday after His labours, on the other. This mediating position led him to attribute creativity to man also; in making men free God appointed them to be His fellow-workers in the realization of His ends. As equal partners with Him in this task they are fully responsible for their deeds, and are at the same time capable of doing wrong. Moral evil is the crux of any theistic system. But since God is immanent in the world, goodness must ultimately conquer evil. Evil is the disturbance of the moral order; it is not a positive principle, with a nature and reality of its own, alongside the good, but is merely relative to this and will accordingly gradually succumb to and disappear in it. "There is some soul of goodness in things evil."[1]

Ward's universe, unlike that of Bradley and Bosanquet, is not a static one but mounts from stage to stage to the highest monad which is God. Like most of his contemporaries he came under the spell of the idea of evolution and worked it intimately into his system. But that idea takes on in a theistic system a meaning very different from the one it bears in naturalism or pluralism. It means no longer the gradual unfolding of what was present from the beginning, but epigenesis, creative synthesis, the continual emergence of fresh possibilities; it indicates a harmony present at the beginning

[1] Shakespeare, *Henry V*, iv, 1.

as well as at the goal, not simply at the end of an advancing process which may have no end at all.

Looking back on Ward's system as a whole we can see that in it Idealism has assumed a new form, assimilating, much more than the other systems we have surveyed, a wealth and variety of ideas which include some that have no intrinsic affinity with the idealistic point of view. There is the same impulse to speculate beyond the limits of experience and seek an ultimate unity, but we fail to get the impression that the synthesis arises out of a genuine consistency of thought. The elements are too numerous and heterogeneous to constitute a real unity and often remain in mere juxtaposition. But this is only another proof of the power of the speculative impetus released by the newly-awakened philosophical interests, driving to metaphysical construction a man whose gift lay rather in the prosecution of scientific research and the examination of philosophical problems in their particularity.

CLEMENT CHARLES JULIAN WEBB (*b.* 1865)

[1899–1922, Fellow and Tutor of Magdalen College, Oxford; 1920, first Oriel Professor of the Philosophy of the Christian Religion, Oxford; retired 1930. *Problems in the Relations of God and Man*, 1911; *Group Theories of Religion and the Individual*, 1916; *God and Personality* (Gifford Lectures), first course, 1919; *Divine Personality and Human Life*, second course, 1920; *Philosophy and the Christian Religion* (Inaugural Lecture), 1920; "Outline of a Philosophy of Religion", in *Contemporary British Philosophy*, edited by J. H. Muirhead, second series, 1925; "Our Knowledge of One Another", in *Proceedings British Academy*, 1930; *Religion and Theism*, 1934; also several works on the history of philosophy and religious thought, and critical editions of John of Salisbury's *Policraticus* and *Metalogicon*.]

Webb is best described as the representative of the philosophy of religion within absolute Idealism. Long connected, both as student and as teacher, with the University of Oxford, he belongs to the Oxford tradition of Green. While still a student he gave his preference to ethical and religious problems. He tells us of the strong impression made on him by Green's *Prolegomena*, and the utterly overpowering effect of Kant's *Foundation of the Metaphysic of Ethics*. On the whole his thought lies nearer to Kant and Fichte than to Hegel. Among his Oxford teachers he mentions with particular respect J. Cook Wilson, though any material influence from such a realistic quarter is extremely improbable. He owed much more to his personal friendship with the Roman Catholic philosopher, Friedrich von Hügel, and was later influenced by Rudolf Otto's *Das Heilige*,[1] which aroused considerable attention in English theological circles.

Webb, then, approached the problem of absolute Idealism chiefly from the side of religion. His special aim was a revision of the metaphysics of Bradley and Bosanquet from the point of view of religious experience and Christian theology.[2] Their religiously indifferent, purely theoretical speculations led them to give an account of the relation of the Absolute and God which was naturally unacceptable to a thinker with a positive and intimate attitude towards religion. For him the Absolute was the object not simply of metaphysical speculation but equally of religious devotion, and he argues that Bradley's and Bosanquet's separation of the Absolute and God, pushed to its last logical conclusions, would take away all meaning from any religion whatever. For religious experience they are and must be identical.

A second problem to which Webb has given close attention is that of the personality of God and its relation to the finite personality of man. Here again he shows that it is only the religious consciousness that can unveil the ultimately personal character of reality, since only in religious experience does man enter into personal relation with the Absolute. Personality must, therefore, be attributed to God; but in a sense somewhat different from man's personality, for the relation of man to

[1] English translation by J. W. Harvey, *The Idea of the Holy*, 1923.

[2] On his relation to Bradley and Bosanquet see the illuminating correspondence between him and the latter in *Bosanquet and his Friends*, edited by J. H. Muirhead, 1935, pp. 211 f., 226 f., 237–47.

man in social experience is one of mutual exclusion, whereas the relation of man and God in religious experience is one of mutual inclusion. We are obliged from the religious point of view to hold that we dwell in God and He dwells in us, that in a way unknown to us God is immanent in the believer, without, however, in any way jeopardizing the independent personality of the finite being. For Webb defends the autonomy of human personality against the denial of its truth and value made by both naturalism and absolutism. In consequence he does not regard religious experience as mystical, as the engulfing of the finite soul in the infinite, but as a relation in which both remain distinct; from which it follows that God, for all His immanence, is at the same time transcendent. He tries to connect and reconcile the two opposite assertions of God's immanence and transcendence by introducing the theological idea of a mediator and of the Trinity, thus making of these a philosophical use. Such and similar unreconciled oppositions in Webb's doctrine are probably due to an intrinsic lack of correspondence or compatibility between absolutism and the metaphysical implications of the Christian religion.

Webb has shown a particular interest in the problem of our knowledge of other selves and of a world of external things. He rules the argument from analogy out of court. Of other selves we have an entirely immediate apprehension, just as we have of God. Our knowledge of other selves cannot be derived from that of our own selves, or of external things, or of the relation between these two, but in some way underlies all these kinds of experience. Another self is never for us simply one object among the rest but is always apprehended as a self-conscious person with whom, in virtue of our own personality, we can enter into direct personal relations.

Personality, then, is the central and dominating idea in Webb's thought, especially in the systematic form he gave to this in his chief work, the two series of Gifford Lectures published as *God and Personality* and *Divine Personality and Human Life*. In the second of these he discusses the expression of human personality in the several spheres of its activity, exhibiting the peculiarities and differences of the economic, scientific, artistic, moral, political, and religious spheres. In general he adopts a middle and eirenical position between Rashdall on the one hand, the fanatical apostle of individual personality, and Bradley and Bosanquet on the other, who sink and extinguish personality in the darkness of the Absolute. But he does not rise to that great originality of thought we admire in Bradley and to a lesser degree in Bosanquet. His philosophy has grown less out of an inner impulse after system than through the exposition and criticism of the ideas of other thinkers. His particular service will probably be found to lie in his having brought down to a soberer plane certain dangerous exaggerations on the part of the Absolutism to which his own sympathies inclined him.

ALFRED EDWARD TAYLOR (*b.* 1869)

[Educated at New College, Oxford; 1891–8, Fellow of Merton College, Oxford; 1896–1903, Assistant Lecturer in Greek and Philosophy, Owens College, Manchester; 1903–8, Professor of Philosophy, McGill University, Montreal; 1908–24, Professor of Moral Philosophy, St. Andrews; 1924, same at Edinburgh. *The Problem of Conduct*, 1901; *Elements of Metaphysics*, 1903 (ninth edition, 1930); "Continuity", "Dreams and Sleep", "Identity", "Theism", articles in Hastings's *Encyclopaedia of Religion and Ethics*, 1911–21; "The Belief in Immortality", in *The Faith and the War*, edited by F. J. Foakes Jackson, 1915, pp. 123–57; "Philosophy", in *Evolution in the Light of Modern Knowledge*, 1925; "The Freedom of Man", in *Contemporary British Philosophy*, edited by J. H. Muirhead, second series, 1925; "The Vindication of Religion", in *Essays Catholic and Critical*, edited by E. G. Selwyn, 1926; *The Problem of Evil*, 1929, a pamphlet; *The Faith of a Moralist* (Gifford Lectures), two vols., 1930 (one vol. ed., 1937); *Philosophical Studies*, 1934; also many books and articles on the history of philosophy.

Taylor received his philosophical education when Oxford was in the grip of the Hegelianizing movement. The first and strongest influence over him came from Bradley. As a Fellow of the same college, he was one of the very few who had the good fortune to come into personal contact with the recluse, and was able through almost daily intercourse to share Bradley's thoughts at the time when Bradley was wrestling with his metaphysic. The thought of the older thinker stamped itself deeply on his own early work. At a much later time, when he had moved far from his early position, he gratefully recorded that the influence of Bradley, "exercised in many ways, must count for the most potent to which my own thinking has been subjected and the most beneficial".[1]

Nevertheless, there can be no question of any close adherence to Bradley or to any other teacher in the early period, still less in the later one. Taylor is not only an independent and somewhat arbitrary thinker but is possessed of a mobile and restless mind. A man of wide erudition, he overflows with knowledge of the most diverse fields, and has an astonishing capacity for assimilating alien spheres of knowledge and ideas. A long array of works in the history of philosophy testifies to the great breadth of his historical knowledge and of his scholarly equipment. One of the leading authorities on the philosophy of the ancients, especially on Socrates and Plato (his large book on Plato and his 700-page commentary on the *Timaeus* stand by themselves in the shoreless sea of Platonic literature in wealth of erudition, pointedness of interpretation, and depth of philosophical understanding); he is almost equally familiar with the secular and religious thought of the Middle Ages, and with the modern and contemporary literature of both philosophy and theology.

Here, however, we are concerned with Taylor as philosopher, not as historian, commentator, and translator. We have had to refer to this aspect of his work only because it has in many ways affected his philosophical thinking. Such doctrine of his own as he has given us bears all over it the traces of his polymathy. At every point it is obvious that this thinker has knocked at many doors and explored many treasure houses, and of the wealth of learning he has found has made a vital and fruitful

[1] In *Contemporary British Philosophy*, edited by J. H. Muirhead, second series, p. 271.

use instead of dragging it about as dead ballast. To trace the ingredients of his thought to their sources would, then, be a useless labour; we should have to begin with the Greeks and end only with the latest vogue of his contemporaries. We must, however, remark that the comprehensive historical knowledge that Taylor has gathered in his ever-open storehouse, fruitful though it has been for his own approach to philosophical problems, has been a burden and a hindrance to the natural development of his thought, on more than one occasion deflecting it from one path to another and depriving it of continuity and unity of aim. It is responsible for those changes, central as well as peripheral, that characterize his philosophical pilgrimage, and that only recently seem to have come to an end, unless some fresh surprise is being prepared for us. In his hunger for knowledge and the capacity to assimilate it he reminds one of his changeful and kaleidoscopic German contemporary, Scheler.

Taylor's two most important philosophical works belong one to the beginning and the other to the end of his literary career. Both deal with ethics. Among the intermediate writings are a comprehensive work on metaphysics which belongs to the early period and several fairly considerable essays, mostly contributions to symposia or composite volumes, which deal with problems in ethics, metaphysics and the philosophy of religion, and which, falling within the last fifteen years or so, express his later position. We shall here first survey his ethics, partly because it is the centre of gravity of his philosophy and partly because his treatment of it at two periods widely removed from each other gives us an admirable opportunity of bringing out the changeful course of his philosophical development.

His first book, *The Problem of Conduct*, with the significant sub-title "A Study in the Phenomenology of Ethics", is in many respects his best philosophical achievement and rightly made his reputation. Even in this early work he reveals himself as a decisive and independent thinker who shrank from neither radical conclusions nor paradox. He does indeed take up some of Bradley's ideas and through acute analysis and skilful dialectic follows them out to their extreme consequences; but it is the sceptical side of Bradley as shown in his *Appearance and Reality* (especially chapter 25 on the Good) rather than the constructive and idealistic phase of the *Ethical Studies* that he follows. Consequently he soon finds himself sharply opposed to the Hegelian school, especially to Green as its chief ethical spokesman. The opposition shows itself most prominently in his separation of ethics from philosophical system in general, and in his treatment of it in a purely empirical way. His primary attack is directed against the linkage of ethics with metaphysics typically represented in Green's *Prolegomena*. "Ethics is as independent of metaphysical speculation for its principles and methods as any of the so-called 'natural sciences'; its real basis must be sought not in philosophical theories about the nature of the Absolute or the ultimate constitution of the universe, but in the empirical facts of human life as they are revealed to us in our concrete everyday experience."[1] Ethics, that is, is a purely positive and empirical, not a speculative science, is necessarily and intimately related to psychology, anthropology, sociology, and similar disciplines, and has the task of describing moral phenomena as we find them in the past and the present, as facts of experience set in a concrete context of situations and conditions.

The first part of Taylor's book is thus a psychological analysis of moral feeling as the spring of conduct and the ground of moral judgment. Here he expressly associates himself with the British XVIIIth-Century theory of moral sentiment (Shaftesbury, Hutcheson, Hume and Adam Smith), and by keeping ethics to the sober level of everyday fact aims at erecting a bulwark against the unreal constructions and abstractions of the Hegelianizing moralists. In every attempt to found ethics on metaphysics he saw the risk of emptying the moral life of its concrete reality, and of burdening the study of it from the start with a purely theoretical structure unable to provide room for all the relevant phenomena. Ethics has nothing to do, for instance, with the timeless and eternal

[1] *Problem of Conduct*, p. 4.

self posited by Green but only with the empirical self embodied in flesh and blood and with the physical, physiological, and psychological circumstances that condition it. Besides the descriptive analysis of moral phenomena, ethics has the further task of tracing the phenomena back to their crude beginnings, of investigating the origin and evolution of moral ideas—what since Nietzsche is known in Germany as the genealogy of morals. In this field Taylor's searching and illuminating analyses have led to admirable results: his discussion of the origin and significance of such concepts as obligation, conscience, responsibility, right and wrong, and moral personality are of permanent value, and do not suffer in the least through the inadequacy of the theoretical presuppositions of the inquiry as a whole. Still, valuable as his ideas and conclusions are taken singly, his reversion to XVIIIth-Century Empiricism was a serious error, especially for a thinker who was reared in the school of Green and Bradley and had tasted of the fruits of Kant and Hegel. Indebted as he was to Bradley, he deliberately turned his back on the latter's *Ethical Studies*, the work in which the ethical views of the German idealists were for the first time, and with profound understanding, expounded in Britain. Taylor's relapse into psychologism and relativism, and also, as we shall see, into hedonism, was an anachronism which neither the acute reasoning underlying it nor the many valuable ideas that emerged along with it (but not out of it) suffice to justify.

Through his rejection of any rational principle, and his restriction of ethics to the facts of experience, Taylor's inquiry is forced increasingly in a sceptical direction and into dialectical difficulties. For the first time Bradley's influence becomes evident in an extremely able transference of the disintegrating dialectic of the first part of *Appearance and Reality* to the sphere of morality. The degradation of the world of experience to mere appearance was bound to have a fateful effect on a purely empirical ethics, and we find in fact that Taylor's empirical theory of morals, like Hume's empirical theory of knowledge, issues in scepticism. For he concludes that our moral tendencies, as soon as they have freed themselves from the primitive moral feeling which is their common root, develop along divergent lines, so divergent that they cannot be reduced again to a general unity. He finds the divergence in a ubiquitous duality of egoism and altruism. Both these attitudes have won moral approval and laid claim to universal worth. We are for ever confronted with two eternally opposite ideas, the one of personal culture, the other of social service, and ethical theory is quite incapable of deciding which of the two is the better. An ultimate synthesis of self-realization and self-sacrifice is utterly impossible.

The consequence is—the argument is obviously circular—that ethics is not a system of rational deductions from a single metaphysical principle but a collection of empirical generalizations which cannot be brought under a coherent system of hypotheses. Ethics, therefore, like physics and all other special sciences, has a merely provisional character. It cannot rise to the enunciation of abiding norms of universally valid principles. It is predominantly irrational. What we call the moral ideal is really a compromise within that polarity of egoistic and altruistic tendencies which holds throughout the moral sphere. And the idea of moral progress is an illusion, for there is no one determinate line of movement, and every seeming advance is balanced by regression.

It is not surprising, then, that Taylor, while rejecting psychological hedonism, as Green, Bradley, Sidgwick, and others had done, took a considerable step towards the so-called ethical hedonism. By this he understood the doctrine that pleasurableness is an essential feature of the morally valuable, and that for all practical purposes we can take its presence as a mark or warrant of the goodness of an act. If the moral has the function of enhancing the energies of life, the pleasant is good in so far as it achieves this function. Ideas such as this, however, bringing morality under biological categories, have only a relative truth. Taylor's dialectical pendulum now swings over to the other side, to do justice to the opposite idea of duty. The categorical imperative in Kant's sense is of course, formally excluded by an empiricist ethic, since it is bound up with a philosophy that rests on *a priori* and absolute principles. Still, there are imperatives. But they are always for individual persons and special situations, and though they can become obligatory upon certain groups of individuals and communities none of them can have an entirely universal *a priori* validity. For the premiss of ethics is that everything that is real is in the long run reducible to a fact of concrete experience. Taylor expressly brings out the agreement of this principle with the fundamental principle of Hume's theory of knowledge, and it must be said that what Hume did in this field Taylor has done in ethics, directing all his efforts towards carrying over into this field a like empirical scepticism, or, if you prefer it, sceptical empiricism. In this connection he outran Hume himself, who, while grounding ethics empirically, had the good sense to shrink from dissolving it sceptically. This makes all the more remarkable the fact that in an epistemological and metaphysical work published only two years later, his *Elements of Metaphysics*, Taylor moved almost completely away from Hume, substituting for sceptical arguments the formulae of absolutism.

The first phase of Taylor's ethic thus ends in psychologism, relativism, and scepticism. There are no positive results. To say only this, however, would be inadequate. The significance of this negative phase is that in it ethical thought is thrown into the restlessness of a dialectical process in which it is forced away from all dogmatic connections only to return to concrete life itself, to do justice to its variety, mobility and discord. No other British thinker has so well brought out the intrinsic dynamic of the moral life, and the antinomies and perplexities that arise in the study of it. In Taylor's dialectical crucible everything is melted. His thought is too supple and mobile to rest in any one position, but in the wealth of the relevant phenomena is ceaselessly carried from thesis to antithesis, to find contentment in none. The scepticism, then, that runs through this pulsating and powerfully thought-out early work, is by no means simply destructive, but is rich in valuable ideas which only await the shaping process.

If the moral life is a compromise and an illusion and includes as part of its essence a certain amount of cant—the word is Taylor's own—the question arises whether we can regard it as a final form of human experience. Taylor tries to answer this question in his final chapter, entitled "Beyond good and bad", which contains a hint of the direction in which his ethical ideas were later to move. Despite the suggestion of the title, the answer is not the one given by Nietzsche. Taylor was, indeed, the first British thinker to feel deeply the fascination of Nietzsche, though we cannot turn aside to discuss in what respects it affected him. His chapter finds the fate of morality in religion. In purely moral behaviour we take the distinctions of good and bad, right and wrong, noble and vulgar, as final, but these rough oppositions are quite inadequate to express certain finer distinctions which lie beneath the surface and are rooted in the heart of things. Besides, the moral ideal has not only not been attained but is unattainable, every apparent realization turning out to be illusory. Moral experience therefore needs to be surmounted at a level that lies above its characteristic oppositions, and this level is to be found only in religious experience. This is the supreme and ultimate expression of practical effort. Its ideal is not something remote and unattainable, an everlasting Beyond, but something already fulfilled and real, not in the ordinary sense, but in the complete and emphatic sense of being the highest reality and the only one that is truly real. The hyperethical attitude of religion takes the form of universal sympathy and willing forgiveness, which, though often in fact basing itself on the morally good, is not necessarily tied down to it.

The later phase of Taylor's ethics, which we have no space to treat with any fullness, is represented by an even more comprehensive but less concentrated work, the title of which, *The Faith of a Moralist*, announces at the outset that the author has found firm ground. Separated from his first book on ethics by a generation, it is a revelation of his unresting advance in the interval to new fields of subject-matter and new sets of problems. The chief addition to his mental equipment is theology, brought about by an extended study of the thought of the Middle Ages; and to his former mastery of the philosophy of classical antiquity he has added a closer acquaintance with the post-classical philosophy of the ancients, especially Neo-platonism. Among the moderns he has moved nearer to Galileo, Descartes, Hobbes, Leibniz, and Reid, and among his contemporaries has made fruitful contacts with Alexander, Varisco, Ward, Royce, Bergson and Whitehead. And he has become indebted in certain important respects to the writings of von Hügel and Webb on the philosophy of religion, and to E. R. Bevan's book *Hellenism and Christianity*.

His new position is best described as ethical theism. Morality is given its ultimate basis in religion and is thought under religious categories. The sparse hints with which the earlier work ended are now systematically elaborated and furnish the theme of the entire inquiry. Ethics is now rescued from scepticism and brought as it were safely to land by the life-belt of theology. But one gets the impression that the primary interest has now passed away from ethics to theism; at any rate, what the protracted discussion is made to lead up to is a new and broadly based moral proof of the existence of God. The change that has come over Taylor's views of the nature of morality is most evident in the changed object of his attack. In the earlier work his main opposition was directed against all attempts to "metaphysicize" ethics, to tie it down to any first principles of a metaphysical order. Now he passes over wholeheartedly to the enemy's camp, for to ground ethics in theism is to bind it to a metaphysic. What he is now attacking—and Taylor repeatedly makes this clear—is secularism, that very limitation of morality to purely human reference which his earlier work was concerned throughout to effect.

All his arguments now converge on the idea that the moral life, however much it is passed in time, and is bound to the conditions of this present world, only acquires its true meaning when it faces towards eternity and is guided at every point by belief in God. It is an adventure that starts in the natural order and ends in the supernatural. With reference to religion this ethic is, of course, heteronomous. But Taylor insists on its autonomy with regard to Nature. This may be illustrated from his discussion of guilt. The feeling we have when we are aware of a wrong we have committed is so different from anything we find below man that we are entitled to regard it as *sui generis* and peculiar to man. Now with the sense of guilt is essentially connected the sense of its inextinguishableness. Guilt cannot be wiped out by any effort or deed, it cannot be "made good", or covered by any punishment. But our sense of its irreparableness is a direct pointer to that intrinsic interweaving of time and eternity which is the distinctive mark of all moral endeavour.

Connected with this is the idea of what Taylor calls "the initiative of the eternal". All genuine morality points beyond our present state by demanding a continual renewal, transformation and rebirth of our personality. We cannot, however, rise above our present achievement by our own effort and by an ideal which is simply an ideal of our own. The initiative to renewal cannot come from the personality to be renewed. It can come only through response to a movement from without, and this movement must come from God. Morality thus presupposes the supernatural as its environment and motive force. This does not in any way abrogate personal effort, but means only that in all our activity we should not remain within the limits of our own resources but look beyond ourselves in order to accept the divine initiative which alone can raise us above ourselves. Taylor's monads have windows, and these windows open on to the infinite.

Immortality is brought within the scope of Taylor's general "moral proof". Immortality means the transformation of the temporal self into the eternal self. The process is a continuous one, and consists primarily in the purification of the self from all its merely temporal conditionedness. It is not, however, a purification that engulfs and annihilates the individual personality in an impersonal Absolute (Taylor is thinking of Bosanquet's theory of individuality), but one that leaves it the richer. The self remains, but moves from its original centre to a new one. As Taylor puts it, in proportion as we give up ourselves we die *into* our true personality. In the Absolute, individuality, far from being extinguished, achieves its maximal expression.

But are not morality and eternal life utterly opposed? Has moral effort any longer any meaning when we have attained our goal? Once more we are confronted with the fundamental difficulty of any ethic whatever, that duality of a perpetually fleeting "is" and an eternally unattainable "ought" which seems to be the very essence of morality. But morality disappears with attainment only when we identify it with the conflict against evil. This, however, is as illegitimate as identifying science wholly with conflict against error. It is possible to imagine a stage of mental life in which, while the process of character-formation is over, the activity that proceeds from the established character is nevertheless continued. Even "in heaven" there is still room for the *vita activa* besides the bliss of pure contemplation. True, we can no longer advance *towards* the good, but there will be plenty of room for advancing *within* it; the good life can actively continue, no more, of course, as a struggle against evil but as a realization of the Good in ever richer and more manifold forms. The fight between good and evil over and the end attained, moral activity still abides. This is the solution of the deep contradiction of morality's "is" and "ought".

Taylor's ethical thought thus passes through two entirely unrelated stages: the first realistic and empirical, dialectical and sceptical, unsystematic and inimical to any metaphysical system; the second, utterly different, rooting ethics in a system of metaphysical theism and making it wholly subservient to this. And in saying this we give an adequate characterization of his later metaphysical thought as well, which is also expounded in *The Faith of a Moralist*. It aims at exhibiting the speculative insufficiency of all merely natural theology and at justifying faith in a supernatural revelation. Taylor's religious faith has travelled as far as his thought. Originally a Methodist lay preacher, he passed into a phase of religious indifference, then moved more and more towards Anglicanism, and now belongs to its High Church wing. Indeed he is in open sympathy with Roman Catholicism, expressing it philosophically in the view that the recent Neo-Scholastic movement is a genuine renewal of the spirit of philosophy, that the thought of Thomas Aquinas is still alive and will be of influence in the future course of philosophical reflection.

We cannot entirely omit an indication, however brief, of Taylor's early metaphysical thought, as expounded in his *Elements of Metaphysics* of 1903. The reader of this work has not to go far before finding here too a deep breach of continuity. A few external links between the secular thought of his first book and the religious thought of his maturity can be traced, but no intrinsic unity. Once more Saul has become Paul. The discontinuity is the more striking when we look backwards, for between his first book and this one there is in spirit and in content a yawning gulf, but in time only two or three years. In both the influence of Bradley predominated. But, as Taylor himself much later emphasized, there were two Bradleys, the one an acute and destructive critic, the other a great constructive thinker, the former forever tearing to bits what the latter had built up; and one cannot resist the impression that in Taylor's early period both these aspects of Bradley were taken over with their opposition unresolved, the first dominating his ethics, the second his metaphysics. His early metaphysics, then, which he denominated "systematic idealism", may be summarily described as Bradley's absolutism minus his scepticism. But it was Bradley's absolutism, left by its author in a very loose form, thoroughly and rigidly systematized. The main divisions of the system were ontology or the general structure of the real, cosmology or the metaphysics of Nature, and rational psychology or the metaphysics of mind and of human society.

The systematization of Bradley's ideas, however, forms only the basis and general framework of Taylor's early doctrine. Mobile, questful, and receptive, Taylor was able to incorporate and utilize for speculative ends a wealth of new material, including whatever was topical at the time. After Bradley, the idealism of Ward and of Royce is the most evident, though more in the general attitude than in details of doctrine. He also took over a considerable part of the psychology, then new, of Ward, James, Stout and Münsterberg, emphasizing the purposive, teleological character of mental life, and using it to combat mechanistic theories. He declared that the mechanistic conception of reality is an inferior and in the long run an untrue view, not holding unconditionally even of the inorganic realm, since the atom itself has a certain degree of individuality, however small this may be, and to that extent cannot be excepted from the thoroughgoing teleological structure of being. These ideas, however, almost forced him to embrace certain important elements of the pragmatism which was then emerging—he certainly made large concessions to it—and it may be seriously doubted whether this linkage of an absolutistic metaphysic with a pragmatist philosophy of life contributed to the consistency and unity of his doctrine. In view of the great tension at the time between the representatives of these two parties, it was at the least a tactical error. Their utter incompatibility, however, soon forced itself on him in a controversy with Schiller, and, driven into a corner, he retracted a considerable part of his pragmatism, which had shown itself in his account of the nature and methods of the positive sciences, in his view of causality and similar general principles as not axioms but postulates (Schiller's recent essay, *Axioms as Postulates*, 1902, had directly influenced him here), in his emphasis on the voluntaristic aspect as present in all experience, and in his rejection of the idea of a disinterested pursuit of truth. His thoughts on the methodology of knowing are almost identical with those of Karl Pearson's *Grammar of Science*. We may note finally occasional agreement with Avenarius's philosophy of pure experience.

Regarding Taylor's philosophical thought as a whole we may say that it is too rich and complex to be apprehended exhaustively or to be brought under a single designation. Illuminated from many sources it glistens with many colours. Again and again it has burnt its boats behind it and pressed on to occupy new realms. But it lacks concentration, leaving the many diverse fields of culture and subject-matter unsubdued to an inner unity. It is a faithful reflection of the deep dissension, philosophical and extra-philosophical, of our time, which by finding its refuge in faith has not thereby become stronger in thought. It is probably the plainest symptom of the extent to which even to-day British philosophy has failed to reach any goal, but is still *en route*.

WILLIAM TEMPLE (*b.* 1881)

[1904–10, Fellow and Lecturer in Philosophy, Queen's College, Oxford; 1910–14, Headmaster of Repton; 1921–9, Bishop of Manchester; 1929, Archbishop of York. *The Faith and Modern Thought*, 1910; *The Nature of Personality*, 1911; *Church and Nation*, 1915; *Plato and Christianity*, 1916; *Mens Creatrix*, 1917; *Issues of Faith*, 1918; *Christus Veritas*, 1924; "Some Implications of Theism", in *Contemporary British Philosophy*, edited by J. H. Muirhead, first series, 1924; *Christianity and the State*, 1928; *Nature, Man, and God* (Gifford Lectures), 1934; also many theological and religious writings.]

Temple received his philosophical education at Balliol College, Oxford, under Edward Caird, who has remained in his memory as the highest example of a man that not only teaches the spiritual life but lives it out. Through Caird he was brought early into contact with the world of idealistic thought within which all his later quest for philosophical clarity has moved. He belongs to that class of philosophizing divines which is more numerous in England than anywhere else, and of which Berkeley was an early and brilliant representative. His philosophy is less the satisfaction of a purely theoretical need than the justification of his religious and theological outlook. Its task is the harmonizing of faith and knowledge, and the theoretical grounding of a theism antecedently fixed.

Temple defines theism as the hypothesis that the ultimate ground of the universe is a will, that this will realizes an end, and that this end appears to us finite beings as good. It is an hypothesis which derives its support from our moral and religious experience. Reality, then, is an expression of the divine will. It has many levels or stages, unified by a single process of development. Regarded temporally the series of stages moves from lower to higher, but regarded from the point of view of its general significance this order is reversed; for although *realiter* the higher presupposes the lower, the lower gives no clue to the meaning of the higher. Determination and meaning move from above downwards, the sense of the lower only revealing itself with the appearance of its next higher stage. *Potentialiter*, therefore, the higher dwells in the lower and then rises out of it to constitute a new stage. There are four main stages of being, strongly distinguished from each other, namely, matter, life, intellect, and spirit; and, to make specific the preceding law of the process, matter only reveals its true nature when it takes on life; and intellect only fulfils its proper function when it comes under the guidance of spirit, which is the highest stage of reality known to us. Here, undoubtedly, we have the influence of the renewed interest in evolution which showed itself later in the emergence theories of, for example, Lloyd Morgan and Alexander, with which Temple's theory in its main outlines closely corresponds.

A doctrine of ascending levels raises the problem of value, particularly of its relation to reality. Is the essence of things exhausted in their mere existence, with values as simply adjectival, or is it the values that are primary? Temple tries to show that the latter is the case. His way of putting it is that only values have substantial reality. They achieve their different forms through embodiment in things. It follows that whatever is real is so in so far as it is informed with value; in other words, in so far as it is good. Now the valuable or the good is simply the correlate of a will, and this will is the creative will of the divine spirit, which alone is self-existent. The world, therefore, is the creation and expression of the will of God. The identification of substance and value leads inexorably to theism.

These ideas find their systematic exposition in Temple's

Mens Creatrix. Here he considers the quest of spirit for a satisfying view of the world under the three forms of science, art, and morality. All three seek after a unification of the chaotic manifold of things. But none of them can achieve it. Only in religion can a unitary world-view be attained, so that religion is the completion of all other forms of knowledge and the coping-stone of philosophic system. Hence to the *Mens Creatrix* Temple adds a sequel in *Christus Veritas*, in which he develops what he rightly calls a Christocentric metaphysic.

For the rest, Temple's philosophical position may be characterized as absolute idealism. Stripped of its theological bonds and its deep attachment to Platonism it is more indebted to Bosanquet, and through him to Bradley, than to anyone else. The primacy of this line of influence shows itself in the alternatives he conceives to be before any philosophy, either to postulate the thoroughgoing rationality (or, at any rate, rational determinableness) of the universe, or to fall back into complete scepticism. The metaphysical rationality of the world carries with it the ethical postulate of its perfect goodness, so that an optimistic world-view results. Such an optimism, we must object, penetrates to the heart of neither the problem of personality nor the problem of evil. It finds no place for the individual, the irrational, and all that militates against value and meaning, except in so far as it can bring them in as functions or appearances of their opposites. It really gives us an Absolute in whose quiescent harmony all such distinctions and oppositions are eclipsed, leaving no trace of the torturing agitation of our factual world and the tragical involvements of our own life. Absolutism has here entered into the safe harbourage of orthodox theology.

The most thorough and comprehensive attempt Temple has yet made to ground and develop his view of the universe is to be found in his Gifford Lectures, *Nature, Man, and God*. Here again, however, what we are given is rather a search for a theoretical justification for prior articles of faith than an independent piece of strict demonstration. There is no essential change of position. His starting-point is now realistic: epistemological subjectivism, for which he holds Descartes' *cogito ergo sum* to be primarily responsible, is rejected in all its forms. In knowing, the mind is concerned not with itself—with its own states as presentations—but with a world that in fact stands over against it. This realism is described as "dialectical", and the development of its dialectical process, together with the prominent place allotted in this to mind, gives it an increasingly Hegelian air, of which the most obvious external signs are Temple's frequent emphasis on his affinity with his old teacher, Edward Caird, to whose memory the volume is dedicated, and his many references to Bosanquet, with whose metaphysic he is, despite differences of detail, in general agreement. The dialectical process culminates in a theism, with a universe regarded as having a "sacramental character". The system Temple here unfolds at length is one of the most impressive statements of Christian theism argued from a predominantly idealistic point of view that recent English thought has produced.

8. COGNATE THINKERS

SIMON SOMERVILLE LAURIE (1829–1909)

[Educated at Edinburgh; Professor of Education, Edinburgh. *On the Philosophy of Ethics*, 1866; *Metaphysica Nova et Vetusta, a Return to Dualism*, 1884 (second edition, much enlarged, 1889) (this and the following were written under the pseudonym "Scotus Novanticus"); *Ethica, or the Ethics of Reason*, 1885 (second edition, much enlarged, 1891); *Synthetica: Being Meditations Epistemological and Ontological* (Gifford Lectures), two vols., 1906; also works on educational theory and practice.

See *La philosophie de S. S. Laurie*, by G. Remacle, 1909.]

The philosophy of the Scotsman Laurie grew almost entirely out of his own mind and consequently cannot be brought without a certain degree of violence under any of the usual general captions. He himself calls it "a return to dualism" (the sub-title of his *Metaphysica*), but the obscurity and impenetrability of his thinking makes it difficult to decide whether the monistic or the dualistic strain (there is a pluralistic one too) is the more dominant. He also called it "natural realism", and this rightly characterizes his epistemological starting-point, which is consciously akin to Reid's position; but it does not by any means apply to the rest of his thought, or to his thought taken as a whole. We may, however, without misgiving, place it within the neo-idealistic movement, even though Laurie himself cannot be said to have been swept into this. There are certainly links with Kant and Schelling, and most of all with Hegel, of whom his knowledge was direct.

But Laurie remains just himself, more so than any other British thinker of his time, and his doctrine, therefore, must be understood in its own light. It is like a soliloquy, a conversation with himself alone, neither heeding others nor proceeding out of any antecedent intercourse with others. For this reason it found scarcely an echo among his own people; the sound of it all but died away into thin air. A solitary enthusiastic apostle,

G. Remacle, has tried in France and Belgium to bring him recognition through the translation and exposition of his works, without finding any response. All this is not surprising, in view of the obscurity, arbitrariness, eccentricity, and originality of both his thought and the manner of its expression. He devised his own terminology, with audacious coinages and unusual word-forms, by no means helpful to the understanding of the reader: in the heaviness of his syntax as well as of his terms he reminds one of Hegel. He was as gnarled and severe as the visage of his own land. But scarcely any of his contemporaries surpassed or even equalled him in power or boldness of speculation beyond the bounds of experience, and in the love of and capacity for system-building. At the same time, only rarely, as in Fawcett (at a much lower level), do we find elsewhere so much visionary fancy and extravagance combined with mystical profundity. Indeed, if we approached him with the conventional ideas of what British philosophers are like we should not find in him a single typical trait; he would impress us rather as a German thinker fallen by accident on British soil.

Of the three works in which his world-view is set forth the first two, the *Metaphysica* and the *Ethica*, are preludes to the third. In this, *Synthetica*, which embodies his mature reflections, all the chords of his thought come together in a powerful and sonorous metaphysical symphony. It opens with a sort of history of consciousness, a "phenomenology of spirit", portraying the stages through which the spirit rises increasingly from the lowest level of organic consciousness, tied to impulse and feeling, to the realization of its true nature. The first stage of consciousness is pure and undifferentiated feeling. The subject has not yet emerged from the mass of objects, but slumbers embryonically in the womb of a general and indeterminate existence. Still, it *is* there, in germ. The next stage is sensation, distinguished as the consciousness of an "other", which is experienced as external; the subject receives external stimuli and apprehends them obscurely. The duality of subject and object has here made its first appearance, and through the process of externalizing its impressions the sensitive subject is now active and not passive only. The stage after this is the highest form of sensation. Laurie coins for it the term "attuition". Intermediate between sensation in the above sense and perception, in it the subject apprehends differences of "things", distinguishing one thing from another, without being able as yet to free itself from the domination of the objective field. In Laurie's own words, attuition is the consciousness of "a many in a single", "a synopsis of the object", "a feeling of the Being of an object which, by reflection or reaction, is placed outside me at its point of origination".[1] When the will, which is pure activity, is added to attuition, which is only "passivo-active", we reach the stage of perception. Here the object is perceived as not simply different from but as opposed to the subject, and it is related by the act of assertion to the unity of consciousness. The final separation of subject and object is achieved, and thereby the stage of reason attained, the intelligence of animal attuition and of human perception being transformed by the emergence of the pure activity of will. The frontier of the sub-rational has been crossed; the subject is now once and for all rational. But of reason the root and form and essence is will. The highest stage of consciousness is a supra-rational intuition in which the original immediacy of feeling is recovered.

This advance of consciousness is conceived dialectically, and is therefore expounded along lines of rational proof. In the second volume, where he passes to his doctrine of God and man and where his speculative power is at its best, we have no longer demonstration, but the revelation of the deepest experiences of a soul in search of God. The problem of God's nature is approached from every side of human experience, convergent searchlights being brought to bear upon it from feeling and will and reason. Hence the prodigality of the attributes that fall from the lips of this enraptured visionary. God is all in all, the one in the many, the identity in difference, the universal, the infinite, the eternal, the fount and womb of things, the great abyss, and immeasurable love, beauty, good-

[1] *Metaphysica*, second edition, p. 6 f.

ness, and truth. But, with all this unconditionedness of being, He does not abide afar off. For a soul like Laurie's, hungering after a mystical union, the purely transcendent God of deism has no meaning: He would be a God who (to retain Laurie's forceful imagery) had gone on a journey or fallen asleep. God is life and activity and creativity as well as being, and must therefore externalize Himself and enter into the temporal order to dwell within the finite spirits He has made. This externalization is a revelation—this "outerance" is an utterance, as Laurie puts it—to His creatures. All this has not to be understood as pantheism. The process is not an emanation but is dialectical; the Absolute includes as part of its essence pure negation, whereby His "other"—the finite, temporal, individual—is constituted over against Him and yet remains penetrated by and included within Him. So that even in mystical union with God, which Laurie depicts in exalted and dithyrambic language, the finite person retains his individuality.

Laurie's doctrine of man refers back to his account of the stages of consciousness. Man cannot remain at the attuitional stage, at which he is simply an animal aggregate of particular desires, impulses, and sensations. Being endowed with reason he aims at the transformation of these unorganized elements into the rational unity of a moral personality. Human experience is a dialectic of will, since it contains essentially a longing for the ideal and the Absolute. The man who fails to follow this volitional dialectic sinks to a lower stage; the man who follows it and realizes his true self participates even in his temporal state in the eternal life of God, and is selected by God to be His fellow-worker in the achievement of His eternal ends. For in this work God has need of man.

At this point Laurie gathers together the threads of his grandiose scheme into a dramatic climax. The negative element of things comes to the fore again in the form of evil. Evil is "the failure of God-creative to realize the ideal of the individual and of the whole *on the plane of Being which man occupies*".[1] It is startling to speak of failure on the part of God, but when we

[1] *Synthetica*, vol. 2, p. 286.

reflect on evil, on the irrational element in the world, on the "everlasting No" (Laurie uses this expression of Carlyle's), we are obliged to leave aside the comfortable phrases of convention. Pain and misery and sin cannot have formed part of the Creator's plan. We are forced to assume, therefore, that the negative principle has somehow proved too powerful for God. Evil, then, is a cosmic fact. As such it must have come from God, but it cannot have come through Him. Laurie, like several of his contemporaries, thus presents us with the idea of a limited God, embarrassed with difficulties, Himself suffering from His own creation, and striving to overcome its imperfections, and for the success of His striving needing the help of man. In this sense finite beings are fellow-sufferers and fellow-workers with Him. Indeed, though they are finite, so closely are they bound up with God that we must postulate their immortality. "A man striving after union with God here and now is, *ipso facto*, making himself immortal, inasmuch as he is bringing his finite spirit within the very life of the eternal spirit and is being borne along in the current of that which cannot die."[1] Man *quâ* man, that is, as a rational being, is divine, and therefore cannot but participate in the divine life. And this is the guarantee of immortality which empirical enquiry cannot, of course, supply.

E. DOUGLAS FAWCETT (*b.* 1866)

[Free-lance man of letters. Lives chiefly in Switzerland. *The Riddle of the Universe*, 1893; *The Individual and Reality*, 1909; *The World as Imagination*, 1916; *Divine Imagining*, 1921 (continuation of preceding); "Imaginism", in *Contemporary British Philosophy*, edited by J. H. Muirhead, second series, 1925 (here he repudiates his first two books); *The Zermatt Dialogues, constituting the outlines of a philosophy of mysticism*, 1931.]

Fawcett's thought stands apart from rational philosophy, just as he himself has remained apart from academic life. It

[1] *Synthetica*, vol. 2, p. 387.

represents a type of philosophy which is relatively rare in Britain but relatively common in other countries. We may call it, using the label that Kant used with much less justice of Berkeley's doctrine, "Fanciful Idealism". He is one of those who "build divers thought-castles in the air" (to borrow again from Kant), flying high above experience. As the titles of two of his later books indicate,[1] Fawcett gives to imagination the central rôle, making it not only the specifically philosophical faculty but also the ground of reality itself. It is his primary metaphysical principle. The world is not will or presentation or reason but creative imagining. In calling his general view "imaginism" he is sensible of his extreme opposition to Hegel's panlogism, and carries his dislike of reason so far as to say at one point, with a touch of pride, "Thus we have got rid of reason".[2] And in truth his philosophy, although it has not quite got rid of reason, is a product of that literary phantasy which it sets up as the first principle of all things.

Despite his boast in the novelty of his view, Fawcett is very much aware of his philosophical forerunners and refers to them repeatedly. Apart from a somewhat faint tendency in Kant, productive imagination first appears as infinite activity in Fichte, and later figures in the Neo-Thomist Frohschammer.[3] Among later thinkers Fawcett feels himself most akin to Bergson, with his doctrine of intuition and creative evolution, and he has rather looser connections with Whitehead, Mackenzie, and Schiller. In its inner structure, however, his thought—or rather his vision—has a closer resemblance to the equally speculative attitude of Laurie than to the thought of any other contemporary thinker. His favourite orientation, however, as one would expect, is to the poets, as men who are able to see more deeply into things than philosophers can. William Blake is for him the "bard of imaginism", and Shelley's pantheistic poems were another frequent source of his ideas.

Fawcett, ever ready to coin new words, calls the essence of

[1] He no longer acknowledges his first two books of 1893 and 1909.
[2] *World as Imagination*, p. 204.
[3] In *Die Phantasie als Grundprinzip des Weltprozesses* (1877).

reality "imaginal", to indicate a conscious activity of which imagination is the nearest human analogue. He coins yet another word for it, "consciring". It is an infinite activity, at once creative and conservative, productive and reproductive, of all that is in the world. Nature is but a phase in the totality of creation: is, so to speak, a divine adventure; and its driving forces are the new, the accidental, the dynamic, the creative, not causal determination with its everlasting sameness, the world of physics being not a real world but a merely conceptual one, an insubstantial spectre in comparison with the concreteness and infinite fulness and variety of the real world.

The original stage of being is envisaged as a static and compact harmony, an unchanging whole in which everything lies only in germ. Fawcett calls it the "great imaginal". From it emerges at one stroke the natural order, in which things become differentiated and opposed to each other and enter into the sequence of time. This process, however, is a disturbance of the original harmony, a metaphysical Fall, or, as Schopenhauer would say, the crime of individuation, and the cosmic principle seeks to escape from this lapse into time and to recover its harmony. The present order of events is the arena of the forces that make for disorder and those that make for harmony. It is the latter, which are to have the victory, that give to the cosmic process its meaning, that is, its creative evolution, its ascent to ever higher orders of being. In this ascent, which is the return of things to the womb of all being, lies salvation from all imperfection, strife and evil. The world we live in is indeed full of suffering and need and sin, but we are justified in assuming that it is capable of making itself better and will eventually, and progressively, help the good to victory.

ERNEST BELFORT BAX (1854–1926)

[Man of letters; barrister; co-founder with William Morris of the Socialist League. *The Problem of Reality*, 1892; *The Roots of*

Reality, 1907; *Problems of Men, Mind and Morals*, 1912; *The Real, the Rational and the Alogical*, 1920; "The Analysis of Reality", in *Contemporary British Philosophy*, edited by J. H. Muirhead, second series, 1925; also translations of Kant and Schopenhauer, a text-book on the history of philosophy, and works on Socialism.

See autobiography, *Reminiscences and Reflections of a Mid and Late Victorian*, 1918.]

In Bax we have a confirmation of the rightness of Green's challenge to the younger generation of the 'seventies to turn their backs once and for all on the doctrines of Mill and Spencer and turn to the works of Kant and Hegel. In his youth he moved entirely within the empiricist circle of Lewes, Bain, Mill, and Spencer, and attended the meetings of the Positivists. Later, on a fateful journey to Germany, he came to know Eduard von Hartmann, and the intensive study that followed of German Idealism in its several forms brought with it a conviction of the ungrounded and superficial nature of the traditional philosophy of Britain. This radical conversion, thus brought about rather by his own direct contact with the originators of Idealism than through its British followers, occurred at the beginning of the 'eighties, and for the rest of his life he remained an idealist. For him, as for Carlyle formerly and for his own contemporary Haldane, Germany henceforward became his spiritual home.

Bax took the fundamental thesis of Idealism to be the principle that there can be no reality out of all relation to consciousness. Consciousness is an indefeasible synthesis of three factors, a "that" which apprehends, a "somewhat" which is apprehended, and the form of thought, which is a reciprocal relation between the two preceding factors. Concrete experience or reality thus consists of at least two elements, a material and a formal, the unity of the two being the ground of objectivity of thought. Regarded more broadly, the primal duality of the real appears as the antithesis of the rational and the irrational, or, as Bax prefers to say, the logical and the alogical. Not that these occur or can occur in separation in concrete experience; but they are clearly distinguishable in the genuine sense that in certain phases of reality now the one and now the other predominates. To the logical belongs everything within the sphere of thought and reason. The alogical is characterized as pure sensation, impulse, and the motive force in all movement and change. The former represents the static, universal and infinite aspects of reality, the latter the dynamic, particular and finite aspects. The one is possibility, the other actuality; the one law, the other chance.

In Rickert's language we may speak of Bax's thought as heterothetic, since it proceeds by the positing of the one and the "other". It is the two together that make up the whole of reality; the abandonment of either would leave nothing but an empty abstraction. The dropping of the alogical factor is what Bax takes, or rather mistakes, to be the leading feature and fallacy of Hegel's philosophy. In his opposition, which he felt to be his main task, to any such monism, he tended to pass to the other extreme, according to the irrational factor the higher metaphysical value. He exhibits the cosmic process as a continual struggle between the two principles, the logical for ever striving to overcome the alogical, but never wholly succeeding. Hence he tends to give the alogical an absolute status, and by identifying it with will concludes to a panvoluntarism which has much in common with Schopenhauer's doctrine. So far he revives the old controversy within German Idealism beween Hegelianism and Schopenhauerianism. His Absolute as Will at the same time brought him into opposition to Bradley's and Bosanquet's conception of an entirely completed system poised in static and blissful harmony over the uneasiness and oppositions of things. Bax's Absolute is a dynamic movement, a continual becoming, a constantly progressive but asymptotic development towards the self-realization of subjective consciousness. The picture bears the marks of Schopenhauer's Will and Bergson's Duration.

The primal opposition within reality shows itself in the ethical sphere as the antithesis of good and evil. But when he comes to work out this application of his general metaphysical principle, Bax falls into a curious contradiction with his metaphysics. For it is not evil but good that now appears as the stronger factor. Evil cannot indeed be quite annihilated; at least the possibility of it must ever remain; but evil in the concrete, as we know it, is transitory and destined to be conquered and extirpated by the good. In the cosmic process, then, there is an original tendency towards the victorious realization of the good, and in experience there is always a balance of good over evil. The goal is goodness, with badness left as nothing more than an empty possibility. Bax here obviously glides unwillingly into the shallow waters of Hegel's and Bradley's optimism, sailing with careless inconsequence round the rocks of Schopenhauerian pessimism on which, had he followed his metaphysical compass, his ship would have been dashed to pieces. To change the figure, he makes a not altogether happy marriage between metaphysical irrationalism and ethical optimism, between a basic doctrine of Schopenhauer and Bergson and an equally basic doctrine of Hegel and Bradley.

Bax's theory of knowledge, which we have no space to expound, moves chiefly along Kantian lines. His philosophy of man's spiritual achievement, which rests on a theory of values more hinted at than worked out, has many points of contact with the ideas of Windelband and Rickert. And his philosophy of society, as we would expect from his staunch adherence to Socialism, connects itself with Marxism, though interpreting it idealistically and therefore rejecting Marx's materialistic theory of history.

The reception given to Bax's ideas in no way corresponds to their worth. He had no influence worth mentioning, and has been virtually ignored by academic philosophers. Having neither studied nor taught in a university and having followed his own way, he has shared the fate of many other outsiders. He was regarded with little favour in the cliquish circles of the universities, and, like Schopenhauer, with whom he had so much in common, felt some resentment against the "professorial philosophy of the philosophy professors".

REINHOLD FRIEDRICH ALFRED HOERNLÉ (*b.* 1880)

[Educated at Balliol College, Oxford; 1905–7, Lecturer in Philosophy, St. Andrews; 1908–11, Professor of Philosophy, Cape Town; 1912–14 and 1920–3, Professor of Philosophy, Newcastle; 1914–20, Assistant Professor of Philosophy, Harvard; 1923, Professor of Philosophy, Johannesburg. *Studies in Contemporary Metaphysics*, 1920; *Matter, Life, Mind and God*, 1923; "On the Way to a Synoptic Philosophy", in *Contemporary British Philosophy*, edited by J. H. Muirhead, second series, 1925; *Idealism as a Philosophy*, 1927.]

Like Merz, German by extraction and early education, but a British citizen, Hoernlé, while a student at Balliol College, Oxford, had Edward Caird as his first philosophical teacher, and acquired from him his own first philosophical leanings. For some years he was Bosanquet's assistant at St. Andrews, and the friendship thus begun endured until Bosanquet's death. It was this thinker whom Hoernlé followed more than any other. "So far as I can judge, I owe to him more than to any other single writer, the essential framework of my own philosophical thinking."[1] For the rest, however, he is beholden to no one school or tendency. His effort has rather been directed towards a marshalling of many minds for a common task, in an attempt to bring about what Bosanquet has called "the meeting of extremes in contemporary philosophy". He sought what he called, following Merz, a synoptic view or attitude, the thinking together of all the various aspects of experience into an organized whole. He regards the philosophical spirit as, in its highest expression, the spirit of totality, so that to philosophize is to think one's own way through to a rational attitude towards the universe as a whole. He does not, however, include in this the construction of yet another system, in which everything is comfortably appointed to a permanent place: not rigidity of system but consistency of attitude is what he desiderates, without bondage to school or dogma.

[1] *Studies in Contemporary Metaphysics*, preface. Muirhead's *Bosanquet and His Friends* (1935) contains many letters from the older to the younger man which throw much light on the philosophical thought and development of both.

Hoernlé's synoptic attitude remains operative in the treatment of special problems. Take, for example, the problem of universals or class-concepts. These he regards, with the Hegelians, not as abstract but as concrete. They represent the apprehension not simply of many things as alike but also of their individual differences within an identical context, so that they may be applied also to the several stages of a developmental series and, indeed, to ideal value-forms. They thus make possible not only descriptive and classificatory judgments of fact but also normative judgments of value.

Since his position allowed him to range widely and freely, Hoernlé took over and assimilated contemporary thought much as he found it. His general attitude is idealistic in the sense that it is speculative and is directed towards the Whole. His doctrine, however, is not distinctively or necessarily idealistic in all its parts, but contains elements drawn from the most diverse systems and tendencies, chiefly within the Anglo-Saxon world of his own day—from Bradley and Bosanquet and other Idealists, Whitehead's philosophy of Nature, Broad's critique of mechanism, J. S. Haldane's biological philosophy, Smuts's "Holism", Holt's version of Behaviourism, Webb's philosophy of religion; and from Meinong, Husserl, and Bergson. His thought is eclectic and conciliatory, and, like all Eclecticism, is attractive rather than compact, receptive rather than original, synthetic rather than creative.

HERBERT WILDON CARR (1857–1931)

[1918, Professor of Philosophy, King's College, London; 1925, same at the University of Southern California, Los Angeles. *The Problem of Truth*, 1913; *The General Principle of Relativity in its Philosophical and Historical Aspect*, 1920 (second edition, 1922); *A Theory of Monads*, *Outlines of the Philosophy of the Principle of Relativity*, 1922; *The Scientific Approach to Philosophy, Selected Essays and Reviews*, 1924; "Idealism as a Principle in Science and Philosophy", in *Contemporary British Philosophy*, edited by J. H. Muirhead, first series, 1924; *Changing Backgrounds in Religion and Ethics*, 1927; *The Unique Status of Man*, 1928; *The Freewill Problem*, 1928; *Cogitans Cogitata*, 1930; also translations of Leibniz, Bergson, and Gentile, and writings on the first two and on Croce. Some of his remains have been published in the American periodical *The Personalist*, vols. 15–17 (1934–6).

Wildon Carr's Idealism has scarcely any connection with that of the British Kantians and Hegelians. Its inspiration and its contents came from other sources. His own career was extremely unusual, one might almost say sensational. While a clerk first in the City and then with a Stock Exchange firm, he attended evening courses at King's College, London, developed an interest in philosophy (with Plato, Berkeley, and Hume as his favourite authors), joined the Aristotelian Society in the second year of its existence, and soon became secretary and one of its leading members. He was in his fifties when an accidental circumstance brought to his notice Bergson's recently published *Évolution Créatrice*, and when he found his interest excited on the one hand in the Idealism of Croce and Gentile, on the other hand in the new physics of Einstein. Henceforward he broke out into a seething activity which expressed itself in an impressive array of philosophical writings comprising translations, expository works, and independent essays in constructive system. In his sixty-first year he assumed as his first academic appointment a chair in philosophy in the University of London, moving seven years later to a similar chair in America and devoting to it the last six years of his remarkable life.

His own philosophical outlook, first developing through expository and critical writings, reached its final formulation in his *Cogitans Cogitata*, a brief but pregnant work. It is a synthesis of the several lines of thought which he had assimilated from without. Among these the dominant place was taken by the metaphysics of Bergson, his first acquaintance with which affected him so deeply that he spoke of it as a philosophical conversion. He was the first to proclaim Bergsonism in England and remained the most zealous of its advocates. In its author he saw the latest of the world's great philosophers and the prophet of a new Idealism of act and creativity. The next influence came from Italian Idealism, which also he did his best to propagate. The final influence came from the new physics. In the controversy that broke out generally after the war over the philosophical interpretation of the Theory of Relativity he ranged himself with those who took a high view of its importance and who attempted to elicit and assimilate its philosophical implications. To bring about an *entente cordiale* between modern physics and modern metaphysics became his chief aim, and in general he repeatedly emphasized the necessity of a close sympathy and co-operation between philosophy and science. He believed that Einstein's theory represented the renewal and verification by the methods of modern science of the monadology of Leibniz, and that the new theory of the atom, in particular the Quantum Theory, was of the greatest importance for Idealism because it took away the ground of dogmatic Materialism, which had based itself on a now antiquated physics. Of the older thinkers he was influenced more by Leibniz than by anyone else; the final statement of his own philosophy in his *Cogitans Cogitata* is, indeed, a theory of monads, which follows that of Leibniz in several important respects. An earlier writing bears the title *A Theory of Monads* and attempts a synthesis of Leibniz's metaphysics with Einstein's physics. In the theory of knowledge his position closely resembles the position of Berkeley, with solipsistic consequences which he did not hesitate to make explicit.

It is clear that this "new Idealism", unlike the older, was scarcely affected by the movement of ideas that began with Kant and culminated in Hegel. Like the older Idealism, it attacked the Materialism, Determinism, Evolutionism, and other forms of Naturalism of the XIXth Century, but its attack was based on the claim that the scientific theories on which they rested had been exploded by the new science of the XXth Century. This was his new ground for substituting creative for mechanical evolution, freedom and spontaneity for necessity, becoming for being, acts for things, life for matter, and intuition in place of discursive understanding.

Carr's system is thus to be ranged with the "philosophies of life" characteristic of the present day, of which Bergsonism has shown itself to be the most fascinating and powerful example. It has affinities with Pragmatism, even though the affinity is not confessed. Its own claim is that it is idealistic (after the manner of Leibniz and Berkeley) in metaphysics, voluntaristic in ethics, modernistic in religion, and relativistic in reference to science. With all its appearance of unity, however, it remains deeply infected by the plurality of its sources, which are too diverse to be susceptible of any genuine synthesis. Carr did not succeed in melting everything that he put into his crucible. The result is at best a conglomerate. Despite his great services, selfless to the point of sacrifice, in the work of quickening philosophical interest and disseminating philosophical culture, he has to be counted an able eclectic rather than a genuine and original thinker. But among all those who have served philosophy as amateurs he is the most attractive and the most deserving of attention.

JOHN THEODORE MERZ (1840–1922)

[Born in Manchester, of German stock on his father's side. Educated at Heidelberg; 1864, *Privat-Dozent* at Bonn, and, 1865, same at Göttingen under Lotze; 1866, settled in England and became Vice-Chairman of the Newcastle Electric Supply Co. *Leibniz* (Blackwood's Philosophical Classics), 1884; *History of European Thought in the XIXth Century*, four vols., 1896–1914; "On the Synoptic Aspect of Reality", in *Proceedings of University of Durham Philosophical Society*, vol. 5 (1920), pp. 45–61, read in 1913; *Religion and Science*, 1915; *A Fragment on the Human Mind*, 1919; also a few early papers in German.

See *Proceedings of University of Durham Philosophical Society*, vol. 6 (for 1915–23), 1925, pp. 215–32, "Personal reminiscences of Dr. Merz", by various writers; and pp. 233–90, "The philosophical work of Dr. J. T. Merz", by R. F. A. Hoernlé.]

Like Belfort Bax, Merz was an "outsider"; after a short spell of academic teaching he entered the world of industry. But in his new sphere he remained faithful to his main academic interest, occupying with the study of philosophy the very scanty leisure which was all that his heavy business responsibilities allowed him. We are told that his chief work, *History of European Thought*, which runs into more than 2,500 pages, was written for the most part in the early hours of the morning, between five and eight o'clock, before he began the heavy duties of his day. He did not escape the usual fate of the outsider: the professional philosophers failed to give him the recognition that he deserved, indeed paid him little attention or none at all.

In this work he shows himself at once the historian and the system builder. In the former capacity he has made himself a name. It is a characteristic product of Teutonic diligence and erudition, felicitously combining thorough and exact research with width of vision and profound historical insight. It is an achievement of the first order. The task Merz set himself was to present in a single picture the spiritual life of the XIXth Century in all its manifold expressions, and although two projected volumes on the poetical and religious ideas of the century never appeared, the four published volumes form a powerful torso, an eloquent testimony to the singular ability and unwearying industry of their author.

In philosophy also Merz planned largely, aiming at the construction of a widely based system, and here, too, he was prevented from carrying his plans to completion. But from such foundations as he managed to lay down the direction in which his thought was moving can be easily seen. The decisive influence upon him came from the German philosophers, less from Kant and Hegel than from Leibniz, Schleiermacher, and Lotze, most of all from Lotze, with whom he was personally associated during his short period of teaching at Göttingen. After his return to England he came under the further influence of the distinctively British lines of thought, especially those associated with Berkeley and Hume and the new form of introspective psychology introduced by Ward and James. The new idealistic movement in Britain scarcely touched him.

His chief endeavour, expressed in his historical and philosophical writings alike, was to reach what he called a "synoptic" view of reality, to see every whole not only in the multiplicity of its parts and relations but also in its wholeness. For him this was the proper task of philosophy, which accordingly resolves itself in the long run, for all its exactitude of detail and strictness of demonstration, into a sort of artistic vision. Hence his special concern was the reconciliation of science and religion, whose separateness and disharmony constituted in his belief a menace to the unity of our spiritual life. To this general problem he applied his synoptic method, as well as to a number of special problems, such as those of the relation of the inner and the outer world, of subject and object, of fact and value. In the spirit of Lotze he tried to resolve the old discord between the needs of the heart and the results of scientific research. He had no contempt for science—he was himself well trained in physics and chemistry—but he saw that all scientific investigation concerns itself not with the whole of experience or reality but with only a very limited aspect of it, proceeding by the methods of selection, abstraction, analysis, and classification, and only at a late stage passing on to synthetic apprehension. Moreover, it studies only facts, not values. The religious point of view, on the contrary, apprehends experience as a whole, fastens on the positive and significant connections within it, goes beyond facts to values, and emphasizes over against the depersonalized world of science the personal character of the special realm which values constitute. The method here is synoptic, and is directed expressly upon the riddle of personality, both human and divine, which natural science is incompetent to solve. In this personalistic emphasis Merz stands near to Lotze.

In bringing this synoptic point of view to bear on psychological and epistemological problems he came into sharp opposition to Hume, for whom, notwithstanding, he had a high regard and to whom he owed a great deal. He pointed out that Hume, in his analysis of consciousness into a bundle of impressions conceived after the analogy of physical atoms, overlooked the simple fact that consciousness is prior to the analysis of it, must first be there to be analysed at all. Merz was thus in cordial agreement with the new psychology of Ward in its substitution of a continuous stream of consciousness for the old aggregate of atomic data, and in its inclusion of emotional and volitional data within the continuum alongside sensations. Reflection on the unity of consciousness led him to the view that the differentiations and distinctions that experience, and experience alone, brings all presuppose a sort of "primordial" consciousness, itself undifferentiated and unbroken and therefore free from such cleavages as that of subject and object or mind and body. That this view closely resembles Bradley's notion of an unmediated experience consisting of pure feeling is obvious. Whether Merz derived it from Bradley or reached it independently is uncertain; but it is clear that it falls naturally and organically within such a system as his own synoptic ideal desiderated.

II

PRAGMATISM

Modern Pragmatism is like a surface painted in many iridescent colours, and it has manifested its influence upon many very diverse provinces of life and culture. It is a general tendency of thought as well as a special philosophical doctrine. As a tendency it penetrates wide tracts of our life, business, and thought in manifold forms with varying intensity. As such it lays stress upon sentiment rather than attempts to outline a definite doctrine; and so it almost eludes historical description. But as a philosophical doctrine it appeared first in a land where pragmatic sentiment is the key-note of life more than elsewhere—in America. There it grew up gradually from modest beginnings which can be traced back to the 'seventies of last century. C. S. Peirce is generally reckoned to-day as the spiritual ancestor and first announcer of modern Pragmatism; but it was the mighty prophet-voice of William James which gave it the whole momentum of his great and powerful personality and brought it from the thinker's study into the world at large. James did not shape Pragmatism into an academic doctrine, but raised it to a spiritual power of the first rank. Because Pragmatism was the expression of a general sentiment it not only carried with it specifically philosophic thought, but became a potent force in the other provinces of intellectual life. In James's life-time Pragmatism as a philosophy established a wide influence over American thought, though without conquering it completely. And to-day, in spite of many opposing influences and in spite of the powerful influx of European ideas, it is the basic philosophy of the New World.

In England Pragmatism has not evoked so hearty a response. About the end of last century it arose less through its own force than through dissatisfaction with dominant modes of thought and found its first utterance in a joint-volume edited by Henry Sturt in 1902 under the title of *Personal Idealism.*

This was the joint work of eight young or middle-aged members of the University of Oxford who a few years earlier (in 1898) had formed the "Oxford Philosophical Society". The contributors at that time were comparatively unknown men; and of them only three have since produced important contributions to philosophy, viz. Stout, Schiller, and Rashdall. Of the rest we need only mention the names: those of the editor, of W. R. Boyce Gibson (later the translator and popularizer of Eucken in England, the producer also of an English edition of Husserl's *Ideen zu einer reinen Phänomenologie*), of G. E. Underhill, of R. R. Marett (subsequently an eminent anthropologist), and of F. W. Bussell. The group cannot be called a philosophical school in the strict sense; nor did they profess a common allegiance to Pragmatism. They were united only in a common tendency of thought and action, manifesting only one positive purpose, the development and vindication of the principle of personality on the basis of experience and with an idealist view of the world. Indeed, the tie which united them was of a rather negative character and consisted in a sharp challenge to the two strongest philosophical fronts of that day: on one side to materialist views, and on the other to Oxford Hegelianism, which was challenged under the title of 'Absolutism'. As Sturt in his introduction points out, what is common to these two opponents is a thorough repudiation of the idea of personality and individuality. While Naturalism teaches that man is a transitory result of physical processes, Absolutism explains him as an unreal appearance of the Absolute. Neither one nor the other can do justice to free, moral, and independent personality. In the recognition and appreciation of this the contributors to *Personal Idealism* unite in their common philosophical creed.

The attack upon such diverse enemies must be carried on with various weapons and with varying force. It is very characteristic that the main shock of this attack is directed, not against Naturalism, which had been often refuted comprehensively and thoroughly both from the philosophical and the theological side, but against the Idealism which might otherwise have been enrolled as an ally against Naturalism. In this way almost simultaneously with the advance of New Realism (Moore's *Refutation of Idealism* appeared the next year) there was made one of the first breaches in the almost unshaken front of the Kantian and Hegelian school; and in spite of Sturt's assertion that the new personalism was only a phase in the development of the philosophy which had reigned for thirty years at Oxford, a clear line of division was drawn once for all between the old and the new Idealism. Later there appeared a much greater separation between the tendency which now appeared for the first time and the old Oxford line of thought, and there developed that great, energetic, and passionate discussion between Pragmatism and Hegelianism which was destined to keep professional philosophers separated for years into hostile camps. The fact that the attack came from Oxford University, where German Idealism had reigned almost unchallenged, heightened the excitement of the conflict and the interest which was taken in it on all sides.

Although the two Oxford Idealisms agreed in their polemic against Naturalism and in the basic conviction that the world in the last resort is spiritual, their subsequent paths diverged widely. It is specially noteworthy that Sturt in the collection of essays edited by him brought forward so often the appeal to experience. For this reason he showed his preference for the term "Empirical Idealism" and did not hesitate to unite in a fruitful synthesis words which according to prevailing views were opposed to each other. Against the Neo-Hegelians the reproach was made that their doctrine failed to do justice to experience and could not be brought into harmony with facts. Two points were mentioned as specially unsatisfactory: first, the manner in which Absolutism criticized human experience not from a human standpoint, but from the fantastic standpoint of an absolute experience; secondly, its intellectualist prejudice which precluded any adequate comprehension of the volitional side of human nature. These two defects involved treating the concept of personality as illusory and therefore neglecting that which the new Idealism regarded as the central aim of its philosophizing.

Appeal to experience and emphasis on the principle of personality formed, then, the common basis upon which the contributors founded their somewhat various contributions. While Stout in an important and influential essay on "Error" presupposed his own voluntarist psychology, Gibson developed his spiritual Idealism and Rashdall a Berkeleian theistic metaphysic (in his essay on "Divine and Human Personality" which adumbrates his later ideas). More pragmatist are the essays of Sturt on "Art and Personality" and above all the basic essay of Schiller on "Axioms as Postulates". This essay marks the real beginning of the specifically British version of Pragmatism, and is thus the central piece of the volume. In it may be recognized almost all the leading ideas which were to be fruitful in the great development of English Pragmatism that so soon afterwards occurred.

While the movement which thus began must be understood primarily as a reaction against Anglo-Hegelianism, and must find in this its immediate explanation, its historical antecedents go back much farther. But we must observe that Pragmatism is not the direct continuation of any special philosophical movement or school, although definite lines of connection with one or another may be traced. It is rather a really new way of thinking, drawn from many sources, which rejected many of the old ideas and assimilated others, but owed its origin to a quite definite spiritual situation and to a peculiar adjustment to exceptional conditions. We need not explore the factual or non-philosophic background of Pragmatism. Within the field of philosophy its place in the great speculative contrasts which stretch through the history of philosophy is plainly evident. If we set in contrast to each other such antitheses as Nominalism and Realism, Empiricism and Rationalism, Voluntarism and Intellectualism, Pluralism and Monism, Individualism and Universalism, Indeterminism and Determinism, a dynamic and a mechanistic view of the world, optimism and pessimism, joy in knowledge and agnosticism, an active and a contemplative way of life, a practical and a theoretical attitude, Pragmatism stands on the side of the former alternatives and opposes the latter. I certainly do not mean that we have here an eclectic selection of more or less consistent standpoints or modes of thought, but that we have a genuine and necessary synthesis, which has sprung from an inward consistency. We have not a rounded, harmoniously balanced, and logically faultless structure of doctrine, but an open mode of philosophizing relatively free from the bonds of system. Pragmatism is not so much a doctrine (still less a system) as a special attitude or adjustment which can adapt itself to every possible form of doctrine. As from its nature it includes a polemical element, it is nourished by repelling no less than by attracting forces; in other words, it is made fruitful by negative influences which provoke contradiction as much as by positive influences.

All this becomes clear if we set forth briefly some of the historical influences which have acted upon it. In the first place some important parallels may be drawn with German Idealism, to go no further back, which sometimes have been drawn by Pragmatists themselves. In regard to theory of knowledge there is a certain agreement with Kant; namely, in the doctrine that understanding prescribes its laws to nature and that knowledge constructs an orderly world from the chaos of the given; but above all, in the doctrine of the supremacy of the practical reason over the theoretical. The relationship with Fichte's activist philosophy may be still closer. Much more than Kant Fichte subordinated the idea of the true to the idea of the good, and made the theoretical fulfil itself in the practical reason. This is thoroughly in accordance with the doctrine of Pragmatism; and in the thought that the world is nothing but the plastic material of our activity (Fichte says "the sensuous material of our duty") both are thoroughly in agreement. For this reason Scheler has justly observed that Fichte may be termed an idealistic Pragmatist. On the other hand, Pragmatism feels itself repelled in every way by Hegel and by every kind of Hegelianism; but this repulsion has been endlessly productive and as a negative ferment has contributed extraordinarily to positive construction. Nevertheless, the cleft between German

Idealism and Anglo-Saxon Pragmatism is very considerable and can hardly be bridged in spite of many well-meaning attempts at mediation.

There were many connections also with native modes of thought, for example with certain doctrines of the older English Empiricism (especially with Hume) and with the Philosophy of Common Sense. The empirical foundation of Pragmatism and the fact that it starts from the healthy understanding of active men point in the same direction. But on the whole the points of difference are much greater than the points of agreement, and occasional agreements are not of much importance in view of the fact that the two modes of thought are widely different in respect of their general intellectual structure, their emotional accompaniments, and their moral tendencies. The case is different with certain tendencies of XIXth-Century thought which may be regarded as direct spiritual ancestors; in particular, the utilitarianism of J. S. Mill, the natural selection theory of Darwinism (one of the most important components of British Pragmatism), the evolutionism of Spencer, to an eminent degree Bergson's doctrine of creative evolution, Nietzsche's extreme activist philosophy of life and power, Pearson's and Mach's efforts to explain thought-processes on the principle of economy, and all systems of thought tending to voluntarism and vitalism. Psychology also contributed a powerful impulse, first as reaction against the mechanistic theory of association and faculties, and then as a positive adoption of the modern voluntarist doctrines of Sigwart, Wundt, Paulsen, and of British and American psychologists with similar views, such as J. Ward, Stout, and James. With all these and with other influences of the last decades, Pragmatism has a real kinship of structure and content, a common philosophic purpose and temper. The purpose of Pragmatism is to avail itself of all these ideas, and by transforming them to combine them into a still higher spiritual synthesis. It is neither that utter novelty, which it professes to be, nor a mere réchauffé of old ideas, as its opponents maintain; but a genuine synthesis of old and new, a focus of attractive and repulsive forces, and a movement which came into being less from purely theoretic interest than from the immediate relations of life itself and its implications with human existence. To life, therefore, Pragmatism may do good service, and accordingly it puts life above thinking, active life above contemplative life, and man, in the fullness of his activities, in his error and striving, willing and dealing, above a one-sided cultivation of him as a merely intellectual being, and above devotion to fanciful ideals which are not embraced by the whole of his being.

FERDINAND CANNING SCOTT SCHILLER (1864–1937)

[Of German ancestry, came to England in his early years, educated at Rugby and Balliol College, Oxford, subsequently Fellow and Tutor of Corpus Christi College, Oxford; for a time lecturer in logic and metaphysics at Cornell University, Ithaca (New York). Latterly Professor in the University of Southern California, Los Angeles. *Riddles of the Sphinx, by a Troglodyte* (anonymous), 1891 (second edition, with author's name, 1894; new edition, 1910); "Axioms as Postulates", 1902 (in *Personal Idealism*, ed. by H. Sturt); *Humanism; philosophical essays*, 1903 (second edition, 1912); *Studies in Humanism*, 1907 (second edition, 1912); *Plato or Protagoras?* 1908; *Formal Logic*, 1912 (second edition, 1931); *Problems of Belief*, 1924; "Why Humanism?" (in *Contemporary British Philosophy*, ed. by J. H. Muirhead, First Series, 1924; *Tantalus, or the Future of Man*, 1924 (German trans., 1926); *Eugenics and Politics*, 1926; *Cassandra, or the Future of the British Empire*, 1926; article "Pragmatism" in the *Encyclopaedia Britannica*, fourteenth edition, 1929; *Logic for Use: an introduction to the voluntarist theory of knowledge*, 1929; *Social Decay and Eugenical Reform*, 1932; *Must Philosophers Disagree? and other Essays in Popular Philosophy*, 1934; Some essays from *Humanism* and *Studies in Humanism*, as well as the paper "Axioms as Postulates", have appeared in a German translation by Rudolf Eisler under the title *Humanismus, Beiträge zu einer pragmatischen Philosophie*, Philosophisch-soziologische Bücherei, xxv, 1911.]

English Pragmatism stands or falls with the personality and work of F. C. S. Schiller. For a generation he was its unwearied champion, its ready defender, and its persistent advocate. As a natural fighter he was always ready for action, always ready to deal blows on all sides. Sometimes he carried the attack into the enemy's camp, sometimes he retreated to a defensive position, sometimes he stepped into the arena with a new offensive. He had complete command of all the weapons which are needed for conflict—of repartee, nimbleness, and intrepidity, of ridicule and irony, wit and humour, of brilliant diction and acute dialectic. Among contemporary British philosophers he was the controversialist *par excellence*, the most agile fighter, the best and liveliest writer. To Schiller philosophy is not a matter of learning, or of strict technical knowledge, or one which is reached by self-searching or shock-tactics, or the satisfaction of theoretic, aesthetic or such-like needs; it was the expression and outpouring of a fresh and free personality; it was more a sport or game than learning, research, or profession of faith.

Schiller was brought up in Oxford, and apart from some excursions to America he made it his headquarters until his death. He began his studies at the University immediately after Green's death, when Hegelianism was in the ascendant; but unlike most Oxford philosophical students of that day he was not carried away by the Hegelian influence, but from the outset opposed a strong resistance to it. He felt quite out of sympathy with Green's *Prolegomena*, which was put before him as an introduction to philosophy, and he felt himself repelled, not only by the new philosophical spirit at Oxford, but by the whole scholastic and unpractical manner in which philosophy (and especially logic) was taught at the University and deflected to purposes of examination. He quickly plunged into the main stream of the Darwinian evolutionary theory and was swept away in the whirlpool of the dominant evolutionary torrent. To it he paid tribute in his first publication which appeared in 1891 and was entitled *Riddles of the Sphinx*. It bore the characteristic sub-title *A Study in the Philosophy of Evolution*, written *by a Troglodyte*. The *Riddles of the Sphinx* belongs to Schiller's pre-pragmatist period, although in many respects it foreshadows his later ideas. In any case his pragmatist attitude was not yet consciously complete, but slumbered in the background of his consciousness.

It only needed the word of release to start into life. But this early work gives striking proof of the unity and consistency of his intellectual development; and he himself made the discovery that even then he was a Pragmatist without knowing it (much more than in *Riddles of the Sphinx* in an essay which appeared shortly afterwards, in 1892, *Reality and Idealism*, reprinted in *Humanism*, Essay vii).

Schiller's work, written in his 27th year, is speculative in the highest degree and attacks with youthful impetuosity the great problems of humanity. Herein there is a great contrast to his later careful reserve towards metaphysical problems and to metaphysics as a constructive science at all. It is a system of philosophy conceived with powerful speculative gifts and worked out with much detail, in which the concept of evolution is the leading thought. Philosophy as the theory of life is a practical and not a speculative affair; and the same is true of the speculative impulse, which in its origin and character is also mainly practical. This bold attempt of a youthful spirit displays at the outset that strongly optimistic view of knowledge which Schiller never surrendered and which he justified later against such disruptive tendencies of contemporary philosophy as agnosticism, scepticism, and pessimism. Simultaneously, Schiller takes up his polemic against the Hegelian system, against "the most ingenious system of illusions that adorns the history of thought".[1] Hegelianism, which puts abstractions in place of realities, because it has itself no contact with reality, is blamed as intellectual charlatanism and despised as the falsest of all abstract metaphysical systems. As against it Schiller demands that metaphysics and metaphysical method should be concrete, should be founded on the exact sciences and on human experience. In harmony with this he says later that all our thinking must necessarily be anthropomorphic (the term 'pragmatic' is not yet in use), that the reality of the personal ego is the basis of all life, and that the individual is the key to the riddle of the world. Personalism is here already brought into connection with pluralism. In contrast with Hegelian and other

[1] *Riddles of the Sphinx*, second edition, 1894, p. 159.

monisms Schiller vindicates the rights of the many individuals against the One, by appealing to the testimony of experience which displays to us a wealth of phenomena and facts and not a distinctionless all-absorbing unity.

On these basic ideas are founded the speculations on the nature of God, to which Schiller gives much space in the constructive part of his work. God cannot be the One which lies behind the many, and cannot be identified simply with Nature or the World. He is rather only one among many other individuals, and therefore his being is limited by the existence of others. From the personality and individuality of God Schiller infers his finitude, a thought which J. S. Mill had already formulated and which we find in many subsequent thinkers. In relation to the world we must think of this finite God both as immanent and transcendent; immanent in so far as he is an all-vitalizing and ever-active power, transcendent in so far as he does not, as the Pantheist holds, disperse himself into the totality of things, but possesses true personality, i.e., transcendent existence over against other individuals. From the standpoint of evolution God is the final aim and highest ideal, the completion of the world-process in the sense of fully harmonizing and reconciling all refractory factors and tendencies. As such Schiller regards the evil and detrimental element of the world. It is that which resists the divine will and, therefore, hinders the advance of evolution. But evil is a necessary element of the world, so far as it is a world of becoming and a process in time. The impulse of world-development moves towards perfection, harmony, and cosmic order, which means that evil is pressed back as the advance proceeds and is finally annihilated. Schiller shapes his evolution-formula in the sense that the world-process leads from a timeless not-being through a temporal becoming to an eternal being. In the eternal being which the becoming of the cosmos develops gradually from the timeless not-being of an acosmic apathy and isolation, we glimpse the vision of a heaven and a peace which is higher than all reason and in which are obliterated the last traces of the pre-cosmic discord of which the battle of life is only a diminished shadow. And this gives the answer to the riddle of the Sphinx.

This early stage of thought, although moving in the atmosphere created by Darwin and Spencer, is distinguished from similar attempts in two essential points: it is anti-naturalist and anti-agnostic. It is inspired by a strong idealist enthusiasm; it does not, like Spencer, halt before the final questions, but draws them into the circle of philosophical inquiry and resolutely tries to answer them. After this incursion into metaphysics Schiller turned to more special provinces and occupied himself with logical, psychological, and epistemological inquiries, in the course of which he found himself pressed more and more into the pragmatist position. This position was reached in almost all essential points in the basic essay *Axioms as Postulates* of the year 1902 (see supra, page 450). As we have seen, it had been anticipated long before in Schiller's own thought; but some powerful external influences were at work to bring it finally to light. The first and most important was contact with American Pragmatism, especially with its most eloquent exponent and champion William James. About the end of the century Schiller fell under James's influence and formed a close friendship with him. Through James he made the final step to a pragmatic system of thought, especially to its psychological, ethical, and metaphysical consequences. The second influence was the new orientation which psychology adopted in the 'eighties and 'nineties and which is marked by the substitution of a teleological and voluntarist conception of mental life for mechanistico-associationist and intellectualist views. This movement, which began in Germany under the leadership of Wundt, found in Anglo-Saxon lands its chief exponent in the psychological researches of Ward, Stout, and also of James. In it, although it is not expressly pragmatist, we must see a powerful ally of Pragmatism, especially of its British form. Schiller was strongly influenced by Ward, not only in psychology, but in his general philosophic views. The third factor to be considered belongs to logic and is especially important for the development of English Pragmatism. Schiller himself gives credit to that neglected logician A. Sidgwick (see infra, page 474) as one of the first to give a new direction to logic, a study which more than any had stood still upon the old paths. Long before the pragmatist movement came into being Sidgwick directed acute (Schiller says 'epoch-making') criticism against the purely formal logic, which made abstraction from real thinking and wasted itself in useless futilities. He called for the extermination of all this artificial abstract machinery directed solely to mental gymnastic and advocated that it should be applied practically and made fruitful in the service of life and science. Schiller, who from the beginning was strongly interested in logic, yielded gladly to these powerful influences, especially as similar movements could be discerned among other logicians (e.g., Sigwart, Wundt, Bain, and Mill) and included them in the pragmatist movement.

Thus it came about that Schiller's Pragmatism established itself mainly in the realm of logic and annexed this discipline as its own domain. This had the advantage of bringing the movement on to a more definite path and of enabling it to prove and establish its method in a definite field of inquiry. Thereby it ceased to be merely an attitude of mind, as it had been predominantly with James, and became more of a definite, articulated, and methodical doctrine (although even with Schiller it is to a considerable extent an attitude or view of life). In comparison with James, Schiller is a stricter, more systematic and disciplined mind, and also more radical and consistent. From logic and the theory of truth connected with it (the kernel of Schiller's doctrine) the light of Pragmatism streams over the other provinces of philosophy: over psychology, the theory of value, the theory of knowledge, ethics, metaphysics, and philosophy of religion. They are all consequences of its basic logical principle, by which they are more or less thoroughly penetrated. Some of these studies, such as the two last mentioned, pass beyond the boundaries of Pragmatism in the narrower sense, but nevertheless are treated in the light of a freer and less constrained application of the principle.

Schiller's efforts for the reform of logic (the most important point of his programme and his deepest concern) extend through all his writings of the last thirty years, from the essay of 1902 to his final treatment of the subject in his *Logic for Use*, and even later (vide the *Transactions of the Aristotelian Society* for 1931 and the essay "The Value of Formal Logic" in *Mind*, vol. 41, 1932). Midway between the two dates lies the comprehensive polemic against the opposing party in the book *Formal Logic* (1912), which was preceded and followed by countless smaller skirmishes in essays, lectures, criticisms, discussions, and reviews.

The character of pragmatist logic as it has been developed by Schiller and others is predominantly polemical, not merely because it encountered at its outset a definite opponent which must be overcome, but because controversy belongs to its essence and cannot be separated from it. So one might say that it would have had to invent an opponent, even if there had not been one ready for it. But the opponent, which was the traditional formal logic that has maintained itself longer and more obstinately in the English university curriculum than elsewhere, was transformed into a perfect caricature and a bogy before which we are expected to shiver in order that the criticism might seem more justified and reform more urgently necessary. Although the opponent which is continually presented to us in pragmatic logic is a mainly fictitious creature, we must not fail to recognize that certain unquestionable excrescences and degenerations are lashed with justice and mortally hit by Schiller's criticism. The distortion of his picture of his opponent increases its utility and is extremely useful for establishing and elaborating his own position, and this is its pragmatist justification.

Schiller's criticism of the traditional logic always circles round the same point. There is no field of logic which is self-contained, separated from all human interests and self-sufficing. There is no truth which could be tied down to a sphere of mere validity or pure value that transcends all reality. And so there is no truth which is eternal, absolutely valid, independent of all human experience or *a priori*. But formal or pure logic has withdrawn itself into the unreality of such a sphere evacuated of all concrete content and severed from all human relationships. By abstracting from all real thinking and contenting itself with the exposition of merely formal rules valid for so-called pure thought, formal logic turns into an empty play of words and ideas and degenerates into mere acrobatics and jugglery which are useless and senseless. It is a contrivance empty of all real substance and completely barren. Out of its need it has made a virtue; it wraps itself in proud exclusiveness and strictly guards its sacred precincts. To justify itself it has invented an ideal, on the basis of which it has built its airy structure, the ideal of truth for truth's sake, or of knowledge for its own sake. But while it advertises truth for the sake of truth and knowledge for the sake of knowledge, it leaves unanswered the question what is the meaning of truth and what is the aim of knowledge.

At this point begins the reform of logic, which is settled immediately by criticism. By criticism it is shown that a logic which excludes real thinking and makes abstraction of the human element degenerates into a useless and meaningless verbalism. But man, as the creator of truth and also of logic, cannot allow himself to be shut out for ever by a creation of his own mind. Schiller emends a well-known quotation—*Expellas hominem logica, tamen usque recurret.* The first and most important need is, therefore, the re-establishment of man in the theory of logic and truth; but not of man theoretically attenuated, engaged merely in thought, judgment, and logical operations; but of man in the completeness of his being, with all his emotions and strivings, feelings and impulses, doings and dealings, purposes, aims, and ends. This means that logic must be bound very closely to the human sciences (anthropology, sociology, biology, etc.), and above all to psychology. Pragmatist logic is, therefore, consciously and emphatically psychological, and declares expressly that pure logic is impracticable. The reproach that it is psychological does not touch it, for it wishes to be nothing else than psychological and its quarrel is with those who make this reproach against it.

We must therefore retrace the path of those who have set out to depersonalize truth and dehumanize knowledge. We must free logic (and philosophy generally) from the curse of intellectualism and from the nonsense of pure thought. Logic cannot be separated from psychology, because all logical structures are products of psychic functions. All truth is humanly conditioned and relevant to human affairs. Truth which is not truth for men and subserves no human aims and interests has no claim to that honourable title. "Has not the time come when Kant's 'Copernican change of standpoint' might at last be put into practice seriously and when Truth instead of being offered up to idols and sacrificed to 'ideals', might at length be depicted in her human beauty and simplicity?"[1] Truth must be serviceable to life, must dwell in our midst, and must not withdraw into some unreality or supra-reality, into some distant and strange region quite alien to life and its concerns.

Now, if truth is a purely human affair, the question about its essence or the mode of its existence is unimportant as compared with the question how definite truths arise, are established, or, as Schiller says, are fashioned. We have to consider the making of individual concrete truths or true judgments. The pragmatist theory of truth concentrates upon a quite special question and intentionally neglects all other aspects of the problem. This question which, I think, pragmatist thinking was the first to raise, runs as follows. How is it that propositions which claim to be true, so often are shown to be false? Is there any criterion by which we can distinguish between mere claims to truth and genuine truths? Thus it is the fact that there are errors which claim to be true, combined with our natural desire to unmask these errors, which forms the starting-point for the pragmatist theory. It views the problem from the beginning *sub specie veri et falsi*, and not merely from the standpoint of the true alone. Within a collection of given propositions we have to distinguish between those which are really true and those which only make a claim to truth; and in reference to the latter we have to examine whether their claim is justified or not, whether they are to be classed as errors or truths. Accordingly,

[1] *Studies in Humanism*, 1907, p. 178.

the examination and verification (validation or establishment) of truth-claims is the proper task of the theory of truth and the final aim of logic. Only when the truth of what it maintains has been certified or tested, when it has stood the trial, is it entitled to enter the kingdom of truth.

We carry out, then, the separation between true and false or, in other words, between recognized truths and not-yet-validated claims, on the basis of the pragmatist truth-test. The truth-test is the selective principle in accordance with which out of the multitude of propositions, statements, assertions, judgments, etc., we choose the useful and reject the useless. We might also say that we evaluate one set as false, the other set as true, in the same way as we evaluate one thing as good, another as bad. True and false are, therefore, closely related to the ethical value-predicates good and bad; the former are the theoretical expressions or correlates of the latter. Thus the problem of truth is amalgamated with the problem of value, the theoretic sphere with the practical. Purely theoretic values cannot be recognized by Pragmatism. All values are practical values and the value of the good is their prototype. At this point there appears the unconditional priority of the practical to the theoretical, the complete absorption of the latter by the former, which is essential to pragmatist philosophy. Truths, therefore, are values, or, better, valuations: true propositions are valuable; false propositions have less value or none at all.

But on what basis do we make our valuations? With the answer to this question, which is the question of the criterion of truth, we reach the heart of Pragmatism. Schiller answers thus: With every question that we put, whether in science or in life, we conjoin a certain purpose or a certain interest. In every science, e.g., we want to know something. If the answers satisfy our questions, if they lead to the fulfilment of our purposes and the satisfaction of our interests, we evaluate them as true; otherwise as false. True and false, therefore, are relative to our aims, relative to the purpose which put the question. In proportion as an assertion satisfies or promotes the aim of the investigation to which it owes its existence, it is true; in proportion as it stultifies or misses this aim, it is false. Assertions must, therefore, be evaluated in the first instance according to their consequences or effects, and according to their influence upon the investigation in which we are interested.

This can also be expressed as follows. An assertion must approve itself within the context in which it is set forth; it must be serviceable, applicable, and useful. It must promote the aim which knowledge has proposed to itself in the given case. It must be victorious in the contest with other less suitable assertions. Thus we come to the well-known connection of truth with utility, and to the famous formula of the utility (or serviceableness or applicability) of truths. As this formula has been the source of countless misunderstandings, and has been continually attacked by the opponents of Pragmatism, either out of malevolence or out of failure to understand it, we must now give a short explanation of its true meaning. I am not undertaking a justification of Pragmatism, but shall merely explain facts which most of the critics leave in obscurity.

First it must be pointed out that no one wants to put truth and utility on the same footing, as though it did not matter whether one said "Whatever is true is useful" or "Whatever is useful is true"[1] The two terms, as Schiller often emphatically says, are not interchangeable. Utility in the exact sense of the word is the *ratio essendi* of truth, insomuch as no truth can be achieved or maintained which has not been proved to be serviceable to some purpose. To be useful is to be a means to an end, and the most diverse ends must be taken into consideration. Moreover, the relation which makes a thing useful must be understood strictly as a relation to its proper, relevant purpose. Finally, we must observe that what is serviceable for one definite purpose may not be serviceable for another. The proposition of the utility of truth can, therefore, only mean that every true assertion is useful, serviceable, applicable, efficacious, and fruitful; but not conversely that everything useful is true. The latter statement would be completely meaningless (although it is often used as an argument against Pragmatism); for evidently

[1] *Logic for Use*, 1929, p. 158.

a lie may be very useful; but that does not make it true. The true, therefore, is useful, but the useful is not always true.

Another common misunderstanding has slipped into the concept of pragmatic utility. Utility in this connection should not be understood in the coarse sense of mere practical or material utility. Utility stands rather in a necessary relation to the context within which a definite purpose is to be realized or a definite aim achieved. Within a theoretical context, e.g., there must be a theoretical establishment of propositions, and their subordination to the general intellectual aim which is here in view. There must be a satisfaction of those value-interests for the sake of which, for example, we pursue scientific inquiries. Even from the pragmatist standpoint we can, therefore, say that those things are true which have knowledge-value or are proved true (verified) within a theoretical context. This line of thought, moreover, coincides finally with the basic pragmatist principle only in so far as theoretic value is not recognized as a self-governing independent entity, but is thought of as based on practical conditions, and subordinate to human purposes. In this sense the gap is bridged between the two apparently widely separated modes of statement, one which speaks of truth as utility, the other of truth as logical value.

The pragmatist truth-theory, which views truth-value as being relative to man as the measure of all things and will not recognize a truth which is not made by man and is valid independently of him, is subjectivist and relativist. But it is not extreme in its individualism; it does not base truth upon subjective arbitrary choice; it tries to give it certain objective foundations. Although the individual is in the beginning the finder and keeper of truth, he cannot decide finally about the value of the truth which he has found. Truth is eminently a social product. To guarantee it needs more than individual evaluation. It must try to win social recognition and become common property. Thus a selection will be made from the mass of individual truths and a fund of truth will be established having a certain objective validity. On this inheritance each new truth-seeking individual enters and recognizes it for what it is, because it has been verified and assured. Objective truth, therefore, is that which in the highest degree has attained to social recognition. The pragmatist concept of truth, which in its origin is individualistic, is thus enlarged and based upon social opinion.

A further step towards objectivization is achieved as follows. Propositions which are recognized as true in reference to a certain purpose, may be proved to be inadequate in relation to a higher intellectual purpose. Their truth upon the lower level is not sublated, but it is transferred to the higher level, to which it serves as a stairway of approach. This holds equally for scientific elements of knowledge and theories which were once approved as true, but now have been superseded by further researches. We must, e.g., regard the three cosmic systems of Pythagoras, Ptolemy, and Copernicus as stages on the way to a progressive approximation to an adequate theory of the movements of the heavenly bodies. Each of them was valued as true in its time, and this truth-value cannot be taken from it. By the later discovery of a new theory the old one was revalued as false. Discoveries of new truths may result in revaluations of older truths. In such a case the new truth is antedated as though it had been established in the past. In this way the establishment of truth remains within the human sphere, and the recognition of antedated theories does not justify us in recognizing a validation which is independent of human recognition.

The pragmatist concept of truth is, as must be evident, thoroughly dynamic. Truth is nothing eternally valid, absolutely constraining, pre-established, and overpowering; nothing stiff and dry-cut, tight and trim, but, like all that is, it is immersed in the process of becoming. It is discovery and invention, the making of what is new and remaking of what is old, it is subject to the struggle for existence, and must ever anew conquer and maintain its rights. As in the biological sphere so also in the theoretic sphere there is a kind of natural selection, an elimination of the worse accredited and a survival of the better accredited. Schiller loves to speak of the great pragmatic principle of selection and of the survival-value of theories.

Truths must be viable, and 'true' in the last resort is not only that which works, but that which works best. Schiller's Darwinism is here plainly evident, and to a large extent his doctrine is nothing but the application of the Darwinian selection-theory to logic. Sometimes the psychological aspect is more prominent, sometimes the biological; sometimes they supplement each other. The latter aspect is especially noticeable in his book *Logic for Use*, where the doctrine of judgment is viewed entirely from this standpoint and where there is developed, not a logic, but a 'biologic' of judgment. The Darwinizing of logic is here elaborated in detail and carried to the furthest point.

Finally the problem of error, the starting-point of the pragmatist theory, has to be fitted into this system of thought. The dynamic character of the truth-concept forbids not only a sharp contrast between false and true, but leads to an almost complete obliteration of the distinction between them. As there is no absolute truth, so there is no absolute error. There are only grades and stages of both which proceed the one from the other and pass over the one into the other.

Error also has had its good meaning and its right to a place in the living process of discovering truth. In the competition of truth-claims with each other it is the victor which is subsequently overcome. When it is recognized as such it must be counted as a false step of our knowing in the achievement of its aim—an ex-truth which was once approved, and now may be replaced by a better. In retrospect it is a preliminary stage of truth, and as such, it still has positive value for knowledge. But even successful truths are short-lived. The quicker a science progresses, the quicker is the accumulation of new truths. And to this process there are no limits, and can be no limits. Error will always change into truth and truth decay into error. We never come upon an absolute.

The first task of logic, then, is to understand and enrich our knowledge already obtained and to discover new knowledge. Definition, proof, inference, etc., are secondary, and in every way subordinate, to that primary task. Pragmatist logic, as

Schiller somewhere says, is a logic of daring and adventure. It starts from a level of being quite different from that of all non-pragmatist logic. This throws a significant light upon its background and the roots from which spring its passionate attack upon the traditional logic, and especially upon Absolutism. There is the contrast between the adventurous, roving, novelty-loving, daring, risking, and fighting spirit, and a tired soul whose thoughts are of peace and security, which has established itself comfortably in a well-furnished system of thought and lies outstretched upon the couch of absolute truth. The contrast is one of temperament, and is, therefore, irreconcilable. At bottom it is the contrast between the *vita activa* and the *vita contemplativa*; between the strong-willed, creative, striving man who shapes reality, and the looker-on, the contemplator, who enjoys in peace.

The development of logic discloses the basic layer of Schiller's Pragmatism. All its other aspects are radiations from the centre to the circumference, and are self-explaining. The pragmatist doctrine of reality is in close agreement with its theory of truth. Most of its detailed statements follow naturally from it. Schiller himself puts them together as follows. Reality which serves as material for science or theory of knowledge is (*a*) not rigid, but plastic and capable of development, (*b*) not absolutely or unconditionally real, but only relatively so to our experience and in dependence on the state of our knowledge. (*c*) Our truth-concept is in continual change, so that (*d*) we frequently reduce to unreality that which, for a long time, has been recognized as real. So we must (*e*) distinguish between original or primary reality which is claimed by everything empirically given, and (*f*) secondary or real reality, and, therefore, we need (*g*) a principle of selection by means of which we can distinguish the two kinds of reality, and give to the higher the rank which is suitable to it.[1]

Pragmatist reality is reality in the strict sense of the word, that upon which we really operate. We find something before us upon which our activity (including that of knowledge, for

[1] Vide *Studies in Humanism*, 1907, p. 214.

knowledge also is a kind of acting) can get going and from which we form or create something, so that the object is transformed. That which we find before us may be called the crude material of reality or ὕλη (in the Aristotelian sense). But we must not think of this as a dead and rigid mass, but as a highly changeable, pliable, shapeable, and mouldable material; in short, as something plastic. In the pragmatist sense, the world is not a ready-made fact, independent of us, but a demand which we make upon the given—a *Tat-Sache* in the original sense of the word, by which language indicates its pragmatist character. We do not stand in humility and submission before the objectivity of the facts, but we encounter reality (in the true sense of the word as that upon which we really work) with energy and enterprise, not only as acting, but as learning men. Even knowing changes the reality which is known. The world, therefore, is, in James's phrase, not to be regarded as a block-universe, but as a plastic entity. Plasticity is the guiding idea of this doctrine of reality. This follows immediately from the anthropocentric world-view of Pragmatism, according to which man is the centre and measure of all things, so that reality also can only be regarded as one of his functions.

In strict language, therefore, Pragmatism cannot recognize an objective reality which is independent of man and not shaped by him. Nevertheless, Pragmatism sees itself compelled to the assumption of such a reality, because it cannot be assumed that man is the creator of all things. Thus it falls into a peculiar antinomy which it cannot resolve from its own principles. It must, therefore, resort to artificial explanations which aim at resolving that which is recognized as objective into the pragmatic process of subjectivization. It can help itself by holding that while we do not create reality in a metaphysical sense we do in an epistemological sense; or by holding that we say that a reality is discovered and not created by us when its behaviour is such that it would be practically inconvenient to ascribe it entirely to our subjective activity. But so far as it brings the pragmatist test into operation upon this objective reality, it contradicts its own definition, and adulterates its objective stability by recourse to Subjectivism.

Pragmatism's doctrine of reality and knowledge is extreme Activism, not far removed from practical Solipsism. Let it be brought up against the formal question: Why is the world not my act? Pragmatism has to reply that it does not approach reality with a question about its constitution or mode of being, but with the question: What am I to do with it, what tasks have I to fulfil with it? This doctrine is an expression of the age of technique and of the Faustian striving inherent in it towards the incessant shaping of things and the continual, progressive subjection of the world to the aims and ends of man. It is the old Baconian ideal of knowledge as consisting of power, in a form suitable to our age. Although it is based on experience it is widely separated from the epistemology of Empiricism, which is satisfied with the passive acceptance of the given. It is more akin to the Idealism of Kant and Fichte with its belief in the creative power of the mind and its doctrine of the shaping of the chaotic material of sense by the power of knowledge. But it recalls the specifically ethical spirit of Idealism to sobriety and puts in place of it the pedestrian purposiveness of instrumental utility. To this extent it stands upon the firm ground of fact in reaction against the idealistic tendency to volatilize the world.

The ethics of Pragmatism has not been explicitly set forth by Schiller. But it stands in the background of all his thinking and may easily be constructed from his logic, theory of knowledge, and doctrine of value. At bottom Pragmatism in all its aspects is ethical and nothing but ethical. It is the philosophy of the practical reason and of its primacy over all other provinces. Its views of ethical practice determine at what spot it shall plant its lever. Of the special ethical problems Schiller has discussed especially the problem of freedom, and his attitude to the alternatives of Determinism and Indeterminism. In accordance with what has been said already, we should expect a full recognition of human freedom and an unreserved acceptance of some form of Indeterminism. We see, however, that Schiller recognizes freedom only to a very limited extent, and makes many concessions to Determinism. His effort is to reconcile the scientific postulate of Determinism with the ethical postulate of freedom, which have fallen into strife with each other. The former is as indispensable for science as the latter is for man. From the moral standpoint we might set before ourselves as an ideal a completely ethical being who possesses the highest degree of freedom, although his action is completely calculable and thoroughly determined. For a completely good man we could dispense with the postulate of freedom; but not for an incomplete or bad one. To him we must grant freedom of action. We must allow him the possibility of improvement, i.e. the possibility of choosing from two alternatives the good rather than the bad. But as our lives are almost entirely determined by habits and other circumstances, and free choice occurs only in relatively few cases, Schiller holds that an extremely small degree of freedom is enough to establish the moral responsibility of man. Freedom must therefore be limited to a minimum, because a world which was free completely, or in a high degree, would be disadvantageous to our action, and would be found uncomfortable. Freedom, however, need not interfere with the order and rationality of the universe. It is no uncontrollable power which upsets all our calculations. The question 'Freedom or no freedom?' cannot be settled from the standpoint of 'all or nothing'. The Determinist has no occasion to fear that a small quantum of freedom will dislocate his whole theory, and an Indeterminist does not need such an excessive amount of freedom as would threaten the order of the world.

This worthless truce established between the opposing parties is not only far from solving the problem, but looks like a foreign body in the flesh of Pragmatism. There is another idea which harmonizes better with the train of thought. From the logical standpoint both postulates may be regarded as valid, not only because they are established by rational arguments, but because they are equally operative in practice. The postulate of Determinism shows itself as extremely fruitful and successful in the sciences, while freedom succeeds in the practical activity of man. As for Determinism, Schiller shows that its origin is due to a subjective need, the vital interest that we have in calculating the future. As anticipation of the future is of the highest practical importance, it was inevitable that a theory should be invented which gave weight to that fact. Which of the two postulates is chosen by an individual cannot be decided on logical grounds, because logically they are equally valid. Our choice must be a completely free one, and this applies no less to the man who chooses Determinism. But this does not confute the Determinist. We may indeed be Determinists because we are "determined" to deny our freedom; but it is just because we are free, that we are free to do so. Thus the whole framework of Determinism is incorporated into the idea of freedom. In the last resort all our convictions, including the theoretical, may be ascribed to the fact of belief and free choice. In every case these precede the rational proof of their truth. The postulate of freedom is primarily an act of belief, and secondarily a theory; and this shows that the functions of our intellect are indissolubly conjoined with those of our will and our moral qualities, and that our understanding works in closest co-operation with our feelings and instincts.

The relation of Pragmatism to metaphysics is one of benevolent neutrality; it neither demands it nor regards it with hostility. It can be presented independently of metaphysics as a method of settling the problems of human knowledge, but it need not be afraid of becoming entangled with it. Schiller has allowed a considerable influx of metaphysics to enter Pragmatism partly implicitly, partly explicitly. The task of metaphysics is to unite in a final synthesis all the data of experience and all the results of the sciences. The theoretic value of such a synthesis can of course be only very conditional. The personal element will play a decisive part here more than in other studies, and no metaphysical world-system can be viewed in abstraction from the personality of its author. In objective value it is far inferior to the sciences. In a sense it is the luxurious indulgence of an excessive desire for knowledge, and it will never be more than a very personal guess about ultimate things.

The metaphysical implications of Schiller's doctrine are briefly as follows. In the first place, the thesis of the plasticity of reality which arose originally from considerations relating to the theory of knowledge leads to metaphysical consequences, especially if it is transferred as a characteristic of all being to the totality of the real. The world is not hard and rigid, but pliable and formable, and accommodates itself to human will as expressed in cognition and creative activity. Moreover, Schiller's world-view is definitely anthropocentric; it is therefore neither cosmocentric nor theocentric. Hence flow two metaphysical consequences, Pluralism and Personalism. Pluralism, which James sought to establish (in his book *A Pluralistic Universe*, 1909), posits the multiplicity of spiritual beings as real, independent, and self-subsisting entities, and maintains the rights of the many as against the One, whether it be God or the Absolute, or any other monistic entity. According to the doctrine of Pragmatism these entities appear in the first place as centres of force and will, as foci of activity, energy, and conscious action. With this doctrine Personalism is most closely combined. Human personality forms the backbone of the pragmatist world-theory. Nowhere can we abstract from it; everything is related to it; and everything must be penetrated with it. It is indivisible (i.e. perfectly individual), and acts continually in the totality of its being and in the mutual relation and complication of its separate functions. It is neither thinking nor feeling, nor willing nor acting, but all of them together. None of its numerous manifestations can be detached from the rest, least of all its intellectual from its emotional and volitional side. Hence Schiller's unwearied battle against Intellectualism in every form, against the attenuation and vaporization of full personality to an abstract product of reason, or to a mere thinking machine. For this reason, in order to restore the full sense of humanity in philosophy, Schiller has revived an old and much-used sobriquet, and given to his doctrine the proud title of "Humanism" (first in the 1903 volume of essays, see the preface). This he meant as a protest against the 'dehumanizing' of philosophical thought, which, as he believed, was always increasing, and against the extrusion from the sphere of philosophy of man as a full and entire personality, as the unity of his interests and instincts, his feelings and expressions of will, his theoretic, practical, aesthetic, and other needs. Simultaneously, he attacked the abstract methods, the mysterious hocus-pocus of philosophical jargon, the fuss of erudition, the futilities of logical drill, the proud exclusiveness and obscure language of academic circles, all tendncies towards philosophical cliques and sects,—in short, the tendency of the whole philosophical profession to turn away from life and ignore the world.

Schiller's pragmatist humanism regards as its highest aim what he calls the 'rehumanizing' of philosophy. In the history of thought he praises for its aptness the old dictum of Protagoras that man is the measure of all things. For this reason he links his own doctrine immediately to that of the Sophists, and calls himself a 'neo-Protagorean'. In his pamphlet *Plato or Protagoras?* he ranges himself on the side of the latter, and defends him against Plato, whose Intellectualism has corrupted philosophy; and in a kind of Platonic dialogue, where he puts his own doctrine into the mouth of Protagoras, he writes a counterblast to the *Theaetetus*, a criticism of Plato from the standpoint of the humanist Protagoras (see *Studies in Humanism*, chap. xiv). But he goes beyond the dictum of Protagoras in making man not only the measure of all things, but their shaper and fashioner; and the parent of truth as well as the creator and fashioner of reality. As thus enlarged, the Protagorean dictum becomes the motto of Schiller's whole philosophy. It is also the central point of the metaphysical outgrowths which have sprung from Pragmatism, including the above mentioned doctrines of plasticity, Pluralism, and Personalism, to which may be added Heracliteanism and Panpsychism. Finally, there stands under its banner the less important philosophy of religion which has for the most part remained floundering in the waters of the XVIIIth-Century "Enlightenment". For the nature of God has also been constructed by Pragmatism according to its ideas, and has had to submit to humanization.

In contemporary thought Pragmatism is to be ranked with vitalist philosophies which, in spite of their various forms, are animated by one and the same impulse. And so Schiller has welcomed everything which has come from this direction to strengthen and support his own philosophic position. For his desire is to lead philosophy back to life, in which alone its strength is rooted. From life philosophy must always renew its energy if it is to do justice to its highest task, the service of man.

ALFRED SIDGWICK (*b.* 1850)

[Cousin of Henry Sidgwick, no profession, author of *Fallacies: a view of logic from the practical side*, 1883; *Distinction and the Criticism of Beliefs*, 1892; *The Process of Argument*, 1893; *The Use of Words in Reasoning*, 1901; *The Application of Logic*, 1910; *Elementary Logic*, 1914.]

English Pragmatism has its only important representative in Schiller. So far as the movement has spread in England, its whole force has concentrated itself in him, and from him it has streamed forth into philosophical circles, and in some degree into those which are not philosophical. The impulse derived from him has acted in different manners in different directions, sometimes destroying, sometimes rousing, sometimes fertilizing. Pragmatist ideas are to be found among thinkers of all schools and tendencies, among friends, enemies, and neutrals; and Schiller himself has with great sagacity traced them everywhere, among his opponents with particular satisfaction. But to Pragmatism, as such, so far as it embodies his own philosophical teaching, not many have adhered, and even these have not been greatly distinguished. The first to be mentioned must be Alfred Sidgwick.

One may say of Sidgwick, whose work is exclusively in the

field of logic, that he thought pragmatically before Pragmatism existed in any explicit form. His first book on fallacies with the significant sub-title *a view of logic from the practical side* goes back to the year 1883. It is the earliest anticipation of that which nearly fifty years later came to full maturity in Schiller's *Logic for Use*. At that time Sidgwick was a complete outsider, who went on his own path alone and unheeded, a path which he has followed consistently ever since. It was not till the rise of Pragmatism that his work was brought out of its original isolation, became incorporated in a greater movement, and received its fitting recognition. To Sidgwick most of all it is due that Pragmatism has taken possession of the field of logic, and has gained its strongest influence there. It is from him that this strong stimulus passed directly to Schiller, and Schiller gladly acknowledged his enduring historical service.

Sidgwick's main effort, which extends through all his writings, is to free logic from its character of a thought-exercise and mental gymnastic, and to apply it practically in concrete cases and definite situations. He tries to apprehend systematically these possibilities of applying logical thinking (inference, judgment, conception, etc.), and to use them upon the given. He refuses (at least in his earlier writings) to abolish the boundary between logic and psychology, and insists on regarding logic as closely connected with grammar, rhetoric, and the art of disputation. He is concerned not so much with the formally regular and correct thinking of the logic books as with real thinking as it takes place in life, in the sciences and in all mental activity. But as this is very liable to error, there is need of an exact and systematic inquiry into the whole range of that by which thought is endangered and threatened. We might describe Sidgwick's intentions by saying that he wishes to reach correct thinking by way of studying false thinking; correct thinking, however, not in its formal purity but in its concrete application. Closely connected with this is the view, which became very important in the development of pragmatist logic, that the formal validity of the conclusion cannot be maintained in view of the fact that the middle term may always be ambiguous when it is applied in concrete cases. For Sidgwick logic is an instrument for combating fallacies (which he tracks down in his first book), a means to the unmasking of ambiguities, multiplicity of meanings, vaguenesses, and indefinitenesses in verbal expression (he wages a conflict like that of Bacon against the *idola fori*), a method of abolishing indefinite concepts, crude distinctions, bad arguments, a criticism of unproved dogmas and unverified assertions. The new logic which he advocates makes, e.g., no claim to complete definitions, but to such as are serviceable for a definite purpose. It helps us in deciding 'Yes' or 'No' in concrete situations, it shows us the difference between good and bad demonstration, it gives us directions for the concrete use of language, for effective disputation, for skilful rhetoric, and so on. Sidgwick therefore advocates a thorough reform of the traditional logical system from the standpoint of considering the difficulties of the real process of thought, and the most important dangers which threaten it—all with reference to its practical application.

HOWARD V. KNOX (*b.* 1868)

[*The Philosophy of William James*, 1914; *The Will to be Free*, 1928; *The Evolution of Truth and other essays*, 1930.]

Captain Knox, a Pragmatist of the purest water, and as such a faithful follower of James and Schiller, is on the left wing of the movement. He is its most pugnacious and bellicose champion, its most convinced apostle, its most enthusiastic missionary. He leads devastating attacks upon the arch-enemy, upon intellectualist logic and absolutist metaphysics, upon Hegelianism and Determinism, upon Green, Bradley, and Joachim. But in his very polemical books and essays there are hardly any new arguments, hardly a thought which has not already been discussed; at the most we find a more convincing and a clearer-cut formulation. His doctrine is almost quite identical with that of his master; though he aims more penetrating blows than Schiller at Determinism, explaining it not only as an error, but as a falsehood, and trying to prove that it is an outgrowth of formal logic. The problem of freedom has a more satisfactory solution with Knox than with Schiller, who has involved himself in compromise. Freedom is based on the human will, and only so far as we exercise will are we free. This, briefly, is the thesis which Knox has developed in a temperamental book entitled *The Will to be Free*.

HENRY STURT (*b.* 1863)

["Art and Personality", (in *Personal Idealism*, ed. H. Sturt, 1902); *Idola Theatri: a criticism of Oxford thought and thinkers from the standpoint of personal idealism*, 1906; *The Principles of Understanding: an introduction to logic from the standpoint of personal idealism*, 1915; *Human Value: an ethical essay*, 1923; *Moral Experience*, 1928.]

Henry Sturt, the editor of the pragmatist manifesto of the year 1902 (see above, pp. 447 sqq.) is also allied with Pragmatism, but not so closely as Sidgwick and Knox. He gives to his standpoint the name of that manifesto, "personal idealism", combining with it the demand that the idea of personality should be restored to all its philosophical rights, and that the most important personal factor, the will, should be adequately recognized. For speculative philosophy there follow two principles, firstly that personal or human experience forms the foundation of all philosophical synthesis, and secondly that this experience is essentially spiritual. From this standpoint (in the book *Idola Theatri*) Sturt has subjected the whole of Oxford thought to a comprehensive criticism, vindicating the idea of personality against the dangers threatened by Intellectualism, Absolutism, and Subjectivism, by Panlogism and Monism. Subsequently (in the book *Principles of Understanding*) he has tried to indicate new paths for logic, which is not concerned with *a priori* laws of thought, but with the real processes of human knowledge, and must therefore be apprehended and treated in its dynamic character.

On this basis he has passed in his two latest works to the discussion of ethical and social questions. Here, however, his thinking does not strike deeply, or raise new issues, while his social outlook shows a certain amount of the bias of a political partisan.

III

THE OLDER REALISM

THE thinkers included in this section, it must be noticed, do not form a definite school or follow a definite tendency. When we include them under the title of 'the older realism', we are simply pointing to the fact that they are connected historically or in doctrine with the later or New Realism, which will be discussed in the next section. Nor are they in general connected with one another, seeing that they have no common philosophical descent, nor have they, as New Realism has, a common opponent to whom they have to show a common front. As they have issued from various camps, so they stand in opposition to various opponents, and the standpoints and interests which they adopt from time to time are diverse. They have a certain connection with each other, though only an external one, insomuch as they can all be brought under the common designation of one of the many variants of realistic thinking, and also because most of them have passed through an idealistic position (principally Kantian criticism), or at least have been more or less strongly influenced by it. It is just this last circumstance which shows most plainly their distance in time and in opinions from the representatives of the younger group who for the most part have made no such transit. In the latter we have the appearance of a new element of thought, in the former the resumption and prolongation of old threads. However, each of the following thinkers must tell his own tale.

SHADWORTH H. HODGSON (1832–1912)

[No profession; lived in London. Joint founder of the Aristotelian Society, whose first president he was, 1880–94. *Time and Space*, 1865; *The Theory of Practice*, 2 vols., 1870; *The Philosophy of Reflection*, 2 vols., 1878; *The Metaphysic of Experience*, 4 vols., 1898; Many essays in *Mind* and in the *Proceedings of the Aristotelian Society*.]

Hodgson's philosophical activity falls within the last decades of the XIXth Century. His first book appeared in the same year as J. S. Mill's *Examination of Hamilton's Philosophy* and Stirling's *Secret of Hegel*. The final and maturest statement of his doctrine appeared before the end of the century. It is included in his four-volume *Metaphysic of Experience*, which, after Spencer's *System of Synthetic Philosophy*, is the most comprehensive work of modern English thinking. What he published subsequently are only some parerga and paralipomena of subordinate importance in periodicals.

The career of this thinker is unusual, and differs considerably from the ordinary development of university professors and teachers of philosophy. A cruel stroke of fortune which fell upon him in the middle twenties drove him into the arms of philosophy, which became to him thenceforward a rescuer and comforter in deep sorrow. From that time for the rest of his long life he applied himself with uncommonly sincere and unwearied devotion to a contemplative life, which was consecrated entirely to the unselfish service of truth. He never occupied or aspired to an academic post, nor followed any profession. Nevertheless, he was no outsider, but as for many years president and member of the Aristotelian Society, in whose foundation he had a prominent part, and as a regular contributor to *Mind*, which without his generous help at that time (in 1876) could not have come into being, he was in close sympathy with the philosophical life and work of his time. He was not only a lover of wisdom, but its magnanimous supporter. In the revival of philosophical life in the last quarter of the last century he took a decisive part, not only by doctrine and writing, but by social intercourse and exchange of ideas, and by creating an organ which stood open to and included all schools of thought.

To place Hodgson in the philosophical development of his age presents considerable difficulty. His thought, which was formed at the time of the almost undisputed predominance of Empiricism, and subsequently could not close itself entirely to new influences, is turned like James both forwards and backwards, standing sometimes in one camp, sometimes in another, sometimes in none at all. There is a symbolical significance in the fact just mentioned that Hodgson's first book appeared at the same time as the *Examination of Hamilton's Philosophy*, which closes one period of thought, and the *Secret of Hegel*, which opens another. Negatively, his doctrine, as he himself pointed out in reference to a special problem (vide *Philosophy of Reflection*, II, p. 173), may be defined by the fact that it is related neither to the school of Hamilton and Mansel, nor to Spencer's Evolutionism, nor to either Comtian or English Positivism, nor to Anglo-Hegelianism, nor to any philosophy permeated or connected with theology. The last of these, to which he was opposed neither from anti-clericalism nor from hatred of religion, but merely from zeal for the discovery of truth, he calls aptly 'Church philosophy'.

As essential constituents of Hodgson's philosophy there remain the traditional Empiricism and a certain modification of Kantianism. On the other hand, he has no connection with New Realism, which did not appear till he had ceased to write; and it cannot be claimed that he was a precursor of this movement. The best term for Hodgson's position is 'critical empiricism'; this expresses its vacillating attitude between the British philosophy of experience and Kantian criticism, and emphasizes its predominant feature and basic character as Empiricism. Its phenomenalist theory of knowledge and a number of other elements indicate that it is firmly rooted in traditional British thought, especially in Hume, while Kantian doctrines have been taken over externally rather than re-thought and incorporated into the system. Hodgson's real attitude to Kant, which underwent many changes, is hard to determine exactly. One critic calls him a weak and half-hearted Kantian, and it is certain that the longer he lived the further he moved away from Kant, and by the end of his career he had stripped away the last remnants of Kantianism. The "critical" spirit which is conspicuous in his early writings dwindles continually, and the result is a complete acceptance of uncritical psychologism, and even physiologism. Another connection with Kant is a certain preference for classifications and rubrics, definitions and divisions, order and schematization, which springs more from a purely formal joy in such things than from an inner compulsion of thought and a definitely marked sense of order, as was the case with Kant.

What is historically remarkable is that in Hodgson's earliest book Hegel, too, is regarded with reverence as a great man. He was thoroughly studied, as is proved by the numerous quotations and a long separate section on his logic (see *Space and Time*, pp. 364–402), but at the same time completely misunderstood, pedantically corrected, forced or bent into Hodgson's own schemes of thought, but given recognition and mentioned with respectful admiration. In this matter the misunderstandings, distortions, and accusations of heresy are less important than the fact that Hegel had come within the mental horizon of England, and was never to disappear from it. Later, when Hegel had been for some time a living power in English philosophy, Hodgson's attitude to him was much more critical and unfriendly, in definite opposition to the growing Neo-Hegelian school. He now regarded Hegel's doctrine as philosophical extravagance, as mere world-construction from pure thought, without any relation to experience. Hegel, Hodgson thought, was the last and perhaps the greatest of the scholastics, and his 'so-called' logic the proper completion of the scholastic mode of thought.

To form a general estimate of Hodgson, the following points also must be noticed. The approach to Hodgson's extensive writings is by no means easy. The reader who has worked his way through these thick volumes, handsomely bound in white buckram, will find hardly enough to reward him for his labour. Their vast length, diffuseness, and verbosity stand in no relation to their philosophical content. Over long stretches one cannot avoid the impression that the author is threshing empty straw, that he is merely a clever manipulator of philosophical terms, not a real solver of problems. For pages technical terms are pushed to and fro, but the investigation stands still or turns in circles; the problems are rolled out and made thin and watery, the real point is lost in a wilderness of trivialities, side-issues, and digressions. I do not mean that this judgment applies to all Hodgson's writing; sometimes he attacks the problems more acutely and produces good and sound analyses, but the prevailing impression is what I have said. For all these reasons Hodgson's doctrine, which was coldly received by his contemporaries, has neither attracted pupils nor left a notable impression (except for some traces of his thought in William James), nor has it influenced posterity. At the present day it is almost forgotten. The broad cemetery of the history of philosophy has received it and assigned it an honourable resting-place.

We may begin the exposition of Hodgson's philosophy with his doctrine of being and consciousness. At the beginning of his early work he firmly rejects the notion of an absolute being separated from all consciousness. All being is being for consciousness; the two coincide completely; one extends so far as the other and no farther. If being is to have an intelligible meaning, it must be an object of consciousness and nothing else. This consistent phenomenalism which stands upon the foundations of Hume and Mill, and rejects the Kantian thing-in-itself and all other forms of the Absolute, is a main pillar of Hodgson's system. At a later stage we shall see how the idea of matter unites with the principle of consciousness, or leads beyond it.

The first and most important task of philosophy is regarded by Hodgson as being the description and analysis of the data or phenomena which are to be found in consciousness. Something similar had been demanded by the classical school of Empiricism in the XVIIIth Century, though carried out with insufficient means. Hodgson's analyses, in which he did his best work, go far beyond the rudimentary attempts of the earlier thinkers in separating, arranging, classifying, and connecting the contents of consciousness and carry the matter a good step further with their subtle distinctions and careful descriptions. In this work Hodgson proposed and performed something similar to the phenomenology started by Husserl after the completion of his system, though without any criticism and theoretic justification of his procedure. He wished to get behind the experience of daily life, and to discover and describe simply the original elements of consciousness in their purity, untouched by thought, custom, experience, and theory. In order to reach phenomena in their pure, immediate givenness, every function of the ego, every synthetic, apperceptive, selective, transforming, or other activity of the subject must be excluded, and it indicates an advance in Hodgson's thinking that from one work to another he tried to carry out more thoroughly this exclusion or isolation of the subjective factor which interferes with the pure data of the problem.

What Hodgson in his chief book calls the metaphysic of experience, arbitrarily distorting the usual terminology, is nothing but a phenomenology of consciousness or descriptive analysis of the data of consciousness. It is the same as what in an earlier book he had called the 'philosophy of reflection'. Philosophy now means questioning consciousness by consciousness as the only means by which being, which cannot be questioned directly, can be brought to our knowledge. Consciousness has the same meaning as experience, for their provinces and boundaries coincide, and what is beyond experience is something with which philosophy can connect no intelligible idea, or in which it can have no interest. Thus all philosophical reflection begins with experience, and remains within its boundaries. Hodgson's doctrine is therefore a philosophy of experience or empiricism, although in a sense somewhat different from the classical meaning of the term.

While the somewhat confused early books *Space and Time* and *Theory of Practice* are seeking with fumbling efforts the path to be discovered later, in the *Philosophy of Reflection* we find for the first time Hodgson's basic positions and the totality of his doctrine. This book, in which Hodgson with extreme self-confidence thought he was inaugurating a new epoch of metaphysics in England, is characterized by the fact that in it Hodgson professes his allegiance to two men whom he regards with ardent devotion, the poet-philosopher Coleridge, to whom he dedicates it as "my father in philosophy", and Salomon Maimon, whom he praises in exaggerated terms as the true successor and inheritor of the Kantian philosophy and of German Idealism generally. To Coleridge he owed the great doctrine of the inner connection between the intellectual and the emotional elements in human nature. Maimon had with his principle of determinability carried forward in the critical spirit the critical school of thought whose founders were Hume and Kant. He thought that all the others, Fichte, Schelling, Hegel, and Schopenhauer, had merely taken over Kant's results dogmatically and built on them their uncritical systems of ontology. Hodgson himself had no other purpose than to go on philosophizing in the path opened by Hume and Kant, and continued by Maimon. Hodgson's enthusiasm, however, for Kant and for Maimon was not of long duration. In his final book of 1898, which sums up his thinking, he was careful to break all the bridges which connected him with Kant; while Maimon, who is not mentioned once, seems to have been completely forgotten. On the other hand, Hume's influence remained strong to the last, though important elements of his doctrine were sacrificed.

While the first principle of metaphysics had given up the Kantian thing-in-itself, reflection upon the original data of consciousness shows that the chaotic 'turmoil' of sensations must be given up also. Such a purely material something, untouched by any formal element, is a pure abstraction which, as such, cannot be found in consciousness. As the original material element Hodgson posits not the ὕλη of Aristotle, completely indeterminate, unformed by categories, but something well known to us, viz. the feelings. The feelings or sensations, as the material which is found in consciousness, are not disorderly or chaotic, but even to primary analysis show themselves as ordered, in their succession and compresence, by temporal and spatial categories. But we cannot regard Space and Time as *a priori* forms of intuition in Kant's sense, which the subject produces for the turmoil of sensations; we should regard them as formal elements which are in consciousness from the beginning, and confront analysis together with the material elements, and in inseparable connection with them. Thus there exists no chaos of sensation; the spatio-temporal, or at least the temporal, order is present in the material sensation before all onset or intervention of the mind. The spatio-temporal elements therefore are on the side of the object, so far as at this primitive stage of experience we can speak of the separation of the subjective and objective sides of consciousness. Analysis of the original or minimal elements of experience discloses therefore in the dynamical continuum of consciousness a combination of three factors which we may distinguish from each other as the material factor of sensation and the two formal factors of space and time or extension and duration, but which we cannot separate from each other.

But we cannot speak of any objective consciousness of sensation; nothing of the sort appears before the stage of perception. There is no stage before perception from which sensation could be abstracted in its purity. Perception is for consciousness the first reality which analysis can reach. Percepts are the true basic elements of reality; they correspond exactly to what Hume calls 'impressions'. Over against them Hodgson places representations or concepts (Hume's ideas) as a separate class of data which are different from the others, not in their content, but in the manner of their givenness. The percepts are distinguished by greater liveliness and intensity, by stronger "enjoyment" and immediate presentness; while we experience representations as derivative and secondary and more weakly "enjoyed." But all contents of consciousness are in the last resort in the mother-soil of perception; it is perception which decides finally about their validity and legitimacy. There is no mode of consciousness which cannot in some way be referred back to perception. This doctrine of perceptions and representations is essentially a revival of Hume's doctrine of impressions and ideas. Through all these discursive investigations into the original data of consciousness and their derivatives there runs like a crimson thread Hume's basic principle, governing Hodgson's whole theory of knowledge, to the effect that all contents of our representations, concepts, judgments, abstractions, etc., can only claim validity if they are referred back to those original impressions which lie at the basis of all our knowledge and thinking.

We have seen that the "Philosophy of Reflexion", although it professed allegiance to Kant's critical spirit, surrendered important components of his doctrine, and in general moved on the empirical paths of Hume. The *Metaphysic of Experience*, a portent in four volumes, where Hodgson gathered into his barns the ripe fruits of his long and devoted life of thought, follows the same lines, but adds some important corrections and additions to the familiar picture and rounds off the whole into an imposing system.

His closer analyses are devoted first to the problem of truth. The mere presence of a content in consciousness and the act of percipient knowledge directed upon it, or, better, the possession of this content in perception, is what Hodgson calls simple perception. In it perceptual content (percept) and perceptual act (perceiving) form a single indivisible unity. From this is distinguished the important idea of reflected perception. When the stream of consciousness flows on, contents which just now were actually present are detained by perception, but no longer as immediately present; they are rather past, or involved with a definite time-factor. Act and content now separate; the percept is perceived as earlier than the perceiving, and as still persisting in the moment of perceiving. Naturally, simple perception is only a limiting case of reflected perception; the latter is the primary and general fact on the basis of which we have consciousness of anything. All perceiving is thus reflective or retrospective; it has the property of holding fast for a while contents which pass by in the stream of consciousness. But we cannot say—and Hodgson attributes special importance to this—that in all this is involved any activity or exertion of the subject. It is true that language is always misleading us to such an assumption when we say *I* am conscious, *I* perceive, etc. In this case, however, the ego is in no way exercised or involved; moreover, we cannot say, as Hodgson at an earlier date said, that in attending we apply ourselves to the newly emerging contents of consciousness, as though on each occasion a new act were necessary when we observe new things. In particular, Kant's transcendental apperception is now definitely rejected as the synthetic activity of consciousness, and the earlier doctrine of attention given up as belonging to Kant. Only that which offers itself to consciousness in simple purity and runs past in the stream of consciousness should be included in descriptive analyses. It cannot be denied that Hodgson in intention comes very near to the procedure of modern phenomenology, although the carrying out of this intention after some good analyses falls back into old constructions and habits of thought, and so falsifies what is simply given.

The new insight obtained by careful descriptions in the field of pure consciousness leads to an important correction of Hume's atomism. Consciousness may be compared to a continually flowing stream, the elements of which do not lie atomically at rest like nuts in a sack, but are like processes in dynamic movement, and drive one another forward. The dynamic character of consciousness is conditioned by the temporal factor which, as we have seen, is inseparably united with each and all of its contents. The temporal element is a factor which is constitutive of everything that is given, and confers duration upon it. It is, as it were, loaded with duration. Time appears here as enduring process in a sense which approximates to Bergson's *durée*, though there appears to be no immediate influence of Bergson's ideas, which in respect of date would be possible. It is evident that herewith the Humian atomism as contained in the doctrine of *minima sensibilia* is quite thrown over. In our consecutive experience there are no such *minima* as separate entities or atoms of consciousness. These are rather products of abstractive thinking which have no reality. From the fact that every state of consciousness has a lowest limit of intensity and duration it must not be inferred that consciousness as a whole consists of states or contents which do not overpass that boundary. Instead of the pulverized, discrete, discontinuous, and static atoms of consciousness of Hume we have the continuous, dynamic, and duration-laden process-contents of Hodgson. And finally in the same connection we have a correction also of the doctrine of presentation and re-presentation (corresponding to Hume's impressions and ideas) insomuch as even the simplest sense-datum must be regarded as a preserved or retained perception, and therefore as a rudimentary recollection; in other words, every impression is also an idea. From this obliteration of the boundaries between original and derived data of consciousness there results a simple and natural explanation of the phenomenon of memory.

Moreover, our presentation of outer objects, or of an outer world, is to be understood primarily as a datum within the field of consciousness, and to be explained or described by means of the analysis of consciousness. While duration is to be regarded as a constitutive character of all phenomena, we see that the spatial element of extension is constitutive only for a definite class of phenomena, i.e. for those which in daily life we call things or objects of the external world. How does the external object come into being? Here Hodgson uses the argument, which long before the days of exact psychological inquiry was used by the acute mind of Berkeley, that the external object is constructed from a combination of visual and tactile perceptions. Not till the percepts of these two senses, which at first are separate, but are in their separateness quite fragmentary and enigmatical, are brought into relation to one and the same place in space, that is when the visual and tactual perceptions are fused into a single complete whole, do we obtain the presentation of a fixed body, which occupies a place in three-dimensional space, and is surrounded on all sides by space. Not till then can we distinguish surface and depth. This procedure is only in part the product of immediate perception; in part it is inferred or thought of on occasion of or in connection with the perceptions of these senses. It must be noticed that here also we cannot speak of any percipient or combining activity of the subject, and therefore not of a separation between the perceptual act and the things perceived.

This constituting of objects completes itself simply as a phase within the one unbroken, complex stream of consciousness. Here again the ego is still completely excluded.

How are we to reach by analysis the presentation of the subject? Hodgson holds that the first glimpse of the subjective is to be found in becoming aware of one's own body, which is distinguished from all other things given in consciousness by the fact that it is continually present, and enduringly accessible to perception. In this way the percipient comes to localize the whole stream of consciousness with all its contents within his own body, and this procedure is basic and decisive for all later experience. It is the first, though not the final, step to perceiving the self as a conscious or percipient being, in which one's own body is given as a real material object, and as an enduring point of relation for all other external things. But pre-philosophic thinking which posits these things absolutely is guilty of a completely unfounded assumption, and so succumbs to a very strong and ineradicable prejudice. Here, as elsewhere, Hodgson is in the strongest opposition to common sense, and especially to every philosophy which bases itself on this uncritical foundation so thoroughly riddled with countless errors and prejudices. Another prejudice of the plain man which is shared by the majority of philosophers is considered by Hodgson in his treatment of the current concept of cause. For it he substitutes the concept of 'real condition' which is of great importance for the inquiries which follow, and which he defines as something on whose appearance something else appears which would not have appeared without the former thing; or, briefly, as a real *sine quâ nôn* antecedent to or co-existent with that which it conditions. Now, according to Hodgson, the only existent of which we know positively that it is a real condition is matter. It is the only source known to us of real conditioning in the course of nature. It is evident that we have here made a leap into the transcendent world from the sphere of pure consciousness which has hitherto been guarded so carefully, and Hodgson's attempt to explain and establish this leap by an analysis of consciousness must certainly miscarry. The insight, he says, that matter is a real condition, and therefore a reality transcending consciousness, is the final result to which the analysis of perception brings us, and therefore that mighty idol of healthy human understanding is fully justified by the facts of experience as they are disclosed in the analysis of consciousness. It does not need any further criticism to see that at this point Hodgson is cutting the ground from under his own feet and smashing up his own system. Like a man imprisoned for years, he has suddenly escaped by violence from the prison of consciousness, and now stands outside free in the wide world.

The phenomenological analyses in the first volume of the *Metaphysic of Experience* contain Hodgson's best work, and are indeed the only thing which assures him an honourable place in recent English philosophy. We can speak only briefly of the extensive discussions of the three later volumes which are founded on this outbreak of the pseudo-metaphysician into the real world. Following his treatment of matter, Hodgson's world-system takes a dualistic form. Matter and consciousness face each other as the two basic factors of all being, and form the world-whole. Their mutual relation consists in this, that matter which at first was born from the bosom of consciousness becomes the real condition on which consciousness with all its modes is dependent for existence; or in common language, matter becomes the cause why consciousness exists at all. This interchange of mutual production and being produced is only possible because the thatness of consciousness is distinguished from its whatness, or consciousness as being or existing from consciousness as knowing or essence. It is only of the first that matter is the condition or cause; while the latter, which is not tied to any material conditions, is itself the subjective aspect of all possible being, including material being. Even these scholastic subtleties cannot, of course, close the rift which splits Hodgson's philosophy into two.

When matter has become independent we enter the realm of the positive sciences, or the world of real conditions.

Philosophy treats of matter so far as it appears to us; science treats of it so far as it appears to us as existing in reality; while matter-in-itself is a creation of the imagination, and therefore has nothing to do either with philosophy or with science. Hodgson goes on to develop a philosophical basis of the exact sciences, and of their basic concepts, such as space, time, matter, number, force, and motion. He moves along strictly empirical paths, and tries everywhere to replace causal explanation with the principle of real conditions.

Thereafter Hodgson advances to the realm of objective mind, and here the articulation of the analytical part of his system becomes still more evident. The first part deals with the analysis of the sensorily given (presentations and impressions); the second part with the analysis of real conditions (the material world, the province of science); the third with the analysis of sensory derivatives (representations or ideas in Hume's sense). The last part of the analytical philosophy describes the structure of the *mundus intelligibilis*, or the realm of thought, feeling, and will. This is the object of the so-called practical sciences which Hodgson in strange conjunction deals with as logic, ethics, and poetics. Logic is the science of the manner in which we must think if we would avoid error. It is a branch of ethics, insomuch as all thought-processes are in the last resort purposive action. Hodgson emphasizes the emotional and volitional character of thought, characterizes judgment as an act of selective attention, logic as an instrument for reaching *de facto* truth, and lays stress upon its practical utility in life and science. Thereby he plays into the hands of the incipient pragmatic movement, to whose early representatives he belongs, and whose revolution in the field of logic (A. Sidgwick and Schiller) he anticipates in important points, and even in their later well-known formulations. It does not appear, however, that the Pragmatists took notice of this alliance. In this connection it is not so much the Aristotelian formal logic as the Hegelian metaphysical logic which appears to be the special adversary.

In ethics Hodgson comes nearer again to Kant in contrast

with the traditional British moral philosophy of Eudaemonism, Utilitarianism, and Hedonism both egoistic and altruistic. The aim of ethics is not the production of individual or universal happiness, but the formation of a harmonious, self-consistent character. Duties, not rights, are the basis of morality. In his doctrine of freedom he takes a mediating position between Indeterminism and, as he calls it, Compulsive Determinism. Freedom does not mean freedom from natural laws, but freedom within them, i.e. freedom in the sense of self-determination. The ethical personality has the power of choosing between presented alternatives and so of acting well or ill. Will means will which is free in and for itself; an unfree will is a self-contradiction. How vacillating and unco-ordinated Hodgson's position is may be seen in the fact that he supports this doctrine of free-will by a confused and quite uncritical neural physiology. The process in which the reasons for or against an action are estimated depends upon the greater or less force of the neural processes which determine decisively the alternative chosen. Self-consciousness, also, which plays a part in this, is, he says, a function of these neural processes. By referring ethical motives to the obscure causation of neural substance Hodgson quite deserts philosophical explanation, and makes nonsense of the sound opinions which he derived from Kant. Here Hodgson drops far behind Hume, whose critical prudence carefully avoided this doubtful way of explanation.

The analytical part of the system leads finally to the constructive part, which nevertheless is likewise based on analysis. The author combines all his earlier results in a single comprehensive conspectus. Is matter, as the condition of all real being, itself unconditioned, or is it perchance subjected to other non-material conditions? Perhaps the material world is only a member of an otherwise unknown order of real conditioning. This consideration opens to us a glimpse into the unseen world as the proper object of constructive philosophy. However we may represent to ourselves the nature of the unseen world, we cannot help thinking of it as continuous with the visible world. Both together form a single order of being. Certainly matter has a beginning in time insomuch as it is dependent upon real though non-material conditions. But this would not exclude its endless extension into the future. It is therefore coexistent with the unseen world which has created and maintains it. Moreover, the unseen world is not so much a postulate of the speculative as of the practical reason, and in this sense is not the cause and support of the material world, but of the moral or conscious world. Similarly, immortality is a moral postulate. Finally, Hodgson is inclined to the assumption that the soul after death may pass first into unknown regions of the material world, since consciousness as its essential characteristic is still dependent upon matter, and not upon matter's non-material conditions. About its passage into the unseen world, however, we know nothing. God as the highest, eternal being we think of as a consciousness similar to our own, but without any of our limitations. He is furnished with power and capacities which immeasurably surpass ours; though without senses, yet with the faculty of a single, all-comprehensive, intuitive power of vision.

Thus are these vague and tentative speculations rounded into the unity of a world-picture. Viewed as a whole, Hodgson's philosophical system, in spite of all its inco-ordinations and weaknesses, in spite of its want of insight and its verbosity, is the respectable and in a sense the imposing performance of a thinker who wrestled with philosophical problems honestly and with remarkable perseverance, whose efforts were not always equalled by his capacity, but were always followed up with the force of his whole personality.

ROBERT ADAMSON (1852–1902)

[Adamson studied at the University of Edinburgh, and was then assistant to Calderwood and later to Fraser. He spent the summer of 1871 in Heidelberg. At the age of 22 he joined the editorial staff of the *Encyclopaedia Britannica*; at 24 (in 1876) he was elected to the Professorship of Logic and Philosophy at Owens College, Manchester. In 1893 he became Professor of Logic in Aberdeen, in 1895 in Glasgow. *Roger Bacon: the philosophy of science in the XIIIth Century*, 1876; *On the Philosophy of Kant*, 1879 (German translation by Schaarschmidt, 1880); *Fichte*, 1881 (in Blackwood's Philosophical Classics); "Moral Theory and Practice", 1900 (contained in *Ethical Democracy*, ed. S. Coit). Posthumously there have appeared the following books: *The Development of Modern Philosophy, with other lectures and essays*, ed. W. R. Sorley, 2 vols., 1903 (separate edition of vol. i, 1908 and 1930); *The Development of Greek Philosophy*, ed. Sorley and Hardie, 1908; *A Short History of Logic*, ed. Sorley, 1911 (largely a reprint of the article "Logic" in the ninth edition of the *Encyclopaedia Britannica*). Also many essays and contributions to the ninth edition of the *Encyclopaedia Britannica* (1875–86); to *Mind* (notices and reviews of the years 1876–98); to the *Dictionary of National Biography* (1885 onwards); to Baldwin's *Dictionary of Philosophy and Psychology* (1901–2); and elsewhere.

Robert Adamson's work was done first and foremost in the history of philosophy. Since Sir William Hamilton he was undoubtedly the greatest philosophical scholar whom the British nation has produced. None of his contemporaries approaches him in the breadth and compass of his learning, none possesses his immense width of reading, his intimate, thorough, and perfectly reliable knowledge of the subject, extending over the whole field of Western thought; none has his comprehensive glance over the whole philosophical development and movement from the Greeks to our own time. His strong and insatiable hunger for knowledge made him even in youth an all-devouring reader, and nothing is more characteristic of him than the fact that at the age of twenty-two he took over the philosophical section of the *Encyclopaedia Britannica* as independent editor, and contributed to it a long series of articles showing in each a profound and detailed knowledge of the subject. In later years he spread his encyclopaedic knowledge by preference over compilations, lexicons, and periodicals without showing the power of collecting them into a great work, and making them further fruitful. His plan of a comprehensive history of philosophy was never carried out owing to his early death; and generally his literary activity lacked concentration, and was split up among several separate undertakings, instead of concentrating upon one. His performance therefore fell far short of his ability; and even his lectures, edited after his death from lecture-notes, offer no adequate substitute for what we might have expected in view of his exceptional ability in historical writing.

This lack of concentration makes it difficult for us to apprehend the essence of his own thought. It is not that Adamson in the copiousness of his erudition stuck fast in historical material and contented himself with being the interpreter of other men's ideas. He had an equally strong impulse to shape things for himself, and historical inquiry was not so much an end in itself (though it was that also) as an occasion for reflection on the problems themselves. But the presentation of what he had himself to contribute to their solution was made mostly in critical explanation of the thoughts of the great philosophers of the past, and not in systematic development of his own. Often, therefore, it is impossible to seize the drift of his teaching directly; we have to pick it out from his critical passages-at-arms with other thinkers. A further difficulty in determining his philosophical position lies in the fact that in the course of years it underwent a continual process of displacement and change; it is true that the several phases do not differ to any considerable extent, but the beginning and end of the change are separated by a wide interval. The displacements and divergencies do not take place by jumps, but gradually and continuously, so that in many cases one cannot say that there has been a change of standpoint, but merely that there have been more or less important modifications within a single tendency of thought.

This tendency, in virtue of which we can, in spite of many

changes, regard Adamson's doctrine as a relatively self-consistent unity, is *Kantian*. He made that his starting-point (if we disregard an earlier attachment to Mill in his student days), and to it he always returned. The "critical" method inaugurated by Kant was through his life the firm, unshakable foundation behind which modern thought should not go. But as since Kant's time philosophy had been enriched with a much ampler stock of experience, to which the exact sciences were continually adding, this foundation, although not thereby basically impaired, must be correspondingly reshaped and enlarged. Adamson's efforts, especially in his later period, were mainly directed to effecting this conciliation between the critical method and the new empirical knowledge gained by the natural and the mental sciences, even at the risk that certain basic positions of Kantianism, its idealism in particular, might have to be sacrificed. This is the explanation and justification of Adamson's transition—which has been emphasized by his interpreters and is plain for all to see—from an originally idealistic position to one becoming ever more realistic. However far the origin and outcome of his thinking may be separated from each other, it must be pointed out against any other interpretation that the path which he followed did not really lead outside the circle of Kantian doctrine, but remained constantly within it, and that though he attempted various and changing interpretations of that doctrine, he never definitely abandoned it. It is therefore right to say that Adamson started from Idealism and turned towards Realism the longer he lived; but this fact is less important than the fact that he was a Kantian throughout his life. As he concerned himself less with speculative than with psychological and epistemological questions, this merely means that he made the critical analysis of experience the basis of his philosophical inquiries, and applied it even in cases where he could no longer concur with Kant's results, and so saw himself constrained to make considerable deviations from them by way of correction. We shall therefore give to the last phase of Adamson's thinking, in which his maturest ideas are expressed, the name of *Critical Realism*, to distinguish his doctrine from the New Realism of Moore, Russell, Alexander, and others, which came into evidence after his death. The philosophical provenance of these two Realisms is so different, and their differences of content so considerable, that it would not be reasonable to try to establish between them a relation which in fact does not exist. Adamson's Realism precedes in time the neo-realistic movement; the latter has neither joined on to Adamson's Realism, nor has it been influenced by him to any extent worth mentioning.

In Adamson's philosophical development, then, there have been two main phases, an earlier idealistic phase and a later realistic phase. The former coincides approximately with his period at Owens College, Manchester, and finds expression in his earlier writings on Kant and Fichte (1879 and 1881), and in his *Encyclopaedia* article on "Logic" (1882). But even within this period there is some preparation for the later change. We cannot fix precisely these intervening stages, since they are not fixed adequately by the published documents, with the exception of the lectures of the years 1886–8 (see G. Dawes Hicks, "Professor Adamson's Philosophical Lectures" in *Mind*, vol. xiii, 1904, pp. 72 ff). The second phase includes approximately his period at Aberdeen and Glasgow, and is first expressed in the Glasgow inaugural lecture of the year 1895 (contained in *The Development of Modern Philosophy*, vol. ii, pp. 3–22) to be fully elaborated in two courses of lectures of 1897–9, of which one develops the main principles of a theory of knowledge in connection with a sketch of modern philosophy from Descartes to Hegel, the other the principles of psychology (vide *ibid.*, i, 283–358, and ii, 161–317). Unfortunately for this last stage we have no fully authentic text from Adamson's own hand. He could neither bring himself to publish his ideas, nor was he accustomed to fix them in writing for his lectures. We therefore have to rely on notes taken by students which we have before us in Sorley's model edition.

Already in the early book on Kant, Adamson had freed himself from the prejudice, at that time widely diffused in England, that Kant's philosophy was identical with his theory of knowledge, and that the latter results in nothing but a phenomenalist Agnosticism which forbids thought to put any questions about the data of experience. From the first he recognized that such a view was completely erroneous, since it separates a single, not very striking and novel aspect of the Kantian theory of knowledge from the rest of his philosophy, and by this separation falsifies or distorts it. Adamson, on the contrary, kept the whole of Kant's doctrine in view, and tried to read Kant's critique of knowledge in the light of this whole. The apparent Agnosticism is for him only a part of that basic metaphysical conception of the unity of reason which dominates Kant's whole system, and finds its most important expression in the teleology of his ethics. Adamson's explanation moves along that general line of Hegelianizing commentary which in the 'seventies was adopted by Green, Wallace, and E. Caird. The powerful intellectual movement, which was set on foot by these men, seized upon him also. But as Adamson's was an extremely realist and sober nature, and had no taste for fine words and inflated language, he was not intoxicated by the idealistic passion of the Hegelians, but preserved that critical self-restraint and prudence which he recognized in Kant much more than in the speculations of his followers. He therefore never became a typical Hegelian, although he could not fail to see the justice of Hegel's criticism of Kant; he could not deny that Kant's keen analytical mind had carried the task of criticism too far, and in his refinements, distinctions, and antitheses had often lost sight of the basic unity and the embracing totality. But he felt himself repelled by the wild and uncritical speculations of certain later Hegelians such as he encountered perhaps in the person of his Glasgow colleague Sir Henry Jones. For in them philosophy had quite lost its characteristic reserve, and became degraded into comforting uplift, or more or less empty sentimentality.

Although Adamson even in his youth was not inclined to follow Kant blindly, he was thoroughly convinced of the surpassing importance of the critical philosophy. The critical method seemed to him to be the only wholesome and fruitful basis for further speculation. "We must resume the problem of philosophy as it came from Kant's hands. No earlier method is now of service; no method that is unaffected by criticism can adequately attempt the problems of modern thought!"[1] For this reason he urged that philosophy should go back to Kant, and wished that his own philosophical work should be regarded as "the legitimate development of what is contained in Kant". Even in his earliest writings he lays stress upon the close connection and mutual influence of speculative thinking and empirical knowledge. Every advance of scientific investigation opens new paths for philosophical reflection, sets it new problems, and demands a review of its old foundations, and no philosophy can prosper which is not in close sympathy with the general conditions of the scientific knowledge which has been reached. Adamson called this the tension between scientific realism and philosophical method. Both often confront each other with hostility or indifference; they are inclined to follow their own paths without paying regard to each other. But those attempts which have been made by science to establish a philosophical world-system (such as those of Spencer and the Darwinians) were condemned to failure from the first, because they posited as absolute a one-sided aspect, that of nature, and therefore could not apprehend the essence of spirit. So this task must be taken up by philosophy and by a philosophy which has opened its doors wide to the new stream of knowledge. Thus only can the tension be overcome which exists naturally between empirical inquiry and philosophical thinking.

These opinions appear at the end of the book on Fichte in 1881. The Glasgow inaugural lecture of 1895, which opens the second phase, takes up the problem at the same point and demands emphatically the revision of idealistic systems on the basis of the new knowledge so copiously furnished by the science of the XIXth Century. The change which came to pass in Adamson's thinking in the intervening years, the change which he himself called a movement from Idealism to Realism, or from Rationalism to Empiricism or Naturalism,

[1] *On the Philosophy of Kant*, 1879, p. 187.

announces itself first in his decided opposition to Kantian Subjectivism. This Adamson regards as the dominant aspect of Kant's theory of knowledge, although Kant himself concerned himself earnestly with a refutation of this standpoint. It is, however, too deeply rooted in his thinking for him to be able to free himself from it completely. It is perhaps not true that the conditions of the possibility of experience are the forms which by the activity of the mind are imposed upon the chaotic material that comes from without. In knowledge, mind is perhaps not the sole determining factor which with a whole armoury of cognitive weapons subdues the given facts to itself. We must rather regard the two correlative sides of the process, the subjective life of the self-conscious spirit and the objectively cognized objects, as alike subject to development and mutual determination. Kant, then, has misplaced the emphasis; he has emphasized unduly the subjective factor and neglected the objective. If we would investigate thoroughly the essence of knowing, we must turn away from abstract ideas to concrete experience. "There is no royal road to philosophic truth; the only route that can be followed is the long and difficult path of facts."[1]

Thus there comes about a displacement of accent from the subjective to the objective side of knowledge, from consciousness to being, or from the abstract to the concrete. Whatever the objective may be, it is certainly not the Kantian "turmoil" of sensations in which the subject must establish order and connection. It is plain that our current antitheses and distinctions of subject and object, form and matter, inner life and outer world, spirit and nature, cannot be maintained against a deeper analysis; that in the basic reality there is nothing corresponding to them which would justify such a separation. They are not original facts, but only subsequent abstractions and constructions of thought or of that factor which does not become manifest till a later stage of development. What we separate and isolate in thinking or in perception is in Reality combined and related. Nowhere in the natural order of things

[1] *Development of Modern Philosophy*, II, p. 18.

do we meet those absolute oppositions and contrasts. There is always the possibility of uniting the parts of our experience and showing their mutual dependence. Reality is a concrete whole or a still unbroken and undifferentiated unity which precedes all the abstractions of thought and in which the subjective and the objective have not yet separated and become mutually independent. All these neat separations and ineffaceable boundaries, such as are characteristic of Kantian thinking, are secondary and derivative; very complicated psychic processes are needed before they can be apprehended at all. Hence results the methodological principle that in primary reality no such absolute divisions can be permitted, and that, therefore, the antitheses of subject and object, soul and body, truth and fact, thinking and perception, and all the rest, have no application. At all events they should not be posited absolutely and opposed to each other as separate provinces of real Being. They are only the names of stages which succeed each other and distinguish themselves from each other in the development of the life of the soul. They can certainly be distinguished from each other in respect of their functions, but in respect of their psychic structure they are at bottom identical. The contrast of fact and truth arises perhaps not from a real opposition between them, but from the contrast between a disconnected isolated part and a connected systematic whole.

The world of understanding which we construct especially in scientific and philosophical thinking is, therefore, a broken, divided, and abstracted world, and so a derived and artificially constructed product. But we cannot halt at this point; we must somehow abolish the boundaries and lines of separation, the abstractions and antitheses; we must recompose the separated members into the unbroken unity of a whole. This may happen in two ways: in one way by speculative philosophy or metaphysics, which advances beyond the splinterings and differentiations of the understanding to the positing of new unities and tries to establish new syntheses. But unity lies not only behind multiplicity but also before it, and therefore a second way is possible, namely, that of regress to the original condition of reality through successive demolition of the structures made by the abstractive understanding. This is the re-establishment of the original experience by excluding all those interpolations and introjections which we, in the course of our spiritual experience, have incorporated in the framework of reality. This latter way, which is not synthetic but analytic, is now taken by Adamson and is thenceforth followed with persevering energy and consistency. The problem which thus presented itself to him, and which he attacked from the side of both theory of knowledge and psychology, is the main concern of his mature thought as it is given in the systematic parts of his posthumous work. Something similar had previously been undertaken in the philosophy of pure experience of Richard Avenarius, apparently without Adamson's knowledge.

The subject-object correlation is, as we have seen, a creation of abstract thinking, in which the objective factor is not given in its original purity, but has undergone manipulation by the subject. This object, which is set over against the subject and at the same time has been created and constructed by it, must be relieved of its subjective trappings and restored in its original non-subjective givenness. We must discover the true features and characteristics of the given contents on the basis of which we were first able to make that antithetic distinction within consciousness. The task is to determine the changing character of objectivity through the series of stages which this concept traverses from the most primitive experience to the most highly developed thinking, though Adamson's interest is directed mainly to the lower stages. Of one thing there can be no doubt, that what appears as objectivity in philosophical systems consists of constructions which are highly notional and abstract; they are correlates and functions of subjectivity on every occasion, and as such are devoid of all concrete content. Examples of this are Kant's thing-in-itself, Hegel's pure being, and Spencer's absolute, mere concepts penetrated with such high generality and so much subjectivity that the proper original meaning objectivity is almost entirely destroyed.

If we go back to primitive experience the question arises: At what point do the provinces of the subjective and objective first separate and become visibly different? Adamson holds that this occurs in space-consciousness. Space or the extended seems to him to be the earliest genetically verifiable characteristic of the objective. Before we can make any other distinctions in the field of consciousness, we experience two kinds of contents, one set of which has the character of extension, while the other is negatively distinguished by lack of that character, but otherwise remains completely undetermined, apart from an element of feeling. Now we can take account of those contents of the objective world which have spatial characters and distinguish them from the non-spatial characters which are states of the subject; and spatial character, therefore, which is connected with certain contents of our sense-experience gives us the first handle for distinguishing the two worlds. Only on the basis of an antithesis between extended and unextended thus experienced or recognized does the consciousness of a self or subject become possible, and consequently the distinction of an inner from an outer world, of ego from non-ego. Space, therefore, forms the pre-condition of consciousness and of the development of mind; but we must not conclude that it is from the very beginning (or *a priori*) a subjective condition of sensory experience, or that through it given contents first become objective. According to Adamson, who here reverses the Kantian position, spatial character, although it may gain subjective importance later in the developed consciousness, is at first nothing but a characteristic connected with objectivity and constituting it.

All further determinations of objectivity are secondary in comparison with the fundamental distinction of extended from unextended contents. Adamson expresses a similar conviction in regard to time. He shows that the primitive form of time-perception is something quite different from the highly developed form of the time-concept which is used in philosophy and natural science. On one side stands the concrete experience of the temporal passage of events, for which the best name is change; on the other side, corresponding perhaps to the empty space of physics, there stand extremely complex and abstract creations of conceptual thought, which are wanting in all the concrete characteristics of primitive givenness. The former is something belonging to the objective state of things; the latter are loaded with subjectivity, that is, products obtained by correlative determinations from the subjective side. Kant's theory of time according to which change is only a characteristic of the subject's inner experience is therefore not acceptable to Adamson. And analogously in regard to causality. Here also the simple experience of the original connection of events is complicated by manifold additions of thought and deprived of its original meaning. The elementary components of that which we in developed thinking understand by the concept of cause are contained already in the simplest forms of sense-perception, and are therefore deeply embedded in that primitive distinction of inner from outer, of subjective from objective. But in Kant's doctrine, however high its philosophical importance may be, the natural order of the genesis of our experience is reversed, insomuch as it everywhere gives precedence and priority to the abstract and general elements over the concrete and particular. Against this Adamson maintains that the definite order which first occupies the place of the objective in the development of our knowledge is in its original form that specific connection of the concrete factors of sense-perception which we have described above. The object is in the first instance that quite determinate, completely independent combination of things, whose resistance we encounter and which in spatial relations of position are experienced as related both to each other and to ourselves. In the genesis of our conscious experience the first thing which we encounter is always and everywhere the concrete.

To this theory of knowledge there runs parallel a more psychological inquiry which lights up things from a rather different angle but arrives at very much the same results. Altogether the line of distinction between theory of knowledge and psychology becomes continually fainter with Adamson. Whereas previously he had defined psychology as a purely empirical study proceeding by the methods of natural science, now it seems to him to be an eminently philosophical study. It is a science of experience, the problems of which are so closely connected with those of logic, theory of knowledge, and furthermore of metaphysics, that it leads directly to the threshold of those studies, which take over the results of psychology for further elaboration.

Adamson's psychology, like his theory of knowledge, is a genetic investigation of the stages of experience and consciousness with special reference to primitive conditions. He rejects both faculty-psychology and atomism, and above all makes fruitful application of the idea of development. He views consciousness as a continually developing process whose changing forms represent the stages of this development. At the primitive stage we find first a related manifold of contents which plainly differ from each other. But in these qualitatively different contents we cannot be said to see any objective entities. For we do not acquire the concept of object till after much more advanced experience; i.e. when we confront a world of things, independent of consciousness, with a subject which knows it. The contents of primitive consciousness stand in relations; but these remain completely unexplained, if we admit so early the assumption of objects. Relations certainly possess no objectivity, and cannot, moreover, be ascribed to a non-sensory synthetic activity of the mind. They present themselves originally quite directly in and with the given terms, and can claim objective existence still less than they. The assumption of objective characters at these early stages is an interpolation which nothing justifies. Similarly, the early correlates of sensations and feelings are here scarcely as yet differentiated from each other. They do not yet stand out in clear separation from the concrete manifold of the given, although certain indications already point to their diversity from each other. Both are characterized by qualitative differences and varying intensity. Not till a later stage do certain contents distinguish themselves plainly as percepts from certain others as feelings, and not till then do we name the one set as objective and the other set as subjective factors of our consciousness. In all these inquiries Adamson is continually concerned with setting aside all later additions and reaching the pure state of experience. Like Avenarius, he wanted to re-establish the natural idea of the world.

In Adamson's doctrine self-consciousness also is pushed out of the central position which it occupies in idealistic systems. Like so much else, it is a late product which we erroneously attribute to the primitive stages of conscious life. A self to which contents are related as to a factor which stands externally over against them is not yet present. It is true that we have to think of the changing contents of consciousness as encompassed somehow with a unity; but this unity is nothing different or separate from the contents; it is therefore not the unity of the self to which they are related. Consciousness is a continuous process within which there are continually changing and qualitatively diverse contents. But these contents are not Hume's, not those bundles of tight and trim "impressions" which, like play-actors, come and go upon the stage. Consciousness is not to be compared to a stationary theatre but to a stream whose waters are always changing, though it still preserves its unity. This continuity is made possible by the fact that we retain the contents of earlier states of consciousness in later states and are able to revive them. Self-consciousness also is subject to development, and advances gradually and by stages from immediate experience. It is neither original nor simple, but is a highly developed form of spiritual life, which does not manifest itself till thought turns back upon itself and becomes reflective. This reflective unity is not an *a priori* form, but has grown from the genetic processes of the spirit in the same way as that vital identity of the subject which as primitive consciousness is its basis and precedes it in time. We see here how far Adamson's psychogenetic inquiries have departed from their starting-point in the Kantian philosophy, and how far for him the problems have been displaced in a direction far remote from Kant. In spite of his rejection of psychic atomism and of the current association-theory, he comes here perilously close to Hume, with whose doctrine of consciousness he agrees in important points, though not in all.

One of Adamson's chief efforts was, as we have seen, to view as a unity all the elements which through the abstractive activity of the mind we think of as separate or antithetic. This may be called the Hegelian feature in his thought. This principle finally determines, though in a quite un-Hegelian manner, his views about the relation of nature and spirit. These also are not absolute entities which confront each other in strangeness or in enmity, but correlative members of an including unity. This unity is the reality itself or the concrete whole which somehow includes both and of which they are manifestations, though its character cannot be more exactly determined. But we must assume that Adamson has viewed the character of reality chiefly under the aspect of nature. The spiritual appears to us at first as opposed to the natural; but this plainly indicates that neither spirit nor nature, if they are contrasted with each other thus in consciousness, has independent being. Spirit can know nature only in so far as it is a part of nature; only so far as it is in a position to know another thing as itself is it a living member of natural being and therefore of the whole of reality. But nature as such cannot be identified with the whole of reality; it is only an aspect of it, although the more important. The life of the spirit is not less necessary for the completeness of the whole than the life of nature. Both grow up together and determine each other in the mutual fulfilment of their being. The development of nature implies also the development of spirit. This metaphysical view confirms the results of his inquiries in epistemology and psychology. We may call it a moderate, critically prudent Naturalism, which has diverged far from its idealistic basis.

GEORGE DAWES HICKS (*b.* 1862)

[Educated at Owens College, Manchester, and Manchester College, Oxford. From 1892 to 1896 studied under Wundt and Heinze in Leipzig, where he took his degree. 1897–1903, Minister at Unity Church, Islington; Lecturer at the London School of Ethics and Sociology 1904–6; Professor of Philosophy at University College, London, 1904–28; retired in 1928. Since 1904 resident in Cambridge, where he has given lectures. *Die Begriffe Phänomenon und Noumenon in ihrem Verhältnis zueinander bei Kant*, Leipzig Dissertation, 1897; "Die Englische Philosophie", in vol. 5 of Ueberweg's *Grundriss der Geschichte der Philosophie*, 1928; *Berkeley* (in the series *Leaders of Philosophy*), 1932; Articles in periodicals, the most important of which are: "Sense-presentation and Thought", 1906 (*Proceedings of the Aristotelian Society*); "The Relation of Subject and Object from the Point of View of Psychological Development", 1908 (*ibid.*); "The Nature and Development of Attention", 1913 (*British Journal of Psychology*); "The Nature of Willing", 1913 (*Proceedings of the Aristotelian Society*); "Appearance and Real Existence", 1914 (*ibid.*); "The Basis of Critical Realism", 1917 (*ibid.*); "On the Nature of Images", 1924 (*British Journal of Psychology*); "The Dynamic Aspect of Nature", 1925 (*Proceedings of the Aristotelian Society*); "From Idealism to Realism", 1925 (*Contemporary British Philosophy*, edited by J. H. Muirhead, vol. ii); "Theory of Knowledge", 1929 (*Encyclopaedia Britannica*, fourteenth edition, vol. xiii.]

Also (published since the present translation went to the press) *Thought and Real Existence*, 1936; *The Philosophical Bases of Theism*, 1937; *Critical Realism, a philosophy of mind and nature*, 1937.

G. Dawes Hicks has concerned himself very largely with problems of psychology and theory of knowledge. His position is a direct continuation of that of Robert Adamson, under whom he studied in Manchester. At a later time he came in Oxford into direct contact with the idealist movement, and then underwent a thorough training lasting several years at Wundt's psychological institute in Leipzig, concluding it with a dissertation on Kant. Kant's philosophy was introduced to him impressively by Adamson, and plays in his thinking a part similar to that which it played in his teacher's. In both it is a starting-point as well as a foundation to be built upon, although many results seem to lead, and have in fact led, far from it. But this is less important than the fact that it is the critical spirit of Kant (though not the letter of his teaching) by which the philosophical attitude of both men is dominated. Dawes Hicks is one of the best Kantian scholars in England to-day, and his theory of knowledge is only to be understood and appreciated as descended from Kant. Like Adamson's, it may best be termed Critical Realism; this marks it off from the New Realism, from which it differs both in origin and in content, and to which it is in many respects sharply opposed. It is the immediate continuation of the efforts undertaken by Adamson, but not carried to completion, to provide a critical and psychologically sound solution of the problem of knowledge.

The main point of difference between Kant's and Dawes Hicks's theory of knowledge consists in this: that the former rests upon subjectivist-idealist, the latter upon objectivist-realist presuppositions. Dawes Hicks rejects above all the view that the object known is a product or construction of the knowing mind. He regards as the centre of the problem the fact that the essence of any act by which we apprehend things consists in a relation to something which in fact is different from the knowing subject. Dawes Hicks's inquiries are directed first and predominantly to the problem of perception, which has been that most frequently discussed by the British theorists of knowledge; for the act of perception is symptomatic and typical of all other ways of knowing or apprehending objects. With Meinong and Husserl, Dawes Hicks first emphasizes the intentional character of perception as of all mental acts. Perceiving is always becoming aware *of* something, or direction *upon* something, as judging is always *about* something. It is essential to all these acts that they intend or indicate some other thing. Analysis of acts of knowing results in the view which is basic for Dawes Hicks's position, that we have here not a production of the object through a whole armoury of categories furnished by the mind, but quite simply what he calls a distinguishing, differentiation, discernment, and comparison of features, characters, and marks which are to be found in the object. When we cognize, we differentiate the features of the object, we discover distinctions in it which we had not noticed at first, and detect relations which we had at first not distinguished. In the act of cognition a something which at first seems undetermined and confused is, as it were, illuminated from within; its content is made manifest in more or less sudden completeness; that content passes from undetermined obscurity into objective clearness. In this the activity or function of mind is not that of generating, creating, or producing, but that of finding, disclosing, discovering, and revealing. It is true that there is an intensive elaboration of the material of knowledge by the subject in the act of knowing. But all the manipulations which we perform on this material tend not to construction but discovery. Cognition doubtless in a certain respect includes an act of synthesis; but this synthesis is not a putting together of the parts of the object. It consists rather in holding together different items of awareness. The essence of an act of cognizing is a process of distinguishing and comparing features which as given are already synthesized and not any creative synthetic activity exercised on the given manifold of experience.

In the perception of an external object we must, therefore, apart from the act of perception, distinguish the content of the perceived object or physical thing from the perceived content or phenomenon. Only the apprehending act and the external object can be termed existent. The apprehended content (usually called 'sensum', 'percept', or 'sensory quality'), on the other hand, is not a third something between act and thing, a psychically existent copy or representative of the thing; it is not an existent but only has being on the basis of the act by which the thing is apprehended. The sensory phenomenon is only a selection from the features which constitute the content of the object, a fragmentary entity as compared with the full content of the physical thing. It is true that we can distinguish logically the merely apprehended or appearing features from those which form the whole content of the object, but we cannot disengage them in reality. Thing and phenomenon are not separated *toto caelo*, and we only learn gradually to distinguish them. The first is a whole which consists of a manifold of attributes and a multiplicity of parts, in which we can distinguish, and thereby apprehend, a great number. But the content of a thing is always infinitely richer and more complex than the content of the features apprehended by perception, and therefore our perceptions are always liable to error, although there is no ground for the assumption that the 'more' of the thing is incompatible with its perceptible features. The favourite antithesis between phenomenon and reality comes, then, to nothing more than a distinction between a fragmentary or partial aspect of the real and its concrete fullness and totality, or between the incomplete apprehension of the real and its complete or total apprehension, if that were possible. The sensory qualities (colours, tones, etc.) are not a structural part or possession of the mind, but are those characters of reality which are isolated and distinguished by cognition. With the cessation of the act of apprehension, the content apprehended, or the phenomenon, ceases to be. It cannot persist in the mind, because, strictly speaking, it never was 'in' the mind. It cannot, therefore, be revived and called afresh into consciousness. What the mind can hold fast and on occasion call up again, what, therefore, has passed into its structure as its true possession, is not the sensory phenomenon, but the contents of its own cognitive act or the *awareness* of its experiences.

Through this third kind of content, that content of the mental act itself which Dawes Hicks saw himself compelled to recognize after he had explained the phenomenal contents as neither psychical nor physical, and therefore as non-existent, the problem of knowledge in relation both to idealist and to Neo-Realist theories undergoes an important complication. His own position requires this in order to explain all those phenomena of mental life which are not concerned with immediately present objects of perception but with the revival or recall of past contents. In the ordinary experience of daily life it cannot be said that we are aware immediately of all the features of an object which we think we perceive directly in their fullness. Rather we distinguish very many of these features with the help of the revival of an earlier awareness of it or of similar objects. The perceptions of mature mind are filled and penetrated by a long series of perceptive acts which, in growing to each new perception, guarantee to it a speedy fulfilment, a fulfilment which would have been effected much more slowly if all the features had to be directly apprehended.

What holds good for perception holds good also for every kind of cognition. Cognition is essentially the same in all its forms, both on its lowest and its highest levels. If we glance over its genesis, we see that there is no break in its development. It is from the beginning a process of separating, distinguishing, and comparing. If we follow back the stages of mental development as far as we will, we always come upon a discriminating activity which, though crude and rudimentary, is still like in kind to that which we find at the higher stages of distinguishing, comparing, and relating. As these acts form the specific character of judgment, the conclusion is that the most primitive and rudimentary kinds of cognitive activity are essentially acts of judging. In the simplest sense-experience judgment, i.e. thought, is already present *in nuce*. We need not, therefore, in this context, describe the higher acts of cognition further; recollection, imagination, fancy, and also conceptual forms such as thinking, judging, generalizing, drawing conclusions, etc., all take place, apart from specific differences, according to the same formula. Intuitive cognition or completely immediate apprehension of contents, not mediated by any kind of act of distinguishing, is not recognized by Dawes Hicks at any stage of development. He therefore rejects as inadmissible Russell's fundamental distinction of 'knowledge by acquaintance' from 'knowledge by description', since for him all cognition, even the simplest awareness of sense-data, is more or less mediated.

In reference to truth Dawes Hicks tries to show that it does not depend on whether it is cognized or not by any individual human mind. But we must not, therefore, call it unreal; he terms its mode of being 'subsistence' in distinction from the 'existence' of psychical acts and physical objects. The truth of the proposition $2 + 2 = 4$ would subsist even though it were not recognized by any consciousness. By thinking we can neither create nor change truth; we can only apprehend or recognize it. For the relation of truth to reality Dawes Hicks accepts to some extent both the theory of correspondence and that of coherence; both come virtually to the same thing and supplement each other. For in the end the point is not that special truths and isolated facts should correspond, but that the whole system of truth should correspond to the whole system of reality, and this means that both systems are self-coherent. This is not the same as saying that the order and connection of truths is exactly the same as the order and connection of things. But the important differences which subsist here in detail need not prevent us from accepting a general correspondence between the two spheres.

Dawes Hicks's theory of knowledge occupies a sort of middle position between that of Kant and that of the New Realists. From the standpoint of the latter it must appear as tinged with idealism in so far as it assures to the activity of mind in all acts of cognition a certain freedom of action, though not a creative function. Some sort of theoretical process constantly takes place through which we apprehend the object. The object cannot be simply given and somehow walk into the mind in full objectivity either by pure acquaintance, as Russell holds, or by mere compresence with the subject, as Alexander holds. But Dawes Hicks's doctrine is distinguished from Kant's by its realistic character; for its basic presupposition is that the object stands over against the subject as an independent entity and that neither in respect of its existence nor in respect of its essence does it depend upon the fact that it is cognized.

THOMAS CASE (1844–1925)

[Professor of Philosophy at Oxford (1889–1910), and President of Corpus Christi College (1904–24). *Realism in Morals*, 1877; *Physical Realism: being an Analytical Philosophy from the Physical Objects of Science to the Physical Data of Sense*, 1888; "Scientific Method as a Mental Operation" (in *Lectures on the Method of Science*, ed. T. B. Strong), 1906; Articles "Aristotle", "Logic", and "Metaphysics" in the eleventh edition of the *Encyclopaedia Britannica*.]

Thomas Case may be regarded as an early precursor of the realistic movement which increased so much in strength after the end of the XIXth Century, although he has no direct connection with the later New Realists. His doctrine attracted little attention and seems to have exerted little influence except perhaps on Hobhouse's early theory of knowledge. Moreover, he came forward in Oxford at a time when Hegel's influence was at its height, and represented a very individual and divergent theory which not only stood in complete contrast to the fashionable philosophy, but showed hardly any points of contact with other tendencies active in England at the time. Though he was a prominent figure in the Oxford of his time, his activity as an author, apart from some unimportant smaller works, was exhausted by a single book which appeared at the beginning of his career.

The title of this book, *Physical Realism*, indicates the direction in which Case's theory of knowledge moves. It calls itself Realism because it assumes a real world of things, independent of the phenomenal data of the senses, which is in principle accessible to knowledge. This cognizable but not perceptible world of things in themselves, in contrast to naïve Realism and the theory of common sense, is equated with the objects of mathematical natural science. Accordingly, the true objectivity of being consists in the known reality of the non-sensory world of physics. Hence there is an antithesis between the sensory, perceptual, or phenomenal world on the one side, and the scientific non-perceptual real world on the other side. Finally, over both there lies the supernatural world of theology as the sphere of divine being.

The physical world upon which by preference Case confers the character of reality naturally cannot be known immediately by us; we must rather infer it mediately. How then does cognition of the transcendent scientific objects come to pass? Here Case proposes a very remarkable and odd theory which, it seems to me, is quite lacking in critical prudence. He thinks that he can solve the problem of knowledge by interposing the sensuously affected nervous system as a medium between physical objects and the data of consciousness. What we immediately perceive, therefore, is not the transcendent or exterior physical objects but the parts of our nervous system which are affected by them, represent them, and are similar to them. The blue, which we see, is nothing else than the optic nerves thus coloured; the warmth which we feel is nothing else than the tactile nerves which have such a temperature. Thus from the blue or warm sense-datum in us we infer to a physical object external to us which is so coloured or so heated. The sense-data, therefore, are immanent but not psychical; they are the physical parts of the nervous system which represent the external world.

The proper opposite of this physical Realism is the subjective or psychological Idealism which has its starting-point in Descartes' assumption that all sense-data are psychic phenomena and descended through Locke's and Berkeley's ideas, Hume's impressions, Kant's phenomena, to its latest form in Mill's sensations. Case, on the other hand, intended a restoration of the genuine Realism of Bacon and the great scientists (Galileo, Kepler, Newton). He means to move along the opposite path which leads not from subject to object, but from object to subject, or, as the sub-title of his book expresses it, he wants to advance by the analytic method "from the physical objects of science to the physical data of the senses". The doctrine professes to be thoroughly objective and analytic.

It must be noticed that in the little book *Realism in Morals* Case developed similar ideals in ethics, but, fearing that his theory might be confused with Materialism, he took particular care to explain that his Realism, so far from issuing in Materialism, harmonized better than any other with Christian theology. Rejection of psychological Idealism, he maintains, is in complete agreement with a recognition of theistic Idealism. It has justly been observed (by Hasan, *Realism*, 1928, pp. 291 ff.) that Case's standpoint directly carries on the Scottish common-sense philosophy and is practically identical with the position of Hamilton and Mansel, although with the characteristic difference that physical science here takes the place of the normal human understanding. But in this very primitive and coarse-fibred theory, which lacks all finer differentiation and shading, we cannot see any advance beyond the thinkers who have been mentioned or beyond Bacon's Realism to which Case loves to appeal.

JOHN COOK WILSON (1849–1915)

[Educated at Balliol College, Oxford, 1873–4; studied under Lotze, at Göttingen; 1874, Fellow of Oriel College, Oxford; 1889–1915, Professor of Logic, Oxford. In his lifetime Wilson (apart from his *Aristotelian Studies*, 1, 1879) published nothing of note. His papers were published by A. S. L. Farquharson under the title: *Statement and Inference, with other philosophical papers*, 2 vols., 1926. This bulky work of over 1,000 pages contains as its most important part his yearly lectures on logic; there are also essays, letters, and discourses, a memoir by the editor, and a bibliography of Wilson's publications.

On Wilson see: H. A. Prichard in *Mind*, vol. 28 (1919); H. W. B. Joseph in *Proceedings of the British Academy* (1915–16); and R. Robinson, *The Province of Logic: an interpretation of Cook Wilson's Statement and Inference* (1931).]

John Cook Wilson, one of the most unusual figures in modern British philosophy and one of the hardest to apprehend, came to Oxford in 1868, attracted by Green's powerful personality, was there caught up in the current of the new movement, went at the end of his student-period to Göttingen to hear Lotze, who was at that time the German thinker most famous and most highly esteemed in English philosophical circles, and after his return to Oxford, where he lived to the end of his life, developed a very intensive and successful activity as a teacher. By the common consent of his numerous followers he was the greatest philosophic teacher in Oxford since Green. His main province was logic, on which for many years he regularly delivered a widely known course of lectures through which a whole generation of pupils passed, conducted as it was with so much skill, enthusiasm, and exactitude. He was less concerned to hand on a definite body of doctrine than to stimulate and carry forward new thought both in himself and in his pupils. He was more concerned with the process than with the result, more with the dynamic movement of thought than with its dogmatic establishment. For this reason he shrank from the final fixation of his ideas, and nothing was less congenial to him than the elaboration of a well-rounded and finished system. This was the reason why he published practically nothing. He was always working over, patching, and improving what he had written. He put his whole force into his teaching and so became one of the most exemplary and impressive philosophic educators and teachers who have worked in England in the last half-century. He might with justice be termed a modern British Socrates.

Wilson possessed an extremely keen and subtle logical understanding whose main strength lay in criticism and analysis. Whenever he attacked a problem he turned and twisted it every way and pursued it into its furthest ramifications without bringing it to a final solution. The finest logical chiselling and filigree-work was what suited him best and to that extent he was a true propounder of difficulties who could plunge into the smallest details and nuances of a problem with delighted, almost passionate devotion, and to whom the discussion of problems always had preference over system-making and the cultivation of principles. But there lay the cause of his weakness, the inability to see anything as a whole and to set it in a wider context. He was so thoroughly convinced that every thing and every problem has first of all its own life and can become intelligible in its own right and not from its relation to other things and problems that he lost sight of the wider whole and became involved in detail. He concerned himself mainly with minor philosophical tasks, i.e. with careful and acute analysis of problems, in which field he certainly did some admirable work. The inexorable demands he made both on himself and on others for perfect candour, honesty, and simplicity of thought freed the philosophic atmosphere of his day from many morbid growths and formed a natural and healthy counterpoise to certain extravagances and lofty flights. As his influence was exercised in Oxford, the citadel of Hegelianism, the fact has special significance.

The best term for Wilson's philosophical standpoint is 'absence of standpoint'; not in a depreciative sense, but in the sense of neutrality towards the obligations which a standpoint involves. His primary philosophical principle was the conviction that there is no such first principle at all. Important as was his idea that the thinker has only to follow out the separate problems, this conceals a certain danger which Wilson could not always escape, the danger that the problems might establish an ascendancy over the thinker and draw him so completely into their power that he could no longer master them, but became mastered by them. Thus often one cannot escape the impression that the well-tempered instrument of his understanding worked rather like a machine which when it is once set going runs mechanically and is capable of threshing empty straw as well as full sheaves of corn. It is said that he possessed an astonishing capacity of discoursing endlessly about unimportant and futile things and exhausting intolerably the attention of his hearers. Ill-natured men even maintained that he could defend a thesis of which he disapproved with the same skill as its exact opposite, so that one was left in doubt which of the two he himself favoured. Moreover, it is characteristic of him that he was always on the war-path, always hunting down some heresy for whose extermination he worked with fanatical industry. When he thought that he had discovered a logical fallacy or a perverted question or a corrupt proof he pursued the mistake like a hunter after his quarry to its remotest lair and did not let go till the situation had been cleared up to the satisfaction of his over-sensitive logical conscience. Even then he usually did not think that the problem was finally settled; he was wont to take it up again on some other occasion and was able to show that it had new aspects, although his earlier analyses seemed to have exhausted it thoroughly. Thus he was indefatigably engaged in the refutation of numerous errors; but his pugnacity seems often to be whim or pique rather than serious business. With special tenacity and perseverance he combated non-Euclidean geometries and symbolic logic, as well as Bradley's theory of judgment, the coherence theory of truth, the subjectivist theory of knowledge, and much else. For the most part he kept to negative criticism, and suggested nothing positive in place of the views which he attacked. Even his life-long preoccupation with the problems of logic led to no reconstruction of the study. More clearly than anyone be recognized the weaknesses and defect of prevailing theories. But he had not the power to give logic a positive impulse and to set it on a new foundation.

As Wilson's thinking was in continual flux, there is great difficulty in finding any sort of definite doctrine in it or establishing any positive results to which it led. Nevertheless, certain constant directions may be indicated by means of which we can set his teaching in its historical context. In regard to this it is important that his thinking grew originally out of the Oxford Idealism and for a long time moved in its path. But in the course of time he moved ever further away from his starting-point in the direction of Realism. This change, as a critic says, took place "with extreme hesitation and without emphasis",[1] so that the point of time cannot be fixed exactly. In the 'nineties Wilson was still greatly under the influence of Kant and Green, and not till the end of the century was the trend towards Realism plainly apparent. But we cannot say that then or even later there was any real breach with Idealism as a world-view or any open polemic against it. The fact rather was that Wilson, according to his custom, set to work on

[1] *Contemporary British Philosophy*, ed. by J. H. Muirhead, ii, p. 339.

some definite points and special problems of the Oxford teaching and tried to show their untenability and inconsistency. But even here he kept to detail and did not venture an attack upon the whole. Thus Wilson became more and more the leader of an opposition which did not try utterly to destroy Idealism by opposing to it an equally comprehensive world-view, but tried to shake it by a series of shrewdly aimed separate strokes. That this opposition came from the home-camp and from within the walls of Oxford increased its efficacy and persuasiveness.

We may show this in the case of Wilson's theory of knowledge. One of his strongest convictions is that philosophers try to explain many things which in their nature are incapable of being explained. Much that is ultimate in our experience is in itself fully intelligible. We therefore set ourselves an utterly perverse question if we try to explain such ultimate things by any kind of relations or appearances which they present. A thing can be intelligible without being explicable, i.e. it explains itself without relation to anything else. This applies especially to the problem of knowledge. Knowledge for Wilson is an ultimate fact which we cannot further analyse or define. Even the attempt to explain it conceals a fallacy because it always assumes that which is to be explained. Knowledge is just knowledge and nothing else. In the last resort there is no such thing as theory of knowledge, at least not in the sense that by it the nature of knowledge can be either determined or explained. Wilson is sceptical of all such theories and shows that they miss the meaning of knowledge if they try to explain it. They say that knowledge is copying, or representing, or constructing an object. But what is gained by that? Must not the copy or representation or construction also be apprehended by knowledge and is not the difficulty thereby simply repeated instead of being removed? Whether we know the image or the thing or anything else, knowledge as such is always presupposed and not explained.

Knowledge, therefore, is *sui generis*, a final unanalysable fact. There are certain further determinations of it, such as perception, thought, and judgment; these cannot explain knowledge, but in some respects they can describe it.

Wilson first rejects the Idealist view that knowledge is the creation of an object. He holds that we do not at all change the object if we apprehend it by perceiving or knowing it. It is incompatible with the idea of knowledge that the subject should exercise any kind of activity on the object or that the object should undergo anything of the kind at the hands of the subject. It is impossible that knowledge should be something merely subjective which could produce the object from itself. Apprehension of an object is possible only so far as that which is apprehended possesses an existence independent of the act of apprehension. This is an essential presupposition of all cognitive acts. Knowledge is therefore a disclosing or discovering of factual relations, not a changing or producing of them. And this takes place by direct apprehension of what really exists and not by any intervening images. Wilson therefore rejects the theory of copying. I cognize the reality because I apprehend it immediately. The fact stands bodily before me. The cognitive judgment is neither the fact itself, nor any image of the fact, nor an apprehension of such an image, least of all mere apprehension as a purely subjective condition, but just apprehension of the fact as real. This indicates the most important features of this Realist theory of knowledge; though, as must be emphasized, Wilson's doctrine is not to be fixed down to any narrow 'ism'. The direction in which the views move, which he reached by mere analysis of the problem, and in which he has influenced some of his pupils, is merely indicated. In any case, Wilson in his later years was counted as the realistic counterpart of Oxford Idealism, and consequently as one of the forces working against it.

In logic, his special field of activity, Wilson shrank equally from finally settling his ideas. His great course of lectures on this subject, the text of which could only be compiled by the editor of his papers with much labour, leaves us almost wholly without a single definite orientation and suggests a geological formation in which several strata are partly intermingled, partly superposed on one another. We can trace the influence of Lotze, whose pupil Wilson had been, or again that of Uberweg, upon which Farquharson has laid stress. It is certain that Wilson, a distinguished classical scholar, expert in both philology and exegesis, learnt much from the Greeks, above all from Aristotle, and had gone through the school of Kant. But all this does not mean much in the case of a man who was quite independent in his beliefs and stood entirely on his own feet. In any case, Wilson tried to keep logic wholly independent of psychology, i.e. free from all dependence on the subjectivity of the thinker, or from any entanglement with psychological points of view, although he did not completely succeed in this. On the other hand, he both laid stress on the close relations between logic and pure mathematics (he was himself a well-trained mathematician, full of original though eccentric ideas), and recognized the high importance of forms of language for logical thinking. He held the view that common linguistic usage contained much more logic than many subtle theories decked out with technical terminology. He therefore preferred to express himself in the speech of ordinary men and avoided all parade of learning and high-sounding terminology. Moreover, he thought it important to put the right questions and to clear up the facts as a pre-condition of every profitable logical inquiry. Above all, in this field also he never buried the war-hatchet and was always in pursuit of fallacies and perverted questions, of obscure and confused thinking. The target of his attacks was chiefly the neo-Hegelian school of Oxford and the theories invented by them. He attacked with characteristic perseverance and passion especially the doctrines of judgment of Bradley and Bosanquet. He wanted to banish the term judgment entirely from logic, because the term included two quite different ways of thinking—namely, knowing and opining. According to Wilson these two are not members of a single logical process within which there are greater or lesser grades or stages of certainty which pass easily into one another, but are in principle separate from each other; inasmuch as knowledge is essentially conjoined with absolute certainty, while opinion is always conjoined with a more or less considerable factor of uncertainty. The term 'judgment' can, therefore, only cause confusion, because it maintains the fiction that there is some sort of common tie between these two completely diverse modes of thought. Moreover, even if a clearly definite sense could be given to the idea of judgment, we could never give a final definition of judgment. If, like Bradley and Bosanquet, we say that it is a relation to reality, we must ask what kind of relation it is; and to that we can only answer that it is the relation of judging. Thus we should be merely turning in circles. Therefore, according to Wilson, not judgment but inference is the central point and proper field of logic, and, as with Aristotle, the doctrine of statement (*ἀπόφανσις*) precedes the doctrine of inference. Instead of the logically irrelevant judgment we must therefore have the theory of the general form of statement and of its several species. This is the explanation of the title of the lecture-course "Statement and Inference". The details of this logic lie outside of our present scope. Here, as everywhere, Wilson shows himself a master of strict, exact thinking, which is keen, often captious and hair-splitting, but always honest and clean-cut.

FOLLOWERS OF COOK WILSON

Cook Wilson's teaching in Oxford has left many traces on modern British thought. But as he had no definite system of doctrine with finished, easily diffusible results, but merely a special way of philosophizing, it is not easy to sum up his influence. In Oxford itself there grew up even in his life-time a sort of Wilsonian tradition, which is still alive. This tradition was carried on by a small group of thinkers, most of whom are still teaching and working in the University of Oxford. But we cannot say that a proper school was formed, because there is no structure of doctrine which can be transmitted. At most there is a kind of *συμφιλοσοφεῖν*, which is continued in Wilson's spirit and with his methods of thought. A further difficulty for the historian lies in the fact that this kind of philosophizing is much stronger in academic teaching than in literary production. These thinkers share with their master his reluctance to formulate and fix their ideas finally by writing. My account is therefore made difficult by the scantiness of the literature; especially for those, standing outside the movement, for whose sake the account is written.

As thinkers who belong to the Wilson tradition we may mention with the necessary reservations the following: H. A. PRICHARD (born 1871), Professor of Moral Philosophy and Fellow of Trinity College (retired 1937); H. W. B. JOSEPH (born 1867), Fellow of New College and Lecturer in Philosophy (retired 1932); SIR W. D. ROSS (born 1877), Provost of Oriel College and Lecturer in Philosophy, all in Oxford; and R. I. AARON (born 1901), Professor at the University College of Wales in Aberystwyth.

Prichard, who is more closely connected with Wilson's thinking than the others, has so far published only a single book, *Kant's Theory of Knowledge*, in which he develops his own theory of knowledge; apart from that he has published only a few essays in periodicals and an inaugural lecture (*Duty and Interest*) in which ethical problems are discussed. That external objects exist independently of consciousness and that they are cognized immediately by sense-perception forms the realistic basis which Prichard shares with Wilson and many other modern Realists. In regard to all inquiries into knowledge his attitude is as sceptical as that of his master; for to make a theory of knowledge without first knowing what knowledge is seems as foolish as to try to learn to swim without going into the water. Inquiry into knowledge always fulfils itself in the act of knowing, and every theory of knowledge must take account of this. Although caution is indicated here, Prichard is more confident and positive in carrying out his views than Wilson. This is to be seen in his analysis of perception from which the problem of knowledge is developed. In strict language perception is objective, i.e. it is a direct apprehension of the object and not of its appearances. If we perceive 'something red', we know that the object of the perception is real, and without having knowledge of its several elements we know further that in its general nature it is spatial. But do the so-called secondary qualities (colour, hardness, and warmth) also belong to the object, as the naïve observer assumes, or are they subjective? According to Prichard, the latter is true. Colour, e.g., is no real property of the thing. It presupposes a percipient subject, and possesses no existence independently of such a subject. The proof which Prichard gives of its dependence is a merely logical one. The subjectivity of sensory qualities is a constitutive mark of the concept of them; in other words, they cannot be thought except as standing in some sort of relation to a subject, and as this is fully evident, we need in this matter no appeal to experience. Thus the decision in an important question about the theory of knowledge is reached by means of pure thought; and, as similar arguments are greatly favoured both by Wilson and his followers, this tendency is rightly termed rationalistic. Herein lies an essential difference between the realistic position of Wilson's school and that of the New Realism.

The surrender of the objectivity of sense-data and their necessary connection with perception entail a further consequence which in the end threatens completely to undermine the foundations of Realism. It is evident that awareness of the spatial character of things, in which the primary quality of spatiality is apprehended as essential for reality, is not really a function of perception, but a necessity of thought. In every judgment of perception spatiality (and therefore reality also) is involved from the first, and is therefore presupposed. Strictly speaking, we cannot say that things *are* spatial, but rather that they must be thought of as spatial, so far as they are perceived. Their spatiality is therefore *a priori*; it is not given to us in the perceptual process or empirically, but is recognized by immediate intuition. The same is true of their reality, the distinctive characteristic of which is spatiality. Here Prichard, in recognizing the *a priori* foundations of experience, advances far beyond his original starting-point; and, though he is here following the guidance of a deeper insight, he is endangering the very principle that he was anxious to establish, the realistic solution of the problem of knowledge.

We must forbear to go into the details of Prichard's treatment of ethical problems. I can only say that his essay "Does Moral Philosophy Rest on a Mistake?" (in *Mind*, vol. xxi, 1912) gave rise in recent days to a very lively and fruitful discussion, conducted mainly by Oxford thinkers, from which there seems to have crystallized a new attitude to certain special ethical problems. The "Oxford Moralists", from whom this new impulse came, have attracted much attention. But these matters are still too fluid to be treated by a historian of philosophy.

Joseph also has passed through Wilson's strict schooling in thought, and shows plain traces of it. But he has moved further from the master, and developed his ideas more independently than Prichard. More than Prichard he has opened his mind to other influences and been impressed by them. This is visible in his first book, his *Introduction to Logic* (1906, second edition, 1916). This excellent and widely read textbook, the best among many similar works, develops a formal logic on an Aristotelian foundation, and avails itself of the later logical researches of Sigwart, Lotze, Bradley, Bosanquet, and, last but not least, Cook Wilson. Next to his teacher Cook Wilson, from whom he learnt his strictness of reasoning and his skill in analysis and in clarifying ideas, Joseph is indebted most to the Hegelians, especially in regard to the main questions of principle. That logic cannot be independent, but must finally be anchored in metaphysics, is a thought which points far beyond Wilson's Formalism in the direction of Absolutism. To this extent Joseph's logic continues the old Oxford tradition and forms the proper antithesis to the mathematical logic of Cambridge. Moreover, we find in Joseph other Hegelian or neo-Hegelian ideas, e.g. in a discussion of the idea of development which is directed against the Biologism of Spencer and his successors, and tries to interpret evolution idealistically.

Joseph's theory of knowledge shows a similar vacillation between Realism and Idealism to that of Prichard, and, like it, is to be traced back to Wilson, as regards both its starting-point and its method. He also starts from the assumption that perception is a direct apprehension of spatial objects which exist independently of the act of apprehension. But critical analysis shows increasingly the untenability of this assumption. It is evident that not only the secondary qualities stand in a necessary relation to the act of cognition, but also the primary. There arises a conflict between the realistic and the rationalistic tendencies which, as in the case of Prichard, comes to the surface in the problem of space. Realism demands the spatiality of the object and its independence of the perceptual apprehension. But Rationalism casts doubt upon the independence of consciousness that spatial determinations are supposed to have. It is the same with other primary qualities, such as resistance and magnitude. Thus Joseph also comes to undermine the original Wilsonian position, and finds himself forced more and more into idealist lines of thought; indeed, into lines of thought which tend more towards Plato than towards Kant. No more than Prichard has he succeeded in solving the problem of knowledge.[1]

The same approach by Joseph to the spirit, though not to the letter of the Idealist tradition showed itself in a little book on ethics (*Some Problems of Ethics*), published 1931, which is connected with the recently mentioned discussion of ethical questions opened by Prichard. In this discussion there have intervened besides Prichard, Joseph, G. C. Field, and above all the well-known Aristotelian scholar Sir W. D. Ross, with a book entitled *The Right and the Good*.[2] In this discussion an attempt is made not so much to erect an ethical system as to analyse and clarify certain basic ethical concepts, such as was undertaken by G. E. Moore, by whose side Ross ranges himself

[1] *Vide* his essays "The Psychological Explanation of the Development of the Perception of External Objects", *Mind*, vols. xix and xx, 1910 and 1911; "On Occupying Space", *ibid.*, vol. xxviii, 1919; and the paper "A Comparison of Kant's Idealism with that of Berkeley", *Proceedings of the British Academy*, vol. xv, 1929.

[2] The discussion is reviewed by J. H. Muirhead in his *Rule and End in Morals*, 1932.

partly with agreement, partly with disagreement. In order to give some idea of the questions discussed in the circle of "Oxford Moralists", we must mention some of the topics dealt with in the writings of Joseph and Ross: they are, rightful and moral acts, act and motive, rightness and goodness, duty and desire, the meaning of right and good and their mutual relation, to what things these attributes belong, the degrees of the good, the morally good, etc. If we label this ethics as intuitionist, we do not characterize it exactly; for its peculiarity is just this, that it is not committed to a definite standpoint, and is concerned mainly with the problems as such, that is, with the clarification of concepts and description of phenomena.

Finally we must mention a discussion of the problem of knowledge, which goes back directly to Wilson's ideas, in Aaron's book *The Nature of Knowing* (1930). In this well-written and careful study Aaron deals especially with the subjective side of the problem, with the act through which knowing takes place, and he agrees with Cook Wilson that in it we have something in every respect elementary and *sui generis*, which can be understood only through itself. Every definition or explanation of this act must, therefore, turn in a circle; it must always come back to that which is incapable of being defined. All that we can do to disclose its nature is to give a plain and accurate description of it which should initially be quite free from metaphysical or other complications. The result of the investigation is that knowledge is nothing but intuitive apprehension of the real. It is something quite simple and immediate, distinct from every other spiritual act, and, wherever it takes place, always one and the same. We cannot call it a process, although psychic processes of many kinds may precede it. As soon as it begins, it is like an illuminative flash of lightning, by which a factual content is instantaneously lit up. Knowledge as such is therefore not subject to error; it is simply infallible. Where there is error it always slips in by another path. Though starting from Cook Wilson's basic ideas, Aaron has developed this problem in an independent way, and shown some new and important aspects of it.

IV

THE NEW REALISM

The New Realism is not a historically rounded movement as the New Idealism is, or as, in a certain sense, Pragmatism is. It is still in course of change; it still includes a possibility of progressive development; its range of problems is still open in all directions. It is the philosophy of the present, and as far as can be foreseen it will still dominate future development, or at least play a leading part in it. The time has not yet come, therefore, to write its history. One can do no more than delimit the field of intellectual life which it has conquered, and characterize and label its most important successes.

We need not spend many words in recounting its history. It is the most recent development of British philosophy, and although it appeared about the same time as Pragmatism, the latter had a longer previous history on American soil and is altogether more transatlantic than European; in England it has only played a brief part as a stranger, and taken no deep root. But the New Realism is a genuinely British growth which has grown in conformity with the best traditions of the indigenous or national philosophy, and though it has taken root also across the ocean, Britain is its native soil. Its difference from the New Idealist or the Pragmatist movement consists just in the fact that it has sprung from the soil, while the others are after all imported, the one from Germany, the other from America. Englishmen themselves for the most part certainly do not admit this to be true, especially in regard to Idealism. They claim that it is in the line of the so-called idealist tradition, which is of great antiquity and within which the New Idealism of Kantian and Hegelian origin is only the latest member. This view cannot be maintained in view of the historical facts. It cannot, indeed, be said that idealistic thinking is foreign to the British; but only that wherever it has appeared as a genuine home-product it has clothed itself (and must continue to clothe itself) in those specific forms which are suitable to the British character. Of this the Berkeleian philosophy is the most striking example. The British character, however, is not suitable to the German garb in which Idealism has in modern times found its classical form of expression; and especially not to the Hegelian garb which the British revival of thought adopted by preference in the last century. It is of deep significance that even within Anglo-Hegelianism forces at once sprang into activity which aimed at discarding this garb and at proclaiming idealist truth in a form better suited to national feeling.

With New Realism British philosophy has found its way home again. It has returned to the track of a tradition whose continuity stretches back to the Renaissance, and which has remained alive till to-day, although for a time it was ousted from its leading position (e.g. in the last third of the past century by the New Idealism). It must be noted that this return to old paths did not take place by a conscious and express resumption of tradition, but took form to all appearance quite independently of old ideas. We do not therefore fall into contradiction if we regard New Realism as a genuine novelty in British thought. For when it appeared, the old tradition, though not completely interrupted, had entered upon a path from which there was no exit. As there was no thought of linking up with the past (I have the evolution-philosophy chiefly in mind) and as there was no revival of the older forms of the tradition, we have before us in fact a new direction of thought similar to that of thirty years previously, when the idealist movement suddenly began. The resumption of the British tradition took place more from internal causes than from any external impulse. It came about more from instinct than from deliberate intention; and it was only later that the thought which was stirred to fresh activity by the New Realism, turned back to its origins and became fully conscious of its connection with the past. Hence it came to pass that it was not from the spirit of the epigoni of the XIXth Century but rather from that of the classical epoch of British philosophy that the revival came. New Realism implies, therefore, although it was unconscious of the fact at the beginning (and even later in some cases), the re-establishment of the true British tradition, the continuation of that which was embodied most purely in the great classical systems from Locke to Hume and Reid; in other words, that which is termed and understood as "British philosophy", to use the briefest expression for it. After what has been said, it will be understood that this is a definite revival, a genuine philosophic renaissance and not a mere handing on or refurbishing of old material; and this will be quite evident in the light of what follows.

To get a clear view of the historical situation another point must be remembered. It was no accident that the new idea broke out just at the time when the Anglo-Idealist movement, after exhausting most of its possibilities, came to a standstill. This fact gains a special importance in so far as New Realism in its earliest utterances (and frequently also in its later course) attacked, *expressis verbis*, the spirit and method of Idealism, and tried to put something quite new and different in its place. Under its leadership was formed that new attacking host which, in alliance with Pragmatism and other foreign influences, made a general assault against the idealist positions, pressed them continually further back, and at last almost completely mastered them. This concentric attack upon the foreign invader, as German Idealism, and especially its Hegelian offshoot, was thought to be in the new philosophic camp, began about the end of last century. On the side of New Realism, apart from the earliest writings of Russell which appeared about that time, it was an essay of Moore's entitled "The Refutation of Idealism" (published in 1903 in *Mind*) which acted like a war-cry. This gave the watchword which was taken up at once by other thinkers; and although the contrast between Realist and Idealist continually lost its sharpness as time went on, and the new movement did not (like Pragmatism) devote itself so much to strife and controversy as to the investigation of problems, the anti-idealist tendency continued, and is still in evidence to-day.

At the present time New Realism and the forces called into activity by it dominate the philosophic field. But the movement is to-day far from being governed by a leading principle or a single leadership. One cannot say that it is uniform in any respect, either in its method, or its field of inquiry, or its aims, or in its inward coherence. Its strength depends not upon its close formation, but upon its openness; not upon its unity, but upon its manifoldness and variety. It is full of inner tensions and contrasts, of inequalities and dissimilarities; it is still in every respect on the march, although we are still uncertain in what direction it is journeying, and whether it will not break up in various directions.

Before we speak of the several representatives of this new movement of thought it is necessary to characterize it briefly, seeing that the short title 'New Realism' tells us nothing about it. 'New Realism' is mainly applicable to the new theory of knowledge which has given the movement its impetus and is its basis even to-day. Above all, it is the problem of perception, to which the attention of British thinkers has been specially given, that has been attacked afresh; with the result that a series of individual and original attempts at solution have appeared and are still appearing. In this point the community of philosophic thought is more plainly apparent than elsewhere, and almost every thinker has dealt with this problem intensively in order to prove his philosophic efficiency. It is a characteristic of this movement that theoretical interests are predominant in it, and that the criticism of knowledge has a leading position over all other departments of philosophic study. Where these inquiries have led and what solutions have been reached, will be shown in the following pages.

Another characteristic of the New Realist philosophy is its strong emphasis upon science. In this it differs from Idealism, which is mainly a world-view, and agrees with the Darwin–Spencer line of thought, which also had a scientific foundation. But this agreement is more accidental than necessary, because the two interests are quite divergent, being in one case primarily philosophic and in the other case specially scientific. The scientific character of New Realism implies refusal to adopt a separate philosophic method. Its method is just that which is common to all science, and philosophic knowledge can be achieved by no other means than those which are applied to the special fields of inquiry. But this does not mean that philosophy is subservient to this or that special department of study. As opposed to them it is rather in a position of sovereignty and makes use of their results only so far as they can help its own tasks and purposes. Although there is in principle no danger that the special sciences will in their growth smother the problems of philosophy, this danger cannot be always excluded in practice.

There are in the main two sciences from which the new philosophy was fertilized in essential matters, mathematics and modern physics (in less degree also biology and psychology). The influence of mathematics preceded that of physics. The latter was not influential before the great changes of the theory of relativity, the quantum theory, atomic physics, etc. These changes had played a predominant part in forming a new picture of the world, and in no other country were they more readily accepted and more fully exploited than in England. Modern physics has left traces on all the movements of contemporary British thought; but it is a merit of the New Realism to have opened itself earlier and more widely to the stream of new knowledge. What biology meant for Evolutionism, physics means for New Realism. The new knowledge fell upon fertile soil and became creative and productive in the new thinking. The appropriation of it leads, especially in the case of Whitehead, to important philosophic conclusions whose range cannot yet be estimated finally.

Like physics, mathematics also furnishes an important constituent of the new doctrine. But this constituent can be distinguished and isolated more easily than the other. It is not so closely united with the whole, but extends only to a special province within which it is operative. This province is logic. Logic has been placed on a completely new basis by thinkers who belong to the realist movement and has been developed as the so-called mathematical or symbolic logic. The new logic, which bulks largely in the philosophic discussions of the past decade, has broken behind it almost all the bridges to the traditional form of the study, and advances dressed in a garb of mathematical formulae, which are intelligible only to a few experts. It is connected with the New Realism by personal union, but it is so special an interest that it cannot be fitted easily into the usual philosophic classification. Although it has often been acclaimed by its champions as the solution of all philosophic difficulties, this can hardly be accepted by those who stand outside the movement. In my opinion mathematical logic represents no important factor in the solution of philosophic problems, and therefore none in the New Realist doctrine, which can be presented and understood independently of it. It seems justifiable, therefore, to separate it from the present section and to treat it by itself (see below, Section v).

The approximation of philosophic to scientific method has this result, that the new philosophy aims more at knowledge of the parts than of the whole, and concerns itself less with comprehensive views than with solid and exact work on details. Or, as its most distinguished representative says in an admirable characterization, it aims neither at pronouncements about the universe as a whole, nor at the construction of an all-inclusive system. It does not treat the world as organic in the sense that from any separate part if adequately understood the whole can be inferred. It does not attempt, as German Idealism has done, to deduce the nature of the world as a whole from the nature of knowledge. It treats knowledge as a natural fact among others and ascribes to it no mystical significance or cosmic importance (see Russell, "Philosophy in the XXth Century", contained in *Sceptical Essays*, 1928, p. 70). It is, as we may say, directed more to solving problems than to making systems; it prefers analysis and description to construction and speculation.[1] It

[1] These lines, which were written some time ago, are fully confirmed by recent developments of British philosophy. At the moment (1934–5), an atomic analysis is the fashion of the day and dominates the whole field of philosophy, starting outwards from Cambridge. Moore, Broad, Miss Stebbing, and others, are leaders in this movement, and many lesser minds follow in their train. A great part of the notable philosophic thinking of to-day follows in this path: "Metaphysics is completely dethroned, and every kind of system-making tabooed",

loves to set to work on a special problem which it pursues and anatomizes in all its aspects; but it is less interested in the connection of the problems and their arrangement in a systematic whole, and in all this it is the true inheritor of the great British tradition. New Realism in its prevailing aspect is critical, not speculative, often sceptical and incredulous; usually sober and dry. It distinguishes itself by freedom from prejudice and strict attention to facts, by clearness and honesty of thinking. Its attitude to metaphysics is sceptical and sometimes hostile. Religion also it usually refuses to touch, treating it sometimes as a neutral, sometimes as an adversary. It shows little interest in anything which transcends experience or cannot be apprehended by means of clean and honest investigation. Here we see that typically agnostic attitude of mind which is found so often in British philosophers.

This characterization has purposely been expressed in the most general terms. In many respects it needs qualification, especially in regard to the most recent phase of the movement, which appeared most plainly about the end of the war. Only one element need be mentioned here, the growth of the speculative impulse, and of a positive attitude towards the great questions of metaphysics, and in particular to those of religion. Thus attention is turned once more to the totality of being, and the

writes one of my British friends. Reaction against all synthetic, speculative, and constructive philosophizing under the pressure of system and holistic views is in full swing. Thinkers have come down from the "high watch-tower" from which Idealists have philosophized and devoted themselves diligently to tasks of detail in order to cut philosophic building-stones and to dig up problems by their roots. This tendency is indicated by the foundation of a new periodical with the significant title *Analysis*, of which the first number appeared in November 1933 (edited by A. E. Duncan-Jones, with the co-operation of L. S. Stebbing, C. A. Mace, and G. Ryle).

It is to be hoped that this is only a passing distemper and that the philosophic pendulum will soon swing the other way; a change of which there are already visible signs, as later pages will show. Philosophy cannot support itself for long on analysis only; otherwise the saying of Goethe will be fulfilled:

"Dann hat sie die Theile in ihrer Hand,
Fehlt leider nur das geistigte Band."

way is opened again to constructive system-making. The great metaphysical systems of Alexander and Whitehead, which have appeared since the war, are examples of this tendency. Whether this new metaphysics which has sprung out of the movement and which, unlike the idealist metaphysics, has a firm foundation in mathematics and natural science, will lead to pluralist or to monist consequences (the former would agree better with the spirit of New Realism than the latter) is of subordinate importance as compared with the fact that metaphysics has once more become a matter of interest. For the subtle analyses of the theory of knowledge or the unpractical formal exercises of mathematical logic cannot serve for long to nourish a philosophy, however valuable both may be in their own place. The new metaphysical wave is creeping forward and has the task of infusing fresh energy into the New Realist philosophy, of assuring it against the dangers of stagnation and of beating the void. Although this cannot be done without many changes, and though it must be accompanied by some internal transformations, it must conduce to the benefit not only of New Realism but of British philosophy generally, of which it is the chief representative. Apart from metaphysics and religion, the great problems of ethics, a province which, apart from the very specialized inquiries of Moore and others, has been unduly neglected by the new philosophy, must once more be considered. Of necessity, this development will then lead, back or forward, to idealist positions, as some existing indications plainly show. For example, the problem of spiritual being, the depth of which has scarcely been plumbed (since it was always exposed to the danger of naturalistic interpretation), has been developed afresh and spirit must be once more restored to its rights. As we may observe in both camps, the idealist and the realist, the advance of thought has the result that boundary-lines tend to be obliterated, and previous tensions are relaxed, or, as Bosanquet's acute mind perceived, that extremes meet on a middle line. The idealistic impulse which even to-day is not exhausted, although the idealist movement is finished, will then have to embark upon a new errand.

Having regard to the incompleteness of New Realism, I have abstained from grouping its thinkers according to historical or systematic points of view. I have arranged them freely, putting the outstanding personalities first and then passing on to the others.

GEORGE EDWARD MOORE (*b.* 1873)

[Educated at Trinity College, Cambridge; afterwards Fellow of the same College, and Lecturer in Moral Science in the University of Cambridge; since 1925 Professor of Philosophy. *Principia Ethica*, 1903, second edition 1922 (new impression 1929); *Ethics*, 1912 and later editions (in the Home University Library); *Philosophical Studies*, 1922 (containing the famous essay "The Refutation of Idealism" of 1903); "A Defence of Common Sense" (in *Contemporary British Philosophy*, edited by J. H. Muirhead, vol. 2).]

In G. E. Moore we have not only the pioneer of the New Realist movement, but also the driving force and dominating personality in all the further course of its development. He has expressed all that is typical and characteristic of the movement in the purest form and the least intermixed with alien influences and factors. His importance lies not so much in stating and establishing a realistic view of knowledge as in introducing a new method of argument and a very peculiar philosophic attitude, whether resulting from or conditioning it. One might say that he has created a new and individual philosophic type which shows many points of similarity to earlier thinkers, especially to those of the classical British tradition, but which is so different from anything that has gone before that we can accord to it the importance of a prototype. In this sense Moore has influenced a series of other thinkers who have followed in his footsteps.

Moore comes from an intellectual environment quite different from that of most of his philosophical co-operators and followers. The latter have started from mathematics and natural science; but he has come from the classics. Exact philological study of the classics generally has left upon his later work as many traces as has his philosophical study of Plato and Aristotle, and he has learnt as much from the maieutic method of Socrates as from any other. As regards its attitude to standard problems, his thinking is rooted in native British traditions. It has been influenced by Berkeley in the direction of negation and antithesis; by Reid in the direction of positive solutions; by Hume in both directions. Of modern thinkers, Bradley and McTaggart have stimulated him in many ways, though he has always vigorously attacked them. He has learnt much both in matter and method from Brentano and Meinong. But all these contacts with the thought of others are of little importance in respect of his own original independent contribution, which must be judged upon its own merits.

It is significant that Moore's literary production is scanty. Apart from a fairly long and technical book on ethics and a shorter one in a popular series he has produced merely a series of essays for periodicals, the most important of which have been made accessible in the collection of *Philosophical Studies*. These deal almost entirely with logic, theory of knowledge, and ethics; it is these three departments mainly in which his thinking has been productive. Metaphysics and similar topics have been excluded on principle from his inquiries.

Before we deal with the doctrine of this thinker we must express our views on the special manner of his philosophizing and upon the foundations of his method. Here we must first of all speak not of the "what" but of the "how" of his thinking; not about the aim, but about the way. His thinking is always "*en route*"; it is not trying to reach a safe harbour or to harvest as much crop as possible, but is content with breaking up the philosophic soil and with liquefying problems. It is undogmatic, unsystematic, and unspeculative. It is sceptical in contrast to the efforts of system-builders after unity, and mistrustful of any supreme principle to which everything must conform. "To strive for unity and system at the cost of truth, is not the real business of philosophy, although that has been the custom in the practice of philosophers."

The basic tendency of Moore's philosophy thus announces

the strongest reaction against the school of Hegel and protests especially against its dogmatism, its tyrannical system, and its frenzied speculation. Before we can apprehend the unity and connection of things, before we can consider problems and concepts in their mutual relations, and in their relation to an encompassing, systematic whole, we must first carefully isolate them from one another, in order to explore their separate existence and peculiar qualities to the utmost and to get clear notions of them. Butler's phrase, prefixed to *Principia Ethica*, "Everything is what it is, and not another thing", is the leading principle which governs all Moore's thinking.

No less characteristic than the isolating study of things in this philosophy is the questioning attitude which it adopts to them. Questioning is its native element, in which it is born, lives, and has its being. In it takes place everything that is important and fruitful in Moore's thought; it is the key to its deepest secret. To it everything is questionable in the literal sense of the word, i.e., worthy of being questioned; and everything depends on whether the question is put rightly at the beginning and whether the questioning process is conducted rightly to a finish. "In all philosophic studies the difficulties and disagreements are mainly due to a very simple cause, the attempt to answer questions before discovering precisely *what* question it is you desire to answer."[1] Here lies the source of countless mistakes, which could easily be removed "if only philosophers would try to discover the true meaning of the question which they put, before they set about answering it".[2] In another passage Moore says:

"I have endeavoured rather to show exactly what is the meaning of the question and what difficulties must consequently be faced in answering it, than to prove that any particular answers are true."[3]

Though we may call Moore the greatest, acutest, and most skilful questioner of modern philosophy, we must add that he is an extremely weak and unsatisfying answerer. When ques-

[1] *Principia Ethica,* Preface.
[2] *Ibid.* [3] *Op. cit.*, p. 223.

tioning is excessively luxuriant, answering must naturally be scanty. Solutions and results are hardly to be expected from Moore, and if they occasionally appear, they are only like crumbs that fall from the master's table. Answers are usually only incitements to new questions, and are therefore only disguised questions, not genuine answers. But in no case must a question be merely a start-off towards a predetermined answer; the meaning of the question is quite autonomous, and is in no way dependent on the answer; the question may possibly carry the answer within itself and the answer may spring out of it at the end of a long journey. Moore therefore is often in complete perplexity regarding the solution of a problem which he has discussed at length with his usual thoroughness and acuteness, or he halts in front of several possible alternatives and leaves it to the reader to choose which he thinks best. We must not be surprised, then, if he says brusquely of a result obtained by painful investigation that it may be utter nonsense, since at the moment of solution new difficulties crop up which may be brought against it.

Evidently this kind of philosophizing is eminently liable to be sicklied o'er with the pale cast of thought and gnawed by the tooth of scepticism. By restoring the true meaning of philosophic questioning, Moore has rendered an inestimable service; he has also put a strong curb upon the exuberant speculations of Hegelianism and Evolutionism, and levelled the path for clean, sober, and practical thinking. But as questioning has become with him an end in itself, and has risen from the position of a technique to that of a fine art, and as its task is that of clarifying problems rather than of solving them, it may evoke admiration but cannot satisfy thought. What Hume said of Berkeley applies to Moore: that all his arguments are purely sceptical, that they admit of no answer and produce no conviction.[1] They confound and agitate the mind, but do not give it peace. They stir up the dust which lies around problems, but they effect no final clarification.

Moore's philosophizing, then, results in an endless chain of

[1] Hume's *Works*, edited by Green and Grose, vol. iv, p. 127.

questions which surround the problem like a swarm of bees, separate, anatomize, disentangle, analyse it and give it precision, pursue it and harry it to its last hiding-place. This over-acute and over-critical thinker is of quite brutal honesty towards himself; he takes nothing upon trust; analyses the simplest and most trivial propositions and cuts them up with the scalpel of his intellect. As a result of this excess of criticism no problem is ever apprehended as a whole and in its systematic relations. It is separated into smaller and smaller parts; but there is no spiritual bond to bind it into organic unity. We have an excessive critical and analytical process of decomposition which leads finally to the complete atomizing and pulverizing of problems.

The best term to describe Moore's method of thought is 'microscopic', in contrast to the telescopic method of the Hegelians. With Moore everything is studied with a strong magnifying glass, so that many details show up which are concealed from the naked eye. This has the disadvantage that wherever the logical microscope is directed, it can examine only a small surface, while everything else remains in obscurity. Thus only separate problems can be studied; these are often probed from various sides till they finally lose themselves in detail or we stand helpless before a number of alternatives. The level of truth thus reached does not go beyond possibilities and probabilities. For the dynamic process of thought is insatiable and will shake even apparently certain results by new objections, or will strengthen and support uncertain results by new evidence. In selecting from the various alternatives, Moore does not so much make a clear decision for or against, but rather weighs the arguments and counter-arguments. As a rule he indicates a preference for one alternative, but he does not completely reject one or adopt another. Thus there results a peculiar contrast between uncompromising efforts at clearness and uncertainty of results. The further the clarification goes the more doubtful is the solution. Critical thinking is inextricably entangled in this antinomy and must renounce a solution, because it cannot sacrifice precision. This means that it can find no satisfaction, but must for ever exhaust itself in a never-resting process.

The importance of Moore's philosophy depends therefore on the method which has been invented by him and employed with such consummate skill. Compared with it the content of his doctrine is inconsiderable. He himself often repudiates earlier 'results', and would like to write his books all over again, when he takes them in hand for a new edition. It is therefore a fruitless undertaking to trace 'stages of development' in his thought and to distinguish several 'periods', each of which represents a new standpoint.[1] Such changes of standpoint can certainly be inferred and documented from Moore's writings, but they are of only minor importance. For the change in Moore's views is not due to the adoption of a new standpoint, conditioned by the facts themselves, but to an acute and consistent method, to its increasing precision, subtlety, and completeness. We should misconstrue the deepest meaning of Moore's thought if we attributed this difficulty to his matter rather than to his method.

This does not imply that several doctrines of Moore's did not influence the development of British philosophy decisively about the end of the century. On the contrary, his teaching was one of the strongest factors in the new movement of thought which arose at the beginning of the new century as a reaction both against idealist and against evolutionist tendencies, and was set in action simultaneously from several sides. In spite of his scanty production and his extreme reserve Moore has given a strong impulse to academic philosophy and contributed in many ways to its fertility. Even to-day he is one of the most influential of British thinkers, whose influence is felt not only in England but in America, especially on the younger generation. But on the continent of Europe he is almost unknown outside technical circles. In conjunction with Russell he is the founder of the school which has arisen in Cambridge and

[1] As Hasan has tried to do in his book *Realism*, 1928, pp. 228–85, where three such periods are distinguished, an idealist-metaphysical, a logical, and a realistic.

has its centre there; and both Russell and Broad own allegiance to him; the former more in respect of matter, the latter more in respect of method. His strict logicality, his unqualified philosophic honesty and sincerity, his effort after perfect clearness and unambiguity, his plain and simple manner of expression, almost free from technical terms, formed an excellent school for a whole generation of philosophic inquirers, which have grouped themselves more or less closely around him, or at least have caught a breath of his spirit.

The doctrine which has influenced Moore's contemporaries most strongly is the realist theory of knowledge, of which he laid the foundations, and which has in him its most impressive representative. He developed it first in his essay "Refutation of Idealism", published in *Mind* in 1903. This is not meant to be a refutation of the idealist world-view as such, but only of the subjectivist theory of knowledge as represented by Berkeley. From this historic essay is usually dated the beginning of the New Realist movement. It was indeed the laying of a foundation-stone. Although Moore has diverged widely from the views there announced, he has persevered in his basic thesis of Realism and tried to build it up and strengthen it by wider researches.

The proof starts from the Berkeleian formula '*esse is percipi*', which is the implicit or overt premise of all idealist theories of knowledge. This formula asserts that everything existent exists only so far as it is experienced (perceived, known, thought of, etc.) or is a content of a consciousness. There is, therefore, between existence and being perceived (Moore concentrates on the problem of perception) a necessary, indissoluble connection, and when the object is made a content of consciousness every distinction between the subjective and the objective is abolished. Moore tries to discover the dangerous fallacy which lies at the basis of this argument. If we have any kind of presentation or sensation we must carefully distinguish two elements: first, the consciousness in relation to which all sensations exist, and secondly the object of consciousness in relation to which every sensation is different from every other.

Consciousness is the element common to all sensations, and always accompanies them. The sensation 'blue' is different from the sensation 'red', and both are different from the sensing consciousness to which they are given alike as objects. We have therefore the sensation 'blue' (consciousness or awareness of something blue) and object 'blue' which are regarded as identical by Idealism. In this identification lies the fatal mistake upon which the whole idealist theory of knowledge is built. The sensation 'blue' and blue itself are not identical, for the former contains more than the latter, i.e. a factor which is also contained in the sensations 'red' and 'yellow'. The object of the sensation is not like the sensation of the object, and therefore the manner of existence of the one is not like the manner of existence of the other. We must therefore apprehend the existence of 'blue' as something quite different from the existence of the sensation of 'blue'; this means that 'blue' can exist without requiring that the sensation of 'blue' should exist.

The subjective factor in the process of sensing is consciousness. Sensing is only a special case of consciousness, just like knowing, experiencing or, as Moore generally says, being aware of something. Being aware stands to something of which it is aware (blue) in a quite peculiar relation. This relation is not that of a thing to a content nor that of a part of a content to another part of it, but is that quite specific relation which is essential to all knowledge and to it only. It is a completely original kind of relation, which cannot be analysed further. We cannot therefore say that when we know 'blue' we have in our consciousness a 'thing' or an 'image' of which 'blue' is the content. To be aware of the sensation 'blue' does *not* mean to be aware of a mental image, and therefore of a 'thing' of which 'blue' and some other element are constituent parts in the same sense in which colour and hardness are constituents of some external object. It means nothing else than to be aware of the awareness of 'blue'. 'Blue' is therefore an object and in no way a mere content of my experience, in the same way as the most independent real thing of which I am aware. We need not puzzle any longer how we get out of the circle of our presentations and sensations to the reality of things. To have a sensation means *ipso facto* to be outside this circle. It means knowing something which as being real is not a part of our experience. Knowledge in the sense of awareness of something is therefore always of such a kind that its object is just the same whether we are aware of it or not. We are as immediately aware of the existence of material things as of that of our own feelings. Both possess the same degree of evidence. Thus Moore's famous refutation of Idealism ends in a commonplace, to the effect that, when we know, we know something, and that which we know cannot be the same as our knowledge. Nevertheless, this plain and simple argument was destined to show itself extremely fruitful in the future. Although towards the end of the last century several realistic essays had appeared (see Chapter III), Moore's thesis was the first to set going the new movement which shortly after was taken up by Russell, Kemp Smith, Alexander, Broad, Laird, and others, and carried forward with much consistency and unity of aim.

Moore has tried in further studies to build up and deepen the realistic thesis which in distinction from other Realisms has been called 'New Realism'. Of eminent fruitfulness for the theory of knowledge initiated and inspired by him was his doctrine of the transparence of the mental act by help of which we are able to apprehend the objectively real. The relation of knowledge is, as we have seen, a unique relation which is different *toto coelo* from all others. By the term 'knowledge' we mean that purely psychic function of being aware of anything by means of which we apprehend immediately what is objectively given, without the interposition of representative or copying images such as the old theory of knowledge argued for, and which were alleged to interpose themselves like a medium between the act and the object. Awareness lights up objects (sensations, presentations, and material things) as it were from within, shines through them, so that they become transparent or diaphanous. We come immediately into contact with them; they are given to us bodily. Knowing, therefore, means apprehension of the objectively real as such.

With the uprooting of the current representationist or image-theory a decisive step was taken in the new direction. As a result a radical reform had to be made in the doctrine of sense-data. A sense-datum is no longer the subjective image in the mind of something corresponding to it objectively; it is the objective something itself. It enters immediately into the mind; the mind shines through it. Thus every argument, empirical or *a priori*, is baseless which purports to show that sensa[1] cannot exist at the times when they are not being experienced. Why should not sensa persist when we shut our eyes or leave the room, provided that the physical conditions remain unchanged? This view not only rests upon a strong instinctive belief, but there are no logical or other arguments against it. It can therefore be regarded as established, although with that merely relative certainty which belongs to all philosophic knowledge.

Moore has taken up the problem of perception and especially that of sense-data and their relations on the one side to the knowing mind and on the other side to physical things in many acute and penetrating phenomenological analyses. By his subtle chisel-work he has shown a series of new aspects in the problem and so made an important contribution to clarifying it, although characteristically he reaches no final result. Compared with all this fine-drawn and painfully exact distinction-finding, all earlier studies of the problem seem to be coarse and rudimentary. One of these trains of argument runs as follows[2]: When I make the perceptual judgment 'this is my hand' I make in the first place a statement about the sensum which is directly given to me, and in the second place about a thing of the external world which I call 'my hand'. Now it is evident that sense-datum and thing, even if I, as Moore does, treat the first as belonging to objective reality no less than the second, are not identical. For the sensum to which the judgment in the strict sense is first related is not my whole hand, but merely that part

[1] This term was introduced by Broad, and has been generally adopted. Moore usually speaks of 'sensibles' or 'sense-data'.

[2] *Philosophical Studies*, No. VII.

of the upper surface of my hand which I directly perceive, and is therefore not the thing as such, but a quite determinate partial aspect of it. So much in general may be conceded. Moreover, Moore regards it as certain that I do not perceive 'my hand' directly; but that when I say I perceive it, I am perceiving something which merely represents it, viz. a certain part of its upper surface. Therefore, if I would express myself precisely, I should say 'This is a part of the upper surface of my hand' and not 'This is my hand'. In any case the demonstrative pronoun 'this' has a different sense in each of these propositions. But now the question arises *what* do I really know about the sense-datum in question when I say, it is a part of the upper surface of my hand. Do I mean to say that it is *itself* a part of this upper surface or that this is not so? In the latter case, then, does it stand only in a definite relation to the part of the upper surface, which possibly is like that which exists between partial aspect and thing (i.e. is representative)?

Moore regards these alternative answers as possible, and between them he makes no definite decision, though the pros and cons can be estimated fairly exactly. The first answer, which has already been alluded to, is that the sensum itself is a part of or is identical with the hand's upper surface. This would mean that I do not perceive *directly* 'my hand' but a part of its upper surface; and therefore that the sense-datum is itself this part and not merely something which stands for or represents it. This view, which Moore thinks very plausible and for which he has a certain preference, encounters difficulties in regard to the phenomenon of double vision. In such a case we certainly have two sense-data, each of which claims to be part of the upper surface; whereas they cannot both be identical with the upper surface *of* which they are sense-data. Thus we come to the second view which stands rather nearer to the old representation-theory. According to this the sense-datum is not itself a part of the upper surface of my hand, but stands in a certain relation to it which Moore regards as original and not further analysable, and of which he merely says that it is such that the sense-datum is an appearance or manifestation of the upper surface of the thing. Moore's theory is therefore representative only in so far as the part of the thing which is directly perceived is representative of the whole thing (and therefore of its non-perceived aspects); but it is not representative in regard to the relation of the sensum to the thing or aspect of the thing. This relation is either that of identity (identity of thing-aspect and sensum) or that of non-identity. In the latter case the relation cannot be more closely determined, because it is an original relation. If the first and second answers are rejected, there remains a third which coincides essentially with Mill's doctrine of permanent possibilities of sensation. According to this the proposition 'This is a part of the upper surface of my hand' means in reference to the sense-datum neither that it is itself this part, nor that it stands in a definite relation to this part, but merely a series of hypothetical facts which we may perhaps express as follows: 'if certain non-realized conditions in the past had been fulfilled, I should then have had certain perceptions, which I have not had; or if certain conditions, which may or may not be realized in the future, were of this kind, then I should have certain experiences.' Against this view some weighty objections may be raised, so that it has at most a certain probability but no unconditioned certainty. The solution of the problem remains open in spite of the most penetrating analysis; apart from the clarification of the matter no proper decision is reached. The intensity of the clarifying process not merely fails to help us to a solution, but even debars us from it.

To sum up we may mention as the most important points of Moore's inquiries into theory of knowledge, on which depends mainly his deep influence upon contemporary thinking, the following. First, the shattering of the equation *esse* = *percipi* (or *percipere*) which exposes the *proton pseudos* of Idealism. *Esse* is freed from the fetters of *percipi* and rendered independent. The existence of a thing does not depend upon its being perceived, and this being-perceived does not imply existence necessarily, still less include it. Perception takes place quite immediately, by direct apprehension of the objectively real, not by the mediation of psychic images which represent the thing "in the mind". But what we apprehend directly in this way are not the things themselves, but sensa or shadowy partial aspects of things from which we form conclusions as to the whole thing or to the real objects as such. All perceptual judgments contain much more than the purely sense-given perceptual object; they are also a disclosure of the non-given or the possibly-given by means of the immediately given, of the whole by means of the partial aspect, or the thing by means of the sense-datum. Finally, we must not regard consciousness as a kind of container into which presentations, sensations, etc., can be thrown like nuts into a sack, but as a purely functional act through which the object is immediately apprehended and made transparent. Although Moore, through the whole course of his inquiries, holds fast to the principle of Realism, its basis becomes ever narrower under the increasing closeness of study. The more the main force of the inquiry centres upon sense-data, the more problematical becomes the reality of things. The result is that Moore gets nearer and nearer the sensationalist Phenomenalism associated with Berkeley and Hume which at the beginning of his philosophic career he set out to attack. That the fact that sensory phenomena hold a predominant place in the discussion is much more important than the diverse interpretation of their mode of existence, and Moore's thought finds its way back to the old British tradition, which suggests that his starting-point was not so far distant from it. In fact, in general the whole movement of New Realism in spite of divergent results in detail and in spite of frequently emphasized opposition does not by its inward structure imply a break with the old tradition, but rather carries it on more strongly and purposefully.

Moore links himself directly to this tradition, and to that Scottish form which diverges from the main line of development and is embodied in the philosophy of Thomas Reid and his school. Like Reid he undertakes in an essay a "Defence of Common Sense", i.e. a recognition of that original knowledge which precedes all inferred and derived knowledge and to which the philosopher is as much bound, and which he calls as much his own, as the plain man. Moore enumerates a series of such evident truths or commonplaces in which the healthy human understanding believes unshakably, although they are often challenged by the philosopher and condemned as wrong. Moore takes himself to be one of those thinkers who regard as unconditionally true the world-picture of common sense at least in its basic features. In any case the propositions on which this world-picture rests must be taken in their ordinary or popular sense. Then and only then is all doubt about their truth banned. So it appears that there are many propositions which we know and understand and the meaning of which is quite unambiguous without our being able to give account of them. Different from the immediate understanding of such commonplaces and belief in their truth is their correct analysis and rational establishment. It is true that we understand the meaning of these propositions but we do not know in what way and for what reasons we know them. We cannot analyse them, and every attempt to anatomize them exactly meets with the greatest difficulties. We must therefore accept them just as they are, without troubling ourselves too much about their philosophical justification. To speak of them with contempt, as so many philosophers do, Moore declares to be the height of absurdity. Here we have a sort of refounding of Reid's philosophy of common sense, strange to say from a thinker whose high critical, analytical, and sceptical powers are hardly inferior to those of Hume, against whose attack upon the views of common sense Reid's defence was directed.

In the field of ethics Moore's ideas have had less success than in that of theoretical philosophy, although in his only two published books[1] he has given special attention to it and has developed it more systematically and consistently than the other. Here also he is the keen and inexorable analyst who goes on his own way independently of all standpoints and cosmologies and of all traditional opinions. Although he has constructed no system, he has tried earnestly by careful

[1] The *Philosophical Studies* is merely a collection of essays from periodicals.

critical analysis to make plain the foundations of ethical thinking and to disclose the problems. He has thoroughly broken up the soil of ethics and has done admirable work in clearing the ground without troubling much about positive results. When any such results do emerge they are generally disintegrated by criticism. In this field Moore is careful to abstain from all dogmatic insistence upon his ideas.

By the term ethics Moore understands the investigation of the question 'What is good' (or bad)? How to define good is the basic problem of any ethics which can claim to be scientific. To adduce valid reasons why we regard this or that as good is the object of ethics. Moore's surprisingly simple answer is, good is good and nothing more. "Good cannot be defined, and that is all that I have to say about it", he declares categorically. This means that 'good' is the name of a simple and unanalysable quality as much as 'yellow.' Both are free of all complexity, and as it is only complex objects that can be defined, the power of definition is checked before such perfectly simple ideas. Good is itself and nothing else. It discloses itself from its own inner essence and cannot be apprehended by determinations derived from any other source. But it is only the predicate 'good' that is indefinable, not 'the good' or the whole of that which possesses this predicate.

The attempt to define 'good' externally or by determinations which are not drawn from its own essence is called by Moore the 'naturalistic fallacy'. Instances of it are those theories which say that 'good' is that which is useful, or what is desired, or produces pleasure. There must therefore be a strict distinction between 'good as means' and 'good in itself'. The first means that the object in question is merely a means to the good or produces good effects; the latter that 'good' is an end in itself and that the object itself possesses the quality 'good', which we in the former case had ascribed to its effects. The two questions, what is the best in itself and what will produce the best possible, are quite different and should be kept absolutely separate.

From this point of view Moore subjects all ethical doctrines infected by the naturalistic fallacy to a penetrating and annihilating criticism. Among these are to be numbered both the naturalistic and the metaphysical theories. Moore calls those theories naturalistic which in the place of 'good' put a property of a natural object and thereby substitute a natural science for ethics. A classical example of this is Spencer's Evolutionism. Spencer sees the good in that which is more highly developed and identifies it with the pleasing. But Moore aptly observes that 'more highly developed' has nothing to do with 'morally better' and that the concept of evolution can throw no light on the basic question of ethics. This holds good equally for all other varieties of Hedonism and therefore for all theories which are built on the principle that pleasure is the only thing which is good in itself. Moore's criticism is directed not only against Spencer's evolutionist Hedonism but against Mills' utilitarian and Sidgwick's intuitionist Hedonism and also against all ethical systems which can possibly be built on this basis; it is his delight to develop the standpoints of his opponents independently of any historical forms of expression in typical purity and to refute them. Thus the great chapter on "Hedonism" (in *Principia Ethica*) offers to us a general settlement with all the forms of the traditional British Ethics such as has often been undertaken from the idealist side; with this difference, however, that the idealist refutations apply to these systems an alien criterion, namely, their own position; whereas Moore's critical explication proceeds from within outwards and rests merely on the criterion of the autonomy of the basic ethical principle.

In reference to the ethical systems based on metaphysical assumptions (the Stoics, Spinoza, Kant, Hegel and the Hegelians), Moore tries to show that they can give no answer to the question, What is good in itself? They also give ethics a heteronomous foundation, by measuring good in each case by their supreme metaphysical principle, which usually involves a relation to a super-sensible reality. Moore therefore refuses to allow metaphysics any more than naturalism to interfere in ethics. Green's *Prolegomena to Ethics* is as far as Spencer's

Data of Ethics from making the least contribution to solve ethical problems.

The result reached so far has been purely negative, and comes to this, that the essence of good is not to be apprehended either by means of pleasure or by any metaphysical principle. But there arises the positive question, what good is intrinsically. This question is connected by Moore with the problem of value which he has dealt with in a separate essay (see *Philosophical Studies*, pp. 253 ff.). Value and value-characters are above all not subjective; they do not spring from a mental attitude of the individual towards the things designated as valuable, but belong to the things themselves and are given with them, and so are objective. The concept of objectivity is not, however, enough to determine them; their special characteristic is what Moore calls their 'intrinsicality'. When we call a kind of value intrinsic this means that the question whether and in what degree a thing possesses this value depends entirely upon the inner nature of that thing. But from other intrinsic qualities of things, such as their colour-qualities, the value-predicates are distinguished by this fact, that they are not themselves intrinsic qualities but merely depend upon them. We must, therefore, in order to determine positively the intrinsically good or valuable, consider what value the things in question have when they exist quite separately from all other things. The method according to which this takes place is that of absolute isolation.

Moore defends the view that by far the most valuable things which we know are certain states of consciousness which we experience in our personal affection for our fellow-men, and in enjoyment of the beautiful in art and nature. These things before all others must be credited with intrinsic value and more than all others they are worthy of pursuit for their own sakes. It is true that the mere presence of anything beautiful has a certain intrinsic value, but in the highest sense a thing does not acquire value till *consciousness* or enjoyment of the beautiful is connected with it. In this simple truth, which is generally recognized as such, Moore sees the basic truth of all moral philosophy. The things just mentioned he regards as the sole criterion of all social progress and as the final meaning of all human action. They are the *raison d'être* both of all virtues and of all public and private duties. Personal affection and aesthetic enjoyment include in themselves all actual and conceivable highest goods. Moore terms them also highly complex organic unities and puts them under a special principle which plays an important part in his ethics. The principle of organic unities means that the intrinsic worth of a whole is neither identical with the sum of the values of its parts nor proportional to it. Therefore it is possible that a quality possessing value may stand in such a relation to another value-quality that the total value of a whole formed from these parts may be much higher than the mere sum of the parts. Conversely, it may be that such a total value may be smaller in value than the sum of the parts or than one of the parts. Thus Moore puts beauty, or rather the appreciation of it, in immediate relation to the morally good. He defines 'beautiful' ('ugly') as that the admiring contemplation of which is good (bad) in itself. That which is always beautiful is also good. But the good is the more original value, and the beautiful is not identical with the good, but stands in close connection with it. The case is similar with personal affection as the basic value of all social relations of men to each other. In contrast to idealist ethics, Moore finds a place for the material qualities of things in the system of values. They also, though they may be without value in themselves, are essential constituents of the moral order, so far as they are known by a human consciousness. Knowledge and knowing also, though they themselves are not values, contribute in a high degree to the realization of value. What we as moral personalities attain by our efforts is and remains the good in itself; and the ethical ideal is nothing other than the *summum bonum* or the good in its highest realization.

This realist ethics combines with its healthy feeling for real life a lofty conception of ethical values. In its attitude and temper it rises high above all naturalistic ethical systems, and in many respects draws near to the ethics of Idealism.

But it keeps free from passion and enthusiasm and avoids no less the severity of rigorism when it pursues the too highly pitched aim of a pure morality of duty.

BERTRAND A. W. RUSSELL (*b.* 1873)

[Educated privately. From 1890 student at Trinity College, Cambridge; 1895, Fellow of the College; 1910, Lecturer. In 1916, because of his pacifist propaganda and his support of conscientious objection, he was removed from his teaching post and afterwards prosecuted for the same reasons and condemned to imprisonment. Russell took up politics, travelled widely in China, Russia, and America, and in 1927 opened a private school. His great literary activity in various fields was undertaken partly to earn a living. In 1931, on the death of his elder brother, he succeeded to the peerage as Earl Russell. *German Social Democracy*, 1896; *An Essay on the Foundations of Geometry*, 1897; *A Critical Exposition of the Philosophy of Leibniz*, 1900, reprinted 1937; *The Principles of Mathematics*, vol. 1, 1903; *Principia Mathematica* (in collaboration with Whitehead), 3 vols., 1910–13 (second edition, 1925–7; the Preface and the two introductions translated into German by H. Mokre under the title *Einführung in die mathematische Logik*, 1932); *Philosophical Essays*, 1910; *The Problems of Philosophy*, 1912 (German translation by P. Hertz, 1926); *Our Knowledge of the External World*, 1914 (German translation by W. Rothstock, 1926); *Principles of Social Reconstruction*, 1916 (German translation by M. Hethey, 1921); *Justice in War-Time*, 1916; *Roads to Freedom: Socialism, Anarchism, and Syndicalism*, 1918 (German translation under the title *Politische Ideale* by E. Gumbel, 1922); *Mysticism and Logic and other essays*, 1918; *Introduction to Mathematical Philosophy*, 1918 (German translation by E. Gumbel and W. Gordon, 1923); *The Practice and Theory of Bolshevism*, 1920; *The Analysis of Mind*, 1921 (German translation by H. Grelling, 1927); *The Problem of China*, 1922 (German translation by M. Hethey, 1925); *The A B C of Atoms*, 1923 (German translation by W. Bloch, 1925); "Logical Atomism" (in *Contemp. British Philos.*, vol. 1); *Icarus: or, the Future of Science*, 1924 (German translation by F. Arens, 1926); *The Prospects of Industrial Civilization*, 1924 (German translation by C. Margolin, 1928); *What I Believe*, 1925; *The A B C of Relativity*, 1925 (German translation by K. Grelling, 1928); *On Education*, 1926 (German translation by F. Schnabel under the title *Ewige Ziele der Erziehung*, 1928); *The Analysis of Matter*, 1927 (German translation by K. Grelling, 1929); *Sceptical Essays*, 1928 (German translation under the title *Wissen und Wahn*, by K. Wolfskehl, 1930); *An Outline of Philo-*

sophy, 1928 (German translation under the title *Mensch und Welt*, by K. Grelling, 1930); *Marriage and Morals*, 1929 (German translation by M. Kahn, 1930); *The Conquest of Happiness*, 1930; *The Scientific Outlook*, 1931; *Education and the Social Order*, 1932; *Freedom and Organisation*, 1934. Also numerous essays in periodicals, collective volumes, etc.]

Of all British thinkers of the present and the recent past none has made himself talked of so much or has raised so great a cloud of dust as Bertrand Russell. Ever since he grew up he has stood in the focus of English philosophic interest and inquiry. He is the most national, conspicuous, and representative, and also the most controversial and problematic figure of contemporary English or Anglo-Saxon philosophy. He is the chief representative of the thought of the last three decades, the strongest spokesman of the philosophic spirit of the English-speaking world of the present time. No one has advanced more strongly than he beyond the borders of his native land or has established himself more firmly in the world beyond. He is the only British thinker of the age who has an international reputation; the only one whose name is known in all countries. To this extent he has succeeded to the inheritance of Spencer, the last world-famous star in the British philosophic firmament, a star, however, which is always growing dimmer. Witness the numerous translations of his books into foreign languages and the general recognition and appreciation of his work wherever philosophic interest is vigorous. In Germany especially Russell's name is well known, both within and beyond professional circles, and although certain schools of thought close their ears to him, his doctrine already (and in increasing measure) is one of the formative factors of German thought. No fewer than seventeen of his books exist now in German editions, forming a record which puts everyone else into the shade, having regard to the fact that of the books of the more notable British philosophers of to-day only very few are accessible in German.[1] This is the decisive proof of the

[1] Of Schiller, Bradley, and Hobhouse one each; of Green, Bosanquet, McTaggart, Alexander, Moore, Whitehead, Ward, Taylor, and Broad, none at all.

power of his influence and the attraction of his name. But we must not overlook the fact that much of this success is due to the activity of the propaganda which has been made on his behalf and in which he himself has had no small share.

When one speaks of Russell and tries to characterize his personality and work one is forced to use superlatives. He surpasses all his philosophical contemporaries in productivity and indefatigability of literary output. So far about thirty independent books have come from his pen, many of them of considerable scope. To these must be added a whole host of fugitive writings, magazine articles, essays in learned and popular periodicals, academic papers, reviews, contributions to collective works, lectures, etc. He is the type of the cosmopolitan *littérateur* and journalist; he has a strong literary gift, facility of speaking and writing, pleasure in and urge to creation, unbounded receptivity; he is quick to hear what others are saying and ready for change, versatile and restless, full of nervous activity. He is one of the freest spirits in England to-day, fully possessed by his convictions, uncompromising and fanatical to the point of self-sacrifice, courageous and open to the point of offensiveness, free from all regard to authority or dogma, full of contradictions and enigmas, deep and superficial at the same time, exceedingly true to his convictions, but at the same time untrue to himself, and enterprising, a fighter with a sure seat in the saddle and skilful at every kind of attack and defence. His books are never tedious; he has at his command a flowing and stimulating style of writing which is often negligent and *outré*, but always impressive and witty; he loves paradox and sensation, and will produce his effect at any cost. It is difficult always to take him seriously, and it is doubtful whether he himself believes everything that he writes. One must be on one's guard not to fall into his snares. He is a sceptic who plays with things with a superior air; he has a flashing and sparkling spirit which loves to lose itself in ingenuities and amuses itself with the fireworks of its own ideas. But he can also be a fanatic, who bolts with an idea and shrinks from no personal sacrifice to make it victorious. He is ready to run risks and sometimes plays for high stakes; his courage is admirable, and so is the tenacity with which he defends a dangerous outpost. But then again we miss the seriousness which is becoming to a philosopher; and there spring up doubts of his genuineness.

It is impossible to-day to pass a final judgment upon Russell as a man and as a philosopher. His work, apart from the fact that it is not yet finished, is too much involved in the controversies of the day and his personality too much "confused by party-favour and hate". So much only may be said with confidence, that he has long since passed the highest point of his development, and that the curve of his spiritual power is on the downward path. The spectacle of his personality and his work up to the outbreak of the war is much more unified and consistent, and in almost every way more pleasing than what it has been subsequently. Almost all his more important work was done before that time, and almost everything that he has produced subsequently is of far inferior quality. A judgment pronounced at some subsequent time would probably make a sharp distinction between his earlier and later work, and while it would allow to the former a high philosophic rank and a real historical importance, would value the latter less highly. We cannot fail to recognize that he has long ago used up his philosophic capital and no longer lives upon his own resources but in great part upon other men's ideas, which he collects indiscriminately and incorporates with his own thinking. He is unparalleled in his capacity for change. Every few years he comes forward with a new scheme of thought, which he sends up like a trial balloon, arouses the curiosity of the philosophic world, and gives it new riddles to solve. Just as he can surprise us by depth and originality of thought, so he can by superficiality; often he fails just where a decisive question needs a decisive answer. What Troeltsch once said of Scheler, that his philosophy is a strange mixture of acuteness, depth, and frivolity, applies also to Russell, whose kinship with Scheler is evident in other respects also. When we take all this into consideration it becomes difficult to regard him as a truly great and genuine philosopher. He seems more like a dazzling flash which for a short time lights things up brightly and then is as quickly extinguished. His services should not be depreciated; but the future will show that in Russell's case much more chaff must be separated from the wheat than with most other contemporary thinkers who are of the same or approximate rank to him.

About his intellectual development we know all that is worth knowing from Russell himself in *Contemporary British Philosophy* (vol. i, pp. 359 ff.) and in other passages of his books. He never had the classical-humanist education usual in England and came to philosophy by way of mathematics and by reflection on the theoretical bases of that science. In pure mathematics he saw at an early date the best and almost the only possibility of discovering truth and of strict scientific knowledge. At 18 years of age he read Mill's *Logic*, without becoming convinced of the empirical basis of arithmetic and geometry. It was somewhat later that he made contact with Hume, the classical Empiricist. The impression which he received from his teaching was extremely strong, and although he at first entered on quite other paths than the empirical, this impression was only driven underground in order to come out later with greater momentum. Hume's influence on the books of the second period is clearly perceptible, but Russell does not associate empiricist or positivist ideas with him, but the attitude of scepticism. We may see in Russell both the renewer of the chief ideas of Hume's philosophy and also the reincarnation of that philosophic type which was represented in classical form by the Scottish thinker. Hume has reappeared in Russell with all his mental qualities, and even the features characteristic of the Enlightenment are to be found revived in him.

As a student in Cambridge Russell came to know idealist systems. He plunged into Kant and Hegel and above all into Bradley's *Logic*, by which he was so strongly affected that for some years he was a follower of Bradley. Later there was added the influence of McTaggart, who was his contemporary at Cambridge, and who of all the Hegelians stood nearest to his own strictly trained mathematical thinking. Of decisive influence for his further development was his acquaintance with G. E. Moore and his new philosophic method which began in the year 1898 and resulted in a complete change of his way of thinking. Russell recognizes this without reservation in the preface to his *Principles of Mathematics*: "On fundamental questions of philosophy my position in all its chief features is derived from Mr. G. E. Moore." Through Moore, who at that time had published only a few magazine articles, Russell not only became an adherent of the new-realist theory of knowledge, but was powerfully influenced in respect of method. At that time Leibniz also came into his field of view and aroused his interest so strongly that he devoted his first philosophic book to him. The book gave quite a new picture of Leibniz; inasmuch as Russell, with emphatic one-sidedness, laid stress upon that aspect of Leibniz's philosophy which previously had been neglected but corresponded with his own views—the mathematico-logical side.[1]

These were the most important philosophic elements by which Russell's future teaching was determined. There was now needed a further impulse coming from outside philosophy to turn his thoughts into that direction in which he was to do his most distinguished work, that of mathematical logic. The decisive influence was supplied by his participation in the Mathematical Congress in Paris in 1900, which he attended with Whitehead. On this occasion Russell became acquainted with the works of the Italian mathematician Peano and his pupils who were aiming at a new foundation of logic upon a mathematical basis and with the technical appliances of mathematics. Peano was directing his thoughts upon a great field of inquiry which now seemed to open itself to a fruitful and exact investigation, that of the exploration of the theoretical bases of pure mathematics by the help of the new symbolic logic. From this decisive impulse, which was strengthened by

[1] The same view was taken by the almost contemporary studies of Leibniz by Couturat and Cassirer.

his friend Whitehead and deepened by the new mathematical discoveries of Weierstrass, G. Cantor, F. Klein, Dedekind, Frege, and others, grew Russell's epoch-making work on the problems of mathematical logic and their combination into an imposing system. These inquiries were first embodied in the *Principles of Mathematics*, and in co-operation with Whitehead were continued and brought to a temporary conclusion in the three-volume *Principia Mathematica*.[1]

Russell's intellectual development was then practically complete. By referring mathematics to logic and by forming a logistic symbolism he disclosed a wide field of inquiry in which his intellectual gifts could reach their fullest exercise. In this field and this alone lies his really important and original work. But, as we shall see, his work in this field is not in the proper sense philosophic, and as all his later work is of far inferior quality, his title to fame as a philosopher shrinks to relatively small proportions. The huge literary productivity which he developed later, and which bears no proportion to its intrinsic value, should not delude us any more than the great vogue of his books and the exaggerated panegyrics of his supporters.

The new intellectual fields which Russell has conquered in the last two decades and the numerous factors by which his restless and unstable mind has been influenced can only be briefly mentioned here. In the first place, like so many of his philosophic contemporaries he fell under the sway of modern physics. The subject in its full compass was appropriated by him with his characteristic power of receptivity and adaptation. He followed it through all its stages from the first beginnings to the latest discoveries of de Broglie, Schrödinger and Heisenberg, popularized it, and tried to make it philosophically valuable and fruitful. Important though his work in this respect may be, it cannot be compared with that which we owe to the truly philosophic sagacity of Whitehead. In regard to the method and theory of knowledge it was the new positivist

[1] The completion of the work in a fourth volume as originally planned can no longer be expected.

theories of Avenarius, Mach, Vaihinger, and others to which as the legitimate heirs of Hume's Empiricism Russell attached himself almost as closely as to Hume himself. Russell has also learnt much from the German phenomenological school, above all from Meinong, with whom he has had critical discussions, and whom he (with others) has brought to the notice of his British colleagues; also from Brentano and even from Husserl, to whom he approximates in many important points. The specifically new-realist character of his theory of knowledge goes back directly to Moore, but was influenced more remotely by Alexander, Percy Nunn, and others. In regard to metaphysics Russell after long hesitation accepted the theory of so-called neutral Monism as it was first represented by James and later by the group of American New-Realists (above all by R. B. Perry and E. B. Holt). In another respect also James has had a strong influence upon Russell, in that he has affinities both with his Pluralism and his radical Empiricism, with his Psychology and his Pragmatism. In regard to Pragmatism, Russell has made from time to time notable concessions, in spite of his expressed disagreement, so that Schiller once thought he might announce his almost complete conversion to pragmatist doctrine. But in this matter Russell, as his custom is, has not finally settled his position, but maintains his characteristic diplomatic attitude, and keeps a way of retreat open for himself wherever he thinks it desirable. In other ways Russell has appropriated many ideas, old and new, derived from philosophy, from the special sciences, and from other sources, often without regard to the question whether they can easily be assimilated. That he allowed himself to be impressed by psycho-analysis and showed sympathy with "Psychical Research" is not so tragic as that he succumbed almost without resistance to the attractions of Behaviourism. It is not, therefore, surprising that he has no understanding of German Idealism, and that even Greek philosophy, the exact study of which is often considered indispensable in England for philosophic education, has received from him no deep consideration or appreciation. As he is wanting in any historical sense and any regard for work in the field of history he would prefer to wipe out the whole philosophic past and to begin anew; he is even vain enough to think that he can play the part of a new Descartes. Sometimes, when he is less heretically inclined, he raises the war-cry "Back to the XVIIIth Century", and indeed it is there and especially in Hume, who, as we have seen, is his philosophic prototype, that the roots of his intellectual power are to be found. He is essentially a typical, though very belated, son of the Enlightenment. His thinking, radical and new fashioned as it professes to be, thus links itself to the great line of British tradition, the last important member of which it embodies.

A brief survey of his intellectual performance is all that we shall attempt. Preoccupation with pure mathematics and logic, i.e. with inquiries into the foundations of mathematics and criticism of mathematical principles, with logistics, symbolism, and so forth—in short, with mathematical philosophy—occupied a great part of his inexhaustible energy up to the outbreak of the Great War. To this stage belong the early writings on the foundations of geometry, on the philosophy of Leibniz, and the standard works *The Principles of Mathematics* and *Principia Mathematica*, both incomplete, or, we may say, the former continued by the latter, and finally the *Introduction to Mathematical Philosophy*, a supplementary work which saw the light in the enforced leisure of a prison cell. Later Russell turned his back almost completely on this field and only occasionally returned to it. Now for the first time he occupied himself in published books with philosophic problems in the narrower sense. The small but important book *The Problems of Philosophy*, which appeared in a popular series while he had the publication of *Principia Mathematica* still in hand, announced his change of interest. To speak briefly, this consisted in the fact that Russell now left the field of pure *a priori* thinking and descended into the actual world of experience. He now concerned himself with the problems which were set before him by experience both theoretically and practically. In regard to theory there followed a series of publications on theory of knowledge, psychology, the philosophy of nature and of mind, and on the general view of the world, etc., beginning with the book *Our Knowledge of the External World* and an important series of articles continued through several years in the *Monist* ("On the Nature of Acquaintance", "Definitions and Methodological Principles in Theory of Knowledge", 1914, "On the Experience of Time", "Sensation and Imagination", "The Ultimate Constituents of Matter", 1915, "The Philosophy of Logical Atomism", 1918). In them is contained most of what Russell later repeated in elaborate form without adding materially to their content, his latest writings aiming mainly at width of treatment and popularization. Of these we must first mention the two parallel works *The Analysis of Mind* and *The Analysis of Matter*; the former dealing with the whole circle of the problems of knowledge and psychology, the latter reviewing modern physical theories in the light of philosophy. In close connection with these are the two popular books *The A B C of Atoms* and *The A B C of Relativity*. Finally there is the feeble recent book *An Outline of Philosophy*, a thin repetition of *The Analysis of Mind* and *The Analysis of Matter*, and at the same time an attempt to summarize the whole of philosophy systematically; and also one of his last publications, *The Scientific Outlook*. Over and above these, out of the great number of his magazine articles, academic papers, lectures, etc., Russell has collected the most important into three volumes, which have been published at intervals of about ten years; namely, *Philosophical Essays*, *Mysticism and Logic*, and *Sceptical Essays*, in which all sorts of subjects are discussed, especially those of theoretic import.

This is not nearly the full tale of Russell's activity as a writer. He has passed into the field of practice and shows himself as fertile and brilliant as in the theoretic field. Russell has taken up almost all the questions which agitate modern life and expressed himself passionately upon them. Here in particular we see him as a fanatical fighter and uncompromising critic; his free spirit leaves nothing untouched which is consecrated by authority and tradition, by custom, faith, and prejudice.

He is one of the strongest awakeners of the sleeping world which this age has produced, an indefatigable reformer, a transmuter of all social, political, moral, and religious values, with an unshakable belief in his mission and an absolute confidence in his own personality. We cannot here describe fully this side of Russell's work, though it is necessary to complete the picture of his character. We need only say this, that here also Russell's personality does not appear in a uniform light, but in many respects broken and distorted. Sometimes we are compelled to admire his high idealism, his courageous pursuit of truth, his boldness, intrepidity, and other excellent qualities; sometimes he disappoints us by his want of seriousness, his biting irony, his frivolous and trifling handling of things. Viewed upon the whole he seems to us, in spite of his reforming zeal and eagerness for novelty, to be more retrograde than progressive, just because he is preoccupied with the ideas of the XVIIIth-Century Enlightenment and the XIXth-Century Liberalism. He pays homage to the ideals of cosmopolitanism and internationalism, individualism and pacifism, and in his passionate struggle against war in his nation's hour of need by refusing to do military service he adopted as his own the pacifist cause, and supported it with all his might. To his credit it must be said that he was moved by no personal advantage; but in freedom of conscience he saw a higher ideal than the plain duty of the individual to serve his country whenever it may call and whatever it may demand. On the other hand, he was one of the few who in the midst of national hatred and national blindness wished that the enemy should be fairly treated. Just as at the beginning he came forward with indignation against the cruel spirit of war, so later he opposed the folly and injustice of the dictated peace, the false allegation of war-guilt, the post-war blockade, and so on.

These activities fall almost entirely in his second period, which begins after the conclusion of *Principia Mathematica*, and is characterized by the fact that interest in the practical questions of life now predominates and that theoretic philosophy also has come down from the ether of pure thinking into the "fruitful depth of experience". It begins in its fullness with the outbreak of the Great War, which shook Russell profoundly and turned his spiritual energies in a new direction. Even in earlier years he had occasionally gone into politics, and at the age of 22 he was for a short time attaché at the embassy in Paris. Even in his younger days also he took a lively interest in social questions. In the mid-nineties he spent some months in Berlin studying the German social democratic movement which was later to retire in discredit from the political stage, and dedicated to it his first book *German Social Democracy*. The Great War in addition to intensive journalistic activity and several fugitive pieces called out three considerable books in which Russell defined his attitude to current movements and recorded his political and social ideas, namely, *Principles of Social Reconstruction*, *Justice in War-Time*, and *Roads to Freedom*, together with the pamphlet *Political Ideals* (1918). In the post-war period there followed as fruits of two journeys to Bolshevist Russia and to China the two books *The Practice and Theory of Bolshevism* and *The Problem of China* (the latter in collaboration with his wife). Later he interested himself in the problem of industrialism (in his book *The Prospects of Industrial Civilization*) and above all in questions of education (*On Education* and *Education and the Social Order* and several essays), a province with which he became familiar by experience in the private school which he founded. A sort of personal confession of faith is contained in the little book *What I Believe*, and in the famous, truly pathetic piece "A Free Man's Worship" (written in 1902 and contained in the collections *Philosophical Essays* and *Mysticism and Logic*). To the province of philosophy of life and practical wisdom belong two earlier books, with which this long catalogue may be concluded, viz. *Marriage and Morals* and *The Conquest of Happiness*, in which the fine literary gifts of Russell's mind soar skywards like sparkling fireworks.

Russell's attitude to philosophy, its nature, method, tasks, and aims, has been determined by the changes through which his thinking has passed. Through all these changes he has held fast to its scientific character and by this idea of science he always guides his course on whatever path he finds himself. For this reason he excludes from philosophy all romance and mysticism, all pathos and heroism, and finally all moral and religious purposes. "It is, I maintain, from science, rather than from ethics and religion, that philosophy should draw its inspiration," he says in one passage.[1] And in another: "Philosophy has erred in applying heroic remedies for intellectual difficulties . . . and so I have been led to doubt whether philosophy as a study distinct from science and possessed of a method of its own is anything more than an unfortunate legacy from theology."[2] Philosophy, therefore, is a very sober, dry, and passionless affair, a matter of the understanding and not of the heart, the unprejudiced and objective inquiry for truth with the means and the methods of the exact sciences. Russell closely follows Moore, to whom he is philosophically more indebted than to anyone else, in understanding philosophy as being primarily the criticism of knowledge and sees its value not so much in the answers which it can give to definite questions, as in the questions themselves by which thought is stimulated and urged forward. "Philosophy, if it cannot *answer* so many questions as we could wish, has at least the power of *asking* questions which increase the interest of the world and show the strangeness and wonder lying just below the surface, even in the commonest things of daily life."[3]

This view we may term the Socratic, since in that old Greek thinker it had its first and supreme embodiment. But athwart this comes another view which does not fully agree with it, soon gains the upper hand, and is decisive for all the early period of Russell's thinking. This is determined by the idea of strictly scientific character, which finds its pattern primarily in mathematical knowledge and its method. All scientific philosophy stands therefore under the banner of mathematics, or, as Russell

[1] *Mysticism and Logic*, 1916, p. 98.

[2] *Contemporary British Philosophy*, vol. I, p. 361.

[3] *The Problems of Philosophy*, pp. 24 f.

finally comes to think, under the banner of logic. All other philosophy, such as we have in the systems of Plato, Spinoza, and Hegel, has arisen from ethical or religious motives. It is subjective opinion and not objective truth; and Russell pushes it aside, regarding it rather as a hindrance than a help to genuine scientific philosophizing. This mathematicism determines Russell's position to the end of *Principia Mathematica*, and in some degree later also. If philosophy is organized according to the ideas of mathematics, or of a new logic which is to be created and closely connected with mathematical ways of thought, it must be a deductive system from general ideas or relations which depends upon a few unanalysable assumptions or axioms. For the rest it proceeds according to the strict laws of mathematics and logic whose methods it uses. This means that philosophy, like pure mathematics, is a strictly *a priori* science, that it concerns itself solely with quite general and abstract concepts and constructions, and that it does not assume the existence of any real being. Complete exclusion of the really existent or empirical world from its field is the main characteristic of this view of philosophy, which Russell expresses by saying that it is not the science of the real but of the possible, not of existence but of being.

Thus philosophy separates itself from all empirical existence, and from all relation to actual experience. Like Husserl's phenomenology, it is indifferent to existence; i.e. everything existential is "bracketed" (a technical term of Husserl's) or shut out from it. Here Russell adopts a similar ἐποχή to Husserl's, although it is less the product of reflection and is less based upon the idea of philosophy itself. Philosophy is the investigation of the *a priori* and generally valid conditions of all possible worlds. Its conclusions are therefore valid for our actual world as for any other which we can possibly think of. This *a priori* philosophy independent of any assumption of actuality and equivalent to pure logic is therefore by no means a creation of purely subjective thinking, but is a strict necessity of thought, the objectivity of which is based upon the very fact that it need not presuppose any kind of actual, i.e. contingent world, but only the totality of all possible worlds which can be thought of as actual. It is evident that here we have before us ideas borrowed from Leibniz, who is to be regarded as the spiritual ancestor of all modern attempts to create a mathematical or logistic philosophy.

The regulation of philosophy by pure logic and pure mathematics, its general and *a priori* character, its deductive-analytic method, and its limitation to the world of ideal being, represent, however, only one side of the task of philosophy. This kind of philosophy shuts Russell in too narrowly, and although it accorded with his ideal, it was too formal, too abstract, and too alien to life, too much wanting in blood and sap, to allow him to go forward with it long. Hunger for experience and desire for living contact with the world forced him to a compromise and brought him down from the proud heights of pure thought to the dim lowlands of experience. He himself acknowledged later that he could not attribute very great importance to the abstract inquiries of his youth. Thus arose a sharp severance between his earlier and his later work, and his conception of philosophy changed correspondingly. To put it briefly, it became traditional; it concerned itself with the customary problems and the usual objects of inquiry. It is true that it still gave the precedence to the sphere of theory, and where increasingly it turned to other fields (ethics, education, politics, civic, social, economic, religious, and other questions) it did not do so with strictly philosophical purposes, but with free literary treatment and exempt from the pressure of any system. Like Nietzsche he jeers at the professional philosopher's slavery to system. He rejects elaborate system-building as being a falsification of truth and as doing violence to facts; and he has himself never troubled about such a thing, just because he would have had to change his system so often. Philosophizing he regards as honest inquiry, while system-making seems to him to be a snare and an adventure which cannot justify itself before the scientific conscience. Thus in his later work he moved ever further along the path of experience, and this implied a close sympathy both with the sciences and with the empirical philosophy. His thought placed itself upon the paths of the British tradition which it now continues in a direct line. It became, moreover, quite in accordance with the tradition, critical, sceptical, and agnostic. In all this it takes over the inheritance of Hume and Mill, and continues it in the light of the progress of the sciences and with the refinements of the new philosophical methods. But in this it is no longer as original and creative as before. Russell the pure logician deserves precedence over Russell the empiricist; it is only the work of the former that marks a stage in the history of British thought and will continue to live in it, however far from it Russell himself has now moved.

Of the nature of his early field, and of the character of his contribution to it, I must give a brief indication. I shall say something later about its historical connections (see pp. 705 ff.). The new mathematical logic, which is also called pure logic, logic of relations, logistics, symbolic logic, or, more briefly, symbolics, was, after a series of more or less important preliminary contributions by others, given a foundation, and completed in its most important parts, by Russell and Whitehead. Russell's work on this extends from about 1900 to 1913, when the final volume of *Principia Mathematica* was published. This book is the generally recognized standard work of the new study; it comprises altogether 2,000 pages and certainly forms one of the greatest efforts of thinking of which our age can boast.

Russell's new logic is mathematical logic, and that expresses its specific difference as contrasted with every other kind of logic which we can call philosophical. It is true that often it shows a tendency to part from its foundation and to develop and shape itself into a relatively independent science which is special rather than general. Thereby mathematical logic has taken the last step; it has broken all the links uniting it to philosophy, and has become a completely independent special study. It is a branch of mathematics, and finds its home in the system of the mathematical sciences. This is due to the fact that it has been practised mainly by mathematicians, and although philosophers like Russell, Whitehead, Broad, and others have been interested in it, this is an accidental personal union rather than a necessary one. It certainly is a different matter, when subsequently, as in Russell's case, the links with philosophy are restored. But for this also there is no necessity, and it occurs more in contradiction to its pure idea than as a development in accordance with its proper meaning. This is admitted by Russell himself repeatedly, though with qualifications. "Mathematical logic, even in its most modern form, is not *directly* of philosophical importance except in its beginnings. After the beginnings it belongs rather to mathematics than to philosophy" (see *Our Knowledge of the External World*, p. 50). The further developments, he goes on to say, though not properly philosophical, are of great indirect use in philosophizing. Still plainer is the following admission in the preface to the *Introduction to Mathematical Philosophy*. "Much of what is set forth in the following chapters is not properly to be called 'philosophy', though the matters concerned were included in philosophy so long as no satisfactory science of them existed. . . . A book dealing with those parts may, therefore, claim to be an *introduction* to mathematical philosophy, though it can hardly claim, *except where it steps outside its province*, to be actually dealing with a part of philosophy" (italics mine). The new logic is, he continues, concerned with philosophy only so far as it declares a great part of the traditional philosophy to be futile and shows the insufficiency of its methods and the untenability of very many of its solutions. It therefore withdraws a series of problems from philosophy, which for a long time has treated them unsatisfactorily (e.g. the problem of infinity and continuity), and takes them into its own charge. After these definite assertions we must meet with scepticism all attempts to show that the new study is relevant to philosophy.

Mathematical logic, therefore, so far as it remains true to itself, has little or nothing to do with philosophical inquiry in the ordinary sense. But it also draws a sharp line of division between itself and that study to which it stands nearest, viz. logic. Everything with which logic hitherto has concerned itself either falls outside its province or is taken over in a completely changed form and restated according to its own ideas. This applies both to the formal logic of Aristotle (with all its developments to the present day) and to the transcendental logic of Kant, the metaphysical logic of Hegel and Bradley, the empirical logic of Mill, and any other there may be. Of all these it is nearest to formal logic, however strongly it may attack its previous form. For it is itself in every respect thoroughly formal; it moves wholly in the realm of pure forms and relations and has nothing to do with the content which fills them. For this reason it is also called relational logic. Thus in its general purpose it agrees with the classical logic of tradition, but goes far beyond syllogistic logic and deals not only with the relation of subject and predicate (for which reason the former logic is often called by Russell subject-predicate logic), but investigates the whole sphere of logical relations and reduces them to their purely formal elements, or, as Russell says, to the logical constants. Logistics therefore implies a huge extension of the field of formal logic. To the traditional practice of logic, which more and more kept turning about its own axis and became rigid and barren, it brought fresh energy and opened the way to new scientific perspectives and possibilities of investigation. "The old logic put thought in fetters, while the new logic gives it wings",[1] says Russell with justifiable pride. It implies an advance in the theoretical field like that of the work of Galileo in the physical; for it is the first to let us know what problems are capable of solution and what problems should, as being illusory, be thrown upon the scrap-heap. Moreover, it supplies us with a method by means of which the genuine problems can be brought to real solutions. In respect of the works of Russell and the other logisticians, the peremptory judgment of Kant that logic has made no essential advance since Aristotle must now be revised. Mathematical logic has in point of fact made such an advance and it has introduced a new era of logical inquiry.

It was said above that the new logic is a branch not so much

[1] *Our Knowledge of the External World*, p. 68.

of philosophy as of mathematics. The converse also of this proposition is true, that mathematics is a branch of this logic; that is, pure mathematics (arithmetic, analysis, pure geometry, the theory of number, etc.) is a branch of pure logic. Russell's doctrine has arisen from reflection on the theoretical bases of mathematics. In this way he came to the decisive thought that mathematics and logic are at bottom identical, and that all mathematical axioms without exception can be reduced to logical principles. This whole way of thinking results in a logicizing of mathematics, and this conversely results in a mathematicizing of logic. But logic is always primary, and mathematics so far as it can be derived from logic is secondary. Moreover, the boundary between the two sciences is so completely obliterated that, as Russell says, one cannot be sure where in *Principia Mathematica* logic ends and mathematics begins. Thus it is the basic idea of the new doctrine that all pure mathematics can, with the help of the logic of relations, be deduced from certain axioms and ideas of formal logic without assuming any new undefined ideas or unproved propositions. Pure mathematics must contain no indefinable quantities apart from the logical constants and consequently no unproved premisses or propositions apart from those which rest exclusively upon logical constants and variables. All mathematical constants are of a logical character; so that when once the logical system is accepted, the whole structure of mathematical doctrine can be deduced from them.

As a result of the basic recognition of the identity of mathematics and logic the essence of mathematics can be determined unambiguously and clearly. Russell's view is opposed especially to the Kantian, which he regards as infected with a fatal mistake, and is to be traced back in essentials to Leibniz. Kant had denied the strictly formal character of mathematics and had said that mathematical knowledge consists of synthetic judgments *a priori*. Moreover, he had both in arithmetic and in geometry assigned an important part to perception, by basing the former upon the pure perceptual form of time, the latter upon that of space. Against this Russell emphasizes the purely analytic and strictly formal character of mathematical propositions. Like logical propositions they are valid independently of all existence; they are completely indifferent to existence or reality, and they need neither contents nor objects. They remain valid even though there were no actual world or, what is the same thing, they can be applied to all possible worlds or to all possible objects. They are completely general and abstract, and they can without any assistance from perception be deduced from each other by purely logical means. Of decisive importance are always the purely formal logical relations which prevail between mathematical propositions and can be gathered or deduced from them. Their basic form is hypothetical; *if* this or that premiss is fulfilled, then there follows with necessity this or that conclusion; or, *if* a proposition is true, then some other proposition is also true. Moreover, Russell (adhering to a dictum of Wittgenstein) speaks of mathematical inference and proof as tautological (which means much the same as analytical). This merely means that every mathematical proof moves according to a purely logical procedure, and that therefore it is nothing but a tautological transformation of that which is contained in the premisses. From any system of presuppositions nothing can be educed but what this system includes in the way of logical relations. Our knowledge, therefore, is not increased or extended to new contents by mathematics, as its tautological determinations are completely empty of content; that is, they are valid solely because of their form. But all this applies only to pure mathematics and not to applied mathematics which Russell rigorously distinguishes from the other kind. We see that in all this the former separation of mathematics from logic is drastically abolished; or, as Russell says, logic becomes increasingly more mathematical, and mathematics more logical. "They differ as boy and man; logic is the youth of mathematics, and mathematics is the manhood of logic."[1]

It is enough to have made plain the basic principle of logistics, viz. the reduction of all mathematical axioms to a

[1] *Introduction to Mathematical Philosophy*, 1919, p. 194.

few fundamental logical ideas. Everything else belongs to detailed execution and lies outside our scope. Only two points call for further notice: one is the doctrine of antinomies, the other the meaning of symbolics or the logical calculus. An important task of the new logistics consists in the effacement of those paradoxes or contradictions which in inquiries into the foundations of mathematics appear at various points (e.g. in the theory of number) and cannot be solved by purely mathematical means. It turns out that these paradoxes are not really mathematical at all, but may be reduced to general logical antinomies. Thus the problem belongs to logic, which, however, at first was not in a position to solve these antinomies. Russell has pointed out a new path. He has succeeded by discovering and applying a very acute and difficult procedure in removing the contradictions (in his own opinion completely, in that of others only partially) and in putting logic (and therefore also mathematics) on an impregnable basis. This procedure is the well-known theory of the hierarchy of types by the help of which logic is freed from all antinomies and should be reduced to a few contradictionless axioms which cannot be deduced from anything (such are the axioms of infinity, selection, and reducibility). Thus at last mathematics is shown to be a completely contradictionless and scientifically unassailable system, and the final reduction of every mathematical proposition to the axioms of logic is completed.

A science which, like logistics, aims at the highest possible degree of rigour, purity, and exactitude cannot, however, use the customary terminology, but must forge for itself a terminological instrument of its own which is suited to meet its demands. Ordinary terminology would be much too stiff and clumsy and vague and burdened with too many presuppositions and prejudices to allow it to express the very fine shades of meaning in logical relations and reasonings with which these inquiries are concerned. Here also mathematics, with its strict and exact language of signs, is the model for the new logic. Thus logisticians have worked out a mode of expressing concepts similar to that of mathematics but suitable to their own purposes, by inventing a great number of symbolic signs and forms by means of which their deductions and proofs may reach the same degree of sureness and unambiguity as those of mathematicians. This notation, the logical calculus, is a kind of calculative operation with symbols, such as is familiar to us in mathematics. The writings of logisticians, therefore, on many pages look like mathematical text-books. Russell (with his collaborator Whitehead) has worked hard at the formation of a language of symbolic signs. He has taken over the well-advanced preliminary work of Peano and supplemented it with the systems of Frege and Schröder. But a good part of his symbolism is of his own invention, for as compared with his predecessors he has so greatly enlarged the field of inquiry that he has had to think of new signs for many concepts which had never before been treated symbolically. In any case, Russell is one of the greatest experts in forming and handling the logical calculus of which he has given a classical formulation which has not been surpassed. In this province also he has contributed more to meeting Leibniz's demand for a universally valid terminology for logical ideas or *characteristica universalis* than any of his predecessors or successors. By this logically complete terminology, of which he says that it consists only of syntax and has no vocabulary, scientific ideas should be freed from all fogginess; sharp and concise designations should take the place of the vaguenesses and indefinitenesses of ordinary speech, and a series of problems should be stripped of the veil of mystery which has enveloped them for centuries; they should be dragged out of the bog of endless controversies and brought to an exact and final solution.

At all times it is the clearness and purity, the strictness and sharpness, the impersonality and universal validity of mathematics which form the ideal of Russell's thinking and investigations. From time to time he indulges in a quite enthusiastic admiration of this cold and sober science, as the following quotation shows: "Mathematics, rightly viewed, possesses not only truth, but supreme beauty—a beauty cold and austere, like that of sculpture, without appeal to any part of our weaker nature, without the gorgeous trappings of painting or music, yet sublimely pure and capable of a stern perfection such as only the greatest art can show. The true spirit of delight, the exaltation, the sense of being more than man, which is the touchstone of the highest excellence, is to be found in mathematics as surely as in poetry" (*Mysticism and Logic*, p. 60).

The rest of Russell's philosophy, which ranges through the whole field of theoretic knowledge (psychology, theory of knowledge, theory of science, philosophy of nature and metaphysics) lacks the resolution, sureness of purpose, and directness which distinguish his logical inquiries. As he often changes his standpoint and allows himself to be determined by every possible external influence, the interlacing paths of its thought with its manifold discontinuities, transformations, and interpolations could be described only by a detailed inquiry showing the history of its development. But this would go far beyond the limits of the present work, and so we must content ourselves with indicating the essential lines of thought from some arbitrarily selected points of view.

First comes the problem of knowledge, in the centre of which, in accordance with British tradition, stands the problem of sense-perception. Here arises the question: How do we construct the external or physical world which is not given to us immediately, but is mediated by the senses? By the term external world Russell does not mean the world of the plain man, but that of physics or natural science, expressing no opinion about its metaphysical status. 'Physical' according to Russell means simply that 'which is dealt with in physics'. The problem reduces itself in the last resort to the question of the mutual relations between the world of the senses and the world of natural science or of the applicability of mathematical physics to sensory reality.

We must, therefore, start from what is given in sense-perception or from sense-data, on which alone our knowledge of the outer world depends. By them Russell understands everything which is found immediately in consciousness, or that which is commonly called 'feeling' in the objective sense of what is felt. In this connection it is important that they are given and that they exist so far and so long as they are given. From them we must distinguish sensibilia which are in no respect different from sense-data except that they are not given to a consciousness or mind. The one class has the character of givenness, the other has not. A sensibile becomes a sense-datum by entering into the relation of givenness or, as Russell says, into that of acquaintance or awareness. So far all sense-data are also sensibilia, in the mode of givenness. There arises the question as to the manner of existence of these two classes of objects. Russell decides the question by saying that they both form the final constitutive elements of the world of natural science, and therefore declares them both to be extra-mental or physical (the sense-data being distinguished from the sensibilia by the fact that we are accidentally immediately aware of them). They are, therefore, not at all subjective or dependent upon the existence of mind or consciousness; though causally they are dependent upon the sense-organs, upon the nerves and brain and therefore upon the body of the percipient. To that extent one might speak of physiological, but certainly not of mental or psychic subjectivity. They stand, therefore, in a necessary relation to the bodily organism. What the mind adds to sensibilia is merely awareness; all the rest is physical or physiological. The sensibilia, therefore, could exist only if there were a body without mind; but the sense-data exist also if a mind is connected with the body. One might say that sensibilia are possible but not actual sense-data; i.e. they represent those appearances which would arise if a perceiving consciousness entered into a definite relation to an object. Although according to Russell sense-data are physical, i.e. elements in the structure of the world of physics, he ascribes to them no persistent existence after they have ceased to be given. But their non-persistence, he argues, is no proof that their existence is mental, but is quite compatible with their physical character. Russell says of this theory (as of most of the others which he sets forth) that it is provisional and not at all finally established, though he thinks that it has advantages over all its competitors. It should merely be the starting-point for clarifying the problem further. Frequently he proposed for one and the same problem several tentative hypotheses, without deciding for any of them, but merely estimating their relative advantages. Thus by not committing himself he keeps his philosophy fluid.

What according to this doctrine is to be understood by a 'thing'? What is given to us is a series of sense-data or, as we might say, appearances of the thing; and the customary view is that the thing is something different from all these appearances, lying behind them. Accordingly, the thing alone is counted as real, while its appearances are regarded as unreal, merely psychical or mental. According to Russell, the opposite is true. It is only the various appearances or views of the thing that are real, while the thing itself has no real existence. It is merely the whole system of all these appearances within which the several aspects are members. Russell calls it a logical construction which has a certain importance in so far as it is neutral to the various aspects of the thing. The assumption of a thing-substance or a thing-substrate is superfluous, although not logically contradictory, because the thing is satisfactorily explained if it is taken to be identical with the totality of its appearances. Thing, substance, matter, and such-like entities are sacrificed by Russell to a very important methodological principle which he invokes countless times, that of logical economy or, as it is usually called in England, Occam's razor, according to which *entia non sunt multiplicanda praeter necessitatem*. In very many cases this principle determines Russell's view of a question, and often decides the acceptance or rejection of a thesis.

A consideration similar to the foregoing in regard to the thing takes us deeper into Russell's theory of knowledge and results in ways of thinking which are closely akin both to Berkeley's theory of vision and to Leibniz's monadology. This is the doctrine of space and spatial perspectives. The case is the same with space as it is with things. An object placed in space can be given to us through various senses, e.g. through sight and touch. The plain man assumes that it is one and the same space in which the object is placed, whether it be seen or touched. For him sight-space and touch-space are identical. This view is rejected by Russell. Different senses have different spaces. Sight-space is quite different from touch-space and only as the result of long experience that certain touch-sensations go with certain sight-sensations do we bring the two into relation. The *one* identical space into which both kinds of sensation fit is not a datum of experience, but a logical construction. Experience only gives us the different spaces of different senses which are united according to laws. Common space may be a convenient mode of expression and also be serviceable for scientific purposes, but it has no real existence.

This argument leads to further and more general consequences. What has been said holds good not only for the various sensory spaces, but for everything spatial. If two persons find themselves in a room and perceive the same objects, it is not true, as ordinary intelligence assumes, that they are in the same space and perceive the same environment. Each percipient lives in his own world and sees the world only from *his* point of view or from his own perspective. In relation to the perspectives of all other persons this perspective is completely closed, like Leibniz's monad, which has no windows that open outwards. Thus Russell says that every individual has his private world which is confined to the perspective perceived by him. The same holds good of space. The different sensory spaces of an observer allow themselves to be combined into a general perceptual space. But this is not the physical space and also not the common space as it exists in the mind of the plain man, but is just the private space of the observer concerned. Everyone takes his own space about with him, and there are as many private spaces as there are perspectives, i.e. as percipient beings. But the private spaces of different persons can be related to each other. It can be shown that certain spatial positions in the perception of one observer are very similar to certain spatial positions in the perception of another observer (two men in one room). We can say then that they are near one another in space or coincide with each other. But this space of which we say that it is common to both observers is *toto coelo* different from the perspective spaces of each individual. It represents only the correlation between them, and is not contained in any of them. We can call it the interperspective space, and we can think of it as composed of the individual perspectives each of which possesses its own private space. It is the system or contents of all the perspectives or private spaces and these are its points or elements. This all-inclusive interperspective space which is *one* only, is the objective or physical space which is the basis of the investigations of natural science. It is strictly to be distinguished from the perceptual spaces which are given to us through the senses. It represents no real fact, but is merely concluded from the sensory spaces which alone are empirically real. It is a logical construction, which rests upon a convention. Thus Russell replaces absolute space, which is dropped as a superfluous hypothesis, with the logical construction of space, which is obtained by a strict deduction from experience.

We need not pursue further the general philosophical consequences which flow from this doctrine of perspective centres and lead to a kind of new monadology, nor need we follow the parallel investigation which Russell makes in regard to the concept of time. It is worth while only to note the general principle to which these and other inquiries lead. Russell is in all this concerned to bridge over the gap between the world of perception, from which he always starts, and the world of mathematical physics, towards which he is always striving. Whitehead later propounds the same problem under the similar title "Sensation and Mathematics", and brings it to a much more fundamental and deeper solution than Russell. The question is: Do any relations exist between the two worlds? or more precisely: Is there logical justification for the inference from the sensory data to the concepts with which natural science works? We have seen that only the perceptual world is immediately given and can be experienced; but that the physical world is inferred or constructed. But this construction does not hang in the air nor is it based on any transcendent reality independent of the senses, but solely on the perceptual contents of the senses. The senses furnish the raw material from which logical concepts are constructed, and these possess exactly the qualities which natural science ascribes to its atoms, electrons, molecules, etc. Russell has carried out this investigation in detail. In acute analyses he has tried to derive the most important and basic ideas of mathematical physics, such as thing, matter, space-time, continuity, infinity, and causality, from sense-data. And in thus employing the methodological instrument of the new logic he has contributed greatly to clarifying these concepts philosophically. On the other hand, there result some important conclusions carrying us back from the inferred world to the world of experience, whereby a great part of the theories of the older Empiricists receives a new and deepened, and for the most part a more complex and differentiated meaning.

Among the problems of Empiricism, Russell has chosen to study above all the foregoing; and apart from Leibniz no early thinkers have had more influence on him than Berkeley and Hume (Locke occasionally, though in less degree). Their influence is so great that often long passages of his books give the impression of being mere paraphrases of their ideas. And though these ideas are often draped in modern physics and the new logic, their origin is plainly visible through the disguise. In this respect Russell is completely rooted in the national tradition, as his own testimony shows: "Perhaps from patriotic bias or from community of national temperament I find more that I can accept, and regard as still important, in the writings of these three (Locke, Berkeley, and Hume) than in the philosophy of their continental predecessors" (*Outline of Philosophy*, p. 255). To mention only a few points: with Berkeley and Hume he shares Phenomenalism both as a starting-point and as a pervading methodological principle; he also agrees with them in basing experience upon sensory data. In spite of his New Realism, he often comes near to Berkeley's Solipsism; he plays a dangerous game with it and sometimes succumbs to it, sometimes presses away from it. Like Berkeley he wages a war of extermination against substance, matter, and other metaphysical chimaeras, and in regard to abstract ideas adopts his Nominalism. With Hume Russell is connected by many ties, among them by his atomic theory of knowledge, which is now termed logical Atomism, and by his strong inclination to associationist psychology, which he—in quite a reactionary spirit—tries to revive and to outbid with Behaviourism. With Hume he agrees, moreover, in his treatment of causality, and in his doctrine of sensations and images which coincides almost completely with Hume's theory of impressions and ideas. The fundamental relation between these two classes of data, the criterion of 'liveliness', the important part which belongs to belief and to custom, all this and much more is in both Russell and Hume. Moreover, the doctrine of recollection and memory plainly shows Humean features, though it is overlaid with Semon's theory of *mneme*. The sceptical and agnostic attitude and the typical philosophical pose which is peculiar to Hume are also inherited from him; and from them springs also Russell's aversion to metaphysics, in spite of occasional incursions into this field.

But nowhere is the relationship more conspicuous or, better, more obtrusive than in the doctrine of mind. Here Russell is completely enslaved by Hume's ideas. The bundle-theory recurs with hardly any improvements, and is finally run to death. In this the agreement is not only of ideas but even of phrases. "When we try to look into ourselves we always seem to come upon some particular thought or feeling, and not upon the 'I' which has the thought or feeling."[1] "A mind is the group of mental events which form part of the history of a certain living body."[2] "As a matter of fact, 'I' seems to be only a string of events, each of which separately is more certain

[1] *Problems of Philosophy*, 1929, p. 78.
[2] *An Outline of Philosophy*, pp. 297-8.

than the whole."[1] "Out of habit the peculiarities of what we call 'mind' can be constructed; a mind is a track of sets of compresent events in a region of space-time where there is matter which is peculiarly liable to form habits."[2] "The subject is a logical fiction." Here Russell, as is shown by these definitions culled at random, actually out-Humed Hume (*sit venia verbo*) and applied dogmatically in all directions an idea which Hume put forward as a cautious hypothesis with sceptical reservations. Nowhere does he fail so badly as in determining the nature of mind and nowhere in him can we discern a genuine and profound understanding for the spiritual world and for spiritual values. In this respect Russell's thinking sinks for the most part into the dullest Materialism and the dreariest reduction of everything to a dead level. After all, there is no longer cause for wonder when in many cases the photographic plate performs the same service as the human mind, and is simply put in place of it.

We turn to one or two more themes drawn from Russell's ample repertoire. We must regard as important the distinction between the two sorts of knowledge, knowledge by acquaintance and knowledge by description. We have acquaintance with something of which we are immediately aware, when no mediating processes of thought, judgment, inference, etc., intervene between the act and the object of knowledge. By description, on the other hand, is meant all non-immediate knowledge, and therefore all our knowledge 'about something', that something is or is not 'so and so'. Both kinds of knowledge are directed both upon particulars and upon universals. In the first place we are acquainted with the data of the external senses, through which our knowledge of the outer world comes to us; but not with the objects themselves, which are the product of various kinds of indirect or mediated knowing. We are acquainted further by introspection with the data of that which Locke called inner sense; that is, with thoughts, feelings, wishes and volitions, and also with things which

[1] *An Outline of Philosophy*, German trans., p. 267.
[2] *Contemporary British Philosophy*, I, p. 382.

were previously data, either of outer or of inner sense; that is, with recollections and memory-images. Probably also, though not certainly, there is acquaintance with the subject-ego as that factor which is aware of things, directs its wishes towards them, has feelings towards them, etc. (though this is not in harmony with the bundle-theory which Russell otherwise always advocates). And finally we are acquainted with universals or general ideas, such as blue, diversity, and brotherhood, a kind of acquaintance which Russell calls 'conceiving'. Knowledge by description we have of objects of daily life, which we project into the external world; of physical objects, which, as was shown, are very complicated constructions, mediated by many various processes of thought; of other souls and of everything through which we are enabled to pass beyond the narrow boundaries of our personal experience. All knowledge by description, if it is to be genuine knowledge, must be referred back to those immediate data with which we are directly acquainted; that is, everything not immediately experienced or capable of being experienced is based on the contents of immediate experience and legitimated by it.

We have seen above that sense-data or perceptual contents form a real component of the physical world. We have seen also that basic concepts of natural science, such as protons, electrons, atoms, and molecules are not understood by Russell as ultimate constituents of the material world, but as complicated logical structures inferred from sense-data which have not the character of reality. Of what stuff does the material world consist? Russell left this question unanswered in accordance with the unspeculative attitude of his earlier books; but he inclined to the view which agrees with his consistent Phenomenalism that sense-data themselves supply the stuff out of which the world is formed. Later, however, the inclination diminished, and he adopted the answer supplied to him both by modern physics and by the metaphysics of Alexander, Whitehead, and others, namely, the idea of *event*. This idea has the advantage that it does not commit us to any general view of the world insomuch as it makes no decision as to whether the nature of the world is spiritual or material. Metaphysically it is completely neutral.

The materials of which the physical world consists are events; and the question arises as to their constitution. Russell, consistently following out his earlier doctrine, calls them perceptual contents. This idea, in contrast with the earlier one of sense-data, is extended in so far as Russell, in addition to the data given to the percipient and those connected with the bodies of other persons, included also data about which we do not know whether they have been perceived or not. Only thus is it possible for him to objectify the sense-data and to incorporate them completely into the system of the physical world. They can now no longer be regarded as something which is essentially distinguished from the processes with which physics is concerned. In this way he arrives at the result that the physical world consists of events, and that these must be thought of primarily as perceptual contents, and secondarily as that which can be inferred from them. He speaks also, however, of physical events which evidently are different from the others and fall under the second class (those inferred from perceptual contents), although we must not understand electrons and protons as being among them. The physical events, which must not be confused with particles of matter, stand in spatio-temporal relations and are determined by causal laws. Their inner character is, however, unknown. We can assume also that perceptual events are connected with them or may appear contemporaneously with them in a relation of compresence. How fluctuating Russell's attitude is towards perceptual contents is shown by the characteristic statement, which is intended to contain his final conclusion: "There is no good ground for excluding percepts from the physical world, but several strong reasons for including them." (*Analysis of Matter*, p. 384).

How completely in Russell all boundaries are abolished between the physical and the psychic, the material and the mental, is shown by the preceding line of thought. He himself has pursued this aim consciously, and it is a peculiar paradox of his doctrine that wherever it treats of mind it threatens to succumb to Materialism; and wherever it treats of matter it flirts with idealistic ideas. As he himself says: "I am of the opinion that matter is less material and that mind is less mental than is commonly supposed." The materialization of mind has been spoken of above. The mentalization of matter stands in relation to similar efforts of modern physics, although it must be doubted whether the increasing desubstantiation or volatilization of solid matter which is going on there really leads to the region of the mental, or whether it does not merely mean another form of material being than that which is familiar to us. Russell takes up this question and commits himself to that fallacy. A piece of matter is for him a logical structure built up out of events and a physical body is defined as a group of events arranged round a centre. Whether there is a substantial core in this centre is quite indifferent. Everything solid is thus broken up into events, and every sort of permanent substance is denied. The causal law which inheres in such a connected chain of events must be expressed by differential equations. What is now left of matter is nothing but a convenient abbreviation for describing certain causal laws which have reference to events. Thus matter, that mistake of classical physics and bugbear of all previous metaphysics, disappears finally from the world. Whether Materialism thereby also disappears from the world is another question which in view of Russell's treatment of mind we cannot answer definitely in the affirmative.

The bridging of the gulf between the psychic and the physical or between the world of perception and the world of physics now leads—and here we come to the critical point of Russell's philosophy—to the bridging of the immemorial metaphysical opposition between Idealism and Materialism. The doctrine which effects this and also contains Russell's rather thin and unoriginal metaphysics is called *neutral Monism*. How small his speculative power is in comparison with that of Bradley, Alexander, and Whitehead is seen in the fact that he has failed to reach a metaphysical position of his own, but has simply taken his doctrine from others and has set it out as a mere prolongation of his former thinking. Neutral Monism, which Russell first viewed critically, and later sympathetically, and finally accepted completely, comes in its modern form from the New World, where it was represented first by James and Dewey, and rather later developed further by the American New Realists, Perry and Holt, who came under the influence of James. This doctrine declares that the stuff of which the world is formed is neither purely mental nor purely material (which would result either in a mental or materialistic Monism); further, that it is not divided dualistically into mental and material, resting upon a primitive antithesis (which would result in some dualistic system), but that the stuff of the world is one and the same and stands in a neutral relation to all these antitheses (neutral Monism). For Russell, as we have seen, mind and matter are no real entities, but merely logical constructions. The world-stuff must therefore be thought of as something much more primitive than either, as something from which they are descended as from a common ancestor, or as something which lies between them. We might also say that neutral Monism, in contrast both to idealist and to naturalistic Monism, is the theory according to which things which usually are regarded as mental or as bodily are not distinguished from each other in their inner character but merely in reference to their exterior arrangement and composition. Thus the duality of mind and matter disappears; there is only *one* world-stuff which lies behind both, or includes both, and which in one definite arrangement is termed mental and in another is termed material. To the concept of this neutral primitive stuff almost all the lines of Russell's thinking converge as to a focal point.

ALFRED NORTH WHITEHEAD (*b.* 1861)

[Fellow of Trinity College, Cambridge, 1911–14. Lecturer in Applied Mathematics and Mechanics at University College, London, 1914–24. Professor of Applied Mathematics at the Imperial College of Science and Technology, London. Since 1924 Professor of Philosophy at Harvard University. *A Treatise on Universal Algebra*, 1898; *The Axioms of Projective Geometry*, 1906; *The Axioms of Descriptive Geometry*, 1907; *An Introduction to Mathematics*, 1908; *Principia Mathematica*, 3 vols., 1910–13 (2nd ed., 1925–7) (in collaboration with Russell); *The Organisation of Thought*, 1917; *An Enquiry concerning the Principles of Natural Knowledge*, 1919 (2nd ed., 1925); *The Concept of Nature*, 1920 (2nd ed., 1926); *The Principle of Relativity, with application to Physical Science*, 1922; *Science and the Modern World*, 1926; *Religion in the Making*, 1926; *Symbolism: its meaning and effect*, 1928; *Process and Reality: an essay in cosmology*, 1929 (Gifford Lectures); *The Function of Reason*, 1929; *The Aims of Education and other essays*, 1929; *Adventures of Ideas*, 1933; *Nature and Life*, 1934.

On Whitehead see Dorothy M. Emmet: *Whitehead's Philosophy of Organism*, 1932.]

If we pass immediately from Russell's philosophy to that of Whitehead, we do so more from an external than from an internal reason, because their two names have been closely connected by their common authorship of *Principia Mathematica*, the basic work on mathematical logic. There, however, ends their partnership, and from now onwards their paths diverge widely, especially in the field of philosophy, where they pursue very different interests and draw continually farther apart. Here Whitehead's doctrine comes into much closer relation to that of Alexander than to that of his former partner, which which it shows only a few unimportant points of contact. And if we measure the work of both in regard to their philosophical importance, that of Whitehead appears to be much weightier than that of Russell. It surpasses also that of most other British thinkers of the present and of the recent past, and, although a final judgment must be left to posterity, it may be said even to-day that very few contemporaries reach Whitehead's high level, and hardly anyone surpasses it. Even when viewed in a more distant historical perspective it is plain that Whitehead's philosophy is one of the highest achievements of British thinking, and may be reckoned as on a par with the great classical systems of the past. But only the future can show whether this judgment of its value, which I give for what it is worth, is justified, and whether Whitehead is really to be reckoned as a new classic in philosophy.

Whitehead's intellectual development has been unusual and peculiar for a philosopher. It falls into three periods which may be clearly distinguished, and are marked by two definite lines of separation. One of them is reflected in his external way of life, in his exchange of a mathematical for a philosophical professorship, which did not occur till he was 63; the other is the change in his central interest. The first period is the mathematical, which is in point of time much the largest and reaches as far as his 60th year. Whitehead is first and foremost a mathematician, and mathematics gave his character its main bias, which even later, when it was forced into the background, has always remained strong and decisive. In this book we must content ourselves with presenting Whitehead's doctrine in its purely philosophical aspect, separated from its mathematical associations.

The first period, marked by a series of important books and papers of purely mathematical interest, finds its culmination in *Principia Mathematica*, written in collaboration with Russell, a gigantic work of thinking and research, by which the system of mathematical logic was founded and placed upon a broad and firm basis. It forms the transition to the next period. Although this also, being concerned with a special science, has little to do with philosophy in the full sense of the word, it led Whitehead nearer to a philosophical attitude. But this was not independently reached by a process of inner development, but was imposed upon him by his collaborator and merely taken over by him. There was needed a further impulse from without to bring him finally into the paths of philosophy and to release him from the fetters of Russell's way of thinking. His awakening from dogmatic slumber resulted, as he himself confessed, from the great changes in the field of mathematical physics that came especially from Einstein's theory of relativity and its criticism of the traditional doctrine of space and time. Whitehead recognized at once the necessity of a philosophical basis for the views now required by the new physics, a basis which could not be furnished by the special science itself, and this led him into the discussion which had broken out vigorously after the Great War about the philosophical meaning of the new knowledge supplied by the relativity, the quantum, and the atomic theories. Of all those who have worked on this subject he has made the most valuable, independent, and original contribution to a truly philosophical understanding and exploitation of modern mathematical physics. Thus the second period of his thought was devoted to the founding and elaboration of a natural philosophy which quite organically (because not hindered or circumscribed by any previous theory) grew from the soil of the newly acquired special knowledge, and among existing philosophical knowledge and methods utilized those which could be easily and naturally fitted into the system of that study. This era of physics and natural science began during the Great War and includes particularly the writings of the years 1919–22, first *An Enquiry concerning the Principles of Natural Knowledge*, in which the basic ideas were first systematically developed then, *The Concept of Nature* in which the new doctrine found its fuller philosophical expression, and finally *The Principle of Relativity* in which the doctrine was discussed from the physical side. It was thus that Whitehead was finally won over to philosophy. The philosophical *eros* was awakened and could thenceforward develop freely. At the same time the period that was here closed produced in principle all the presuppositions which were to serve as the basis of all his later work in philosophy.

From natural philosophy, which at this stage is to be taken not in the speculative but in the purely empirical sense, Whitehead's thinking advanced to metaphysics. In the third period of his development (or, better, the unfolding of his great spiritual gifts), while closing his previous line of thought, he has produced a constructive scheme which, in boldness of speculation, depth of insight, fullness of vision, and width of culture excels almost everything which the whole of British philosophy has hitherto produced. But Whitehead does not belong to the type of 'airy architects of manifold thought-worlds', 'dreamers of feeling or reason', wild and conscienceless speculators, or arbitrary system-makers. His metaphysics rather grows with iron consistency from the firm foundation of his mathematical mode of thinking, his knowledge of natural science, and his previously acquired philosophical insight, and at the same time fills itself with the whole wealth of metaphysical knowledge from Plato and Aristotle to Bergson and Alexander. It is certainly a unique example in the history of philosophy that an inquirer trained in the most exact studies (mathematics and physics) should in advanced years rise to the height of a metaphysical world-system which harmonizes with those studies and takes them up into itself as its inevitable presupposition. Whitehead's thinking, in fact, has so far outgrown its previous limits that it now occupies itself with problems of mental science and takes up questions of culture, history of philosophy, education, and other matters.

The literary activity of this period includes the books published from 1926 to the present day (1934); first the arresting work *Science and the Modern World*, in which the new direction first appears, then the two smaller works made up of lectures, *Religion in the Making* and *Symbolism*, then, best of all, *Process and Reality*, the deepest, most difficult, richest, and most concentrated of Whitehead's books, which contains his metaphysics or cosmology in strict conceptual development, and in a specially devised dark and cryptic language, a book with seven seals for most of his contemporaries and for every reader who does not make the severest effort of thought and go through it in the sweat of his brow; finally the three books which should be treated either as prolegomena or paralipomena, *The Function of Reason*, *Adventures of Ideas*, and *Nature and Life*, in which the doctrine of the main book has been in many respects completed, extended, and felicitously annotated and explained, and which may serve as keys to *Process and Reality*, although they cannot unlock all the secrets of that oracular work.

The understanding of Whitehead's doctrine encounters extraordinary difficulties because most of his books are composed in a very difficult technical language, which often conceals rather than reveals their meaning. In this Whitehead diverges from the great majority of his philosophical countrymen and approaches nearer to the German model, with its notoriously clumsy terminology overladen with technical terms. Even where, as in the later books, Whitehead is not using mathematical symbols, his diction bears plainly the stamp of mathematical thinking. It is spare, severe, and sober, uncompromisingly practical, and lacking in all rhetorical adornments and all literary grace. It is rich in newly minted words and it forms for itself a new vocabulary, in which it takes little account of the established meaning of words, which it changes arbitrarily in the service of its own purposes. Another cause of difficulty in understanding him is that his terms are subject to change, even within his own usage, and often change their meaning abruptly from one book to another without the writer thinking it necessary to inform the reader. His terms achieve their meaning in their actual use, and as his thinking has been in continual movement and has never been established dogmatically, his ideas also in their verbal formulation lack firm definition and take part in the movement by which his thought is driven forward to ever new positions. A typical example of such manifold change of meaning is the basic term 'event', which as Whitehead's thought advances is filled with new and often greatly changed meaning from one book to another. Thus Whitehead's verbal idiom reflects the profundity of his thoughts, a profundity to whose ultimate depths the plummet even of his own understanding can reach only with difficulty. This gives the impression of a dark storm-cloud which from time to time is lit up by a lightning flash, which makes its outlines visible, but not what is concealed in its midst. Thus Whitehead's philosophy appears to us (as to all critics and interpreters who have dealt with it) as a gigantic cryptogram at the deciphering of which whole generations will work because—so much may be said even by those who stand so near in time—it is a product of high genius, true originality, and deep penetration. Human thinking has been enriched by it with new views, brought into new connections, and so been carried forward upon its path. The following account, in view of the difficulties which have been mentioned, must content itself with a very provisional and sketchy outline of this philosophy, and is far from claiming to exhaust it thoroughly or to pass any final verdict upon it.

The mathematical and logistic side of Whitehead's work belongs to his pre-philosophical period, and can here be left out of account. The books of his second period are the first to be philosophically relevant; this we have called the period of his natural philosophy. But as what is dealt with here is not the speculative metaphysics of nature, it would be better to speak of it as a philosophy of the natural sciences. But it must be observed that the earlier philosophy of nature and the later cosmology are not to be put into separate compartments, but that many threads of connection pass from one to another and maintain the union between the two phases of thought. We have seen that Whitehead's philosophical doctrine sprang from the new physics, and it must be added that it is penetrated by this spirit in all its stages and in all its basic views. Our account therefore begins with the criticism which Whitehead continually directs from the standpoint of the new against the old or classical physics and the habits of thought which have arisen from it.

First comes the concept of simple location, against which Whitehead's criticism is primarily directed. Upon it is based the mechanical world-picture of the XVIIth Century as it was formed by Newton, and remained in force till the threshold of our own time. By this Whitehead understands the view according to which a piece of matter takes up an unambiguously determined location in space so that it is fully characterized if one says that it is to be found at a definite finite place or region in space and endures during an equally definite finite period in time. According to this view, one can fix the relation of a material body to space-time by saying quite simply it is just where it is, independently of any essential relation to any other regions of space or to any other periods of time. The piece of matter stands isolated in a position in space-time and there is needed for its explanation no reference to other regions of the space-time system. Whitehead points out that on such a view we are dealing with a schema which is highly abstract and artificial, to which in concrete experience no reality corresponds. Among the primary elements of our experience of nature no element can anywhere be found which possesses this character of simple location. But the service of Newton to science is not thereby in any way diminished, for it is just upon this extreme abstraction that the strength of the classical physics rests and the unanticipated progress of scientific thought which was made possible through it depends upon that abstraction. The mistake of the Newtonian system consists only in this, that these simply located material bodies have been taken for concrete things from which in reality they are different *toto coelo*. Thus we have a substitution of abstract locations for concrete facts, which in science has proved fruitful; in philosophy, on the contrary, devastating. Whitehead calls this "the fallacy of misplaced concreteness", a mistake which sprang inevitably from the idea of simple location. Accordingly, one of the most important tasks of philosophy is the criticism of such scientific abstractions, and Whitehead himself has done excellent service in this field.

A train of ideas parallel to the foregoing leads on to the criticism of philosophical abstractions, and here it is in the first instance Hume's Sensationalism in which Whitehead points out a mistake exactly similar to that just mentioned. Hume's name meets us in his books at every turn. He reckons the Scottish philosopher as one of the greatest formative influences of the modern mind, but usually adopts a critical attitude towards him and has done more to uproot and overcome the mode of thinking represented by him than his numerous other critics; and this just because Whitehead's criticism is not applied from without but from within, because it has grown from the soil of Hume's own system. Whitehead shows that Hume's "simple impressions" are just as much intellectual abstractions as the material bodies of physics, and that what Empiricism regards as the final concrete components of experience cannot be verified by experience. Hume's pure sensations are divested of all spatial and other relations to other sensations, and where a connection is established with the remaining factors of experience, it is purely external and accidental. It is true that the impression represents logically the simplest thinkable element of a physical datum, and to this extent Hume's procedure is a masterpiece of abstract concept-formation; but it is a mistake to claim physical priority for this highly developed product of abstraction, as Hume and his successors have done. On the contrary, we ought to put every empirical datum into the context of our whole concrete experience and to apprehend it in conjunction with this. The pure sensation is to be found nowhere in this experience, and therefore the empirical philosophy, although it professes to base itself upon experience, is fundamentally non-empirical. We shall see how what at first sight seems a purely negative result, leads on to a positive piece of insight.

Whitehead's attack upon inveterate habits of thought and false abstractions is next directed sharply against another deeply rooted principle of thought, namely, what he calls the "theory of the bifurcation of nature". In this he has undoubtedly scored a great success and has been widely judged to be in the right. The principle of the bifurcation of nature has its historical origin in the doctrine of simple location and just like Hume's sensational theory of perception results from the world-picture of mechanistic physics. By it Whitehead understands the doctrine according to which the system of nature is regarded not as a unitary organic whole but as split into two isolated and disconnected parts: the one the reality of which we become aware in perception, and the other the reality which is regarded as the cause of our perceptual world. On the one side nature is posited as a cause or as what we call the primary qualities of nature (molecules, electrons, atoms, matter, ether, etc.); on the other side as an effect or as that which we call the secondary qualities (colours, tones, feelings, etc.). As the meeting-point of the two realities stands the mind, viewed from which causal nature is to be regarded as influent, while nature as perceived is effluent. Hence results the bifurcation of nature into an appearing and a non-appearing reality, of which the one is localized in mind or consciousness while the other carries on its own separate existence which lies in a world which transcends consciousness. In other words, the bifurcation theory divides the totality of being into a reality which does not appear and appearances which are not real. Against this Whitehead urges that causal nature is a metaphysical chimaera, and the nature which appears is an artificial abstraction, and instead of the bifurcation assumes a single unitary system of coherent relations which embraces impartially primary and secondary qualities, molecules, and feelings. It is not the duty of philosophy to inquire into the cause of the things which are known, but to determine their character, and therefore the character of the nature which appears; the adjectival phrase 'which appears' can therefore be discarded; since there is only *one* nature, that which is given to us in perception. From perception Whitehead's new doctrine takes its start and remains within it to the end. For knowledge of reality is one and the same from the most rudimentary sensations to the highest scientific hypotheses. The latter are based on the data of perception and everything perceived is to be found within nature. To philosophy falls the task of exploring the coherence of things, so far as they are perceived; and there are no other things than those which we encounter in perceptual knowledge. It is evident that Whitehead's starting-point is closely akin to the phenomenalist position of Berkeley, Hume, and the majority of Empiricists, and that his reliance on feeling is similar to Hume's foundation of all the data and structure of knowledge upon impressions (in spite of the different conformation of the basic factor in each case).

It is important to make as plain as possible Whitehead's position at the stage of natural philosophy. As yet no metaphysical questions are here involved. We are not dealing with the question what is in the mind and in nature, nor with the psychological or other relation between subject and object, nor with their status in the realm of reality, but merely with the effort to set forth the various kinds of relations and connections which prevail between the entities which we perceive as existing *de facto* in nature. Colours, tones, and toothaches stand as regards their character of reality upon exactly the same footing as molecules and electric waves. They are all given to us only by perception and to that extent they find themselves equally 'in nature', or, as Whitehead expresses it figuratively: "All we know of nature is in the same boat, to sink or swim together."[1] Thus Whitehead rejects the so-called theory of psychic additions, a less radical variation of the bifurcation-theory; in other words, the inclusion of mind in the philosophy of nature as a factor which alters the character of the perceived data by subjective additions. To mind (subject or consciousness) there belongs no precedence over the other entities, and on this ground Whitehead expressly calls his doctrine a reversal of the Kantian position. In Kant's distinction of appearance from thing-in-itself he sees a striking example of the bifurcation-hypothesis, and in his doctrine of mind as the lawgiver of nature he recognizes the typical mistake of psychic addition. For Kant the world emerges from the subject;[2] for Whitehead, conversely, the subject emerges from the world (hence he uses instead of 'subject' the term 'superject'). Mind raises itself from the background of the world given to it and constructs its own concepts progressively in accordance with the relations which it finds there. Whitehead's standpoint as natural philosopher (which here perhaps means the same as theorist of knowledge) is outspokenly realistic and naturalistic; although, as we shall see, nothing is prejudged thereby against the future metaphysician. Whitehead represents, moreover, a peculiar, almost unparalleled, synthesis of Realism and Phenomenalism in giving to the principle of phenomenality or perceptual immanence an objectivist turn and shielding it from the subjectivist meaning which is usually given to it. His doctrine is subjectivist only in so far (here again agreeing with Hume) as it allows nothing into the philosophical system

[1] Cf. *Concept of Nature*, p. 148.
[2] *Process and Reality*, p. 123.

which is not present as a factor in subjective experience. This Whitehead with his usual arbitrariness in the use of philosophical terms calls the ontological principle, and sums it up in the statement: "apart from the experiences of subjects there is nothing, nothing, nothing—bare nothingness."[1] We can now understand what is meant when Whitehead opposes to the critique of pure reason a critique of pure feeling; that is, of feeling in the sense of the basic factor of impressions as the starting-point of all our knowledge of nature.

In Whitehead's natural philosophy Subjectivism and Objectivism are intertwined in a very peculiar fashion. It starts from perception and therefore from subjective experience, and yet is anxiously concerned to exclude everything subjective from its field. Mind is as it were equally included in natural philosophy and excluded from it, and therein natural philosophy is essentially different from metaphysics, in which this exclusion is cancelled. Thus a clear division is made between the two studies, and Whitehead expresses this by saying that natural philosophy has to do merely with investigating what is perceived, while metaphysics includes consideration both of what is perceived and of the perceiver. To it, therefore, are assigned the problems of the mind which have no place in natural philosophy. One might be tempted to accuse Whitehead here of a bifurcation such as he has reproached other thinkers with. This is the thesis which has become famous, that nature is closed to mind; or, as Whitehead puts it, nature is completely self-contained or self-sufficient. But the question how it is possible that natural philosophy should break off all relations with mind, though all its knowledge is conditioned by the percipient subject, receives no satisfactory answer from him. For with the concept of the 'percipient event', which he puts in the place of the subjective principle, the excluded mind is smuggled in again through a back-door; and all his efforts to incorporate this factor, which he characteristically also calls 'percipient object', into the system of nature and therefore to objectify it, fail in view of the fact that the subjec-

[1] *Process and Reality*, p. 234.

tive cannot be changed into the objective by a piece of philosophical jugglery. He is thus unable against his own theory consistently to carry out the exclusion of mind. He often falls into the 'heterogeneous' way of thinking instead of persisting in the 'homogeneous' way demanded by him.

To turn to some basic thoughts of Whitehead's philosophy of nature: it was shown above that the view of nature as a mere aggregate of entities, which are independent of each other and each of which is capable of isolation, is untenable. Such a system would be completely accidental. According to it there would be space without time, and time without space, and although space and matter are thought of as standing in relations, time is carefully kept apart from them both. Now everything depends on viewing the elements and factors thus fenced off from one another as inwardly united members within an inclusive whole, the realm of nature. Thus there can be in nature nothing existing by itself, nothing which could be what it is except as an ingredient in the totality of nature. There can be no space without time and no time without space, and similarly no space-time without matter or substance to fill it. In every natural entity all these factors must be included; they cannot stand merely in external relations to one another, but they must penetrate one another inwardly. Hence there arises the question about the constitution of such an entity, especially about the constitution of the ultimate basic factors of reality. Whitehead's answer is that nature consists of a network or web of *events*. This is the term which he puts in the place of the old concept of substance or matter, so that the latter undergoes a radical transformation, or is thrown completely overboard. The concept of 'event' is the foundation and stands in the focus of natural philosophy and everything else is determined and illuminated by it. This concept had already been used by others in a philosophically pregnant sense, but Whitehead was the first to give it a central place and to endow it with new significance as one of the basic and most fruitful ideas of the new view of the physical world. But in what follows I propose to disregard this in order to indicate the place that he assigns to it in its purely philosophical sense as the centre of his exposition.

An event is everything which, as it commonly said, eventuates or occurs. As such it is a matter of fact or an actuality; i.e. it is simply that which it is here and now and nothing else. It occurs somewhere and somewhen, and it is therefore not only temporal, as it is usually understood to be, and originally also by Whitehead, but it is also spatial. It has both spatial extension and temporal extension or duration. Its spatiality and temporality do not confront each other as separate factors, but are interwoven. It is therefore better to term it a spatio-temporal unity than a spatial *and* temporal unity. The event is the most concrete finite entity; it is self-contained and demarcated against other events; i.e. it is of atomic character.[1] But this does not mean that it is isolated from its fellows or stands in merely external connection with them (like the material bodies of the older physics and Hume's impressions). It stands rather in relations of the closest connection with all other events and finally with the whole universe. This principle of finding a place for even the smallest and least important event in the totality of things, this mutual connection between all the things which happen in the world, was expressed by Whitehead in very exact, mathematically determined form, as the basic category of 'extension'. Every event extends over other events which are contained in it as parts, and it is itself contained as a part in other events which extend over it. For example, the journey of a cart through a street is a part of the whole life of this street; the life of the street extends over the journey of the cart. Similarly, the revolution of a wheel of this cart is a part of the event which is constituted by the journey of the cart, which extends over the revolution of the wheel. But the same relation holds good for stable objects which show neither movement nor change. These also Whitehead, differing

[1] Emphasis upon its atomic character appears more definitely in his metaphysics. At the stage of natural philosophy the continuous character is predominant, and the atomic appears merely as an ideal limiting case, which is demanded by mathematical considerations, but corresponds to no perceptual experience.

from common usage, calls 'events', and it is of the highest importance that he views them not merely as spatially extended, but as bodies extending through a definite time-duration, i.e. as events. For example, the continuous existence of a house extends over that of a brick of the house and similarly the existence of the house during a year extends over that during a day, and the existence during a day over that during a second. The event therefore is determined in its nature by the quality of 'extending over'. Events overlap one another. This basic relation holding good between events may be thought of as infinitely prolonged in both directions. Every event which is contained in others possesses, however small its extension, the capacity of extending itself over others. Moreover, every event in which others are contained, however great its extension, enters in its turn into other events, and is embraced by them. The capacity of 'extending over' has no boundaries, and goes forward in both directions to infinity. This is the principle of the uninterrupted relation of extension.

The concept of extension, like that of event, is of basic importance for Whitehead's philosophy. It has also a bearing on metaphysics (although it is later supplanted in metaphysics by the concept of process); for the unity and continuity of nature and the interlocking of its parts spring from it. It is also more original than space and time, both of which presuppose extension. Extension as such is the basis both of spatial and of temporal extension and is therefore neither spatial nor temporal. It is the basic relation between events, and space and time are only partial and special expressions of it. In order to study as exactly as possible the relation of extension and the problems connected with it, Whitehead has invented a very difficult and complicated method which he calls the method of extensive abstraction.[1] In many respects it recalls MacTaggart's principle of determining correspondence (see pp. 372 ff.). This method, which uses the language of mathematics and mathematical logic and therefore is not

[1] Later, in *Process and Reality*, where he develops it afresh, he calls it "extensive connection".

directly intelligible to non-mathematicians, is highly appreciated by those who are competent to speak and is regarded as having the greatest importance for the new philosophy of nature. Broad sees in it the "prolegomena to every future philosophy of nature",[1] and defines its purpose as serving to "bridge the gaps between the crude facts of sense and the refined concepts of mathematical physics".[2] And in fact Whitehead's philosophy is a peculiar mixture of concrete perception and mathematico-physical (or mathematico-logical) conception. Mathematics and sense-perception are here most closely woven together and Whitehead evidently holds the view that mathematical relations disclose themselves directly in sense-data and can be read off from them. Mathematics appears here in the function of a mediator between the data of perception and the exact concepts of physics, as an ally of that radical Empiricism which was represented by Hume with his demand that everything conceptual and abstract should be legitimated by showing its origin in impressions. One might say, then, that Whitehead's power of perception was greatly enhanced by his mathematical knowledge and his capacity of thinking in strictly mathematical relations. But the question still remains undecided whether such heterogeneous ways of knowing can be summoned at all to fruitful co-operation, and whether the philosopher does not yield to an illusion in thinking that he can bring this to pass. We can, however, spend no more time over the very special questions which are connected with the problem of extensive abstraction, and merely wish to draw attention to this basic feature of Whitehead's philosophy.[3]

To return to the doctrine of events. We have seen that events are spatio-temporal entities. But this does not mean that they exist at a given time and a given place and consist of

[1] *Scientific Thought*, 1923, Preface. [2] *Ibid.*, p. 39.

[3] For further information on this matter I would refer to the instructive essay by Edgar Wind, to which my own account is indebted: "Mathematik und Sinnesempfindung. Materialen zu einer Whitehead-Kritik", in *Logos*, vol. xxi, 1932, pp. 239–80.

changes in a given persistent material. This view is completely transformed. Space and time are merely relations between continuously extended events and are only accompaniments of events, not composing their essence. It is therefore wrong to say that nature is in space and time; on the contrary, space and time are in nature. Both exist only because things happen, and these happening things are primary and constitute nature. A further characteristic of events, which concerns their mode of existence, is that they are never at rest but continuously move forward and in a certain degree go past us, but do not properly change. They change merely in their relations to coming events, by which they are taken up, but not in their essence. Such a change is called by Whitehead a passage. Events therefore pass into other events or perish in them; but they cannot change. They are either what they are or they cease to be. They are not permanent, but in constant movement or flux, and therefore the world is not a block-universe; it does not stand still but is in uninterrupted forward movement. Whitehead calls this 'creative advance', because no state of the world is ever repeated but new possibilities are always being born from the bosom of nature.

In this way we anticipate the metaphysics which already enters in a marked way into natural philosophy with the doctrine of the creative advance of nature. But first we have to note the presence of the important concept which is correlative to event. Besides events we are in sensory perception aware of a second category of data, viz. objects; which means that both categories are necessary to constitute nature. But becoming aware of objects is different from becoming aware of events and Whitehead calls it 'recognition', whereas events are apprehended by us immediately in the act of perceptual experience. Recognition of an event is therefore impossible, because as essentially fleeting it never recurs. Recognition is an awareness of identity, and thus we can recognize only such elements as do not merely pass by and disappear, but which recur; i.e. can as identical re-enter perception. But we must observe that immediate sensory recognition is only a limiting case, and that in all actual recognition intellectual processes (such as comparison, judgment, etc.) are concerned.

Objects, therefore, in contrast to events, from which they are utterly different are the permanent factors of nature. But both stand in relation to each other. We can view concrete nature neither as a mere passing-by of events without objects, nor as a mere collection of objects which are not related to events. Each would be an inadmissible abstraction. The relation of objects to events is called by Whitehead 'ingression', and corresponding to the variety of objects there are various kinds of ingression. In contrast to events objects need not be different from each other; they can make a fresh appearance as one and the same at different points of space and time. But in distinction from events they can change without thereby impairing their permanence. They merely enter into a new relation to passing events. The permanence of objects also implies that in the strict sense of the word they stand outside of space and time. Only in an indirect or derived sense in virtue of their relations to events can one say that they belong to space-time. This implies that they lack the main characteristic of events, extension. Extension is a relation which obtains only between events, but has no application to objects. One cannot say, therefore, that objects consist of parts; for, if this were so, they would be able like events to extend over other objects, which is essentially impossible for them. The essence of an object, moreover, is not dependent upon its relations; these may be different without seriously affecting its self-identity. But to an event its relations are essential; they spring as it were out of its interior; it is just as it is related and apart from that is nothing.

In ordinary thinking the distinction between these two basic entities of natural being is not drawn at all or is made very uncertainly. It can, however, be realized even by the understanding of plain men. An external object which comes into our field of vision is firstly this once-occurring, never-to-be-repeated experience belonging to its immediate present;

but it is further that self-identical something which we can have repeated continually in perceptive experience and view as identical (in spite of more or less change) with that which was presented in earlier experience. The object so far as it is experienced is the event which is different at every new act of experience; because nature meanwhile has moved forward and stands in changed spatio-temporal relations. The thing before us, so far as it discloses itself in the new experience as identical and as identical appears afresh, is the object. Objects can therefore recur on all possible occasions, and therein lies their permanence. But this is not to be understood as duration, since objects stand in no direct relation to time (or space-time).

After all, it is not easy to get a clear idea of Whitehead's concept of object. As he takes from the object the character of extension and therewith the capacity of partition, and therefore just that characteristic which since Descartes' time in his doctrine of the *res extensa* has been recognized as belonging essentially to all natural reality, he has thereby made the object so unreal that it can hardly be united with the idea of a natural existent. It has therefore been justly observed (by Wind, *loc. cit.*, p. 253) that it would be much better if we were permitted to explain Whitehead's object from the standpoint of the universal concept. In that case a series of difficulties would at once disappear and in fact Whitehead himself in his metaphysical writings has in many ways favoured this explanation. What he later calls 'eternal object' certainly, as we shall see, comes very near to what is commonly understood by the Platonic idea. But here upon the plane of natural philosophy this explanation must be rejected as contrary to Whitehead's meaning. For here by objects he means really (or naturally) existent and concrete things, things which are given in experience and are realized in events. There can be no doubt about this if we examine more closely the kinds of objects which he distinguishes from one another.

Objects may be divided into three main groups: 1, sense-objects; 2, perceptual objects; 3, scientific objects. The first are the simple sense-data, such as colours, tones, smells, touch-feelings, a blue spot of colour, something loud, etc. They correspond more or less to Hume's impressions, and Whitehead, like Hume, understands by them the primary factors of the external world of things, the ὕλη or basis of all our knowledge of nature. The whole structure of natural knowledge rests on them; they are the foundation of the whole building or the building-stones which lie ready for its construction.

While sense-objects can with comparative ease be combined with Whitehead's theory of objects, perceptual objects present greater difficulties. By this term Whitehead understands the ordinary objects of daily life as they are given to us in perception; such as tables, chairs, trees, and mountains. They are the result of ordinary experience or the ordinary conjunction of definite sense-objects in a definite situation. Two classes are distinguished: the illusory and the non-illusory or physical objects of perception. The latter are justified practically rather than theoretically; for they are the objects of our daily use, and as such useful and advantageous for life. Theoretically, on the other hand, they are less satisfactory, because their boundaries are too vague and their identity is for the most part undetermined and confused. Philosophical criticism cannot remain contented with these impure and ambiguous forms; when it is directed intensively upon them, they slip away under our hands and break up either into pure sense-data or into objects of exact scientific thought. With them above all the basic distinction of object from event disappears, as they are furnished with marks which belong only to events. In reference to them there can be no question of carrying out this distinction strictly and systematically. They are logically confused, but *de facto* present because they are given in perception and are indispensable for practical life. Thus at this point Whitehead's theory falls into a serious dilemma which points to a source of error: either the concept of object is wrong or at least too narrow, because this important and practically undeniable class of objects finds no place in it; or these objects are no true objects, because they conflict with that conception; or perhaps the mistake lies deeper still, in the basic distinction of object and event.[1]

With scientific objects as the third class, the course of the theory becomes smoother. They are the atoms, molecules, electrons, etc., of physics which are not immediately perceived but are inferred because of their capacity to express the causal character of events. Every scientific object stands in a special relation to every event in nature. It expresses the character of the object, as it is postulated by Whitehead, purely and truthfully. For it is evident that an electron, e.g., has neither parts nor extension, although it evokes both on its entry into an event. In any case Whitehead, when he claims for scientific conceptual structures the same existence *in rerum natura* as for other objects, moves far away from the theory (held by Pearson, Mach, Poincaré, and many others) according to which they are interpreted as short-hand expressions invented by science or as formulae of calculation to which no empirical reality corresponds.

Thus upon the plane of natural philosophy, as we may say summarily, nature appears as having a structure similar to that of the four-dimensional continuum of the relativity-theory. In this connection it is important that the fourth dimension or the time-factor comes into the foreground in a dominant position and gives its stamp to the whole. Moreover, in agreement with physical theory this factor is firmly woven into the fabric of space, and united with it to form a unity, the unity of space-time which thereby becomes constitutive for the system of nature. This view is contained focally in the fundamental concept of event. From a philosophical standpoint Whitehead's doctrine on this matter stands nearer to that of Alexander than to that of Bergson, in which the time-character is equally dominant, though not in connection with the space-character, but in opposition to and isolated from it. In other respects Whitehead stands in very close intellectual relationship to these two great metaphysicians of our day, to whom he

[1] For suggested solutions of this difficulty compare the admirable explanations of Wind, *loc. cit.*, pp. 255 ff.

joins himself as a third ally. This shows itself much more in metaphysics than in natural philosophy, which is his own domain and in which he gives proof that he is rooted in mathematical and physical modes of thought. But even upon natural philosophy, from which above all metaphysical prejudices should be excluded, the coming metaphysics throws its shadows in advance. This occurs especially in the idea of the creative advance of nature, in the thought that its real character is becoming, or, as Whitehead prefers to say, "becomingness", that it finds itself in continued transition and unceasingly enters into new situations. If in the doctrine of objects mention is made of their permanent or static character, this is done with much less emphasis and with much less metaphysical significance. If anything is said of the duality of nature it is understood that the dynamic preponderates over the static element, or the event over the object, in both of which these antagonistic and at the same time complementary aspects are embodied. But all the threads of Whitehead's philosophy and all the phases of its development converge in the central concept of event. It is, looked at from the place at which we stand, viz. at the transition from natural philosophy to metaphysics, *chargé du passé et gros de l'avenir*. For into it, as that which bears the whole structure of the theory of nature, not only have mathematical modes of thought and all modern physics been poured, but it bears in its womb the anticipation of the metaphysics that was to follow.

Apart from these anticipatory hints, metaphysics breaks on us for the first time in the book *Science and the Modern World*; though here not yet in systematic development, but in a complicated confusion of deep and pregnant thoughts *de omnibus rebus et quibusdam aliis*. Speculations on the philosophy of history and civilization and views of the history of intellectual development are here interpolated among Whitehead's own doctrines, or conversely, if you will; and these doctrines are displayed from various viewpoints and in various lights. We will deal first briefly with the development of natural philosophy which here appears in a new and altered garb. Whitehead now adjusts his doctrine to the newly introduced concept of the organic, and therefore calls it the organic theory of nature or the *philosophy of organism*. Instead of the matter of the older physics and instead of the events or objects of his earlier phase (for this basic distinction is still maintained, though carried through less strictly) Whitehead now substitutes organism. Nature appears as organic both as a whole and in its several parts and elements. The structure of the organic contains in itself the element of capacity for development in the sense of the creatively new or emergent. It is embodied not only in biological organisms or living creatures, but also in inorganic matter down to its smallest parts. The electron itself has an organic structure. It possesses a definite individuality, and we must even allow it to have a life-history which reaches through a multiplicity of events and is different from that of other electrons. These primary entities which cannot be further divided are called by Whitehead primates. We recognize plainly their organic character, although their life-history and individual structure are almost completely hidden from us. Atoms and molecules, then, are organisms of a higher type in which a quite definite organized unity is already discernible. In larger aggregations of matter, in those which science calls inorganic bodies, there supervenes a disturbance of the organic principle. It here disappears into the background in order to come back fully into view at the higher level of living creatures. The life-history of these organisms can be followed through all their phases, and their individualities stand out plainly from each other.

In the developmental process of nature two different aspects can be distinguished, adaptation and creative power. On one side we see an environment with organisms which adapt themselves to it. Herein lies the truth of Darwinism, which is, however, only a partial truth. For on the other side we see organisms with the capacity of making their own environment and shaping it creatively. In this, however, the individual organism is almost powerless, and therefore it needs the company of co-operating organisms in order to achieve this purpose. The environment now appears no longer as firm and fixed, but as shapeable or plastic. Ordinary mechanistic evolutionism fails in so far as it neglects this second aspect, which is the deeper and more comprehensive, and a new light is thrown upon the idea of evolution whereby its full truth is first revealed. Whitehead does not wholly reject the mechanistic view, but he subordinates it to the organic, and because he does justice to both views he sometimes calls his theory organic mechanism. This theory, however, does not extend merely to organisms in the narrower sense, but also to the totality of natural entities and therefore also to primary structures. Although it may be admitted that electrons run their course according to mechanical laws, it makes an important difference whether this occurs inside or outside of a living body. Electrons, molecules, atoms, etc., are therefore different in their structural character according to the situation in which they run their course mechanically, and the organic principle in entities which appear to us as predominantly mechanical is manifested through the fact that these entities are organically combined with the situation in which they find themselves.

Whitehead also adjusts the organic theory to modern physics and believes that in it there is directly expressed what modern physics assumes in regard to the ultimate entities of nature. As a matter of philosophical history he connects it with Leibniz's theory of monads in which he sees a confirmation of his own organic view. Like the monads, Whitehead's primary entities are thoroughly organized ultimate real unities, but they are different from monads in that they are not closed against other entities, but are rather opened wide in virtue of the inner relations which spring from them and unite them with the rest of the world. Whitehead therefore rejects the windowlessness of the monads and the idea of pre-established harmony. For there is no need for a harmony established from without or by a *deus ex machina*; since everything which should be brought by it into harmonious unity springs out of the inner essence of the monads and must be understood from their own nature. Whitehead, indeed, more than any other British thinker of the XIXth and XXth Centuries (except, perhaps, Wildon Carr) has had recourse to the treasures of Leibniz's philosophy and brought them again to notice; just as he loves to take guidance from the other great metaphysical systems and thought-constructions of the pre-Kantian epoch, from Descartes, Spinoza, Locke, and Hume. Thereby he has inaugurated a kind of renaissance of pre-Kantianism which at the same time implies a renunciation of Kant and all German Idealism, because unimpregnated with the spirit of natural science. Nevertheless, this great movement (like almost all in the history of philosophy) has not passed by without leaving traces upon his thought, although its influence is shown more by way of repulsion than by attraction.

On the basis of natural philosophy, Whitehead erects a speculative system which aims at nothing less than a complete and comprehensive cosmology in which the world is viewed as a unitary whole. To him metaphysics is an intensive effort of constructive thinking or speculative reason, which seeks to show that the plurality of individuals can be combined with the unity of the whole, and further that the world demands its union with God and God his union with the world. Thus is introduced the theme to the working out of which all Whitehead's further efforts in philosophy are directed—efforts of a speculative reason which in Whitehead (as in Alexander) has displayed a vigour scarcely reached previously in the history of British thought. For British thought in its predominant aspect is unspeculative and anti-metaphysical, mainly because it bases itself upon experience and in its methods and aims follows the model of exact science. But with Whitehead there is an effort to overcome this ancient and inveterate contrast between experience and speculation, science and metaphysics, insomuch as his thinking accepts both the contrasting members and demands their systematic reconciliation. This last phase of Whitehead's philosophy implies no break with his earlier work. It is metaphysics in the best sense of the word and with consciously speculative aims, but replete with experience and full of the scientific spirit. We may indeed say that with Whitehead speculative thinking does not spring from blind impulse but is highly conscious of itself and of its value. It is not so much speculative impulse as speculative reason; i.e. it takes a reflective attitude to that which it achieves from inner necessity. Whitehead's metaphysics shows none of the bashfulness that British thinkers so often display in their speculative efforts. It is metaphysics speaking in the robust tones of perfect conviction and full of devotion to the study. Hardly ever has speculative reason been more highly valued by a British writer or more thoroughly understood than by Whitehead, as we can see from his little book *The Function of Reason*. It appears here as connected most closely with the highest functions of the human mind; it is not only the completion of all our efforts in the special sciences and philosophy, but also the element which drives them forward and shows us ever new possibilities of thought. Without it all intellectual life would sink into stagnation. Its function consists in making thinking creative and maintaining it in creative process. In this sense he ventures upon the bold and liberating phrase: "The rejection of any source of evidence is always treason to that ultimate rationalism, which urges forward science and philosophy alike."[1] In this way, though against his will, he becomes an ally of Hegel, whose philosophy he despises chiefly because he cannot free himself from the common prejudice that Hegel set himself above the science of his day, and so plunged forward into vacancy.

For the understanding of Whitehead's constructive philosophy it is important to notice that it is not a systematic structure with neat compartments, finished outlines, and symmetrical subdivisions; this would be in contradiction with his completely undogmatic way of thinking, which is never at rest, but continually fluid, open, free, and thoroughly personal in its attitude to the problematic aspect of things. He is not so much a great system-maker as a seer of genius, and his want of systematic power is fully compensated by the depth and width of his vision, by his wealth of ideas, and the persistent

[1] *The Function of Reason*, p. 50.

and penetrating energy of his thought. What he has said of Plato, his revered philosophical master, that he was the greatest of metaphysicians but the poorest of systematic thinkers, applies *mutatis mutandis* to himself.

Whitehead's metaphysics, which can only be sketched roughly (so that the final important results will be apparent, but not the equally important path which leads to them), moves like almost all great metaphysics round the central problem of the relation between the many and the one, change and duration, becoming and being, facts and forms, evil and good, necessity and freedom, or, briefly, between the world and God. In its highest cosmological inquiries it deals with the primal antithetic character of all existence and the overcoming of it. Its final aim is, therefore, the *coincidentia oppositorum*. His whole philosophy, as one might say, has as its framework the idea of antithesis or polarity; however various the forms in which it is expressed, it is always present and with it the eagerness of the thinker to transcend it in an ultimate unity—not, however, in the sense of establishing a monotonous uniformity which results in the extinction of one pole or the other, but rather in the sense of establishing equal rights for all. Transcendence of antithesis does not mean annihilation of one factor or the other, or absorption of one by the other; it means rather reconciliation of tensions, balancing of contending parts, and establishment of equilibrium between them; in short, it means synthesis.

In his natural philosophy, as was shown, this dichotomy of the world was expressed in the antithetic concepts of event and object, and in the tensional relation between them. In his metaphysics it appears first with rather different terminology in the antithesis between actual entities and eternal objects. These represent the metaphysical correlates of the former; i.e. they mean upon the plane of metaphysics the same thing as the former upon the plane of natural philosophy. The characteristic changes of meaning, which here appear, are therefore conditioned by the changed point of view. Whitehead defines actual entities, which he often calls "actual occasions", as "the final real things of which the world is made up".[1] In respect of their reality they are all "in the same boat", although in respect of their function and value they manifest important differences. There is no sense in going behind them in order to find something more real. They include the whole realm of reality or actuality and God belongs to them just as much as the most trivial bit of existence in any part of space. They are, as he once says, "drops of experience",[2] which are complex because each of them includes in itself all the others, or is contained by them as a component. Actual entities are never finished or closed, but are in continual process; or, as Whitehead also expresses it, they are concrescences, i.e. combinations of many things into a new unity. They are real, individual, and separate things, not in the sense of fixed objects but in the sense of moving events. They come into the flow of happenings from other entities, endure for a while and then pass into others. Every single one of them brings something new into the world. The world is changed and enriched by them in however small a degree and this enrichment is creative. But their disappearance does not imply the extinction or annihilation of something which once existed; the condition of the world is not impoverished. For every actual occasion in its downfall objectifies itself in another by which it is taken up and in the concrescence of which it forms thenceforward a constructive factor. Thus its peculiar existence is not lost even after the extinction of its actuality but is preserved for all time in the framework of the world. Whitehead calls this the objective immortality of actual entities which is as essential to them as their fleeting and transitory character and in no way conflicts with it.

The doctrine of actual entities embodies the Heraclitean element in Whitehead's cosmology. Everything is fleeting, the world is in becoming; it is an eternal process. But the stream of happening does not flow away simply; it does not merely flow past in order to cease to be and to make place for new flowing; all the past is gathered up by it and borne along

[1] *Process and Reality*, p. 24. [2] Ibid., p. 25.

with it. It is made broader and deeper by it and continually rises in its flow. Thus the Leibnizian element is indissolubly bound up with the Heraclitean. Every present happening of the world is, like the monad, charged with all the happening of the past (*chargé du passé*) and bears all the future which potentially rests within it and waits for actualization (*gros de l'avenir*). Bound up with both is the Bergsonian motive, in so far as the process is creative and produces ever new possibilities; as also the emergence-theory of Alexander, which is merely a variant of Bergson's.

The character of the world of being is not exhausted in the domain of the real and actual or the flow of things. In addition there arises in and out of it the domain of the possible or the permanent which is the original province of metaphysics. As everything actual is real or actualized only so far as it proceeds from the possible and is selected from it, it follows that the final explanation of the specific character of actual occasions lies in the analysis of the specific character of the realm of possibility. This is put forward as the world of transcendent entities or eternal objects. An exact definition and explanation of what Whitehead understands by this is not easy and would take us too far. In any case the concept of object when compared with its correlate in natural philosophy has undergone an immense broadening and deepening, though at the expense of its clearness. It is so greatly overladen with metaphysical knowledge and vision that it is hardly possible to disentangle all the threads which are woven together in it or to interpret all the wisdom which is hidden in it. A considerable element of Platonism is certainly incorporated in the doctrine of the eternal objects, as in the whole of Whitehead's cosmology, which, according to his own admission, is under a great debt to the mythical speculations of the *Timaeus*. But in accordance with the individual character of Whitehead's philosophy, which adopts no alien doctrine without recasting it, the relationship to Plato remains thoroughly indefinite, nor can the eternal objects be simply identified with Plato's ideas, but have their own specific mark. But the Platonic view can give us a fair indication of their meaning; and if we interpret them in the sense of universals, or of Lockean ideas, or of logico-mathematical forms of highest generality, or of categories or *a priori* factors in Kant's sense, each interpretation contains a greater or smaller kernel of truth. From all this it is evident that Whitehead by the concept of eternal object understands the formal as opposed to the factual, the ideal as opposed to the real, the general as opposed to the particular, the abstract as opposed to the concrete, the enduring as opposed to the changing, being as opposed to becoming; in short, the potential as opposed to the actual. The last aspect is the predominant one, especially in regard to metaphysics, and includes the others within itself. The eternal objects form a class of categories of existence and are defined as "pure potentials for the specific determination of fact, or forms of definiteness".[1] Their metaphysical status is that of possibilities for the realization of the factual or actual. The realms of the possible and the real stand, therefore, in a necessary relation to each other; and this relation is that of ingression, i.e. the possible passes into the real or makes its realization possible, and is therefore a precondition of the real coming into existence. The metaphysical principle of "reciprocal immanence", a basic principle of the organic philosophy, determines also the relation between eternal objects and actual entities.

Whitehead's metaphysics is not like those of Bradley and Alexander, an orderly system, which can be presented in a continuous train of thought, but is more like a labyrinth in whose countless paths one easily loses one's sense of direction, or like a complicated knot which can be disentangled only with difficulty. We will try to unfasten this knot by setting forth in conclusion the thought on which almost all its threads converge and in which they at the same time find their crowning completion, the idea of God. The idea of God is rooted fast in the whole of Whitehead's system, and is no supplementary addition which it could dispense with without serious loss. Whitehead's philosophy thus includes a strong religious ele-

[1] *Process and Reality*, p. 29.

ment, and although it is free from all dogmatic ties and develops to the end entirely from its own systematic assumptions, it has announced its sympathy with positively religious schools of thought, and is recognized and appreciated by them. In this respect it merely takes over the idealist inheritance of the past, insomuch as, like Idealism, it aims at a reconciliation of philosophy and religion, and is able also to satisfy the soul of the believer. Even apart from this, many various idealist elements are to be discerned in it; and Whitehead's general attitude of mind is altogether in favour of this tendency. It is thus intelligible that people have sometimes seen in him the champion of a new Idealism, which follows quite another path than that of Kant and the neo-Hegelians, but comes to much the same thing in the end. Whitehead himself is conscious of this when he says in the preface to *Process and Reality* that he finds himself in sharp opposition to Bradley's doctrine, but that the final results on both sides are not very far apart.

Whitehead's metaphysics, as we have seen, circles round the problem of the bi-polar relation of real and possible, becoming and being, actual entities and eternal objects. Over against the unlimited potentiality of the eternal forms stands the limited actuality of realized or temporal happening. The latter proceeds from the former by reason of a selective process, through which, out of the fullness of possibilities, only one definite reality receives embodiment and enters into the temporal process. If all the possibilities were realized, there would be no orderly world, but merely a complete chaos. Thus the question arises why there results from the creative cause of being just this world and no other, and why out of the unlimited fullness of possibilities just this happening is actualized. The primal creative cause through which all coming-to-be springs and which impels everything which has become real to ever new forms and events is called by Whitehead creativity. This embodies his basic metaphysical principle and it would be natural to assume that he identifies it with God. But that is not so. Whitehead rather understands by creativity the pure substantial activity at the basis of things, which is completely formless, without any definite character, without any limitation, but quite general and abstract. The pure possibility of the eternal objects stands in opposition to this purely active creativity, which precedes all real happening, and therefore all creation. If we must ask whether the world of things can arise from the co-operation of these two factors, unlimited possibility and abstract creativity, Whitehead answers no, and points out that the two together could never produce a definite something, a something real. Actuality rather presupposes a restriction or limitation both of unlimited possibility and of unbounded creativity. It is at this point that he brings the divine principle upon the scene. The primary function of God is nothing but just this restriction of general creativity—i.e. what Whitehead calls the "primordial nature of God". According to Whitehead God is not that primary creativity destitute of form and determination, but the first, original creation which proceeds from it. As such the divine principle is itself creative. It is the metaphysical reason of all things, real as well as possible, those which are actualized as well as those which are waiting for actualization. But it presupposes the general metaphysical character of creativity as *its* cause; it is the primal embodiment of this power, insomuch as it is the first thing which restricts it or gives it form. In this sense God is neither a merely ideal possibility nor a creativeness without aim or restraint, but a real, actual Being. He is the creator of all things, the cause why a world exists at all, why it comes from possibility into actuality and why from the unbounded fullness of possibilities of world-becoming, a determinate world has become and advances upon the path of becoming. God in His original character is, therefore, the *ratio sufficiens* of the world, or, as Whitehead expresses it, the principle of concretion.

This, as has already been shown, indicates the real character of everything which really exists. It asserts that everything which exists includes in its existence the totality of all being. It implies that nothing in the world is isolated or independent, but that everything partakes of all others and is intimately bound up with them. This is the universal immanence of things, the fact that they dwell in one another and mutually fulfil one another. Therein consists their eminently concrete character, 'concrete' being understood in the original sense of the word as 'grown together'. Things grow together with each other and every one of them grows with the whole remaining content of the world. In this emphatic sense concretion means the same as concrescence. That the organization of things is such and that the world is orderly—a cosmos not a chaos—is due to the primordial nature of God, who, though Himself not concrete, is the origin and source of all concrete actuality.

God in His original, or as Whitehead also puts it, conceptual nature is transcendent of the world. He is the unalterable principle, complete in Himself and eternal. In this original character He has no immediate participation in the becoming of the world; He is not immediately interwoven with it. But the nature of God possesses not only an original but also a consequent character. It is bi-polar and in this second character it streams out into the world and enters into the creative process of becoming. God in His derived function is immanent in the world; they are helpful to each other, and as the world cannot maintain itself, so God cannot dispense with the world. We can therefore speak of God's ingression into the world or, conversely, of the world's ingression into God. Both processes mean the same; i.e., that the creativity which is the origin of all being and takes its starting-point from God, streams out into the world and returns to Him. And as God in His primary function is the principle which tames and limits the primal creativity, so is He in His secondary function the orderly and formative principle in the world. As all order is according to Whitehead in the first place aesthetic order, God is the measure of it, and therefore He is also called the poet of the world. This God is nothing static and complete, not mere contemplation of the pure forms. He is ceaseless becoming, operative power, creative impulse, and He is the organ of the eternal renewal of the world and the unresting creative thrust by which all the becoming in the world is informed and driven forward. It is evident that these ideas are very closely related to the dynamic concept of God as represented by Bergson, Alexander, and the Pragmatists.

What is to be said about God, the world, and their mutual relation may now be expressed in a final survey of the cosmos through a series of antitheses which apparently contradict one another but just for that reason contain the whole truth. Whitehead sums up his metaphysics in the following striking propositions: "It is as true to say that God is permanent and the world fluent, as that the world is permanent and God is fluent; that God is one and the world many as that the world is one and God many; that in comparison with the world God is actual, eminently, as that in comparison with God the world is actual, eminently; that the world is immanent in God as that God is immanent in the world; that God transcends the world as that the world transcends God; that God creates the world as that the world creates God" (*Process and Reality*, p. 492). A final quotation may be given which lights up and summarizes the whole of Whitehead's cosmology: "Neither God nor the world reaches static completion. Both are in the grip of the ultimate metaphysical ground, the creative advance into novelty. Either of them, God and the world, is the instrument of novelty for the other" (*Ibid.*, pp. 493 ff.).

SAMUEL ALEXANDER (*b.* Sydney, Australia, 1859, *d.* 1938)

[Studied in Melbourne and Oxford, and in 1882 became Fellow of Lincoln College, Oxford; in 1893, Professor of Philosophy in Victoria University, Manchester; retired in 1924. In 1930 received the Order of Merit. *Moral Order and Progress: an analysis of ethical conceptions*, 1889 (third edition, 1899); *Locke*, 1908; "The Basis of Realism" (*Proceedings of the British Academy*, vol. vi, 1914); *Space, Time and Deity*, 2 vols., 1920 (second edition, 1927); *Spinoza and Time*, 1921; *Beauty and other forms of value*, 1933. Also numerous articles in professional periodicals. On Alexander see P. Devaux: *Le Système d'Alexander*, 1929.]

Next to Whitehead, Alexander is in his work and influence the strongest philosophical force which Anglo-Saxon thinking has produced since the war. What Bergson means for French philosophy, that Alexander means in many respects for British philosophy. But he stands less conspicuously above his environment and has been much later in coming to maturity and in attaining an influential position than his more famous French contemporary, born in the same year. The influence of Alexander's doctrine, moreover, has been so far confined to the Anglo-Saxon world, and within this to professional philosophical circles. It has not passed beyond the English-speaking community nor has it influenced other departments of intellectual life. The world-wide extension as well as the manifold influence upon different provinces of general culture of the Bergsonian philosophy have been denied to it. Although Alexander is inferior to Bergson in power and originality of thought and is far behind him in mastery of language and literary brilliance, yet his speculative power of vision and thought is very considerable, and his system of ideas is not unlike that of the Frenchman. Among British philosophers he is one of the greatest and boldest system-makers, and among the moderns Whitehead, Bradley, and McTaggart are the only men to compare with him in respect of the impulse to the formation of a comprehensive world-system.

In his philosophical descent he belongs to two different camps, the idealist and the naturalist. In Oxford, where he spent many years as student and Fellow of his college, he was unable in spite of an inner repulsion to withdraw himself from the idealist revival of the neo-Kantians and neo-Hegelians. He felt the powerful influence of Green and Bradley, traces of which are still visible in his mature thinking, although this has moved in quite another direction. But at the same time he was overtaken by the wave of Darwinian evolutionism which finally carried him away and brought him in the end to a naturalistic position. Thence, turning backward, he attached himself to the old national tradition, firstly to Hume's Empiricism, and then forward to modern mathematical physics, the philosophy of Bergson and the theory of knowledge of the New Realists (Moore, Russell, and the Americans). But what is of special importance for his doctrine and gives it a quite specific character is the fact that here for the first and only time since Spencer the ideas of the realist-naturalist-empiricist school have been used by a highly speculative mind with real systematizing power to form a unified world-scheme and an imposing articulated structure of thought. The fact that Alexander's philosophic vision ranges freely over the whole, and that he wishes to form a system and delights in speculation, he probably owes to Idealism. But, unlike most thinkers of his way of thinking, he has not simply ignored the idealist movement, but has passed right through it. It was in the first instance the idealist and especially the Hegelian movement which set free new speculative forces in England, forces which have now developed themselves in the opposite camp. Thus Alexander takes over Hume's empirical philosophy, but not his scepticism; Spencer's evolutionary philosophy, but not his agnosticism; the theory of knowledge of New Realism, without halting at it, using it only as an organ or a foundation for his metaphysics; and the physical theory of relativity, but not without a speculative evaluation and a subordination of it to his own system. All the components which enter into this doctrine have been welded into a unified system, which may show a flaw here and there, but viewed as a whole represents one of the strongest and most consistent systems of thought which have appeared in Great Britain.

Alexander's doctrine came late to maturity and has been presented in a single great work, the two volumes entitled *Space, Time and Deity*. This is composed of Gifford Lectures, which were delivered during the Great War, and has exercised a great influence since its publication in 1920. In the lively discussion which arose upon its appearance it was hailed by supporters and opponents as a philosophical event of the first rank and has since struck deep roots into the most diverse schools of Anglo-Saxon thought. Compared with it the rest of Alexander's writings are of subordinate importance. Except the early book *Moral Order and Progress*, which was written a generation earlier and has a certain independent importance in his philosophical development, they are mostly prolegomena or paralipomena in relation to his main work. *Moral Order and Progress* dealt with the problems of ethics long before his own system was formed and without essential connection with it. A short account of it must therefore be given here, especially as it is characteristic of the development of British philosophy under the influence of Darwinism.

The task of ethics consists in the analysis of moral concepts and presentations, and its basic problem lies in investigating the meaning of good and evil, right and wrong. As ethics in its essence is social, it concerns itself also with the relation of the individual to the world around him and with his place in the social community of which he is a member. But ethics is not only the description of moral phenomena and facts; it is also a normative science which has to determine the value of moral facts on the basis of the ethical ideal, and to examine the question of moral progress. Alexander's ethics both in its basic ideas and its detailed explanations, is a thorough application of evolutionist categories to the moral life and takes the side of the numerous biological moral theories which appeared in the train of Darwinism and were expressed most forcibly in Leslie Stephen's *Science of Ethics* (1882). In the most important points Alexander agrees with this book, though he has developed his arguments independently (see pp. 135 ff.).

He adopts the idea of natural selection and tries to apply it to the field of human conduct as the proper sphere of morality. Here we have not to consider, as we have among animals, the struggle for existence among individuals which is completed by the extermination of the weaker and the survival of the stronger members of a species as the best adapted to the environment. We have rather to consider the struggle of moral ideas which compete with each other and of which the more effective and vital according to the law of selection overcome the weaker and suppress them. Extermination of a rival in this case does not mean his physical annihilation, but his spiritual suppression by the power of persuasion which belongs to the stronger moral ideal. The origin, development, and maintenance or destruction of moral ideas proceeds according to the same law as the parallel processes among species of animals, i.e. according to the law of natural selection. But what is the meaning of this law in the moral world? According to what criterion can we distinguish the stronger moral ideal from the weaker, and finally the good from the bad? This criterion is found by Alexander in the concept of equilibrium, which is decisive for his position. This means that the goodness and rightness of a moral action consists in this, that the various elements (motives, impulses, and inclinations) which are in combination and mutual antagonism balance each other and thus adapt themselves to each other; in short, that they are in a condition of equilibrium. The moral ideal means nothing else than the adjustment of the elements to the ideal order within a whole which has been brought into equilibrium, and the approbation or recognition of an action in the moral judgment bases itself upon just this fact. There is, therefore, no need to assume the existence of a separate moral sense through which we make judgments about moral actions. The moral sense is rather the natural sense which finds itself in equilibrium or in unison with the moral ideal. Or, looking at the matter from the point of view of the moral agent, we may say that the feelings from which a moral action springs are not a special class of feelings, but simply ordinary feelings in the condition of harmonious adjustment. In its application to social life this means that we have reached an equilibrium between ourselves and our fellow-men or between individual and community similar to that between the elements of our being.

The ethical end is thus the equilibrium of moral conduct, and this is both the object and the norm of human action. It is, Alexander thinks, superior to all other ideals postulated by ethics, insomuch as it includes all of them in itself, the ideal of perfection, of self-realization, of the principle of the greatest happiness of the greatest number, and that of social vitality. In all these we are concerned with the harmonious balance of the forces of the moral and social life. Where this balance does not exist, the ideal of the good is not attained. Evil is defined by Alexander as that which in the struggle with the good is rejected and vanquished. When we condemn a bad action we merely mean that the norm according to which it is regulated is not that which prevails in the present condition of society, and that therefore it upsets the social equilibrium of this condition. What was formerly good may now be evil if the moral standard has changed meanwhile. The rejection of an action means the defeat of an ideal which has succumbed in the struggle with a successful variation, and the latter is just the new species which has prevailed and thereby established the now prevailing norm. But just here arises the problem of moral progress. Progress is essential for morality. There can be no absolute, unchangeable ethical principles since life, from which ethical standards spring, is in a continual process of development. Every moral ideal is only a brief halt in the passage from one ideal to another. Since new conditions and relations are always arising, the moral equilibrium also must continually be established anew. The essence of morality is therefore not static, but dynamic, it is uninterrupted development. This idea is emphasized more strongly by Alexander than even by Spencer, who held that ethics becomes more nearly absolute in proportion as the adjustment of man to his environment advances, so that at the end of the development a condition of complete adaptation is reached for which absolute moral standards prevail (see above, p. 109). But for Alexander adaptation means a common action of the individual and his environment, in which both sides conform to each other. As the environment changes like the individual the act of adaptation is not one-sided, but a selective process on both sides. But this implies that every adaptation is perfect adaptation and that the good of the moment is the absolute good. All moral behaviour so far as it is right under given conditions is absolutely right, and we cannot imagine any higher degree of absoluteness. From these considerations there results as the highest principle of morality the thought of free service or voluntary co-operation of the members of a community for the welfare of the whole, and as a moral maxim the simple precept "make the world better than thou hast found it".

At this early stage, then, Alexander's thought moves completely along the lines of the then fashionable principles of Darwin and Spencer. Like Nietzsche, Simmel, and many other contemporaries he paid a tribute to this movement in his ethics. The later development of his doctrine does not imply a complete divergence from it, but an emancipation from its more literal sense under the dominant influence of the new philosophical environment, by which his own creative powers were first set free. Between his early books and his main work there lies an interval of thirty years which, apart from a small book on Locke, is occupied only by a series of short essays. In some of these the new ideas already announce themselves which later are systematically brought together in *Space, Time and Deity*. Thus Alexander's most characteristic contribution did not fully appear, or exercise its deep influence upon contemporary philosophy, till after the Great War. We may pass over the writings which lie between the earlier and the later stages and turn to consider the main work in which Alexander has harvested the fruits of his long and ceaseless meditation.

We may begin by trying to sketch his theory of knowledge as far as possible separately from its metaphysical implications. His position is, as has been mentioned, a link in the chain of the New Realist movement which was begun by Moore and Russell shortly after the end of last century and carried on by a group of American thinkers in *The New Realism* of the year 1912. Since Locke the theory of knowledge has been studied in British philosophy as an independent science or department of philosophy, which stands upon its own foundations, though often, especially in empiricist and realist systems, it has been combined with general philosophical inquiry. But in this respect there comes a notable change with Alexander. As the centre of gravity of his doctrine lies in his metaphysics he rejects the primacy of theory of knowledge and treats it merely as a kind of introductory chapter to the much wider considerations of metaphysics. This greatly diminishes its importance, causing it to depend for its basis ultimately upon philosophy as a whole.

Wherein consists the essence of knowledge? Alexander describes it with startling simplicity as a relation between two entities, a subject and an object or a consciousness and a thing. If we ask what kind of relation this is, it shows itself to be nothing but simultaneous presentness of the two components of knowledge or, as Alexander expresses it, as compresence or togetherness. The relation is exactly the same as that between two physical objects; e.g. between the table and the floor upon which it stands. Knowledge comes into existence only when one of the two components which is compresent with the other is a subject endowed with consciousness. It makes no difference to the relation whether a subject confronts an object, or whether two objects or two subjects confront each other. The sole point is whether the two components are together. The knowledge-relation therefore has no special dignity or peculiarity; it is the simplest relation that we can imagine, just that of compresence. This definition of knowledge, which, Alexander holds, is reached by mere introspection, implies the presupposition that the knowing subject is not something *sui generis*, which is different in principle from the objects known, or transcends them in any peculiar manner, but only an existent thing among other existents, or a thing among things in a common world. The metaphysical consequences which are implicit in this, will become apparent later.

The results for theory of knowledge which spring from the above are as follows. The object as such is completely independent of the subject or of the mind, with which it can enter into a knowledge-relation. It is a non-psychical entity which is not further affected or modified by the presence of a consciousness. It is existent or real whether it stands in the knowledge-relation or not; this makes no difference to its being. On the other hand the subject is dependent upon the object as its original material. Consciousness is always consciousness *of* something, *of* an object. The little word "of" is the expression of compresence. When I perceive a tree, then I and the tree are together. The togetherness of the tree with myself is experienced by me as my togetherness with the tree. So far Alexander's doctrine is not different from ordinary Realism, at least in its formulation. In what follows, however, it goes far beyond it by a further development which implies a radical change. He explains not only objects as such, or things in themselves as physical realities transcending consciousness, but also percepta or sensa which are commonly reckoned as existing in consciousness and as psychic phenomena which picture or represent the things of the external world. It is an error to separate the perceived thing from its perceptual image or content, or to localize the latter in consciousness, the former outside of consciousness. The images of things are rather the things themselves or parts of them. They are therefore not psychic, but physical like the things themselves. They are the various perspectives under which we perceive objects. In perception we choose from the totality of the perspectives of one thing one or more, according to the position of the observer in reference to the observed object. The real thing is identical with the totality of the perspectives contained in it; it is that from which the perspectives are chosen by the perceiving subject. Therefore the perspectives are not unreal; they are only partial and in their mode of existence are physically real like the whole from which they are taken.

Alexander, therefore, carries objectivism or realism to the furthest extreme. Everything which in any way confronts the subject, or which in the act of knowing is given as compresent, is put "outside of the mind" and assigned to the physical world of things. His doctrine is the radical converse of Berkeley's subjectivist theory of knowledge; not *esse* = *percipi*, but *percipi* = *esse*; not things = ideas, but ideas = things. There are no ideas which are not things, or at least do not belong to things. This applies not only to perceptual contents or to Hume's impressions, but also to everything which Hume included under the term "ideas", and therefore to the presentations of memory, of expectation, of imagination and fancy, and to fictions and illusions, and finally even to all conceptual constructions, such as abstractions, universals, logical and mathematical symbols, etc. We may illustrate this by memories and illusions. In memory we have not to do with presentations which refer back to the past or represent it. We are dealing rather with the past itself and not with its image or representative in consciousness. We experience the past immediately as past; it carries, as Alexander says, a mark upon its forehead which announces its pastness. Pastness is a datum of experience which we apprehend directly, and therefore is an object which is compresent with us as past. Even illusions are perspectives of the real world and not pure creations of the spirit. But they are distinguished from sensa by the fact that they are referred to things to which they do not really belong. They are constructions which do not stand in their right place, which have been displaced or placed awry, and therefore are somehow dislocated—a dislocation which is the work of the mind. They are therefore subjective in reference to their origin, but objective in reference to their mode of existence. Here also the mind creates nothing new, but only arranges what is already there, puts it into new and peculiar relations, chooses perspectives in unusual ways, etc. But the elements from which all these constructions are composed are things or thing-aspects of the real physical world. Apart from a small but very important correction, this doctrine agrees precisely with Hume's theory of impressions and ideas. It is a revival of Hume's basic principle that every idea, though it may be never such an airy construction of fancy or remote abstraction of thought, is in the end constituted out of impressional elements and based upon them. Knowledge can bring these basic elements into ever new connections, but it cannot in principle get away from them. Alexander's correction of Hume consists merely in this, that he determines the mode of existence possessed by impressions and ideas differently from Hume; he holds that they are not psychic phenomena, existing "in" consciousness, but physically real and independent of consciousness. We might say then that nothing has been changed but the existential character. Alexander's theory of knowledge is the purest Humism; but it is not Phenomenalism; it is rather extreme, not to say brutal Realism. But the final intentions of this doctrine can only be understood from the point of view of his metaphysics.

Another important distinction is drawn by Alexander in relation to the mode of apprehending subjective acts and objective things. These come to our consciousness in different ways. The ego apprehends its own psychic acts in experiencing or "enjoying" them; while it perceives or contemplates physical objects. We cannot isolate our own ego as an object of contemplation and set it over against ourselves or apprehend it objectively by an act of perception. We can only live through it and through its acts. The earlier definitions are therefore to be extended to mean that in every experience the mind both "enjoys" itself and contemplates its object; so that we have two strictly different existents, which are connected with each other by the relation of compresence. Every experience is a piece of the world, which consists of these two existents in their togetherness. One existent, the enjoyed, experiences or enjoys itself as part of its life; the other, the contemplated, is experienced by that which enjoys itself. Thus it is evident that in spite of all efforts to delimit the subjective as opposed to the objective, mind is in the end drawn down to the plane of the objective, and that Alexander's doctrine when thought out consistently ends by agreeing with Hume, and results in the well-known bundle-theory, according to which the ego is composed of the sum or collection of its experiences and is nothing beyond this.

But Alexander's theory of knowledge is only the prelude to his metaphysics, and can only be understood through it. Metaphysics is the basis of his whole philosophy; all the lines of his thought converge upon it and are gathered up in it. It is Alexander's deepest interest and his most important, original, and influential contribution. It is science and system, cosmology and speculation in one. Regarded historically, it is the direct continuation of the comprehensive system of Spencer. It is the latest and ripest fruit on the tree of the great evolutionist movement and probably its completion. It reaches indeed the highest summit which the national tradition can reach. Compared with Spencer it is closer in its concentration, bolder in speculation, more constructive, and more positive in result, but for that reason narrower in its empirical basis, less replete with exact knowledge and with less bearing upon cognate inquiries. It has been called an ambitious work of imagination, and this is in certain respects a just judgment. Alexander, however, would have it be regarded as a strictly scientific inquiry. The *method* of philosophy is empirical and is in no respect different from that of exact science. Only the *domain* of philosophy is wider and more comprehensive, insomuch as it includes not only empirical reality, but its non-empirical or *a priori* features, as well as those problems which arise out of the relation of the empirical to the *a priori*. Thus the character of philosophical inquiry is defined as the empirical study of the non-empirical. As systematic metaphysics, philosophy, moreover, is directed upon the totality of the universe. It investigates its first and final cause and has the task of viewing our knowledge of the universe critically and arranging it systematically. It is also an investigation of the meaning of our existence and the meaning of the world.

The central element of Alexander's metaphysics is the now famous doctrine of space-time. According to his own admission, this concept takes the place of the absolute in idealist systems. But there is the characteristic difference that the absolute of the Hegelians means the highest expression of the universe, while Alexander's is its lowest. Naturalistic metaphysics, therefore, represents the exact converse of the idealistic. Its centre of gravity rests entirely upon the lowest plane of being. This metaphysically is the most important point, and is the focus from which all the rest emanates and to which it returns. Space-time is the primal matter or ὕλη of all things. It is the matrix which lies behind everything, the begetter and producer of all finite being. Things are merely differentiations of this primal material. Such is the fundamental hypothesis of this metaphysics.

We may ask the question how Alexander came to this peculiar view of the basis of Being as space-time, a view which has so far not occurred to any thinker in the whole history of philosophy (with the single exception of the Hungarian philosopher Palágyi, see below). There can be no doubt, and Alexander occasionally mentions the fact, that this idea is connected with modern mathematical physics and that only through this connection could it become relevant to philosophy. Though Alexander himself has not been trained in physics, he has boldly taken up the hints of the theorists of relativity who have made a basic change in our conceptions of space and time and of their mutual relations. But we have here no exact adoption or exploitation of the physical theories of Lorentz, Minkowski, and Einstein, but merely a general suggestion transferred to metaphysics and infused with Alexander's own creative ideas. Alexander himself wishes his concept of space-time to be understood in a thoroughly metaphysical sense and therefore it is not worth while to enter upon an inquiry as to the agreement or discrepancy between it and its physical counterpart. This only need be said here, that apart from the relativity-theory Alexander's space-time metaphysics is unthinkable. It is unthinkable also apart from Bergson's doctrine of time as *durée réelle*, which also forms an essential constituent of it. That the problem of space-time was in the air *before* the development of the relativity-theory and was waiting for philosophical formulation is proved most plainly by the writings of the Hungarian thinker Palágyi. As early as 1901 he developed a philosophical theory of space-time in which Alexander's ideas were in many respects anticipated. But this we may disregard, as there has evidently been no direct influence of the one thinker on the other (see J. A. Gunn, *The Problem of Time*, 1929, pp. 208 ff.).

What, then, are we to understand by space-time hypostatized into primal matter? How does a construction composed of the two categorical forms of arrangement, space and time, come to be raised to such metaphysical dignity? It is clear that here we have not to do with the ordinary views of space and time, and still less with a mere combination of them into an artificial whole, but with an original synthetic vision of a supreme unity in which the components are shaped into a creative novelty. We can imagine that the following or a similar dictum of Minkowski's may have released the igniting spark in Alexander's mind: "From henceforth space in itself and time in itself sink to mere shadows, and only a kind of union of the two preserves an independent existence" (see Einstein, article "Space-Time" in *Encyclopaedia Britannica*, 14th edition, vol. xxi, p. 105). Alexander similarly explains space and time taken by themselves as mere abstractions from unitary space-time, abstractions which can indeed be made by thought, but which in reality do not belong to things. In things there is neither mere space, nor mere time, but only the most intimate interweaving or welding of the two, their complete union with, through, and in each other. We may ask if this can be proved. But, as Alexander expressly declares, we have here nothing to do with deduction or construction, but merely with seeing, discovering, and disclosing things and relations which are given in experience—a procedure which may with justice be termed phenomenological description or analysis in Husserl's sense.

Space and time, then, are closely related and dependent on each other. One needs the other for its completion, has reference to it, and without it is nothing or at most an empty abstraction. There is no space without time and no time without space. Space is in its essence temporal and time spatial, or, as Alexander also says, space is full of time and time is full of space. Space and time present themselves to us as infinite and continuous wholes composed of parts; the latter we call points and moments. If we consider time purely in itself, i.e. according to its purely temporal character, as in physics, it manifests itself at first as successiveness, i.e. as a string of discrete moments, of which some are earlier, others later. We cannot speak of a binding together of the several moments, or of a persistence of an earlier in a later or of a past in a present. Rather every moment at the instant of its coming into being disappears and vanishes for ever. Time as successiveness would be a mere now which would have to be continually created afresh. The pure temporality of time would leave no room for the continuity of time, and would indeed conflict with it. In reality we experience time not as pure successiveness, but as a continuum of moments, or as a duration of the successive. Real time is successiveness within duration. Time as such is, therefore, incomplete and in need of supplementation. To ensure the togetherness of past and present, earlier and later, it needs a continuum which is not contained in its purely temporal character, and is something in principle different from it. This 'other' of time is space. Space supplies to time the continuum through which the binding together of its parts takes place and so rescues it from its mere 'nowness'. Space must necessarily reinforce time in order to solve the contradiction between mere succession and true continuity. Time is, therefore, spatial insomuch as it is more than pure temporality, i.e. in so far as it is real time, or duration.

But space also cannot dispense with time. Taken by itself space would be a whole of coexistence and continuity in which no parts could be distinguished. As pure spatiality it would be a mere emptiness. Everything that it contained would be swallowed up by it. Things in their multiplicity and diversity would be extinguished in it. But the empirical continuity of space shows itself to be incompatible with its second empirical characteristic, the distinctiveness of the parts which it contains. But this latter characteristic is not supplied by the all-togetherness which is the special quality of space in its purely spatial character. There must, therefore, be some form of existence which, although not itself spatial, distinguishes and delimits the parts of space from one another. This other form of existence is time. It has to provide space with that element without which space would be complete emptiness. Without space there would be, then, no binding together in time, while without time there would be no points of space to be bound together. Thus it follows that there can be no moment of time without a position in space and no point of space without a moment of time. A point of space occurs at a definite moment of time, and a moment of time includes a definite point of space. There are, therefore, no such things as points or moments in themselves. There are only point-instants or pure events. Just as little are there pure space and pure time; there are only time-space or space-time, i.e. a continuum of point-instants or pure events.

These views are different from Bergson's theory of time in one decisive point. Bergson's whole effort is directed towards divesting time of its spatial character and presenting it in its complete purity as duration. Alexander, on the other hand, sees in the spatialization of time an essential character of it. Bergson's *durée réelle* is a complete despatialization of time, i.e. release of time from the spatial bonds which fetter it, and thereby achievement of its pure essence. In Alexander's doctrine just that is made essential to time which Bergson denies to it, namely, spatialization, i.e. the complete interpenetration of space and time to the point of forming a new unity, space-time. In spite of this basic difference, Bergson has contributed much to Alexander's metaphysics.

The development of the concept of space-time is the foundation of Alexander's metaphysics. Space-time is the primal stuff of the world; it is like a vast matrix from which the totality of things or the world is born. It is the unity which includes every sort of differentiation. But it is also the essence of things after they have emerged from this matrix, after their separation into definite and diverse shapes and forms. Even when it splits up into the multiplicity and manifoldness of things it penetrates and fills them with its essence. Without it nothing can endure and nothing happen. But it is not only the factual but also the *a priori* logical presupposition and condition of all that is empirically and all (not only material but also mental) that exists finitely, and therefore itself super-empirical and infinite. We might call it also the categorial framework of the world or the all-embracing medium, or the universe in its primal form, or the one or the absolute or finally God. We cannot get behind the space-time unity and we must think of God Himself as taken up in it.

Alexander usually calls his absolute the original stuff (ὕλη). But from the foregoing it is evident enough that we must understand this term not in its literal but in a metaphorical sense. Above all, we must not understand it in the sense of matter or think that Alexander has hypostatized matter to be the essence of things, and has succumbed to ordinary materialism. According to his doctrine, matter is something quite secondary, belonging to the empirical world of the finite and like everything really existent generated by the primal stuff, but not suited to furnish the essence of being. On the other hand space-time, as we shall see, stands much nearer to the material than to the mental, although it is distinguished from both by its *a priori* character, and it will be seen that mind is taken to be a function of matter and not matter a function of mind. Moreover, it is just the spatial component of the primal stuff which points to its kinship with matter. Thus we may call Alexander's metaphysics most appropriately naturalistic, because it is organized entirely with reference to the categories of natural science, and as materialistic in a refined or disguised fashion in order to mark its difference from the ordinary crass materialism.[1]

This is fully justified by the fact that in further characterizations of the character of space-time the temporal component gains the predominance, while the spatial retires into the background.[2] In one passage it is said that we must think of space as generated by time, since time is the source of movement. Pictorially expressed, space can be represented as the trail of time, but not conversely, because space has no movement

[1] See *Space, Time and Deity*, vol. ii, pp. 49 f.: "Of the familiar types of existents, material existence is possibly closest to space-time and the stuff of reality may therefore most easily be conceived on the material analogy; for the phrases 'stuff of things', 'the matrix in which things are precipitated' are all physical descriptions."

[2] The purely theoretical derivation of the concept of space-time in no way creates a prejudice in favour of one of the components; it is only when considered metaphysically that time preponderates over space, as is indicated by the term space-time, not time-space.

in itself. It throws a light upon the proper sense in which the primal stuff is ultimately to be understood that occasionally instead of space-time the term movement is introduced. Space-time is said to be a system of movements and movement is called the only quality which is possessed by the otherwise qualityless primal stuff. But this movement which comes to pass in space-time must be understood as pure movement, because it precedes the origin of material things, and is not a mere relation between things which exist already and which may be said to be in motion. Pure movement is something ultimate, preceding all separateness, and like space-time, is called a stuff from which things are made. This doctrine seems like a revival of the cosmological speculations of the old Ionian thinkers, and reminds us of the world-fire of Heraclitus and the primal vortex of Empedocles and Anaxagoras. In fact, Alexander's metaphysics viewed from this point seems like the last and most grandiose embodiment of Heraclitean thought. Movement is the essence of the world, not only in its primal stage, but also after finite being has assumed definite forms. The primal movement, from out of which things have been flung as from an ever-revolving whirlpool, communicates itself as impulse or nisus also to empirical happening. For Alexander there is no firm and fixed being, nothing which is absolutely at rest. "If anything were at rest, everything would be at rest and space-time would lose its meaning."[1] What we call rest is likewise movement, for a resting body is in movement relatively to space-time. All things are entangled in the eternal unrest of becoming. Everything is living movement and restless development. The universe is through and through a history in the continually flowing stream of happening. Thus time triumphs finally over space.

Within the framework of the space-time theory Alexander has also developed an elaborate doctrine of categories, which he himself has declared to be the central point of his metaphysics. Apart from their space-time filling, empirical things possess a great number of characters and qualities, among which two

[1] *Space, Time and Deity*, 1927. Preface, p. xii.

classes can plainly be distinguished; those which change from thing to thing, and those which belong essentially to all things. The former, those which change, are called qualities; the latter, those which are constant, are categories. Qualities are empirical characters; categories on the contrary, as the essential and universal constituents of everything which is given in experience, are *a priori*, non-empirical, or categorial characters. Following Kant, Alexander calls them also categories of experience, and therefore in a wider sense also empirical, just as he called philosophy the empirical investigation of the non-empirical. They are the necessary scaffolding of all empirical reality, everywhere interwoven, penetrating and filling everything. Their most conspicuous quality is this capacity of penetration which extends not only to external, material things, but also to spiritual and psychic life. They are not subjective forms of the mind or mere functions of the understanding which are applied to things, but objective factors which constitute things and are given with and in them. They are that which remains when things are divested of their sensory and other qualities. In their origin they stand—an important fact—in close connection with the primal stuff. They are the basic forms or qualities of space-time in so far as it has streamed out into the finitude of existence and has taken shape in particular phenomena. Space-time itself as the infinite matrix of everything finite, is not yet shaped categorically. But simultaneously with the earliest appearance of separate things the categorical penetration begins.

From the number of categories dealt with by Alexander we select causality only as an example. Hume's greatest service consists in having purified the concept of cause from all anthropomorphic and obscurantist associations. But his atomism prevented him from reaching the kernel of the problem. He cut through the sole bond which unites cause and effect and then was unable to find the unity which he himself had destroyed from the beginning. Alexander gives a very simple and clear description of this category with the help of the concept of movement. Space-time as the system of movements is a continuous system, within which every movement is continuous with every other. Causality is nothing else than this relation of continuity between two different movements. That which in order of time precedes the movement into which it is prolonged is the cause; the other is the effect. Causality is therefore continuity of two substances within a space-time whole. It is transition of movement, which does not mean that the cause disappears in the substance which is acted upon, but only that it is added to the movements which are already present there.

The space-time doctrine forms the foundation of Alexander's system; the doctrine of categories is its immediate consequence. To it is attached the very important doctrine of order and of the problems of empirical existence. This section is continued in the doctrine of Deity with which the system concludes. In the third book the investigation advances into the wide field of experienceable reality. This investigation is guided by the clue of a new and dominating thought which is one of the main pillars of the system and in the sequel has not only proved itself extremely fruitful, but has even enjoyed a certain fashionable vogue. It is the thought which has been developed in the doctrine of Emergence or new appearance. This is the formulation of a general cosmic law of development and of an arrangement and connection of stages of being from a new point of view. Historically, this doctrine represents an up-to-date continuation and deepening of Spencer's evolutionary philosophy as was previously Bergson's doctrine of creative evolution, from which it received an immediate impulse, and of which it may be regarded as the British counterpart. Before Alexander and contemporaneously with him Lloyd Morgan was led to a similar theory by considerations predominantly biological. Alexander is directly indebted to him, but we still owe him the service of giving the new idea a metaphysical application by incorporating it firmly in his system.

Empirical things are groupings of elements within a limited space-time field, which itself is a part or section of the infinite continuum of space-time in general. In other words, they are complexes of pure events or movements in manifold grades of complexity. Moreover, they are filled with all those categorial characters which penetrate inwardly every piece of finite space-time, and pour out from the essence of primal matter into the empirical world. They are also in possession of separate, continually changing and self-renewing qualities, whereas we must think of primal matter as qualityless, unless we recognize pure movement as its sole characteristic quality. The categories are only the general scaffolding or skeleton of the world; only through qualities do things obtain colour and shape, tone and timbre. Then only do they weave the variegated carpet of life, in whose many-hued brightness we delight. This living world of things now comes into existence, breaking forth mysteriously from the primal background, at a definite point of time. There arise complexes or constellations of elementary parts which group themselves into unitary forms and shapes. There arise stages of being each of them provided with special characteristic qualities. In the course of development there arise on the basis of the elementary processes by new arrangement and grouping of elements new qualities and ever new stages of being of a higher order. Alexander describes this process in the following terms. The processes of one stage are a-processes with the quality A. A special grouping of these processes arises as a new process, ab, whose quality is B. Although the ab-processes are also a-processes, they are not that only, but stand upon a plane different from the a-processes which represents the next higher plane of being. The higher quality emerges from the lower plane of existence and has its roots in it. But it raises itself above it and no longer belongs to it, but arranges its possessor in a new order of being, for which separate laws of behaviour prevail. The newly arising quality is called by Alexander "emergent", and the process of arising "emergence". Thus mind emerges from the sphere of life, and life from the inorganic realm. This process rests upon the raising of the elements of which the lower plane consists to greater complication and differentiation. How this creative process comes to pass in the individual we cannot explain. We must accept it as an empirical fact, to be reverenced with natural piety.

On the basis of the foregoing ideas Alexander sketches his cosmological system of Emergent Evolution. The empirical world rises from the primal background of space-time, into whose unfathomable depths it sinks its roots. Space-time presents itself as the world-substance, which remains after all emergent qualities and categories have been subtracted. It is an all-present and all-penetrating continuum or a fluid of pure movements with a space-time character. We call the lowest phase pure qualityless movement. Between it and the next level the empirical universe assumes its basic structure. Observation here fails us almost completely. But we may assume that pure movement passes over into movement filled with matter and that mechanical matter (electrons, atoms, and molecules) represents the first level of the world of experience. To the purely space-time relations there is now added a new quality, materiality, and it is clear that the primary qualities of matter precede the secondary. There follows the plane of physico-chemical existence, where probably chemism is a new quality which emerges from the physical order. Between each of the layers here sketched there may be intervening members, and even within each layer there are progressively ascending stages. Within the physico-chemical processes and continuous with them there develops a new quality, life. This is not an epiphenomenon of matter, but emerges out of it. Alexander rejects the theory of neo-vitalism, according to which there is a separate stuff of the organic, such as Driesch's entelechy. Organic stuff belongs completely to the physico-chemical sphere; if the particular kind of constellation which produces life were known, it could be analysed completely into physical and chemical processes. There is no sufficient reason for severing the continuity between the material structure and the emergent order of vital structure. Life and matter are not separated from each other by an unbridgeable cleft. Here there is clearly a conflict between continuity and emergence. If the stages pass continuously into one another then the intervention of what is creatively new, the element which really emerges is hard to understand. Moreover, we can see plainly the tendency to explain things from below, the explanation of higher qualities by the lower levels, so that the apprehension and determination of the creatively new in its specific quality comes out boldly. Alexander's thought is here completely involved in the materialistic ideas of the older evolutionary movement.

This becomes still more evident when we pass to the next higher plane which is termed comprehensively consciousness or mind. Mind occupies no exceptional position within the process of emergent evolution. It does not soar above the realm of nature, but is firmly embedded in it. This means that it is held by the ruthless iron grip of the system. Mental processes develop from the organic structures of the vital sphere and within these from the physiological conditions of the nervous system. There is therefore need for a particular constellation of vital or neural structure in order that mind may arise. A mental event does not correspond to every neural event, but every mental event includes in itself the emergence of a new characteristic feature. Nature has created the new quality, mind, from certain physiological conditions. This quality is not itself physiological; but it lives, works, and exists in physiological conditions. Mind is therefore something both old and new; vital, but not merely vital; rooted in neural processes, but rising above them. Here also Alexander emphasizes the continuity of all spiritual life with earlier stages, immediately with the neural processes of the brain, mediately also with lower organic and inorganic phenomena.

In another connection Alexander has attached the doctrine of mind still closer to the bases of his system, and has united it directly to his doctrine of space-time. Here he advances considerably in naturalizing and materializing mind. He does not hesitate to speak of mind itself as spatio-temporal, and of a special mental space-time, manifesting the same features as physical space-time and identical with a part of it. Its spatial and temporal components are similarly related to and penetrated by each other, as we have seen in the case of primal matter. Mental space-time is a finite section of the infinity of space-time in general. We must think of mental processes not only as elapsing in time, but as filling space, or, at least, as localized at a definite position in space. Space, therefore, stands in as close a relationship with mind as with matter; the mental is no less extended than the material. The higher mental self is on all its planes merely a continuation, unfolding, and refinement of the bodily self. The particular locality at which the processes of the soul take place is identical with the neural substance of the brain. Psychic experiences occupy different places in mental space. The experience of a present event occurs at a different place from that of a past or future event. But as experiences can change their positions (when, e.g., something present becomes something past) experienced space is also full of experienced time, and, conversely, experienced time is distributed over experienced space. The past is not extinguished by the present, but leaves its traces on it. The present is penetrated by the past and this penetration is identical with that of space by time. Only now can we understand what was set forth above in the theory of knowledge, that the knowing subject or consciousness is only one thing among other things in a common world, and that the psychic contents (perceptions, images, fictions, and concepts) in their mode of existence belong to the physically real world. In the light of metaphysics this means that they are all involved in space-time conditions. The apparently brutal realism of the theory of knowledge finds its support and explanation in metaphysical materialism.

Finally, the close union of the bodily with the mental justifies further a highly speculative conclusion which is calculated to obliterate the basic thought of the emergence-doctrine, or at least to weaken it considerably. In order to view the various orders of empirical existence from a single standpoint, Alexander introduces a sort of world-formula which is based on the analogy of the unity of mind with body. This formula, which makes no claim to exact truth, but only to be a fruitful hypothesis, says that time as a whole and in its parts stands to space as a whole and its corresponding parts in a relation similar to that of mind and its bodily basis; or, briefly, that time is the mind of space and space the body of time. Alexander therefore assumes that in the matrix of all being, space-time, there is an element, time, which relatively to the element, space, has a function similar to that of mind relatively to its bodily counterpart. This formula is applicable to the other levels of being. The emergent quality of a level appears, then, as the mind of this level, and the level itself as the bodily stuff from which the new form emerges. But in this case material existence is not merely material in the sense in which matter is opposed to mind. Even matter includes an element which corresponds both to the bodily and the psychic, and which constitutes the materiality of matter, whatever this may be. Although matter is not animated in the same sense as an organism is, yet it contains an element which in it plays a part similar to that which life plays in organic structure or consciousness in the human person. Thus Alexander sees himself constrained to the conclusion that a chain of affinity encompasses the whole universe, and that there is no existence the constitution of which does not in some way or other correspond to ours as the highest known to us in the world-plan. There is, therefore, nothing dead or inanimate in the universe, and we must view space-time itself as somehow animated and endowed with life. Alexander's doctrine, therefore, ends in a panvitalism or pampsychism, which is sharply opposed to the strictly empirical foundation on which he professed to build his metaphysics. Although this speculation too is evidently inspired by upward-looking ideas, it is plain that it inflicts a mortal wound upon the emergence-doctrine. For now the boundary between the two levels is to a large extent obliterated and the fruitful thought of the emergent as the creatively new loses all its importance.

With mind the system of emergent development reaches the highest level which is accessible to human experience. But there remains a further province which is not immediately connected with the foregoing arguments and therefore needs separate treatment. This province, which springs directly from the mental sphere, is the realm of values. Alexander, using an original terminology, calls values the tertiary qualities of things and in ordinary fashion understands by them the true, the good, and the beautiful, and their respective contraries. Both the primary and the secondary qualities had been completely separated by him from the knowing subject and referred to the objective sphere. They belong to things quite independently of whether they are realized by a consciousness or not. This is inevitable in such an extreme objectivism as Alexander's. Even the secondary qualities owe their existence neither to mind nor to the sense-organs, but inhere materially in external objects. Colour, e.g., is present if the necessary physical conditions (presence of light) are fulfilled. But this does not hold good for the tertiary qualities or values. Here Alexander acknowledges expressly as necessary the relation to the consciousness which realizes the value. The rose is red whether it is seen by me or by another; and it makes no difference whether there are eyes to see it or not. But the proposition that the rose is red is *true* only if it is stated by me or by someone else, or if the quality 'red' is attributed to the rose by one or more perceiving subjects. Truth and reality are therefore clearly to be distinguished. The fact as such stands beyond the alternative true or false, beyond all subjective conditionality. But the truth of the fact holds good only in relation to the subject which cognizes it. Values are, therefore, not qualities of things but creations of the mind; though this does not mean that they are not real. Although they are dependent upon the valuing subject, they inhere in objects which exist in reality apart from the subject. They are new characters of reality, although not qualities in the proper sense, but just values which arise through the connection of mind with its object. Colour, which I experience as beautiful, belongs as colour to the object. But its beauty is added by me to it as a new characteristic when that connection takes place on the ground of which it gives me aesthetic pleasure.

Values, accordingly, among all emergent qualities are the

only ones which are not objectified. Their subjectivization is not annulled by the fact that Alexander makes them dependent not upon the individual but upon the collective consciousness. The knowing individual cannot possess truth for himself alone; truth exists only in so far as a majority of individuals make their contribution collectively to the whole system of true propositions; while error means expulsion of the erring individual from the intellectual community. The individual cognizes truth only so far as he is the representative of the social spirit. The same holds good *mutatis mutandis* for the other provinces of value. Sociality is, therefore, a fundamental character of all values as much as subjectivity is. If we consider the mutual relations of the individual value-qualities, it is plain that they are all included in truth-value, insomuch as this has as its object reality in its totality. Truth represents the whole of reality. Goodness is the highest revelation of finite existence which is known to us. Beauty occupies a middle position between the two, insomuch as the aesthetic spirit neither follows reality in the way the theoretic spirit does, nor shapes reality in the way the moral spirit does, but unites both, freely rendering back the real with beauty for its form.

The doctrine of values is freer from the fetters of system than most of the other parts of Alexander's metaphysics. On the other hand, in the doctrine of Deity the system resumes all its rights. This is a termination and rounding-off of the metaphysical system much more than it is a knowledge or vision of God. It is much less a question of what God is than a question of what place and function remains for Him in a universe so constructed. One who has immersed himself in Alexander's work must be almost in a position to construct his teaching in advance. We can deduce it from his doctrine of emergent evolution. Of the empirical qualities which have emerged from being in continually ascending stages mind is only the highest which we know so far. There is, therefore, no reason for the assumption that the hierarchy of qualities is exhausted with mind. When from the womb of infinite time ever new forms are born and ever higher qualities emerge, matter from the primal stuff, life from matter, mind from life, the development is not finished therewith. Beyond the plane of mind new qualities will arise. The cosmic nisus will carry the development to a higher level of being than all that has gone before. This new emergent quality is called by Alexander, Deity. It is the next higher quality beyond the highest which has appeared so far, viz., mind. But as the lower level cannot properly apprehend the higher, we men cannot penetrate to the essence of God as the bearer of the quality of Deity. We can present it to ourselves only through analogies from empirical experience, as though we were ourselves gods.

These considerations lead to the following results. From all empirical beings which are finite and limited God is distinguished by His infinitude. But the infinitude of God is empirical in contrast to the *a priori* infinitude of space-time. This means that God cannot yet be in full possession of Deity, for then He would be a finite being beyond which there could be further development. God's is not a real, fulfilled, and completed nature, He is not a level of existence in which a development has terminated or ever can terminate. God, as actually existing, is not a finished Being but an eternal Becoming; not a consummation but an urge or nisus. God has not yet reached His godhead; if He had reached it He would cease to be God. He can never realize the idea of Himself; He finds Himself continually on the way towards this idea. He is, as Alexander says, the ideal God in embryo. There is no actually infinite entity whose specific character would be deity. God means rather nothing but the eternal striving towards deity, which fills the whole universe and penetrates it and leads upwards to ever-higher forms. God is therefore the proper and final meaning of the ascending developmental process of the universe. The world in its infinitude is pregnant with deity and strives unceasingly towards it. The continual change and movement of things through the divine nisus moves ever upwards, towards ever higher, richer, and more perfect forms. God is the eternal drive of the world, which never comes to an end, but is ceaselessly pushing further forwards on the path of emergent evolution.

The question of the immanence or transcendence of God Alexander tries to answer with the help of the world-formula according to which every level of being stands to the next higher in a similar relation to that of body and mind. In the nature of God also we can make this figurative distinction between His body and His mind. In that case both immanence and transcendence are contained in the concept of God. God is immanent in the world in relation to His body, but transcendent in relation to His mind or deity. Yet this argument does not seem to be in harmony with Alexander's doctrine elsewhere, but looks like a mere play of ideas. His theology is thoroughly pantheistic and his concept of God is so completely involved in the texture of the world that all his efforts to save the transcendence of God and to justify theism against pantheism are in vain.

Finally, another argument points in the same direction. God thus described cannot be the God who has created the universe. He is rather Himself a creation of this universe, and therefore not the whole of the universe but only a part of it. According to this doctrine the true creator of the universe is space-time, and God, like all other beings, is merely a creature of the primal stuff; he is certainly the highest which has so far appeared, but still only a creature. If we view God as that being to whom all things owe their existence, then we should reverse the order of the world and consider the primal cause of being in the light of its highest empirical quality. The concept of a creative God would be merely a hybrid mixture of a creative space-time with that of the quality, godhead, which is made by it. Moreover, God is not eternal and raised above time; but, as is said in another passage, a birth of time and exists in time; since timelessness is for Alexander a meaningless idea, and eternity is only the incessancy of forward-pressing evolution.

We need not follow out further the other ramifications of Alexander's theology, and the problems connected with it (e.g. those of evil, freedom, immortality, etc.), in order to see that his speculative boldness has led him on to paths which take us very far from true insight into them. Manipulation of ideas in the interests of a system could hardly be carried further than in this last part of his metaphysics, and although the attempt is made to bring these vain speculations into harmony with the demands and ideas of the religious consciousness, there can be no doubt that the problems have been violently handled by him through excessive zeal for system in a manner which often leaves a painful impression and fails to reach any living relation with the object. However much we may admire and appreciate the high speculative qualities of this world-scheme—its boldness, its breadth, its tenacity—we must reject as ill-judged its attempt to explore a region which is unexplorable. Spencer, whose greatest successor Alexander is in our own time, halted before the Absolute in silent humility and reverence; this behaviour seems to us to be more honest, pious, and honourable than the impetuosity and violence with which Alexander tries to overcome it.

CONWY LLOYD MORGAN (1852–1936)

[Educated at the Royal School of Mines in London in mining and works-management, then under Huxley in biology. Then followed five years (1878–83) as Lecturer at a South African College. From 1884 Professor of Zoology and Geology at University College, Bristol; 1887–1909, Principal of the College, later Vice-Chancellor of Bristol University. *Animal Life and Intelligence*, 1890; *Introduction to Comparative Psychology*, 1894; *Psychology for Teachers*, 1895; *Habit and Instinct*, 1896 (German trans., 1909); *The Interpretation of Nature*, 1905; *Animal Behaviour*, 1908; *Instinct and Experience*, 1912 (German trans., 1913); *Herbert Spencer's Philosophy of Science*, 1913; *Emergent Evolution*, 1923 (first volume of Gifford Lectures); "A Philosophy of Evolution" (*Contemp. Brit. Philos.*, ed. by J. H. Muirhead, First Series, 1924); *Life, Mind and Spirit*, 1926 (second volume of Gifford Lectures); *Mind at the Crossways*, 1929; *The Animal Mind*, 1930; *The Emergence of Novelty*, 1933.]

The philosophical work of Lloyd Morgan is connected very closely to that of Alexander by the idea of emergent evolution.

The relation of the two is that of a true συμφιλοσοφεῖν, a community of thought such as exists between Bradley and Bosanquet, Whitehead and Russell, and James and Schiller. Neither of them is a pupil of the other, but both are masters, who in their works supplement, help, and urge forward each other. In view of the close intertwining and constant mutual influence of their ideas it is not always easy to demarcate clearly their shares in the result at which they have arrived. The threads run back and forth and are woven into a whole which belongs equally to both. Nevertheless, there are important and characteristic differences, in which their various origin, their idiosyncrasies, and the special emphasis of their thinking are represented. Alexander has grown up almost entirely within the philosophical *milieu*, and has only slight contact with the positive sciences. Hence his boldness in metaphysical flights which are made in the sphere of pure speculation unhindered by exact studies. Morgan on the other hand is a genuine scientist and specialist who had occupied himself with several specifically scientific fields of study, in some of them making original contributions, before he gave free rein to his early-developed taste for philosophy. Apart from his training as an engineer, which he did not follow up, and from his thorough training in biology under Huxley, his professional work made it necessary for him to master such various subjects as physics, English literature, constitutional history, geology, and zoology. Later he devoted himself to psychological investigations, which resulted in numerous writings by which different branches of the science were powerfully stimulated and advanced. In the province of animal psychology especially, Morgan's inquiries, supported by exact experiments, have resulted in epoch-making advances. From them the behaviouristic movement, as its founder, Watson, expressly acknowledges, received its decisive impulse. All the relevant inquiries of the American school go back to him and move along the path indicated by him. But we cannot pursue further the more special side of Morgan's work in this and other fields, closely connected though it was with his philosophical thinking. Although his speculative gifts have not been cramped directly, they have been kept under restraint, and he has been protected from over-hasty generalization. Critical prudence and careful consideration, which we often fail to find in Alexander, characterize every step which Morgan has made beyond the limits of exact science into the realm of philosophical speculation. In this way, apart from some early tentative steps it was not until late in life that he reached a comprehensive synthesis of his ideas. After long inward preparation and maturation this was achieved in the publication of the Gifford Lectures delivered in 1922 and 1923, which contain the final formulation and systematization of his philosophy. As with Alexander, this and the influence it has exercised belong in the main to the post-war period, although the literary activity of both thinkers reaches back into the XIXth Century.

In what follows I shall sketch Morgan's philosophical doctrine in its maturity, as it has been developed in the books of the post-war period, and shall lay special stress upon those points in which they are characteristically different from similar trains of thought of Alexander.

In the first place it is important that the common metaphysical Naturalism, which with Alexander owes most to Spencer, and with Morgan owes most to Huxley, is connected with a very different theory of knowledge as its basis. While Alexander's doctrine of knowledge moves upon the paths of New Realism, Morgan, who is more strongly rooted in the British tradition, goes back to earlier national principles, to the Phenomenalism of Berkeley and Hume. But his doctrine, although in the main it is in harmony with Hume's position, is expressed in a much more differentiated and clearly defined form than in the thinkers of the XVIIIth Century. Morgan may be said to have formed a philosophical terminology which is extremely strict and definite and handled with great skill, and has introduced many new and striking terms which have enabled him to express his ideas in an extremely precise and pregnant form; in this respect acceding to the demands and taking over the traditions of exact science by which his whole system is penetrated.

In particular he rejects the uncritical New-Realist obliteration of the distinction between object of knowledge and real physical thing.[1] With Hume he asserts that everything which can be known is enclosed within that narrow circle which we call our consciousness. In the attitude of knowing we are limited to the world of given phenomena; we know nothing about an external world of things. It is true that we can postulate their existence as a hypothetical assumption, but it cannot be established by exact proof. According to New Realism, the thing, so far as it is a cognized object, is identical with the thing which stands outside that cognitive relation and exists entirely by itself. It is, as Alexander says, simply present to the cognizing subject or is together with it, and this presentness or togetherness makes no difference to its external character or inner structure. According to Morgan's Phenomenalism, we must understand by the object everything which, as he says, accrues to the physical thing from the fact that it enters into a cognitive act of the subject. But this accretion is added by the mind, and therefore none of our feelings, perceptions, presentations, etc., belong to the physical thing as such, and they are, therefore, in their mode of existence not physically real, but psychically phenomenal. Mind, accordingly, is not merely the observer which only contemplates things as they are in themselves, but the co-operator which shapes the objective world into that which it is. The object is a construct in the construction of which mind has a prominent share. To this extent Morgan professes himself to be in accord with Idealism. In the cognitive process we must therefore make the cardinal distinction between the objective thing which is a construction of psychic designations, and that upon which these designations are projected, viz. the merely 'acknowledged' or postulated but unprovable non-psychic thing which exists in its own right, quite independently of anything with which we invest it, and which merely represents the skeleton of that

[1] In strictness, this detail concerning Morgan is out of place here; but the close connection with Alexander's doctrine seemed to indicate that it should be mentioned at this point.

which cognition clothes with flesh and blood. Cognition is a synthetic process consisting of the physical influx of the thing and the projective psychic relation to the object, as well as of a very complex system of intervening processes. In another passage Morgan illustrates the act of cognition with the help of an arrow. The feathered end of the arrow is embedded in a person (the subject) while the pointed end is directed to a something (the object). The object is a centre upon which many arrow-heads converge. The arrows are the references of the subject to the object. The object is the something to which reference is made by the subject. There are three kinds of such references: the percipient, the perceptive, and the reflective. Our usual experience is penetrated by reflective references; but these rest upon perceptive, and the latter again cover the percipient. By reflective references (activity of the mind) the world which is given to us immediately in feeling and perception is greatly changed and divested of its original character. In scientific thinking we use predominantly arrows of reflection while children and animals have almost exclusively the two other kinds of arrows in their quiver. The arrow-points of every kind stick in that which we call the external world. But this, so far as it is hit by an arrow or is referred to by a subject, is a psychic world. This does not mean that there was no physical realm of nature before a cognizing being appeared, but only that the physical order only came into the circle of experiences at the moment when such references could be made. Everything which comes into a circle of relations—shapes, colours, tones, values, ideas, and everything else—is of mental or spiritual nature. The physical or material remains outside this circle and cannot as such be known, but merely 'acknowledged' in its existence or believed to exist.

The phenomenalist theory of knowledge is, like Alexander's realist theory, only a member in the system of naturalistic metaphysics. This in its structure is emergent evolutionism, in a more comprehensive sense than even with Alexander. Morgan has not only exploited speculatively the idea of emergent development, but has based it scientifically on copious empirical material and completely systematized it. What with Alexander is a speculative hypothesis is with Morgan a strict demonstration on the basis of empirical facts. Morgan's service consists in the fact that he has freed this fruitful idea from the fetters of Alexander's system-making and has set it upon its feet, though not without involving it in new relations or imposing upon it the burden of a system.

In substance this idea is, of course, not new. What is new is only the philosophical range which Alexander and Morgan have given to it. Both thinkers make reference to the inventor of the term 'emergent', G. H. Lewes, who in his *Problems of Life and Mind* (1875) used it for the first time (see above, p. 121). In J. S. Mill's *Logic*, still earlier, a similar idea is developed, though in other terms; and later we find it in W. Wundt, J. Ward, and many others. But it was through Bergson's idea of creative evolution that the doctrine of novelty became widely known and made its way into England, where, by a similar reaction against the mechanistic evolution-theory, Alexander and Morgan became its most influential champions.[1] Emergent evolution is a new, important, and specifically British variation of Bergson's creative evolution.

Morgan's conception of this doctrine starts from the idea that progress in the development of any entity consists not in a continuous equable advance, but is accomplished by stages or leaps; so that there are critical turning-points at which the development hastens forward and new qualities and connections arise, the presence of which cannot be deduced from the previous course of things. It is this advance by stages or sudden appearance by leaps of new characters that he calls emergent evolution. The essence of the emergent consists in this, that its features cannot be anticipated from the stage out of which it appears and that before its appearance no operative causes can be seen which could bring it into being. Viewed from later

[1] To-day it has representatives in the most diverse camps, Idealists, Realists, and Pragmatists; such as Schiller, Broad, Wildon Carr, Hobhouse, McDougall, Smuts, and, in America, Sellars, Dewey, Spaulding, Brightman, and others.

stages it is probably open to scientific interpretation and can to a certain extent be exactly described and explained. But why the emergent emerges we cannot explain, even from the higher stage. We must simply accept it as a fact in that unprejudiced agnostic attitude of mind which is fitting to scientific investigation.

We can say also that the emergent does not result from the existing factors of evolution. Morgan, therefore, puts as correlate to 'emergent' the term 'resultant', as Lewes had already done, and formulates the relation of the two thus: through resultants there is continuity in the advance of the development; through emergence advance in the continuity. While the emergent *a parte ante* is not predictable, the resultant can be exactly determined beforehand and calculated. Evolution fulfils itself both in resultant and emergent processes; but certainly not in the former only. Organic life is not something which was already latent at the stage of the inorganic and needed only to come forth from its concealment and unfold itself. It is rather something new in principle which suddenly appears without any evident cause for its presence. Morgan's doctrine is therefore a continued energetic protest against the older mechanistic conception of evolution which contented itself with the interpretation of evolutionary processes as resultants and thought it was able to calculate in advance the whole course of events from the lowest stages by the algebraic summation of components. He points out, however, that the emergence doctrine which he puts in place of the mechanistic interpretation, is not a mere speculation but an exact scientific theory, which can be verified by facts of experience. It is, as he says, thoroughly naturalistic, and needs no principles of explanation which cannot be got from the course of evolution itself on the basis of pure fact. For this reason he cannot accept Vitalism, since this works with ideas which are introduced into the system of nature from without, and cannot be proved from it. Such ideas as Bergson's *élan vital*, or Driesch's entelechy, or McDougall's psychic entity are not compatible with scientific thinking and should therefore be rejected.

But Morgan's strict Naturalism or purely scientific attitude is pierced by himself, widened, and carried forward by a mode of treatment which, as he thinks, is not excluded by the previous mode and is not in contradiction with it. This is the philosophical or metaphysical mode. It hardly appears in his earliest books, in which Morgan still talks of the "blue mist of metaphysics". It came to him very late when he was elected Gifford lecturer, and had to cast up the whole sum of his thinking; although, as we must admit, a certain seed of speculation was already visible at an earlier time. Moreover, with Morgan Naturalism frees itself from its agnostic fetters and becomes speculative, though in a way different from Alexander's. With the latter we have before us from the first a naturalistic metaphysics, i.e. a constructive synthesis which arises from a naturalistic view of the world. With Morgan on the other hand we have a scientific Naturalism on which metaphysical speculation is imposed as a sort of second story. The two provinces here face each other in isolation and there is no bridge leading from one to the other. Let us give to science what belongs to science, and to metaphysics what belongs to metaphysics; but let us not confuse them lest both should suffer harm. Thus Alexander's system is made at one casting, and unified by a single point of view, while through Morgan's there is a rift which separates it into two parts which are clearly differentiated as substructure and superstructure.

The superstructure rises from the substructure through the following consideration. We can explain the appearance of an event from two points of view; firstly, from the natural course of things themselves, i.e., from the order of nature out of which it proceeds, without asking about the cause which generates it. This point of view is that of natural evolution, and its methodological principle is that of scientific investigation. But we can make inquiry about this cause, or author, to which it owes its being; we can consider it from the viewpoint of the agency which has generated it, whether it be human, divine, or otherwise. Thus there are two radically different modes of treatment or principles of explanation which Morgan distinguishes as the scientific or natural and the dramatic or supernatural. The natural interpretation does not exclude the dramatic. We can accept both without contradiction and pursue them in detail independently of each other.

In a rather different line of thought what Morgan here calls the dramatic interpretation shows itself to be the properly philosophical explanation of the universe. To philosophy falls the task of outlining a constructive scheme of the world, a scheme of the highest reflective thought which includes in itself the achievements of the scientific point of view, but, without falling into conflict with science, leads beyond it, and sets forth those constitutive features of reality which scientific thinking cannot apprehend because of its incompleteness. In constructive philosophy speculative hypotheses are not only permissible but indispensable. Morgan's system is constructed upon three such permissible hypotheses or assumptions. The first is that which met us when we were dealing with theory of knowledge, the assumption of a non-mental physical world of things or events which exists in its own right and is in no way dependent upon the fact that it is perceived or thought of by a consciousness. We can regard this world as a four-dimensional space-time system of relations which proceeds upon a natural plan, and whose several stages develop in an ascending hierarchy according to the law of emergent evolution. The physical series of stages includes electrons, atoms, molecules, crystals, organic cells, organisms, etc.

The second assumption we may call the correlation-hypothesis. It maintains that there are no physical events which are not also psychic, and no psychic events which are not accompanied somehow by physical events. There exists a thoroughgoing correlation between the psychic and the material world. Neither of them exists independently of the other; they are separated from each other neither temporally nor spatially. They stand in the relation of concomitance, i.e. of constant togetherness or mutual reference. Physical and psychical processes can be distinguished from each other, but not separated. There is neither a simply physical nor a simply psychical world, and so not two worlds, but one only, which viewed from top to bottom is of a psycho-physical character. This assumption, it is true, cannot be verified thoroughly by facts, but it suffices that it is at least not refuted by them. For the evolutionary doctrine there results the consequence that the physical and psychical are present together at all stages and that therefore neither the psychical suddenly appears at a definite stage of the evolution, nor is the physical wholly absent at any stage, even the highest, nor can either be inferred from the other. They do not belong, therefore, to the emergent qualities, but are universal, constitutive characters, which determine all things and events. We need not lay stress upon the difference between this doctrine and that of Alexander; it is self-evident. But how can it be reconciled with the theory of emergent evolution in which were distinguished three main stages of development, matter, life, and mind? Can we speak in any pregnant sense of matter and mind, if at one time they are explained as stages of evolution, at another time as universal characters of all being and happening? It is clear that correlation-hypothesis and emergence-doctrine, and therefore philosophy also and science, have fallen into a sharp conflict which Morgan with all the resources of his thinking cannot reconcile. Superstructure and substructure are not in accordance and experience refuses to follow the lead of speculation.

The third assumption, already touched upon above, which is indispensable for a comprehensive world-scheme, is that of an operative power or activity, which is behind all happening and is the cause and impulse of all things. This assumption springs from the question about the primal cause of being and of its constitution, a question which no serious philosophy will ever be able to evade. The specialist investigator, such as the physicist, the physiologist, and the psychologist, does not need to come to any decision about this question. His position is agnostic; he does not deny the primal cause nor does he assert it. But it presses upon the metaphysician and demands an answer. Morgan answers it to the effect that the whole process of development points to a divine author, and the revelation of a universal divine purpose. Constructive thinking postulates the concept of an activity or causal principle, a concept which is dispensable and indeed embarrassing for the naturalistic attitude; and this causal activity is to be understood in a quite general sense, as an activity which manifests itself in all particular actions and happenings. It is omnipresent and is manifest in each one of the manifold phenomenal forms of the course of development. The source of all this operation is the creative activity of God. God, accordingly, is not the *terminus ad quem* of the genetic, evolutionary interpretation, but the *terminus a quo* of the dramatic explanation. God is the universal spiritual substance which we can view also as a personality. He is therefore not, as in Alexander's system, the quality which stands upon the highest stage of the evolutionary pyramid, but the operative power of which all emergent qualities from the lowest to the highest stages are only an expression and revelation. In an isolated passage Morgan speaks of this power as 'logos', and thus puts his doctrine into close relation with Platonism. In another connection he draws nearer to Alexander's doctrine where he speaks of the stage of deity which surpasses all others in wealth and fullness, and distinguishes from it God Himself, who rises as the highest ideal even above this stage, and so brings to a conclusion from above the scheme of development.

Thus Naturalism and Theism join hands in alliance. The same arrangement of facts which we can interpret strictly in accordance with Naturalism, furnishes us also with an example of universal divine purposiveness. The naturalistic interpretation is completed by the spiritual explanation. There are not two orders of reality, however, but only one single realm of being, which is both natural and spiritual, and is founded upon a final substantial unity. Morgan's monistic profession of faith means that there is advance in cosmic development, and that in the end this is equivalent to saying that God is all in all, although in diverse modes and grades of revelation. There can be no doubt that Morgan's concept of God presupposes a larger element of faith than Alexander's; although it is less consistently thought out and less firmly fitted into the framework of his system.

Morgan's excursion into metaphysics, as we may call his doctrine of assumptions, is a sign how little exact science and the naturalistic-empirical philosophy which proceeds from it find satisfaction to-day in renouncing the attempt at a solution of the problems which involve a general theory of the world. Agnostic modesty, in any case, is no longer in fashion, and the fresh wind which has swept through the land with the idealist movement has had its influence upon those schools of thought in which hostility to metaphysics has been inherited from generation to generation in accordance with ancient and inveterate tradition. Morgan's speculative attempt seems to us, therefore, like that of Alexander, to whom he is considerably inferior in philosophical importance, as a notable sign that the philosophical spirit is once more undertaking a bold flight where a little while ago it had contented itself with a modest *ignoramus* or *ignorabimus*.

CHARLIE DUNBAR BROAD (*b.* 1887)

[Student of Trinity College, Cambridge, then Fellow of the College; afterwards Lecturer at the University of St. Andrews and Professor of Philosophy at Bristol; then returned to Cambridge as Lecturer in Philosophy at Trinity College, and since 1933 as Professor of Moral Philosophy in the University. *Perception, Physics, and Reality*, 1914; *Scientific Thought*, 1923; "Critical and Speculative Philosophy", 1924 (*Contemp. Brit. Philos.*, ed. by J. H. Muirhead, First Series); *The Mind and its Place in Nature*, 1925 (second edition, 1929); *Five Types of Ethical Theory*, 1930; *Examination of McTaggart's Philosophy*, vol. i, 1933, vol. ii, 1938; *Determinism, Indeterminism, and Libertarianism* (Inaugural Lecture), 1934. Numerous papers in periodicals.]

C. D. Broad is the most conspicuous and influential thinker of the younger generation of philosophers whose education belongs mainly to the pre-war period but whose work has appeared only subsequently to the war. He was trained in the philosophical *milieu* of Cambridge, where a less unified and consistent tradition has prevailed than in Oxford, but where in recent years a series of important men have worked, who have had a decisive influence upon philosophical circles in England. If we mention as the most distinguished Sidgwick, J. Ward, Moore, Russell, Whitehead, McTaggart, and Johnson, Broad has received from all of them (except perhaps from Ward) more or less enduring impressions, and most of them have been his immediate teachers. Among other thinkers to whom, as he himself confesses, he is under great obligations, may be mentioned Stout, Taylor, Alexander, and Dawes Hicks. On the other hand, the contribution which both the great philosophers of the past and the foreign thinkers of the present have made to the formation of his doctrine, is much smaller. His doctrine is drawn almost entirely from modern British ideas and is a typical product of British thought. Larger and more decisive factors are supplied by the natural sciences, especially by modern physical and biological theories, of which Broad has a wide knowledge, although he has never carried on research in the special sciences on his own account. His thorough mastery of these and other provinces of knowledge (especially of mathematical logic) shows itself in the content and still more in the method of all his philosophical writings.

Before we consider the content of his doctrine, we must try to grasp the peculiar features of his philosophical character and of his method. For we have in him a highly interesting and in many respects novel phenomenon, as a man, judgment upon whom must take into consideration not only the content but also the structure of his thought and the psychological idiosyncrasy which his type of philosophy reveals. He has himself given us some notable indications pointing in this direction (see *Contemporary British Philosophy*, First Series, pp. 80 ff.). His is an extremely practical, sober, and passionless nature, without deep feeling for the products of artistic, musical, and poetic genius, and without any personal relation to religious or mystic experience. Everything which serves to uplift and agitate the spirit, or springs from feeling or sentiment, or rises upon the wings of fancy, is alien to him. He has no use either for any science of spiritual life or for a philosophy which is dominated by it. He is sceptical of philosophical system as of everything which represents a general metaphysical or speculative view of the world. He despises all philosophical extravagance and rhetoric, and all that savours of enthusiasm and edification. He has a horror of all thinking which is expressed in vague, confused, and obscure language, and he sets himself the highest ideal of terminological exactitude and definiteness of verbal expression and complete adequacy of speech to thought. He makes much use of mathematical symbols or logical signs in order to reach the highest degree of unambiguity and definiteness of ideas of which philosophical thinking is capable. Mathematical physics is, therefore, the science which serves him as the model of philosophical method.

What tasks remain for philosophy if it is neither a general view of the world nor a guide for the conduct of life, neither systematic nor speculative nor metaphysically constructive? Broad defines its field in two ways. Its most important function consists in subjecting to a scrupulously exact analysis the concepts which are used uncritically in common life and in the sciences, such as thing, substance, quality, number, change, cause, movement, person, etc., to determine their exact meaning as terms, and to show their mutual relations. The second function goes hand in hand with the first and consists in subjecting to a strict examination the concepts and propositions thus analysed and purified from obscurity, to adduce and consider every objection which can be brought against them; in short, to expose them to a regular cross-fire of critical questions till they show themselves to be completely invulnerable and entirely purified of all obscurity and ambiguity. What Broad here demands he has carried out fully in his philosophical investigations. He is describing merely the method which he has himself adopted with the greatest conscientiousness. All this is included by him under the concept of critical philosophy, by which he understands his own philosophy and which for him includes the whole circuit of philosophical investigation. It is clear that upon this view logic is the fundamental part of philosophy, and that all other branches are subject to its strict regulation. Thus ethics, for example, is quite analogously defined as that part of critical philosophy which has to do with the analysis of the confused ideas of daily life about good and evil, right and wrong, duty and responsibility, etc., to examine their presuppositions, to define them exactly, and to refine them critically. It is the phenomenology of the moral consciousness, without any metaphysical presuppositions or deductions, without setting up any ethical ideals or standards of value; and so is not a normative but a purely descriptive and analytic science of the empirical facts and relations of the moral life. In this province also, which he has dealt with in a book which is mainly historical (*Five Types of Ethical Theory*), Broad goes to work *sine ira et studio.* He is merely the cool and passionless observer and the contemner of all ethical agitation, deep feeling, or uplift. Nothing is more characteristic of the dry coolness and impassivity of this typical Englishman than the following passage: "A healthy appetite for righteousness kept in due control by good manners, is an excellent thing; but to 'hunger and thirst after' it is often merely a symptom of spiritual diabetes."[1] It is no wonder that he vastly over-estimates the good average work of Henry Sidgwick and sees in him the model ethical thinker, and that he is so far from understanding the significant figure of Green, whose "comforting aroma of ethical uplift"[2] he dislikes.

In so far as a philosophy that goes beyond scientific criticism has any meaning, Broad calls it speculative philosophy. In general he thinks little of it, although he does not deny that it has some value. It has brought into discredit genuine or, as he calls it, neutral philosophy; for it is dependent upon our emotional life, and is more a product of fear and hope than of exact, unprejudiced thinking. It can never attain to the strictness and certainty of critical philosophy. If it is to have any value it must presuppose criticism and build only upon its foundation. At best it is more or less felicitous guessing; but it may in

[1] *Five Types of Ethical Theory.* Preface.
[2] *Five Types,* etc., p. 144.

the future reach greater importance, when critical thinking has advanced further. Beside metaphysics and the general theory of the world, theology and mysticism are relegated to this province.

It is characteristic of Broad's position that in his hands the distinction between critical and speculative philosophy becomes that between Realism and Idealism. But in an incautious moment, when he is led less by critical prudence than by real insight, he rises above his own position and recognizes the relative right of both by contrasting impartially their respective advantages and disadvantages. In this connection he observes that the characteristic mistake of Idealism is that it cannot see the trees for the wood, while Realism cannot see the wood for the trees. Whatever we may say as to the justice of this aphorism, it is evident that by it Broad has illuminated in a flash his own philosophical position. As a typical representative of a mode of thinking which is realistic in this sense, his philosophizing is devoted almost entirely to detail and seldom rises to wide comprehensive views over a great assemblage of phenomena. This can be seen, not only in the content of his doctrine, but in his peculiar method of treatment, which in a high degree bears the impress of his personality, although in many respects it seems to be related to that of Moore.

Inquiry into any problem leads first through a series of conceptual dissections and clarifications to a minutely careful descriptive analysis which is carried to a point at which a preliminary clarification of the problem is attained. But now in the manner of a cross-examination there begins a flood of critical questions, and the answer which apparently had been safely reached is thrown once more into the crucible of criticism, where, at white heat, it is completely reduced to its elements and worked up for a further analysis. It is shown that all the factual, scientific, and logical possibilities are far from being exhausted. New arguments and points of view arise and produce new alternatives and theories which like a thick net surround the problem and envelop its kernel. Broad can never do too much in discovering and exposing such possible alternatives and perspectives. His keen, critical, analytic mind throws light upon the furthest recesses of a problem and anatomizes it to the furthest point possible. Only after the problem has been explored in all its possibilities and probabilities and has been spread out before the astonished reader in minute detail, does his critical mind make a last and decisive assault on the problem which has now become ready for solution. Among the alternative theories which are considered for solution and have already been fully developed there now begins the great business of elimination. The several alternatives are once more examined most rigorously and their strong and their weak points carefully estimated. Debit and credit are balanced against each other and recorded. Some alternatives are rejected at once; others are conditionally accepted; and a third set are accepted tentatively; a fourth set with certain limitations. Some are allowed a lesser, others a higher degree of probability. As ever new arguments are thrown into the scale and the cross-fire of criticism grows ever more intense, this struggle for existence of theories mounts finally to a dramatic *dénouement*, and ends in a kind of race in which many fall upon the track, others collapse a little before the winning-post, while a few fly past the post victoriously. Even among the victors there are gradations according to the higher or lower number of points which they earn, and by none are all the conditions fulfilled which may ideally be imposed.

This is the process of selection which is almost invariably used by Broad and applied by him with great technical skill and profound knowledge. The theories which compete with each other are generally constructed logically and only occasionally taken from actual cases or from the history of science. This offers the advantage that they are disentangled as clearly as possible from the rest of the problem in every case. In one case which we shall adduce here as an example of the method just described, that of the study of the relation between mind and matter, Broad has set forth no less than seventeen possible theories, has reviewed them one after the other, in order to decide at last in favour of that theory which he calls 'emergent materialism', though not without many reservations and parentheses and not without conceding to many others a more or less well-founded right to exist (see *The Mind and Its Place in Nature*, chap. xiv). This kind of philosophizing suffers, one may say, from an excess of conscientiousness and a want of decisiveness. In trying to examine everything in order to keep the best, it falls into an ocean of detail and loses itself in the abundance of possibilities. Thus not seldom it reaches the opposite of what it wanted to reach; and instead of clarifying the problem renders it obscure. If one judges it by its results, one cannot escape the impression that a vast expenditure of keen thinking and genuine inquiry has been made for the most part fruitlessly. For in the end most questions are left undecided, unless we choose to call a decision the somewhat higher coefficient of probability with which one theory is invested in preference to another. Not only the actual decision is wanting, but also resolution to make a decision; and a virtue is made out of a necessity, when this failure is raised to the rank of a principle. Such a philosophy is like the game of diplomacy where the main purpose is to settle nothing finally, but always to leave open a great number of possibilities. It is, as Broad himself confesses, profoundly sceptical; not in the sense of destructive negation, but in the sense of lacking the will to make a positive avowal. It is sceptical both from antipathy to dogmatism, and from excess of critical caution. Therefore it moves by preference in the shallows of probability, without ever reaching or wishing to reach the firm ground of certainty. Broad expressly raises probability to a methodological principle and herein is a typical representative of Empiricism. Philosophy is, as he declares in opposition to Kant, far from being able to answer its questions with certainty. It must content itself with investing its arguments with the highest possible degree of probability, and often it will not succeed even in this. This cautious modesty indicates the completely unspeculative character of his philosophy which in the manner of the special sciences takes up particular problems only, and aims at a preliminary solution, mainly in the sense of a clarification of the problem, without troubling itself how the problems are connected systematically on taking a view of the whole philosophical field. "I can at most," says Broad in one passage, "claim the humble (yet useful) power of stating difficult things clearly and not too superficially."[1] And this goes straight to the root of the matter.

We cannot undertake the task of following the numerous paths of investigation which Broad's thinking has cleared for itself. As the method which leads towards the results is always more important than the results themselves, and as we have already given a general indication of those results, we must content ourselves with a selection. The problem of knowledge with Broad, as with almost all the thinkers of the realist school, is in the foreground of his interests, and in particular it is the problem of sense-perception which dominates the field. Broad as usual distinguishes three factors: 1, The sensations or mental acts which he as a rule calls states of mind; 2, their objects, the sensa; 3, physical objects. Of particular importance is the exact determination of the nature of sensa and their relation on one side to mind and on the other to physical objects. First arises the question whether and how far the sensa can be termed mental. It is shown that the question in this form admits of no clear-cut answer. It is extremely complex and separates at once into a series of further questions which need preliminary clarification. In any case the view is rejected that sensa as such are states of mind. On the other hand the question whether they are at least dependent upon mind requires a thoroughgoing analysis. The dependence may be of an existential or of a qualitative kind; and for both kinds weighty arguments may be brought into play. Here also Broad stops short of a definite decision, but the view of qualitative dependence upon mind seems to him to have greater weight than that of existential dependence. The latter would mean that sensa can exist only as objective constituents of sensations. On the other hand he says that we can adduce no valid reason why spots of colour or sounds should not exist without being per-

[1] *Scientific Thought*, p. 6.

ceived. So he comes finally to the conclusion, indecisive despite many safeguarding clauses, that sensa depend partly upon the position of the body which senses, partly upon the mental states which they condition. For the assurance of existential mind-dependence sufficiently plausible reasons cannot be adduced. On the other hand definite facts support the view that they can to a certain extent be called qualitatively mind-dependent. Occasionally Broad's expressions are more cautious and involved and often a painfully conquered position is undermined by some fresh argument. There is always open a wide field for the further activity of thought. And so we are often justified in asking whether we are engaged in some subtle game of diplomatic intrigue, or in the attainment of true philosophical insight.

The second question concerns the relation of sensa to physical objects. It is highly important, because the physical world or nature, so far as it is accessible to our knowledge, is rooted in the sensory world of phenomena, and because we are therefore able to reach the former only from the latter. All thinking about natural science, so far as it reflects upon itself, is vitally interested in this question, and Broad has devoted to the subject a comprehensive book (*Scientific Thought*) which testifies to his mastery alike of the old, the new, and the newest physical methods, and is one of the most important which have been written on the philosophical treatment of modern mathematical physics. He there attempts to clear up the relations between sensory and physical objects by wide and penetrating investigations which take account of all possible aspects of the problem, as well as the exact meaning of what we should understand by physical place, form, size, movement, duration, etc., and the sensory correlates on which they are based. He attempts to determine the ontological status of sensa chiefly by the aid of the concept of space-time, to which, however, he does not ascribe any metaphysical meaning, but understands in a purely empirical sense. Two possibilities present themselves by reason of the fact that sensa are somehow involved in spatial and temporal relations. They either inhere in regions of physical space-time or we must assume particular sensory space-times within which they exist. If the first is true the inherence of sensa in physical space-time must be quite different from that of physical objects. Either there is only one meaning of inherence and many different space-times, or there is only one space-time and many meanings of inherence. In the latter case we must assume physical space-time to be fundamental; in the former case we must assume a plurality of diverse though somehow interconnected space-times. It is significant that Broad, faced with the important question of the connection of the phenomenal world and reality, halts before alternatives. He himself is not able to give a definite answer but contents himself, as he says, by setting out some facts which may be important data for a solution of the problem.

Broad tries in another way to settle the problem of perception which he has taken up in different forms. The descriptive analysis of perception shows us, if we consider it freed from its mental and material implications, four diverse factors: there is the sensum (speck of colour, flash in the visual field, noise, etc.) which here is not characterized as a mere datum, but as an event; then the perceptual act or sensation now called situation (e.g., this noise is being sensed); to this is added the sensory field or the spatially greater whole of which the particular sensum is a specially conspicuous or differentiated part (for sensa do not exist as isolated atoms like Humean impressions); and finally the sensory history, since every sensory field extends through a longer or shorter temporal duration and therefore has a history. A sensum, e.g., a certain coloured spot, is a feature standing out from within a visual sense-field and this again is a sensorily coloured continuum of coexisting visual sensa. The visual field is a small section of a larger whole which is a visual sensory history. The situation in which I find myself when I perceive extends, therefore, in many respects beyond that which my senses immediately disclose to me. Broad calls this the exterior relation of the situation and he distinguishes the epistemological object, as that which offers itself immediately to the senses, from the ontological (or physical) object, as the correlate of the sensory object in the physical world. This theory is realistic in so far as to be perceived is unessential to the existence of physical things but is something which from time to time happens to them without causing any alteration in their qualities. The perceptual situation points beyond itself in three ways. In the first place spatially, because I never become aware of the whole surface or extension of a physical object, but always of a part of it only; in the second place temporally, because perception always apprehends merely one or a few moments out of the total duration of the object or out of its history; thirdly in respect of quality, for it always happens that only certain qualities of the thing (as colours in vision) are revealed while others remain concealed or disclose themselves under other conditions or in a changed situation. The perceptual situation, therefore, is characterized by the fact that only a small spatio-temporal fragment of the ontological object literally enters into it and that only a small selection of the qualities of this fragment belongs to it as a sensory phenomenon.

In this connection finally must be mentioned the important part which is played by the term *event* in Broad's doctrine. This concept is taken from the philosophy of Whitehead, from whom Broad has borrowed much, though he has handled it independently in detail. By event Broad understands some very diverse things: a spot of colour, a flash of lightning, a motor-car accident, the life of Bismarck, and the chalk cliffs of Dover. The specifically historical element which usually is connected with this expression does not appear in this case. An event is anything which has any sort of duration; it does not matter how long it lasts or whether the temporally contiguous stages are qualitatively similar or different. Every sensum and every physical object is an event; the former a shorter, the latter a longer event. The boundary line between event and thing or object is completely obliterated. For there is no object which is without duration in time or without a history. Duration in time corresponds to extension in space, and as we can perceive no extended points, so we can observe no merely momentary events. Every object is identical with its whole history. So soon as we equate it with a momentary part of its history we exclude the always important factor of time and so fall into mere abstraction. For an object without duration could not exist at all. Duration belongs to it essentially. A thing is therefore nothing but a prolonged event which elapses within a characteristic space-time unity and whose course is marked either by qualitative similarity or by continuous qualitative change.

The older theory of knowledge as far back as Descartes' *res extensa* had considered physical bodies entirely under the spatial aspect of extension, and had almost completely overlooked the temporal factor. Broad allows a fundamental importance to the latter under the influence both of Bergson and Whitehead and of the relativity-theory. By interpreting 'things' as 'events' he restores to the time-dimension its due rights in regard to external objects and even gives it the primacy over the dimensions of space. Both change and duration are indissolubly connected with the time-factor. Change means succession of events in a definite direction which is irreversible. Continuity of direction which corresponds to the continuity of spatial order, however great its difference from it, is guaranteed by the duration in which the events occur. Duration, therefore, means the unity, change the diversity within the temporal succession. Without change or alteration we should not become aware of the temporal factor, however thoroughly this may penetrate those events in which we observe no change. The temporal series possesses as its typical order, which is different from that of space, an inner direction; this means that time flows in *one* direction and cannot flow backwards. From these definitions there results the important consequence that time as change or becoming is always bringing forth new events, and that therefore the sum of existence in the universe is always increasing. The capacity of calling new events into being is the basic feature of the universe as becoming. So far as an event becomes, it enters into the totality of being and increases it by a new feature.

The doctrine of the primacy of time over space leads necessarily, as with Bergson and Alexander, to the doctrine of new appearance or emergence. To this theory, which was planted upon British soil by Lloyd Morgan and Alexander, and has become fashionable there, Broad has given a turn peculiar to himself and correspondent to the general tendency of his philosophy. This doctrine was also reached by methodical selection, through discussion of the relation between life and mind. In considering the specific behaviour of living organisms there present themselves three types of theory: substantial Vitalism, biological Mechanism, and emergent Vitalism. Substantial Vitalism, which is embodied in Driesch's entelechy-theory, is eliminated at once. For such a mysterious factor as the entelechy cannot be verified empirically, as it cannot be isolated and transferred from a living to a dead body. It is therefore to be regarded as a pure assumption which we do not need for the explanation of the phenomena of life. More weighty reasons may be adduced in favour of the mechanistic theories. Mechanism satisfies best of all alternatives our aesthetic and logical interests inasmuch as it sets forth a law of composition which embraces all phenomena and so attains the highest measure of unity and simplicity of explanation. But here precisely lies the tendency to over-simplification and therefore the danger of straining the facts. If at definite stages new types of law make their appearance, we must loyally recognize the fact.

It is emergent Vitalism that is victorious in the conflict of competing theories, standing for the attempt to heal the ancient quarrel between Mechanism and Vitalism. This theory is confirmed more strongly by chemical than by mechanical phenomena. Its essential point is that the behaviour of a connection or compound which has not been "verified" cannot be predicted merely from knowledge of its elements in isolation. As applied to a living organism, which Broad calls a compound of the second order, or a combination made up of elements which are already compounded, this law means that no knowledge of the manner in which the components of such a body behave in isolation or in other inorganic wholes is sufficient to enable us to anticipate the characteristic behaviour of an organism. We have no right to assume that the laws which have been discovered for inorganic complexes can be transferred straightway to organic relations or the latter to mental phenomena. Breathing, e.g., is a basic indication of vitality and cannot be derived from any knowledge of non-vital wholes. On the basis of this theory we can, it is true, assume that matter, e.g., has a natural tendency towards that structure, the emergent characteristic of which is vital behaviour; but we cannot reduce vital structure to nothing but the chemical components of which it is constructed. Thus at every level we have new and irreducible qualities, and everywhere in nature there is apparent the general tendency that entities of any order should under certain favourable circumstances combine together to produce entities of the next higher order. Instead of a thorough structural unity and universal submission to law in all natural phenomena, such as Mechanism advocates, emergent Vitalism posits a hierarchy of many ascending levels and orders with ever new qualities, structures, and uniformities which are *sui generis* and not deducible from lower levels.

In a subsequent connection, where Broad investigates the problem of soul and body and tries to determine the nature of mind, this doctrine is developed speculatively still further, and leads finally to the theory of emergent Materialism which comes out victorious from a contest with no less than sixteen competing theories. This emergent Materialism is not very different from ordinary Epiphenomenalism, according to which the mind is a concomitant phenomenon of the body. It explains all normal psychic and mental phenomena satisfactorily, but needs certain modifications in regard to the explanation of abnormal and parapsychological phenomena such as telepathy, multiple personality, intercourse with spirits, etc. In accordance with it Broad defines mentality as an emergent quality of a compound composed of a living brain and a nervous system to which there is added a further constituent which is not always destroyed at once by the break-up of the brain and nervous system. This constituent Broad calls the psychic factor, and he ascribes to it the capacity of persisting for a time after the death of the organism. Possibly this psychic factor will manifest itself as material, although with a materiality different from the usual one. It is true that Broad does not believe in the immortality of the soul in any metaphysical or religious sense, but merely in the persistence of this psychic factor and in the possibility of its reincarnation in a new organism, after it has for a time led a free, disembodied existence. He therefore allows a certain probability to the primitive doctrine of metempsychosis.

Without examining more closely these highly speculative ideas we may say that Broad's mind, otherwise so critical and sceptical, has under the influence of Occultism and Spiritualism allowed itself to be manœuvred into a dangerous position, a position which is hopelessly irreconcilable with the foundations of his thinking and his inquiries. That an intellect so cool, sober, and calculating, which detests all speculative and emotional obscurity owing to its excess of critical endowment and intellectual training, is unable to offer sufficient resistance to the seductive siren-voices of Occultism and psychical research is a fact so astonishing that we can here do no more than put it on record.

JOHN LAIRD (*b.* 1887)

[Studied in Edinburgh and Cambridge, then Lecturer in St. Andrews, Professor in Nova Scotia and Belfast; now Professor of Moral Philosophy in the University of Aberdeen. *Problems of the Self*, 1917; *A Study in Realism*, 1924; "How our minds may go beyond themselves in their knowing" (*Contemporary British Philosophy*, ed. by J. H. Muirhead, First Series, 1924); *Our Minds and their Bodies*, 1925; *A Study in Moral Theory*, 1926; *Modern Problems in Philosophy*, 1928; *The Idea of Value*, 1929; *Knowledge, Belief, and Opinion*, 1931; *Morals and Western Religion*, 1931; *Hume's Philosophy of Human Nature*, 1932; *Hobbes* (Leaders of Philosophy), 1934; *An Enquiry into Moral Notions*, 1935; *Recent Philosophy*, 1937.]

The Scotsman, John Laird, a very prolific philosophical writer of the younger generation, attaches himself in his theory of knowledge to the New Realists and follows in general the path marked out by Moore and Alexander. His doctrine, however, is distinguished from the typical forms of New

Realism to this extent, that it adheres more closely to the British tradition of the XVIIth and XVIIIth Centuries, and tries expressly to maintain the continuity between the older and the newer thinking which at the beginning of the movement appeared to be broken. It is above all the ideas of Locke, Hume, and Reid which Laird has tried to incorporate with and to turn to good account in the new thinking. Refusal to indulge in speculation characterizes his doctrine as it does that of almost all genuinely British theorists of knowledge from Locke to Moore, Russell and Broad, and it is in the first instance the traditional problems of theoretic philosophy to which his inquiries are directed. So far he has paid little or no attention to metaphysical questions, and he is as much opposed to Hegelian Absolutism as most of the philosophers of his school. His literary fecundity and the multiplicity of his interests have hindered rather than promoted the clear and precise development of his ideas, and the philosophical content of his books is often overlaid with historical excursuses and rambling discussions, which miss the point of the matter and are wanting in philosophical restraint and severity. Nevertheless, he occupies a considerable position among the thinkers who have come forward subsequently to the Great War.

Laird starts from the questions raised by Locke and Hume about the theory of knowledge. In the central place he puts the problem of sensory perception and regulates all his views by it. From the outset he professes a decidedly realist theory of knowledge and rejects every subjectivist and phenomenalist solution of the problem of knowledge, and therefore both the position of Locke which wavers between Realism and Phenomenalism and the definite Phenomenalism of Hume. Knowledge does not move within the narrow circle of our consciousness, but is essentially determined by the fact that whenever we apprehend an object we step beyond ourselves and apprehend a transcendent reality. The table, which presents itself in sense-perception, is not, as Hume argued, a mere perceptum or aggregate of phenomenal qualities, but a real and transcendent existent, which discloses itself in determinate phases and features, and is independent of the act of perception through which we apprehend it. According to the general thesis of Realism, knowledge, therefore, is a kind of discovery, through which we come into immediate relation with the things of the external world. These are given directly to the mind, and as such enter into consciousness. Laird lays special emphasis on the immediacy of the apprehension of external objects and tries to determine more exactly the essence of this basic fact of all cognition. What, then, is immediately perceived? According to the theory of sensationalist Atomism we perceive sense-data and nothing else. This theory is right, so far as it goes, but it is incomplete in its description of what is really given to us in perception. We perceive not only naked sense-data or mere facts, but also important indications which point beyond the mere factuality of the data, give them meaning and importance, and arrange them in wider connections of the most various kinds. Laird, therefore, distinguishes the data which are important or significant from those which are purely sensory. The former he calls signs, the latter facts; though it must be observed that this distinction implies no actual division. For every fact is *qua* fact charged with meaning and therefore is also a sign pointing beyond the mere datum; and every sign is not a mere sign, but is also something factual as being an object standing over against the subjective act of perception and independent of it. The phenomena of meaning also are objective data and therefore immediately perceptible, just like colours and tones. What we perceive are in the strict sense neither pure facts nor mere signs, but sign-facts. This only means that every sense-datum is coloured by a meaning which points beyond it and this colouring of meaning forms a constitutive factor of every perception. Laird goes so far as to objectivize the meaning-factor itself by calling it literally a part of the reality of the observed thing which is independent of mind.

His position in reference to the problem of perception, and, in a wider sense, that of knowledge, is as follows. Perception is the becoming aware of a sensory complex which encounters the mind directly. This complex is a sign-fact which has significance of meaning as well as extension, duration, colour, or tone; and this meaning belongs to it as inalienably as solidity, extension, and all the rest. By the factor of meaning, Hume's atomism is overcome so far as the transitory, ever-changing, and interrupted sense-data are formed into continuous and enduring objects, which on their side point to wider complexes of continuities and finally to the continuum of a physical world which includes and unifies all external things.

Thus the philosophical theory of perception issues in the view of simple or naïve Realism and is strengthened and confirmed by common sense. It is significant that Laird allows great importance to common sense in regard to all philosophical problems. Wherever a scientific or philosophical doctrine has reached an *impasse* or is halted before several alternatives, common sense must give the decision and judge between the true and the false. It is the task of the philosopher to follow from afar the view of the plain man and to submit to his judgment, although there may be powerful reasons against it. Philosophical thinking grows out of critical reflection upon what healthy human understanding has already concluded, and is in the end nothing else than the scientific establishment of this conclusion. Laird here takes over the inheritance of his more limited countryman Thomas Reid, and carries on directly the work of the Scottish school. Within the New Realism he stands closest to Moore, whose defence of common sense has had a direct influence upon him.

From the basic fact of the theory of knowledge, that in sense-perception we immediately apprehend data full of meaning (sign-facts) which are parts of the physical world and point to other parts of this world, all the further consequences result. We encounter the same world in remembrance and in imagination. The objects of remembrance are not contemporaneous memory-pictures of past events; the previous events themselves enter directly into our consciousness. Moreover, the objects of imagination are not mere subjective-psychic constructions; they are, just like those of perception and remembrance, objective facts and therefore parts of the physical world. They also possess extension, duration, form, colour, etc. They are distinguished from perceived objects merely in respect of their meaning. They are relatively detached from the connection of the order of things constituted by perception. As pure facts they are exactly that which they appear to us to be, viz., spatial, temporal, physical, etc. But their spatiality and temporality is not that of the world of perception. Their meaning assigns them no abiding-place in this world, but puts them outside of it in a separate fictitious world which is no less objectively real than the other.

In his doctrine of mind Laird keeps equally far from metaphysical speculation and turns once more to the view of common sense which he tries to purify critically and clarify with the help of psychology. We must take mind as we find it. What we find first is consciousness. Of this we are aware immediately as a fact, and we can investigate it while we observe it. Such observation is performed by means of introspection. It is the simple method of Locke which Laird follows in essentials. It is evident that my consciousness is not a character of the things which I perceive or think of or imagine. It is quite simply my becoming aware of these things and of the feelings and efforts which accompany it. But consciousness is always consciousness of something, effort towards something, etc. In its primary function it always points beyond itself to something standing objectively over against it, whether it be a thing or not a thing. But it must not be identified with the object. It is essentially different from it. It can also be directed upon itself and become objective to itself. But even then consciousness and becoming aware of consciousness are to be carefully distinguished. By introspection we are able to apprehend the self in its main features; it presents itself as a continuum of states and activities of consciousness, although we can observe directly only fragments of it. To this extent it is like empirical things. And like them it is extended by inference on the basis of fragmentary data which are accessible to us introspectively and which disclose their essential structure. But personal identity is not unchangeable substance or uninterrupted existence, but continuity of character and function. It is the most individual entity which we encounter in the whole circle of being. That the personal self belongs to a greater whole and is bound up with it, need not be denied; but this question has no decisive importance for a realist philosophy. For this it is enough to know that the self is a unity which persists through a series of conditions and processes each of which demands and sustains the others. Beyond that it need ask no questions.

In a later work (*Knowledge, Belief, and Opinion*) Laird has extended his inquiries far beyond the traditional problem which centres in the theory of perception, and has taken cognizance of the theoretical field in its full extent. Beyond the field, called in the narrower sense cognition or knowing, he has discussed thoroughly the fields of belief and opinion, and their relation to each other and to knowing. These three—knowing, belief (in Hume's sense), and opinion—include the whole theoretic side of human activity. Even the lower planes of certainty, such as belief, opinion, assumption, probability, etc., are not left to blind chance, but are accessible to the penetrating power of reason. Knowing is characterized by completeness of conviction or perfect certainty. But belief also is assent, which involves a high degree of certainty. The certainty of belief is called by Laird merely psychological, that of knowledge is logical, i.e., well grounded or shown to be immediately evident. The determination of the middle plane or belief is, therefore, not easy. It cannot be demarcated clearly either on one side or the other. It represents the upper boundary of opinion and the lower boundary of knowledge. Laird fixes its position mainly on the side of knowledge by claiming for it such cases as, in reference to their certainty, admit no shadow of doubt, but are yet neither self-evident nor demonstrable. His extensive investigations into these questions have not led to a satisfactory explanation of the matter. As often elsewhere he does not press forward to a decisive and exact view. His want of strictly systematic thinking is not made good by the abundance of the details which are adduced or by the wide extension of the field of inquiry.

The same is true also of his treatment of other fields than that of theory, especially that of ethics, which he has studied from the standpoint of the idea of value. The basic thought of his theory of knowledge is applicable also to the field of value. When we call a moral action or character good or bad, we ascribe to it positive or negative value. But values belong to them in the same way as redness belongs to the cherry. Aesthetic values also inhere in certain things under certain conditions as objectively as any other qualities, primary or secondary. Laird's realistic value-theory therefore advocates the unconditional objectivity of values and puts them upon the same plane as all other qualities of things. In a separate book (*The Idea of Value*) he has attempted to determine and mark off the axiological field in its whole compass. But the problems here are so diluted and attenuated, the want of philosophical thoroughness, concentration, and systematic power is so noticeable, that we may be excused from following up the matter further. Here as elsewhere Laird has tried to master a province to which his philosophical capacities are hardly equal.

SIR T. PERCY NUNN (*b.* 1870)

[Professor of Education in the University of London (retired 1936). *The Aim and Achievements of Scientific Method*, 1907; "Are Secondary Qualities Independent of Perception?" 1910 (*Proceedings of the Aristotelian Society*, N.S., vol. x); "Scientific Objects and Common-Sense Things", 1924 (ibid., vol. xxiv); "Anthropomorphism and Physics", 1928 (*Proceedings British Academy*, vol. xiv).]

In common with Russell and Moore, Percy Nunn has developed a realistic theory of knowledge or perception which is notable mainly because it embodies the characteristic features of New-Realist thought in typical purity. Nunn's doctrine represents a kind of average resultant of the many shades of thought which are to be found in the works of Russell, Whitehead, Moore, Alexander, Broad, and the Americans, but is closer to the special variety which is due to Alexander than to the other thinkers of the school. It is true that in this case there is no reference to the metaphysical background from which Alexander's theory of knowledge rises and it must be noticed that Nunn put forth his most important ideas before Alexander and independently of him, and that only certain later formulations are indebted to the extension of the doctrine effected by Alexander. Of the same kind is his relation to Russell who also is under a considerable debt to Nunn, and whose doctrine in its extension has reacted fruitfully upon him.

The essential elements of Nunn's theory are as follows. All sensory phenomena belong collectively and severally to the objective aspect of things; both the primary and the secondary qualities of bodies are "really in them", whether they are sensorily perceived or not. They exist just as they are apprehended in the act of perception; in other words, the conditions by reason of which perception of qualities takes place at all do not affect the character of the apprehended qualities in any way. Hence follows the denial of any psychic entities provided with the function of representation or copying which intervene between the act of knowing and the thing; this implies rejection of the current image- or representation-theory. Even feelings (e.g. toothache) are uncompromisingly assigned to the objective sphere by Nunn. They also are objectively existent, quite independently of whether they appear in the individual experience of a feeling subject or not. The pain which arises from a toothache has the same existence as a feeling of colour or size. However often it may become the experience of a subject which endures it, it has also objective existence apart from this experience. It can both precede and outlast the experience. Even illusions, fictions, and fancies are not as regards their elementary components merely psychic creations, but real existences; although the grouping and combining of them is the work of the mind. All perceptual data are extra-mental; they can enter into the subject-object relation, but their character is not in any way affected or changed thereby. Wherever this relation takes place, the apprehending subject stands in immediate contact with the object as such, or with its bodily presence and not with a psychic intermediary.

Nunn's Realism, however radical it may seem, is nothing but the direct continuation of the classical sensory Phenomenalism of Berkeley and Hume. Only a small correction is made in it, insomuch as the sensa which form the basic substance of reality are given a physical instead of a psychic character. Otherwise everything remains as it was. In a separate discussion which Nunn devotes to the difference between the objects and things of science and those of ordinary life this is plainly evident. If we analyse what we commonly call things, we can discover nothing but sensory data together with the manifold forms of their connection. But the sense-data, from whose syntheses the things of daily life are constructed, are the primary factors of reality, and there is no sense in looking for anything behind them. Therefore we cannot with our scientific concepts penetrate into a region beyond the sensory world and apprehend a reality of higher grade (or indeed absolute reality). On the contrary, scientific objects are in regard to their mode of existence of quite secondary character; they are derivatives from the world of ordinary experience and are based upon sensory things, in accordance with which they are organized and after which they are modelled. All the claims of physicists that their world represents the true reality of which the ordinary world is only the appearance must be rejected. The scientific world is not a new order of things, which allows us to see behind the sensuous veil of phenomena, but rather a manipulation performed for special purposes on the things of sense which are the basic factors of real being. The latter are the primary factors; the former are secondary constructions.

Thus Nunn's researches on "The Aim and Achievements of Scientific Method" which he made in an earlier book of 1907, stand in immediate connection with his sensationalist theory of knowledge. The New Realist elements of his doctrine have here entered into a fruitful conjunction with the ideas on the method of science which belong to Pearson, Poincaré, and Mach, and from them result some important views of the nature and formation of the concepts and hypotheses of natural science. In scientific thinking we are not dealing with a mere copy of sensory reality; we are becoming consciously aware of it and remodelling it according to principles which ensure economy of thinking and according to the postulate of pragmatic objectivity. The postulate consists in this, that the boundless wealth and manifoldness of the primary sense-world is by artificial selection and simplification replaced by a conceptual order of things, and that this transformation is made from a pragmatic standpoint, and is determined by the purposes which are special to human activity. The aim of forming scientific concepts is to make the objective world of sense-perception intelligible by methodical aids to inquiry, and to rationalize it thoroughly not from mere desire of knowledge, but in order to master the world by the human mind, and to make it useful for our service. Scientific concepts and hypotheses are never ends in themselves, but always means to the economical presentation of the sensory facts. Although they are founded on ordinary judgments of experience, they go far beyond them and constitute a world *sui generis*, which follows its own laws, and is directed towards its particular purposes. Although in these ideas we may see the influence of recent theories, they go back ultimately to the old Baconian demand that the essence of knowledge should consist in the power which it gives to men over things.

NORMAN KEMP SMITH (*b.* 1872)

[Studied at the University of St. Andrews, later at the Universities of Zürich, Berlin, and Paris. From 1896 to 1902 Assistant to Adamson at Glasgow. From 1906 to 1916, Professor of Philosophy at Princeton, U.S.A. Since 1919 Professor of Logic and Metaphysics at Edinburgh. *Studies in the Cartesian Philosophy*, 1902; *A Commentary to Kant's Critique of Pure Reason*, 1918 (second edition, 1923); *Prolegomena to an Idealist Theory of Knowledge*, 1924; "The Nature of Universals", 1927 (*Mind*, vol. xxxvi); *Kant's Critique of Pure Reason* (Eng. trans., 1929; abridged ed., 1934); "Is Divine Existence Credible?", 1931 (*Proceedings British Academy*, vol. xvii); Edition of *Hume's Dialogues Concerning Natural Religion*, 1935.]

Norman Kemp Smith, who, by translating and annotating the *Critique of Pure Reason*, has done invaluable service for the knowledge and understanding of this book, which is so fundamental for modern thought and for Kant's philosophy generally, stands in regard to the theory of knowledge near to the New Realism, and adheres mainly to the doctrine of Alexander and Stout. The title of his chief systematic work (*Prolegomena to an Idealist Theory of Knowledge*) should not lead us astray. For, in fact, his doctrine belongs entirely to the New Realist school, and that which in this case is called "Idealist" is rather an emotional background in the form of a belief in a world of spiritual values than a theory immediately connected with his epistemological views or resulting from them. It is nearer the truth when Smith, in the course of his argument, frequently emphasizes his "truly realistic standpoint".

In his case, as in that of most British writers on the theory of knowledge, the problem of sense-perception stands in the foreground of interest. Of what kind are the sensa which form the content of our acts of perception? is the main question. According to the view of the plain man (naïve Realism) they are qualities of external things and exist in these themselves. As such they are accessible to everyone, and therefore we can term them objective and public. According to the popular doctrine of representative perception they are pure data of consciousness, and therefore subjective and private. According to Kemp Smith, who rejects both views, they are events which are conditioned by physical, physiological, and possibly also by psychic factors. They are not accessible to a number of percipients, but to one only. He calls them, therefore, objective and private. His thesis comes to this, that sensa, although the private possession of the percipient, are not necessarily "in the mind" or mental states, but objective occurrences which belong integrally to the system of the physical world and appear within the spatio-temporal continuum. We must ascribe to them much more physical than psychic existence, although it must be conceded that they are psychically conditioned in many ways. Looking at the matter in reference to the categories of space and time, he holds that sensa have temporal continuity, but not spatial extension. In sense-perception we have not to do with a process mediated by psychic images which represent or copy physical objects; we have direct apprehension of the real, material world which is independent of consciousness. Sensory knowledge is therefore in the true sense objective.

Sensa form the content-factor of our experience and experience is altogether impossible without them. But no less important for the existence of knowledge are the formal or uniform factors, the categorial relations and the intuitional forms of space and time. These are not contents, but *a priori* forms for the organization of the extremely variable sensory material. Only if all three factors co-operate can knowledge come into existence; namely sensing, categorial thinking, intuiting on the subjective side, and sensa, categorial relations, and space and time on the objective side. In the act of perception we have before us a twofold process, the elements of which mutually condition, penetrate, and complete each other, viz., sensing, and intuiting or becoming aware of the sensory material through spatio-temporal intuition. Both are effected immediately. Just as we deal with sensa as it were face to face, and in them apprehend directly what is objectively real, so do we intuit the specific character of space and time as fundamental and constitutive features of reality. Space and time are real factors in the process of sense-perception, but are not themselves of a sensory character. They are just conditions of the possibility of apprehending sensa and are, therefore, *a priori* and formal. If we, as J. Ward did, assume a sensory field which is a continuum, then it must be observed that what is sensory in the strict sense is just not continuous, and that the continuous is not sensory. It is by the formal and non-sensory characters of space and time that the variable sensory material of sensa is organized into a continuum.

In these views we can catch a glimpse of Kant's fundamental ideas. Kemp Smith's intensive study of Kant's theoretic philosophy which is embodied in his two unsurpassed books on

Kant, has left considerable traces on his own thinking. He wishes, however, to interpret the doctrine of the German philosopher more in the realist than in the idealist sense, and as purified from all subjectivist elements in order to ensure the objective meaning of knowledge. He recognizes the spontaneous character of conscious activity in certain respects, but sees this not in the engendering of the object, but in the latter's self-disclosure. In the further course of his inquiry, however, he enters upon paths which lead far away from Kant's transcendental basis of the theory of knowledge and end in naturalistic, biological, psychological, and pragmatic views.

The naturalistic bias in treating the problem of knowledge shows itself in the fact that here the brain (occasionally also, following Ward, a "psychoplasm") acts as subject in the theory of knowledge and has to fulfil a double function. It is a condition of awareness generally, and also a condition of the appearance of sensa. By reason of the former function, the world is disclosed as a public world in its constant, uniform factors; by reason of the latter this public world is experienced in a perspective suited to the practical needs of the individual. The process of knowledge shows itself to be a vital function which in the totality of the individual life has a task similar to that of instinct. It is evident that knowledge cannot possibly be adequate to the infinite manifoldness and complexity of reality, and that in the process through which the external world of things enters our consciousness a great part of their content is lost. We can transfer to knowledge only an infinitesimal fragment of their immensely rich content, and even this only in a changed, usually a simplified, form. But the principle of selection according to which the mind acts in this case is determined by biological purpose or usefulness. We do not need to know more than fits us for the battle of life and the maintenance of our species. Selection, on the basis of which we shape the fullness of world-material into knowledge, is effected from the standpoint of the maintenance and promotion of life, and we must be thankful to Nature that she has so arranged this for our welfare. Knowledge both upon its lowest and its highest plane is an eminently practical affair and is in its character, its task, and its boundaries mainly determined by non-theoretical needs and interests.

Kemp Smith's doctrine of knowledge, although it is in several points influenced by Kant, is thoroughly in accordance with the national tradition. Older and more recent ideas both from philosophy and from the special sciences are skilfully introduced to solve the problem. These ideas in part go back to Hume, to whose doctrine Kemp Smith many years before the formation of his own theory gave a naturalistic interpretation (see *Mind*, vol. xiv, 1905); partly they are of Darwinian origin, partly they are taken from the important physiological researches of H. Head, to the philosophical importance of which Scheler and Cassirer in Germany and Delacroix in France have drawn attention; but above all they are derived from the modern psychological theories of Ward and Stout, and from the New Realism of Moore, Whitehead, and Alexander. Kemp Smith, by introducing old ideas into the stream of the contemporary movement, has enriched the theory of knowledge with some new and fruitful points of view.

CYRIL E. M. JOAD (*b.* 1891)

[Head of the Department of Philosophy in Birkbeck College of the University of London. *Essays in Common-sense Philosophy*, 1919 (second edition, 1933); *Common-sense Ethics*, 1921; *Common-sense Theology*, 1922; *Introduction to Modern Philosophy*, 1924; *Introduction to Modern Political Theory*, 1924; "A Realist Philosophy of Life", 1925 (*Contemporary British Philosophy*, ed. by J. H. Muirhead, Second Series); *Mind and Matter*, 1925; *The Meaning of Life as shown in the Process of Evolution*, 1928; *The Future of Life, a Theory of Vitalism*, 1928; *Matter, Life, and Value*, 1929; *The Present and Future of Religion*, 1930; *Philosophical Aspects of Modern Science*, 1932; *Counter Attack from the East: the Philosophy of Radhakrishnan*, 1933; and many other writings.]

Together with Broad and Laird, C. E. M. Joad belongs to the younger thinkers who have taken their places in the New

Realist front, although his place is much lower than theirs. It is only in respect of his abundant literary activity that he excels all living philosophers except Russell. For although he is still well under 50, he can look back on about a dozen and a half philosophical works, an average of more than one a year. But it cannot be said that this formidable record of production is proportionate to its intrinsic value. His production rather reflects in typical form the spiritual restlessness and nervous excitement of the post-war period. its distraction and want of balance, its fussing and fumbling, its hurry and flurry.

About his philosophical development Joad himself tells us that, although as an Oxford student he was brought up in Idealism, he always felt himself repelled by this school of thought, and even then had a preference for Realism. Thus he became a Realist, at first "a more or less naïve Realist in the style of Meinong", and later advanced "to the extreme position, which is known as New Realism". To this he was drawn by the influence of Russell, to whom he felt a stronger allegiance than to anyone else, although to-day he differs from him in some important points. Russell's influence was exercised at first and exclusively in regard to the theory of knowledge, but was soon complicated by a series of other influences for the most part of different character, which impelled Joad towards metaphysics and aroused in him the ambition to construct a great philosophical system and to solve the world-problem at the first assault. The bold and precipitate attempt was condemned to failure because it was undertaken with inadequate means and by an immature mind. Only in later years, after he had passed through the worst period of storm and stress, has Joad attempted to subject himself to discipline in thinking and to justify his ideas carefully (especially in the two longer books, *Matter, Life and Value*, and *Philosophical Aspects of Modern Science*), although his impetuous nature does not seem to be as yet sufficiently tamed and a real clarification of his thinking has not yet been attained.

However, the ground-plan is already quite plain. His Theory of Knowledge moves as was said upon New Realist lines, but instead of limiting itself to mere analysis, it pushes forward beyond its own boundaries and develops into metaphysics. In all knowing Joad distinguishes the act of apprehension from the object which is apprehended. The act itself is psychic; it is a pure activity of the mind as such without any definite content, and its only function consists in awareness of some datum. But this activity is, however it may seem, purely passive. It merely accepts the object and cannot alter it under any circumstances. On the other hand the object, whatever it may be, is independent of the act; its mode of existence is in no way influenced by its being apprehended. Whether apprehended or not, it is and remains transcendent of the act. As object it is purely objective and essentially different from the subjective act of the mind; which means that it is non-mental. The separation between subject and object is here carried through as thoroughly as possible; and this is done at the expense of the former which is reduced to the quite empty function of becoming aware.

The main emphasis of this theory of knowledge is put upon the object, and its most important part is the theory of objects formed by Joad, which is undoubtedly the best of all his ideas so far. The activity of the mind in all knowledge is one and the same, viz., mere direction upon the object in the form of awareness. It is therefore "intentional." The objects, on the contrary, to which the mind is directed are extremely diversified and essentially different from one another. Joad first distinguishes three kinds: 1 Sense-data; 2, physical objects; 3, scientific objects. Physical objects he calls common-sense objects, and means thereby the ordinary things of the external world. We have first the sensory experience of the physical world which can be apprehended immediately by sense-data. These alone possess existence in the proper sense; they exist as material objects which constitute the physical world unaffected in any way by the circumstance that an act of apprehension has been directed upon them. But the act of apprehension can be directed upon them only, and not upon physical and scientific objects. Of the two latter we are not aware immediately but only circuitously and because of the former. The relation between the latter and the former consists in this, that in the apprehension of sense-data we have the occasion to think of physical and scientific objects. In other words the material world of the senses guides the mind to the non-material world of objects which are thought of. These, therefore, become apprehended not through a sensory act but through an act of thought, and here also the radical division of subject from object is justified. This means that physical and scientific things are objective in the same manner as sense-data. They are in no way changed and nothing is added to them by the acts of thought which apprehend them. The world which is thought of exists independently of its being thought of. Thinking is nothing but apprehension of non-material things, just as sensory perception is apprehension of material things. We therefore do not perceive the things of the external world through the senses, but we apprehend them through thinking. This procedure has become so familiar to us that we do not realize this but think wrongly that we perceive them. The difference between physical and scientific objects is not a matter of principle as is that between these two and sensory objects. Whether the awareness which is occasioned by the apprehension of sense-data directs itself upon physical or upon scientific objects depends, Joad thinks, merely upon the level of development which has been reached or upon the purpose connected with it. Knowledge of physical objects serves mainly for practical ends; by them we replace the purely private worlds of sense-data by a world of public objects common to us all. The world of science first discloses itself to the human mind at a relatively high stage of development, viz., when the pressure of necessary vital needs relaxes and the mind gains leisure for the disinterested study of things. Scientific objects grow out of physical objects as a result of an ever-advancing process of abstraction. By scientific thinking they first become divested of secondary qualities, and of all the other qualities which adhere to the sense-data of the physical world. The higher the formation of scientific concepts is carried the poorer objects become in sensory content, and this process leads finally to their being rendered completely empty. Joad holds the opinion that this uncompromisingly realistic theory of knowledge and of objects does not contradict the results of modern physics and is indeed necessarily required by them. He therefore regards all attempts at an idealist interpretation of the most recent physical theories as mistaken, and rejects the inferences drawn therefrom by Eddington and Jeans, as well as those drawn by Russell, which point in this direction.

We can deal more briefly with Joad's metaphysical speculations, although they occupy a much larger space in his books. His earlier writings offer the picture of a very wild and frivolous eclecticism or, as we might say, a philosophical soup compounded arbitrarily and indiscriminately of every sort of herb. It is speculation without responsibility and without bridle. Whatever catches his eye and is favoured by fashion is eagerly picked up and pasted together into a world-system. The only thing is to get a "comprehensive synthesis". Thus Joad adopts vitalistic and neo-vitalistic and also evolutionary ideas. He is intoxicated by Bergson's doctrine of *élan vital* and creative evolution; he is enthusiastic for life-force, the stream of life and new emergents; and apart from the strong infusion of Bergsonism there are ideas of Samuel Butler and Shaw, Driesch, Lloyd Morgan, and Alexander, which point in a similar direction. Moreover Schopenhauer's voluntaristic metaphysics and aesthetics, James's pluralism and Freud's psychoanalysis contribute threads to Joad's skilful fabric and furnish him with bright, fresh colours, while shades of grey are interwoven with dry and sober analysis of knowledge in the style of Russell and Moore. And finally, to change the metaphor, the structure is crowned and completed by a sort of Platonic doctrine of ideas.

In later days Joad has given more thought to self-criticism, and especially in the book *Matter, Life and Value* he has welded the structure of his ideas more firmly and given it more consistency. As the title indicates, he presents a pluralist (more precisely triadic) world-scheme and reduces all being to the three primal principles of matter, life, and values. No one of them can be reduced to the others, or explained by them. They must be recognized as independent entities; they are as it were in water-tight compartments which are closed fast against each other. Thus matter is the principle which confronts life; it is the *brutum factum*, on which the stream of life breaks and which it penetrates without ever being able to take it up completely. And as not everything real can be reduced to material being, so it cannot be included completely in life. Life is flow and movement, coming into being and passing away, and ever new creative transformation. But that is not the end of it. There is still a third realm beyond the stream of life in which the eternal unrest and movement of life comes to a stop, a realm of the enduring, changeless, and complete, that of values. Here at last we reach true reality. Joad puts the world of value so high above the other provinces of being that there is no bridge between them. He fixes it in a transcendent realm of Platonic Ideas (all through the book he is very Platonic) and rejects every suggestion that they are immanent in life. Values are objective qualities and like everything objective are completely independent of their realization in a mental act. They persist in their transcendent existence and do not come down to us even when we turn to them in knowledge or experience. The doctrine of the duality of knowledge thus makes its appearance anew, and so does Realism, which here is given its axiological completion.

WILLIAM ERNEST JOHNSON (1858–1931)

[Fellow of King's College, Cambridge. Lecturer in the University of Cambridge (1893–98 in Education, 1896–1901 in Moral Science, 1902–31 as Sidgwick Lecturer in Moral Science). *Logic* (Part I, 1921, Part II, 1922, Part III, 1924). The contemplated Part IV was never completed. Some sections of it on "probability" were published in *Mind*, vol. xli, 1932.]

W. E. Johnson, whose philosophical work was limited to the field of logic, had no definite connections with any school of thought ("he was pupil of no school, and had no ambition to be the master of one", says Broad of him) but in the main followed his own path. His *Logic*, an ambitious but never-completed work, is certainly one of the notable British books in the field of logical inquiry and for the post-war period might claim an influence almost as great as that of Mill's logic for the middle, and Bradley's and Bosanquet's for the end of the XIXth Century. It is, however, not easy to fix the exact historical standpoint of his logic, since he did not start from any definite presuppositions in general philosophy, but merely trod the path of inquiry and let himself go just where the path led him. This unfettered, purely matter-of-fact study of logical problems certainly improved his book, but on the other hand stood in the way of a clear direction and purpose for his inquiries. Johnson's work therefore may be regarded not so much as a milestone in the history of English logic as a cross-road at which many routes intersect. Thus as regards formal logic he drew upon the classical Aristotelian tradition, while as regards what he called material logic he took Mill as his starting-point. He was not uninfluenced by Bradley's logic, although he did not adopt its Hegelian tendency, and above all he was profoundly influenced by the mathematical logic of Russell and Whitehead, though he met it also with critical reserve and kept at a distance from it on decisive points. This is plain from purely external evidence in that he often used the language of symbolical formulas, and in an exhaustive discussion investigated the foundations of mathematics and its relation to logic. He did not, however, confine himself to the treatment of purely logical problems, but made the boundaries of his study as wide as possible, by discussing questions of theory of knowledge, method and general philosophy, and occasionally by entering upon metaphysical controversies. He was a master of exact terminology, and introduced a series of very felicitous neologisms, using instead of vague, ambiguous, and worn-out terms definite and logical expressions (e.g., instead of the pair of concepts, "particular and general" he used the more definite logical terms "substantial and adjectival"; for "subjective" and "objective" he used to say "epistemic" and "constitutive"; for "substance" "continuant", etc.). But what he demanded for logical terms, viz., unconditional definiteness and unambiguity, was not always fulfilled by his own, It may be mentioned as a curiosity that H. W. B. Joseph, when he put the question "What does Johnson understand by a proposition?" discovered no less than twenty different meanings of the word (see *Mind*, vol. xxxvi, 1927, and vol. xxxvii, 1928). He also, in this resembling Kant, devoted himself to the careful preparation of antitheses, of skilfully constructed divisions, of distinctions, delimitations, etc., and loved to invent technical terms for them. He had a definite dread of publication (even the *Logic* owed its appearance to strong external pressure). He was a very self-centred thinker who paid little regard to the work of his contemporaries, and had great mental energies which in spite of a life-long struggle against ill-health continued to be fresh and active to the end.

After these general remarks we can give only a brief glance over his work, rich as it is in content. Johnson, like Mill, defines logic as the analysis and criticism of thought, in which no other aim may be pursued than the attainment of truth. The question here is not about the content of thought, but about the mental attitude or activity of the thinker, and this distinction between thought and thinker leads to treating logic under a twofold aspect, the objective and the subjective. The latter is the epistemological aspect, through which the theory of knowledge comes to be included in logic; the former aspect is called the constitutive, and has reference to the content of knowledge. The content again can be considered both from formal and from material or empirical standpoints. Thus we can, e.g., among certified propositions distinguish those, the formal, which are believed through pure thinking and others, the empirical, which are believed because of real experience. Here it must be noticed that there are no propositions which are based solely upon experience, but only such as can be established with the help of experience. Thus logic is divided into a formal and a material part. The first treats of the ordinary objects of formal logic (parts i and ii of Johnson's book), but with considerable divergence from the traditional order and important changes of content. At the beginning stands the proposition as the unit from which the whole system of logical principles can be developed. In the place of the ordinary doctrine of concept and judgment stands the doctrine of the proposition. By proposition Johnson understands that of which truth and falsehood can be significantly predicated. Johnson, therefore, in opposition to the majority of modern logicians, starts from the proposition, not from the judgment, and from this standpoint unrolls a great number of formal logical problems (such as those of negation, of proper and class-names, of enumeration and class, of identity, of the important distinctions of determinable and determinate, of adjective and substantive, of "continuant" and "occurrent", of the laws of thought, of relation, etc.). To this is conjoined in the second part the doctrine of demonstrative inference, both of deductive and inductive inference. All deductive inference rests upon two principles, the applicative and the implicative. Both principles are applied in the syllogism. Syllogism is first set forth in its ordinary formal development (categorical syllogism), then is extended in the light of the concept of function, and so introduced among the problems of the logico-mathematical theories. Questions such as those of symbolism, of function, of magnitude, of pure mathematics and its relation to logic, of the difference between pre-mathematical and mathematical logic are investigated here, often combined with criticism of Russell's theories. There follows the doctrine of induction as the process through which a general conclusion is reached by reason of particular instances as premisses. Four kinds are distinguished: intuitive, summary, demonstrative, and problematic. Here, as all through the third part, Johnson carries on Mill's work and criticizes his theories, and there can be no doubt that he has made important advances beyond the earlier methods and conclusions.

The third part treats of "the logical bases of science", and logic thus enters upon its material division. Ontological concepts such as substance and causality, matter and mind, are introduced and discussed, and the separation between the standpoints of theory of knowledge and ontology becomes uncertain. Out of the multitude of topics we may mention the specially characteristic treatment of the problem of substance. Johnson attempts to free the concept from its metaphysical implications and to establish as far as possible its purely logical character. The metaphysical concept of substance on account of its ambiguity is replaced by the much more definite concept of the substantive; this concept including not only what is usually termed substance, but also the concept of process or event. By substantive we must understand everything existential. Within the category of existence we may distinguish two sub-categories, according as that which exists continues or ceases to exist. Thus we get the important distinction between "continuants" and "occurrents". More precisely the "continuant" is determined as that which persists through a limited or unlimited section of time, during which its inner states and its outer relations may change into other "continuants" or remain unchanged. In this sense the manner of existence of mind is "continuant," but that of a toothache is "occurrent". Everything which has the character of process (occurrent), which also includes event, must be related to one or more continuants, even though the connecting link between two processes, apart from their purely spatio-temporal relations, is always the "continuant" itself. This basic distinction involves a series of other problems of material logic. As there are physical and psychic "continuants", there arises the problem of material and psychic being and their mutual relations and, as "continuants" stand in causal relation to each other, there is also the problem of causality. The categories of substance and causality are viewed by Johnson not as two different categories, but as inseparable factors of a single category; neither can be understood without the other. Within causality there is, moreover, the fundamental distinction of immanent and transient causation. That concept of relation which constitutes the unity of a single "continuant" is viewed as determined by immanent causality; while a multiplicity of non-identical "continuants" which all belong to one and the same province of reality is determined by transient causal relations. All this need not be considered further here, but it may be evident already that, in comparison with the classical formulation of this problem by Hume, Johnson's explanation seems to be extremely complicated, differentiated, logically refined and deepened, although this often takes place at the expense of that clearness which distinguishes Hume's thinking, and which has such an elementary charm in comparison with Johnson.

In the fourth part the problem of probability should have been attacked in the same thorough and comprehensive fashion; but Johnson was able to complete only a few sections. Thus the whole remains a torso which testifies to an amazing power of thought. His influence already has been considerable, but may not exercise its full power till some future date.

With Johnson's work the original logical research of the present-day reaches its highest point, so far as it does not, like symbolic logic, stand quite outside of tradition. But in addition there is an almost boundless wealth of logical literature; countless class-books, hand-books, text-books, books of exercises, elementary and advanced logics, special investigations and comprehensive treatises, usually upon an Aristotelian basis, less often upon an empirical, Hegelian, pragmatic, or other basis. This abundance, apart from the evident natural gift of the English for the study, is to be explained by the fact that logic is still an important subject in the examinations for university degrees. From the mass of these writings, so far as they have not met us in other connections, we may select for mention one work which may with better right than many similar books be regarded as the classical presentation of Aristotelian logic. This is *Studies and Exercises in Formal Logic* (1884; fourth edition, 1906, new impression, 1928), by JOHN NEVILLE KEYNES (born 1852). This widely-used class-book, which has been established in England for half a century, presents us with a thorough treatment of all formal logical inquiry from Aristotle to the present day. In it logic appears as a special study quite separate from the other departments of philosophy, and as possessing its own strictly defined province of inquiry. Its strength (and at the same time its weakness) lies in its assured advance towards the status of a special science, which consciously pushes aside all questions of ultimate principle. Finally may be mentioned here the important work of the well-known economist JOHN MAYNARD KEYNES (born 1883), son of the logician, on Probability (*A Treatise on Probability*, 1921, German translation by F. M. Urban, 1926). It is one of the most exemplary and exhaustive monographs upon a special problem, which it investigates and illustrates in all its relations and aspects with profound learning and admirable command of the subject.

After this excursion into logic we may turn back once more to New Realism. From a large number of *di minorum gentium* we may choose the following for brief consideration: L. A. REID (born 1895, Professor at Armstrong College, Newcastle-upon-Tyne), H. H. PRICE (born 1899, Professor of Logic, Oxford), and J. E. TURNER (born 1875, Reader in Philosophy at the University of Liverpool).

Reid in his book *Knowledge and Truth* (1923) reviews the whole New Realist theory of knowledge (English and American) and tries, while criticizing it somewhat adversely, to reach a standpoint of his own in regard to the nature and relations of knowledge, truth, and error. Knowledge and truth are, as he shows, not things which are different *toto coelo*, but are closely bound together and illustrate each other. Knowledge is determined as an activity by which the mind apprehends something which is given. It is therefore not a static condition, in which the cognizing subject merely has presentations which state, represent, or copy something outside of itself. Knowledge is essentially prehension of the real, and every cognitive function includes the immediate relation of the mind to reality, even when the knowledge as such is mistaken. In knowledge we come into direct contact with the objectively real, and, as it were, work our way through to it. This Reid calls the transitive character of knowledge. Truth is basically the same thing, but with the difference that in this case the apprehension of reality is successful and adequate, while knowledge may miss its object. So far as knowledge is true it is the apprehension of a complex reality or of a part of it, as it really is. The solution of the problem of error follows easily from these definitions. Error is the false arrangement or application of real facts and relations. To err is that act of knowledge in which a predicate is related to a datum and a judgment formed from it which is not an apprehension of the complex fact which was originally connected with the datum. Beside theoretic experience Reid considers aesthetic experience both in the last chapter of the above-mentioned book, and in a separate book on aesthetics (*A Study in Aesthetics*, 1931), and moral experience in *Creative Morality* (1937).

In his book *Perception* (1932), Price deals with the central problem of the New Realist theory of knowledge, perception. This investigation, which, without committing itself to any definite theory, has much in common with the views of Moore, Russell, and Broad, aims at a sort of phenomenology of sense-perception, and therefore at clearing the phenomonen of perception from a number of confusing theories and laying its nature bare by simple description and exact analysis. In carrying out this process of purification it tries to prove not only the inadequacy of the naïve-realist view, but above all to refute the so-called causal theory of perception as the most popular and pernicious of philosophical theories. By this Price understands the view that sense-data are caused by external things and that perceptual knowledge consists in an inference from an effect to a cause. Such a relation between sensa and things is not consistent with the results of phenomenological inquiry. This in the case of sense-perception first shows that material things are present to the senses, and that therefore the relation which prevails in this case should be described according to a phrase of Moore quite simply as "belonging to". Price, then, in some penetrating descriptive analyses, without regard to the inquiries of the German phenomenological school, which are so important in this connection, deals with the character and the mode of existence of sense-data, with the perceiving consciousness (in regard to which he distinguishes two different grades, that of acceptance and that of assurance), with the exact determination of the relation of sense-data to external objects, of the various sense-data to each other (which he tries to clarify by the concept of family), with their origin, etc.

Turner's position in regard to theory of knowledge as developed in the book *A Theory of Direct Realism, and the Relation of Realism to Idealism* (1925) is closely akin to the doctrine of Alexander, in which it makes some small corrections. Here also Realism is carried to the furthest extreme, when sensations are assumed to belong to the physical world of things. They are *in* things or parts of them, and no change is made in them by the occurrence of perception. They are, even when they appear in the perceptual act, physically real. But we must distinguish between normal and abnormal sensations, and although their mode of existence is not affected thereby (so as to imply that the former are taken to be real, the latter to be merely apparent), yet there is an essential difference in the fact that the normal are completely identical with the really existent, while the abnormal are only imperfectly identical and that the former reveal exhaustively and quite adequately the reality which presents them, while the latter do so partially and inadequately. Although this Realism professes to be more realistic than almost every other, viewed in a longer perspective it appears merely as a preliminary stage to an idealist metaphysics in the Hegelian, or rather in the Anglo-Hegelian style. Turner comes near to this in another book, in which he tries to reach a metaphysical standpoint of his own; a standpoint which approximates to Bradley's way of thinking, but partly changes and distorts it, partly misinterprets and falsifies it.[1]

[1] See *Personality and Reality*, 1926, to which there is a continuation entitled *The Nature of Deity*, 1927. Other books by Turner are *The Revelation of Deity*, 1931, and *Essentials in the Development of Religion: a philosophical and psychological study*, 1934.

How true it is that idealist and realist thinking in the most recent days no longer move upon separate paths, but often meet and try to accommodate their differences and to weld themselves together, we have often had occasion to notice. We will, therefore, mention finally a philosopher whose doctrine especially illustrates this. A. C. EWING (born 1900, Lecturer in Moral Science in the University of Cambridge), one of the ablest and most promising thinkers of the younger generation, to whom we already are indebted for three excellent books (*Kant's Treatment of Causality*, 1924, *The Morality of Punishment*, 1929, and *Idealism; a critical survey*, 1934), is in the main allied with the New Realists, but is at the same time connected by "deep sympathy" with the New Idealist movement. The latter he has in the last-mentioned work subjected to a comprehensive and penetrating constructive criticism, especially on its theoretical side. The criticism has the main purpose of reconciling the inner tensions of both schools of thought, and of introducing important elements of Idealism into the New Realist doctrine. The high importance of what modern British philosophy owes to the New Idealist school finds eloquent expression in this book of one of its keenest critics; and from it we can see with especial clearness what a strong influence this school has upon contemporary thinking, though it has itself almost completely disappeared. Ewing's criticism mentions three main services of "inestimable value" which the realist reaction against Idealism has achieved. It has: (1) Shown that the true character of knowing is a finding and discovering rather than a generating and producing. This truth, which has been too long obscured by the idealist theory of knowledge, does not, however, justify us in postulating logically the complete independence of the object from the cognizing subject. Though idealist arguments for the mental character or dependence of reality in mind are invalid and the problem of knowledge can be solved only by the method of Realism, a kind of methodological Idealism can be combined with it. Hence it follows, (2) that the theory according to which the physical world exists independently of any experience cannot be proved strictly and is exposed to many difficulties, but is at least accessible to a judicious philosophical inquiry. Such inquiries have already given great help in the problem of perception. But still more important is (3) the demand for a careful and exact analysis of the problems, a demand which has been too much neglected by idealist thinkers because in their eagerness for synthesis they have pushed on over-hastily to a solution of the world-problem. It is right to prepare the ground for the solution of the great metaphysical problems by scrupulously exact detailed analysis of special problems. In the course of this section we have seen how far this demand has been met by the work of the New Realists. The further results to which Ewing's criticism of Idealism has led cannot be considered here. It is enough to point out that in the main they lie in the direction of New Realism. But Ewing's thinking avoids all extreme formulations and tries to reach a kind of middle position between the contending parties.

V

MATHEMATICAL LOGIC[1]

By "mathematical logic" is meant here the various attempts to renew formal and analytical logic in the spirit of mathematics and by means of mathematical terms and methods. It is a movement which assumes an increasing importance throughout the period of which we treat. Both the first suggestions for the establishment (or re-establishment) of a mathematical logic in the middle of last century and, indeed, in part earlier still, and the later development that took more explicit shape at the opening of the present century derive mainly from the work of British thinkers; and even to-day, when the movement has become an international one, the British share in it remains of the first

[1] The expressions 'pure', 'symbolic', 'algorithmic' or 'algebraic' Logic, or 'Logistics', 'Symbolics', and 'Logical Calculus' differ only in slight nuances of meaning and are here taken as equivalent. As regards this section the author wishes it to be clearly stated that he feels far removed from the subject with which it deals, and is therefore very well aware of the inadequacy of his treatment of it. The full understanding of the matter requires a training and proficiency in mathematics which the author does not command. For this reason in particular, among others, no detailed examination of the problems has been attempted, but only a general survey and orientation of the field. The author has consulted those works which were the original sources of the movement, so far as he could understand them, but it must be expressly stated that, in contrast to the rest of the book, this section relies preponderatingly upon literature at the second remove—upon comment and exposition. The following works have proved of special use in this connection: C. I. Lewis, *A Survey of Symbolic Logic*, 1918; C. I. Lewis and C. H. Langford, *Symbolic Logic*, 1932; L. S. Stebbing, *A Modern Introduction to Logic*, 1930 (second edition 1933); J. E. Salomaa, *Idealismus und Realismus in der englischen Philosophie der Gegenwart*, 1929 (esp. pp. 163–188); Ralph M. Eaton, *General Logic*, 1931; R. Carnap, *Abriss der Logistik*, 1929; J. Venn, *Symbolic Logic*, 1881 (especially the Introduction); J. B. Rieffert, *Logik*, 1925 (in Dessoir's *Lehrbuch der Philosophie*); W. Dubislav, "Die Philosophie der Mathematik in der Gegenwart", 1932 (*Philos. Forschungsberichte*, No. 13); in addition, the relevant articles in the latest (fourteenth) edition of the *Encyclopaedia Britannica*. Full bibliographies are given by Lewis and by Stebbing.

importance. In confining ourselves to a very superficial survey in the form of a short historical review of this subject of so many ramifications, we are well aware that we are doing less than justice to its significance. The only excuse for so cursory a treatment is that we are here concerned with a very specific discipline, whose connection with the movement of philosophy as a whole is not close and whose philosophical import and relevance is even to-day a matter of much controversy. We cannot accept the claim of the over-enthusiastic devotees of mathematical logic, that this is the ground upon which philosophy as such must join issue, and upon which, indeed, its very fate must be decided. Nor can we admit that the last word has been spoken upon logic, however radically the subject has been transformed and improved by the mathematical logicians. What they have done is, rather, simply to constitute a new branch on the main trunk of logical science, a branch full of significance and extensive in its reach, but drawing nourishment far more from the soil of mathematics than from that of philosophy. That the new discipline lies closer to the heart of mathematics than to philosophy is, indeed, shown by the fact that it grew in the first instance out of mathematical interests and discussions, and was established and developed by mathematical investigators. Accordingly, if the excessive claims of mathematical logic are rejected and its philosophical relevance duly limited, this is only to endorse and affirm the more emphatically its services in its own special domain.

It is to be agreed, then, that so far is mathematical logic from being able to claim the whole of philosophy, or even the whole of logic, for its province, that it occupies a quite specific and precisely assignable place within the logical system, and that the remaining branches of logic, as well as the other philosophical disciplines, have altogether a right to a place beside it. There would, indeed, be no need to mention so obvious a fact were it not that the new discipline has sometimes presumed so far as to imagine itself in a position to take over the whole business of philosophy as its sole heir, and to jettison all that philosophy has hitherto achieved. Nor is its attitude to the earlier achievements of logic itself very different. In the first zest of discovery the mathematical logicians were inclined to break down the bridges and to overlook the historical connections uniting their study with traditional logic. Above all, the former was presented as the authentic counterpart and antithesis of the Aristotelian tradition, the overthrow of which was to be regarded as one of its main purposes. As against this, we have to maintain what, in point of fact, is of late being more and more clearly recognized even in the mathematical logicians' own camp—that Aristotle's formal logic is in truth the precursor of theirs, which is not only not opposed to it, but is in essentials the first fulfilment of its deeper meaning. As Riehl justly remarks: "Thus Aristotle is the first founder of algorithmic or mathematical logic, the logical calculus," and in the same sense Miss Stebbing, one of the most recent representatives of the school, writes that "Aristotle's theory of the syllogism is the first attempt to demonstrate the formal principle of deduction." The ideal of pure logical form is the goal alike of the Aristotelian and of mathematical logic, and the two are only to be distinguished by the difference of the degree in which they approach this goal.

Accordingly no sharp line of division can be drawn between "old" and "new" logic. The latter has its source in the former; that is to say the purely formal Science of Order (as Logistics may be termed) is derived from the analysis and criticism of thought by continued generalization and abstraction. The transformation of classical into mathematical logic means just this perfected process of generalization and formalization resulting in pure form emptied of all content and of every concrete object. The pursuit of this tendency inevitably drove logic into the arms of that science in which the ideal of pure form is most perfectly fulfilled, viz., Mathematics. And conversely, when Mathematics began to pay attention to its own fundamental principles it had resort to this logic which enabled it to become aware of its own essential nature. The result was a close sympathy between the two sciences, leading on the one hand to the "logicizing" of mathematics, on the other to the "mathematicizing" of logic. But all this was already implicit in the programme of Aristotle, though it never received explicit expression and was only in part systematically carried out. And in Aristotle is already found one essential characteristic of the new logic, namely the use of symbols instead of verbal terms ("ideograms" instead of "phonograms"), so that not even in its symbolism has Logistics anything new in principle; what is new being merely the comprehensiveness and strict system with which the symbols, introduced from mathematics (especially algebra) or resembling those of mathematics, are applied.

Nevertheless, the new logic does, from the formal standpoint, signify a notable and distinct advance on the classical. It means that the essential idea of logic has been more purely worked out, its range enormously extended, its methods systematically overhauled, and its means of expression thoroughly reformed. From the standpoint of mathematical logic the Aristotelian logic is shown to be defective in the following points: (1) in its restriction to a single mode of deduction, viz., the syllogism; (2) in its failure to devise an adequate symbolism for logical relations; (3) in its faulty analysis of these relations (see Miss Stebbing, *Encyclopaedia Britannica*, 14th ed., vol. xiv, p. 331).

The traditional syllogistic logic represents only a relatively small section of the field surveyed by mathematical logic, and it was only with the discovery of non-syllogistic types of deductive inference that new and hitherto unsuspected possibilities were laid open to logical inquiry. It was the same with the discovery and analysis of a greater variety of logical classes, types, propositions, functions, etc., which are involved in deductive inference and may be indicated by precise conceptual symbols, so as to make possible a sort of quasi-mathematical calculus. But as already stated, all this represents no *essential* difference from the accepted logical tradition, whether regarding its subject-matter, or its methods, or its purpose and goal. The difference is one of approximation only: in the closer approach which the new logic makes to the principle of ideal form, which is the directing principle for the science of logic throughout.

We may now define mathematical logic, marking with Lewis the following as its essential characteristics: (1) Its subject-matter is that of logic of whatever form, that is, the principles of rational or reflective process in general in contrast to principles which pertain exclusively to some special branch of such rational process. (2) Its tools are provided by an "ideographic" symbolism, in which every separate symbol stands for a single relatively simple and quite explicit concept, the ideal being the exclusion of all non-symbolic language. (3) Among the ideograms are presented certain variables which have a quite determinate range of meaning. (4) Every system of symbolic logic is developed deductively, that is, all its theorems are derived from a relatively small number of first principles, expressed in symbols, by operations precisely formulated or at least formulatable.

There is a wide divergence of opinion as to the philosophical and general value of Logistics, from an absurdly exaggerated self-esteem on the one side to utter rejection on the other. Logistics is assuredly not a subject to be studied by everyone. It demands a special, essentially mathematical, endowment, a sure mastery of its method, technique, and symbolism, and above all a high degree of training. It is not easy to get an objective judgment upon it either from the ranks of its devotees or from those who stand aloof from it: the latter cannot penetrate its secrets, the former suffer mostly from a morbid consciousness of superiority. In the creative pioneer works at any rate (e.g., that of a Frege, a Peano, a Russell, and a Whitehead) we have culminating achievements in pure formal thinking which are hardly to be surpassed. Reason (*ratio*) celebrates here as in mathematics its most exalted triumphs, and the spirit of rigorous scientific precision attains its finest possible development. But this spirit has become wholly disembodied and has broken behind it every bridge uniting it to life and concrete experience. And so we are often reminded of Bradley's comment on the "unearthly ballet of bloodless categories", or of Windelband's sharp condemnation when, glancing at the logical calculus, he speaks of it as "a spacious exercise ground for the gymnastics of a sterile ingenuity".[1] We do not wish to accept this last estimate, though it certainly contains a grain of truth. For we cannot ignore the fact that, besides much mere intellectual agility and conceptual gymnastics and besides the delight in the game of logic and in purely formal exercises, a considerable amount has been achieved by really serious scientific work. A series of problems which logic had hitherto worked at in vain or which had never come within its purview have been successfully tackled and in part solved by mathematical logic. It has only proved inadequate where it was occupied with specifically philosophical problems; for we cannot admit that it can itself usurp the place of philosophy. Logistics has retired to a lonely and remote island and assumed sovereignty over it, but no road leads back from thence to the familiar ways of everyday life and thought. It is "gray theory" and the "golden tree of life" cannot grow "green" in its territory. It is also noteworthy that some of the most original thinkers of the school, like Russell and Whitehead, have latterly turned away from mathematical logic and reverted to more customary methods of philosophizing, whence we may perhaps conclude that the former is easily exhausted and can give no genuine lasting satisfaction.

We shall now attempt to give a short sketch of the historical development of mathematical logic, with special reference to that part of it associated with the work of British thinkers.

Although, as we have seen, mathematical logic is a descendant of the formal logic and analytic of Aristotle, Leibniz was the first man to announce its programme consciously and explicitly, and to demarcate clearly its subject-matter. He set out the need both for a universal scientific written language (*characteristica universalis*) using symbolic signs instead of words, and for a rational calculus (*calculus ratiocinator*) to proceed by the help of these in a quasi-mathematical fashion. And the conception of a *mathesis universalis* that should serve as the basis for a *scientia generalis*, an all-inclusive methodology grounded in mathematics, already expresses the intimate union between

[1] See Windelband, *Lehrbuch der Geschichte der Philosophie*, 5th ed., 1910, p. 536.

mathematical thinking and that of scientific philosophy. Leibniz himself only carried out a small part of this programme, but his genius surveyed the whole extent of symbolic logic with all its possibilities and grasped its essentials; and already in Leibniz are found most of the nodal points to which subsequent investigation was able to attach itself. In the XVIIIth Century various attempts were made along the same lines, e.g., by Lambert, Holland, Ploucquet, and Castillon, but no noticeable advance beyond Leibniz was achieved. It was not till the XIXth Century that "logistic" ways of thinking came again markedly to the front, and this time the first impulse to the study in its revived and more thorough form came from England. In the first half of this period British writers were not only pioneers in the development of logistic theory, they were for several decades the only ones to occupy themselves with it.

We may record as the earliest attempt of the period to put logic upon a new basis that of GEORGE BENTHAM (1800–84), nephew of Jeremy Bentham and known otherwise as a botanist, who in 1827 published his *Outline of a New System of Logic.* The main point of this, as of other similar efforts to modernize logic, was the correction of the traditional doctrine called the "quantification of the predicate". This principle became much better known through the work of Sir WILLIAM HAMILTON, the head of the Scottish school (see above, pp. 33 ff.), whose work *Lectures on Metaphysics and Logic* lent an important stimulus to the new logic, though he cannot be accounted among its avowed representatives. Without knowing anything of Bentham's previous work Hamilton sought to show that the predicate of a proposition or judgment can be quantitatively determined in the same way as the subject had hitherto alone been determined. In this way logical propositions could be expressed in the form of equations, and for this Hamilton showed a preference for geometrical figures and algebraical symbols. The inferences that were to be drawn in the new way suggested calculations with given magnitudes exactly determined, naturally recalling the processes of mathematics, which thus moved into the purview of logic. Hamilton's importance for the subsequent development of logic is, indeed, limited to the stimulus he gave in this respect, which incidentally has so little of originality that it can be traced back at least as far as Leibniz. The principle of the quantification of the predicate, credit for the priority in which became the matter of a lengthy and barren controversy, was discovered by Hamilton in 1833 and recognized in its complete form and publicly taught by him at the latest in 1840 (see Appendix vi of his *Lectures on Logic*, vol. ii, pp. 251–323). THOMAS SPENCER BAYNES (1823–87), a disciple and assistant of Hamilton, pursued the same line of thought further, and long before the appearance of Hamilton's lectures on logic published his *Essay on the New Analytic of Logical Forms* (1850). Earlier still, WILLIAM THOMSON (1819–90, later Archbishop of York) had expounded Hamilton's position systematically in his *Outline of the Laws of Thought* (1842, sixth edition, 1860).

But all these and other logical writers of the mid-nineteenth century were merely preliminary skirmishers. The credit of having led the new logic to a decisive new departure belongs to the two mathematicians De Morgan and Boole, especially to the latter. AUGUSTUS DE MORGAN (1806–71), Professor of Mathematics in the University of London, was the author (apart from a number of works on pure mathematics) of the following works bearing on our subject: *Formal Logic: or the Calculus of Inference, necessary and probable*, 1847; *Syllabus of a proposed System of Logic*, 1860; as well as a series of important papers on logic that appeared in the *Transactions of the Cambridge Philosophical Society* between 1846 and 1863. De Morgan, like Hamilton, was concerned with the quantification of the predicate, but his mathematical ability was greater than Hamilton's, and in many respects the development of mathematical logic owed more to him than to any of his predecessors. But he stood still more or less firmly in the jurisdiction of Aristotelian logic, which provided the starting-point for his inquiries and which it was his endeavour to revise in important respects, so that he entered the new domain with some hesitancy and many of his reforms were incompletely carried through. But he advanced a definite stage on the road to the symbolization of logic, and thereby to its approximation to mathematics. He attempted to break down the prejudice which earlier logicians had felt against the introduction of mathematical methods and to justify the application of such methods to logical processes. He discovered new forms of syllogism and new classes of propositions, and set forth a penetrating analysis of the copula "is", whose employment hitherto he explained to be logically defective and which he expressed by a variety of symbols according to the relation it establishes or the function it performs. And it was in fact in respect of the doctrine of relations that De Morgan went furthest in anticipating future developments. He distinguishes, for instance, between transitive, convertible, and correlative relations, a distinction which was to show how very fertile it would prove only much later. And in recognizing the importance of the concept of relation he laid the foundation-stone of the logic of relations that was to be extensively developed in the future by Russell and others.

Still more important than De Morgan is his contemporary, GEORGE BOOLE (1815–64, Professor of Mathematics at Queen's College, Cork). The investigations of the two men appeared upon the scene almost simultaneously; in fact, by a coincidence, the first of Boole's writings that here concerns us, *The Mathematical Analysis of Logic*, was published on the same day as De Morgan's *Formal Logic*. An exact comparative account of Boole's writings is to be found in Lewis's *Survey*, pp. 389 ff., and we shall here mention only the chief of them, *An Investigation of the Laws of Thought* (1854), also republished as the second volume of the *Collected Works* (ed. Jourdain, 1916). If we have recognized Leibniz as the first discoverer of Logistics, Boole is by general consent to be accounted the second, and he deserves all the more credit for having obviously built up this science in a comprehensive and systematic fashion by the power of his own mind unaided by any acquaintance with what had already been done by others. Being first and last a mathematician he bothered himself little about logic in its wider bearing, and so in establishing the new discipline he has been impeded hardly at all, or at least much less than any of his predecessors, by traditional prejudices. It may be said that Boole was the first who really succeeded in transferring into Logic in the grand style algebraic notation and mathematical processes of calculation. He was the first to devise a complete and efficient calculus and to apply a symbolic language really fit to be used and systematically worked out. In this he became a model for all later workers in this field, who are all more or less closely linked up with his work. Of the mathematical sciences it was in particular algebra whose methods and signs Boole applied to the service of Logic, becoming thus the founder (if we disregard the anticipatory work of Leibniz in this matter also) of the so-called Algebra of Logic—that special branch of mathematical logic which was subsequently carried to its highest point by Schroeder. Thus through the work of Boole mathematics and logic were welded fast together. He only so far mistook their relationship as to regard mathematics as the primary and logic as the secondary science, whereas later inquiry proved that the converse is the correct order of ranking. Boole held that the supreme principles of thought were in form mathematical, and he represented them in the guise of equations with an algebraical notation (e.g., the laws of Contradiction and Excluded Middle). Boole's importance, then, rests on his thoroughgoing mathematicization ("algebraicization") of Logic. To-day when more modern, more exact, and better constructed systems have replaced his, his work has merely an historic significance, but there is no doubt that it represents a chief turning-point in the history of Logistics.

The labours of the next thinker to be considered were of less pioneer interest for mathematical logic than those of Boole, but were fertilized by him and show a further advance in the same direction. WILLIAM STANLEY JEVONS (1835–82, from 1866 to 1876 Professor of Philosophy and Political Economy in Owens College, Manchester, 1876–80 Professor of Political Economy in University College, London), had a many-sided and capacious mind, and, in addition to his work in Logic, made outstanding contributions to all the scientific fields of study in which he was interested. He is one of the most important

British economists in the XIXth Century, and represented a theory that is based upon the principle of utility as its central idea, and is thus in general line with Benthamite Utilitarianism. Yet these investigations, too, were closely connected with his work in logic and mathematics, in so far as he applied mathematical and statistical methods to economics much more comprehensively and much more successfully than had hitherto been done. His aim was to turn economic theory by the help of mathematics into an exact science (see his essay *A General Mathematical Theory of Political Economy*, 1862, and his large work *The Theory of Political Economy*, 1871). Even in the field of more abstract theoretical analysis his interests were much wider than Boole's; besides logic in the narrower sense he treated of the Theory of Knowledge, the Theory of Statistics, the Doctrine of Probability, and above all the problem of the Methodology of the Sciences, which (especially in his book *The Principles of Science*, 1874) he investigated as thoroughly as Whewell and Mill before him and Pearson after him. His remaining logical writings are: *Pure Logic, or the Logic of Quality apart from Quantity*, 1864, *The Substitution of Similars*, 1869, *Elementary Lessons in Logic*, 1870, *Studies in Deductive Logic*, 1880, and *Pure Logic and other minor Works*, 1890 (posthumously edited by R. Adamson and H. A. Jevons).

So far as concerns the algebraical treatment of logic, Jevons is a disciple of Boole, from whom he takes his starting-point. But in certain points he goes beyond his master, modifying his system in ways which in many, if not in all respects, mark a definite advance. Thus Jevons is convinced that the fundamental science is not algebra, but logic, and although he likewise avails himself of an algebraical notation yet he is careful to take into account the special logical relations, and not to adopt the symbols of mathematics simply as such but to endow them with a specifically logical connotation. He recognized (though his practice did not always accord with the recognition) that the application of algebraical signs to logical relations ought not to be determined purely from the standpoint of mathematics, and that the science of thought was subject to other laws and conditions than that of number. And so he came to see that logic is not to be subordinated to algebra but *vice versa*, expressing this point of view by proposing to treat algebra simply as a fully developed logic. On the other hand Jevons went so far in the application of calculative processes to logic that he constructed a "Logical Machine", by means of which one might draw the appropriate conclusion from given premisses in purely mechanical fashion (a picture of it is given in *The Principles of Science*). A further advance upon Boole is in the simplification he made in the Sign-system (which he called the "Logical Alphabet") and the calculus, whereby he got rid of the intricacy of Boole's system and made the whole procedure more easy to grasp and to work. Subsequent study profited by this simplification and based itself more frequently on Jevons's system than on that of Boole. Furthermore, Jevons went considerably further than his predecessors in the Quantification of the Predicate and in transforming every logical judgment or proposition into an exact equation. Like them, he took exception to the narrowness of the Aristotelian logic, showing how small a part the syllogism plays among the many other possible forms of deductive inference. Thus in place of syllogistic he put forward a very much more general and more fundamental theory of the process of inference, which he called the Principle of the Substitution of Similars and which secured wide attention. In its simplest form this principle runs as follows: "Whatever holds true of something equally holds true of what is like it."[1] This amounts to saying that in its most general form inference consists in the substitution of one identical term for another. All logical propositions are statements of identity or must permit of being reduced to such; their basic form is expressed by the equation $A = B$, and this form underlies also those propositions which only state a partial or in some way limited identity. This doctrine led to an acute discussion of the possibility of applying the mathematical sign of equality in the sense of the logical copula, in which Jevons acknowledged that this sign could not simply be taken over in its mathematical function, but must be interpreted

[1] *The Substitution of Similars*, 1869.

in accordance with the special relationships of logic. For the rest, Jevons was to his contemporaries the leader of the opposition both to traditional logic and to the empirical logic of Mill, both of which he combated stoutly, while in the field of mathematical logic continuing that course of development that leads from Boole to Schroeder.

Mention may be made in this place of the nearly contemporary logical work of JOHN VENN (1834–1923), which apart from a number of contributions to periodicals (for which see Lewis, *op. cit.*, p. 405) is comprised in the following three writings: *The Logic of Chance*, 1866, *Symbolic Logic*, 1881, and *The Principles of Empirical or Inductive Logic*, 1889. Of these the second has here the greatest importance. Like Jevons, Venn set himself the task of making good the defects of Boole's system, and he went further than either in his search for new ways and means of arriving at a symbolic language that could really be used. It is to be noted in this connection that, as Venn himself complains, mathematical logic was still dominated by a most bewildering diversity of signs and sign-systems, that nearly every logician devised a system for himself, and hardly any one of them took over one already in existence. In this respect real improvement had to wait until *Principia Mathematica*, though even to-day the chaos of symbols has not been altogether reduced to order. But how devastating the chaos in his day was Venn illustrated by citing no less than twenty-five symbolic notations for one and the same type of judgment (see *Symbolic Logic*, p. 407). One notable point in Venn's theory is that he opposes the obliteration of the boundary between logic and mathematics and again sharply distinguishes the domain of each. He does not subordinate either to the other, but recognizes that each has structural differences and laws of its own. He aims at preserving logic from the danger of "mathematicization", while at the same time pursuing its symbolization (in the last resort through symbols borrowed from mathematics). He repeatedly emphasizes that all his investigations rested on purely logical foundations and that even the logical calculus he employed was wholly independent of mathematical methods of calculation. He treats symbolic logic and mathematics as branches of a single symbolic language, which have some, though only a few, laws in common. Only, mathematical "symbolics" has up to now progressed far further than logical. And he stands opposed to the then prevailing view in holding that the customary logic had not been in any way superseded and deprived of its force by mathematical logic, but that it retained its educational value (which Venn in point of fact rated highly), and had also other advantages that warranted its separate existence. He treated the new logic simply as the further development of the old along the path of progressive generalization. And finally it is to be noted that while regarding letter symbols as the aptest for the operations of logic, Venn introduces alongside of them a second kind of symbolic representation new to Logistics, viz., the diagram, using geometrical figures such as circles and ellipses. Venn's diagrams, which have attained a certain reputation, represent the relations of logical classes as they were treated of in Boole's and later in Schroeder's Algebra. Its principle consists in representing classes by objects so related that all the relations possible between the classes may be indicated in the same diagram.

In several respects Venn's logic stands apart from the general line of development and takes in part a course of its own. The algebraicizing of logic inaugurated by Boole, marking it off as a special branch within the general history of symbolic systems, is, after Jevons, most powerfully represented in numerous studies of the American mathematician and philosopher CHARLES SANDERS PEIRCE, one of the most significant thinkers of the New World. It was carried further in new variations and modifications by investigators like ALEXANDER MACFARLANE, ROBERT GRASSMANN, HUGH MACCOLL, Mrs. C. LADD-FRANKLIN, and others, and took finally its classical and conclusive shape in the work of ERNST SCHROEDER, especially in his three-volume treatise, *Vorlesungen über die Algebra der Logik* (1890 to 1895).

A second line of development, which likewise can be traced back as far as Leibniz and his idea of a *mathesis universalis*, leads on to the important labours of the German Frege and the Italian Peano, which lie at the foundation of mathematical logic in its modern form, and finally to the classical formulation of the entire discipline by Russell and Whitehead. This development, which at first took place principally along mathematical paths and was strongly influenced and promoted by the discovery of non-Euclidean systems of Geometry, is closely bound up with important new discoveries in the sphere of present-day mathematics, such as the theory of Quaternions of the Irish mathematician Sir W. R. Hamilton, the so-called Theory of Extension of H. Grassmann, the Theory of Aggregates of G. Cantor and the Theory of Number of R. Dedekind. It grew out of a preoccupation with the bases and essential nature of mathematics, and led to the recognition of the logical character of mathematical concepts and axioms. Frege's work came first in time. His book ***Begriffschrift*, *eine der arithmetischen nachgebildete Formelsprache des reinen Denkens*** appeared as long ago as 1879, and five years later came *Die Grundlagen der Arithmetik, eine legisch-mathematische Untersuchung über den Begriff der Zahl.* But the symbolic script developed in these writings was so obscure and difficult to grasp that it remained wellnigh unnoticed by contemporary inquirers. And it was only many years later (1901) that Russell rediscovered Frege and realized the deep significance of his work, which, therefore, only began to bear fruit for research when the former had already taken a path similar to Frege's but found independently of his writings. Frege was the first who succeeded in developing a logistical form of arithmetic, and in deriving arithmetic from purely logical premisses. He showed that the basic concepts of mathematics are to be reduced to the fundamental Laws of Thought, and that mathematics must thus be anchored in logic. Through this and other central discoveries Symbolic Logic was brought to awareness of itself and to a more reflective attention to that to which all its labours had hitherto been directed.

Frege's second book marks a new stage in the development of mathematical logic. But as this work remained, as already stated, almost entirely unknown and without influence, historically the credit of having opened the new chapter must be assigned to another work published eleven years later, viz., the well-known *Formulaire de Mathematiques*, by G. Peano, and his Italian collaborators (it appeared in five volumes between 1895 and 1908). I shall not here attempt to describe this work, but it was through it that Russell was directly influenced to turn his thought to mathematico-logical problems, and it thus became the source of that system of Logistics to which all previous currents have been tributaries, and which shows this discipline in its most advanced structure and in what may well be its definitive form. I mean the system of Russell and Whitehead. It is set forth in the three volumes of *Principia Mathematica* (1910–13), an achievement of thought of monumental magnitude, epochal in its significance, in which the whole prolonged labours of their predecessors as far back as Leibniz came to fruition and fulfilment. This is, in fact, the completest, the most comprehensive, maturest, and closest-knit system which the entire movement has yet produced. It might well be called the "Critique of Pure Reason" of the movement, alike in regard to work of past thinkers which it has completed, and to the challenge which it will be called to meet in the future. If ever the term "classic" were justified it is so of the work of Russell and Whitehead. As we have already expounded as much as was necessary in this connection when discussing the philosophies of these two thinkers, further mention in this context is superfluous. We will content ourselves here with quoting the important passage with which the authors open their book: "The mathematical treatment of the principles of mathematics which is the subject of the present work has arisen from the conjunction of two different studies, both in the main very modern. On the one hand we have the work of analysts and geometers, in the way of formulating and systematizing their axioms, and the work of Cantor and others on such matters as the theory of aggregates. On the other hand we have symbolic logic, which, after a necessary period of growth, has now, thanks to Peano and his followers, acquired the technical adaptability and the logical comprehensiveness that are essential to a mathematical instrument for dealing with what have hitherto been the beginnings of mathematics. From the combination of these two studies two results emerge, namely (1) that what were formally taken, tacitly or explicitly, as axioms, are either unnecessary or demonstrable; (2) that the same methods by which supposed axioms are demonstrated will give valuable results in regions, such as infinite number, which had formerly been regarded as inaccessible to human knowledge. Hence the scope of mathematics is enlarged both by the addition of new subjects and by a backward extension into provinces hitherto abandoned to philosophy" (Preface to *Principia Mathematica*, vol. i, p. v).

It cannot be said that the system of Russell and Whitehead has already been outgrown, though since it was published the work of further developing mathematical logic has been prosecuted more intensively than ever. For such work, wherever it has been performed, stands throughout under the sign and under the powerful impress of that system. Accordingly we shall only indicate briefly the further course of the movement in England. The names of two thinkers deserve special mention, who in their own way have continued the investigations of Russell and Whitehead with certain modifications and additions, Wittgenstein and Ramsey. LUDWIG WITTGENSTEIN is an Austrian by birth who has been for some years domiciled in England and has held a professorship in Philosophy in the University of Cambridge. In 1922 he published his *Tractatus Logico-Philosophicus*,[1] a book that made something of a sensation in philosophical circles on its appearance, and was described by Russell himself in an Introduction which he contributed to it as an important event in the world of philosophy. It is for the ordinary reader a book sealed with seven seals, of which the significance is only to be revealed to the most esoteric devotees, and which, as it seems to us, embodies a very peculiar combination of rigorous mathematical and logical thought and obscure mysticism. It

[1] First published in 1921 in Ostwald's *Annalen der Naturphilosophie*. The English edition of 1922 contains both German and English versions.

treats in the first place of the logical structure of propositions and the nature of logical inference, passes next to theory of knowledge, the principles of physics, and problems in ethics, and finally lands in the region of mysticism. Thus it brings the findings of symbolic logic to bear upon various branches and problems of traditional philosophy, and attempts to show how these problems and their solutions have their sources in ignorance of symbolic methods and in the misuse of speech. Accordingly the book expresses a growing demand for a language that shall be logically perfect, and rejects the claim of ordinary linguistic methods to be able to master the problems of philosophy. Wittgenstein himself acknowledges that "to the great works of Frege and the writings of his friend Russell he owes in large measure the stimulation of his thoughts".[1]

He expresses the nature of logical truth more uncompromisingly than ever before, by defining it as tautological, i.e. as true on the ground of its mere form. Mathematical truth, similarly, is to be held to be tautological, so that both logical and mathematical propositions are pure tautologies. One further point may be noted as significant. Russell's deductive system, which had set itself to demonstrate the identity of pure mathematics and pure logic by deriving the axioms of mathematics from a few primary logical laws, came to a stand before certain axioms (e.g., the so-called axiom of Reducibility and that of Infinity), which it was not able to show to be strictly logical in character. It is one of Wittgenstein's services to have pointed out a way to overcome these difficulties of Russell's system, and thereby to have made a notable contribution to the enterprise of reducing mathematics to logic without remainder. For the rest, Wittgenstein's influence upon the school of philosophical thought centred at Cambridge is most potent, although the literary manifestation of it cannot easily be determined.

The same current of thought is exemplified also in the work of Frank Plumpton Ramsey (1903–29), a young Cambridge mathematician who represents Logistics in its latest phase, and from whose genius great things would have been expected, but

[1] *Tractatus Logico-Philosophicus*, 1922, p. 28 f.

for his early death. Fragmentary papers, both published and unpublished, were collected and edited by R. B. Braithwaite under the title *The Foundations of Mathematics and other Logical Essays* (1931). Ramsey was under the dominant influence of Wittgenstein, and his work in the judgment of Russell, who wrote a detailed appreciation of it (see *Mind*, vol. 40, 1931, pp. 476–82), represents by far the most important contribution to mathematical logic since the appearance of the *Tractatus Logico-Philosophicus*. More particularly Ramsey set out to achieve a reconstruction of the system of *Principia Mathematica* which should start by abolishing the principle of Reducibility and thereby build up a completely rigorous deductive system comprehending every branch of mathematics and in a position to display its entire identity with logic as the science of pure form.

The representatives of mathematical logic form to-day a definite group, and occupy an ever-increasing space in the philosophical life of England. One has only to turn over the pages of certain technical philosophical periodicals during the last few years to be convinced of their assiduous activity. Such periodicals for pages together are crammed with symbolic formulas and often resemble mathematical textbooks more than philosophical texts. We must be content to mention a few other names, the bearers of which have come to the front during the last few years, and belong, for the most part, to the younger generation; e.g., R. B. BRAITHWAITE (King's College, Cambridge), A. E. HEATH (University College of Wales, Swansea), C. A. MACE (Bedford College, London), G. RYLE (Christ Church, Oxford), JOHN WISDOM (University of Cambridge), A. E. DUNCAN-JONES (University of Birmingham, Editor of *Analysis*, see above, p. 535 n.), MAX BLACK (London University); also, C. D. BROAD, of whom we have treated in another place. In conclusion, two others require more than merely nominal mention. L. SUSAN STEBBING (*b.* 1886, Professor of Philosophy in Bedford College, University of London) has in her important and influential book *A Modern Introduction to Logic* (1930, second edition revised and enlarged,

1933) and in other papers done less for the constructive development of the new discipline than for the comprehensive presentation of it in a form worked out to fit the needs of students. She stands in near relation to the Cambridge philosophical circle, and her researches are rooted in the soil of the Logistics of Russell and Whitehead, though as regards method she is also indebted to thinkers such as G. E. Moore and C. D. Broad, and as regards the content of her work especially to W. E. Johnson's developed logic (see above, pp. 694 ff.). But in contrast to most exponents of Logistics she is in very much less radical opposition to earlier logical tendencies, and while going strongly counter to all metaphysical and pragmatic logic she endeavours to do full justice to traditional Aristotelian logic, and even in certain respects to the empirical logic of Mill. She brings into prominence the close connection in content and the historic continuity between the doctrine of Aristotle and that of symbolic logic, and is by no means disposed to break down all bridges uniting the present with the past. It is, indeed, astonishing to see in her work with what intensity a woman's mind has penetrated the mysteries of the logical calculus, and what an expert mastery it shows of the methods and formulas of this difficult science. Miss Stebbing stands in the front rank of the younger representatives and disciples of Logistics, and to-day she exercises a strong influence upon the course which the study of this discipline is taking.

The final stage in the development of Logistics is that represented by *Language, Truth and Logic*, by ALFRED J. AYER. In this book motives drawn from diverse systems and tendencies cross and intertwine, and give rise to a new variation of mathematical logic such as has, hitherto, had no parallel. Ayer's doctrine, like the others, stands under the influence of the system of Russell and Whitehead, as developed by Wittgenstein. But besides this, it draws in important points upon the earlier empiricism of Berkeley and Hume and also stands in close relation of kinship to theories of the Vienna circle, especially as developed by M. Schlick and R. Carnap. The so-called "Logical Positivism" of these thinkers here flows for the first time into British Logistics expressly and explicitly, and it is bringing about a new ferment of future significance. This is first shown in the proud claim to furnish final solutions to the problems of philosophy in so far as they are genuine problems. The analytic method—so Ayer believes with the most imperturbable assurance—will sift once for all the grain from the chaff, by unmasking the pseudo-problems and revealing the genuine ones by means of mathematically strict and rigorously compelling definitions. But by "chaff" Ayer understands wellnigh everything that has appeared in the history of philosophy up to date, in fact all the endless and barren controversies over metaphysical, theological, and ethical problems. For the future these are to be cut out of philosophical inquiry, and therewith the everlasting strife between schools and tendencies which for so long filled nearly the whole history of philosophy will come to an end. Either the questions in dispute are logical ones and then they admit of clear and unambiguous answer; or they are non-logical and then they are dismissed as metaphysical. For all metaphysical assertions are nonsensical, and, therefore, without interest for the philosopher who seeks truth and clarity. Real philosophy (as Wittgenstein also teaches) is not so much a doctrine as an activity. It is concerned with the way we speak of things and its function is "to elicit the consequences of our linguistic usages". This function is performed in the medium of logical analysis, and that, in turn, in the formulation of definitions. And so we reach the contention that all philosophical propositions are linguistic propositions, and that convention is here of decisive importance. The principles of logic are linguistic conventions.

If all metaphysical propositions are excluded as nonsensical or non-significant, there remain only significant propositions as the sole object worth philosophical inquiry. But all significant propositions fall into two groups: they are either pure tautologies or empirical hypotheses. The first yield us no knowledge of facts, they are "non-factual", i.e., they are purely *a priori* and analytic, and are all tautologies. The latter, on the other hand, deal with facts (are "factual") and are synthetic. But a synthetic proposition is only significant if it is empirically verifiable. And this means that it never has more than hypothetical certainty, whereas analytic propositions are necessary and certain. Thus a proposition is analytic, if it depends simply on the definitions of the symbols it contains whether it holds good or not, and is synthetic if this is determined by facts of experience. It is clear (and Ayer has indicated as much expressly) that in all the contentions here maintained there gleams the fundamental distinction drawn by Hume between "relations of ideas" and "matters of fact", and this distinction has found here its philosophical renewal. But in other ways too Empiricism is resuscitated in Ayer's teaching, in the extremely phenomenalist standpoint he adopts with regard to empirical problems, seeking, for instance, to solve the problem of perception, of the Self, and other such from a purely phenomenalist position. Thus in this its latest phase British Logistics incorporates in itself both the logical Positivism of the Vienna Circle and important elements of the classical English Empiricism, and achieves a new synthesis, the significance of which it will be for the future to decide.

VI

THE PHILOSOPHY OF NATURAL SCIENCE

THE relations between Philosophy and Science have never been closer in any country than in England. Since the efflorescence of the exact sciences in the XVIIth Century there has been an almost uninterrupted process of cross-fertilization between the two fields. It would be easy to show in a historical inquiry how continuous this process has been, and it would then become clear that philosophy has received far more than it has given, while science on the contrary has been more often giver than receiver. In dealing with earlier periods we had more than once occasion to notice this relation of reciprocal influence as it concerned the XIXth Century, and the chapter on the evolutionary-naturalistic tendency presents continuous evidence of a unique sort of this living interchange between the scientific investigator and the speculative thinker. At that time (and indeed, earlier, in isolated instances), there came into prominence two phenomena typical of the intellectual life of England: on the one hand the investigator of nature putting forward a philosophy, on the other the philosopher practising scientific investigation, or, at least, keenly interested in it. Both of these have to-day, indeed, more than ever before, plenty of representatives, in fact they are figures characteristic of the situation of the moment. In section iv of this part of the book, it was with representatives of the latter tendency (the scientifically-minded philosopher) that we were mainly concerned; in this section, on the other hand, we have to bring together a number of scientists who illustrate the former tendency, while leaving many without mention. We are not so much concerned with specialist investigators who, being in touch with the philosophical movement, have from time to time dealt with speculative problems, as with those who have left their special field and proceeded to develop independent philosophical thinking, and even a *Weltanschauung*, of their own.

There are in the first place two groups of the special sciences which have proved particularly fruitful in fertilizing English philosophical thought, namely the sciences of biology and mathematical physics. Naturally the group exercising the stronger attraction over philosophy will be that which owing to new methods or aims of scientific inquiry is itself at the focus of general interest. Thus in Newton's time it was mathematical physics, in Darwin's zoological biology that radiated its powerful influence over the contemporary movements of philosophy. With the opening of the XXth Century came a fresh shifting of interests, due to the re-awakening of new philosophical energies through the transformations that were taking place in the fields of mathematics, physics, and chemistry. Contemporary philosophy, in so far as it has any scientific orientation, is thus markedly affected by the new departure which has been brought about through the researches and discoveries of these sciences. Besides this the biological impulse is still exercising its influence, though in a lesser degree: it is the vitalistic development of this science rather than its earlier mechanistic form that has been bearing philosophical fruit in recent years.

There is, finally, one further point to note. The sciences hitherto mentioned all belong to the group of *natural* sciences. And, in fact, an Englishman means by the term exact science, and even by the word science, standing alone, the sciences of nature exclusively; which explains why the *Geisteswissenschaften*, the scientific disciplines of scholar or historian, have been for long so less relevant to philosophy than the natural sciences. They have never, or at least relatively seldom, been envisaged by British philosophers as forming a distinct group of cognitive activities meriting the name of science, and were not therefore, as in Germany, brought really within the scope of philosophical critical inquiry. And even where, as by Mill, they were made the subject-matter of philosophical discussion, they were nearly always regarded from the point of view of natural science. When one considers, for example, how much German thinkers have been occupied with the problem of history, both as regards the methodology and the subject-matter of the study, it is astonishing to find how little of all this there has been in England. History is the stepchild of British philosophy, which has yielded no explicit philosophizing about history, neither a methodology of history as a science, nor interpretations of universal history in the grand style, nor a speculative metaphysic of history, apart from incidental contributions, which, of course, are not lacking. That is why the problem of "historicism" (*Historismus*) has never become really acute in England. The point of view of the natural sciences has always been dominant and remains so to-day.

SIR OLIVER LODGE (*b.* 1851)

[The famous physicist. The following writings, among others, contain his speculative and philosophical views: *Life and Matter*, 1906; *Man and the Universe*, 1908; *The Survival of Man*, 1909; *Reason and Belief*, 1910; *Beyond Physics; or The Idealisation of Mechanism*, 1930; *My Philosophy*, 1933.]

In the long line of natural scientists who have turned to philosophical speculation, and who are so characteristic of the England of to-day, Sir Oliver Lodge occupies a prominent place, and, at the same time, he is almost a prototype of them all. His great personal popularity and the enormous vogue of his many books have given to this typical figure a significance far beyond specialist circles, and deeply interested the general public in him. He still remains one of the best-known and most widely read "lay", i.e. unprofessional, writers on philosophy, and he has contributed more than any other to the spreading and popularizing of scientific theories and philosophical thoughts. Neither has anyone shown a better or more penetrating estimate of the need for a rapprochement and reconciliation between knowledge and faith, which is always alive in England, both in more educated circles and among the general public. Furthermore, his position has a special significance from the fact that he has brought the whole weight of his personality and his standing as a professional scientist not only to support the exact investigation of occult phenomena, but to take himself a positive part in this investigation. This alliance from the camp of strict natural science was of great importance to the "Psychical Research" movement that had its origin in the 'eighties, and contributed more to the establishment of a scientific outlook in this field than the adherence of outstanding representatives of philosophy, psychology, and general literature.

Two souls dwell side by side in the breast of this thinker, the one directed to the exact investigation of physical nature, the other pushing out beyond the domain of physics to more comprehensive interpretations of the grounds of being and the underlying realities. "The Physical aspect of the Universe", and "Beyond Physics", are the titles of two of his essays that are symptomatic of the dual character of the man himself and of his work (they appeared in *Philosophy*, vol. vii, 1932, and vol. iv, 1929). Thus in him a genuine spirit of scientific investigation and a speculative daring are combined in a unity that is not inwardly in equilibrium, and there is besides a strong tendency to a credulous enthusiasm that springs from a genuinely religious and devout mind. His main concern is to overcome the opposition between science and religion: but he is not satisfied with a mere truce between them, he strives for a genuine alliance and positive collaboration. He rejects the theory of "water-tight compartments", i.e. that there are two regions hermetically closed to each other and merely tolerating one another; he would prefer to base faith upon knowledge and anchor knowledge in faith. But the fusion of the two cannot be accomplished either from the side of science or from that of religion, but requires a mediating factor reconciling the two. This mediating function belongs on the one side to poetry, on the other to philosophy.

An antecedent condition, however, for the reconciliation of science and religion (which latter Lodge identifies with its highest historical manifestation, Christianity), is the resolution of other sharp contrasts pervading the universe, especially the dualisms of matter and life, and matter and spirit, or as Lodge prefers to call them, the realm of physics and the realm of psychics. The world of nature and the world of spirit are not any more than science and religion cut off from one another in water-tight compartments, but are mutually involved and interpenetrating. The scope of physics has, therefore, to be extended widely enough to find a place for the phenomena of life, mind and spirit. Natural science is not restricted to nature in its merely mechanical or metrical aspect (Eddington), nor to its mathematical aspect (Jeans), but includes also the biological, the teleological, and the psychological and psychical, indeed every path of whatever kind that leads to the investigation of truth. Now one such path leads from occult and spiritualistic phenomena into science and beyond into philosophy, and Lodge has himself opened wide the door to the procedure of "psychical research". His speculations upon pre-existence and survival, his belief in telepathy and apparitions and even in the existence of angels and the like point in this direction. In part they are recognized by him as metaphysical speculations, but in part, too, they are covered with the mantle of science. In addition there is in Lodge a strong influx of religious ideas, for the most part made to yield a speculative interpretation (as in his discussions of the meaning of the Incarnation), and the philosophical view of the world resulting from all this is a kind of monistic idealism, which finds its crown and culmination in theism. But all this cannot be claimed as genuine philosophy and has accordingly met with but little respect at the hands of professional philosophers. Lodge is rather the typical "philosopher of the people", whose public is the "general reader". For his task as a popular educator stimulation and inspiration and edification are more important than rigorous thinking. Frequently this otherwise exact and conscientious physicist assumes the rôle of Sunday preacher, and he is better able to discharge his mission in that capacity than by employing, be it never so subtly, the conceptual apparatus of the philosopher. But even in his entries upon philosophical ground he has certainly earned credit that ought not to be undervalued, for his service in having undertaken to reawaken a sense of the importance of the great questions of philosophy and metaphysics among wide sections of the people, and to harmonize religion with the claims of science and vice versa.

SIR ARTHUR STANLEY EDDINGTON (*b.* 1882)

[Professor of Astronomy at Cambridge. *Space, Time and Gravitation*, 1920; "The Domain of Physical Science", 1925 (in *Science, Religion and Reality*, ed. by J. Needham); *The Nature of the Physical World* (Gifford Lectures), 1928; *Science and the Unseen World*, 1929; "Physics and Philosophy", 1933 (in the journal *Philosophy*, vol. viii); *New Pathways in Science*, 1935.]

Prominent among the distinguished investigators of nature who have occupied themselves with philosophical problems is Sir Arthur Eddington, the famous Cambridge astronomer. Of special philosophical importance are his epistemological and methodological discussions of the nature and the limits of scientific conceptions, and his extremely vivid and lively description of the nature of the physical world. We are clearly to realize that the world of ordinary experience or of daily life is *toto coelo* different from the world within which the investigations of the physicist proceed. The latter presents us with things utterly desubstantialized and dematerialized, a radical transmutation of their sensory qualitative content into purely quantitative measurements and derivates of these. The physical world of electrons, atoms, quanta, events, movements, spatio-temporal continua, etc., is a mere realm of shadows or a skeleton of reality, divested of all the variegated manifoldness of life and under the domination of the grey formulas and symbols of mathematics. Here the disenchantment of the world has reached its culmination. If we translate some object of our environment into the language of physics, we are left with nothing but a "set of pointer-readings".[1] Where everything is measured, reckoned, counted, and weighed, there is no longer a place for the individual and the concrete. Physics can in its field correlate only one quite special aspect of the external world of things: it excludes all remaining aspects, not because they are less important, but because they lack the special quality of measurability and ponderability, or because they are not amenable to treatment in terms of quantity. Viewed from this standpoint

[1] *The Nature of the Physical World*, p. 254.

the cleavage of Reality into a material and a spiritual sphere appears superficial compared with the much profounder cleavage into a world that is metrical and a world that is non-metrical.

But this aspect, cut out of a greater whole and determined according to the criterion of measurability, now shows itself to be a strictly self-enclosed region or a self-sufficient system entirely detached from all other world-aspects, and, indeed, owing its imposing importance and extent precisely to this one-sided isolation. Eddington displays this enclosed character of the methods of physics in the form of a circle or cycle, in so far as the single determinate formulations are linked together in a cyclic series that always returns to its starting-point. The conceptual constructions of natural science turn out to be an endless chain of mutually involved definitions, and not (what philosophical methodology had hitherto for the most part assumed it to be), an edifice built tier on tier like a pyramid, proceeding by a continuous series of determinations, each more general and comprehensive than the last, to one final and supreme universal formula that should include under itself all phenomena whatever.

The world of symbols with which physics deals represents only a fragment of the whole of reality. Physics is confined within narrow limits and its very strength depends upon this its self-imposed limitation. But "life would be stunted and narrow if we could feel no significance in the world around us beyond that which can be weighed and measured with the tools of the physicist or described by the metrical symbols of the mathematician".[1] Thus Eddington strives to escape from the confines of the world as given in physics and seeks to do justice to that more inclusive totality that underlies this partial fragment of the real. But his leap out of physics into metaphysics cannot be allowed the same significance as his penetrating insight into the structure of the physical world and the methods of its investigation. His exposition in the wider field is that of the typical philosophical amateur, who enters the domain of philosophy

[1] *The Nature of the Physical World*, p. 317.

because of his own inner need or because the fashion of the time demands it, without stipulating in this domain for the same high standards of exact training and strict scientific thinking which he claims for the field in which he has shown such mastery as an investigator.

It is the world of consciousness that, as Eddington holds, constitutes the background of the physical world of measurement and number. A simple reflection is enough to lead us out of the region of physics and open our eyes to a quite new and fundamentally different world, the consideration, namely, that after all the physical investigator himself cannot as a being who thinks, measures, experiments, defines, and seeks the truth, be treated merely as quantity (as physics is bound to treat its object); and that physics can give no answer to the question how it is that a certain class of atoms constituting the human brain are endowed with consciousness and the power to think. Thus consciousness gives us the key to the constitution of metaphysical reality and the essential nature of Being as a whole. This is spiritual in kind as every conscious process must be, though it does not need to attain everywhere to the relatively high level of explicit consciousness. Here Eddington introduces the dubious conception of "mind-stuff", taken over from Clifford, but applied rather differently, by which he means us to understand "the aggregation of relations and relata which form the building material of the physical world".[1]

Mind-stuff, which we must think of as a sort of consciousness, only with the inclusion of the fore-conscious, the subconscious, and the (so-called) unconscious, forms the substratum of everything there is: but as matter is already to the highest degree dematerialized we cannot of course really speak of any "stuff" in the case of mind. "Mind-stuff", accordingly, whatever else it may be, is that which is not to be measured, weighed or counted, and if we ultimately represent the primal basis of the universe as a divine all-embracing Spirit or Logos, this, too, can then only belong to the sphere of the non-metrical. Thus the world of spirit occupies a fundamental position, differing from

[1] *The Nature of the Physical World*, p. 278.

all other orders of being, outside or behind the machinery of the physical world, and does not signify simply a phenomenon that manifests itself from time to time, occurring within the world of the inorganic at a late stage in the evolutionary process.

Naturally, we must think of the physical world as standing in some sort of relation and connection with its background, the spiritual world, however much it presents itself as a system completely shut off from it. But Eddington goes further and finds that the most recent results of physics support or at least suggest the view that there is a certain structural kinship between the two. Hitherto, the opinion has prevailed that in the realm of nature necessity rules, and in the realm of spirit, freedom; according to the principle of causality every natural event is determined according to strict laws, so that we can accurately predict the future event from the past. Now, however, the most recent researches in the field of Quantum Theory have gravely shaken the causal principle; it has been shown that the great laws which up to now have been accounted valid as causal laws are really only statistical rules. We have even to admit a certain measure of indeterminacy in the occurrences that take place within the atom. A strict determination has once and for all lost its validity in theoretical physics; indeterminism has penetrated even the physical world. But from this it results that on the one hand the assumption that mind or spirit is subject to the laws of nature is seriously weakened, and on the other that mind is able to abrogate these laws for the material world. The dethronement of the principle of causality has brought the two worlds nearer together.

Finally, the spiritualistic metaphysic which is here supported by the findings of the scientific mind, favours the project ot bringing science and religion to a friendly accord. Eddington, it is true, expressly refuses to base religion upon any specific results of scientific research, but he holds that the transformations which modern physics has brought about in the scientific view of the world have removed certain hindrances which have hitherto stood in the way of a reconciliation between them. It is more an emotional sympathy with religion than a clear insight into the deep underlying connections that sustain it.

Eddington's excursion into the field of philosophy is noteworthy in two respects, quite independently of its theoretic value: it affords gratifying evidence that the universal domination of scientific thought is to-day being seriously shaken by leaders in the work of specialist investigation, and it has shown that the view of the world established upon this sort of foundation need not necessarily be a form of Naturalism, but may also issue in Idealism.

For the rest, Eddington has the credit of having understood how to interest a wide public in scientific and philosophical questions, and to keep this interest always fresh and alive. His brilliant gifts as a writer, his lucid, vivid, and popular style which renders even the most difficult matters intelligible, have contributed much to this result and secured a wide publicity for his writings both at home and abroad. But no special importance attaches to his philosophy. It is neither more nor less than the brilliant dilettantism of a scientist who, though evincing an interest in philosophy, has little aptitude in the truest sense for philosophic thought. It is enough to point to Whitehead to bring out clearly the difference between the two things.

SIR JAMES HOPWOOD JEANS (*b.* 1877)

[The well-known mathematician, physicist, and astronomer, Professor at the University of Cambridge. *The Universe Around Us*, 1929; *The Mysterious Universe*, 1930; *The New Background of Science*, 1933.]

Sir James Jeans is another celebrated scientist who has of late years turned to the battleground of philosophy and enrolled himself among the philosophizing physicists, and the comment above made upon Eddington applies *mutatis mutandis* to him also. He seeks in his excursions into the speculative region to give a *mathematical* interpretation to the universe. Like Comte he puts forward a sort of law of three stages, according to which the efforts of the human mind to explain nature and to penetrate its mysteries pass through three phases, the animistic or anthropomorphic, the mechanistic, and, finally, the mathematical. The animistic interpretation was dominant until the beginning of modern times when it was dissolved by the mechanistic age, of which Galileo and Newton laid the foundations and which maintained its supremacy until the threshold of the XXth Century. The mechanistic view of the world received its deathblow from the theory of Relativity of Einstein and the modern mathematical physics that developed as its consequence. It has become evident that the mathematical explanation is incomparably better adapted to the real being of nature than the two before mentioned, even taking into account that it in its turn has not made genuine contact with essential reality and like the others is a way of interpreting the cosmos thought out by the mind of man. The book of nature is written in the language of mathematics, and everything points to the belief that the universe has been created by a pure mathematician and not, as it were, by a mechanical engineer on the analogy of a machine. Consequently we must consider it as consisting of pure thought. The question whether objective reality has substantial or ideal existence falls into the background in comparison with the fundamental fact of its essentially mathematical character. But Jeans understands by "mathematical" the entire realm of pure thought and not any special discipline.

The world outlook of "Panmathematicism," however, as represented by Jeans, lacks final clarity because it has not been thoroughly thought out. Sometimes the mathematical interpretation of the universe appears to be simply a principle for the economizing of thought, enabling us to attain much more success in interpreting reality than when we think about it in biological or mechanistic categories. The mathematical approach is, relatively to our present knowledge, the simplest and most complete that we know, and, therefore, approximates more nearly to truth than all other interpretations hitherto attempted, even though it can make no claim to finality, and cannot grasp the essence of things as such. It is merely the best alphabet hitherto devised in which to reveal the mysteries of the universe. Sometimes, on the other hand, the mathematical character of the world is hypostatized ontologically, and the methodological principle is replaced by metaphysical speculation. We discover in the Cosmos traces of a Being like ourselves, with a capacity for the most highly developed thought, a thought so pure and exact that for want of a better term we can only conceive it under the pattern of mathematics. We must, therefore, represent to ourselves the builder of the cosmos in the guise of pure thinker or mathematical genius, on the strength of the manifold signs which he has imprinted on his creation, and the world itself as a great creative thought conceived by him. That is the conclusion to which the results of modern physics point. Mind appears to-day no longer what it seemed in the world-view of the mechanists, an accidental and tardy intruder in the realm of matter; but rather as the creator and controller of all material being. We are beginning to surmise that matter does not exist in its own right, that it is rather the creation and revelation of that spiritual or intellectual principle which we have perforce to represent to ourselves on the analogy of pure or mathematical thinking. That is why the mathematical formula expresses the ultimate meaning of Being more profoundly than any other type of interpretation. Thus Jeans's speculations also, like Eddington's, issue in a sort of idealistic philosophical outlook, if the term idealism be used to denote the dominance in the universe of the intellectual or spiritual principle, and this in turn interpreted as the Logos that finds its embodiment in the thought of the mathematician.

SIR JOHN ARTHUR THOMSON (1861–1933)

[The famous zoologist and biologist, Professor of Natural History in the University of Aberdeen. Among his numerous works the following are important for our purpose. *The System of Animate Nature* (Gifford Lectures), 2 vols., 1920; *What is Man?* 1924; *Science and Religion*, 1925; "A Biologist's Philosophy", 1925 (*Contemp. Brit. Philos.*, ed. by J. H. Muirhead, Second Series); *Purpose in Evolution*, 1932.]

Another member of the class of scientific investigators who took to philosophy was Sir J. A. Thomson, whose starting-point was biology. He, too, was convinced that science cannot of itself fashion a picture of the world, and can never do more than cut out separate sectors from the totality of the Real and examine them in isolation. But above and beyond this is the well-warranted demand and need to grasp the universe in its totality with all the appearances and aspects it contains. It was in the bringing about of such a synoptic view over reality as a whole that Thomson saw the true task of philosophical thinking.

Science and philosophy are wholly distinct fields of study. The former asks the questions What? and How? Whence? and Whither? but cannot ask for the final causes of phenomena; the question Why? is the prerogative of philosophy. Science, again, is a description of natural facts, while philosophy is their interpretation from a teleological point of view. Yet naturalistic description and teleological interpretation are not mutually exclusive, they supplement each other as two distinct ways of treating of nature.

Now, if we survey nature as a whole, synoptically, we see that three orders of fact are clearly to be distinguished: first, the realm of inorganic nature or the "cosmosphere"; second, the realm of organisms or the "biosphere"; and third, the realm of man and human societies or the "sociosphere". Since the biosphere occupies a central position between the other two, to biology must be assigned the key position in philosophical inquiry into world problems. Thomson maintained the autonomy of the sciences corresponding to these three orders, more particularly that of biology. Not that the several regions are isolated from one another; rather, they interpenetrate and overlap one another, and the biosphere is enclosed by the cosmosphere as the sociosphere by the biosphere. Therefore, from the biosphere access is possible both to the cosmosphere below it and to the sociosphere above it.

Now, seen from this standpoint, the ancient dispute between mechanism and vitalism loses its meaning. It is no longer a question of deciding for or against either, but of securing a point of view that overcomes both by including both. The biologist must, as Thomson put it, steer between a metaphysical Scylla and a materialistic Charybdis; that is, he must on the one hand carefully avoid concepts that are not scientifically verifiable, such as "vital force", "entelechy", or "élan vital", and on the other hand beware of confining the organism in the meshes of purely mechanistic categories. Thus Thomson represents a biological doctrine that he called "methodological vitalism". Such a theory has to pay due regard to the entanglement of organic life in the physical and chemical conditions of the material sphere (biophysics and biochemistry): but its primary task is to work out and elaborate the specifically biological categories—as, for instance, the capacity of organisms to store up experience and to behave purposively. But on the opposite side the biologist must also include in his inquiries the mental or psychical factor, which appears at every level of organic life, however different its various manifestations. According to the old doctrine of Aristotle there can be nothing at the end of a process of development which was not in some sense already there at its beginning, even if only potentially. Thomson therefore, like James Ward, inclined to a restrained Pampsychism. Although the factor of mind can be detected only relatively late in evolution, yet we must assume that it has been present from the very beginning. There are thus no purely material or physical phenomena and no bodies that are merely corporeal; for all organisms are, according to the level they occupy in the evolutionary process, either mind-bodies or body-minds, as the corporeal or the spiritual element in them predominates.

The methodological vitalism of Thomson thus abandons the supposition of a special vital factor like the "entelechy" of Driesch. But in contrast to the theories of the mechanists Thomson laid stress on the teleological structure of all organic life. The thought of an end or goal can be brought into connection with the facts of science. We observe purposive behaviour and a striving after ends throughout the entire course of organic evolution. This suggests, though it cannot strictly demonstrate, the hypothesis that purposiveness is not merely immanent in evolution, but that there is a supreme purposeful Being, transcendent of the world, in whom every purposive happening has its origin. The entire cosmos is the creation and expression of a divine principle or of a supreme Reason, whose wise intentions are realized in everything that happens whether in the inorganic world, the organic, or the world of men. Thomson's philosophy, as expressly developed in his *System of Animate Nature*, culminates in theism, and takes its stand with the other divers attempts recently undertaken in this direction from the ranks of the natural scientists.

JOHN SCOTT HALDANE (1860–1936)

[Brother of Lord Haldane, the Hegelian; distinguished physiologist and biologist, Director of the Mining Research Laboratory at the University of Birmingham. "The Relation of Philosophy to Science", in collaboration with R. B. Haldane, 1883 (in *Essays in Philosophical Criticism*, edited by A. Seth and R. B. Haldane); *Mechanism, Life and Personality*, 1913; *The Sciences and Philosophy*, 1929 (Gifford Lectures); *The Philosophical Basis of Biology*, 1931; *The Causes of Evolution*, 1932; *The Philosophy of a Biologist*, 1935.]

A similar position to that of J. A. Thomson was also adopted by J. S. Haldane, but he, while likewise starting from specialist research in biology and physiology (especially in the physiology of respiration), proceeded to a more comprehensive philosophical synthesis. We find his standpoint already suggested in an early essay, of which he and his brother Richard Burdon Haldane were joint authors, which appeared in that first common manifesto of the British disciples of Kant and Hegel, the *Essays in Philosophical Criticism*, of 1883. In that essay Haldane was already trying to demonstrate that organic phenomena cannot be grasped in their real nature if biological experiments are based on solely mechanical conditions. In the period that has since elapsed he became one of the most powerful and best-known champions in the fight against a mechanistic biology.

Haldane's Vitalism (generally called "Neo-Vitalism" to distinguish it from earlier forms of the doctrine) postulates the autonomy of scientific biology, and bases this upon the fact that with organic life an entirely new factor comes into existence, determined by a type of law different in principle from the mechanical laws of material phenomena and not to be understood by merely physical and chemical methods. Every attempt to reduce living creatures to "physico-chemical machines" must fail, owing to the fact that an organism does not admit of being taken to pieces and put together again like a mechanism, but is an autonomous whole that forms and maintains itself both as regards its internal structure and its external activity and relations with its environment. The life of any organism can only be described as the behaviour of a structure which is an entirety, and cannot be analysed into the sum of the separate elements of behaviour of its parts taken severally. A point of importance here is that environmental processes must be brought into relation with the biological process taken as a whole, and thus organic life is to be considered as an active unity which embraces its environment and is manifested not only in the mutual relations between the parts of the organism but also in those between the whole organism and surrounding nature. Biological behaviour is manifestly purposive and implies effort to attain ends, and, therefore, a large part of biological investigation is taken up by the teleological method.

In his interpretation of the living entity as a self-maintaining whole, Haldane, like Thomson, came very near to the biology of Driesch. He rejected, however, Driesch's substantial Vitalism, or the doctrine of Entelechy, according to which organic processes are to be explained by the operation of a special factor not subject to physical or chemical laws. But he is still more opposed to the view that life is a mechanical process. A mechanical system can neither grow of itself nor reproduce another system of the same type. The idea of a mechanism that continually sustains and renews itself is in itself a contradiction. Moreover, organic processes are throughout so complex and differentiated that a purely mechanical explanation of them appears to be utterly inadequate. The scope and range of the mechanistic theory remains restricted to what we can construct after the fashion of machines. But in its application to purely physical and chemical entities also it is only a sort of useful shorthand or a highly abstract working hypothesis yielding formulas that are extremely imperfect representations even of the behaviour of atoms and molecules. The worlds of physics and chemistry are mere abstractions from objective reality, or at best, stages in the approach to a complete theory of reality. These sciences analyse and dissect, but do not treat the objects with which they deal as wholes. Their methods and principles have, therefore, no validity for the far more concrete science of biology, which is essentially an attempt to grasp wholeness. Haldane, therefore, assigned to biology a higher and more inclusive place in the system of the sciences than to the purely physical disciplines. Thus the sciences according to Haldane's teaching form a graded hierarchy, the position of each corresponding to the degree of abstraction which it attains. The more our experience is divested of its concrete content through a process of artificial abstraction the further removed will the relevant science be from the meaning of the whole, and from a philosophical interpretation of Reality. But Biology stands much nearer to concrete experience than the physical disciplines do, and therefore it leads by a much shorter road than they do to a philosophical cosmology. The resulting order of the sciences based on the progressive extension of the process of abstraction, begins with psychology and passes through biology and chemistry to physics and mathematics.

The psychological level or layer of experience is thus built upon the biological, as the biological upon the physical. The world of psychology is interpreted by Haldane as a concrete mental world of personalities, which means that personality extends over the entire range of experience. In the physical world this is not realised, for that is an abstraction, of the greatest use for certain practical purposes, but not to be revealed by experience save in a very restricted and partial aspect. By personality we mean in the first place individual personality, but this does not exhaust the idea, which includes not only what is individual, but the endeavour for the good, the search for truth and joy in beauty. When then we interpret experience in its ultimate and highest aspect we reach the conception of an all-inclusive personality as the realization of all that we meet with in the highest values, and only in this is the true reality of our experience brought to its consummation. But this is to tread upon the ground of religion, whose essence consists in recognizing this all-inclusive personality as God. The Universe is thus a world of spirit or mind in which the activity of God is everywhere and always being revealed. It is symptomatic of the changed outlook of the time that here too is a scientific investigator whose speculations lead to an idealistic and spiritual view of the world, connected both epistemologically and metaphysically with the doctrine of Berkeley, and like that issuing in the theistic conception of God.

JAN CHRISTIAN SMUTS (*b.* 1870)

[The South African General and Statesman. *Holism and Evolution*, 1926 (new and revised edition, 1936); Article "Holism" in the *Encyclopaedia Britannica*, 14th edition, 1929.]

In the "Holism" (from ὅλος = whole) of General Smuts the category of wholeness or totality is set at the centre of a philosophical interpretation of the world which takes its place in the general line of the cosmological and biological systems of Bergson, Alexander, Lloyd Morgan, Boodin, Driesch, J. S. Haldane, J. A. Thomson, and others. Historically considered it is linked up with Aristotle's doctrine of form and matter and with Leibniz's theory of Monads. The concept of wholeness or totality as established by Driesch to be the fundamental category of the organic world is first extended in its scope by Smuts (who is likewise emphatic that without it we cannot explain the determinate unity of organic behaviour and organic evolution) to apply to the realm of inorganic matter as well, that is to all natural objects, inanimate no less than animate: it is then further extended to cover psychical, mental, and cultural phenomena; structural "wholes" are found not only in human personality, but in the systematic forms of Science, Art, Literature, Society, and Religion, and besides these in Truth, Goodness, Beauty, Love, etc. Finally, the concept of Whole is elevated into a universal metaphysical cosmic principle. It provides us with a key to unlock all the more perplexing problems of philosophy, the right definition of the relation of effect to cause and of freedom to necessity, the problem of individuality and likewise the problem of soul and body. In conclusion it proves specially fruitful for the notion of evolution. Holism in its final intention aims at an all-embracing system of evolution, which is presented in more or less close connection with Bergson's Creative Evolution, Alexander's Emergent Evolution, and Boodin's Cosmic Evolution. But Smuts tries to complete and improve all these evolutionary concepts, once again through the principle of Wholeness. The Universe that is evolving creatively is a universe of Wholes, and it is in the ever new fashioning and creating of such Wholes that Smuts sees the real meaning of the cosmic process. The concept of the Whole, however, cannot be rendered conceptually self-evident without remainder, but is enveloped in the veil of the non-rational: and the same is true of the questions bound up with it, such as the question how new wholes perpetually come into being, and the question whether Reality as such has the character of Wholeness. We must accept all these things with "natural piety" and not presume to penetrate to their ultimate ground. "Everywhere it is the Whole, even the apparently smallest and most insignificant whole, that is the real miracle which hides within it the secrets we grope after in our thought and our conduct."[1]

By way of appendix mention may be made of two younger biologists, J. H. Woodger (*b.* 1894) and Lancelot Hogben (*b.* 1895). Woodger may be termed a "Holist", in Smuts's phrase, though in his book *Biological Principles, a Critical Study* (1929) and elsewhere he stresses more strongly than Haldane and Smuts the heuristic significance of mechanistic concepts and hypotheses. Among the Holists exceptionally well instructed in philosophy, he is the specialist in the theory of science, and pursues a meticulous analysis into the scientific terms used by

[1] Article "Holism", *Enc. Brit.* (14th ed.), vol. xi, p. 643.

the biologist, now and then availing himself of the language of symbolic logic. He rejects both vitalistic modes of thought such as Driesch's, and also the reference of specifically biological problems to the inorganic categories of physics and chemistry, and sets up a hierarchy of scientific problems corresponding to the levels of reality which are studied by the several scientific disciplines. Thus in declining mechanism and vitalism he demands what he calls a "biological biology", that is a strict adaptation of biological concepts to the facts with which biology has to do. He wishes to devise methods and concepts to suit the facts, and not force the latter into a pre-arranged scheme, as is the way of all over-acute, one-sided theories. In his general philosophical position Woodger stands close to neo-Realism and also to the doctrine of Whitehead.

As evidence that mechanism in Biology still finds representatives to-day, we have the doctrine of Lancelot Hogben, as developed in his book *The Nature of Living Matter* (1930). Hogben does indeed abandon in many respects the mechanism of the older school, but the core of his inquiry into the nature of life is to be found in the contention that biological problems can only be rightly handled by the aid of mechanistic, i.e. physico-chemical methods. Indicative of this is the term he employs, "living matter", instead of "life". He draws an important distinction, based on Russell, between the "public world" constructed by material concepts and accessible to everyone, and the "private worlds" which are the diverse pictures of the world of single individuals. There is only one public but many private worlds. The former Hogben calls ethically neutral, as it is one and the same for all. It is in the latter that moral and aesthetic values come to hold good, and Hogben includes with these vitalistic and holistic theories, which can only frame such private worlds, and no public world. Hogben's doctrine threatens to obliterate the differences elaborated by the vitalists between the realm of the inorganic and that of the organic, and between the sciences of physics and biology. It may be termed a "neo-mechanist" theory and stands in the sharpest contrast to all we have been concerned with hitherto.

VII

PSYCHOLOGY AND KINDRED STUDIES

THE development of British Psychology follows a more or less straight course from its first beginnings down to near the end of the XIXth Century. It proceeded on a line parallel to the empiricist philosophical tradition—or, better, it is interwoven with this and to a great extent coincides with it. What seen from the philosophical side is termed empiricism is from the standpoint of psychology associationism. The mechanical-atomistic association-psychology, as expressed in the classical systems of the XVIIth and XVIIIth Centuries, was continued in the XIXth particularly by the two Mills, enriched by Darwin and Spencer with a new strain—the evolutionary—and brought to a conclusion by Bain and Sully, the latest stragglers of the movement. To-day it belongs to history, and it might be paradoxically maintained that it is only still alive in so far as it continues to receive its death-blow at the hands of psychological doctrines that have superseded it. It is obviously merely being kept alive artificially in order to meet the polemical needs of modern psychologists, and it will presumably continue to discharge this function for a while longer.

The crisis of exhaustion which afflicted the older psychology after the death of J. S. Mill came to a surprising and even dramatic end through the celebrated attack launched in 1886 by JAMES WARD, whose article on Psychology in the ninth edition of the *Encyclopaedia Britannica* in that year felled the old tree as by a single vigorous stroke of the axe. This exposition (which Ward had anticipated by several shorter essays between 1875 and 1886) clearly and unambiguously records the turning-point in the development of psychological science, and dates the beginning of the new phase of British psychology. Nothing makes this more clear than the fact that Bain, at that time the most important representative of the older school, immediately[1] set himself to defend his doctrine, and while acknowledging the high value of the new teaching drew a sharp line of division between it and his own. This is the point at which the streams part to flow in different directions, never to be reunited. It does not matter what name we give to this new development of psychology: we may call it voluntarist or activist or organic or teleological or hormic, or contrast it as "Psychology with a soul" with the "Psychology without a soul". It suffices to say that in fundamentals and in nearly all essential points it is in opposition to the earlier interpretation of psychical and mental life, although it does not break radically with tradition and, indeed, not infrequently shows its connection with it in respect of method. But taken as a whole, the change is so great that we can speak of an entirely new departure.

Ward's service in the renewal of psychology has been already appraised in another context (see pp. 400 ff.), and here we need only remind the reader of what was then said. The path which he took, and which was also that taken about the same time by William James, whose *Principles of Psychology* appeared in 1890, leads straight forward to the present day, in close connection with certain parallel currents in philosophy (Bergsonism, Pragmatism, etc.). This may be termed the main road of contemporary British psychology in so far as it is rooted in philosophical soil and stands out against a general philosophical background. The two most important British psychologists, G. F. STOUT and W. McDOUGALL, share Ward's general outlook and have worked at psychological problems mainly in his sense of the term. The accounts that follow, however, will be devoted not only to their psychology, but to their work as a whole, which passes over into the philosophical field.

GEORGE FREDERICK STOUT (*b.* 1860)

[University Lecturer in Moral Sciences in Cambridge, 1894; Lecturer in Comparative Psychology in Aberdeen, 1896; Reader in Mental Philosophy in Oxford, 1898. From 1903 to 1936 Professor of Logic and Metaphysics in the University of St. Andrews.

[1] In two articles in *Mind*, 1886 and 1887, vols. xi and xii.

Analytic Psychology, 2 vols., 1896; *A Manual of Psychology*, 1898, 4th ed. 1929; "Error", 1902 (in *Personal Idealism*, ed. by H. Sturt); *The Groundwork of Psychology*, 1903; *Mind and Matter*, 1931 (first part of Gifford Lectures). Also numerous articles in technical journals the most important of which have now been published under the title *Studies in Philosophy and Psychology*, 1930.]

Liberation from the bonds of the idealistic school in the narrower sense is even more a characteristic of G. F. Stout than of Ward. This is evident especially in his renunciation of speculative solutions and rounded systems, that is, in his departure from the Hegelian interpretation of life and the world of thought and in his exaltation of philosophy as a scientific investigation. Thus Stout's hitherto published work is concerned almost exclusively with the fields of Psychology and theory of knowledge, while the discussion of metaphysical questions (including those of ethics and philosophy of religion) is kept for the present in the background and is to be dealt with in a subsequent work already announced. It is, therefore, impossible to decide definitely so long as this work is not before us to what philosophical school Stout's doctrine belongs—and it does not seem in place to attempt to label his thought with this or that designation. It is rather an exemplary instance of what Bosanquet called 'the meeting of extremes in contemporary philosophy', i.e. the ever-strengthening tendency towards a mutual rapprochement or assimilation of modes of thought formerly in sharp opposition to one another. In Stout we have a "meeting" of pragmatist, realist and idealist motives; the first dominates a comparatively early stage of his thought and more and more recedes into the background; his psychological and epistemological position, as well as his method of investigation, may be called realist, while Idealism characterizes certain consequences drawn from his position and the general background of his doctrine as a whole.[1]

[1] We should have been justified in treating of Stout's doctrine in the section allotted to the older or newer Realism; whereas it does not seem right to classify it with the idealistic movement, in spite of certain elements that point in that direction, as Dawes Hicks has done

It is in the first place significant that Stout's philosophy, like Ward's, is anchored in the psychological researches to which he has devoted a large part of his life-work, and to which all that he published in book-form up to the age of seventy solely belongs. His three comprehensive works, among which the earliest (*Analytic Psychology*) is specially noteworthy, take a place in the psychological literature of the time comparable to that of James's *Principles of Psychology* and Ward's *Psychological Principles*. Together with these two, Stout is one of the pioneers of Anglo-Saxon Psychology after the barren *impasse* of the earlier empirical type of theory. He has an outstanding share in the renovation of the science, both in regard to the exact investigation of its special problems and in regard to its general philosophical orientation. He understands by Psychology the study of the mind or of mental phenomena, that is of the higher functions of beings endowed with mind. Its method is, in contrast to other branches of human knowledge, subjective or introspective, and its task is to set out systematically the laws and conditions determining the course of the psychic life of individuals. This life, however, consists not in the sum of separate data, states, or occurrences, but is characterized by the special kind of unity which persists both before and beyond the single psychical facts, and is radically different from every unity in the world of material things. Thus there is *a* mind in the sense of the unity of consciousness, not merely mental states and processes, and psychology is the science of this mind. Stout accordingly rejects expressly the psychical atomism of the earlier English school or 'psychology without a soul', just as he rejects the amalgamation of physiological with psychological inquiries. For him the two are to be kept sharply distinct, each being a science with a subject-matter of its own.

Hand in hand with his rejection of the atomic structure of mental life goes the rejection of the mechanical course of its

in his presentation of modern British philosophy in the fifth part of Ueberweg's *Grundriss*. Treatment of it in this place needs no special justification if we regard it as more important to identify the actual content of a doctrine than to pigeon-hole it under this or that heading.

processes. Stout accepts the fundamental positions of Ward, to whose teaching he owes more than to any other though he later passed far beyond it, and co-operates with him in the liberation of psychological thought from the bonds and fetters of the natural sciences. He exhibits the psychical realm as *sui generis*, with a structure and structural laws of its own, and abandons the mental mechanics and 'mental chemistry' of earlier psychologists. In particular he presses the *teleological* character of this structure into the foreground of the picture, and shows in how high a degree all psychical processes and the entire apparatus of the association of ideas are subordinated to vital interests and endeavours. It is always personal interests and not impersonal forces which determine the associations that come about. The essential character of psychic life is its effortfulness and purposiveness; it is dominated through and through by conative factors, instincts, impulses, volitions. And Stout, like Ward, recognizes the pre-eminent significance of attention; with attention, the conative factor which had hitherto been treated purely 'theoretically', i.e. without reference to practice, enters psychical phenomena. He shows how indispensable a factor (though one that had hitherto been unduly neglected) attention is for the right understanding of perception, and how fundamentally it determines all perceptual activity. The new and important discoveries promoted by Stout in this field will remain one of his lasting services, and psychological investigation has been to a high degree stimulated and fertilized thereby.

The method of Stout's psychology is that of descriptive analysis of the data presented in consciousness. It has nothing to do either with physiological or with experimental psychology, nor yet with anything akin to these. Furthermore, it eschews all speculative hypotheses and interpretations—which, of course, does not mean that it is not grounded in philosophic thought, but that it deliberately keeps in the first place all philosophical theorizing in the background. It is a straightforward, careful, and detailed description of conscious phenomena in the field of pure experience, and it often attains to penetrating analysis in the style of Meinong and Husserl. Though Stout is not a conscious adherent of Meinong's theory of the objective or of Husserl's 'phenomenology', yet his method of investigation is closely related to that of these thinkers, and his results are often similar to theirs. When later he became acquainted with their writings and with those of Brentano, Lipps, Külpe and Messer, he himself felt conscious of the kinship, and thought that in his first work he had independently of their influence done a service to analytical psychology not unlike their own. The same thing is true of his epistemological inquiries, which likewise have frequent points of contact with Lipps, Meinong, and Husserl, whether such agreement was due to their influence or not. Thus, to give one example, he adopts as his own Husserl's doctrine of 'intention' and 'intentional acts', when he interprets the unity of self-consciousness as essentially a unity of intentional experience, which is essentially co-determined by the unity of the 'intended' object.

To sum up, we may now define the character of Stout's psychology as follows: in so far as it is voluntarist it follows the trend of thought of which Ward and Wundt were the pioneers and which had been carried further by James and the Pragmatists, and thereby severs itself as radically as do these thinkers from the traditional English psychology with its intellectualist and atomistic point of view and its mechanistic theory of association. Furthermore, in so far as it practices descriptive analysis of a quasi-'phenomenological' kind, it is linked up with (or at least resembles) the pure psychology of consciousness of the German schools; in addition—a point not yet mentioned—it stands in close relationship to modern 'Gestalt' psychology; and, finally, it exhibits not a few points of contact, in matter and in method, with the native empirical tradition, in spite of its definite rejection of and hostility to this tradition as regards its fundamentals. Here, as everywhere, Stout is the trustworthy researcher, knowledgeable and solidly devoted to the matter in hand, which he seeks to advance not so much by startling insights and dazzling *aperçus*, as by sober and tenacious labour.

As has been already remarked, Stout's philosophy remains a still unfinished system. But its ground-plan and the main lines of its structure are already plainly recognizable, and its most important parts are already completed. It is very characteristic of this cautious and circumspect thinker, so averse to committing himself to final conclusions, that he began by always tackling only single problems, carrying their solution forward to a certain (for the most part provisional) point, while remaining long unable to bring himself to attempt a comprehensive and connected treatment of them. And even this tardy decision was not due to any impulse of his own, but was imposed upon him from without through his nomination to the Gifford Lectureship—a Foundation, by the way, to which in addition to its other services we owe more than one philosophical *system* which would otherwise never have seen the light. Twelve years more were needed for the production in its definitive book-form of the first part of these lectures, while the concluding second part is even yet (1938) unpublished. And so it came about that Stout, building his philosophy stone by stone, gave expression to his thought in an impressive series of contributions to periodicals and symposia dealing with special topics, and was in his seventy-first year before he issued his first complete philosophical volume.

In what follows we can only select a few out of the many problems with which he has dealt, without attempting to trace the manifold changes through which his thought has passed, if only for the reason that they do not involve any real break or radical alteration of standpoint, but are minor improvements and retouchings in regard to the problems treated. The result is many instances of vacillation and qualification in matters of detail, the outcome of a scrupulous care to do justice to every feature of the matter under investigation, to subject them all to ever more precise and accurate analysis, and to view them from every possible angle so as to take into consideration all objections in the course of the inquiry. Solutions are thus prepared piecemeal, and step by step, but scarcely ever finally achieved, so that there remains always an open horizon ensuring ample room for further investigation.

We may take as the first problem for discussion—and no

particular order will be followed—that of Error. Stout treated of this in his contribution to the joint volume *Personal Idealism*, the early manifesto of the pragmatist movement, with which he at that time was in close sympathy (see pp. 447 ff.).[1] Error is a special case of what Stout calls mere appearance. By appearance he understands the 'imaginary' object, and by the 'imaginative' attitude that in which the subject stands neutral to the alternative reality or unreality. We have to do with mere appearance when anything is thought as having a character which does not belong to it independently of the psychical process through which it is apprehended. It is thus a qualification of the apprehended object not of the apprehending subject. Error arises whenever that which is merely apparent is thought of as belonging to an independent real, or whenever psychical conditions cause the mere appearance not to be cognized as such but to be presented as though it really existed. Error has a high significance for our practical life, in that the adventure of knowing is involved in it, without which we could not come to apprehend truth. The risk of error, that is, the readiness to dare thinking what is untrue among the alternatives offered for our acceptance, is an antecedent condition both for right conduct and for true knowledge. Capacity for error is a theoretical and practical necessity without which we could neither know nor act, let alone really live in the full sense. Truth and error are thus not in absolute opposition nor do they belong merely to the theoretical sphere. Both are rather essentially relative to the psychical conditions of the cognitive or active subject, i.e. to human interests. With this thought Stout, as is obvious, anticipated the kernel of the pragmatist theory of truth, as it was later developed *in extenso* particularly by Schiller.

Apart from psychology, the problems which have chiefly benefited from Stout's keen analytical understanding have been epistemological ones. He enters fully into the inheritance

[1] His psychology already contains some notes that accord with Pragmatism. None the less, Stout is not to be counted among the adherents of this doctrine: the pragmatist phase of his thought, as expressed in the contribution above mentioned, is merely an episode.

bequeathed by classical British Philosophy since Locke as regards the general situation constituting the problem of knowledge, and treats in a new way the same objects of inquiry which were the concern of the thinkers of the XVIIth and XVIIIth Centuries. Only everything here is far more complicated and differentiated, the methods more refined in their working, the critical analyses more exact, and the philosophical inquiry has acquired a special and precise technique. In spite of this Stout is carefully anxious not to lose contact with the normal human understanding and to establish his theories in accordance with the opinions of the ordinary man or to secure his confirmation of them. Here the influence of Reid is apparent, and particularly of G. E. Moore, the modern renewer of Reid's 'common sense'; and it is often to this common sense that Stout makes his final appeal as regards the acceptance or rejection of a theory.

A question with which Stout has dealt repeatedly and with special thoroughness is the problem, so hallowed by tradition, of our knowledge of the external world, and more particularly that of the sense-perception of external objects. Here, too, his ideas have undergone many modifications, and it must suffice to indicate their final phase. According to the older theory we perceive the objects of the external world by means of the ideas in our consciousness, produced by these objects, and in some way corresponding to or representing them. Things are assumed to be material, ideas on the other hand, *quâ* contents of consciousness, psychic or mental. Stout designates these ideas of the earlier epistemology more precisely as sensa, and he has now to determine rightly the character and mode of being of these sensa. He tries to show that the essence of sensa is not exhausted by the fact that they are representations or copies of objects which transcend consciousness. Rather they are, over and above their 'being' in the psychic sense, real existents which constitute an integral portion of what we understand by the 'material world'. But this 'material world' must not be equated with *physical* existence; it has to be conceived more widely, so as to include within it sensory appearances. The world of matter thus includes both the world of sense (sensa) and the transcendent world of 'physical objects',—and this view fully coincides with the opinion of common sense. We must represent the sense-worlds of different individuals as continua, and these continua as specially differential parts within one world-continuum which comprises them all and upon the existence of which they are dependent. The single sensa are modifications within the sensory continuum of the experiencing individual. Knowledge of sensory data and of physical objects is equally direct, the only difference between them being that while the former enter into the actual experience of the individual, the latter do not. Objects are, as Stout puts it, known phenomenally, sensa are directly experienced, but both are in reality bound together as components of one and the same unbroken unity. They are different not in respect of the kind of existence that is theirs, but in respect of the kind of apprehension we have of them. To guarantee the truth of a 'sensum' it is enough to show that it is given immediately in the course of experience; in the case of a physical thing we have to show the mutual coherence of perceptual data within a system. The oar in the water does not only appear bent, but is in fact, bent, *quâ sensum*; the 'bentness' belongs to actual experience and is so far real. 'In reality', however, i.e. *quâ* physical object, the oar is not bent, but straight, because when it is given its place in the coherent context of other facts it is its straightness not its bentness that is established. The possibility of successful action is also a component belonging to this coherence; we can only row effectively with a straight oar.

This consideration throws also a new light upon the problem of primary and secondary qualities. It is not correct to say that the former qualify things and the latter sensa, nor that—as Berkeley tried to prove against Locke—both alike are simply 'in the mind', but rather that the secondary qualities qualify not merely sensa, but also objects as such, being physically real as the primary qualities are. The physical world also is everywhere pervaded by secondary as well as by primary qualities. The sole important difference between the two consists in the fact that the criterion of coherence is applicable throughout to the primary, but only very restrictedly to the secondary qualities. But it must be strongly emphasized that both are integral parts of one sole inclusive whole, viz. the world-continuum or the closed universe of being in which everything that exists is contained. From all this it follows that sensa are not mental but *material*, though not *physical* entities. In this way Stout marks his doctrine off from the sensationalist realism of Alexander, who treats sensa as physical objects, as well as from the sensationalist idealism of Berkeley, who treats physical objects as sensa or 'ideas' 'in the mind'.

In all this the thought of the all-including reality-continuum or coherent systematic whole is the only neo-Hegelian motive to be met with. But this, too (in a discussion belonging to an earlier phase of Stout's thinking), is characteristically transformed so as to be interpreted more in empirico-realist than in absolute-idealist fashion—that is, more in the sense of Hume than of Bradley. The theory of absolutism had set up coherence —the systematic interrelatedness of the components to the totality of knowledge—as the only valid criterion of truth, and Stout also concedes to this doctrine a high significance. But he does not recognize this as the sole criterion, but adds another which he calls *immediacy*. A cognition is either mediate or immediate; the former, in so far as it is reached by logical inference or in some analogous way; the latter, in the case of self-evident propositions ($7+5=12$) and also in the direct apprehension of actual given presentations (e.g., joy as actually felt or a sensory percept in the moment of being perceived). The pure datum is immediately certain, even though it stands in relation to other data from which it cannot be separated. And so the touchstone of truth—for instance, the truth of judgments—can never consist merely in their coherence with other true judgments equally borne out by the cognitive system. The judgments that support one another on the basis of their mutual coherence require besides a relatively independent support derived from themselves. And this support, the further back we trace the process of knowledge, will be continually found to lie in some sort of immediacy, whether that of feeling and sensation, of self-evident certainty, or of both together. True knowledge in the sense of systematic knowing is only possible if there is an incessant stream of new material in the form of feeling and sensation flowing in upon our cognitive consciousness, a stream of data of which we become immediately aware and which only then become coherent and incorporated in a system of relations. All mediate and indirect elements in knowledge radiate likewise, as Stout says, from a central core of immediacy, which forms the point of departure and the original condition for all further knowledge. The return from the mediated to the unmediated which we call verification or the appeal to facts, is as essential for the progress of knowledge as the advance from the unmediated to the mediated which we call interpretation or explanation. Immediate knowledge does not become the less immediate because it passes through various stages of mediate process.

The views thus summarized are significant for their reinstatement in its rightful place of the material ('hyletic') factor in knowledge, unduly neglected by the Hegelians. Stout's appeal to immediacy is the close counterpart of Hume's appeal to the impression, and Hume's demand that every idea which lays claim to truth must be verified in an original datum is the implicit assumption underlying Stout's argument, as set out above. Husserl's doctrine of the sensory ὕλη also might be compared with it, and may have influenced it, although Stout does not refer to this expressly. His polemic is mainly directed against Bradley and Joachim, in whom he sees the most consistent champions of the notion of coherence. All things considered, here, too, it is evident that Stout's thought cannot be brought under any formula of the schools, and exhibits comparatively few ties with that of other thinkers, but that in the main it makes in the same direction as Brentano, Meinong, Husserl, Lipps, and Külpe in Germany, and as Alexander, Broad, Moore, and W. E. Johnson in England, although Stout occasionally makes use of idealist elements. What amounts to much the same thing, he is more concerned with working out special problems than with erecting a system or constructing an interpretation of the world as a whole.

In conclusion we must mention a line of thought in which the latest phase of Stout's philosophy finds expression, and which reveals certain features of his cosmology usually kept in the background, namely, his doctrine of the embodied self. He is here concerned with defining the relation of body and soul, and with the solution of the psycho-physical problem. In this case, as elsewhere, we are first of all to seek an answer in the plain experience which the individual has of himself and his own body. Apart altogether from the fact that I can perceive my body as an external object like everything else in the external world, I become aware of it primarly in my self-consciousness, and I know that no one but myself can become aware of it in this way. Thus and only thus have I an absolutely immediate experience of the unity of body and mind as inseparable factors of my own indivisible being; I apprehend myself as an embodied mind or as a body-mind unity. What self-consciousness reveals is not mere mind or mental phenomena, but mind and body in one, and this unity in self-consciousness must be taken as an ultimate given fact not admitting further analysis and not to be reduced to anything else. The psycho-physical problem is, therefore, presented at the outset in a wrong light, if body and soul are first of all contrasted with each other as separate entities, and the inquiry then undertaken as to their reciprocal relation or interaction, or as to the nature of the unity they form. What has been once so incorrectly torn apart cannot afterwards be glued together again even by the subtlest arguments. This is just the original error, the πρῶτον ψεῦδος, of the Cartesian philosophy which dominates the entire history of modern thought, namely, that it split this primary unity into a dualism and was then unable to heal the breach or close the fissure it thus had made.

Stout believes that in this doctrine of the embodied self also he finds himself in full agreement with the opinions of ordinary men—just as in general he holds that a philosophy cannot be finally acceptable which cannot be justified at the bar of common sense. He rejects, therefore, alike metaphysical spiritualism and its counterpart metaphysical materialism, and does not admit that the special sciences have the right to decide upon this question. They have, indeed, the task of treating both sides (the psychical and the physical) separately, but on that very account they are incompetent to solve the psycho-physical problem. Its solution is to be found in the original unity and wholeness of the embodied mind, and this can only be exhibited by philosophy. Thus different sides of Stout's doctrine may now be grasped from one unifying point of view; it is the idea of solidarity which everywhere is forced to the front. Just as earlier he sought to show the solidarity of sensum and physical object, so now he seeks to show that of soul and body and in a wider metaphysical setting also the solidarity of individual and the world, of matter and mind.

The metaphysical *aperçus* which Stout has allowed himself in his hitherto published writings tend in the direction of an idealistic solution of the cosmic problem. In the universe of being the spiritual principle occupies a predominant and fundamental position. The mental and spiritual is something primary and underivable from anything non-mental. We must, therefore, suppose a universal and eternal mind unfolding and expressing itself in the world of finite and changing things which we call Nature. But this mind cannot be ascribed to Nature itself or identified with it, for Nature is not a unity stable and at rest in itself and, therefore, it is not the totality of being. It has no status in its own right, but points beyond itself to a Being different from, and transcending it. And this Being must be an eternal and all-embracing spirit, by which the processes of Nature are pervaded, and to which they owe their essence and their meaning.

WILLIAM McDOUGALL (1871–1938)

[Formerly Reader in Mental Philosophy in Oxford, then Professor of Psychology first in Harvard University, at present in Duke University, Durham, U.S.A. *Primer of Physiological Psychology*, 1905; *An Introduction to Social Psychology*, 1908 (twenty-second edition, 1931); *Body and Mind, a History and a Defence of Animism*,

1911; *Psychology, the Study of Behaviour*, 1912 (sixteenth edition, 1928); *The Group Mind*, 1920 (second edition, 1927); *National Welfare and National Decay*, 1922; *An Outline of Psychology*, 1923; *Ethics and Some Modern World Problems*, 1924; *An Outline of Abnormal Psychology*, 1926; *Modern Materialism and Emergent Evolution*, 1929; *The Energies of Men: A Study of the Fundamentals of Dynamic Psychology*, 1932; *Religion and the Sciences of Life*, 1934; *The Frontiers of Psychology*, 1934.]

The voluntaristic psychology inaugurated by Ward and continued by James, Stout, and others finds its most forcible embodiment at the present time in the work of W. McDougall. This outstanding investigator, who has been working in the United States since 1920, is, indeed, the most important living British (and in the wider sense Anglo-Saxon) psychologist, with the possible exception of Stout, who excels him in acuteness of critical analysis, but not in respect of the wide scope of his scientific interests nor yet as regards the measure of his influence over the entire Anglo-Saxon world. Moreover, McDougall's Psychology differs from Stout's, to which it comes nearest in value and importance, in being far more deeply rooted in a general philosophical outlook and far less preoccupied with matters of detailed analysis. It is always seeking to advance to problems of more comprehensive scope and to reach a standpoint which shall be philosophical in a wide sense. This standpoint, to which we may apply provisionally the arid catchword 'voluntarism', is always latent in McDougall's psychology, underlying and determining it in every part, and controlling even its most specialized lines of inquiry. To this is due the clear orientation, unmistakable pattern, and singleness of aim which distinguish his doctrines from most other present-day types of psychological investigation.

McDougall's work is only exceeded in its range by that of Wundt and of James: it covers the most diverse fields of psychology and extends beyond to the problematic issues of epistemology, logic, ethics, metaphysics, religion, and the general interpretation of life. Psychology is, however, its focus —comprising branches of the study as different as experimental and physiological psychology, animal and child psychology, the study of the individual and the social mind, of occult and abnormal phenomena, of character national and personal, and of the psychic life of primitives. McDougall has recourse to all methods, empirical and introspective, analytical, descriptive, and behaviouristic; he discusses questions of first principle (as those of the essential nature and structure of the mind and the relation of body and soul); he treats of psychology both in respect of its theory and its practical applications; he undertakes polemical examinations of opposing schools and tendencies;—in a word, he pursues psychological research in every direction, and ploughs over the entire field in its fullest extent. In all this we must specially emphasize his contributions to social psychology, for this is the section in which he has achieved his most important success (in the two works *An Introduction to Social Psychology* and *The Group Mind*, of which the former has passed through twenty-two editions). Wherever his researches provided the lever, the result has been fruitful and stimulating, and though they have certainly blazed new trails, yet their chief merit is to have led psychology back to older and tried paths, keeping it from cul-de-sacs and by-ways of error, while making the fullest use of its modern acquisitions.

Historically the standpoint of this psychology is easy to define. McDougall has, indeed, himself repeatedly exhibited the historical presuppositions of his doctrine and marked it off precisely from those of his opponents.[1] If one takes a bird's-eye view of the development of psychology one may distinguish two sharply contrasted tendencies, which McDougall, borrowing the well-known distinction drawn by Nietzsche, terms the Apollonian and the Dionysian. These terms denote very much the same difference as the expressions 'psychology without a soul', and 'psychology with a soul'. The decisive point is, whether the concept of the soul is maintained in any pregnant or genuine sense, or whether, on the other hand, it is broken up into a sum of psychic events or experiences and thereby destroyed. In the

[1] Most plainly in the essay "The present chaos in Psychology" which appeared in the *Journal of Philosophical Studies*, vol. v, 1930.

ormer case we are concerned with an interpretation of mental ife as basically an organic unity (whether substantial or functional or in some other way); in the latter, with mental life as mechanism. McDougall traces back the mechanistic current in psychology to Democritus, the organic to Aristotle, and shows how the two currents pursue their courses alongside one another almost uninterruptedly through the entire history of the western mind, and strive against one another for mastery. In modern times the line of the mechanistic interpretation starts with Descartes and proceeds (at first markedly predominant) *via* Newton's philosophy of nature, Spinoza's pantheism, the thought of the deists and of the 'enlightenment', Locke's doctrine of 'ideas', the associationist psychology of the XVIIIth Century (Hume, Hartley) and of the XIXth (the two Mills, Spencer, Bain, Herbart), thence on *via* Comtism, Darwinism and even neo-Hegelianism down to the present time, where it has had its last flowering in the doctrine of emergent evolution, in Behaviourism ("a poor misshapen and beggarly dwarf"), in Russell's *Analysis of Mind* ("Russell . . . reduced it to the lowest level of banality"), and in other intellectualist and avowed or veiled materialist tendencies. The 'Dionysian' countercurrent can in the philosophy of the modern period at first only be seen in isolated instances, in Böhme and in Pascal; then it appears more strongly represented in the Romantic movement both among the poets (Goethe, Wordsworth, Coleridge) and among philosophers in Germany (Schelling, Oken), in Scotland (Hutcheson, Dugald Stewart), sporadically even in France (Maine de Biran), and in a distorted form in Bentham's Hedonism. The stream gathers force in the systems of writers like Schopenhauer, E. von Hartmann, Lotze, Nietzsche, and flows out into the world of to-day through many irrigating channels, as embodied in the philosophy of Bergson, in Psycho-analysis, in Pragmatism, in Vitalism, in the personalist psychology of W. Stern, in the philosophical psychology of Spranger, in the *Verstehende Psychologie* of Erismann and Jaspers, in the 'Gestalt' theory of Köhler and Wertheimer, the characterology of Klages and Prinzhorn, finally in the work of Ward and Stout,

Brentano and Külpe; James and Münsterberg (though confusedly and vacillatingly in the case of the last-named).

If this review seems too elaborately worked out, it is none the less true that McDougall's doctrine issues in a renewal of the old Aristotelian notion of the soul and is linked up with the entire psychological heritage of the Aristotelian tradition, while in a negative direction it represents an uncompromising challenge to every type of naturalistic and mechanistic, sensationalist-atomistic, as well as intellectualist psychological theory, to all psychophysical parallelism, and to every explanation of the psychical by the aid of physical categories. In interpreting the soul as an animating principle and mind in the sense of life, with which it is coextensive though not identical, biology—the vitalistic not the mechanistic biology—is demonstrably an important gateway into psychology, and vital processes acquire a significance that throws much light upon psychical processes. Biological categories, such as organism, wholeness, entelechy, vital force, are shown to be far better suited to the investigation of the 'psyche' and its phenomena than the categories of physics and chemistry can be, which originate in the utterly different domain of inorganic matter. Thus McDougall's psychology is strongly influenced 'from below' by the views of a vitalistic biology while it reveals 'upwards' the standpoint and outlook of the 'mental sciences', and so satisfies one of their fundamental demands—that the higher must not be interpreted in the light of the lower, but vice versa. We do not, however, find in McDougall any sharp line of demarcation between the three levels of life, mind, and spirit. They for the most part pass over into one another, and illuminate one another so that their boundaries become obliterated. This is especially the case with the mental and the spiritual principle, which are only feebly, if indeed at all, distinguished from each other.

It is not, then, surprising that McDougall should devote a substantial volume (*Body and Mind*) to the 'defence of Animism', understanding by this nowadays discredited term nothing essentially different from the spiritualistic-teleological interpretation of psychic life, which his other books also represent though with less emphasis upon the general philosophical implications of the doctrine. Animism presents the contrast to Materialism carried to its extreme point, and here, too, it is the 'materialist dogma' that McDougall is passionately contesting, hunting it down in its most secret hiding-places. The realm of the organic from the level of life up to the level of spirit is determined by quite other than merely mechanical factors and laws; everywhere in it we come up against teleological principles like meaning, intention, purpose, aim, etc., and the higher we rise in the scale of development the more do these principles hold the field. The human soul is throughout determined by them, that is, it is more than the stream of consciousness, and cannot be thought to consist of elements, fragments, atomic particles, fortuitously combined. Rather it represents a unity of quite another kind, to which there is no analogy in the realm of physics. The unity of the individual consciousness is a fundamental fact, and we must conclude from this that there is a ground and basis for it which is quite other than its changing contents. And this is what is meant when we speak of the psychical subject, the self, ego, mind, or spirit.

That consciousness is not exhaustively given in its content, sensory or other, is evident from the fact that one of its most essential features is *meaning*, and it is to be noted that this is just the feature which mechanistic psychology of associationism has grossly neglected. The unique character of 'meanings' is due to this—that they have no physical correlate in the nervous system. Every psychical activity—perception, thought, judgment, or whatever it may be—is carried out in the interplay of meanings, and these form the real bond of connection between the impressions received and the psychic state which the impressions evoke. For the mere passive acceptance of impressions could evoke no reaction in the soul; a factor of meaning must enter in, and only by it can the impulse find release in an action corresponding to the impression. Consciousness, as McDougall is constantly protesting with emphasis. is not exhausted by the data which we apprehend by introspection and are capable of describing; beyond these it contains a something more, extremely hard to grasp or describe, a sort of residuum from which the contents of consciousness derive their meaning. But this bestowal of meaning represents by far the most important function, indeed constitutes the essential core, of consciousness. It is a conscious activity that is directed upon an object with intention, and to be conscious of anything does not signify merely a passive possession of it, but an active achievement accomplished upon it. In this the genuinely dynamic character of consciousness becomes apparent, a character which we may indicate by a static expression and call the meaning belonging to consciousness. Viewed thus, the contents of consciousness are simply the medium or impulsion that brings the activity into play and determines its direction: they constitute at once a challenge and a stimulation to it.

But at the same time the venerable faculty-psychology receives its death-blow. For it is not true that the life of the soul is 'a composite product of the faculties of knowing, feeling, and willing, each of them accommodated in a separate compartment; but each mental process is at once knowing, feeling, and willing, and according as one or other of these aspects is dominant we speak of acts of perception, states of feeling, or impulses of will. So, too, what we call thinking is by no means a merely theoretic process, but at the same time emotional and volitional, indeed the volitional factor plays a decisive part in it. The will to know is a presupposition of all knowledge, and thus cognition is a process whereby the will works through to its goal, and the acquired knowledge is the satisfaction of reaching this goal. Throughout there is, accordingly, an eminently active or pragmatic element at work, and one might well interpret the fundamental intention of McDougall's psychology as the attempt to translate everywhere the static into the dynamic and the passive into the active. It may be said that the efforts of nearly the whole of British psychology since the time of Bain have been directed to the one aim of transcending the associational mechanism that is so deeply rooted in English thought, though most psychologists never got further than half-way to the goal. But of all the endeavours in this direction McDougall's is certainly the most radical and consistent. For here we have a complete recasting of the basic assumptions of the associationist psychology, a root-and-branch reform, which makes itself felt even where the results reached and the expressions employed appear to resemble those of the associationists. For even in such cases there has been a significant shift in the accent; the text has been transposed into a different key. To give another example of this, the sensations furnished us in perception are no ready-made articles waiting to be applied for in our consciousness, but qualities of experience which first come into existence on the basis of the reaction of the mind to a physical stimulus. Their association is not the result of their being presented to the senses simultaneously or in immediate succession: it only comes about if the mind perceives them as related, and this in turn, only in so far as its interest is diverted to them as being so related, that is, in so far as they arouse its activity in some way. It should be already plain enough how closely this doctrine approximates to Pragmatism: what follows will make this plainer still.

It is significant that in a little book published in 1912 (*Psychology, the Study of Behaviour*) McDougall cut himself free from all psychology of consciousness and presents his results from the entirely new standpoint of *behaviour*. Psychology is now defined as the positive science of the behaviour of living beings. Here, then, the term behaviour emerges for the first time in a pregnant sense, and before the establishment by the American John Watson of the 'behaviourist' psychology which has raised such a dust, for this only began to appear a year later. It is, however, important to point out that the two theories have nothing in common but the name, that on the contrary they are diametrically opposed. McDougall sees in Watson's Behaviourism the final and most absurd sprouting of that long series of mechanistic theories against which he is chiefly at war.

The reason for defining psychology as the study of behaviour is that living beings are thereby distinguished from inanimate things. For according to McDougall's 'animistic' point of view, the field of psychological investigation extends over the totality of things endowed with life and therewith also with soul. Changes in dead or inorganic things are accomplished through mechanical processes, whereas changes in the organic world occur in the way of behaviour. The latter is distinguished from merely mechanical occurrences by being not determined from without, but self-determined from within—something that pursues ends from an inherent power and is able to realize purposes of its own activity. There are thus two types of change affecting external objects, the purely mechanical type and the type of purposive action or behaviour. It is the business of psychology to investigate these activities or modes of behaviour of an organism in which it is active as an entirety, as a single unity, in contrast to physiology, which only studies the processes of parts or single organs of the organism. Behaviour is defined more closely by a number of criteria, as, for instance, spontaneity of movement, persistence of activity independently of the continuation of the impression through which it was released, the cessation of movements as soon as a specific change in the situation has been attained, etc. But by far the most important mark of behaviour, which underlies all the others, is its *purposiveness*. Purposive action is such as is dominated up to a certain point by the foresight of its consequences; the purpose is more or less clearly anticipated. In this sense all psychical behaviour as such, and in a special degree all mental activity, is purposive: purposiveness constitutes its essence, and is shown to be the most fundamental of all psychological categories. On this account McDougall expressly calls his doctrine 'purposive' psychology in contrast to all mechanistic or, as he also puts it, 'mosaic'-psychology.

This conveys the gist of his contention, and it is merely a matter of terminology when he introduces instead of 'purposive', the expressions 'conative' or 'teleological', or occasionally also 'hormic' (derived from the Greek ὁρμή, impulse). In calling his the 'hormic' theory he means simply that in all organic, psychic, and mental life, and in all animal and human behaviour there is an original vital nisus towards purposive action, which at first works out in terms of instinct, then at higher levels of organic development is directed to ever more conscious and intelligent paths. McDougall rightly recalls the kinship between the 'hormic energy' and Schopenhauer's will to live, Bergson's *élan vital*, and the *libido* of the pyscho-analysts, the vital force of the vitalists and so on. It does not need to be pointed out that in this doctrine strong stress is laid on instinct, and that intellect and reason are interpreted not so much in terms of what they themselves are as in terms of the category of the instinctive, from which, according to McDougall, they arose. The difference between instinct and intellect is that between the inborn urge to purposive action and the capacity to improve and enhance the original disposition by utilizing past experience. The carefully worked out account of the instincts and their relations to the emotions is one of the most valuable contributions to psychology which we owe to McDougall; it is the central pillar supporting the whole structure, equally for the psychology of the individual and for his social psychology. We conclude with a paragraph which clearly expresses the high significance he assigns to action of an impulsive or instinctive kind:

'The instincts are the prime movers of all human activity; by the conative or impulsive force of some instinct (or of some habit derived from our instincts), every train of thought, however cold and passionless it may seem, is borne along towards its end, and every bodily activity is initiated and sustained. . . . All the complex intellectual apparatus of the most highly developed mind is but . . . the instrument by which these impulses seek their satisfactions, while pleasure and pain do but serve to guide them in their choice of the means. Take away these instinctive dispositions with their powerful impulses and the organism would become incapable of activity of any kind; it would be inert and motionless like a wonderful clockwork whose mainspring had been removed or a steam-engine whose fires had been drawn. These impulses are the mental forces that maintain and shape all the life of individuals and societies, and in them we are confronted with the central mystery of life and mind and will' (*Introduction to Social Psychology*, p. 44).

Apart from Ward, Stout, and McDougall two other thinkers

should be mentioned here, L. T. Hobhouse and C. Lloyd Morgan, who both rendered services of the highest merit to psychological research both in special fields and more generally. Though they cannot be counted as belonging without qualification to the trend of thought hitherto discussed, they are in sympathy with it in several points; for the rest, they follow each their own way, in both cases to destinations of outstanding achievement. We need only recall here the pioneer researches of Morgan and the no less important work of Hobhouse in the field of animal psychology, the work of both in comparative psychology, and Hobhouse's labours on problems of social psychology. Of their works already referred to in a different context the following are here specially relevant: by Morgan: *Animal Life and Intelligence*, 1890; *Introduction to Comparative Psychology*, 1894; *Habit and Instinct*, 1896; *Animal Behaviour*, 1908; *Instinct and Experience*, 1912; *The Animal Mind*, 1930; by Hobhouse: *Mind in Evolution*, 1901; article "Comparative Psychology" in *Encycl. Brit.*, 14th ed., 1929; *Development and Purpose*, 1913 (rev. ed. 1927); *Morals in Evolution*, 1906; *Principles of Sociology*, 1918–24. As we have treated of both thinkers in another part of this work this short reference to them here may be sufficient (see above, pp. 150 ff., and pp. 651ff.).

A special part of the field is covered by the investigations of A. F. Shand (1858–1936) on the psychology of character, as laid down in his *Foundations of Character* (1914, 3rd ed., 1927), a book that has already come to rank as a classic. Shand sets himself to show what are the constituent factors of human character, what relations obtain between them, and how they are in turn related to the unity or whole person. He indicates first three components of character that are clearly to be kept apart, which he terms instinct, emotion, and sentiment, and which correspond to three levels of mental development, that of the animal, the child, and the human adult. The first of these stages is the most perfect in respect of its organization, but at the same time the most fixed and rigid, since the intellect only exercises a very slight educative influence over it. The second is merely a transitional stage between a lower and a higher form of organization, helpless as such and in need of guidance. The third is more plastic and comprehensive in scope than the other two, but its organization remains ever incomplete: only at this stage do reflection, reason, and self-control come into their own.

The three factors which are found severally in their characteristic features in the three stages of evolutionary history are somehow also found together in the character of a single human being, and the unity of character is determined by their synthesis. First we are confronted by the problem of the relation between instinct and emotion.[1] Instinct is, like habit, to which it is most closely akin, a very stable, orderly, peaceful function which exhibits such slight variation in its behaviour that we are able to foresee its outcome. Emotion, on the other hand, is unstable and disorderly and emotional acts always carry with them an element of surprise. When emotion and instinct are combined the latter shows a tendency to moderate and quiet the former. The value of emotion as against instinct consists, first, in the reinforcement it brings to master a given situation, and secondly in the fact that it possesses a much more complex and more adaptable system. All great changes of character have their origin in emotions. While, according to McDougall, every instinct has a separate emotion associated with it, which must be regarded as the stable element in the instinctive transaction, Shand reverses this view by seeking to show that on the contrary the instinctive represents the constant factor in the activity of an emotional system.

Thus the instincts result in a certain measure of control over the emotions. But the genuine function of control cannot be exercised from a lower system, but lies in the hands of a higher and more inclusive one, such as admits a much more adequate expression of the self than does the rudimentary function of instinct. This is the system of the sentiments, the most important of which are love and hate. The sentiments are that part of the

[1] This problem—one frequently discussed, by the way—was made the subject of a symposium between McDougall, Shand, and Stout, ta a meeting of the Aristotelian Society, see *Proc. Arist. Soc.*, N.S. XV, 1915.

character by which all the rest are ruled and controlled, authoritative over both instincts and emotions. They are the real organizing centres of character or its organs of control. They regulate the emotions, whether by weakening those that are too strong and strengthening those that are too weak, or by suppressing those that are harmful, that is, excluding them from consciousness and inhibiting their return, for a part of character cannot be destroyed like an object in the outer world, but only repressed or suppressed. In conclusion we have to distinguish yet another factor belonging to the group of sentiments from the basic sentiments of love and hate, namely conscience, whose very uniqueness makes its interpretation difficult. Shand defines it as the repository of that part of the moral views of the community in which the individual has grown up and which he has taken over as authoritative. As a living force in the character it grows as a man's experience of life grows, and rises above the subjectivity and partiality of the other emotions to a really objective and normative power.

But the phenomenon of character is not exhausted in its whole range and depth by all that is manifested *actually* in terms of instincts, habits, impulses, appetites, emotions, and sentiments which in their manifold mutual relations give expression to its synthetic unity. The *potential* factor of character, its background and underlying foundations, extend far beyond that part of it which is visible and accessible to interpretation. This is the eternal riddle which it is beyond our power to solve and in which all 'characterological' inquiry finds its limit.

We have still to mention CHARLES E. SPEARMAN (*b.* 1863, Professor in the University of London, retired 1931), and the works in which the main fruits of his investigations are garnered: *The Nature of Intelligence and the Principles of Cognition* (1923), *The Abilities of Man, their Nature and Measurements* (1927), *Creative Mind* (1930) and *Psychology down the Ages* (1937). Spearman has devoted himself chiefly to the psychology of cognition and intelligence and his endeavour is to raise this discipline to the rank of an exact science in the sense of physics, and to discover methods on the basis of which psychical phenomena may be measured and mathematically determined. He holds that all psychical events, like all physical events, can be referred to a small number of principles admitting of exact formulation, and he terms this view 'neogenesis', in distinction from the earlier faculty- and association-psychology. He thus develops three primary neogenetic laws: (1) apprehension of experience, (2) eduction of relations, (3) eduction of correlates—which concern the qualitative aspect of the cognitive processes, and five further principles of a quantitative kind. In all this a good deal reminds us of the old rules of association, despite the difference of formulation and despite the author's conviction of the entire novelty of his theory. Spearman has also subjected the nature of human intelligence to a thorough examination, having recourse equally to experimental methods and exact measurements. His 'theory of the two factors' is well known. He distinguishes two factors in all the mental capacities of man, a 'general' and a 'specific'. The general factor while it varies freely from one individual to another remains the same in regard to all correlated capacities within one and the same individual. The specific factor varies not only from one individual to another, but also from one capacity to another in the same individual. In this way he aims at founding a psychology supported by experiment and based upon laws and principles experimentally deducible by strictly mathematical methods.

The work of JAMES DREVER (*b.* 1873, Professor of Psychology in Edinburgh) tends in a similar direction. He has brought psychology into the service of educational science, and, like Shand and McDougall, has endeavoured to elucidate the relation of instinct and emotion. Drever rejects the thesis that all instinctive activity necessarily includes emotional excitement, and holds that an emotion is only experienced when the instinctive impulse is either advanced or impeded in attaining its end, and that certain instincts, such as imitation and play, are not associated with any corresponding emotion. (Cf. *Instinct in Man, a Contribution to the Psychology of Education* (1917); *The Psychology of Industry*, 1921; *An Introduction to the Psy-*

chology of Education, 1922). Finally, of the younger authors who have acquired a name, we may mention ROBERT H. THOULESS, Lecturer in Psychology in the University of Glasgow, and his books *An Introduction to the Psychology of Religion*, 1923; *Social Psychology*, 1925 (2nd ed., 1927); *The Control of the Mind*, 1927; *Straight and Crooked Thinking*, 1930.

Among the foreign tendencies which have more or less strongly influenced British psychology the following three may be specially considered here: Behaviourism, the Gestalt theory, and Psychoanalysis.

The doctrine of the American, JOHN B. WATSON, the founder of Behaviourism, has aroused much notice in England though it has not found any genuine representation there. It was on the whole rejected by British science, since despite its new dress it was recognized to be a straggler of the old mechanistic tradition, which the development of Psychology since Bain had rendered obsolete. Traces of its influence were to be found here and there and it is to be noted that so outstanding a thinker as Russell (and in a lesser degree Broad also) was not able to escape from its attraction altogether. The attitude of English psychologists to the German 'Gestalt' theory is much more positive. This was all the more favourably received because it was fighting the same battle against associationist Mechanism in which British psychology since Ward saw itself involved. The chief writings of Koffka and Köhler are available in English editions and are studied with interest and profit; the word 'Gestalt', for which no suitable English equivalent has commended itself, has even been adopted as a technical term.

Psychoanalysis also has had a victorious campaign in England, and indeed its popular success has been greater than that of any other movement since Darwinism. It has taken root more deeply in England than in the German lands, and its influence extends throughout the widest circles and to the most diverse fields of mental life. The works of Freud, Adler, Jung, and other psychoanalysts are translated into English and widely disseminated. The most powerful impetus came naturally from the founder of the movement, but Jung also has, at least in academic circles, won much notice and esteem. The leading British adherent of psychoanalysis is the physician Dr. ERNEST JONES, President of the Institute of Psychoanalysis and of the British Psychoanalytical Society, and from among many others may be mentioned T. W. MITCHELL, likewise a physician and editor of the *British Journal of Medical Psychology*. Professional philosophy also has not remained unaffected by this tendency of research, although to its honour it should be said that in general it has maintained a reserved and critical attitude and has remained immune from severe infection.

This, however, cannot be said to the same extent of another movement, much older, wider in scope and more influential even than psychoanalysis, which here demands cursory mention, namely, parapsychology, or as it is called in Anglo-Saxon countries, Psychical Research. However much one may be inclined from the standpoint of philosophy to reject the movement, yet the successful founding of the 'Society for Psychical Research' in 1882 must at any rate be given the credit of having undertaken to guide the wild and unbridled speculations of the occultists and spiritualists on to the highway of scientific method. This foundation came about mainly through the efforts of F. W. H. MYERS (1843–1901), the most important figure in the long series of 'Psychical Researchers', and its success was due to the co-operation of R. Hodgson, E. Gurney, F. Podmore, and Henry Sidgwick, who became its first president. Other outstanding members in the early years were A. J. Balfour, Andrew Lang, Mrs. Sidgwick, and the poet Tennyson. The Society is to-day in a highly flourishing condition; it has set itself to the task of investigating in a strictly scientific way parapsychic (and with greater reserve paraphysical) phenomena, such as clairvoyance, telepathy, thought-transference, mediumism, psychometry, cross-correspondence, hypnosis, crystal-gazing, apparitions. It issues regular reports (*Proceedings*, hitherto over forty volumes) and a monthly periodical (*British Journal of Psychical Research*). Two works ranking as classic are *Phantasms of the Living* (2 vols., 1886, abbreviated edition, 1923), jointly published by Gurney, Myers, and Podmore, and chief of all the pioneer labour of Myers: *Human Personality and its Survival of Bodily Death* (2 vols., 1903, abbreviated edition, 1926 and 1935). There was genius in the conception of this work and as a performance that delved deep it is undoubtedly the most important achievement of parapsychological investigation up to the present time. The great problem which was here attacked in comprehensive fashion following upon the labours of Schopenhauer, E. von Hartmann and Fechner, is that of the Unconscious or Subconscious, i.e. the entire field of phenomena which lie below the threshold of consciousness. Myers coined for this the phrase the 'subliminal self', since become famous, and found therein the thread of Ariadne which was to lead him safely through the labyrinth of psychic abnormalities and bring under one unifying concept phenomena as various as sleep, dream, memory, hypnosis, hysteria, hallucination, chromatic hearing, telepathy, clairvoyance, etc. Hereby the conception of the self and of human personality was enormously extended and a valve opened upon the entire world of the subliminal, through which it could break in in full flood, so that the supraliminal realm of consciousness was able to appear as only a relatively small section of a psychic totality immeasurably expanded. Next to this work in importance come the writings of FRANK PODMORE (1855–1910), *Apparitions and Thought-Transference* (1894), *Studies in Psychical Research* (1897), and, above all, *Modern Spiritualism, a History and a Criticism* (2 vols., 1902), an extensive and basic work evincing great versatility which at the same time strikes a strongly critical and sceptical note as regards the so-called facts of the occult.

The voluminous writings of the other 'researchers' need not be further noted here, but we may add the names of some other notable personalities who joined in the effort of the movement and helped to augment its momentum. Besides the philosophers Sidgwick and Balfour who are considered in another context in this book (pp. 83 ff. and pp. 780 ff.), the movement enlisted the sympathies of such well-known physicists as SIR WILLIAM F. BARRETT (1844–1925), SIR WILLIAM CROOKES (1832–1919), and SIR OLIVER LODGE (see above, pp. 729 ff.), of whom the last-named in particular has contributed greatly to spreading an interest in these matters through wide sections of the public. The following are among the relevant writings: by Barrett, who was experimenting on thought-transference as early as the 'seventies, *Psychical Research* (1911), and *On the Threshold of the Unseen* (1917): by Crookes, *Psychic Force and Modern Spiritualism* (1871), and *Researches in Spiritualism* (1874): by Lodge, *The Survival of Man* (1909), and *Raymond, or Life and Death* (1916), and many others. Among psychologists none has pointed to the high significance of this field of study more untiringly than McDougall and its cause was greatly furthered also by W. James's investigations into the psychology of religion and other subjects. From this source, too, Pragmatism acquired a certain occult strain, which is likewise apparent in its chief British representative, F. C. S. SCHILLER (see *Studies in Humanism*, 1907, ch. 17, and *Problems of Belief*, 1924, pp. 66ff.). And even in the realist camp we meet with agreement, sympathy, and even actual preoccupation with these matters, as, for instance, in the writings of Russell and Broad. No special note need be taken of the fact that here and elsewhere there are frequent lapses in the critical circumspection and reserve which are demanded on this dangerous ground; it hardly redounds to the credit of modern British philosophy that so many thinkers and investigators who have otherwise to be taken seriously have on this ground proved so over-venturesome.

VIII

THEISM AND PHILOSOPHY OF RELIGION

In this chapter no more than in the corresponding section iv of the first main division of this book shall we be undertaking a complete or exhaustive presentation of the religious thought of the more recent period. Rather we are simply to consider some specially striking forms of the religious consciousness as manifested in the last and the present generation apart from those currents of thought of which we have already treated. Here as before, we do not intend to push the inquiry too far into the domain of theology. We shall mainly select for consideration those thinkers who, although their chief interests are theological, must also be regarded as of significance for philosophy. We shall thus exclude whatever is put forward within the limits of traditional ecclesiastical or denominational belief, whether liberal or orthodox, Anglican or Nonconformist, without having any philosophical character or note of its own over and above this, as well as the numerous attempts from the religious side, mostly stereotyped enough, to reconcile Christian doctrines with modern science. From this point of view we shall have no special interest in the theistic attempts and systems of A. M. Fairbairn, A. B. Bruce, H. Wace, H. M. Gwatkin, the Duke of Argyll, J. Lindsay, G. Galloway, F. R. Tennant, and many others. But we must also exclude all those with whom we have already dealt in another connection, first and foremost among these being the neo-idealist writers who have bestowed specially intensive attention on the problems of religion and religious philosophy, partly because of its strong ecclesiastical connections and partly from the character of its speculation. The reader is, therefore, asked to refer back at this point to earlier comments, those, for instance, passed upon the doctrines—theistic through and through or culminating in a type of theism—of E. and J. Caird, J. Ward, Pringle-Pattison, Rashdall, Sorley, Laurie, Taylor, Webb, Temple, and others. In regard to religious speculation other contemporary tendencies to a large extent recede into the background when compared with the idealist movement.

In this connection we must not omit to mention what was by far the strongest stimulus given in recent times to philosophy of a religious cast, in so far as this did not grow up within the communion of one or other of the Christian Churches, namely, the lectureship founded and endowed in the late 'eighties in the Scottish Universities by Lord GIFFORD. According to the directions of Gifford's will, these lectures were to have as their subject-matter 'Natural Theology in the widest sense of the word'; they demanded an inquiry into the ultimate ground of being, pursued in a spirit of scientific philosophy, and expressly renouncing supernatural sources of knowledge; an inquiry into the question of the existence, nature, and attributes of the Divine, the relations in which man and the universe stand to deity, the meaning of our existence, etc. The lectures were not to be bound by any restrictions, but were to submit these problems to discussion, and where possible to solution, in a genuine spirit of research and with the methods of critical scientific thought. This stimulating seed fell upon a fertile soil. The greater part of the output of speculative thought in Great Britain since 1888, when the first Gifford Lectures were given, bears the name of this magnanimous foundation, whether as directly releasing it or as providing the framework into which it was fitted. This is true in regard not only to the quantity, but also to the quality of these lectures, and though there may well be much chaff among the grain, yet the most outstanding achievements of speculation are found under the aegis of the Gifford foundation. Thinkers of the most diverse camps and tendencies here found utterance and gave frequently of their best; and nomination to the Gifford Lectureship signified for many the opportunity to round off their thoughts into a comprehensive system, and for others that of disentangling and liberating their thoughts for perhaps the first time. The greater part of the better-known names in modern British philosophy are represented in the long series of Gifford Lectures.[1]

[1] A complete list given in *A Bibliography of David Hume and of Scottish Philosophy from Hutcheson to Balfour*, by T. E. Jessop, 1938.

This section may well begin with one of these lecturers, the celebrated statesman and Parliamentarian, the Earl of Balfour.

ARTHUR JAMES (EARL OF) BALFOUR (1848–1930)

[*A Defence of Philosophic Doubt, being an Essay on the Foundations of Belief*, 1879; *Essays and Addresses*, 1893; *The Foundations of Belief*, 1895; *Theism and Humanism*, 1915; *Theism and Thought*, 1923; *Essays Speculative and Political*, 1920. Cf. *A. J. Balfour as Philosopher and Thinker*, ed. W. M. Short, 1912, a good selection from Balfour's works.]

Lord Balfour is one of the most notable examples of the type, not uncommon in England, of the philosophizing statesman; but his thinking is not to be so essentially connected with the core of his personality or with his work as politician and statesman, as is that of his contemporary, Lord Haldane, also an embodiment of the type who shared the same speculative interest. The imposing series of Balfour's works, an astonishing achievement for a man whose life was spent in labours in the service of the State, is the typical expression of an amateur of keen intellectual alertness who pursues philosophy neither for professional reasons nor because of a profound inward disturbance of mind, but from the need of an intellectual orientation and conspectus, and perhaps also as a pleasant way of passing the time. It is difficult to include his doctrine within any specific school or tendency, and we had better call it in quite general terms Theism, which indicates its foundation in religious faith. But this tells us very little so long as the special character of this theism is not more precisely determined. Sometimes a kinship with the views of Mansel, the disciple of Hamilton, has been noted in it, and as we shall further see important links may be found between it and ideas of Berkeley and Hume. There are even certain points of relationship between it and Kant and Hegel, even though, in spite of having passed his philosophical student years at the very time when the German systems of thought were awaking to new life, Balfour felt no deep or lasting sympathy with German Idealism. What he primarily has in common with the older generation of Kantians and Hegelians is the campaign he wages against the same enemy, Naturalism.

His first philosophical book (*A Defence of Philosophic Doubt*), which aroused at the time but little notice, is one of the earliest attacks upon the Naturalism that was still almost all-powerful in the 'seventies, and upon its allies, Agnosticism, Positivism, Empiricism, Materialism, Darwinism, etc., though the means it employs is strangely enough the weapon of sceptical method furnished by the armoury of Hume. A superficial judgment based upon the title of the book accordingly saw in the young thinker a sort of Hume *redivivus*, and for long afterwards the label of sceptic stuck to Balfour. But the sub-title ought to have been enough to warn the reader that this pseudo-sceptic was less concerned with the defence of philosophic doubt than with the establishing of religious belief. The stage of rational doubt is for Balfour rather merely the preliminary to rational certitude which has its firm anchorage in the tenets of religion. Balfour's procedure resembles that of Berkeley a hundred and fifty years earlier, in his campaign against the infidel mathematicians. Berkeley had denied them the right to sit in judgment upon the simple truths of the Christian mysteries and faith in miracles, when the differential calculus was based upon similar absurdities and contradictions. And so Balfour seeks to show that universally acknowledged axioms of scientific and philosophical thought, as the principle of the uniformity of nature or belief in a transcendent world of things, are not subject to the tribunal of critical thought, cannot therefore be proved on rational grounds, but rest upon a non-rational foundation, that is, upon faith. He calls such dogmas, supposed to be strictly demonstrable and postulated by the sciences, 'inevitable beliefs'. They form the presuppositions both of the sciences and of practical life, and their basis is neither theoretic argument nor perceptual observation but intuitive probability. An element of authority, springing from the needs of practical life, is involved in the foundations of even the exact sciences, and in his first work, as also later, Balfour glorifies authority at the cost of reason—perhaps a symptom prognosticating his subsequent leadership of the Conservative Party! There is evidently a striking agreement between this and Hume's famous criticism of scientific, and especially causal, thinking, and Balfour goes as far as Hume in pushing his sceptical analysis of the rational bases of philosophy and science, according to which psychical processes like instinct, habit, and association take the place of logical grounds.

Up to this point, Balfour follows faithfully in the steps of the great XVIIIth-Century sceptic. But we shall not forget that what he was avowedly fighting was not the exact sciences as such (though he *was* in certain respects opposed to their claims) so much as the general philosophical world-view which boasted of its close connection with these and was founded upon them, namely, Naturalism. It is to be noted that Balfour sought to fight this philosophy, ostensibly strictly scientific in origin, by arguments of a 'misological' (i.e. sceptical) kind. He rightly pointed out that though philosophy should be the adjudicator of science, naturalistic philosophy is merely its servant.

A later work upon *The Foundations of Belief* caused something like a philosophical sensation in England, becoming for a time the focus of philosophical discussion and passing through numerous editions. In it Balfour developed the position he had already reached and added the more positive side of his doctrine. This is clearly expressed in the sub-title—'Notes for an introduction to the Study of Theology'. The only change from the standpoint in the former book is that the sceptical note is definitely less emphasized and reason comes to some extent again into her own. It now became more plain that the earlier sceptical position had been merely a mask, a superficial attitude. Hume's scepticism is doubt born of unbelief or at least of indifference, and is directed equally against science, philosophy, *and* religion: Balfour's is a scepticism directed simply against the scientific reason, and is born of belief, that is it springs from a profound attachment to and faith in the fundamental truths of religion. Can we satisfy our intellectual needs through the philosophical interpretation of the world offered by Naturalism, when it has been shown that this is based upon similar presuppositions and assumptions, equally of the nature of 'faith', as the spiritual or theistic view of the world to which it is opposed? And, if such is the case, why should we not prefer the theistic interpretation to the naturalistic, seeing that the former can, in addition, satisfy the higher needs of our life, and particularly our aesthetic, moral, and religious needs? In conclusion, Balfour is not content to assign to science and to theology what severally pertains to each: he tries to show that every philosophy or science is impossible which does not borrow from theology. For science, too, must postulate a rational ground or ultimate cause of the world, and at that point becomes dependent upon theology. Science no less than ethics and other disciplines will be the more rational and the more comprehensible theoretically, the more it is comprised within a theological framework. The entire edifice of science thus requires a theistic interpretation. These lines of thought bring out more evidently than elsewhere the amateurishness of Balfour's philosophy with its *penchant* towards dilettantism. The sceptic who threatened to shake the firm foundations of scientific knowledge here appears in his true rôle of a preacher, fighting Naturalism like the Evil One, and again and again indicating the one thing needful. Such a reconciliation of faith and knowledge is philosophically untrue, and cannot maintain its ground before the analysis of the critical thought by whose help Balfour himself professed to obtain his results. How inferior is this unwholesome confounding of different domains to the honest, consistent, and uncompromising criticism of Hume!

The later writings, *Theism and Humanism* and *Theism and Thought*, delivered as Gifford Lectures, add almost nothing new to the expositions already given. They merely broaden the basis of the argument and develop a general doctrine of the aesthetic, ethical, and intellectual values. They seek to show that whole spheres of human culture require for their support the notion of God, whether their object and concern is beauty or goodness or knowledge, and that humanism—and in 'humanism' Balfour includes the entire achievement of human culture as manifested—finds its crown and culmination in theism.

WILLIAM RALPH INGE (*b.* 1860)

[Educated at Eton and King's College, Cambridge; Master at Eton, 1884–88; Fellow of King's, 1886; Fellow of Hertford College, Oxford, 1889; Incumbent in London, 1905–7; Professor of Theology in Cambridge, 1907; Dean of St. Paul's, 1911–34. *Christian Mysticism*, 1899 (2nd ed., 1912); *Faith and Knowledge*, 1904; *Studies of English Mystics*, 1906; *Truth and Falsehood in Religion*, 1906; *Personal Idealism and Mysticism*, 1907; *Faith and its Psychology*, 1909; *Speculum Animae*, 1911; *The Philosophy of Plotinus* (Gifford Lectures), 2 vols., 1918 (3rd ed., 1929); *Outspoken Essays*, vol. i, 1919, vol. ii, 1922; "Philosophy and Religion", 1924 (*Cont. Brit. Phil.*, edited by J. H. Muirhead, First Series); *The Platonic Tradition in English Religious Thought*, 1926; *Christian Ethics and Modern Problems*, 1930; *God and the Astronomers*, 1933; *The Eternal Values*, 1933; *Vale*, 1934.]

The statesman Balfour, although a personality with an interest in philosophy and an enthusiasm for religion, was certainly not one of the intellectual and spiritual leaders of his time. Such a one we meet again upon Protestant ground, in the prominent and sharply characterized figure of a Dean of St. Paul's Cathedral. Dr. Inge is not only one of the foremost and most enlightened men in the Anglican Church, he is, in addition, one of the intellectual leaders of the British nation. As one of the chief representatives of contemporary British culture, he is a man of comprehensive knowledge, deep erudition, a finely trained mind and a penetrating understanding, expressing itself in pithy and weighty language. As he is in critical opposition to the dominant spirit of the time, so as a philosopher he follows a lonely sequestered path of his own. He does, it is true, stand within the idealistic camp, not, however, to the extent of adhering to any contemporary school or tendency or swearing by the dicta of any modern philosopher, but only in so far as he seeks to revivify the idealistic thought of antiquity and incorporate it with modern ideas. Thus his point of departure is neither Kant nor Hegel nor any of their British successors and followers: he has chosen a new one hitherto little noticed, from which to construct his own philosophical and theological view of the world. This point is in respect of philosophy, neo-Platonism, in respect of theology, mysticism, or, to put it better, on the one hand the neo-Platonic metaphysics, on the other the neo-Platonic mysticism. These two, philosophy and theology, are for Inge in no wise either separate or merely parallel studies, but form a single indivisible unity of which now the one aspect is more plainly in evidence and now the other. Fundamentally, they are one and the same—philosophical theology or theological philosophy, according to our mental orientation.

Inge's peculiar significance for present-day philosophy is thus founded on his renewal and reawakening of the doctrine of Plotinus, and his success in revealing the intellectual stature of this inscrutable and forbidding thinker. His work upon Plotinus in two volumes owes its origin less to the antiquarian interests of a scholar (though the scholarship of the work is genuine and thorough) than to quickening contact and sympathy with a congenial spirit. Inge calls himself expressly not the expositor and critic of Plotinus, but his disciple. Plotinus is to him a guide to right thinking as well as to right living, and his doctrine no dead conceptual system but a living spiritual force which has its message even for our own day. 'I have lived with him for nearly thirty years, and have not sought him in vain, in prosperity or adversity', he writes at the end of a ten years' long immersion in the depths of Plotinus's philosophy.

What were the causes that made it possible for the work of this late thinker of the ancient world to rise again to new power and influence, and set yet another 'neo-ism' alongside neo-Kantianism, neo-Hegelianism and all the rest, a 'neo-Plotinism', or if the term may be permitted, a 'neo-neo-Platonism'? It is evident that this reawakening primarily grew out of theological interests. Inge's researches into the history of early Christianity led him, as they led Troeltsch, to recognize the vital significance of neo-Platonism for the origin and formation of Christian theology. He saw that in the mighty historical process of blending and fusion through which in the first Christian centuries the Church took over and administered the heritage of ancient culture, neo-Platonism constituted the real nodal point at which the dying culture of Hellenism combined with the primitive Christian outlook to form the synthesis we call the Christian Church. But the Church, into which the ripest wisdom of the ancient world had flowed from the philosophy of Plotinus, became from that time on the sole bearer of western Civilization. It was, in fact, not the beginning of the Middle Ages, but the final creative fulfilment of classical antiquity. The old Civilization and the new religion stand in a real continuity, and it is, therefore, impossible to cut Platonism out of Christianity without shattering the latter into fragments. Christianity, Platonism, and Civilization are inextricably interwoven, and stand or fall together.

This is the point of view from which the central importance of Plotinus is to be understood. According to Inge he is one of the greatest figures in the history of thought, the most significant of all genuinely religious philosophers. In his presence we confront one of the few world-embracing personalities, whose rôle in the history of the human mind has even to-day not been fully played out. He stands at one of those great critical turning-points at which fresh life is engendered and fresh creative forces unloosed from the transition from old to new. His doctrine is a profound mind-pervaded religion, which is based in part upon philosophical thinking, in part upon intimate personal experience. Its whole content streamed into the life of the Church and has remained alive in it to this day. That is why, as Eunapius wrote, 'the altars of Plotinus are still warm even to-day', and the only possible solution of the religious problem of our time is based upon that new synthesis into which neo-Platonism and Christianity entered in the third and following centuries. Inge, therefore, entirely agrees with Troeltsch that in the future development of Christian philosophy as in the past the Plotinian ferment will be of determining significance.

This is particularly true for that side of the religious life the renewal of which Inge has especially at heart—the mystical. Plotinus is for him the classical representative for all time of mystical philosophy, and he refers back all Christian Mysticism to him. But Mysticism must not be confused with mere visionary enthusiasm and has nothing to do with the extravagances of an unbridled fancy or of confused and glutted emotional excess. It is protected from such identification by its origin in a strict school of thinking which can be traced back beyond Plotinus to Plato. Genuine Mysticism includes philosophical thought, with which, indeed, it is at bottom identical. It is either the endeavour after an ultimate objectively valid truth or it is nothing. The mystic aspires to know God, and if possible to see Him face to face. If his experience is always concrete and individual, its value is not merely subjective, but lies in the fact that it is the revelation of a universal and eternal truth. The mystic vision is, therefore, a spiritual philosophy demanding the co-operative activity of all psychical factors, thinking, feeling, and willing. Only if, and when, his whole personality is enlisted in the search for God is a man truly able to become what is else but a dormant possibility in him, that of being sharer in the divine nature and citizen of the spiritual world. Accordingly reason is in some sense involved in every submersion in mystical experience. It is meaningless to appeal to a super-rational faculty, so long as reason is taken in its true sense, i.e., as Inge puts it, as the logic of the whole personality. Therefore every revelation which transcends the reason and claims to be able to get outside it is a dangerous aberration from the right path of mystical experience. What we have to transcend if we want to make any progress in the knowledge of the divine is not reason but the shallow rationalism that bases itself on a formalist logic and is totally incapable of attaining spiritual insight into things. Inge's position is, therefore, sharply opposed to Harnack's: the latter defines Mysticism as Rationalism applied to a sphere that lies beyond Reason; while Inge defines it as Reason applied to a sphere that lies beyond Rationalism.

Psychologically Inge interprets the mystical impulse as a disposition innate in man's nature, and refers it back to what he calls the raw material of all religion and perhaps also of all philosophy and art, namely the obscure consciousness of a higher being beyond our own which we yet feel to be a part of our very self. Religious Mysticism is accordingly to be defined as the attempt to realize and make actual the presence of the living God in the human soul and in external nature, or more generally, as the attempt to make present to oneself in thought as well as in feeling the immanence of the temporal in the eternal and of the eternal in the temporal. Moreover, Inge has investigated Mysticism also in all the rich variety of its historical manifestations, back to the Bible and on into modern times, in his earliest book on *Christian Mysticism* and in his *Studies of the English Mystics* which was its sequel; and apart from his chief interest in Plotinus he has in particular pointed to Meister Eckhart as the greatest speculative mystic of the Middle Ages.

Turning to Inge's own philosophy, it must first be emphasized that the real import of his work is not in this but primarily in his having focussed the intellectual life of England upon historical forces and powers which had hitherto been in part buried and hidden, in part merely the research work of scholars, and in part still not even brought within sight at all. Present-day English philosophy (if we may confine his influence to this field, which, of course, does not exhaust it) owes him a noteworthy widening of its cultural horizon, the sharpening of its vision for far views over space and time, a training in genuine thought about and insight into history and the philosophy of civilization. Inge seems to me to feel more vividly than any other contemporary British thinker that philosophy is not a self-sufficient detached affair, but an organic member of the general culture of the mind, in which it is included and which is operative in it. It is world-wide in scope, penetrated by history and potent for life in a far profounder sense than Pragmatism and the current philosophy of life can even remotely hint at. From this point of view Inge's reaching back to Plotinus and the neo-Platonic Mysticism appears as no capricious renovation of some one thinker or period of thought but as the opening up of a spiritual world eternally valid which was made manifest in a crucial crisis of history and found its classical embodiment in a personality of outstanding eminence. It is strange that the English Hegelian school drew so sparingly upon the historical and cultural content of Hegel's work; otherwise they might already have learned from the German master what Inge, on whom Hegel made almost no impression, has taught them—ample horizons and wide intellectual vistas in philosophical thinking. It is to Troeltsch in particular that Inge owes his own finer insight in this direction, and he honours Troeltsch as one of modern Germany's profoundest thinkers. Both possess a wide range of culture and a panoramic view in the philosophical interpretation of history, and in these respects no English philosopher to-day seems to me to be Inge's equal.

The philosophy of this 'Christian Platonist' (as Inge prefers to call himself) is the resultant of these factors in the history of the human mind and human culture which have become alive in him. His own thinking has been chiefly kindled at this fire; these are the influences that have shaped it. But it has also been open to fruitful stimulations from his contemporary philosophical *milieu*—or to put the matter otherwise, the old fundamental problems have been thereby clothed in a modern vesture more in accordance with the times. But the substance is and remains 'Christian Platonist'.[1] Philosophy is according to this no mere affair of scholarship or scientific research, no mere attempt to satisfy a theoretic impulse or an aesthetic need, nor yet an index to practical life, but rather a commitment and direction of man to the blessed life, and, therefore, in essence religious and theocentric rather than scientific or ethical or pragmatic or aesthetic. The call to philosophy means a call to a dedicated life; all authentic and elevated thinking is charismatic or sacramental.

The real domain of philosophy is not facts but *values*, not what 'is' merely *quâ* 'existing' but what 'is' *quâ* 'counting' and 'holding good'. Reality is defined as neither merely psychical nor merely material, but as a realm in which thought and being, fact and value are inseparably combined, so that neither of the

[1] This applies also to his last substantial work, *God and the Astronomers*, in which he examines modern theories of physics and seeks to square their results with his own doctrine; as, for instance, the law of entropy, which he maintains not only does not imperil his Christian-Platonist theism, but on the contrary may be held to give it more impressive support and justification.

two has existence without its correlate. The real world is a coherent organic-unity, timeless and spaceless, but including within it all events in space and time in their relations to the world, i.e. *sub specie aeternitatis.* The essence of reality is spiritual, and spirit is revealed to us in values: the spiritual world is a realm of values. The values are the attributes of true Being. Things are only real in so far as they participate in values. But values are not ideals or guiding principles, not something merely belonging to the subject and imputed to things, but genuine components of reality and so objective, existing in their own right, not made by us, but eternal and transcendent. They are the most real of realities, which amounts to saying that they are the primary attributes of deity. The realm of values is threefold: it comprises the true, the good, and the beautiful. These three are the highest forms of reality of which our mental vision can have cognizance. They are absolute and fundamental and cannot be blended or harmonized. They belong to a super-temporal and super-spiritual sphere of being of which the world of ordinary experience is but a feeble reflection, and they obey their own laws. The realm of values is exhaustively given in the true, the good, and the beautiful; in explicit contrast to Windelband and Otto, Inge rejects the sacred as a separate value constituting the sphere of religion, at least in the sense of giving it a place co-ordinate with the other values. These are, rather, indications of a higher unity lying beyond or above them and to which they are only the upward leading paths. This unity beyond knowledge and existence is the absolute or the Godhead. But God reveals Himself to us only in the mystical experience by intuition. The values are the triple constellation through which the supreme being manifests its existence and will. Inge terms the Deity also the value of values, thus bringing out their subordinate relation to it.

Inge's conception of God coincides with that of Christian theology. God is the creator of the cosmos, who lives independent of the world and *above* it. The world owes everything to God, God nothing to it. That is the essence of the relationship, and not that God is *in* the world, for such a doctrine would lead to regarding God and the world as equal in value, or to the diluted pantheism which is the religion of English Hegelianism. Inge recoils from this doctrine and reverts to the theory of creativity and the transcendence of God. On the other hand he makes contact with the absolutism of Bradley in his treatment of the problems of human personality. He distinguishes individuality from personality; the former is the lower, the latter the higher stage of human existence. To attain to our true self we must overcome our separate, self-centred, merely individual being and become spiritual or rational beings to whom alone pertain true personality and inner unity. But since a human being has no single self-subsistence, but is only truly human when he shares in the life of the whole of which he is a part, there results the paradox that he has always to be winning his personality afresh, that is, that he must lose it in order to save it. Most of all is this so when he approaches the Deity in the mystic vision, whereby his personal being is utterly transformed so that God may think, will, and act *through* man freely and unimpededly of his own spontaneous willingness. Inge expresses this by saying that the human soul has an independent value but no independent existence. It is clear that Inge with his mystical presuppositions was no more able to master in thought the problem of personality than Bradley was, seriously as he has laboured at its solution.

A similar remark might be made also on his attitude to the problem of evil. At first here, too, he stands in sharp opposition to the shallow optimism of many Hegelians, and acknowledges the wickedness and suffering in the world in all their gravity. Man cannot of his own strength overcome the terrible power of iniquity; deliverance from evil can only come to pass through the grace of God and the substitutionary suffering of Christ. On the other hand his philosophical discussion of the problem cannot give theoretic satisfaction, mainly because it approximates to precisely that optimistic outlook which cannot be reconciled with the general character of Inge's thought. So he in the end accepts Bradley's solution as that which involves us in fewer contradictions than other theories, namely that it is best to deny the absolute existence of evil and to treat it as mere appearance which belongs necessarily to the realization of moral ends as a vital activity. It need not be said that he is well aware of the danger of such an interpretation—that of blunting unduly the evil power of sin, and drawing the sting that is of its essence.

In conclusion, to complete the mental picture of this outstanding and influential personality mention must be made of two further essential characteristics. His conservative temper leads Inge to erect a dam against all those contemporary currents which he comprises under the term 'misology', by which he means the despisers of reason, prominent to-day in many fields and in the most diverse camps, but especially where modern philosophy of life is the thême. In the XIXth Century he recognizes misological tendencies in the philosophies of Schopenhauer, E. von Hartmann, and Lotze, in our own day primarily among the advocates of Pluralism and Pragmatism like Howison, James, Royce, Balfour, Kidd, and the so-called 'Personal Idealists', but also in the poetry of Browning and in modernist theology. His attack is especially sharp against the anthropocentric and 'anthropolatrous' view of the world of Pragmatism, against that self-centred philosophy which makes man and his interests the measure of all things: he calls this a provincialism of thought. It is a striking thing that it is Inge the mystic and intuitionist who wages this war against the irrationalisms and anti-intellectualisms of our time: a plain indication of how strictly the mystical element of his thought is controlled in the forms of reason.

But the enemy whom most of all Inge arraigns is the enthusiasm of the present age for evolution and its fanatical faith in progress. Again it is noteworthy that a thinker so soaked in culture and with a mind so rich in the fruits of education should have lifted his warning voice against the *soi-disant* achievements of modern civilization, and even have been driven to moods of pessimism. Inge's 'cultural pessimism' has penetrated the public mind more than any other side of his intellectual influence and earned him the *sobriquet* of 'the gloomy dean'.

He is convinced that the over-mechanization of our life has not furthered, but impeded the growth of the inner qualities of man, and that what we so proudly call our 'progress' means the degradation of our race and the loss of our true spiritual goods. There has been no progress in the past, nor may we expect progress in the future. The idea of a *progressus ad infinitum* can neither be justified in thought nor give us any ground for consolation. How should progress in an infinite whole be possible? The superstition of progress which has held the western world under its sway for a hundred and fifty years and to which Hegel and Comte fell victims as Darwin and Spencer did likewise, is a bastard philosophy, a spurious product of our time with its complacent idolatry of humanity. So Inge confronts all the illusion of progress and the intoxication of evolution with his reiterated belief in the eternal values which are projected from the primary basis of being into our temporal sphere. They alone are the pivotal points and guiding stars of our willing and acting and the meaning of our life.

BURNETT HILLMAN STREETER (1874–1937)

[Canon of Hereford from 1915 to 1934, Provost of Queen's College, Oxford, from 1933, and Reader in Early Church History in the University of Oxford from 1927. *Immortality*, 1917; *The Spirit*, 1919; *God and the Struggle for Existence*, 1919; *Reality, A New Correlation of Science and Religion*, 1926; *The Buddha and the Christ* (Bampton Lectures), 1932.]

While Dean Inge, dissatisfied with the so-called conquests of modern civilization, reaches back to the philosophical wisdom of the ancient world, and in a way quite out of harmony with the spirit of the age seeks from thence to renew and deepen the intellectual life of the present, Canon Streeter goes precisely in the opposite direction by fully endorsing everything in science and philosophy which is seasonable to-day and bringing it into accord with his religious thought. Thus in his book *Reality*, the clearest expression of his philosophical standpoint, he endeavours to reach 'a new correlation of science and religion', a synthesis which ventures to bring both the results of modern physics and biology and the metaphysics of Bergson into harmony with Christian theism. Mathematical physics appears here as an ally against the materialist-mechanist view of the world ('Mechanomorphism', as Streeter calls it), and against its scientific and philosophical presentation as much as against superficial popularizations of it. Streeter opposes to mechanomorphism, according to which the world is to be viewed as a gigantic machine, an anthropomorphism of a more exalted kind than the crude acceptance of the figure of man as the measure of all things, an anthropomorphism for which the ideal man is the ectype or image of God. But, above all, we have here the influx of Bergsonism into the theistic interpretation of the world, forcing more and more into the background the absolutism of the Hegelian school, with which Streeter had at one time been in close sympathy. The universe appears according to the analogy of life as an organic system of parts in dynamic movement, while 'life' (which here as with Bergson has a value laid upon it that goes far beyond mere biological 'living') appears as a creative principle. There is not that destructive struggle for existence which Darwin had seen in it, nor yet that blind will to power, which it appeared to Nietzsche to be, but a 'creative strife', in which life is continually renewing itself, a productive making and co-making whereby new and higher values are constantly being engendered. Of this force the highest expression is found to be not struggle and conflict but collaboration and love. Streeter sees in love the true symbol of the creative activity, and so far he can say that in love is revealed the ultimate meaning of the cosmic process. This standpoint also defines the metaphysical ground of being which is identified with the deity. God is not a static state of being, or inert principle, but the eternal creative force, who did not make the universe once and for all in order to let it pursue its course according to mechanical laws, but is in perpetual and vital operative activity within it. We can only represent this supreme active being to ourselves under the similitude of an absolutely perfect personality, a final sublimation of what we ourselves are at the highest level of our being, and as such we must ascribe to Him that concrete synthetic character which is connoted by the concept of individuality. This God is the living God and His essential attribute is like that of all life, love. Thus this line of thought leads back to that idealistic theism which is essentially equivalent to the demands of the Christian religion.

The religious philosophers hitherto considered belong like their spiritual kindred of the idealist school to Protestantism, whether within or without the Anglican Church. Turning now to religious philosophy that is Roman Catholic in origin, we recognize at once the deep cleavage that separates the two. It is significant that as in a previous section (see p. 185) so here, it is a Catholic thinker who takes the leading place in the contemporary philosophy of religion. Friedrich von Hügel took over the heritage bequeathed by Cardinal Newman, and refashioned it in the spirit of the XXth Century, in the sense in which a piece of inherited property is transformed by creative adaptations into a new profitable source of income. We therefore find in the figure of von Hügel the most important religious thinker of the last generation, the counterpart to that of the great requickener of XIXth-Century religious faith.

BARON FRIEDRICH VON HÜGEL (1852–1925)

[Catholic lay theologian and religious philosopher, born in Florence, of German father and Scottish mother. His youth was spent partly in Austria, partly in Italy and Belgium. Hügel attended neither school nor university, but was educated privately, and carried his education further for himself. Later, in the 'seventies, he took up residence in England, where he lived till his death with a few interruptions (nine winters in Rome) as an independent writer and student (cf. *The German Soul*, pp. 121 ff., where he gives autobiographical details). *The Mystical Element in Religion as Studied in St. Catherine of Genoa and Her Friends*, 2 vols., 1908 (second edition revised 1923); *Eternal Life, a Study of Its Implications and Applications*, 1912; *The German Soul: Two Studies*, 1916; *Essays and Addresses on the Philosophy of Religion*, vol. 1, 1921; vol. 2, 1926 (cheap edition, 1928 and 1930 respectively); *Selected Letters, 1896–1924*, edited with Memoir by B. Holland, 1927; *The Reality of God*, *and Religion and Agnosticism*, edited by E. G. Gardner, 1931 (contains his literary remains); *Readings from F. von Hügel*, selected by A. Thorold, 1928.]

Only a part of Friedrich von Hügel's character and work as a thinker belongs to philosophy, and his figure cannot therefore be presented to the reader in its entirety, but only in some of its emanations. It is not out of place to offer an appraisement of him for the reason that there is unanimous testimony that in him we have to do with 'the profoundest thinker among the theologians of England to-day' (W. R. Inge), 'the greatest lay Roman Catholic theologian, indeed the greatest mind of which the Catholic Church can boast since Newman' (F. Heiler), 'the greatest, perhaps even the only great religious thinker of the twentieth century' (Loisy), 'one of the most significant religious personalities of the present time' (Troeltsch). No framework in which we try to enclose it is ample enough for the breadth and depth, wholeness, purity, and genuine sanctity of this remarkable personality. It is not exhausted in the deeply fixed anchorage in Catholicism, nor in the strong leanings toward Mysticism, nor in the scholar's researches in the field of scientific biblical criticism, nor in any other form of systematic scientific activity, nor in metaphysical and philosophical knowledge, nor in relations with the Modernist movement. It was in every respect *sui generis*, and all these several modes of activity were fostered by something central in it and brought to fruition by drawing upon the man's whole being. His personality while present in all these, can neither be identified with any one of them singly nor yet with all taken together. The best characterization of Hügel's quality and work is accordingly that conveyed by the term by which he himself professed to define the peculiar character of the Catholic Church, the term 'comprehensiveness', which must be taken as connoting—a point made by Heiler—not only universality, but also harmony, balance, and freedom from partiality or exclusiveness.

Hügel's position within, and attitude towards, the Roman Catholic Church is in this respect typical. It cannot be said that his whole effort and output in thought and conduct can be made to coincide absolutely with Roman Catholic doctrine and observance. He was indeed a devout son of the Church, who willingly submitted to her commands and subjected his writings to her *imprimatur*. Yet there were features in his personality not to be comprised by Catholicism even in its widest interpretation. Though he well recognized the high importance of all that we may call the body of the Church—its external organization and observances in particular—yet again he had also a deep understanding of the solitary wrestlings of the soul, its needs and its distresses—of the true inwardness of a God-seeking man, and thus of the individual side of the religious life, as expressed most purely in Mysticism. He knew that genuine belief is possible outside of, as well as within, the Church organization, and that important as the institutional factor may be it does not cover the religious life in all its full extent. But above all and for all his submission to the authority of the Church in other matters, he was unwilling to stint his right to pursue free inquiry. His profound sense of the historical element in religion, combined with genuine scholarship and the spirit of research, made any compromise for him on this point inadmissible. Thus his contributions to biblical exegesis and to the history of religion and dogma are a service to strict scientific criticism. In none of them did he when treading dangerous or controversial ground allow himself to be guided by anything but the spirit of truth and knowledge. And seldom has anyone realized with greater pain than von Hügel, one of the Roman Church's greatest and most loyal sons, how narrowly that Church seeks to limit and check the free flight of the mind. Again and again he complained of the lack of freedom of spirit and of the intolerable restrictions upon the research work of scholars, and he remained full of admiration, and doubtless silent envy also, of the great achievements of Protestant scholarship which had no such fetters to impede it. Here, indeed, is the deepest root of his glowing veneration for so pre-eminent a figure in research and scholarship as Ernst Troeltsch, as well as for other Protestant theologians.

And finally his tolerance. This, too, went far beyond the measure permissible to a strict Catholic, and was as active in his practice as it was claimed and maintained in his theory. Men of the most diverse kind came and went in his house in Kensington: Roman Catholics and Anglicans, Lutherans and Dissenters, Quakers and Freethinkers. He stood in personal relations to a whole series of important personalities of the most various camps and tendencies in the old world and the new. His influence was more far-reaching among Anglican laymen and theologians than among his own co-believers. By the Roman Church he was not so much recognized (let alone prized at his true worth) as silently tolerated. What would have been unpardonable in a priest was excused in a layman. Yet there has seldom been a more eloquent advocate, a sincerer panegyrist, or a more obedient son of the Roman Catholic faith than he. Heiler calls him 'a wonderful embodiment of the Catholic essence, a genius of the Catholic idea'. But just because he embodied the essence and the idea of Catholic Christianity in such purity and profundity, the coarse actuality of the Church as he found it hurt him, and he it. This drove him also, at least for a time, into the Modernist movement, with whose leaders—especially Loisy and Tyrrell—he was bound in close friendship, and of which he was called the lay bishop. But here, too, it became evident that he was greater than the cause in whose service he enlisted. When the movement was swept into radical currents, he withdrew from it and remained loyal to the Church with which he was from the first in greater inner accord than with any reformist or secessionist endeavours. So in spite of his passing connection with Modernism we must beware of finding in him a Modernist in any pregnant sense: on the contrary, his views in the philosophy of religion and in theology show an expressly anti-modernist character.

Hügel's universality, shown outwardly in his parentage, his education and life-history, is manifested wherever we meet him. The space in which his mind and spirit move is not to be hedged in by any narrow boundaries. In whatever categories, or in whatever region we seek to enclose him, we always only grasp a part of his expansive and comprehensive nature. He is a genuinely 'ecumenical' man, who despite his strong bonds with the Catholic Church moves into a region in which denominations are transcended and all Christians are at one. His strong and firm faith is not only a precious possession of his heart, but also a cognition of his mind that is constantly being renewed. His Church allegiance is not merely the acceptance of an inherited traditional value, but the free movement of a spirit controlled by strict regard for the canons of science and objective investigation. His understanding of the divine grows out of a comprehensive mundane culture; his piety is neither dogmatic nor ascetic, but open to sensuous enjoyment and related to everything true, good, and beautiful in the earthly life also. He has been called the holy scholar, and the phrase does in fact excellently express the most important components of his nature. He was fond of designating Hellenism, Christianity, and science as the three essential constituents of modern western man. Is he not himself a marvellous embodiment and synthesis of these three elements which are alive in him in beautiful harmony and balance: Hellenism as the aspiration for beauty, fullness and harmony of life, Christianity as the world of higher revelation and deep inward faith, and science as the domain of iron law disclosed in untiring investigation and by the lucid processes of thought?

Hügel's philosophy in the narrower sense can only be understood in relation to his mind and personality in their wholeness. It is the religious man's struggle for truth and clear understanding, not an interest to be satisfied along with others but an affair of the whole man demanding the engagement of the entire personality and born both of the stress of knowledge and the abundance of life. It did not grow out of any school and belongs to no philosophical current, but rose out of the creative depths of his being. It incorporated all the wealth of his scholarship and learning in secular and spiritual matters, and reflects the elevation and ripeness of his culture. It is in the final sense a divine wisdom, for all the problems about which it turns are illumined by this its ultimate meaning.

This divine metaphysics already irradiates the epistemological foundation of Hügel's thought, which is the weakest side of his doctrine, a by-product, simple and almost primitive in character. In all experience three factors are operative, subject, object, and the thinking function that is the bridge between them, and of these it is above all the second that seems important to Hügel. The object is that which is the given in an absolute sense, that which simply exists outside our consciousness, the transcendent reality which confronts or, better, comes to meet the subject as the 'wholly other', that which can never be merely a product or function of thinking, but which we apprehend because we come upon it, or come up against its pressure and resistance. It is *there*, whether we are aware of it or deny it or doubt it, accept it or reject it; all such subjective acts presuppose it already present. It is of the essence of knowing from the first that trans-subjective reality is in principle accessible to the knowing mind. Hügel, therefore, rejects all subjectivist solutions of the problem of knowledge, solipsism, idealism, immanentism, phenomenalism, etc., and declares for an uncompromising objectivism or realism, which he himself qualifies as 'critical', though at bottom it is naïve enough. He holds that this realism is to be found in Plato and Reid, in Lotze and Külpe, as well as in other contemporary thinkers.

The real, then, is given us in immediate self-evidence as the 'more than merely subjective'. It discloses itself to human experience in different ways and in different forms and gradations. Two points of view are significant as deciding the level or status of a given real: the clearness with which we apprehend it and the wealth of content which it presents to us. In the mathematical sciences we are concerned with purely formal and abstract relations, numerical or spatial. These are given us in complete clarity and distinctness; their transmission from one subject to another is accomplished with ease and directness. They are completely transparent, because they involve no affirmation of specific realities. But the higher we rise in the scale of being and the more manifold and complicated the relations in which things are enmeshed become, by so much does their content grow in richness and concreteness. But such richness of content is not to be apprehended with the same compelling clarity, or transmitted so easily, as purely formal patterns of relation; all higher reality is inexhaustible to cognition in the measure of its concreteness and complexity. What, however, is lost in clarity is gained in vividness, fecundity, and richness of meaning. Together with this goes a certain vagueness and obscurity in the manner in which we become participants in such reality. This takes place in the 'profounder sciences', above all in history and the mental sciences, where we encounter life individual and concrete, and where we employ entirely different criteria and methods from those of mathematics and the investigation of nature. Similar ideas were developed under the influence of Windelband's and Rickert's methodological inquiries into the conceptual basis of the 'natural' and the 'cultural' sciences; and had early aroused Hügel's notice. He expressed joyful agreement with them in a lecture delivered in 1905 (*The place and function of the historical element in religion*, printed in *Essays and Addresses*, II, pp. 25–55). He later recast his ideas in a form better fitted to his doctrine, but the main features of Rickert's methodology of the sciences still shine through them.

Reverence for reality, the humble acceptance and acknowledgment of it from the lowest level to the highest—this is a characteristic feature of Hügel's thought. On every side transcendent reality surrounds us, from every quarter the trans-subjective impinges upon our human existence. We encounter it in special fullness and vital meaning in the specific forms of the true, the good, and the beautiful, in these worlds of value which are equally not of our own creating but are grasped by us as objective reals and become the subject-matter of logic, ethics, and aesthetics. But the supreme revelation of the trans-subjective is provided in religious experience, and the reality of God surpasses every other reality. And so we come to the field which was from the first peculiarly Hügel's own, the core and focus of his philosophy, which he was always endeavouring to illuminate from his continually deepening knowledge and experience.

The conception of God fits in easily with Hügel's theory of knowledge and of the real; or perhaps it would be better to put the matter the other way about, for the theory of knowledge was only worked out to supplement the doctrine of God, and for the sake of it. It is his idea of God that sets the other parts of his system in their true light, and not *vice versa*: here, also, the central thought is that of the *givenness* of God. 'Religion, even more than all other convictions that claim correspondence with the real, begins, proceeds, and ends with the Given, with existences, realities, which environ and penetrate us, and which we have always anew to capture and to combine, to fathom and to comprehend' (*Essays and Addresses*, First Series, p. xiii.). The existence of the Divine Being cannot be deduced *a priori* from pure reason or demonstrated from any facts of nature or human life. All such considerations are forestalled by God's being already there, that is, his givenness means at the same time his provenience, and this forms the ultimate guarantee for the existence of all other 'givens' or realities of a lower order. The Divine Being is thus pre-given or provenient in a double sense, first in contrast to all interpretations in terms of knowledge or subjective experience, and second in contrast to every other more or less objective 'given' real.

Givenness and provenience are the two most important facts that can be established about the being of God. They affirm that God is a stupendous Reality independent of all knowing and feeling, of vision and experience, prior to every other entity, conditioning and containing it; a reality the most exalted and perfect that we can conceive, in comparison with whose wealth and plenitude of life, force, intensity, and concreteness all other reality that we know pales into empty illusion. As Hügel likes to express it in a figure, it overflows from the limitless abundance of its own inexhaustible richness. But this signifies for the knowledge of God, that we always carry in us a profound obscure feeling of this all-surpassing reality, but that we can only very imperfectly grasp it by way of our conceptual reason. The knowledge of God is not a matter of clear thinking, strictly defined concepts and metaphysical perspicacity; it cannot be lifted to that high level of rational, self-evident, compelling clarity with which we apprehend mathematical relations. It will always be obscure, confused, and mysterious, but on that very account infinitely rich, fertile, and productive. Knowledge of God is distinguished not by lucidity but by vitality. It is like a field of light, at the centre of which is a power of luminous radiance, while the margins grow dimmer the further you get from the source of illumination. Far as we may be able to push forward in our knowledge, these margins will always remain in darkness.

None the less, Hügel's philosophy is very far from running aground in any sort of agnosticism. On the contrary, it is bold enough in ever finding new descriptions and determinations of the Being of the Absolute, and enjoys pushing knowledge on into the ultimate depth of metaphysics. Furthermore, its supreme and sole aim is the illumination of the divine foundations of being. Its centre of gravity is wholly theocentric. All other problems repose on this and are lit up by it. In continuing to follow the determination of the being of God we shall be unfolding the philosophy of Hügel in its entirety.

Thus with the popular thought of the omnipresence of God as point of departure we may deal with the momentous problem of time and eternity. As in every great metaphysics the absolute is thought of in Hügel's doctrines as timeless, spaceless, extensionless. But its eternity or timelessness—which, rather than 'spacelessness', is here our main concern—is interpreted as contemporaneousness or simultaneity. We must represent to ourselves the life and character of the deity under the figure of 'all at once' or 'all together', the *totum simul*. But simultaneity signifies not an empty form but a maximum of unity in diversity and diversity in unity. In this sense it is the adequate expression of supreme beauty, absolute truth, and perfect goodness. All this shows us the nature of the Absolute as pure being, or as pure function or energy, as *actus purus* in the sense of St. Thomas Aquinas and the schoolmen. Expressed negatively it means that God is neither process nor evolution nor succession, that all this after it has entered into Him is superseded and erased. The opposite to be contrasted with simultaneity is found in succession or temporal sequence, of which Hügel distinguishes two kinds, mere 'clock-time' and duration. He means by the former purely mathematical or astronomical time, which simply lapses and is not charged with any concrete filling; by the latter, more or less what is included in Bergson's *durée réelle.* This is the true form of time *quâ* experienced in the concrete, the time in which all genuine history lives and moves, in contrast to the mere lapse and passage of events in inorganic nature or in the animal world. Duration signifies not merely succession, but a perpetual overlapping and interpenetration of temporal moments or meaningful experiences. What endures is capable of intensification, concretization, and concentration, and may approximate continually nearer to a sort of simultaneity. Succession and simultaneity thus stand to one another in a definite relation, that of stages in a development; the more successive frees itself from mere sequence and passes into a reciprocal interpenetration or duration, the nearer it approaches simultaneity. Human life, in so far as it is a true life of the mind and not a mere animal living from moment to moment, thus moves in the intermediate region between mere clock-time and pure divine simultaneity and has its adequate form in duration. Consequently durational time forms no sort of barrier between us and the eternal life of God but is on the contrary the means and the medium whereby we come to experience and know that life in the most vital way. The temporal projects upward into the eternal and is superseded by it as soon as every element of successiveness is transformed by the way of the enduring into the simultaneous.

But in turn the eternal impinges back upon the temporal. This leads to a new characteristic of the divine, namely the notion of God as immanent as well as transcendent. But how is the immanence of God to be harmonized with His transcendence in such a way as to avoid a contradiction in thought? We have seen that God is the richest and fullest reality that we can present to ourselves. But we can consider this reality in two ways, now from within and now from without, while leaving its unity unimpaired. Seen from within the divine nature is Being at rest in itself, centred in itself, drawing on its own plenary inner life: this is the divine 'aseity', what we may also call God's absoluteness, an old notion of the schoolmen which Hügel here revives.

But this does not exhaust the divine nature. The absolute God can, by a free act of will, leave His aseity and fashion a world which although it is His creation and in many respects expresses His nature is yet totally other and different from Him in essentials. The absolute God thus becomes a Creator God, His inner life becomes outward action, His superabundant Reality overflows and streams down into the world He has created, penetrates, sustains, and controls. God is then 'given' and reveals Himself *in* the world also. In it He became flesh, in it He is immanent. But the idea of the divine Immanence is to be kept pure from every pantheistic dilution, from every pretence to equate God with the universe. Immanence means simply the universal fact of the Incarnation, the 'descent' of the divine into the limitations of creaturehood, without compromising in the least His real transcendence. The incarnation or self-externalization of God is accomplished most visibly and manifestly in the Son of God becoming man. But this is not confined to the historical manifestation of Jesus, but relates also to the entire Church which is the body of Christ and therewith the continued incarnation of the Son. But the Church is a historical phenomenon, and so God reveals himself further in the life of history, above all in the history of the Christian Church and the Saints, and to a lesser extent also in secular history. But the highest assurance of God is given us in religious and especially in mystical experiences; though in the sciences and arts also, and finally in nature, the divine becomes visible—in these instances, however, only as a feeble shimmer rather than a radiant certainty, the divine signature rather than the divine given presence.

For Nature is the other of God, that sphere of being upon which His presence impresses itself least potently, as also may be said of animal and human life to the extent in which it moves in the paths of nature. In this sphere are to be found in only too great profusion, sorrow and pain, sin and guilt, evil and ugliness—just the things which are alien to and not to be unified with the divine nature. The problem of evil, the hardest stumbling-block for every theistic metaphysic, troubled Hügel throughout his life, and he could neither accept any one of the current solutions of it nor find one of his own that was theoretically satisfying. Above all he held himself aloof from all shallow optimism or every frivolous attempt to argue away or belittle the fundamental fact of evil, and he therefore felt repelled by the cheap arguments of the Hegelians, a school for which in general, both in the doctrines of Hegel himself and still more in those of his British disciples, he felt an express aversion. He recognized the full gravity and difficulty of the problem, and saw in evil not merely the absence of good, but a positive force, a radical perversion of good. Sometimes he expressed the opinion that there exists between good and evil an ontological difference in so far as evil cannot be to the same extent fully and concentratedly evil, as good can be good. He held good to be in general more powerful than evil, just as he held happiness to be stronger than misery. But he did not mean this to weaken the fundamental character of negation in the world. So he was honest enough to confess that faced by the perfect wisdom, goodness, and power of God no theoretically satisfactory argument has ever been or can ever be found to explain the reality of evil. We must accept it for what it is, and the only possibility of finally resolving the difficulty lies in the field of practice in enlisting all our power to overcome evil and turn it into an instrument of good.

But do the sun-spots of evil in any way dim or diminish the splendour of the divine sun? Are sin and guilt, are even sorrow, pain, and anxiety in any way to be connected with the nature of God? Hügel raises this question in an explicit form for the reason that in contemporary British philosophy it was frequently answered in the affirmative. Thus the notion of the finitude of God was accepted by thinkers as different as Mill, Schiller, Sorley, Rashdall, and others, and it carried with it the assumption that God is a suffering Being who like man can feel pain and compassion. Hügel could not harmonize this opinion with his own exalted view of God. He was convinced that suffering while not identical with sin belongs in its ultimate ground to the kingdom of evil just as sin does. But because he could not connect God with anything negative he excluded suffering also from His nature. 'We will not allow in Him the presence of any evil, whether sin or only pain, whether actual or only possible.' He accordingly represented the Absolute as pure, unmixed, overflowing joy, as an ocean of bliss in which there is not a single drop of sin or suffering and not even the possibility of them. But since man yearns not only for a higher being to share his joy and happiness, but also one to feel with him in his pain and suffering with sympathy and pity, God sent his Son into the world and laid upon Him the burden of the suffering of humanity. In the Passion of Christ suffering is like a wave-crest breaking against the very glory of God, but this itself remains untouched by it. With regard, then, to the distribution of sin and suffering in the world, the result reached by Hügel is the following: while man is involved in sin and susceptible to suffering, Christ is free of the former, but subject to the latter; God, however, is immune from both.

We close this notice of Hügel's metaphysics with a brief discussion of the problem of freedom, which stands in close connection with the problem of evil. Hügel distinguishes two kinds of freedom, the perfect and the imperfect, the former being the freedom of God, the latter that of man. Against the often expressed view that sin is the price which man must pay for the freedom of will bestowed upon him by God, Hügel argues as follows. It is true that man has the capacity of choosing between good and evil, and that he on that account often falls into sin. Human freedom is thus a freedom of choice between two or more alternative options. But we are not free because we have this power of choice, but notwithstanding it. True freedom has nothing to do with the capacity to will evil instead of the good. So long as we can sin we are only free in a most imperfect sense. Did we possess perfect freedom there would not only be no actual evil, there would not even be the possibility of any. But no answer can be given to the question why God made men such as to be exposed to evil choices. We only know that genuine freedom simply consists in expressing our true being as fully as possible and without any external compulsion. But sin is the negation of our true being and therefore freedom to sin cannot be genuine freedom, but only a feeble reflection of that highest form of it, which belongs to God alone. We may sum up Hügel's teaching as to freedom in the saying of Augustine: *posse non peccare, magna est libertas: non posse peccare, maxima est.*

Hügel's metaphysics which we have here considered in detachment from his other interests was by him developed not as a closed system, but in the wider context of his studies in theology, biblical criticism, and Church history. These are not only the fields in which he achieved his best and most significant results; it is in them also that he sowed broadcast his most fertile seeds of thought. We must content ourselves here with some indications of his teaching as to the essence of religion in general and of Christianity and the Church in particular. Religion is not concerned with human thinking, but with superhuman reality, not with the production of what should be but with the acknowledgment of that which is. It is not the work of man but the deed of God. Its essential mark is givenness, or, as Hügel with his predilection for abstract word-making puts it, 'isness'. This distinguishes it from morality, for the imperative character of which he employs the term 'oughtness'. The object of religion is, like that of knowledge, transcendent reality, and the transcendence with which religion has specifically to do is called for the most part Trans-subjectivity or Super-humanity, or, again, simply Otherness. Religious experience as the mode of apprehending the religious object is always inadequate to it, or, to put it otherwise, the objective factor markedly outweighs the subjective. The manner in which the religious object becomes visible to human insight is the revelational; it is always the outcome of the objective factor, and is the self-disclosing of its givenness. The correlate of the revelation on the side of the subject is self-evidence or the immediate discernment of the self-revealing reality. This need not be clear and distinct; it is mostly obscure and mysterious, but none the less certain on that account. Religion is thus, in Hügel's phrase, qualitatively 'evidential' and 'revelational'.

A further very important thought in Hügel's philosophy of religion, which runs like a crimson thread through all his writings, is the distinction he draws between three elements of religion. These are: (1) the institutional-historical; (2) the critical-speculative; (3) the mystical-volitional. He derives them from the three basic forces of our inner psychic life, which he calls the sensuous, the rational, and the ethico-mystical. The first element corresponds to the indubitable experience of sense-perception, the second to clear and distinct thinking, and the third to the warm faith tested in action. Hügel links up this distinction with a doctrine of Newman's, according to which all genuine religion (and not least Catholicism) draws nourishment from the three domains of politics, philosophy, and piety, and its true nature only comes to fulfilment in the synthesis and equilibrium of the factors springing from these very different domains. The philosophical side of religion is supplied by metaphysics, as has been indicated above. In addition Hügel derives from the principle the right to investigate religious sources and documents in accordance with the strictest scientific methods, the justification, therefore, of biblical criticism and the scientific study of the Scriptures. He wishes the Church not simply to permit free historical inquiry but to encourage it, and in no circumstances to forbid it. For the Christian religion is based, he holds, like every other, upon historical facts, and to ascertain these and subject them to scrutiny, the same method must be used which is applied to the facts of secular history.

Hügel now turns his attention to the institutional and mystical character of religion, especially of Roman Christianity which he has always before his eyes as the most ideal type of religious life. The institutional side—and despite a certain secret predilection for mysticism he gives weighty consideration to it—is the incarnation of the divine in the world, its descent from transcendence to the immanence of temporal and earthly existence. It is the shape which the infinite seeks to take in the finite, spirit in matter, the necessary in the fortuitous present place or present time, and this taking of shape and body is accomplished most visibly and perfectly in the Church. This is the external, sacramental, or historical aspect of religion, and it will include whatever is not merely subjective and personal experience of the individual, whatever belongs to the religious life in community, passing on as an inheritance from generation to generation and finding expression in Churches, groups, and sects, in organizations and established observances. In this sense religion is a social force locked up in ecclesiastical institutions; it rests upon the tradition of historical life and is itself an historical structure that grows out of and is enmeshed in the tissue of events in the world.

Two elements in religion which are necessarily implied by its institutional character are given a specially prominent place by Hügel—its historicity and its sensible aspect. Even if the object of religion is the super-temporal and super-sensible reality of God, this does not mean that the religious life moves in a sphere of pure spirituality and stands in no connection with finite existence. On the contrary, religion and history are so far from being in mutual opposition that the former expressly involves and includes the latter within itself if it is to come to its true fulfilment. But this is only possible when history is rightly understood, as no mere succession or series of processes, but as the theatre of super-temporal powers and values which find in it embodiment and expression. In so far as the historical is thus indissolubly bound up with objective values it has already overcome mere temporality in its here and now, and stands in the form of time as duration, demanding as foundation and background that pure simultaneity in which all functional process and all event have been transformed into creative deed. Strands of Rickert's theory of value and Bergson's theory of time have found a place in this line of thought, and opened a path to the understanding of history and the significance of historicity which was still locked to thinkers whose orientation was determined by the natural sciences.

But it is not only with history that religion is in full accord: the sensible world, the life of body and matter, is also in no contradiction with it. Religion, it is true, is a life of the spirit, but Hügel is never tired of emphasizing that everything spiritual must embody itself in the sensible and be kindled by it in order to become apprehensible in human experience. The ideas that we have of non-sensory or spiritual realities are never mere abstractions of thought, but are combined in some way or other with sensory stimuli, images, or memories, or come to us on occasion out of these. Hügel finds the epistemological justification for this emphatic stress laid upon the sensory basis of all higher mental or spiritual life in Hume's familiar doctrine of impressions and ideas, and he seeks to show that what appears to us the most fugitive, fortuitous, and transient of reals, the sensory fact, is indispensably necessary to frame even the simplest idea of something abiding and enduring, and ultimately to frame that of eternity and God. The purity of the soul does not exclude the sensory and the corporeal, but requires them as its necessary ingredients. The body is the indispensable companion of the mind and each is equally incapable of being set free from the other. There is neither pure spirituality nor pure corporeality, but always that unity of body-mind or spirit-body in which both are mutually implicated and functionally related. Thus corresponding to the process of the corporealization or incarnation of spirit, which Hügel used a rich variety of expressions to indicate, there is, on the other side, the process of the spiritualizing of the corporeal or sensuous, which means, however, not its suppression or obliteration, but only its higher development with full maintenance of its own peculiar character. Or, in Hügel's own fine words: "The higher bends down to, attracts the lower; the lower rises on tip-toe towards, thirsts after and finds and wills the higher" (*Essays and Addresses on the Philosophy of Religion*, second series, cheap ed. of 1930, p. 107). Not even the life of the blessed, therefore, can Hügel think of as utterly freed from everything material, corporeal, or sensible, but as somehow still in contact with it, appropriating it and affirming it at a higher level. By this line of thought he finds expression for all the joyful delight in the senses which pertains to the Roman Catholic.

But it would be to mistake the nature of religion to consider it merely as external institution. It is also and no less directed inward, a personal experience of the individual soul; it is subjective experience as much as it is objective observance. Hügel treats of this side of religion under the concept of mysticism. In his great work on St. Catherine of Genoa he subjected 'the mystical element in religion' to a penetrating examination, and endeavoured to illuminate and interpret it from every side. Expert scholarship, perspicacity of mind, and spiritual insight combine in this most important of Hügel's achievements to produce a work which has scarcely a match in the modern literature of Mysticism.

Mysticism is, according to Hügel's definition, the intuitive and emotional apprehension of the religious object as an objective reality in the sense of an infinite spirit and perfect personality realizing itself in the eternal values of the true, the good, and the beautiful, and active in them. Mysticism is the inner experience of the actual presence of the divine in human consciousness, not as a mere subjective state of mind but as a felt awareness of the transcendence of God in contrast to all human and finite existence. It is also the hallowing and pervading of the finite being, soul and body, by the indwelling of the divine spirit. Furthermore Mysticism has no meaning as a phenomenon in isolation, but only when combined with the rational and institutional side of the religious life. The mystical element may not claim self-sufficiency or cut itself off from the other elements of religion. In every religious exercise it must be present as a part of the whole, but not as an exclusive aspect presuming to be the whole. Such a pretension Hügel terms pseudo- or exclusive Mysticism; it is a view that comes perilously near to Pantheism, in which all distinctions between transcendence and immanence, and infinite and finite, threaten to be confounded. There is, therefore, also no specifically mystical organ of cognition, through which the mystic under conditions of ecstasy might become the recipient of a higher revelation of the eternal than the normal religious man could have. Rather, Mysticism *is* normal to religious life, as are all the other forms in which religion is manifested; the only difference being that in it the divine proclaims itself in ways of a special sort though open to every man. Conditions of ecstasy are only abnormal phenomena accompanying the mystical experience, and do not belong to its essence, as is commonly supposed. What is essential is only the first-hand experience of the individual soul that the unearthly divine power dwells within it, penetrating and charging it with the living breath of its spirit. Mysticism is also a form of the incarnation of the higher being; but this time not in external observances and organizations of the life of the community, nor yet in rational systems and speculations of metaphysical thought, but as a personal experience in the roots of the soul, and as the direct and immediate apprehension of deity in the deep places of the human heart.

GEORGE TYRRELL (1861–1909)

[*Lex Orandi*, 1904; *Lex Credendi*, 1906; *Through Scylla and Charybdis*, 1907; *Christianity at the Cross-Roads*, 1909.]

The Modernist movement, with which Hügel had been for a time closely connected without being definitely absorbed in it, drew into its vortex George Tyrrell, the most considerable Roman Catholic thinker of the first decade of the century next after Hügel. Tyrrell, who was the guiding brain of British Modernism, passed from the Anglican into the Roman Church at the age of eighteen, entered the Society of Jesus soon after (1881), occupied a teaching post in Moral Theology in Stonyhurst College in 1894–96, and in 1906, after his conflict with the Church, was expelled from the Society, suspended from the priesthood, and finally excommunicated. He, like his French colleague Loisy, was a man in whose passionately combative nature the tensions of the time could not be kept from breaking out, and he fought his battle with the dogged resolution of a will supported by firm faith in a good cause; he had for armour a wide scholarship, and he was specially gifted in the freedom and mobility of a very alert mind. It was the great disappointment of his life that the community to which he had committed his destiny proved not to be the *milieu* in which such eminent qualities of mind could operate effectually. It is questionable whether his membership in the Roman Church and the Jesuit Order really accorded with the innermost attitude of his mind, and one can only express surprise that under these circumstances the conflict with his order was so late in coming to an open breach.

The tensions and contrasts that meet and clash in Tyrrell's soul are reflected in the course of his mental development. At first through his education by the Jesuits he was led deeply into the study of scholastic theology and philosophy, and first among his teachers was St. Thomas Aquinas, who not only became his accepted authority, but awoke in him the power of thought by opening and unlocking his mind. Then followed a period in which the doctrine of Newman became a formative experience for him and had a most liberating influence upon him. But the decisive turning-point was not fully reached until Friedrich von Hügel entered his life. Under Hügel's guidance he became for the first time acquainted with modern views, both with the biblical criticism and apologetic of German liberal theology and with the endeavours of French Modernism and reformative Catholicism. And with this he had found his own path, which he henceforth followed to the end with unswerving courage and resolute energy.

The great problem which Tyrrell strove to solve presented itself to him as the resolution of a polar opposition which while it appeared to him in varying shape remained fundamentally the same. This is the tension between outward and inward religion, between the visible and invisible Church, between theology and revelation, between progressive and conservative principles, between tradition and scientific truth, between scepticism and dogmatism, between Catholicism and the modern world: and so on. He desired, as he expressed it in the title of one of his books, to steer between the rock of Scylla and the whirlpool of Charybdis, that is 'between a crippling dogmatism admitting no improvement and an all-engulfing scepticism and negation, between an authority which nullifies personality and an individualism which destroys society'.[1] In this sense modernism meant to him the equating of faith in the Roman Church

[1] See E. Wolff's preface to the German translation of *Through Scylla and Charybdis*, p. 10.

with confessed belief in the modern world, or, what amounts to the same thing, the reconciliation of a perfect loyalty to the fundamentals of the Catholic tradition with an equal loyalty to the claims of scientific truth and moral sincerity. This was the basis of his demand for a critical testing of theological principles instead of their acceptance on authority.

This critical examination proceeds for some distance on similar lines to the views of J. H. Newman. Like Newman, Tyrrell distinguishes two possible ways of considering things, the natural way of thinking from the scientific and philosophical, or the concrete apprehension from the conceptual and abstract. The advantage of the latter is that it reduces into order the bewildering medley in which the things of experience are presented, throws their differences into clear relief, and puts them where they belong in a system of concepts. But its truth is merely hypothetical; it only holds for the domain of the abstract, and it is only able to apprehend its object piecemeal, never as a whole. The more abstract and universal its concepts become, the poorer they become in content and the remoter they are from the infinite wealth of meanings and relations which reality in its concreteness exhibits. On the other hand, the alternative way of apprehending suffers from a certain blurred confusedness in its cognitions, a lack of clear-cut distinctions and orderly arrangement; but by way of compensation it is capable of really penetrating into its object, and of grasping it in its entirety instead of piecemeal, so as to realize exhaustively all its wealth and fullness of life *in concreto*. It stands in immediate contact with the reality of things, and therewith also with their truth. Now since both these modes of knowledge are imperfect they must reciprocally complete one another; but there can be no doubt that Tyrrell, no less than Newman, unconditionally assigns precedence to concrete over abstract cognition, and that (again like Newman) he is thereby driven to accept conclusions of an anti-intellectualist sort. Tyrrell's scepticism with regard to Reason, which he inherited with so much else from Newman, became still more notably intensified when late in his life he became acquainted with Pragmatism and its way of thinking. Similar trends had already been latent in his own doctrine, but they became now precipitated in explicit and assured form. How great was the sympathy with which he regarded pragmatist ideas is shown in a paper he wrote in 1905 in which he defined his attitude to Pragmatism.[1] He certainly does not even here surrender that freedom of mind which distinguishes every position he adopts, and so he was only willing to recognize the positive and not the negative principle of this, in those days, novel doctrine. But, in spite of thus keeping to some extent aloof he did in fact agree with James and Schiller in the point of decisive importance, as, for instance, that truth is nothing on its own account, but has always to serve practical interests, that it must be verified in life and conduct, that the fruitfulness of a hypothesis is the strongest if not the only proof of its correctness, and so on. Such and similar thoughts penetrated even into his theory of religion, or, at least, found their corroboration in it.

In this field also Tyrrell constructed his doctrine upon the basis of an idea of Newman's, namely that of mental (spiritual) development. Like Newman, Tyrrell was looking for a *via media* between scholastic theology and modern science, or, he was fond of saying, between the old theology and the new. For by new theology he understood a discipline proceeding according to the canon of modern scientific method. But this means that theology cannot be a rigid system of fixed, already formulated dogmas which can neither be shaken nor tampered with. It is rather a living, fertile and progressive science, subject to the same laws which all our mental life obeys, and more particularly the law of development of forms and methods with the passage of time. But this is what justifies the demand of historical criticism for a testing scrutiny of its results upon the basis and with the means which contemporary knowledge puts at its disposal. The fact remains, however, that Christian dogma and Christian philosophy of religion have developed and evolved in history; that, for example, the Church of the present

[1] "Notre Attitude en face de Pragmatisme", in the *Annales de Philosophie Chrétienne*.

day is far more enlightened in its theology than the Apostolic or Medieval Church was.

Theology is one part of the outward form which the Christian religion has made for itself. It is to be sharply distinguished in principle from the inner religious substance and content of Christianity, which is revelation and also, in an extended sense not fully elucidated by Tyrrell, dogma. While theology has its source in natural knowledge revelation is of divine origin and is based upon a special supernatural gift of Grace. It is, therefore, eternal and unshakable, admitting no change or modification and subject to no temporal process: it is always one and the same ('semper eadem', as the title of two of Tyrrell's essays says). It is the concrete reality of religion, and speaks the plain, unmistakable language of truth, which the man of simple piety can often understand better than the theologian and philosopher who think in abstract concepts which have been emptied of reality. It is superior to all rational knowledge, even that of theology, and is antecedent to it in time. Thus the relation between religion and theology is to be defined in the same way as that between art and art-criticism, between logical thinking and the science of logic, language, and grammar; the former existed before the latter, which is in each case only its subsequent conceptual interpretation. Theology must, therefore, continually be measured and tested afresh by the original revelation if it is not to be too far sundered from the real substance of religion. In order to be living and fruitful it must become conscious of the profound difference between a revealed kernel of religion exalted above all change (the *depositum fidei*) and the kernel's shell, developed from the application of reflective thought upon it.

This modernist teaching is in every way more firmly fastened and anchored to religion than is Liberal Protestant theology. With the latter Tyrrell did not go beyond half-way. He withdrew support and indeed actively opposed it at the point where it brought under criticism what was for him beyond challenge—the credal substance of the revealed doctrine of salvation. His most vigorous attack is that in his posthumous book *Christianity at the Cross-Roads*, in which the influence of Albert Schweitzer's eschatology is considerable. He conceded to the theologian full freedom of theorizing and inquiry, but not freedom to undermine the very foundations of faith, upon which the whole edifice of theological science is erected. He demanded of him an intellectual burden no heavier than the pious acknowledgment of the fact that Christianity arose from an original supernatural initiative of a divine power. He sought a middle way between Protestant Liberalism and Catholic Dogmatism, between exaggerated Modernity and a too rigid Medievalism, between unbridled licence and servitude of the thinking mind. He found it in a truth, simple and yet profound, the synthetic combination of the unshakableness of faith with the capacity of Christian doctrine or theology for progressive development.

ENGLISH NEO-SCHOLASTICISM

That the neo-Scholastic movement aroused a far weaker reverberation in predominantly Protestant England than in other European countries, such as Germany, Italy, France, and Belgium, is a fact that explains itself. Moreover, no outstanding thinker has appeared in its ranks and succeeded in winning a hearing from a wider public. Thus it remained essentially restricted to Catholic circles, and even here for the most part confined to academic studies within theological seminaries and colleges. None the less, scholastic and neo-scholastic literature has in the last ten years swollen to considerable proportions; since Leo XIII's Encyclical *Aeterni Patris* (1879) there have been printed not only numerous translations but many original works. Inasmuch as for the most part this literature consists in a renovation and revival of the old scholastic teaching, with, of course, its adaptation to modern views, rather than in any independent intellectual achievement, we may be content here merely to name the most important authors and their works, leaving out of account the translations of the works of continental neo-Scholastics (such as Cardinal Mercier, de Wulf, etc.) whose influence has done much to further the movement.

First and foremost mention must be made of the spaciously planned but never completed work, *The Metaphysics of the School*, by THOMAS MORETON HARPER (1821–93), only three of the intended five volumes of which appeared in print between 1879 and 1884, and which presents the Thomistic metaphysics in systematic form. A few years later a series of manuals was published under the editorship of R. F. CLARKE, which evinced a stronger sympathy with modern thought, mostly by way of a critical examination of contemporary tendencies. The following volumes appeared in these 'Manuals of Catholic Philosophy': *Political Economy* (1892), by C. S. Devas; *First Principles of Knowledge* (1888) and *General Metaphysics* (1890), by John Rickaby, S.J.; *Logic* (1889), by R. F. Clarke, S.J.; *Moral Philosophy* (1881), by Joseph Rickaby, S.J.; *Natural Theology* (1891), by Bernard Boedder, S.J.; *Psychology* (1890), by Michael Maher, S.J. The most prolific neo-scholastic writer to-day is PETER COFFEY, Professor of Logic and Metaphysics in Maynooth College, Ireland (*b*. 1876). We owe to him a system of philosophy based on a Thomistic foundation, broadly planned and fully worked out, which is much used for instruction in Roman Catholic theological seminaries, but has hardly aroused any notice outside their walls: *The Science of Logic*, 2 vols., 1912; *Ontology*, 1914, and *Epistemology*, 2 vols., 1917. We may also mention the Jesuits, LESLIE J. WALKER (*b*. 1877) and M. C. D'ARCY (*b*. 1888), both actively at work in Campion Hall, Oxford, where their influence both as teachers and writers makes itself felt also beyond the borders of the Roman Catholic Church. Walker is the author of a work on *Theories of Knowledge* (1910, second edition, 1911, and several subsequent impressions) which won serious attention among professional philosophers. It examines the epistemologies of Absolutism, Pragmatism, and neo-Realism, and aims at reconciling mutually conflicting views while itself attempting to solve the problem of knowledge in a realist sense. If Walker in this work takes his starting-point from Aristotle and St. Thomas, the reason is simply that he regards their doctrines not as finally closed, but as in a high degree capable of development and admitting of being combined with modern scientific knowledge (see also *The Return to God: a Catholic and Roman View*, 1933). M. C. D'Arcy[1] also was able to secure a wider than a merely Roman Catholic reading public with his two excellent books on *Thomas Aquinas* (1930) and *The Nature of Belief* (1931). In the former he tries to present the living interconnection of Thomistic thought with the problems of modern philosophy and therewith its continued generative power; the latter is a keen discussion of the problem of belief, much influenced by Newman's *Grammar of Assent*, the thoughts in which here awaken to significant new life. Finally, the scholastic philosophical standpoint provides the general framework for the thinking and investigations of FRANCIS AVELING (*b.* 1875, Reader in Psychology in the University of London), whose work is mainly in the field of psychology (*On the Consciousness of the Universal and the Individual*, 1912; *The Psychological Approach to Reality*, 1929; *Introduction to Psychology*, 1932), but who has also published some works of general philosophical import ('Some Theories of Knowledge', *Proc. Arist. Soc.*, 1914; 'The Thomistic Outlook in Philosophy', *ibid.*, 1924; *Personality and Will*, 1931).

Among professional non-Catholic philosophical circles the neo-Scholastic movement has hitherto aroused but little interest; one cannot recognize any effect worthy of mention from this source upon the philosophical currents of to-day. The greater number of lay thinkers appear unaffected or even repelled by it,[2] with the single exception of A. E. TAYLOR (vide pp. 412 ff), who brings to bear on medieval philosophy not only the interest of a scholar, but also that of a systematic thinker, and is endeavouring to draw from the Scholastic, that is the Thomistic, mind and spirit a renewal of modern thought similar to that which the neo-Scholastics of the Continent are also seeking.

[1] Not to be confused with C. F. D'Arcy, Anglican Archbishop of Armagh and Primate of Ireland (*d.* 1938), who is likewise well known as the author of several philosophical works.

[2] Cf. the expressions used on this point by several British philosophers in the volume edited by J. S. Zybura, *Present-Day Thinkers and the New Scholasticism*, 1926, Part 1, ch. 2.

INDEX OF NAMES